100
Most Popular
Picture Book
Authors and Illustrators

POPULAR AUTHORS SERIES

The 100 Most Popular Young Adult Authors: Biographical Sketches and Bibliographies. Revised First Edition. By Bernard A. Drew.

Popular Nonfiction Authors for Children: A Biographical and Thematic Guide. By Flora R. Wyatt, Margaret Coggins, and Jane Hunter Imber.

100 Most Popular Children's Authors: Biographical Sketches and Bibliographies. By Sharron L. McElmeel.

100 Most Popular Picture Book Authors and Illustrators: Biographical Sketches and Bibliographies. By Sharron L. McElmeel.

100

Most Popular
Picture Book
Authors and Illustrators

Biographical Sketches and Bibliographies

Sharron L. McElmeel

2000
Libraries Unlimited, Inc.
Englewood, Colorado

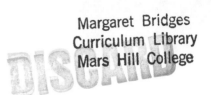
Libraries Unlimited, Inc.
P.O. Box 6633
Englewood, CO 80155-6633
1-800-237-6124
www.lu.com

Library of Congress Cataloging-in-Publication Data

McElmeel, Sharron L.
    100 most popular picture book authors and illustrators : biographical sketches and
bibliographies / Sharron L. McElmeel.
        p. cm. -- (Popular authors series)
    Includes index.
    ISBN 1-56308-647-6 (cloth : hardbound)
        1. Children's literature, American--Bio-bibliography--Dictionaries. 2. Authors,
American--20th century--Biography--Dictionaries. 3. Illustrators--United
States--Biography--Dictionaries. 4. Illustration of
books--Bio-bibliography--Dictionaries. 5. Illustrated children's books--Bibliography. 6.
Picture books for children--Bibliography. I. Title: One hundred most popular picture
book authors and illustrators. II. Title. III. Series.

PS490 .M395 2000
810.9'9282'03--dc21
[B]
                                                                        00-023181

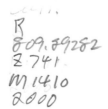

For Jack who makes this possible.

Contents

Introduction

SHARING AUTHOR INFORMATION
AND MOTIVATING READERS

One of the most effective ways to motivate young readers to read more is to connect the reader with a favorite author or illustrator and to provide some background information about that person. Educators, in their efforts to promote reading, often create the need for students to respond to a book through activities that create a visible sign of their having read and understood the book. However, one of the most valuable responses to a book is for the reader to want to read another book by the same author or a book illustrated by the same illustrator. When readers begin to make connections between the author or illustrator and what they are reading, they will begin to make connections that will promote more reading and hopefully their own writing and artistic efforts. Connecting the writer or illustrator to the books he or she has created will help develop readers, writers, and artists.

This book is intended to provide information about the authors and illustrators of the picture books most read by young readers. While picture books are often thought to be for the very youngest of readers, they hold much utility for the older reader as well. The older reader will be able to understand the multiple layers of meaning, to compare and contrast plots and themes, and to emulate the art and the literary style. The basic information given in this book is biographical, accompanied by a selected book list, and suggestions for further reading. Other reference sources have included these popular authors and illustrators, often through a multivolume set of references written over a period of years. Thus, in order to obtain information on the most popular authors/illustrators being read, one must have access to several volumes of a reference work. Even with that access, the information for those authors initially profiled early in their career is seriously out-of-date. The information included in this book has been researched and every effort has been made to have the information as up-to-date and accurate as possible.

For more than a dozen years I have profiled authors and illustrators in books and periodicals. I have interviewed hundreds of authors/illustrators and have heard many of them speak at national or state conferences. For those included in this book, I have relied heavily on my previous writings, interview notes, and notes from their presentations at various conferences. Quotes included in this book are from these sources. Further research brought information up-to-date in regard to recent books and future plans. While I have included selected book lists as part of each profile, I did so only to provide readers with some titles to associate with the author. New books are being added each publishing season. Those readers wishing to have a complete and up-to-date list of a particular author's or illustrator's publications can now access that information in minutes by going to the Library of Congress's Catalog on the World Wide Web at <http://catalog.loc.gov>. The suggestions for further reading include periodical articles and, where appropriate, Web sites which will provide more information about the author/illustrator and his or her books. Do keep in mind that while Web sites can provide up-to-date information about authors and illustrators and their work, the site can also disappear very quickly. All the Web sites listed in the book were accessible during the three months before the manuscript was completed. I cannot vouch for their continued presence. Once you access the Web site, you may wish to print a hard copy of the site and archive a personal research copy in an appropriate file for future reference. If a World Wide Web address is still accessible but the address has changed, a search using one of the many search engines will often yield the new URL.

Some of the choices of authors and illustrators for inclusion in this book seemed obvious. Throughout my career as an educator I have worked with more than 12,000 young readers choosing and selecting books to read and enjoy. Authors such as Dr. Seuss (Theodor Seuss Geisel) have enjoyed a level of popularity for several decades. Some names are new on the list—and most likely will not be as long lasting as Seuss. Eric Carle has been a constant for several decades. He was also at the top of the survey which we used to confirm selections for the list.

The list of authors selected for inclusion in this book were based, in general, on the results of a survey conducted nationwide in 1997—a survey designed to identify the 100 most popular authors and illustrators in children's literature. Responses to the survey came from teachers and students. The results of the survey were originally reported in *Library Talk* (January/February 1998).

The 1997 survey was based on a survey conducted by Don Gallo in 1988. In the spring of 1989, Don Gallo published the results of a 1988 survey of forty-one educators who had served as officers of the Assembly on Literature for Adolescents (ALAN) of the National Council of the Teachers of English. Gallo's format provided the model. We (Lin Buswell and myself) decided to expand the survey to include books aimed at younger readers and to expand the population invited to participate.

The first step was constructing a preliminary list of picture book authors and illustrators—a major task. As with all surveys, favorites of individuals might not have shown up on the preliminary list and several of those sending in surveys added notes about a favorite author that had been left off the preliminary list. When choosing authors and illustrators to share with young readers, there seems to be as many sets of criteria as there are authors and illustrators. No one person or group of people can create a list of authors/illustrators that all children must read before they pass through a specific age or grade. Any list compiled would most assuredly leave out some local favorites—every choice is relative. Unless every author/illustrator who ever wrote or illustrated a children's book could be included on a preliminary list, someone or some group must make a preliminary selection and that selection is bound to reflect the biases of the group making it.

There was an attempt to make the selections as diverse and representative of the current trends in children's literature as possible. The list was narrowed using the input of hundreds of educators and students. Once this survey was published in the national journal *Library Talk*, completed forms began to come in. The survey attracted participants—students and educators—from forty-one of the United States, two Canadian provinces, and Saudi Arabia. More than 3,000 completed surveys were submitted. The results were significant in that clear patterns began to emerge. Dr. Seuss was at the top of the list—being marked as recognized by a little over 90% of the respondents. No one other author garnered recognition by more than 90% of the respondents. The next group—Marc Brown, Eric Carle, Tomie dePaola, Steven Kellogg, Mercer Mayer, Beatrix Potter, and H. A. Rey—was recognized by 50–89%. The next seven—Frank Asch, Eve Bunting, Joanna Cole, James Marshall, Bill Peet, Jack Prelutsky, Chris Van Allsburg—were recognized by 40% or more of the respondents. The rest were recognized by a smaller percentage of respondents; none were recognized by less than 15% of the respondents. Other authors were included based on years of observation, and informal interviews with young readers.

The authors, because of the types of books or the nature of the biographical information, demanded a slightly different treatment. Some of the book lists, I felt, needed to be annotated with a brief indication of the book's topic/theme, while other book lists seemed to be self-explanatory based on the title or on the author's chosen genre. So, while each author/illustrator's chapter has standard information (a biographical sketch and a section titled "Books and Notes"), the Books and Notes section will vary depending on the author/illustrator. In the same way, the suggestions for further reading vary depending on what is available. I have, in each case, attempted to provide information that will entice readers into the books mentioned in conjunction with each author/illustrator.

This book, while initially conceived to include 100 of the top picture book authors and illustrators, actually contains information about several husband and wife teams that have collaborated extensively to create books. While many of these teams also have created books individually and this individual work is significant, it seemed that much of their work and personal lives are so interconnected that to profile them separately would have resulted in much duplicated information. Thus, I decided to discuss some husbands and wives in a single profile, so this book actually contains information about a few more than 100 authors/illustrators.

I hope you will find that the biographical information provides connections for young readers—connections to a particular author or illustrator and to her/his books.

Sharron L. McElmeel
Cedar Rapids, Iowa

Verna Aardema

Courneye Tourcotte, Master Photographer

New Era, Michigan
June 6, 1911–May 11, 2000

📖 *Who's in Rabbit's House?*
A Masai Tale

📖 *Why Mosquitoes Buzz in*
People's Ears

ABOUT THE AUTHOR

Verna Norberg was born in New Era, Michigan, on June 6, 1911. She was third in a family of nine children. During her childhood in New Era, she often scurried away from an unfinished job of drying dishes to scour the neighborhood for children to whom she could tell stories. Verna wrote her first poem at the age of eleven. When her mother read it, she said, "Why Verna, you're going to be a writer, just like Grandpa VanderVen." That was the first time Verna had been noticed for anything positive, and at that moment, she decided she would be a writer, just like her great-grandfather. When he died, he left an unfinished book manuscript written on squares of brown wrapping paper.

Verna began writing little stories and "asking God to help me to become as good a writer as Gene Stratton-Porter." In high school, she wrote school news for the weekly newspaper. Once she completed high school, she entered Michigan State College (1929–1934), where she majored in composition and journalism. After college, Aardema was a "stringer" for the local daily, *The Muskegon Chronicle*. She held that position for twenty-one years, some of which were spent teaching in an elementary school. For twenty-four years, she taught first- and second-grade children.

In 1937, Verna married Albert Aardema. After their son and daughter, Austin and Paula, were born, Verna often told them stories and eventually began to write the stories down. Her first children's story was one she made up to get her baby daughter to eat. She sold that story to *The Instructor* for $35. It appeared in the January 1959 issue. She sent the same story to book editor Alice Torrey at Coward–McCann. The editor liked it and suggested she use the story as the first chapter in a novel for young readers. Aardema could not think of a second chapter, so she proposed that she retell a collection of African folktales. The editor accepted, and Aardema began researching and writing her first book, *Tales from the Story Hat* (Coward–McCann, 1960). Several more books followed. Aardema continued to teach and write until 1973, when she retired from teaching to become a full-time writer.

Her fascination with Africa and the stories that came from that continent have inspired her to spend hours researching and reading stories that she thought she would like to retell. Elements from the story "Why the Bush-Fowl Calls at Dawn and Why Flies Buzz," which was retold by Kathleen Arnott in *African Myths and Legends* (Walck, 1963) inspired some of the elements in *Why Mosquitoes Buzz in People's Ears* (Dial, 1975). Aardema's neighbor's dog, who drooled at her screen door while she was frying meat, inspired the Sloogeh Dog, featured in an African story, who drooled at a rich man's gate.

In 1974, Aardema's husband, Albert, died of cancer. The following year, she married Joel Vugteveen, a dentist. Both had grown up in New Era. For many years Verna and Joel Vugteveen's home was in the woods on the shore of Mona Lake in Michigan. When Verna was not writing, she was preparing for the more than thirty speaking and storytelling engagements that she had each year. For fun and to keep in shape, she and her husband also swam 10 laps a day in their clubhouse pool. They also rode bicycles for two miles nearly every day.

In 1984, Aardema relocated in North Ft. Myers, Florida, where she continued to enjoy swimming and riding bikes. On August 5, 1992, eight years after moving to Florida, Aardema suffered a stroke and became confined to a wheelchair. Verna Aardema died on May 11, 2000. She is survived by her son, Dr. Austin Aardema; her daughter, Paula Dufford; six grandchildren; and five great-grandchildren.

BOOKS AND NOTES

Many of Verna Aardema's tales use onomatopoeia—words that make a sound like the action they represent. *Why Mosquitoes Buzz in People's Ears* is a fine example of a text using onomatopoeia. Aardema has retold many African tales—tales from the Ashanti, Kenya, Rwanda, Liberia, Zanzibar, and various other locations. Many notable artists, including Leo Dillon and Diane Dillon, Marc Brown, Susan Meddaugh, Victoria Chess, Ellen Weiss, and Marcia Brown, have illustrated her books.

Anansi Does the Impossible! An Ashanti Tale. Illustrated by Lisa Desimini. (Atheneum, 1997).

Anansi Finds a Fool: An Ashanti Tale. Illustrated by Bryna Waldman. (Dial, 1992).

Jackal's Flying Lesson: A Khoikhoi Tale. Illustrated by Dale Gottlieb. (Knopf, 1995).

The Lonely Lioness and the Ostrich Chicks (Knopf, 1996).

This for That: A Tonga Tale. Illustrated by Victoria Chess. (Dial, 1997).

The Vingananee and the Tree Toad: A Liberian Tale. Illustrated by Ellen Weiss. (Warne, 1983; Puffin Books, 1988).

FOR MORE INFORMATION

Books

Aardema, Verna. *A Bookworm Who Hatched.* Illustrated by Dede Smith. (R. C. Owens, 1992).

Web Sites

University of Southern Mississippi, de Grummond Collection: Verna Aardema Papers. URL: <http://avatar.lib.usm.edu/~degrum/findaids/aardema.htm> (Accessed March 2000).

Allan Ahlberg
Janet Ahlberg

◆ Word/Visual Play ◆ Folklore (Literary) ◆ Humor

Croydon, England
June 5, 1938

Huddersfield, England
October 21, 1944–November 15, 1995

📖 *The Clothes Horse and Other Stories*
📖 *Each Peach Pear Plum: An I Spy Story*
📖 *The Jolly Postman*

ABOUT THE AUTHORS

Janet Ahlberg was born in 1944 in Huddersfield, England, but she grew up in Leicester. Allan Ahlberg was born in 1938 in Croydon, England. They met in Leicester while both were training to become teachers at the Sunderland College of Education. They married in the 1960s. Allan taught for ten years and even became the headmaster of a village school. Janet never did teach. She knew it wasn't for her, but she said illustration wasn't her first choice either. After earning her teaching certificate, Janet followed a second course of study and took a graphic design course at Leicester School of Art. For a number of months, she worked as a paste-up and layout artist for a woman's magazine, but she didn't like the job.

About that time, Allan was offered a temporary headship in Oxford. The couple moved there, and Janet began doing freelance artwork. When they moved back to Leicester, Janet continued her freelance work. Janet said that in early 1985, "We sold our first published collaboration, *The Brick Street Boys* (Heinemann) and then did not sell anything for eighteen months. Our friends worried about us. We never worried, though. We had no responsibilities. Jessica wasn't born yet and Allan was teaching, so we just kept going." Soon, however, publishers began to regularly accept their work, and Allan became a full-time writer. They regularly collaborated to create books. Allan created the text, and Janet illustrated it with exquisite watercolors. *Each Peach Pear Plum: An I Spy Story* (Viking, 1979) and *The Jolly Postman* (Little, Brown, 1983) were two early collaborations.

The Ahlbergs viewed their books as a unit—a marriage of words and pictures. They bantered back and forth about their ideas, discussing and modifying them. Together, they designed each book's format, determining details such as the width of the margins and the size of the font. They even co-wrote the blurb for each jacket's flap—no detail was too small.

In addition to his collaborations with Janet, Allan also wrote lengthier fiction. Sometimes André Amstutz or Joe Allen Wright worked with the Ahlbergs. André Amstutz was Janet's former teacher and was greatly admired by both Ahlbergs for his wit and economy. Their first collaboration was the Brick Street Boys readers, published in 1975 (Heinemann). They were spoofs on the Janet and John (Dick and Jane) readers.

The Ahlbergs had a special knack for building many layers of meaning into their books. The young reader will notice the apparent themes of the stories, whereas older readers will notice the juxtaposition of word play and illustration within a simple story, creating a rich backdrop that requires knowledge of traditional literature.

Using the traditional "I Spy" game, the Ahlbergs created a visual character hunt that plays throughout the pages of *Each Peach Pear Plum*. The imaginary landscapes that Janet created included inhabitants based on characters from folk and fairy tales. The book builds on characters from Mother Goose and other traditional folk characters beginning with Little Tom Thumb. Each picture that follows hides a new character somewhere in the design. As Cinderella stands on the stairs, the Three Bears are shown peeking in the window. The illustration featuring Little Bo-Peep acknowledges her presence and ends with "I spy Jack and Jill." Hidden in the Bo-Peep picture are Jack and Jill. Successive verses and illustrations feature a host of other familiar faces. This book earned the Ahlbergs the 1978 Kate Greenaway Award, England's equivalent of the Caldecott Medal for illustration.

The Jolly Postman is a tale that plays on several levels as well. A jolly, plump postman carries letters from one storybook character to the next. The book actually contains the letters, postcards, advertisements, and invitations that are sent to each recipient. Goldilocks uses her childish writing to compose a letter of apology to the Three Bears. B. B. Wolf, Esq. receives a very formal legal letter from attorneys Meeny, Miney, and Mo informing him that he must leave Grandmother's cottage. Various other fairy and folk characters appear in the tale.

They used the technique masterfully in a book titled *Jeremiah in the Dark Woods* (Viking, 1987). The story is about Jeremiah Obadiah Jackenory Jones and his grandma's jam tarts. The Ahlbergs managed to include three bears, seven dwarfs, five gorillas, a frog prince, some sleeping beauties, a wolf, a dinosaur, a mad hatter, a crocodile with a clock in it, giant beanstalks, four firemen on a fire engine, and a number of other images.

The Clothes Horse and Other Stories (Viking, 1988) features figurative language, challenging readers to use their intellect to unravel word riddles. Allan Ahlberg wove his stories around phrases such as "life savings," and "jackpot." Each story explains, in farce, the meaning behind each of the phrases. The woman who is saving bits and pieces of her life does so by wrapping up parts of her life to savor later, when she is seventy. She sometimes reaches back into her life savings to bring out a special day or week from her past. When she dies, there is only one unused package left, "Half an hour, age four."

The Ahlbergs' first five years of creating books brought them enough success that they were able to move to a new home, complete with a garden and fruit trees, in a suburb of Leicester. Their daughter, Jessica, was born in 1979. When Jessica was eleven months old, Janet sketched out the idea for *The Baby's Catalogue* (Kestrel, 1982), which completed a trio of early baby books. The book was a runner-up for the Kate Greenaway Award.

Janet Ahlberg died of cancer on November 15, 1995. Her husband and their daughter survive her. They still live in Leicester, England. Allan Ahlberg continues to write books for young readers. André Amstutz , the couple's good friend, illustrates his books, although other illustrators also work with Allan.

BOOKS AND NOTES

The books on which Janet Ahlberg and Allan Ahlberg collaborated are generally picture books, conceived first as an idea and then fleshed out with visual images. Because Allan was able to create the text more quickly than Janet could create the illustrations, Allan often worked with other illustrators to create books—most often, for intermediate readers. Since Janet Ahlberg's untimely death, Allan has continued to write and create books reminiscent of those books he created on his own, prior to Janet's death.

Books by Allan Ahlberg and Janet Ahlberg

The Baby's Catalogue (Little, Brown, 1982).

The Bear Nobody Wanted (Viking, 1992).

It Was a Dark and Stormy Night (Viking, 1993).

The Jolly Pocket Postman (Little, Brown, 1995).

The Jolly Postman, or, Other People's Letters (Little, Brown, 1986).

Books by Allan Ahlberg

The Better Brown Stories. Illustrated by Fritz Wegner. (Viking, 1995).

The Black Cat. Illustrated by André Amstutz. (Mulberry, 1993).

The Giant Baby. Illustrated by Fritz Wegner. (Viking, 1994).

Mockingbird. Illustrated by Paul Howard. (Candlewick, 1998).

Monkey Do! Illustrated by André Amstutz. (Candlewick, 1998).

The Mysteries of Zigomar: Poems and Stories. Illustrated by John Lawrence. (Candlewick, 1997).

The Pet Shop. Illustrated by André Amstutz. (Mulberry, 1993).

FOR MORE INFORMATION

Limited information can be found on book jacket flaps. No articles, books, or Web sites were located.

Martha Alexander

◆　Bears　◆　Drawing and Imagination

Augusta, Georgia
May 25, 1920

📖　*Even That Moose Won't Listen to Me*
📖　*Nobody Asked Me If I Wanted a Baby Sister*

ABOUT THE AUTHOR/
ILLUSTRATOR

Martha Alexander was born on May 25, 1920, in Augusta, Georgia. She spent her first nine years in that state, where she often visited a ninety-three-year-old former slave who told her stories of her grandfather's boyhood. In 1929, Martha's family moved to Cincinnati, Ohio. A teacher in her new school encouraged her drawing, and later a high school history teacher encouraged her further. He allowed her to draw historical pictures for extra credit.

After high school, Alexander attended the Cincinnati Academy of Arts. It was during those years that she became acquainted with the magic of paintings by Paul Klee and Marc Chagall and with Leonardo da Vinci's portrait of Mona Lisa. She came to understand that art could evoke strong responses from viewers and that complete stories could be told through pictures. It was then that she began to think about creating children's books.

In 1943, Alexander married a painter. As a member of the U.S. military, he was sent overseas during the first years of their marriage. When he returned, the couple and their young daughter, Kim, settled in Honolulu, Hawaii. Their son, Allen, was born three years later. During their sixteen years in Hawaii, Alexander focused on silk-screening and creating murals. Some of these murals were commissioned for pediatrician's offices and for children's waiting rooms.

In 1959, the couple divorced, and Alexander decided to try her hand at creating children's books. She sent some samples of her work to a friend in New York. Before long, she had moved to New York City and was working in the illustrating field. Supporting her two children was a struggle as she illustrated stories in teen and women's magazines. It wasn't until 1965 that she actually submitted some samples to a children's book publisher. The editor at Harper & Row liked her work and encouraged her to author a book that she could illustrate. By 1968, her first book, *Out! Out! Out!*, was published. This wordless book tells the story of a boy and an uninvited pigeon that he lures out of the house. Later that year, a book with text, *Maybe a Monster*, was published.

Alexander has said that she begins the process of creating a book by making a dummy of it. She folds about thirty pages into the form of a book and then fills the pages with pictures and words as they come to her. Many of her books have little or no text. She uses pictures to convey the story. Books such as *Blackboard Bear* (Dial, 1969) sometimes contain as many as fifteen pages with no text.

Like many other authors, Alexander's stories come from her surroundings. *Blackboard Bear* came about after she spent three days with relatives and listened to an imaginative four-year-old nephew explain how his brave father had rescued him. Later, the four-year-old handed his aunt twelve imaginary baby kangaroos to hold for him. Upon returning home, the dummy for *Blackboard Bear* formed the beginning of that popular classic tale.

When Alexander's then two-year-old granddaughter suggested that her new baby sister go live with Grandma, Alexander parlayed the idea into a new book, *Nobody Asked Me If I Wanted a Baby Sister* (Dial, 1971), in which Oliver attempts to give away his baby sister but realizes that she really needs him—only Oliver can stop her from crying. Oliver decides to take his sister home, and to keep her.

After decades in New York City, Alexander moved to Sag Harbor, New York, and later to the Northwest, first to Oregon and then to Washington. It was in Oregon where she met the moose that became the main character in

Even That Moose Won't Listen to Me (Dial, 1988). Alexander eventually moved to Olympia, Washington.

Alexander's children and grandchildren—Lisa, Christina, Leslie, Mia, and Scott—are now grown, but she continues to search her childhood and the childhood of her family and friends for more story ideas.

BOOKS AND NOTES

Many of Martha Alexander's books are simple narratives, often with minimal texts. A majority of her stories are told with illustrations created with pencil and delicate tempera paints. She uses the characters' gestures and actions to help tell her stories.

And My Mean Old Mother Will Be Sorry Blackboard Bear (Dial, 1972).

While feeding his teddy bear, Anthony manages to leave a trail of sticky honey all over the kitchen floor. Anthony's mother sends him to bed, and Anthony vows to run away.

How My Library Grew by Dinah (Wilson, 1983).

Dinah and her teddy bear get dressed and watch the bulldozers work to build a new library. Each day she watches, and months later when the library is built, Dinah has a surprise for the library—a book called *How My Library Grew*.

Lily and Willy, Willy's Book, Where's Willy, Good Night, and *Lily* (Candlewick, 1993).

Two friends make their first appearance of several titles.

No Ducks in Our Bathtub (Dial, 1973).

David's mother is a "mean old crab" since she has decided that their apartment should have no bugs, no pigeons, and no ducks. But what will happen when the "fish" eggs he brings home are something more than any of them expect?

You're a Genius, Blackboard Bear (Candlewick, 1995).

Another of Alexander's books featuring the bear who comes off the blackboard and becomes a real bear—at least in the little boy's imagination.

FOR MORE INFORMATION

Limited information can be found on book jacket flaps. No articles, books, or Web sites were located.

Sue Alexander

◆ Friends ◆ Plays

© Marilyn Sanders

Tucson, Arizona
August 20, 1933

📖 *Nadia the Willful*

📖 *Witch, Goblin and Ghost's Book of Things to Do*

ABOUT THE AUTHOR

Although she began writing at age eight, it wasn't until Sue Alexander was married and a mother that she began to cultivate a writing career. She discovered that writing stories for children made her happier than any other kind of writing, so she has steered her life's work in that direction. Since her first book was published in 1973, she has written dozens of books.

Sue was born in Arizona but spent her childhood years in Chicago. Books were an important part of her life. She was a voracious reader as a child and even today will often make a phone call to a friend so she can read aloud a particularly interesting piece of writing she has found. Her elementary classmates often listened intently as she read a selection from a story she had written.

When she went to college, Sue planned to prepare for a career in journalism. After she wrote a news story and turned it in, however, she would rewrite the endings to fit her idea of how the story should have ended. Eventually, Alexander began to write entire stories for herself.

Initially, Alexander's writing wasn't for children, but she found that writing for children brought her more joy and satisfaction than other types of writing. Her first exploration of children's fiction came about when she went to the library to find plays with parts for two children. When she could not find plays for two parts, she sat down to write her own. She decided to submit the plays, *Small Plays for You and a Friend*, to a publisher.

Alexander's stories are built on incidents from her life. For example, *Nadia the Willful* (Pantheon, 1983) is taken directly from her own life, although the setting is not. Alexander had read about the rigid standards of behavior, language, and family roles in the formal Bedouin culture. She researched the Bedouin culture to develop a general feeling for it, which made the writing much more controllable. The popular story also has been translated into French, in which the title is *Leila*.

There are several memorable characters in Alexander's books. She has written several titles about a keen sleuth named Muriel. Among her cases is one involving a queen's missing lanterns and a dragon that is threatening a kingdom. For several years, Alexander had a special book character in her files. The right story just did not seem to evolve for him, so Goblin stayed in the file drawer. Finally, after about three years, two more characters, Witch and Ghost, joined Goblin. It was seven more years before Alexander found the right story for the three characters. Pantheon Books published *Witch, Goblin, and Sometimes Ghost* in 1976. Several more books featuring these three characters followed. In one of the titles about the three friends, *Witch, Goblin and Ghost's Book of Things to Do* (Pantheon, 1982), one of Alexander's author friends, Sid Fleischman, created a magic trick for Goblin to perform in the book. Fleischman is a Newbery Award winner (*The Whipping Boy*; Greenwillow, 1986) who was once a magician. He still enjoys dabbling in magic. When Alexander asked him to develop a trick for Goblin, he did. The results appear as "Goblin's Magic Trick." Mr. Mysterious, as he appears in Alexander's book, bears a strong resemblance to Sid Fleischman.

Sue Alexander is married to Joel Alexander. They have two sons, Glenn and Marc, and one daughter, Stacey. Their children are now grown with homes and interests of their own. Alexander and her husband enjoy traveling, although they do not get to pursue this interest as much as they would like. Alexander is very much involved in the Society of Children's Book

Writers and Illustrators (SCBWI), for which she provides support for her fellow writers. She and her husband reside in Canoga Park, California.

BOOKS AND NOTES

The strength of Sue Alexander's books is the interesting characters she develops. Nadia shows the tenacity to persevere and remember her brother. Witch, Ghost, and Goblin show the strength of their friendship as they share everyday experiences. Muriel is a detective who rivals Donald Sobol's Encyclopedia Brown and David A. Adler's Cam Jansen.

Nadia the Willful. Illustrated by Lloyd Bloom. (Pantheon, 1983).

Small Plays for You and a Friend. Illustrated by Olivia H. Cole. (Scholastic, 1973; Clarion, 1974).

What's Wrong Now, Millicent? Illustrated by David Scott Meier. (Simon & Schuster, 1996).

Who Goes Out on Halloween? Illustrated by G. Brian Karas. (Bantam, 1990; Gareth Stevens, 1998).

Witch, Goblin, and Sometimes Ghost. Illustrated by Jeanette Winter. (Pantheon, 1976).

World Famous Muriel. Illustrated by Chris Demarest. (Little, Brown, 1984; Dell, 1988).

FOR MORE INFORMATION

Articles

Lachtman, Harold. "Authoress Wows Her Toughest Critics in Stockton Visit." *The Stockton* (California) *Record* (November 17, 1983): 22–23.

Aliki (Aliki Brandenberg)

◆ Dinosaurs, Nonfiction ◆ Friends ◆ Family Relationships

Wildwood Crest, New Jersey
September 3, 1929

📖 *Digging Up Dinosaurs*
📖 *How a Book Is Made*
📖 *Medieval Feast*
📖 *My Visit to the Zoo*

Val Lambros

ABOUT THE AUTHOR/ILLUSTRATOR

Aliki Liacouras was born on September 3, 1929, when her family was on vacation in a small town near the New Jersey seashore. Her parents, Stella Lagakos Liacouras and James Liacouras, were natives of Greece, and Aliki spoke Greek before she spoke English. Her childhood was spent in Philadelphia, Pennsylvania, and later in Yeadon, Pennsylvania. She began to draw as a preschooler. She liked to create pictures of her own family and of Peter Rabbit's family. She liked the fact that the families had something in common: both included three girls and a boy named Peter.

After high school, Aliki attended art school and then became a freelance artist. In 1956, she decided to travel to Europe to sketch and paint. She set out to explore her Greek heritage and then ended up in Florence, Italy. While browsing in a Florence bookshop, she met her future husband, Franz Brandenberg, a native of Switzerland. The following year, 1957, the couple was married and then settled in Berne, Switzerland. While there, Aliki Brandenberg discovered that William Tell was Swiss. That bit of information resulted in her first book, *The Story of William Tell* (Faber & Faber, 1960; Barnes, 1961). The year the book first was published, Aliki and Franz Brandenberg moved to New York. There Aliki began to focus in earnest on her career in children's books. From the time her first book was published, she became known to her readers simply as "Aliki." Franz Brandenberg became a literary agent; later, he began to write as well. While living in New York, the Brandenbergs had two children, Jason (b. April 15, 1964) and Alexa (b. June 7, 1966).

During the next decade, Aliki Brandenberg published many titles, including biographies and other topics of interest to young readers. Her informational picture books helped set the standard for publishers. She wrote about places, as in the title *Alaska: A Book to Begin On* (Holt, 1962) and about science topics, such as *My Five Senses* (Crowell, 1962) and *Bees and Beelines* (Crowell, 1964). She also told the stories of well-known people in titles such as *The Story of William Penn* (Prentice-Hall, 1964; Simon & Schuster, 1994) and *A Weed Is a Flower: The Life of George Washington Carver* (Prentice-Hall, 1965; Simon & Schuster, 1988). She also retold folktales, such as *Three Gold Pieces: A Greek Folk Tale* (Pantheon, 1967).

In 1977, the Brandenberg family moved to London, England, where Aliki continues her book career. They settled in a five-story townhouse in Regent's Park. The Brandenbergs' house is much like the other twenty houses on their short road, except for the bright red door and flourishing backyard garden. Aliki works on the top floor of the house, often in solitude. She considers herself both a workaholic and a perfectionist. Sometimes she works sixteen hours a day, for months on end, to complete a book. Once or twice a year, Aliki travels to the United States to confer with her editors.

Aliki's earlier books often were filled with incidents from the lives of her children. In 1983, when her children were teenagers, their faces were featured in the illustrations on the front and back covers of *A Medieval Feast* (Crowell, 1983). Her fiction also has been based on incidents from her own life. Mary Bloom, from *At Mary Bloom's* (Greenwillow, 1976), is a real person. *The Two of Them* (Greenwillow, 1979) includes episodes based on actual events, and Aliki now wears a ring with a large, green stone, much like the one worn by a child in that story. *We Are Best Friends* (Greenwillow, 1982) came out of experiences of her children during the time they left the United States, leaving their friends behind, to settle in London. Alexa's birthday—June 7—provided the title for *June 7!* (Macmillan, 1972).

Aliki's interest in a given topic and her desire to learn more about it contribute to her work as well. All of her information books require research. *A Medieval Feast* (set in the 1400s) is the result of Aliki's love for baking and cooking and of her desire to do a book about England and English history. She researched what people in fifteenth-century England ate and wore, as well as what they grew in their gardens. The research and her writing consumed all of her time for twenty-four months, twelve hours a day. Her reading included more than sixty books and resulted in six thick files.

How a Book Is Made took even longer to create. Although she knew much about the publishing process, she still had to research some of the more complicated aspects of it. Aliki wanted to inject a measure of humor into the book, so she turned all of the characters into cats. The feline characters provided a level of lightness to the topic and allowed Aliki to include her editor, Margaret Clark, without drawing her as a person.

A trademark of Aliki's books is her knack for telling two stories in one. Often, a text tells one story while speech "bubbles"—usually in the form of hand-written text, labels, and notices—supplement the main text with humor and incidental information. She uses the technique to include even more snippets of information, to point out details, and to amplify an idea. She writes biographies of American heroes and retells Greek folktales. She manages to draw her children, husband, parents, aunts, uncles, and other relatives and friends into her illustrations for both fiction and nonfiction titles. Her husband, Franz, has included the same collection of relatives in his books as well. Their children, Jason and Alexa, became the models for his "Edward and Elizabeth" books.

Aliki says, "All books come from a spark, like a firecracker going off." One book that is actually two books in one, *Marianthe's Story, Painted Words: Marianthe's Story, Spoken Memories* (Greenwillow, 1998), tells an immigrant child's story. The first story "is about an immigrant child and her experiences in the classroom. Book Two is her story when she learns to tell it in words." Like the character, Aliki is bilingual. The story developed after she was talking about her language abilities with a librarian. After their discussion, Aliki sat down to write another book that she had in mind, "but this one fell out on paper."

Another story came to Aliki in a similar way. The book, *William Shakespeare and the Globe,* came about when Aliki and Franz were visiting the Globe exhibition in London. Aliki's sister-in-law said, "Why don't you write a book about this? It's archaeology." Aliki had actually thought of the idea but had dismissed it. When her sister-in-law used the word archaeology, Aliki says she could "relate to that word, having written about dinosaurs and fossils, etc. I decided I'd do it if I could include all that I wish to. Why do we never learn to walk away . . . ?" HarperCollins released the book in 1999 for the 400th anniversary of the Globe.

Of her family Aliki says, "I have a great family, starting with my parents (their bodies are gone but their souls remain). My husband, Franz, is loyal and understanding and cleans up all the mess I make in the garden and the kitchen. Our son, Jason, went to the New York University Film School and is a script writer/director/musician and could succeed in painting, too. Our daughter, Alexa, has written and illustrated two books, illustrated two more, and is trying for more. We all have difficult lives of freelancing in the arts. You've got to LOVE it."

Aliki and Franz used to travel in Europe every summer. They also have traveled in the United States, Mexico, and Egypt. "I have to travel a lot because everyone I love—friends and family—live in the States. That allows plenty of time here to work, but missing them is not easy. I visit schools because I love children and teachers and feel it's my duty to go whenever I can. My teachers gave me so much; it is my way of giving back. I go on tours for my books and to conferences and so forth."

The Brandenbergs have been residents of England for more than two decades. They enjoy the theater, music, films, and their friends. Aliki spends her time creating books, traveling, and enjoying her family.

BOOKS AND NOTES

In addition to illustrating her own books, Aliki illustrated books for other writers earlier in her career. The majority of her recent illustrative work is for books that she has authored, although she continues to illustrate books written by her husband, Franz Brandenberg.

Aliki has revised some of her books to include full-color illustrations and, in some cases, to revise the illustrations, including more females and a diversity of cultures. For example, in *Digging Up Dinosaurs,* the paleontologist on the front cover of the 1981 edition was male; the 1988 revision has a female paleontologist on the cover instead. Other dinosaur books were revised to reflect scientific name changes for some dinosaurs.

Aliki also has contributed to two anthologies that benefit the environment and the homeless. Aliki contributed text and illustrations to *The Big Book for Our Planet,* edited by Ann Durell (Dutton, 1993), and contributed illustrations for *Home: A Collaboration of Thirty Distinguished Authors and Illustrators of Children's Books to Aid the Homeless* (HarperCollins, 1992).

Information Books

Corn Is Maize: The Gift of the Indians (Crowell, 1976; Harper Trophy, 1986).

Digging Up Dinosaurs (Crowell, 1981; revised 1988).

The King's Day: Louis XIV of France (Crowell, 1989).

A Medieval Feast (Crowell, 1983).

My Five Senses (Crowell, 1989).

My Visit to the Dinosaurs (Crowell, 1969; Harper, 1985).

Picture Book Fiction

Best Friends Together Again (Greenwillow, 1995).

Christmas Tree Memories (HarperCollins, 1991).

I'm Growing! (HarperCollins, 1992).

Marianthe's Story, Painted Words: Marianthe's Story, Spoken Memories (Greenwillow, 1998).

My Visit to the Zoo (HarperCollins, 1997).

Those Summers (HarperCollins, 1996).

FOR MORE INFORMATION

Web Sites

University of Southern Mississippi, de Grummond Collection: Aliki Brandenberg Papers. URL: <http://www.lib.usm.edu/~degrum/findaids/brandenb.htm> (Accessed March 2000).

Mitsumasa Anno

◆ Mathematics ◆ Folklore ◆ Word/Visual Play

Tokyo, Japan
March 20, 1926

📖 *Anno's Journey*

📖 *Topsy-Turvies: More Pictures to Stretch the Imagination*

ABOUT THE AUTHOR/ILLUSTRATOR

Mitsumasa Anno, the internationally popular Japanese writer and illustrator of children's books, is known simply as Anno to most of his readers. Anno was born on March 20, 1926. His parents operated a bustling inn, located in Tsuwano, a small historic town in western Japan. While other school children learned how to copy pictures from books, Anno's teacher taught his class to create drawings from their imaginations. Once, they were encouraged to illustrate the tale of Urashima Taro, a Japanese folk character who had been to the Sea God's palace. Another time, the students drew images of what they wanted to be when they grew up. Many of his teachers encouraged Anno and the other children to observe the natural world, and Anno learned how to sketch and draw directly from nature.

Anno spent his early years near the town of Tsuwano but left to attend high school. He dreamt of becoming an artist and continued to draw and paint. He also thought about becoming a professional player of *go*, a Japanese game similar to checkers. During World War II, he served in the army and later went to Paris, where he visited the tomb of Van Gogh and read books by Maurice Escher. Anno later graduated from Yamaguchi College and taught art before beginning his own career as an artist.

Anno has said that his interest in children's books began as a labor of love. In the past few decades, this interest has become a full-time career, and Anno works six hours a day illustrating children's books. He creates his illustrations with watercolors.

Anno produces three types of books. The first type features numerical references and optical illusions. *Anno's Alphabet* (Crowell, 1974), for example, features what appear to be normal objects in normal environments, but a closer examination reveals that nothing is quite what it seems. For example, a hatchet handle is part of a tree trunk, a typewriter has only one letter, and a tube of orange paint disappears into the artist's palette. Anno also likes to play with scale in his illustrations. In *The King's Palace* (Collins, 1979), a king wants his possessions to be bigger than those of anyone else. His toothbrush is so enormous that it takes two people to move it. Anno's detailed drawings help bring a sense of normalcy to such objects, a task that few artists could accomplish.

The second theme typical of Anno's work is travel, and the books in this category are pictorial records of his own trips—with many creative additions. These wordless travel books take readers through Europe (*Anno's Journey*; Philomel, 1978 and *Anno's Italy*; Philomel, 1980), Great Britain (*Anno's Britain*; Philomel, 1982), and the United States (*Anno's USA*; Philomel, 1983). Anno cleverly hides images and characters in these books. Readers quickly spot well-known characters, but others are significant only to Anno himself. For example, Judy Taylor, an editor at a prestigious publishing house, was extremely helpful to Anno when he was gathering images for *Anno's Journey*. In appreciation, Anno included Taylor's house in *Anno's Britain*, among those of well-known people such as Arthur Rackham, Kate Greenaway, and William Morris.

Each of Anno's journey books is filled with expanses of fields, rivers, towns, castles, country fairs, gardens, and cathedrals. Dozens of characters populate each illustration. They take part in numerous activities, from running races and fighting duels to dumping tea into Boston Harbor. In *Anno's Britain*, Anno arrives by boat and travels the countryside. While there, he meets a copper craftsman, a tinker, Prince Charles, and Princess Diana. He also visits the Tower of London, the Loch Ness Monster, Shakespearean characters (King Lear and the Merchant of Venice), and storybook characters (Peter Pan, Tinkerbell, Alice in Wonderland, Jack and the Giant, Winnie the Pooh, and Toad from *The Wind in the Willows*). In *Anno's USA*, he follows a similar format. His boat takes him first to Hawaii and then on to the San Francisco Bay. Anno travels by horseback across the continent. Along the way, he meets historical figures such as John Muir, Betsy Ross, and the Wright Brothers. He also encounters other popular characters such as King Kong, Dorothy from *The Wizard of Oz*, and Superman.

A third type of book, characteristic of Anno's work, features the retelling of classic folk stories such as *Kitsune ga hirotta grimm dowa* (The Grimm Tales That the Fox Gathered).

In Japan, Anno has received several awards, including the Minister of Education Award for Encouraging New Talent of Art and the Shogakukan Award for Illustrations for Children. He has received several citations and awards in the United States for his work as well. In 1984, he received the international Hans Christian Andersen Award for illustration.

Anno lives with his wife, Midori Suetsugu, in Tokyo. Together, they raised a daughter, Seiko, as well as a son, Masaichiro, who co-authored and co-illustrated three of Anno's recent books. Anno believes that *Anno's Counting House* (Ju-nin no Yukai-na Hikkoshi) has received the most favorable response from his readers. When asked what he is doing now, Anno simply replies, "I'm living peacefully."

BOOKS AND NOTES

Those of Anno's books that feature numerical references and optical illusions were inspired by Anno's study of the work of Maurice Escher. Often his illustrations encourage the reader to question what is "normal" or real, much as the work of Escher does.

Books Written and Illustrated by Mitsumasa Anno

Books with Optical Illusions

Anno's Faces (Philomel, 1989).

Anno's Magical ABC: An Anamorphic Alphabet. Co-authored with Masaichiro Anno. (Philomel, 1980, 1981).

Anno's Masks (Philomel, 1990).

Anno's Sundial (Philomel, 1987).

Topsy-Turvies: More Pictures to Stretch the Imagination (Philomel, 1989).

Upside-Downer: Pictures to Stretch the Imagination (Philomel, 1971; 1988).

Folklore Retellings

Anno's Aesop: A Book of Fables by Aesop and Mr. Fox (Orchard, 1989).

Anno's Twice Told Tales: The Fisherman and His Wife & the Four Clever Brothers (Philomel, 1993).

Socrates and the Three Little Pigs. Written by Tuyosi Mori. (Philomel, 1986).

Journey Books

Throughout each of the wordless journeys, Anno teaches the reader through illustration about each country (or in the case of *Anno's Journey*, about Europe).

Anno's Britain (Philomel, 1982).

Anno's Italy (Philomel, 1980).

Anno's Journey (Philomel, 1978).

Anno's USA (Philomel, 1983).

Math Books

Anno's Math Games (Philomel, 1982, 1987).

Anno's Math Games II (Philomel, 1990).

Anno's Math Games III (Philomel, 1991).

Miscellaneous

The Animals: Selected Poems. Poems by Michio Mado. Illustrated by Mitsumasa Anno. Translated by the Empress Michiko of Japan. (McElderry, 1992).

FOR MORE INFORMATION

Books

Morse, Samuel Crowell (Translator and Adapter). *The Unique World of Mitsumasa Anno: Selected Works, 1968–1977* (Philomel, 1980).

Caroline Arnold

◆ Animals, Nonfiction

Pittsburgh, Pennsylvania
May 16, 1944

📖 *African Animals*

📖 *Koala*

📖 *Stone Age Farmers Besiege*
   the Sea

📖 *Zebra*

Arthur Arnold

ABOUT THE AUTHOR

If someone had told Caroline Scheaffer that she would grow up to write children's books, she would have been as surprised as anyone. Born in 1944 in Pittsburgh, Pennsylvania, Caroline spent the first ten years of her life in a settlement house in Minneapolis where her parents, Lester L. Scheaffer and Catherine Young Scheaffer, were social workers.

During her summers, she often visited at a Wisconsin camp called Camp Hodag, named for a monster with the head of an ox, the feet of a bear, the back of a dinosaur, and the tail of an alligator. Campfire stories included legends about the Hodag. At camp, she saw many wild animals. She watched deer leaping through the underbrush and porcupines scurrying up trees. She wanted to learn about these animals and was delighted whenever she uncovered a fact that she considered amazing or unusual. She loved to read and especially liked the books of Maude Hart Lovelace and Carol Ryrie Brink, as well as the pioneer stories that Laura Ingalls Wilder wrote.

When Caroline was an adult, her mother found some writing that she had done at school. One piece discussed how to make maple syrup, and another (written when Caroline was in first grade) told of a train ride the family took from Minneapolis across the Mississippi River to St. Paul. She noted that the trip cost 14¢, and "when you push a button the seat will go back."

Arnold has said that she wrote little other than school essays when she was young, but she did keep journals of some of her experiences. Once, the family went on a camping trip to Glacier National Park in Montana. Caroline kept a journal. When the family returned home, they used photographs that they had taken and Caroline's journal to create an album of the trip. "I now realize," says Arnold, "that this was my first photo essay. I still enjoy choosing photos from a trip and making them into a story."

At age twenty, Caroline left for college with plans to become a painter. In 1966, she earned a B.A. from Grinnell College in Iowa. At the age of twenty-three (in 1967), she married Arthur Arnold. A year later, she earned a master's degree in art from the University of Iowa. For the next ten years, Caroline Arnold worked with young people as an art teacher. She did not start writing children's books until she was more than thirty years old, but she began to gather inspiration for her writing many years before. In 1971, for example, the Arnolds lived in East Africa for four months. Arthur Arnold was doing scientific research at a national park in western Uganda. During those months, Caroline Arnold had daily encounters with wild animals. She had the opportunity to observe lions lolling in the grass, giraffes eating from the leafy treetops, and cheetah cubs playing with their mother. There were warthogs rooting in the ground and marabou storks swooping down to steal freshly cleaned fish. She noted how the animals behaved in the wild and learned how scientists studied them.

Arnold kept a written journal of her experiences. She also wrote letters to friends and family, and the couple took many photographs. Years later, these notes and photographs became part of her extensive research for a book. Her family had saved the letters she wrote from Africa, and those, too, became part of the material that helped her to write the text for *African Animals* (Morrow, 1997).

When her children, Jennifer and Matthew, were young, Arnold often illustrated books for them. Soon, she realized that she could write the stories to go with the illustrations. It wasn't long before publishers noticed her work. One of her first books, *Electric Fish* (Morrow, 1980), was selected an Outstanding Science Trade Book by the Children's Book Council and the National Science Teachers Association.

Eventually the family moved to Los Angeles, where Arthur Arnold worked as a neurobiologist, teaching animal behavior at the University of California at Los Angeles. By now several of Caroline Arnold's manuscripts had been published.

In 1983, the Arnold family traveled to Australia. They spent part of their trip on Heron Island on the Great Barrier Reef. Caroline Arthur, an amateur photographer, took many photographs, and when the family returned home, she realized that she had another book.

Earlier, Arnold had met a woman in a writing class whose husband was a professional photographer named Richard Hewett. When a publisher asked Arnold to write two books, one about koalas and another about kangaroos, she asked Hewett if he would like to collaborate with her. Arnold and Hewett traveled to Australia and spent two weeks in a wildlife park. Morrow published both books in 1987. The titles were named Outstanding Science Trade Books. After this initial success, editors asked Arnold and Hewett to collaborate on more animal books.

As Arnold and Hewett's animal series developed, they attempted to write about animals from different parts of the world. The books are published in pairs. For each pair, Arnold writes about animals that live on the same continent or, in some cases, even in the same environment. Arnold often chooses to write about endangered wildlife because she feels it is important for children to realize the plight of these animals.

Because of the time and expense involved in each project, Arnold and Hewett often visit zoos and wild animal parks to gather information and to take photographs. These animals are more accustomed to interaction with people, and Arnold and Hewett are able to get closer to the animals, especially the baby animals that often become the focus of Arnold's work.

Once Arnold identifies a subject for a book, she and a photographer (often Hewett, but she does work with others), select a zoo or wildlife park that will provide appropriate opportunities for photography. Her next step is to do background research, take notes, and prepare a basic outline. The notes and outline provide the photographer with a list of pictures they will need. Sometimes the photographer has the opportunity to capture an image of something neither of them could have predicted. Those photographs may suggest changes for Arnold's text. Once the book, text, and photographs are complete, Arnold and her partner submit the completed manuscript to their editor.

Arnold's interest and curiosity are most often the impetus for her writing, but sometimes someone suggests a topic to her. Her childhood interest in fossils, and later in the La Brea tar pits, gave her the idea to do research for *Trapped in Tar: Fossils from the Ice Age* (Clarion, 1987). After her editor read that book, she suggested Arnold write another one about dinosaurs. The editor came up with the idea after reading a reference in Arnold's book to fossils found at Dinosaur National Monument in Utah.

Not all of Arnold's books are about nature, however. Both of her children play violin, which inspired *Music Lessons for Alex* (Clarion, 1985). Jennifer and Matthew appeared in the photographs for this book and have appeared in other books as well. Matthew's interest in soccer gave Arnold the idea for *Soccer: From Neighborhood Play to the World Cup* (Watts, 1991).

Most of Arnold's books are nonfiction, but she has written one fiction book, *The Terrible Hodag* (Harcourt, 1989), which was inspired by her days around the campfire at Camp Hodag. By 1996, Arnold had written about many subjects, ranging from lions to dinosaurs and from sports to archaeology. She had ninety-eight books published since 1980.

In 1997, four more books were published, pushing her list of published books over the 100 mark. *Stone Age Farmers Beside the Sea: Scotland's Prehistoric Village of Skara Brae* (Clarion, 1997) is the result of a vacation in Scotland. During that 1992 trip, the Arnolds visited the Stone Age ruins in the Orkney Islands. The trip provided Arnold's text, which was accompanied by Arthur Arnold's photographs. The third book, a collaboration with Roger Hewett, was written about bobcats. The pair had been working together at a zoo for another title, *Fox* (Morrow, 1996), when they discovered a pair of bobcats. While Hewett waited for the kit foxes to wake and move about their enclosure, he photographed the bobcats. Those photographs became the basis for their 1997 book, *Bobcats* (Lerner).

The fourth 1997 book came about when Arnold's work with photographer Robert Kruidenier was displayed together in a museum exhibit concerned with the plight of California birds. Kruidenier worked with an organization called HawkWatch International, a team of volunteers and scientists that help endangered birds. He had spent several summers in the Goshute Mountains of Eastern Nevada trapping and banding migrating raptors. Arnold knew Kruidenier's photographs would make a great book. To write the book, she had to visit the Goshute Mountains herself. Kruidenier invited her to accompany him on his next visit to the mountains, so Arnold rented a backpack, borrowed a tent, and flew to Salt Lake City where her adventure began. From there, she traveled to the trailhead at the bottom of the mountain.

Arnold intended to take notes and observe other people working. Before long, however, she was recording data, running errands, and sometimes even handling the birds. As she began to understand the process, she listed new topics that she could cover in her book. Although Kruidenier already had many photographs available to accompany the manuscript, they discussed possible additions. Kruidenier took more photographs during Arnold's stay in the Goshute Mountains. Later, the collaborators worked together to layout the text with the photographs.

In 1998, Carolrhoda published Arnold's 103rd and 104th books: *Mealtime for Zoo Animals* and *Children of the Settlement Houses*. Arthur Arnold continues to work as a neurobiologist at UCLA. Their daughter, Jennifer, is a linguist at Stanford University, and their son, Matthew, is a medical student at the University of California at Davis. When Caroline Arnold is not working, she enjoys a variety of pastimes. She plays tennis once a week and likes to garden and watch movies. On weekends, the Arnolds often hike or bird watch in the mountains north of Los Angeles. They also like to travel and gather new ideas for books.

BOOKS AND NOTES

The majority of Caroline Arnold's books deal with animals. Many are photo essays. The texts are well organized and provide a variety of information, including how animals live in their natural habitat and in captivity. The focus often is on the young of the species.

Books Written by Caroline Arnold

Animals

Bat. Illustrated by Richard Hewett. (Morrow, 1996)

Camel. Illustrated by Richard Hewett. (Morrow, 1992).

Elephant. Illustrated by Richard Hewett. (Morrow, 1993).

Flamingo. Illustrated by Richard Hewett. (Morrow, 1991).

Monkey. Illustrated by Richard Hewett. (Morrow, 1993).

Prairie Dogs. Illustrated by Jean Cassels. (Scholastic, 1993).

Sea Turtles. Illustrated by Marshall Peck III. (Scholastic, 1994).

Miscellaneous

Caroline Arnold has written about holidays, extinct animals, and ancient historical sites, as well as about contemporary topics that her children have suggested. Some of these books are listed below.

Dinosaurs Down Under and Other Fossils from Australia. Illustrated by Richard Hewett. (Clarion, 1990).

Dinosaur Mountain: Graveyard of the Past. Illustrated by Richard Hewett. (Clarion, 1989).

Juggler. Illustrated by Richard Hewett. (Clarion, 1988).

Music Lessons for Alex. Illustrated by Richard Hewett. (Clarion, 1985).

Trapped in Tar: Fossils from the Ice Age. Illustrated by Richard Hewett. (Clarion, 1987).

FOR MORE INFORMATION

Web Sites

Caroline Arnold Web Site. URL: <http://www.geocities.com/Athens/1264> (Accessed March 2000).

Frank Asch

◆ Bears ◆ Poetry

Somerville, New Jersey
August 6, 1946

📖 *Here Comes the Cat!*
📖 *Popcorn*
📖 *Shadow Bear*

Jan Asch

ABOUT THE AUTHOR/ILLUSTRATOR

Frank Asch has described himself as a country kid who enjoyed playing in nearby woods and exploring the brook. One of the few days that Frank Asch recalls having had an interest in school occurred during high school when he walked into the art room and saw a bulletin board captioned "Frank Asch—One-Man Show." The board was covered with his drawings.

Asch grew up in Somerville, New Jersey, and then went on to study art at the Pratt Institute and Cooper Union in New York. While Asch was at Cooper Union, Maurice Sendak helped to interest him in creating children's books. But Asch did not move straight from art school into illustrating and writing children's books. Both he and his wife, Janani (Jan), are trained

Montessori teachers, and in addition to accepting teaching assignments in New Jersey and India, they have performed as storytellers and puppeteers. He and Jan were both involved in children's theater, and their stage name was "the Bellybuttons." They wrote their own material, and Jan was in charge of the music.

Eventually, Frank Asch's interest in creating books began to develop. His first book, *George's Store* (McGraw-Hill, 1969), features a main character who is a lot like Asch's Uncle Jack. *Elvira Everything* (Harper, 1970) came from his experiences living on Ludlow street, a center for the wholesale toy business. His own dog, Rebecka, inspired a book titled *Rebecka* (Harper, 1972) His poems in *City Sandwich* (Greenwillow, 1978) came from his years of living in New York, and his interest in Yoga resulted in *Gia and the Hundred Dollars Worth of Bubble Gum* (McGraw-Hill, 1974). Asch says, "My books grew out of my paintings. Instead of painting one painting at a time, I preferred to paint a series, showing form and colors progressing from canvas to canvas. There is a very thin line between my work and my life."

Young readers are most familiar with Frank Asch's picture books, especially his "bear" books, but he has also written several books for older readers. In the late 1980s, Asch began an ongoing collaboration with a Soviet illustrator, Vladimir Vagin. The first book they created was *Here Comes the Cat!* (Scholastic, 1989). At the time, neither could speak the other's language, although Vagin now lives in the United States and speaks English.

One of Asch's most popular characters is a little bear who has starred in *Moonbear* (Scribner, 1978), *Mooncake* (Prentice-Hall, 1983), and *Bear Shadow* (Prentice-Hall, 1985). In 1998, Asch said he was "currently working on another 'bear' book called *Moonbear's Dream*. He said the book, "was inspired directly from a dream I had. I often give over my creative problems to my subconscious. I just study the problem and then take a nap or wait a day and the solution [comes]." *Moonbear's Dream* was published by Simon & Schuster in 1999.

Asch says that he does not think it is "accurate to say that I make up stories out of my head," even if it seems that way at times. "There's always some experience, relationship, or involvement in the real world that supports any flight of fancy I might take in a story."

Even his poems come from experience. *Cactus Poems* (Harcourt, 1998) took Asch to the desert where he camped for several months. That experience helped him create the poems but "in turn has influenced my fiction picture books for younger children, giving them more of a realistic flavor in subtle ways."

Today the Asch family lives in a small country town in Vermont, where they raised their son Devin, who was born in 1979. The family cuts their own wood and raises much of their food in a big garden. Together they enjoy horses and skiing. Frank Asch is a full-time writer who averages two to three books a year.

BOOKS AND NOTES

Many of Frank Asch's books feature a simply drawn bear who observes the moon and wonders at the everyday things that are around him. Asch fishes, makes friends, and observes nature. He also writes poetry and continues to encourage and mentor his friend, artist/illustrator Vladimir Vagin.

Books Written and Illustrated by Frank Asch

Little Bear Books

Baby Bird's First Nest (Harcourt, 1999).

Barnyard Lullaby (Simon & Schuster, 1998).

Good Night, Baby Bear (Harcourt, 1998).

Moonbear's Books (Little Simon, 1993).

Moonbear's Canoe (Little Simon, 1993).

Moonbear's Dream (Simon & Schuster, 1999)

Moonbear's Pet (Simon & Schuster, 1997).

Moondance (Scholastic, 1993).

Sand Cake (Gareth Stevens, 1993).

Poetry

Cactus Poems. Illustrated by Ted Lewin. (Harcourt, 1998).

Sawgrass Poems: A View of the Everglades (Harcourt, 1995).

Collaborations

Dear Brother. Co-created with Vladimir Vagin. (Scholastic, 1992).

The Flower Faerie. Co-created with Vladimir Vagin. (Scholastic, 1993).

Here Comes the Cat! Co-created with Vladimir Vagin. (Scholastic, 1989).

Insects from Outer Space. Co-created with Vladimir Vagin (Scholastic, 1994).

FOR MORE INFORMATION

Books

Asch, Frank. *One Man Show* (R. C. Owen, 1997). Illustrated with photographs by Jan Asch.

Jim Aylesworth

◆ Folklore (Literary) ◆ Friends ◆ Family Relationships

Jacksonville, Florida
February 21, 1943

📖 *The Completed Hickory Dickory Dock*

📖 *My Son John*

📖 *Old Black Fly*

📖 *Shenandoah Noah*

ABOUT THE AUTHOR

Scott Campbell

Jim Aylesworth was born in Jacksonville, Florida on February 21, 1943, but he lived in many places during his childhood, including Alabama, Texas, and Indiana. At age fifteen, he and his family ended up in Hinsdale, Illinois, and he graduated from Hinsdale Central High School in 1961. Four years later, he graduated from Miami University in Oxford, Ohio, with a B.A. in English. He returned to Hinsdale and began a career as a stockbroker.

After five years, Aylesworth realized that he did not like what he was doing. The year was 1970, and all of his friends were "doing their own thing." Aylesworth began to consider what he really wanted to do. Kids kept coming into the picture. He took a job in a theater at night and worked as a substitute teacher during the day. He returned to school to earn a teaching certificate.

As a substitute teacher, he usually was sent to a junior high school, but one day he was assigned to a second-grade class. That was a turning point for Aylesworth, and he began to consider teaching younger children. He began teaching first-grade students in Oak Park, Illinois, in 1971, and in 1978, he earned a master's degree in elementary education from Concordia College in River Forest, Illinois. He taught first graders for twenty-five years, until he retired (in 1996) to become a full-time writer.

During his teaching years, Aylesworth regarded "story time" as his favorite part of the day. He has said, "I've read hundreds and hundreds of books out loud to my kids, and decided I would like to be more of a part of the world of books." At first he simply wished he could write a book, but he finally got up the nerve to try it. For years, he collected rejection slips. These letters accumulated to form a pile of about six inches, but he persevered. In 1980, his first book, *Hush Up!*, was published by Holt, with illustrations by Glen Rounds.

Aylesworth says that he shares a fear with many other authors—that he will one day run out of story ideas. Of course, that hasn't happened yet, and Aylesworth says the ideas seem to be all around him. The premise of *Siren in the Night* (Whitman, 1983) came from a true experience where his family's peaceful sleep was interrupted by the startling sound of an approaching fire engine. The sight of a lady dressed up on a Sunday morning inspired *Mary's Mirror* (Holt, 1982). Some book ideas just seem to flow for Aylesworth, but he says that others resist being recorded on paper. He worked on *Shenandoah Noah* (Holt, 1985) on and off for five years before finally completing it.

His writing has parodied such common nursery rhymes as *My Son John* (Holt, 1994) and *The Completed Hickory Dickory Dock* (Atheneum, 1990) and has introduced memorable new characters. *Shenandoah Noah* is a classic character, as is the old black fly that meets the natural consequences in *Old Black Fly* (Holt, 1992).

With their two sons fully grown, Jim and his wife, Donna, moved from Hinsdale to Chicago where Jim continues to write. He travels extensively to speak to children in schools and at book events across the United States. For many summers, he returned to Concordia College to teach a course in children's literature and occasionally is an adjunct faculty member at other colleges in the area.

BOOKS AND NOTES

When Jim Aylesworth writes, he likes to produce rhyme, rhythm, and repetition. Although he feels that plot is important, his main focus is on the sound of his words. If a book reads well out loud, it meets his goal as a writer.

Aunt Pitty Patty's Piggy. Illustrated by Barbara McClintock. (Scholastic, 1999).

The Completed Hickory Dickory Dock. Illustrated by Eileen Christelow. (Atheneum, 1990).

The Full Belly Bowl. Illustrated by Wendy Halperin. (Atheneum, 1999).

The Gingerbread Man. Illustrated by Barbara McClintock. (Scholastic, 1998).

Hanna's Hog. Illustrated by Glen Rounds. (Atheneum, 1988).

Hush Up! Illustrated by Glen Rounds. (Holt, 1980).

Mary's Mirror. Illustrated by Richard Egielski. (Holt, 1982).

McGraw's Emporium. Illustrated by Mavis Smith. (Holt, 1995).

My Sister's Rusty Bike. Illustrated by Richard Hull. (Atheneum, 1996).

My Son John. Illustrated by David Frampton. (Holt, 1994).

Old Black Fly (Holt, 1992).

One Crow: A Counting Rhyme. Illustrated by Ruth Young. (Lippincott, 1988).

Shenandoah Noah. Illustrated by Glen Rounds. (Holt, 1985).

Siren in the Night. Illustrated by Tom Centola. (Whitman, 1983).

Splash! Illustrated by Jason Wolff. (Atheneum, 2000).

Teddy Bear Tears. Illustrated by Jo Ellen McAllister-Stammen. (Atheneum, 1997).

Through the Night. Illustrated by Pamela Patrick. (Atheneum, 1998).

Wake Up, Little Children: A Rise-and-Shine Rhyme. Illustrated by Walter Lyon Krudop. (Atheneum, 1996).

FOR MORE INFORMATION

Web Sites

Jim Aylesworth—Teacher, Author, Lecturer. URL: <http://www.ayles.com> (Accessed March 2000).

Molly Garrett Bang

◆ Family Relationships ◆ Folklore

Princeton, New Jersey
December 29, 1943

📖 *The Grey Lady and the Strawberry Snatcher*
📖 *Ten, Nine, Eight*
📖 *Wiley and the Hairy Man*

ABOUT THE AUTHOR/ILLUSTRATOR

Molly Garrett Bang was born in Princeton, New Jersey on December 29, 1943. Her father, Frederick Barry Bang, was a research physician; her mother, Betsy Garrett Bang, was a medical researcher. Her mother was a translator as well, and she later authored several books that Molly illustrated.

Molly Bang has fond memories of discovering Arthur Rackham's illustrations in her parents' library. She loved looking at his work and even then wanted to illustrate children's books herself. After her graduation from high school, Bang attended Wellesley College, earning a B.A. degree in French in 1965. She did not want to be a French teacher, so she went to teach English at Doshisha University in Kyoto, Japan. One reason Bang chose to go to Japan was her interest in Japanese art. After eighteen months, Bang returned to the United States and studied at the University of Arizona (M.A. 1969) and Harvard University (M.A. 1971) for a master's degree in Oriental Studies.

Bang's parents later lived in Calcutta, India, and Molly visited them there. She remembers listening to folk stories by lamp light at early dusk. She spent eighteen months living in Calcutta and Bangladesh, where she illustrated health manuals for rural health projects for UNICEF and Johns Hopkins Center for Medical Research and Training. Her next assignment was as a civil servant in Mali. After twelve months, she returned to illustrating health manuals for village health workers and midwives. The basis for the development of the manuals was the folk literature of the area. That experience sparked Bang's interest in folklore from various cultures.

Bang later worked for the *Baltimore Sun* as part of its reporting staff. That job ended when she was laid off. If they had kept her on staff, she might never have written a children's book.

Bang had difficulty getting her first work published. It was a whimsical story of a strawberry snatcher who tries to take strawberries from a lady (later known as the Grey Lady), but as he follows her from shop to shop, he finds some blackberries instead. The book had no words, and editors thought children would not be able to relate to all the color and the odd-looking creatures. They said there was no market for her work, that it was "too scary" and "too much in the Japanese manner." No one wrote the way she illustrated.

Bang says "one has to search for the right publisher for a given idea—there is always one out there." So she decided to compile her own collection of stories; a collection that would suit her style of illustration. That first compilation was *The Goblins Giggle and Other Stories* (Scribner, 1973), which was followed by a second collection, *Men from the Village Deep in the Mountains and Other Japanese Folk Tales* (Macmillan, 1973). The second compilation was translations of stories she heard during her time in Japan. The works that followed were, for the most part, derived from her experiences in Japan, Indian, and Bangladesh. Bang collaborated with her mother to produce four books. The books are translations or adaptations of Indian and Bangladeshi tales. Finally, her first work was published as *The Grey Lady and the Strawberry Snatcher* (Four Winds, 1980). It became a bestseller and was named a 1981 Caldecott Honor Book.

Bang's illustrations vary from watercolor on gray construction paper, which she used for *The Grey Lady and the Strawberry Snatcher*, to collage illustrations using recycled magazines as in *Chattanooga Sludge* (Harcourt, 1996), to three-dimensional dioramas used for *One Fall Day* (Greenwillow, 1994). When she illustrated *Men from the Village Deep in the Mountains and Other Japanese Folk Tales*, she used the Japanese Sumi style but later evolved to include a diversity of media in her work.

Each of the books Molly Bang has illustrated have been set in regions or countries where Bang visited. The lone exception is *Tye May and the Magic Brush* (Greenwillow, 1981), which is set in China. Her experiences are important parts of her work. Before illustrating *Wiley and the Hairy Man* (Macmillan, 1976), for example, Bang spent three months riding through the south on a motorcycle to familiarize herself with the people and the region that inspired the African American tale.

After authoring several original stories, Bang renewed her interest in folk literature when she adapted a Japanese tale, "The Crane Wife," by retelling the story as *Dawn* (Morrow, 1983). In this adaptation, a shipbuilder marries a mysterious woman, who makes him promise never to look at her while she weaves. Bang replaces the crane with a Canadian Goose.

Bang later retold *The Paper Crane* (Greenwillow, 1985), a tale of a mysterious man who enters a restaurant and pays for his dinner with a paper crane that magically comes alive and dances. The crane helps the restaurant attract customers, but when it becomes a thriving business, the crane loses its magic.

For many years, Molly Garrett Bang lived with her husband, Richard Campbell, and their daughter, Monika, on Cape Cod in Massachusetts. She was a reporter and editor with the *Woods Hold Passage*, her hometown newspaper. Now she divides her time between Falmouth, Massachusetts, where her parents live, and California, where she is interested and involved in environmental concerns.

BOOKS AND NOTES

Molly Garrett Bang has illustrated folktales retold or translated by her mother Betsy Garrett Bang and has retold her own versions of folktales. She also has written and illustrated original stories, some of which focus on environmental issues. She illustrates using a variety of media, including watercolor, collage, and dioramas.

Folklore

The Buried Moon and Other Stories (Scribner, 1977).

Dawn (Morrow, 1983).

The Demons of Rajpur: Five Tales from Bengal. Written by Betsy Bang. (Greenwillow, 1980).

The Old Woman and the Rice Thief. Written by Betsy Bang. (Greenwillow, 1978).

The Paper Crane (Greenwillow, 1985).

Tuntuni, the Tailor Bird. Written by Betsy Bang. (Greenwillow, 1978).

Tye May and the Magic Brush (Greenwillow, 1981).

Wiley and the Hairy Man: Adapted from an American Folktale (Macmillan, 1976).

Environmental Fiction

Chattanooga Sludge (Harcourt, 1996).

John Todd attempts to clean up the toxic waters of Chattanooga with a living machine.

Common Ground: The Water, Earth, and Air We Share (Blue Sky, 1997).

Discusses a village where too many people are consuming too many resources.

FOR MORE INFORMATION

Web Sites

Molly Bang. URL: <http://www.mollybang.com> (Accessed April 2000).

Graeme Base

Amersham, England
April 6, 1958

📖 *Animalia*

📖 *The Eleventh Hour: A Curious Mystery*

📖 *My Grandmother Lived in Gooligulch*

Earl Carter

ABOUT THE AUTHOR/ILLUSTRATOR

Graeme Base was born in Amersham, England. His family first lived in Beaconsfield, Buckinghamshire, and later moved to Weymouth in Dorset. In 1966, the family moved to Melbourne, Australia, where Base has lived ever since. His was a happy childhood, except for some rough times in primary school because he was one of the few English boys in the Australian school.

Graeme Base read books by J. R. R. Tolkien, Kenneth Grahame, and A. A. Milne. Each had an influence on him. By the time he was twelve, he had started to tell people that he would be a commercial artist when he grew up. He also discovered books illustrated by Sir John Tenniel, the illustrator of

Lewis Carroll's "Alice" books, and Ernest A. Shepard, the illustrator of A. A. Milne's *Winnie the Pooh*. In high school, Base discovered Salvador Dali. After high school, Base spent three years at the Swinburne College of Technology studying graphic design, earning a Diploma of Art in 1978. He then began working as a commercial artist, but "got sacked . . . for incompetencies." At the time, he also was playing in a rock band. His future wife, Robyn Paterson, was singing with the band.

Base began talking to art editors and taking his artwork portfolio to publishers. One editor suggested that he do something with an Australian theme, so he wrote and illustrated *My Grandma Lived in Gooligulch*. It was published in Australia in 1983 and Abrams published it in the United States in 1990. In 1995, Abrams released a pop-up version of the title. John Baker and Keith Moseley created the paper engineering, and it features Grandma riding atop a kangaroo, flying through the air in the mouth of a pelican, and popping up from among the ocean's waves. Dozens of native Australian animals and birds populate the tale.

The art editor who suggested Base's Australian work expressed interest in another piece. The art for "Hairy Hog" eventually became part of *Animalia* (Abrams, 1987). The art took Base three years to complete from the time the editor expressed an interest in the book to the finished product. Penguin Publishers in Australia printed 11,000 copies, almost double its usual run. Even before its official release date, the publisher went back to print an additional 10,000 copies. A week later, they printed 10,000 more copies and soon they decided to print an additional 25,000 copies. By 1989, the book had sold nearly a half million copies.

The publisher sold U.S. rights for the book to Abrams for $10,000 at the Frankfurt book fair. The representative for the U.S. publisher happened to be browsing at the Australian publisher's booth when he spotted Base's book. Spin-offs from the book resulted in an *Animalia Coloring Book* and an *Animalia Wall Frieze*, as well as posters of individual spreads from the book.

The great success of *Animalia* brought Base more job offers. Macmillan asked him to do two stories for its reading series. One of the stories he illustrated was Lewis Carroll's *Jabberwocky* (Abrams, 1989). In the United States Abrams released the work as a trade book in 1989. The book spawned another version, *Lewis Carroll's Jabberwocky: A Book of Brillig Dioramas* (Abrams, 1996).

Shortly after the *Jabberwocky* book, Base began working on a book about dragons that he had been considering for several years. As he was working on the dragon book, another idea emerged, a mystery story in pictures. *The Eleventh Hour: A Curious Mystery* (Abrams, 1989; Puffin, 1997) features clues hidden in the illustrations. The original idea had eleven animals attending an eleventh birthday party on November 11. They played eleven games and then the lights went out. At first, he had two basic ideas for the mystery. The first was that the dog would be dead; he rejected that idea. The second idea was to have the ostrich's jewelry stolen. He rejected that idea as well. Instead, he decided to have the animals rush to the feast, at 11:00 AM, and find the food missing. To gather images for this book, Graeme Base and his wife traveled extensively in Asia, Africa, and Europe. He said, "I traveled overseas in 1987 collecting ideas for *The Eleventh Hour*, and spent a month in the game parks of Kenya and Tanzania. It was an incredible experience to travel through herds of zebras and wildebeest and see giraffes, rhinos, elephants, lions, cheetahs, hippos, crocodiles, and even a leopard all running free in the wilds of Africa! I hope to return there one day."

Inspiration for other illustrations in the book came from Base's travels as well. He used St. Peter's Basilica in Rome as the model for the entrance to Horace's house. Paintings at the Uffizi Gallery in Florence, Italy, inspired the borders, and the rug is one that Base purchased in Istanbul. Indian motifs are included in the chess game. To provide a record of images he would like to use, Base photographs things he sees during his travels. He also draws small pencil sketches. The sketches and photographs help him create the final illustrations for his books.

Base's travels have provided him with some interesting experiences, too. He says, "We . . . traveled through northern India, where we thought we were going to be murdered by a taxi driver but were mistaken; Nepal where we thought we were going to die of exhaustion but finally reached the end of the trek; Europe where we thought we were going to be run over by several crazy European motorists, but they missed us; and U.S.A., where we thought we were going to die of overeating but ran out of money."

The Eleventh Hour was published in Australia in 1988. After completing the art for the book, Base returned to his dragon book. In early 1989, he decided that twelve dragon pictures would become a calendar. His work on with dragons continued, and in 1996, Abrams published *The Discovery of Dragons*. In this book, a Victorian scientist, R. W. Greasebeam, shares with readers the "rare" correspondence he has uncovered—correspondence that documents the discovery of some of the world's most spectacular dragons. Greasebeam has discovered "original" letters from a Viking, who wrote his notes on a piece of hide while pillaging Europe in the 9th century, and the delicate calligraphy of Soong Mei Ying, who wrote of her observations on precious vellum in the 13th century. Professor Greasebeam also finds the befuddled correspondence of a scientist, who used the world's first type-writer to write to his fiancée from the depths of Africa.

The Sign of the Seahorse (Abrams, 1992) was set totally underwater and inspired by "three weeks spent snorkeling and scuba diving in the Galapagos Islands, Martinique, and Australia's Great Barrier Reef." It was on this first dive that he found himself surrounded by the "stunning world of a coral reef." He says he "suddenly knew exactly what my next book would be. The title came next, as was the case with *The Eleventh Hour*, which only left me with the problem of coming up with a decent story."

Base describes his writing schedule as "very erratic." Sometimes he works all day, sometimes all night, and "sometimes not at all." Describing his creative process, Base says, "My paintings are done on illustration board with watercolors and transparent inks, using brushes, pencils, technical drawing pens, a scalpel (for scratching). I also use a very special tool called an airbrush, which actually sprays colors onto the board (very handy for painting skies and mist and breath from horses' mouths). I do exhaustive rough drawings and detailed designs before embarking on the finished art. I present my concept first, then the dummy, and finally the finished product." British artists who Base admired as a child, such as Sir John Tenniel, Ernest A. Shepard, Maxfield Parrish, and Robert Ingpen, have greatly inspired Base, as has the American artist, Michael Hague.

Base often puts personal references or images in his paintings. In *Animalia*, he drew himself in each illustration—as a boy in an orange and yellow striped sweater. He also includes a tiny letter *R*, for Robyn, in most of his illustrations, and in September 1990, the month his first child, James, was born, Base began including a tiny letter *J* in illustrations as well.

Base's life in Melbourne is "extraordinarily hectic, exciting, exhausting and very rewarding from a creative point of view." Although he has enjoyed traveling extensively for the past twenty years, he says that he has lived in Australia "since the age of eight and intends to be there well into the next century." Base's list of favorite things includes Vegemite, Norway blue, leopards, and playing the guitar. The guitar playing and his earlier association with a band might have been the inspiration for one of his books, *The Worst Band in the Universe* (Abrams, 1999).

Base continues to travel, gathering images for his lush illustrations. He lives and works in Melbourne in a house near the sea with his artist wife, Robyn, and their children: James (b. 1990), Katherine (b. 1993), and William (b. 1995). Base's main hobby is writing and playing music. He says, "I write most of my music on guitar and keyboards, using a computer to record the songs, and hope one day to spent a lot more time on this interest. Whenever

I need a break from my illustration work, I pick up the guitar or pick out a tune on the piano." If he were not a full-time writer and illustrator, Base says he would "love to work as a musician."

BOOKS AND NOTES

Each of Graeme Base's books are heavily illustrated with lush and exotic images. He creates incredible imaginary worlds that will intrigue readers of all ages.

Animalia (Abrams, 1987).

The Eleventh Hour: A Curious Mystery (Abrams, 1989; Puffin, 1997).

Jabberwocky: From Through the Looking Glass (Abrams, 1989).

Lewis Carroll's Jabberwocky: A Book of Brillig Dioramas (Abrams, 1996).

My Grandma Lived in Gooligulch (Abrams, 1990; 1983).

My Grandma Lived in Gooligulch: A Pop-up Book. Paper engineering by John Baker and Keith Moseley. (Abrams, 1995).

The Sign of the Seahorse: A Tale of Greed and High Adventure in Two Acts (Abrams, 1992; Puffin, 1998).

The Worst Band in the Universe (Abrams, 1999).

FOR MORE INFORMATION

Limited information can be found on book jacket flaps. No articles, books, or Web sites were located.

Jan Brett

◆ Folklore ◆ Folklore (Literary)

Hingham, Massachusetts
December 1, 1949

📖 *Annie and the Wild Animals*
📖 *Berlioz the Bear*
📖 *The Mitten*

ABOUT THE AUTHOR/ILLUSTRATOR

Jan Brett was born and raised in Hingham, Massachusetts. She had many animals, including horses, dogs, cats, guinea pigs, and rabbits, and she spent a lot of time drawing them. She especially liked horses and drew them over and over again, trying to perfect her work. She also liked to read.

In the late 1960s, Brett attended the New London Academy (now Colby-Sawyer College), and in 1970 she attended the Boston Museum of Fine Arts School. She spent much time in the museum and marveled at the paintings of landscapes that filled rooms, as well as the stone sculptures, delicately embroidered kimonos, and ancient porcelain. Her illustrations are filled with images based on her experiences at the museum and with animals, as well as images she has gathered during extensive travel and research.

In 1970, Brett married Daniel Bowler, whom she divorced in 1979. They had one daughter, Lia. *Woodland Crossings* by Stephen Krensky (Atheneum, 1978) was illustrated by Brett under the name of Jan Brett Bowler. Her later books are published using the name of Jan Brett. In 1980, Brett married Joseph Hearne, a musician with the Boston Symphony Orchestra.

Daughter Lia's desire for a pet wolf or moose planted the seed for Brett's illustrated story, *Annie and the Wild Animals* (Houghton, 1985). The story tells of a little girl whose pet cat disappears in the woods. Over a period of days, a succession of wild animals visits the girl. Through the story, Brett is able to explore the differences between wild animals and friendly pets.

Ideas for many of her other books came from experiences in her life. Jan Brett once met a little girl, Miriam, who was very unusual. Miriam was very curious and Brett thought that her face could have come out of the past. She decided to put Miriam into a book. Miriam's sense of adventure brought about Brett's version of *Goldilocks and the Three Bears* (Putnam, 1987), in which she used Miriam as her model for both Goldilocks's spunky personality and her physical features. Brett's pet mouse, Little Pearl II, was a model for a mouse that readers can find in *Goldilocks and the Three Bears* and for the mouse that appears in *The Mitten* (Putnam, 1989).

Three teacher friends suggested that Brett retell *The Mitten* because they thought she would like to draw the animals and the snowy scenery she could include in the story. When she began to search for the story, she talked with an Ukrainian woman named Oxana Piaseckyj, who helped Brett by translating eight different versions of the story into English. One of the versions had the animals crawl into an old pot, which breaks into bits when too many animals squeeze in. A violent ending was included in another version that told of a hunter who goes back to find his lost glove filled with animals and subsequently blasts it with his gun to have food for his family's dinner.

After hearing different versions, Brett created a retelling that included the important aspects of the tale but gave the story a new twist at the end. Because the story was Ukrainian in origin, Brett and her husband, Joe Hearne, went to the Ukrainian section of New York City to find out what a Ukrainian house looked like and to gather other information about the Ukrainian culture. One of the guides at the museum suggested that the clothes should look too big because clothes often were handmade and had to last a long time. Clothes often were handed down from one wearer to another as well. Brett also learned that Ukrainians often hang a water jug on their fence to tell those passing by that they are welcome to help themselves to a cool drink and that a stork's nest on the cottage roof was thought to bring good luck. These elements became part of her book.

Brett had to decide whether to have the animals wear clothing and whether the animals should talk. She felt that the little boy should not talk if the animals did. She decided to use a hedgehog in the story, but hedgehogs live only in Europe, so she traveled to England to research hedgehogs and ended up adopting three at St. Tigglywinkles Wildlife Hospital and bringing them back to the United States with her.

At the suggestion of her art director, Brett used models for the people in *The Mitten*. The model for the little boy, Nicki, was one of Brett's neighbors, Tad Beagley, who seemed full of energy. Tad climbed trees, jumped walls, and leaped into the air so that Brett could take pictures. Baba's model was Brett's mother, Jean. Brett changed her mother's shiny brown hair to snowy white and put a long braid on her head. The Ukrainian home was filled with traditional ceramics, a fireplace, and coral beads. Some of Brett's research indicated that Ukrainian women would have worn a headscarf, so Brett put one on Baba. Later in the book, to make Baba look friendlier, Brett took the scarf off Baba's head and put it on a peg. Afterward, Brett learned that the custom of wearing a headscarf was old-fashioned and that some people considered it sexist, so she was glad she had made this change.

A research trip to Caribbean island of Martinique provided the images for the background setting of Edward Lear's *The Owl and the Pussycat* (Putnam, 1991). Brett's choice of settings came from a friend's sailing excursion to the area. The friend intended to stay only a short while, but he stayed for ten years. During her visit to Martinique, Brett saw many fishing boats in colors such as pink and azure blue that would not have been found in New England. Many women wore white blouses and skirts with white petticoats. They also wore brightly colored turbans, tied in a traditional fashion. Turbans tied with one point indicated that the wearer was single. Two points indicated that the wearer had a boyfriend, three points indicated marriage, and four points indicated that the wearer was married but loved attention.

The owl in the story is a worker on a sugarcane plantation who has just been paid. The pussycat owns her own little shop, one similar to many of those on Martinique. Pussycat is surprised at Owl's proposal. They go to sea in a pea-green boat with the name "Promise" on its side. Beneath the boat, Brett depicted a pair of yellow fish who have their own story. In Lear's original manuscript for *The Owl and the Pussycat*, the "bong tree" was drawn more like a "palm tree." Eventually she discovered a tree that looked as if it had ping pong balls all over it. She knew that was what a "bong tree" should look like. Brett depicted the Piggy, who was to marry the Owl and the Pussycat, as a beach comer (one who used to have a nine-to-five job); Brett's Turkey is a pompous individual.

For *The Wild Christmas Reindeer* (Putnam, 1990), Brett began with an idea about the North Pole. She drew on her childhood images of Santa Claus and the elves and an imaginary Santa's Winter farm. She wanted the reindeer to be important to the story, so she began to think about the problems that might develop if Santa asked an elf to prepare the reindeer for Christmas Eve. Brett thought about her own problems with her horse, Westminster. Sometimes when "Westy" would not do what she wanted him to do, Brett got angry and lost her temper. That only made things worse. Brett soon learned that if she remained calm, things improved. She had the same thing happen to the elf girl, Teeka, and the reindeer.

Teeka's image was modeled after a special girl named Natalie. Natalie acted out all of the things that Brett imagined Teeka would do in the story. Brett watched Natalie's movements and took photographs and drew sketches of her so that she could create realistic illustrations. The original drawings of Teeka depicted her with the same long hair and graceful curls that Natalie had. But Brett's editor suggested that the long hair made Teeka look too modern, so Brett redrew the images to show Teeka with shorter hair.

Research in museums in Norway brought images for the beautiful designs on sleighs, clocks, spoons, harnesses, and blankets. Brett discovered that caribou of North America and the reindeer in Europe are varieties of the same animal, so she conducted research at the University of Maine, where the scientists were studying caribou. Brett was able to get very close to the caribou. She even was able to find out what a caribou's tummy looked like so that she could show Lichen, one of the reindeer in her book, upside down. She decided the reindeer she was writing about were probably the great-great grandchildren of the ones that Clement Moore wrote about in *The Night Before Christmas*. This allowed her to name the reindeer, instead of using the traditional names for Moore's reindeer, and give each one his or her own personality. One reindeer, Tundra, liked being first and saw himself as a noble leader. The pure white and chubby reindeer was named Snowball. Crag was sometimes called "Crab" when he was too grumpy. Twilight was dark and mysterious, and Heather was easily frightened. She had big, brown eyes. Brett noticed that each caribou or reindeer's antlers are different, so she created each of the reindeer drawings with their own distinctive antlers. Bramble was named for the shape of his antlers. Because the seventh reindeer would often get started and forget to stop, he was named Windswept. The last reindeer was named Lichen because of the moss-like markings on his coat.

Brett's enjoyment of the Boston Symphony inspired *Berlioz the Bear* (Putnam, 1991). Her husband plays the double bass for the symphony, and Brett began to speculate about what would happen if something very small crawled into his bass and began to play. She learned that weather sometimes affects the musical instruments; for example, Joe's 300-year-old bass produces a loud and annoying buzz when it becomes too dry. Brett developed a story line about an orchestra composed of bears that have a problem getting to a town festival.

To gather the images for this story, Brett accompanied the Boston Symphony Orchestra on its tour to Europe and took a side trip to Bavaria. Brett and her husband went to a May Day festival in the hopes of being able to observe a town celebration, the kind often held in the town square. They were fortunate to find a concert in Grunwald. Brett sketched and photographed the costumed Bavarians as they raised the May Pole, as well as the orchestra as it played and the people dancing and enjoying *weisswurst*. The couple searched for a decorated band wagon similar to the ones they had seen depicted on posters and carvings, but they could not locate a real one until they visited the village of Bad Tolz. The folk museum in that village had a real cart. When they returned to Massachusetts, they had a scale model of the cart constructed so that she could use it as she painted her illustrations. She found an especially endearing plow horse in Bavaria, one that looked as if it really wanted to be in her book. The schnauzer that appears in the book is her neighbor's pet, Gretchen. When it came to the bear characters, Jan Brett looked toward the Boston Symphony. In her drawings, she lengthened her husband's nose, rounded his ears, covered him with fur, and he became Berlioz—the star of the book. The reddish bear was modeled after the symphony's clarinetist, Tom Martin, who is tall and lanky. The trombonist, Norman Bolter, became the dark bear with the expressive eyes; the blond drummer, Tom Gauger, became the blond bear; and the Boston Symphony's cellist, Martha Babcock, became a bear who plays the French horn; Babcock's husband, Harvey Seigel, became a violin-playing bear.

A tale about a cat named Comet, told in *Comet's Nine Lives* (Putnam, 1996), was set on Nantucket Island, once a famous whaling village. Information about lightship baskets, turks head bracelets, sailor's valentines (shells), scrimshaw, navigation lights, sea glass, Nantucket reds (shorts, jackets, skirts, and hats made from faded pinkish red cloth), weather flags, and messages in bottles came from a visit to a Nantucket whaling museum and the Nantucket area. In the book, Brett included a self-portrait (her illustration of a Siberian husky, Perky, is supposed to be Brett herself), a hedgehog, and a sea captain who pops up in the border panels of the book.

The success of *The Mitten* contributed to a sequel of sorts, but *The Hat* (Putnam, 1997) had an origin all its own. She says, "The idea for *The Hat* came to me after a curious incident with our pet hedgehog, Pudge." One day, when Brett discovered Pudge was missing, she searched in all the dark, small places and finally located her in a slipper sock on the floor. Somehow, she had gotten in the sock, and because of her prickles, Pudge got stuck in the woolen stitches. A pair of scissors provided the necessary rescue equipment. The image of Pudge stuck with a stocking on its head like a hat gave Brett a beginning for the next book, *The Hat*. Brett traveled to Denmark and ended up putting the weather she encountered into the book. Several other images contributed to the illustrations. The Danes have a custom of flying red and white pennants similar to the Danish flag. Brett liked how the pennant looked against the sea and put one in her book. A friend, Sara Carty, and Brett's own daughter, Lia, modeled for the little girl named Lisa. Brett's friends, a mother and daughter named Lise and Lisa, are natives of Denmark. They helped Brett with authenticity of her images. The character is named for them. Images of thatched roofs, a gander, knitting patterns, and lovely landscapes came from Denmark as well. A character in the book, a cat named Luther, actually lives in New York with Brett's editor, Margaret Frith.

The idea for *Armadillo Rodeo* (Putnam, 1995) came about when she heard of an encounter a woman had with a characteristically near-sighted armadillo and the woman's tennis shoe. It took imagination and a trip to Texas to create the images of sagebrush country, red boots, and life on a Texas ranch for this tale of an Armadillo and her four youngsters.

When Brett creates a book, she starts with what she feels is the most difficult part—writing the story. In each of her stories, something happens that causes a change. In *The Mitten,* it is a sneeze. In *The Wild Christmas Reindeer,* it is Teeka's evolution from bossy to helpful, which in turn changes the reindeer's behavior. In *Berlioz the Bear,* a bee sting causes the stubborn mule to get the bandwagon to the festival on time. After she completes a story line, Brett creates a book dummy, a simple version of the book. She uses a cartoon style that doesn't take too much time. The dummy gives her the first impression of what her book will be like. During the process of creating the book, changes take place that contribute to the final version. After planning spaces for the words, Brett creates a pencil sketch for the final version. She often uses photographs to help construct the paintings. For *Berlioz the Bear,* she asked each of the symphony members whom she intended to feature as a bear in her book, to attend a photo session in which each was photographed going through the actions that take place on each frame of the dummy. By using her photographs of characters, photographs of the settings from her travels, and her preliminary sketches, Brett is able to paint the characters in their setting. Her art tools are simple: pen and ink, small brushes, watercolors, good light, and imagination. She uses a very small amount of water on her brushes to keep the colors from running together.

Many of Brett's books are created with borders. The borders give her an opportunity to add additional images and ideas that she cannot easily put into the main frame of the story. For example, in *The Mitten*, the borders show Nicki trudging through the woods, while the main picture focuses on the animals and their efforts to squeeze into the lost mitten. In the border art, Brett shows Nicki scaring different animals out of their hiding places. On the following page, the animal that Nicki has scared out appears in the mitten scene. Because the animals grow larger throughout the book, the green branches serve as a marker to indicate the animals' size. The borders of *The Wild Christmas Reindeer* show the activity in Santa's workshop as the calendar marks the days during the time Teeka is training the reindeer. The borders of *Annie and the Wild Animals* tell a second story by showing the cat and what is happening to her in the woods while Annie is trying to lure the cat back into her yard by placing corn cakes at the edge of the woods. The borders eventually show the kittens that are born and mature in the hollow tree. In the final pages of the book, the cat and her kittens move from the hollow tree (and the border story) to arrive back in Annie's yard (and the main story frames) where Annie welcomes them all home. The side borders for *Berlioz the Bear* depict the authentically dressed concert attendees as they arrive in the town square. The top border shows two rabbits as they set up the town square for the festival and the concert. The borders of *Comet's Nine Lives* feature the sea captain and signals from the lighthouse actually spelling out a message. *The Hat* has decorative borders as well.

Brett's art is quite intricate, taking her about an hour to do one inch or about two days to complete a page. The art for *The Mitten* took four months to complete, and the art for *The Wild Christmas Reindeer* took five months. She tells young artists that some people draw certain things better than others do. She says she cannot draw motorcycles or bridges very well, but she especially enjoys drawing animals and is proud of them when she finishes. Her books are filled with animals and intricate designs.

Brett lives with her husband, Joseph Hearne, in Norwell, Massachusetts. Their combined family includes three daughters, all grown. During the summer months, Brett and Hearne move to a cabin in the Berkshire Mountains. There Brett is able to paint in a setting near a shimmering lake surrounded by birds and wild animals, and Hearne plays with the Boston Symphony Orchestra at the nearby Tanglewood festival.

BOOKS AND NOTES

Jan Brett travels extensively and researches the architecture and costumes of many countries for images that may appear in her work one day. "From cave paintings, to Norwegian sleighs, to Japanese gardens, I study the traditions of the many countries I visit, and use them as a starting point for my children's books." In many (if not all) of her books, Brett includes a hedgehog. In *Armadillo Rodeo*, a sideboard on a truck entering a ranch includes a picture of hedgehog because a real hedgehog would not be found living in Texas.

Books Illustrated by Jan Brett

Happy Birthday Dear Duck. Written by Eve Bunting. (Clarion, 1988).

The Owl and the Pussycat. Written by Edward Lear. (Putnam, 1991).

Scary, Scary Halloween. Written by Eve Bunting. (Clarion, 1986).

Woodland Crossings. Written by Stephen Krensky. (Atheneum, 1978).

Books Written and Illustrated by Jan Brett

Annie and the Wild Animals (Houghton, 1985).
Annie's cat is missing, but she eventually finds her cat and more.

Armadillo Rodeo (Putnam, 1995).
Set in Texas, a mother armadillo and her four young ones hope to find excitement—and they do.

Berlioz the Bear (Putnam, 1991).
Berlioz and his band attempt to get to the town square to play. When the stubborn donkey refuses to pull the wagon any farther, a bee that has been buzzing in the bass violin comes to the rescue.

Christmas Trolls (Putnam, 1993).
The magical world of trolls comes to life at one of the most decorated seasons of the year.

Comet's Nine Lives (Putnam, 1996).
The tale of Comet the cat and nine of his exploits.

The Hat (Putnam, 1997).
A literary tale patterned after the folktale "The Mitten."

Trouble with Trolls (Putnam, 1992).
The troll world is filled with exploits and humor.

Books Retold and Illustrated by Jan Brett

Classic tales are retold and given new vibrancy with Brett's detailed illustrations, which provide visual information not given in the text.

Beauty and the Beast (Clarion, 1989).

Goldilocks and the Three Bears (Putnam, 1987).

The Mitten (Putnam, 1989).

Town Mouse, Country Mouse. (Putnam, 1994).

FOR MORE INFORMATION

Articles

Harayda, Janice. "All the World's a Model: Illustrator Jan Brett Entices Children's Eyes." *Cleveland Plain Dealer* (May 19, 1991): 1–H, 6–H.

"Jan Brett Invited to Paint White House Easter Egg Roll." *Nantucket Inquirer* (March 31, 1988): 1.

Mehren, Elizabeth. "Every Picture Tells Her Tale." *Los Angeles Times* (April 27, 1994): E3, E8.

Spitz, Jane Tamburri. "Illustrator Takes on a Christmas Classic." *Boston Globe* (December 8, 1986): 47, 49.

Sumner, Jane. "The Troll Lady." *Dallas Morning News* (December 7, 1993): 5C, 7C, Family sec.

Web Sites

Jan Brett's Home Page. URL: <http://www.janbrett.com> (Accessed March 2000).

Norman Bridwell

◆ Animals ◆ Family Relationships

Kokomo, Indiana
February 15, 1928

Mark Lovewell

📖 *Clifford, the Big Red Dog*
📖 *Clifford, the Small Red Puppy*
📖 *The Witch Next Door*

ABOUT THE AUTHOR/ILLUSTRATOR

Norman Bridwell was a freelance illustrator of filmstrips and slides for corporations when a bad year came. He had little work and a new baby to feed. His situation nudged him to try his hand at book illustration. He gathered samples of his work and made the rounds of more than twenty publishing houses. Not one editor was interested. Finally, he met a young editor, Susan Hirschman, at Harper & Row, who later moved to Greenwillow Books. Hirschman told him that it was highly unlikely that any publisher would choose him to illustrate its books. His art just wasn't special enough, she said. She looked through his portfolio and pulled out a sketch of a baby girl and her horse-sized bloodhound and suggested that perhaps he should write his own story—and perhaps the picture of the girl and dog could suggest the story.

With that suggestion, Bridwell went home to write a story. First, he changed the bloodhound to an "all-around dog" and made him even bigger—as big as a house. Emily Elizabeth went from a two-year-old to a six- or seven-year-old. He named the girl after his young daughter and named the dog "Tiny." His wife thought Tiny was a dumb name for a dog, however. She suggested "Clifford," so Clifford it was.

The manuscript was written in three days. The dog was painted red simply because Bridwell had a jar of red poster paint on his desk. Eventually, he submitted the manuscript to Grosset & Dunlap. A freelance reader, Lilian Moore, read the manuscript but decided that it wasn't right for Grosset. She suggested that it might be of interest to Scholastic to include in one of their book clubs.

Three weeks later, Scholastic accepted the book, and *Clifford the Big Red Dog* (1963) was published. The first printing met with moderate success, and they contracted for two other books and then published *Clifford Gets a Job*. Beatrice Schenk deRegniers, an editor at Scholastic, decided that those Clifford books were enough. Eventually, Scholastic reissued the first Clifford book through its book club; this time, the response was overwhelming—so overwhelming, in fact, that deRegniers called Bridwell and asked him to write another book about Clifford. She told him, "I can't just take Clifford soup. Don't turn in any old story with Clifford stirred in. It has to be a real story."

Bridwell distills this story into a few sentences. "I set out to be an illustrator," he says. "Nobody liked my art enough to give me a book to illustrate. I had to write a book of my own. I picked a sample picture I had done—a girl with a big red dog—and I wrote about them. It turned out to be 'Clifford the Big Red Dog.'" In 2000, Clifford turned thirty-seven years old.

Bridwell was born in Kokomo, Indiana on February 15, 1928. As a youngster, he spent a lot of time making up stories. "I didn't write them down. I drew pictures or acted the stories out with dolls or lead soldiers."

Bridwell attended John Herron Art Institute (1945–1949) and the Cooper Union Art School (1952–1953). While attending art school, he began his career with a lettering company in New York City as a messenger and later became an artist-designer for Raxon Fabrics Company (1951–1953) and an artist for the H. D. Rose Company (1953–1956). Bridwell became a freelance artist in 1956.

As of 1999, Bridwell had written more than 150 books—about sixty have been published. His most popular titles are those featuring Clifford the Big Red Dog. Many of his Clifford titles have been translated into several other languages. In Canada, Clifford is known as Bertram, in Germany as Samson, in Denmark as Sofus, and in Italy as Piccoli. Clifford has become a Scholastic icon and is used in much of their literature; he is also a logo on their Web site.

Bridwell used his daughter, Emily Elizabeth, as a prototype for the little girl in the Clifford books, and his son, Timothy, wanted his own book, too. Timothy became a character in *The Witch Next Door* (Scholastic, 1966), one of Bridwell's best selling titles.

One of Bridwell's most faithful fans was a second-grade boy, Eddie Stalling, who wrote to Bridwell several times each year. By the time the boy was a fifth grader, he wrote Bridwell and asked him to write a book "for fifth graders." Bridwell responded by writing *How to Care for Your Monster* (Scholastic, 1970), which he dedicated to Stalling, and *Monster Holidays* (Scholastic, 1974). Stalling grew up and became a forest ranger in Alaska. Recently, Bridwell dedicated one of his Clifford books to Eddie Stalling's children.

For twenty years, the Bridwells lived in New York City. Nine years after their first vacation to Martha's Vineyard, they became permanent residents of that island, where they live in a modest house with red shutters and a Clifford-red door. Their car is Clifford red, too, with a license that reads "Clifrd." Frequent trips to New York City keep Bridwell in contact with his publisher, but the island provides the respite that allows him to create more books. He also speaks to schools and libraries across the United States. In 1995, he was part of an International Schools tour that took him to Spain, where he spent several days meeting with students in Madrid, Barcelona, Valencia, Bilbao, and Las Palmas.

Bridwell's wife is an artist who creates watercolors and prints. Their afternoon strolls to the beach and the picturesque surroundings of their hometown lend themselves to artistic inspiration. Their daughter, Emily Elizabeth, does ceramics and dolls and is the mother of the Bridwell's "lovely granddaughter, Alissa B. Merez." Timothy has studied movie making. When Bridwell is not "doing books" he likes "to read—poetry, humor, or history." The Bridwell's take care of their granddaughter one day a week, and "When we are home on Martha's Vineyard, we enjoy evening beach walks, photography, and classical music and jazz."

BOOKS AND NOTES

When Norman Bridwell first created Clifford, the illustrations were black-and-white line drawings with only Clifford shown in color. The books were produced in a standard rectangle shape. As the book industry has progressed, so have the Clifford books. Most of the books are now square in shape. Scholastic editors also decided that Bridwell's drawings should be colorized, and they solicited candidates to do the work. Rumor has it that Bridwell applied, but the job went to someone else! Bridwell continues to draw black-and-white drawings for new titles, but another artist fills in the drawings with color.

Books Written and Illustrated by Norman Bridwell

Clifford Books

Clifford and the Big Storm (Scholastic, 1995).

Clifford, the Big Red Dog (Scholastic, 1985).

Clifford, the Small Red Puppy (Scholastic, 1985).

Clifford's ABC (Scholastic, 1994).

Clifford's Big Book of Stories (Cartwheel, 1994).

Clifford's Big Book of Things to Know (Scholastic, 1998).

Clifford's First Valentine's Day (Scholastic, 1997).

Clifford's Furry Friends (Scholastic, 1996).

Count on Clifford (Scholastic, 1985).

Miscellaneous

How to Care for Your Monster (Scholastic, 1970).

Monster Holidays (Scholastic, 1974).

The Witch Goes to School (Scholastic, 1992).

The Witch Next Door (Scholastic, 1966).

FOR MORE INFORMATION

Articles

"Author's View." *Scholastic BookTalk* no. 4 (May 1988): 6.

Levine, Beth. "The Day I Hope My Son Won't Remember (A Rainy Day Activity for a Mother's Sanity)." *Redbook* 187, no. 3 (July 1996): 125.

Videos

The World of Norman Bridwell Featuring Clifford the Big Red Dog (Scholastic, 1990). VHS 25 mins.

Craig Brown

◆ Animals ◆ Farm

Sharron L. McElmeel

Fairfield, Iowa
September 4, 1947

📖 *The Patchwork Farmer*
📖 *Tractor*

ABOUT THE AUTHOR/ILLUSTRATOR

Craig McFarland Brown is the son of Jane Louise Brown, a teacher, and Carl Conrad Brown. He was born in Fairfield, Iowa, on September 4, 1947. After his parents' divorce, he and his sister, Barbara, grew up with their mother in a rural farming community near Tama, Iowa.

Brown describes his daily routine from about the third grade on as "leaving the house early in the morning to bike out into the country where I spent the early part of the day drawing and painting things I saw." When the noon sun signaled midday, he would return home to play baseball or go swimming. Later in the evening, he would browse the magazine rack at the local soda fountain where he found things to read. The fantasy world of Jean and Laurent deBrunhoff (authors of the books about Babar) and the Beatrix

Potter stories featuring Peter Rabbit and other small creatures contributed to Brown's dreams of becoming an artist.

He began to realize his dreams shortly after he graduated from high school in 1965. Brown left Iowa to attend the Layton School of Art in Milwaukee, Wisconsin. It was during these years that Brown's dream of being an artist began to merge with his growing interest in children's books.

Brown soon developed an interest in stippling technique, the use of dots to create the lines and shapes within a picture. He describes it as "the idea of working with dots to make things darker or lighter, depending on the separation between the dots." He adds that his interest in the technique "was developed while attending art school and during visits to the Chicago Art Institute where each visit started and ended at the paintings of Georges Seurat." Georges Seurat is the French painter who first used the painting style known as pointillism, which is similar to stippling.

His dream of being a children's book illustrator was put aside for a few years as Brown and his wife struggled to support themselves and their two children. For sixteen years, he worked in advertising by day and created images for his illustration portfolio by night. He was able to attend a workshop on children's book illustrating, conducted by Uri Schulevitz, in New York. Schulevitz's work influenced Brown's style, as did the work of children's book artist Maurice Sendak and the renowned American painter Grant Wood. Schulevitz's workshop provided ideas to help Brown refine his portfolio, and soon he returned to New York to present his art work to publishing houses. His portfolio work was in black and white, but the publishers said they wanted color.

Brown "returned home and began to add color to my work." Later, he returned to New York with his "colorized" portfolio, and within four months, he was offered a contract to illustrate a book. The publisher that offered the contract wanted the illustrations in black and white, so Brown returned to creating black-and-white illustrations. The final result was his first illustrative work for a trade book, *The Talking Bird and the Story Pouch* by Amy Lawson (Harper, 1987). His next two books were for Rockrimmon Press, a Colorado publisher.

Eventually, Brown proposed his own story to publishers, a minimal-text story to be told using illustrations. This work, *The Patchwork Farmer* (Greenwillow, 1989), is about a farmer who rips his overalls. Each day, he goes out to the fields to work and then must mend his pants at night. Then he returns to the fields the next day. At the end of the book, the farmer is shown in his patchwork overalls beside patchwork fields that resemble those through which Brown bicycled during his childhood. The book,

Brown suggests, shows how hard farmers work and is intended to "respect that work ethic."

Brown is one of the few artists to use the technique of stippling to illustrate his books. His illustrations are created using a multistep process. During the planning stages, he creates thumbnail sketches and preliminary drawings. Once he has determined the composition of each illustration, he draws the final illustrations. He uses a special blue paper to transfer the drawings onto a textured artboard. The blue line drawings guide where he lays the dots (stippling) to form the final illustration.

Brown's next step is to add the color. By using his fingers to apply pastel over the stippling, he is able to control the color. He uses different erasers to create highlights. The colors are added from light to dark. After Brown applies each color, he sprays the paper to prevent one color from fading into another. Although Brown primarily uses stippling in his work, he has used watercolor as well and currently is working on other techniques that he might use in the future.

The five titles that Brown has authored and illustrated honor the rural existence that was part of his childhood. *The Patchwork Farmer* was the first title in which both the story line and the illustrations were his creation. Brown's next book, *My Barn* (Greenwillow, 1991), is a tribute to the old barns that are disappearing from the Midwestern landscape. *My Barn* includes authentic sounds that animals make and shows children the structure of a barn.

Brown then wrote and illustrated *City Sounds* (Greenwillow, 1992). When he was growing up, his maternal grandparents lived nearby, and Brown spent many hours at his grandfather's chicken hatchery. Baby chicks from the hatchery were shipped to farmers all over the United States through the U.S. Postal Service. The chicks were sent in cardboard boxes with air holes and shipped just like any other package. The chicks became part of *City Sounds*, as Farmer Brown heads to the city and the post office to pick up his shipment of baby chicks. The final scene shows the farmer opening the box and hearing the final sound portrayed in the book—the peeps of the chicks.

In 1994, Brown paid tribute to the springtime energy and activity on a farm. The story of budding trees, blooming flowers, and new baby animals comes to a happy climax when the farmer's wife has twins. That book, *In the Spring* (Greenwillow, 1994), quickly became a favorite title among young readers.

Tractor (Greenwillow, 1995) is among Brown's best works. It pays tribute to the Iowa landscape and the farmers who make it productive. Beginning readers can read the text, which is peppered with occasional uncommon words, such as the names of the machines: manure spreader, harrow, cultivator, and so forth. A glossary at the end of the book includes these terms. Brown successfully charts the seed's progress from fertilized soil to roadside vegetable stand. The illustrations expand the text's meaning by showing the other recipients of the farm's bounty. Deft observers will notice that a family of robins oversees the whole enterprise, and the robins' survival techniques mirror those of the farm family.

Brown's experience and reverence for farm life are apparent in his writing and illustration. *Tractor* is dedicated to Verlyn Strellner, an expert on tractors, who was one of Brown's best friends during his childhood. The idea for *Tractor* came during a speaking tour of ten Iowa schools and an appearance at the annual Iowa Educational Media Association's conference. During an evening's road trip to Iowa City, Brown says he "noticed an old tractor sitting in a field, sketched it quickly, and next to the drawing, I made a notation about an idea for a tractor book." At this time, Brown was living in Colorado, so when he returned, he acted on the idea, and the book was published by Greenwillow in 1995.

Brown's illustrations have been described as "gently colorful and cheerful." Those same words can be used to describe the artist himself. Craig Brown regularly visits schools. He has made several extensive tours throughout the Midwest but has shared his writing and illustrating techniques with children as far away as Seoul, Korea, where he spent two weeks visiting American schools in Seoul, Osan, Taegu, Pusan, and Chinhae. The school days were filled with talk about his books and excited readers. In his free time, he visited art galleries, shopping districts, and historic temples and buildings. He also wondered what the native Koreans thought about his standard attire—cowboy boots and a ten-gallon hat. He found that Korea had Burger King, KFC, and Wendy's, so when he wasn't in the mood for kimchee, he could retreat to something familiar. His flight back home took him just thirteen minutes by clock time—thanks to the recovered day made possible by the International Date Line. In real time, the journey took twenty-four hours and thirteen minutes.

Brown continues to visit schools and libraries and to speak at conferences throughout the United States while working on more books. In 2000, he is working on the art for *Three Weeks Later*, a book about an Amish barn raising, which will be published by Greenwillow.

Brown lives in a studio apartment in Colorado Springs. He has a daughter, Heather, and a son, Cory. Whenever he is not teaching or working on creating books, he says, ". . . spare time is spent with my children and friends in the mountains, hiking, biking, camping, and fishing . . . whenever I go into the mountains I take my writing and art supplies. I so enjoy writing and illustrating, that it seems natural to mix both with the outdoors, much as I did as a child riding my bike in the rural countryside of Iowa." Among his favorite things are hot tea and salads, colors in shades of lavender and purple, classical music, and jazz.

BOOKS AND NOTES

Craig McFarland Brown has used his full name on a couple of his books, but most are published using only his first and last names. His first illustrated book featured black-and-white illustrations, but his more recent titles have featured colored work. His illustrations are characterized by the stippling that is a unique illustrative method in the field of children's literature.

Books Written and Illustrated by Craig Brown

City Sounds (Greenwillow, 1992).

In the Spring (Greenwillow, 1994).

My Barn (Greenwillow, 1991).

The Patchwork Farmer (Greenwillow, 1989).

Tractor (Greenwillow, 1995).

Books Illustrated by Craig Brown

Big Thunder Magic. Written by Craig Kay Strete. (Greenwillow, 1990).

A modern Native American story about small Thunderspirit, who rescues his friend Nanabee, the sheep from the city zoo. The chief, Nanabee, and Thunderspirit return to the Pueblo wondering why they wanted to go to the city in the first place.

Cucumber Soup. Written by Vickie Leigh Krudwig. (Fulcrum, 1998).

Ten ants go out for a safari looking for food. Upon returning, they find a cucumber on top of their anthill. *Cucumber Soup* takes readers on a backward counting trip from nine noisy mosquitoes to one teeny tiny fly.

The Gossamer Tree. Written by Toni Knapp. (Rockrimmon, 1988).

Four mice invite some insects in from the cold, and together they celebrate Christmas.

The Ornery Morning. Written by Patricia Brennan Demuth. (Dutton, 1991).

A cumulative tale that has the farm animals refusing to do their jobs until the farmer refuses to feed them.

The Six Bridges of Humphrey the Whale. Written by Toni Knapp. (Rockrimmon, 1989).

The true story of Humphrey, a whale that got turned the wrong way in the San Francisco Bay and needed to be rescued.

FOR MORE INFORMATION

Articles

McElmeel, Sharron L. "Author & Artist Profile: Craig Brown." *Library Talk* 7, no. 2 (March/April 1994): 15–17.

Web Sites

Craig McFarland Brown. URL: <http://www. geocities.com/Craigbrown_2000> (Accessed March 2000)

Marc Brown

◆ Family Relationships, Fiction and Nonfiction

© 1995 Rick Friedman

Erie, Pennsylvania
November 25, 1946

Arthur Adventure Series
- *Arthur's Chicken Pox*
- *Arthur's Eyes*

Arthur Chapter Books
- *Arthur and the Scare-Your-Pants-Off Club*
- *Arthur's Mystery Envelope*

D. W. Books
- *D. W. the Picky Eater*
- *D. W.'s Lost Blankie*

The Dino Life Guides for Families
- *What's the Big Secret?*
- *When Dinosaurs Die*

ABOUT THE AUTHOR/ILLUSTRATOR

Marc Brown was born in Erie, Pennsylvania, on November 25, 1946. His parents were LeRoy Edward and Renita Toulon Brown. Marc attended school in Mill Creek, Pennsylvania. During his growing up years his grandmother Thora and her mother, Brown's great-grandmother, "told us the most wonderful stories." The best stories were usually spooky, and Thora took out her false teeth when she told those. Brown never dreamed that he would grow up to tell stories of his own, but that is just what he did.

Thora also encouraged Brown's passion for drawing. She saved his artwork in a bottom drawer of her bureau. Brown knew that his art was important because his grandmother saved very few things. Later, it was Thora who provided educational funds that helped Brown pay his tuition to the Cleveland Institute of Art from 1964 to 1969. Years later, Brown's grandmother became the inspiration for Grandmother Thora in the books about the friendly little aardvark, Arthur. Brown reached back into his childhood for other characters, too. Inspiration for D. W. and Francine came from his three sisters: Bonnie, Colleen, and Kimberly. Buster evolved from Brown's best friend in elementary school, Terry Johnson. The Brain is based on his first close friend Allan. Mr. Ratburn is a manifestation of the "meanest algebra teacher ever." In real life, he had green hairs in his nose and never combed his hair. His eyes followed students all over the room. He slinked around the classroom in the same sports jacket and tie everyday. The tie glowed in the dark and had "Welcome to Niagara Falls" on it. The children were asked to wait outside the room in alphabetical order and to walk into the room in single file, sit down, and look straight ahead. They called the back row "death row." Test papers were announced with names and grades. No one wanted to go to the black board for fear of having the answer wrong. When Mr. Ratburn was introduced in *Arthur's Teacher Troubles* (Little, Brown, 1986), Brown made Ratburn considerably nicer than he was in real life.

At the age of seventeen, Brown played Artful Dodger in *Oliver* and designed the set for the play. Later, Brown attended art school and held a variety of jobs. He drove truck, was a short-order cook, a college professor, a soda jerk, an actor, a chicken farmer, and a television art director.

On September 1, 1968, Brown married ballet dancer and college teacher Stephanie Marani. Their two sons, Tolon and Tucker, were born in 1972 and 1975 respectively. One night, Brown was telling a bedtime story to Tolon. Most of Brown's stories involved animals, and that night, the story he told happened to be about an aardvark who hated his nose. That story became the basis for the first published book about Arthur, *Arthur's Nose* (Little, 1976). He went on to write more than twenty picture books about Arthur and several chapter books featuring Arthur and his friends.

In 1977, Brown and his first wife divorced. He met Laurene Krasny in 1982, and they married on September 11, 1983. Marc Brown is both an illustrator and writer. His artwork has developed with the help of his editors.

Brown has said that it took him ten years to "unlearn all the superficial techniques I spent five years learning at art school." He began illustrating to satisfy himself and other adults but soon learned that he must consider the children who would be reading his books. His first editor, Emilie McLeod, helped him to concentrate on the visual framework of a story and to remove excess.

Brown and his friend, Stephen Krensky, collaborated on a book titled *Dinosaurs Beware!* (Little, Brown, 1982). Later, he collaborated with his wife, Laurene Krasny Brown, using the same dinosaur characters. Laurene, a psychologist, had conducted research in children's television, and she was aware of the difficult life situations that modern children face. Dealing with divorce brought about *Dinosaurs Divorce* (Little, Brown, 1986). The dinosaur characters made the topic a little softer for younger readers, but it was intended to help children, such as Brown's own two sons, deal with divorce. Eventually, the dinosaur characters became the characters in the series The Dino Life Guides for Families which included guides for traveling, dealing with death, and talking about sex with young people.

Events in the Browns' life often are reflected in books about Arthur. *Arthur's Baby* (Little, Brown, 1987) and Arthur's new baby sister, Kate, came about the same time Laurene and Marc's baby daughter, Eliza, arrived in the Brown household. Some of Arthur's adventures come from Brown's own childhood. *Arthur's Valentine* (Little, Brown, 1980) was Arthur's first holiday book. In third grade, Brown was infatuated with Patricia DelPorto, a girl with curly hair and long eyelashes. She became Sue Ellen in *Arthur's Valentine*. Books celebrating Christmas, Thanksgiving, Halloween, April Fool's Day, and other family celebrations soon followed, as did books about birthdays and family vacations.

Brown's three children have inspired many stories. He also gets suggestions from children he meets in schools or other places he visits. Tucker suggested *Finger Rhymes* (Dutton, 1980) when he was in nursery school, and the boys told Brown some of the riddles that were included in *Spooky Riddles* (Random House, 1983). They sometimes visited the cemetery across the street from their home to tell silly, spooky riddles.

Once Brown is ready to act on an idea, he begins to write on lined paper, sometimes rewriting a story thirty times. He rewrites the story, reads it to his family, and makes a thirty-two-page storyboard for the pictures. At this point, he decides what words are needed to say what the pictures cannot and what pictures are needed to say what the words cannot. Once Brown is ready to create the illustrations, he uses Sharpie® pens, watercolors, and Primas color for detail. He draws images in his books from his own surroundings.

The movie house and even the cemetery shown in some of his books are from his hometown. He includes the names of his children and his wife in many of his illustrations. In some books, he includes other references to places he has been. He mentioned Cardinal School and Briggs School in Maquoketa, Iowa, in *Arthur's Christmas* (Little, Brown, 1984). In *Arthur's Baby*, Brown labeled each of three nursery cribs with the names of his children. Presents are delivered and labeled as having come from "Holidaysburg, PA" and "Duncanville, PA," places from which presents might have, in real life, arrived for Eliza Brown. On a bulletin board filled with family notes is a paper captioned "Hingham History," reflecting the reality of the Brown residence in Hingham, Massachusetts. Arthur's house is similar in many ways to the white, two-story house where the Browns live. A change in the chairs used in the Brown's kitchen is reflected in *Arthur's Baby* and *Arthur's Teacher Trouble*. The same kitchen is depicted with the new chairs in one of the books.

Sometimes Brown uses unique end papers or dust-jacket covers to foreshadow events and set the mood for the story within. For example, in *D. W. All Wet* (Little, Brown, 1988) the patterned end papers set the mood for the story with items that might be associated with a day at the beach. The back of the dust jacket for *Arthur's Teacher Trouble* has row after row of pastel-drawn alphabet letters. The letters appear to be in random order, but a careful look will uncover more than twenty-five words in a word-find puzzle, each relating to the story or to Arthur. The puzzle design does not appear on the paperback edition.

Brown lives with his wife and their daughter in Hingham, Massachusetts. Summers are spent on Martha's Vineyard. Tolon and Tucker are grown now. Brown enjoys fixing houses, growing things (his favorite plants to grow are things to eat, especially raspberries), and exploring the history of his town.

BOOKS AND NOTES

Marc Brown has created more than 100 books for young readers. He has written and illustrated many of them, collaborated with his wife on others, and has illustrated books by many other writers, including those of Mary Blount Christian and Verna Aardema.

Arthur Adventure Series

Arthur Writes a Story (Little, Brown, 1996).

Arthur's Chicken Pox (Little, Brown, 1994).

Arthur's Computer Disaster (Little, Brown, 1997).

Arthur's Eyes (Little, Brown, 1979).

Arthur's First Sleepover (Little, Brown, 1994).

Arthur's New Puppy (Little, Brown, 1993).

Arthur's TV Trouble (Little, Brown, 1995).

Arthur Chapter Books

Arthur Accused (Little, Brown, 1998).

Arthur and the Crunch Cereal Contest (Little, Brown, 1998).

Arthur and the Scare-Your-Pants-Off Club (Little, Brown, 1998).

Arthur Makes the Team (Little, Brown, 1998).

Arthur's Mystery Envelope (Little, Brown, 1998).

Buster's Dino Dilemma (Little, Brown, 1998).

Locked in the Library (Little, Brown, 1998).

The Mystery of the Stolen Bike (Little, Brown, 1998).

D. W. Books

D. W. the Picky Eater (Little, Brown, 1995).

D. W.'s Lost Blankie (Little, Brown, 1998).

The Dino Life Guides for Families

Dinosaurs to the Rescue (Little, Brown, 1992).

What's the Big Secret? (Little, Brown, 1997).

When Dinosaurs Die (Little, Brown, 1996).

Miscellaneous

The Family Read-Aloud Christmas Treasury. Selected by Alice Low. Illustrated by Marc Brown. (Little, Brown, 1989).

Monster's Lunch Box (Little, Brown, 1995).

Oh, Kojo! How Could You? Written by Verna Aardema. Illustrated by Marc Brown. (Dial, 1984).

Perfect Pigs. Written by Marc Brown and Stephen Krensky. (Little, Brown, 1993).

Read-Aloud Rhymes for the Very Young. Selected by Jack Prelutsky. Illustrated by Marc Brown. (Knopf, 1986).

Rex and Lilly Playtime. Written by Laurie Krasny Brown. Illustrated by Marc Brown. (Little, Brown, 1995).

Scared Silly! A Book for the Brave (Little, Brown, 1994).

Swamp Monsters. Written by Mary Blount Christian. Illustrated by Marc Brown. (Little, Brown, 1993).

FOR MORE INFORMATION

Articles

"Children's Books: In the Studio with Marc Brown." *Publishers Weekly* 240, no. 20 (May 17, 1993): 32.

"Happy." *People Weekly* 47, no. 19 (May 19, 1997): 164.

"Meet the Author: Marc Brown." *Instructor* 105, no. 4 (November 1995): 60.

Videos

Meet Marc Brown (American School Publishers, 1991). VHS 19 mins.

Marcia Brown

◆ Folklore

Sharron L. McElmeel

Rochester, New York
July 13, 1918

📖 *Cinderella*
📖 *Once a Mouse*
📖 *Stone Soup*

ABOUT THE AUTHOR/ILLUSTRATOR

Marcia Brown's interest in illustrating children's books began early in her career and continued into the early 1940s when she was teaching English and dramatics at Cornwell High School in New York. In 1943, she left teaching to become an assistant librarian for the rare book collection at the New York Public Library. She stayed there until 1948 and completed four books during that time. Her first book, *The Little Carousel*, was published in 1946 by Scribner. Years later, in 1975, Brown described her experience with this book during a presentation at a book conference in Iowa City, Iowa. She said, "I had to go somewhere. I had heard Alice Dalgleish speak and admired the Scribner list, so I made my way to Alice's office. She was too busy to see me.

There I was, armed with the completed dummy form and in such a high pitch that I burst into tears. I left the office and walked around the corner to Viking. But there I found Viking tied up with an elevator strike, and Miss Massee's office was on a high floor. So, rather than climb, I decided to wait for Miss Dalgliesh, who took the book. I've been with Scribner ever since."

The setting for *The Little Carousel* came from Brown's own life. At the time, she was living on Sullivan Street in an Italian district of Greenwich Village in New York City. The little carousel actually did arrive in the neighborhood, an event Brown viewed from her apartment window. In 1947, *Stone Soup* (Scribner) was retold and illustrated. It was the first of Brown's books chosen as a runner-up for the Caldecott Medal. Eventually, her illustrative career would be honored with six Caldecott Honor Book citations and three Caldecott Medals.

Brown was born in 1918, in Rochester, New York. Her father was a minister, and the family moved quite often. Brown and her two sisters, Janet and Helen, often visited the public libraries in the towns where they lived. All three sisters loved books, reading, and music. The girls would find the library before their parents "had the china unpacked." They read fairy tales by the Grimm Brothers and Charles Perrault, as well as the literary tales of Hans Christian Andersen. They read tales retold by Howard Pyle and fairy tales collected by Andrew Lang. It is no wonder that, years later, more than twenty-five of Brown's books would have some association with folklore.

After high school, Brown studied painting at the Woodstock School and then at what is now the State University of New York in Albany. From there, she went to the New School for Social Research, Art Students' League, at Columbia University. After teaching and then working at the New York Public Library, Brown began to focus on her book career.

Brown lived most of her adult life in New York City and Connecticut, but she traveled all over the world. Over the years, she gathered stories and experiences in Europe, the Virgin Islands, Hawaii, East Africa, Mexico, Denmark, the Near and Middle East, the former Soviet Union, the Far East, and China. In 1953, she taught puppetry at University College in Jamaica. Ideas for her books often came directly from her travel experiences, and her illustrative techniques were as varied as her travels. She came to use watercolors, wood and linoleum blocks, paper cuts, photography, and pen-and-ink sketches.

The illustrations for one of her last books, *Shadow* (Scribner, 1982), were developed with meticulous detail, even though pain from arthritic hands prevented her from using the wood blocks she wanted to use. Instead, she developed a technique using cut-paper figures for the people and animals. Photographs she had taken in Africa suggested the characters' body positions. She formed backgrounds by printing wood blocks in white on translucent paper to suggest memories, spirit images, and ghosts. Halfway through this project, Brown became ill and was forced to abandon the work for a year. When she resumed work, she developed a method of blotting to suggest a land scarred by its history. Fragments of paper pasted together formed the landscape. Her painstaking artwork for *Shadow*, an African prose poem by Blaise Cendrars (pseudonym of Frederic Sauser-Hall), resulted in her third Caldecott Award.

Although some of her books have been reissued, her illustrative career ended in the mid-1990s. She was awarded the University of Southern Mississippi Medallion in 1972, and she donated many of her manuscripts to the de Grummond Collection, which is housed in the McCain Library and Archives at the university. Her good friend since her days at the New York Public Library, Helen Adams Masten, possessed the press sheets from *The Little Carousel* and donated those as well. For a number of years, Brown and Masten had their own homes but shared a New York City apartment as well. In the 1960s, Brown had a home in West Redding, Connecticut. She had a studio of her own design built there, which contained areas for painting, woodcuts, drawing, photography, sewing, and flute playing. Throughout her life, Brown has enjoyed music, ballet, opera, reading, and travel. Her trip to China in 1985 stimulated her interest in nature photography, as well as the painting, calligraphy, and languages of China.

In 1993, Brown moved to the West Coast to escape the harsh eastern winters. Before she moved, she donated the bulk of her work to the University at Albany. The collection is now housed in the M. E. Grenander Department of Special Collections and Archives and includes more than seventy-two linear feet of material. The following year, Brown donated $10,000 toward organizing, cataloging, and preserving her papers.

In May of 1996, Marcia Brown accepted an honorary doctorate of letters from her alma mater. At the time, Brown was living in Laguna Hills, California. Her studio was a brief walk from her home, and she said she planned to continue working on children's books. She said she didn't "know of many artists who retired."

BOOKS AND NOTES

Marcia Brown has used many techniques for illustrating her work. In her presentation in Iowa City, Brown said, "The need for variety is a matter of temperament. I could no more stand using the same style art in book after book than I could [stand] eating the same food every day." The books listed below often include information regarding the media used to create the illustrations. Her books are noted both for their variety of media and their spare texts. Her characters are filled with magic and enchantment.

Books Written and Illustrated by Marcia Brown

All Butterflies (Scribner, 1974).
An alphabet book with woodcut illustrations.

The Bun: A Tale from Russia (Harcourt, 1972).
A variant of the common runaway tales. Illustrations are pen-and-ink sketches.

Dick Whittington and His Cat (Scribner, 1950).
Linoleum block prints in gold and black complement the tale of a poor orphan boy and his cat.

How, Hippo! (Scribner, 1969).
Four-color woodcuts illustrate this tale of Little Hippo, who is born in a clump of papyrus stalks at the edge of a cool river.

Once a Mouse: A Fable Cut in Wood (Scribner, 1961).
Two- and three-color woodcuts illustrate this 1962 winner of the Caldecott Medal.

Stone Soup: An Old Tale (Scribner, 1947).
Three French soldiers trick a village. Red and black drawings suggestive of peasant art are reflective of the village setting.

Books Illustrated by Marcia Brown

Anansi the Spider Man: Jamaican Folk Tales. Written by Philip Sherlock. (Crowell, 1954).
Anansi tales from West Africa, where Anansi is the beloved rogue, the trickster.

Cinderella or the Little Glass Slipper. Written by Charles Perrault. (Scribner, 1954).
The traditional French version of this fairy tale. Brown used gouache and crayon to create these illustrations.

Shadow. Written by Blaise Cendrars. Translated by La Feticheuse. (Scribner, 1982).
From the storytellers of East Africa comes this tale of a sorcerer, whose images are brought forth through the brilliant shadows of their surroundings.

FOR MORE INFORMATION

Articles

Brown, Marcia. "1992 Laura Ingalls Wilder Award Acceptance Speech." *Journal of Youth Services in Libraries* 5, no. 4 (Summer 1992): 363.

Brown, Marcia. "Organized Wonders: Laura Ingalls Wilder Acceptance Speech." *The Horn Book Magazine* 68, no. 4 (July 1, 1992): 429.

Web Sites

University of Southern Mississippi, de Grummond Collection: Marcia Brown Papers. URL: <http://www.lib.usm.edu/~degrum/findaids/brownmar.htm> (Accessed March 2000)

Anthony Browne

Sheffield, Yorkshire, England
September 11, 1946

📖 *Gorilla*
📖 *Willy the Wimp*
📖 *Zoo*

ABOUT THE AUTHOR/ILLUSTRATOR

Anthony Edward Tudor Browne was born on September 11, 1946, in Sheffield, Yorkshire, England, to Jack Holgate Browne and Doris May (Sugden) Browne. He grew up in Hipperholm, Yorkshire, England, near Halifax. Browne's father was a teacher who spent many hours drawing pictures and playing drawing games with Anthony and Anthony's older brother, Michael. Anthony drew both comic pictures and battle pictures; sometimes, the humor crept into his battle scenes in the form of surrealistic jokes.

Anthony Browne entered Whitcliffe Mount Grammar School in 1957 and then entered Leeds College of Art in 1963. After college, in 1967, he became a medical illustrator at the Manchester Royal Infirmary, a job he kept for three years. Although he thought the job stifled his humor, imagination, and creativity, he does credit this time with helping him to "use [watercolors] in a more controlled way than is usual." Browne now uses watercolors in all of his illustrations.

From the job at the infirmary, Anthony went on to join the world of advertising. He describes this work as boring and high-pressure, and it still did not allow him the freedom to draw "happy" pictures. His next job, with a greeting card company, allowed him to draw "happy teddy bears and happy cats." During the fifteen years that he designed greeting cards for Gordon Fraser Gallery, he began to illustrate children's books. A friend and co-worker suggested that he stabilize his income by submitting some of his illustrations to editors at magazines or in the children's book field. An editor, Julia MacRae, saw promise in his work. Soon, *Through the Magic Mirror* (Hamilton/Julia MacRae, 1976; Greenwillow, 1977) became his entry into children's books.

His illustrations quickly became noted for their trademark use of creative color, finely drawn details, and inventive, surreal humor. He began to write and illustrate books, using his early years as seeds for his stories. As a child, Browne had enjoyed *Alice's Adventures in Wonderland*, and he later illustrated a version of that story by Lewis Carroll. When *Alice's Adventures in Wonderland* (Knopf, 1988) was published, he left his work with the Gordon Fraser Gallery to become a full-time author and illustrator. As he continued his career in children's books, his childhood love of folklore brought him to illustrate his version of *Hansel and Gretel* (Julia MacRae, 1981). He created a contemporary setting with the stepmother in a leopard-skin coat, smoking a cigarette; there was even a bottle of Oil of Olay® on the dresser.

Browne's love of comic books probably contributed to the image of "Super Gorilla" that he created for *Gorilla* (Knopf, 1983). The image actually began as a greeting card featuring a gorilla holding a teddy bear. How did the image get from greeting card to book? Browne says, "It is impossible to really remember how the idea [for the book] came about. I just try to make my books as rich as possible—to have more than one level."

Browne's awareness of sports heroes spawned the development of *Willy the Wimp* (Knopf, 1984) and *Willy the Champ* (Knopf, 1985). When his readers wrote and asked for more books about Willy, he complied. One book, *Willy the Wizard* (Knopf, 1995), features Willy as a small, "outsider" chimp who loves soccer but can't afford soccer "boots" (the English term for cleats). Willy goes to all the practices, but none of the big, burly teammates will pass the ball to him. Then a ghostly stranger plays great soccer with Willy and gives him a pair of soccer boots. Willy plays ball very well with the boots on, but then, during the championship game, he forgets the boots—and still plays like a champ. Undoubtedly, the focus for this book came from Browne's son's interest in playing soccer.

Piggybook (Knopf, 1988), one of his most controversial books because of its message about women's and men's roles in the family, is said to have been based on a real family, to some extent a family like the one in which he was raised. Interestingly enough, Mrs. Piggott bears a resemblance to his wife, Jane.

The children in *The Tunnel* (Knopf, 1989) have definite similarities to Anthony and his brother. In fact, there really was a tunnel that they went through as children. He also managed to include some subtle illustrative visual references to Hansel and Gretel's trek through the woods to the witch's cottage.

Browne's gorilla shows up in many of his books, including *Willy the Wimp* and *Willy the Champ*, and he became a central character in *Willy and Hugh* (Knopf, 1991). The gorilla makes an appearance in *Changes* (Knopf, 1990) and in *Kirsty Knows Best*, (Knopf, 1987) a book written by Annalena McAfee. The gorilla even managed to sneak into *The Tunnel*.

A Walk in the Park (Hamilton, 1977) was Browne's second published book. As his career developed, he wanted to revisit the illustrations from this book. He had always liked the story but felt the illustrations could have been much better. He did not just want to reillustrate the book, however; he wanted to develop both the writing and the illustrations. He writes, "I had wanted for some time to write a book from the point of view of different characters in a story. I like the idea of showing that the world looks very different from inside someone else's head. At some stage (probably very early in the morning when I couldn't sleep) I must have brought these two ideas together, and out of them came *Voices in the Park*" (DK, 1998). He developed the story around Mrs. Smythe and her son, Charles, who take their dog, Virginia, to the park. Mr. Smith and his daughter also take their dog, Albert, to the park. Soon, voices (perspectives) begin to emerge. The dogs immediately begin to play together, and the people interact. Browne says, "I had been working for some time on the illustrations when I gradually realized that something wasn't quite right, however, and one day I found myself doodling with one of the finished illustrations. I started painting over one of the faces, and it turned into a gorilla. I had a mixture of feelings. I didn't want to do another gorilla book—it didn't seem necessary or relevant to the story to make them gorillas—but it worked. Suddenly, the illustration was lifted; it became more child-friendly . . . I changed the other characters and it worked for them too. In a peculiar kind of way, it made them more real, more human. And it made the whole book funnier. I was very reluctant to tell my publishers, so I took the pictures to my editor with great trepidation. But she felt exactly the same way as I did. I was delighted. I still haven't worked out why it works, and in a way I don't want to, but it does show that quite often the best decisions I make are more to do with instinct than intellect."

Each of Browne's books has plenty of interesting aspects. In *Kirsty Knows the Best*, for example, he foreshadows the ending of the story by placing a round shape with antenna-like projections on almost every page. There is a flying mouse with butterfly wings, a child's picture that comes alive, and a black shadow that is really the gorilla. The trees are formed as composites of other strange and interesting shapes, which is where the gorilla shows up in this book. The *Piggybook* is filled with visual images that slowly transform almost everything into a pig symbol. The gorilla makes his entrance early in this book, appearing as a picture in a newspaper in one of the first double-page spreads. Sally Grindley's *Knock, Knock! Who's There?* (Knopf, 1985) is a wonderful vehicle for Browne's ingenuity. Each time a knock is heard at the door, the little girl imagines it is one frightening creature after another. The ever-changing wallpaper gives amble clues as to who will be the next creature at the door (of course, the gorilla was the first to frighten her). But in the end, it is just Father with a cup of hot chocolate. Browne's forte is his ability to create imaginative illustrations.

After receiving many letters asking for more books about Willy, Browne responded by writing *Willy and Hugh*. More recently, Browne has created *Willy the Dreamer* (Candlewick, 1998). In 1998, he called that book, "perhaps the most enjoyable I've ever worked on and as a consequence, I'm now making a companion piece, *Willy's Pictures*, which is supposed to be Willy's drawing book, and shows his versions (hopefully funny) of famous paintings." Further, Browne says, "[The book] is a sequence of pictures which celebrate dreaming, some of my favorite paintings and . . . bananas. I think that maybe some of this enjoyment shows through, at least I hope so." Browne has said his own favorite among his earlier books is *Gorilla* but that he received many more letters from children about his Willy books. One letter from a child, Jan Brett in Australia, was addressed simply to Willy and said, "Dear Willy, you don't have to be big and strong, just watch where you're going." Since that time, Browne says he "has three favorites—*Gorilla, Zoo* (Knopf, 1992), and my new book, *Willy the Dreamer*."

Browne works at home. His schedule is fairly typical; he usually works form 9:30 A.M. until about 6:00 P.M. When working on the early stages of a book, he considers it less like writing a story and more like planning a film.

He makes a storyboard and then works out how to tell the story in thirty-two pages. He uses mostly watercolors but occasionally chooses gouache for overpainting or inks and crayons for a lighter effect, as he did for the Willy books. When asked what contemporary artists he admires, Browne says, "I like many British picture book authors and illustrators, but my two favorites are both from the USA: the great Maurice Sendak and Chris Van Allsburg."

Browne is married to Jane Browne, and they live in a historic seventeenth-century house in the English county of Kent, close to the sea. The Brownes have a son, Joseph, and a daughter, Ellen. Jane is a violinist and violin teacher. Like Anthony, she also is an illustrator of children's books and has five published so far. Her first book, published by Crown Publishers in 1991, was a song book called *Sing Me a Story: Action Songs to Sing and Play* and included thirteen songs with words and music to share with young children. Each of the songs relates to a nursery rhyme or fairy tale.

Anthony says, "We spend a lot of time together. The children are musicians, so I hear them play in concerts frequently. Joe plays the violin and saxophone. Ellen plays the cello and flute. Joseph is a keen rugby player, soccer player, and cricketer, so I spend a lot of time watching him. I play cricket for the village team in the summer, swim, love films and books, and travel extensively in connection with my work."

In 2000, Anthony Browne became the first United Kingdom candidate to win the prestigious Hans Christian Andersen Award for Illustration. The award is an international award given for a candidate's body of work.

BOOKS AND NOTES

Anthony Browne's artistic medium is usually watercolor that is semi-moist or concentrated liquid. He does not use tubes of paint. Maurice Sendak and surrealists René Magritte, Max Ernst, and, to some extent, Salvador Dali, have influenced his work. Browne describes the surrealists as juxtaposing seemingly normal objects. Browne uses bold, rich colors and clear outlines that are often set against white backgrounds. His images mix the realistic with the fantastic. He includes a combination of impossible pictures, surrealism, parody, and ironic images in his illustrations, often to make social commentary.

Books Written and Illustrated by Anthony Browne

About Willy

In *Willy the Wimp*, Browne introduced the chimp character who uses masculine fantasies of body building and aggression. Browne parodies those fantasies through the anthropomorphic character of Willy. Willy has gone on to demonstrate his compassion and perseverance in five more titles.

Willy and Hugh (Knopf, 1991).

Willy the Champ (Knopf, 1985).

Willy the Dreamer (Candlewick, 1998).

Willy the Wimp (Knopf, 1984).

Willy the Wizard (Knopf, 1995).

Zoo (Knopf, 1992).

Miscellaneous

Anthony Browne often uses his illustrations to invoke moods. In *Gorilla*, the child's sense of isolation is emphasized by the chilling, impersonal illustration of Hannah and her father sharing breakfast. Colors accentuate the sense of detachment. The mood seems to change with the excitement of the night before her birthday, and Browne changes small things in the illustrations: the top of the banister post is carved into a gorilla head and the picture near the stairs is a portrait of a gorilla in a Mona–Lisa-like pose.

Alice's Adventures in Wonderland. Written by Lewis Carroll. (Knopf, 1988).

Bear Goes to Town (Doubleday, 1989).

Bear Hunt (Doubleday, 1990).

The Big Baby: A Little Joke (Knopf, 1994).

Changes (Knopf, 1990).

Gorilla (Knopf, 1983).

Hansel and Gretel. Retold from the Brothers Grimm. (Julia MacRae, 1981).

I Like Books (Knopf, 1988).

Kirsty Knows Best. Written by Annalena McAfee. (Knopf, 1987).

The Little Bear Book (Doubleday, 1989).

Piggybook (Knopf, 1988).

Things I Like (Knopf, 1989).

Through the Magic Mirror (Hamilton/Julia MacRae, 1976; Greenwillow, 1977, 1992).

The Tunnel (Knopf, 1989).

Voices in the Park (DK, 1998).

A Walk in the Park (Hamilton, 1977).

FOR MORE INFORMATION

Web Sites

ACHUKA—Children's Books UK. "ACHUKA's Special Guest #2." URL: <http://www.achuka.co.uk/absg.htm> (Accessed March 2000)

ACHUKA—Children's Books UK. "The Anthony Browne Interview." URL: <http://www.achuka.co.uk/abint.htm> (Accessed March 2000)

Ashley Bryan

Sharron L. McElmeel

New York, New York
July 13, 1923

📖 *Ashley Bryan's ABC of African American Poetry*

📖 *The Dancing Granny*

ABOUT THE AUTHOR/ILLUSTRATOR

Ashley Bryan wrote his first book when he was in kindergarten. His teacher taught him the alphabet. He wrote the ABCs and created an illustration to accompany each letter. She taught him to put a cover on the book and to stitch the binding. As he learned to read and write, he created many other books and had produced hundreds of books for family and friends by the time he was in fourth grade. His elementary school years also instilled in him a love of reading and reciting poetry. He says, "We would study a poem for two or three weeks, until we could feel from deep inside us what the poet wanted to say." Now when Bryan visits schools, he recites the poetry of many of his favorites, such as Langston Hughes, Paul Laurence Dunbar, Gwendolyn Brooks, and Eloise Greenfield, as well as poems he has written.

Ashley Bryan was born in New York City, on July 13, 1923. He grew up in the "toughest of New York City neighborhoods." His parents were born in Antigua, West Indies, and emigrated from there shortly after World War I. Bryan and his three brothers and two sisters were all born and raised in the Bronx. He filled his childhood with reading and writing. His earliest childhood memories include those of hearing his mother sing and seeing the many birds—at one time, more than 100—that his father kept in cages on bookshelves of the family's Bronx apartment. In 1946, he was a student at Cooper Union Art School in New York and won a scholarship to paint in Maine. He earned his degree in art from Cooper Union that same year. Later, he majored in philosophy at Columbia University and received a degree in 1950. He went back to live in the Bronx while he taught at Queens College. During this time, Jean Karl, an editor at Atheneum, heard about his work and visited him in his studio. She looked at all of his book projects for family and friends and sent him a contract to create his first book, *Moon, for What Do You Wait?* (Atheneum, 1967). The book was a collection of one-line poems by Indian poet Sir Rabindranaht Tagore, collected by Richard Lewis.

After teaching at Queens, Bryan went on to become an artist in residence at Dartmouth College in New Hampshire. In 1973, Dartmouth offered him a permanent position on its faculty. For more than a decade, he lived in Hanover during the school year, teaching drawing and painting as a professor of art. In 1946, while an art student at Cooper Union, he had found the Cranberry Isles off the coast of Maine. Islesford was a small fishing village in the Isles. In later years, he loved the quiet existence on the island and returned there each summer.

Bryan continued to read and enjoy the poetry of Paul Dunbar and others, as well as to seek stories from the people and places around him. He began to retell some of his favorite African folk stories. In 1971, he collected five of those stories in a book, *The Ox of the Wonderful Horns and Other African Folktales* (Atheneum, 1971). He illustrated the stories with tempera paints. His tendency to intersperse paintings in red, black, and ochre with black-and-white paintings is shown in the end papers. Bryan has used several different techniques in his various books. In some, he has used vibrant watercolors; in others, he has used block prints. The illustrations in *The Adventures of Aku* (Atheneum, 1976), *Beat the Story-Drum, Pum-Pum* (Atheneum, 1980), and *Lion and the Ostrich Chicks* (Atheneum, 1986) may appear to some to be block or silk-screen prints. In fact, the illustrations are paintings. Bryan feels that original artwork created as paintings reproduce better. Nonetheless, he did create the illustrations for his volumes of spirituals with linoleum blocks to emulate early religious block-printed books. Initially, he thought he would have to use wood blocks, but the cost of good hardwood would have been immense, and he would have had difficulty transporting such heavy and bulky material between Dartmouth and Islesford. He settled on unmounted linoleum because it was lighter and much cheaper, it would not splinter, and, most important, it allowed him to achieve the detail and effect he wanted.

In *It's a Wonderful World* (Atheneum, 1995), a song book written by George David Wiess and Bob Thiele and illustrated by Bryan, Bryan used brilliantly colored scenes of a puppet show acting out each stanza of the song. A featured character in the puppet show is Louis "Satchmo" Armstrong, who popularized the song.

Bryan collects African stories, sometimes only a paragraph or two. There are more than 900 dialects in Africa, so he uses translations, written in French, German, or English, as his source material. Bryan's motifs are brief, skeletal ideas that are not yet stories. He says, "I take these motifs from anthologies or in scholarly studies and work to bring them in to the oral tradition of story telling." He rewrites each of his books until the rhythm is perfect. He strives to create a special relationship between the words, rhythm, and sounds. The songs he collects in his books are meant to be sung.

The text of a book determines the technique and medium Bryan will use to illustrate it. He creates roughs from which he works the finished illustrations. He has illustrated all but one of his books. His friend, Fumio Yoshimura, illustrated Bryan's retelling of *Sh-Ko and His Eight Wicked Brothers* (Atheneum, 1988), a Japanese tale. During a 1991 interview, Bryan explained how the collaboration came about: "My friend Fumio Yoshimura had done extensive brush paintings to Japanese legends. When I saw the large amount of beautiful brush paintings, I asked him if I could retell one small part of the Sh-Ko story. I wanted children to see the Japanese style of brush painting from this fine artist, since books introduce children to the art of the world."

When Bryan illustrates his own books, his family often inspires him. His grandmother, Sarah, came from Antigua for a visit and stayed 20 years in New York before she returned. She inspired the illustrations of the grandmother that accompany "Somebody's Knocking at Your Door," a song Bryan included in *I'm Going to Sing: Black American Spirituals, Volume II* (Atheneum, 1982). She also inspired the retelling of and illustrations for *The Dancing Granny* (Atheneum, 1977), which came from the Ashanti tradition via the West Indies.

While Bryan's grandmother was in the United States, she often watched her great-grandchildren dance. Once she figured out the pattern, she joined in, built her own patterns onto theirs, and then out danced them. Bryan's grandmother became "The Dancing Granny." When Bryan illustrated *The Dancing Granny*, he based his illustrative style on his study of the Japanese brush painting in the work of his friend, Hokusai. Through his brush strokes, he achieved the illusion of movement that he sought for the story. *The Dancing Granny* fairly whirls off the page as Granny dances through the story.

Whenever Bryan recites or shares a story or a poem, he feels there must be a sense of connection. When the story or poem he is sharing comes from a book, he always holds the book so the listeners connect with the printed version as well. "Whatever the voice does, it lives in a book."

Bryan has lived in France and Germany and has traveled to England, Italy, Spain, Yugoslavia, Greece, Israel, Malaysia, Indonesia, Bali, Kenya, and Uganda—always in search of a story. After teaching at Dartmouth for nearly fifteen years, Bryan retired in 1995. He currently lives on Islesford, the island he discovered many years ago as a college student. His home is filled with surprises. He displays toys in every nook and corner—on the tables, in display cases, and on top of doorframes. The toys have come from all over the world.

Art is a dominating presence throughout his home. Innovative paintings hang on the walls, he always has new art for a book or two in the making, and he has created glorious paintings with papier-mâché and bits of glass he has collected along the beach. Glass decorative panels are like stained glass windows, not unlike those in a church. His innovative use of glass brought him a commission at St. John's Church in the Bronx to create a replacement window depicting the Resurrection after a window was lost in a fire.

In addition to his toy collection and his art work, he collects colorful and expressive hand puppets, some of which he has created from materials collected on the beach, including driftwood, seashells, and so forth.

Bryan's island home is remote. When he travels away from home, Bryan must catch a ride on a mail boat to a little town on the coast of Maine, Northeast Harbor, just south of Bar Harbor on Mount Desert Island. Then he must travel by car to Bangor, Maine, and then fly out to his destination. His visitors must take the same route in reverse to reach Bryan's home.

Bryan's status as professor emeritus at Dartmouth has allowed him to have much more time to tell stories, write poetry, and to travel and visit schools.

He is "always working on retelling African folktales. I loved poetry and folktales of the world . . . still do."

BOOKS AND NOTES

Ashley Bryan's books include books of poetry, folktales, and songs. Many of the stories, songs, and poetry come from his childhood experiences. Others, particularly some of the folktales, come from his travels to the continent of Africa where he has gathered many of the tales he retells. He gathered favorite tales from three of his books into a new compilation, *Ashley Bryan's African Tales Uh-Huh* (Atheneum, 1998). The fourteen stories in the collection were previously published in *The Ox of the Wonderful Horns* (Atheneum, 1971); *Beat the Story-Drum, Pum-Pum* (Atheneum, 1980); and *Lion and the Ostrich Chicks* (Atheneum, 1986). The following titles are all written and illustrated by Ashley Bryan unless otherwise noted.

All Night, All Day (McElderry, 1991).

Analeesa Lee and the Weaver's Gift. Written by Nikkie Grimes. Illustrated by Ashley Bryan. (Lothrop, 1999).

Ashley Bryan's ABC of African American Poetry (Atheneum, 1997).

Ashley Bryan's African Tales Uh-Huh (Atheneum, 1998).

Carol of the Brown King: Nativity Poems. Written by Langston Hughes. Illustrated by Ashley Bryan. (Atheneum, 1998).

Climbing Jacob's Ladder: Spirituals from the Old Testament (McElderry, 1991).

It's a Wonderful World. Written by George David Wiess and Bob Thiele. Illustrated by Ashley Bryan. (Atheneum, 1995).

Sh-Ko and His Eight Wicked Brothers. Illustrated by Fumio Yoshimura. (Atheneum, 1988).

Turtle Knows Your Name (Atheneum, 1989).

FOR MORE INFORMATION

Articles

Marantz, Sylvia, and Kenneth Marantz. "Interview with Ashley Bryan." *Horn Book* (March/April 1988): 173–79.

Raymond, Allen. "Artist, Writer and Teacher: Ashley Bryan." *Teacher K–8.* (May 1995): 36–39.

Web Sites

Harrison Elementary School: Author Links. "Ashley Bryan." URL: <http://www.cr.k12.ia.us/Harr/Bryan.html> (Accessed March 2000).

Simon Says Kids: Meet the Brains. "Ashley Bryan." URL: <http://www.simonsays.com/kids/mtb.> (Accessed March 2000). Use the search function to find "Bryan."

Telling Stories with Pictures: The Art of Children's Book Illustration. "Artist: Ashley Bryan." URL: <http://www.decordova.org/decordova/exhibit/stories/bryan.html> (Accessed March 2000).

Eve Bunting

◆ Family Relationships ◆ Friends ◆ Community

Hans Gutknecht

Maghera, County Derry, Ireland
December 19, 1928

📖 *Ducky*
📖 *Smoky Night*
📖 *The Wall*

ABOUT THE AUTHOR

Ireland, Scotland, and the United States (California) have all been home to author Eve Bunting. Anne Evelyn "Eve" Bolton was born in Ireland in 1928, the daughter of Sloan Edward and Mary Bolton. Her father was a product merchant. From the age of nine, Eve attended a boarding school in Belfast. She tells of air raids over England from the German warplanes and hurried trips to the shelters.

In 1945, she graduated from Belfast's Methodist College and entered Queen's University, where she met Edward Davison Bunting. They married on April 26, 1951 and soon moved to Scotland, where they lived for several years. Together they had three children: Christine, Sloan, and Glenn.

In 1958, the Bunting family left Scotland for the United States. They settled first in San Francisco where Ed's brother was living. After about a year Ed, was offered a job as a hospital administrator in Los Angeles, so the family moved to Pasadena. The have lived in the same home, on a lovely tree-lined street, for more than thirty years. The dining room looks into the backyard gardens and the swimming pool. Eve Bunting became a naturalized citizen of the United States in 1967.

When her children grew up and left home, Bunting began to think about what she would do. It was then that her writing career began to bud. "In 1971," she says, "I was facing the 'empty nest syndrome' with no prospects of much that would be worthwhile or entertaining for me for the rest of my life. At that time, I didn't know of the wonder of grandchildren."

Bunting spotted a Pasadena City College brochure and a course called Writing for Publication. "I'd always liked to write, though I had never in my wildest dreams considered 'being a writer.' It worked out well." To date, she has had more than 180 titles published. She usually publishes as Eve Bunting but has also used the pen names "Evelyn Bolton" and "A. E. Bunting."

Bunting has written books for every age group from preschool to young adults. She has also published a number of articles and short stories. For a time, she also taught writing classes at the University of California.

Bunting says that she writes "when I feel like it, but fortunately I feel like it everyday." Each day, she spends four to five hours writing. She says she doesn't "need a computer or a fancy desk" to write her books. She works in the library at her house. Each piece of information is carefully thought out before Bunting begins the actual writing. After writing her notes, she types the story on a typewriter. Using a pencil and paper, she jots down her many ideas for characters and plots. With a wry nod to today's technological world, she describes the point of her pencil as the "character insertion subunit" and the eraser as the "character deletion subunit." She writes on only the left side of the paper, saving the right side for second thoughts and insertions. After writing her first draft, she reads the story into a tape recorder in an effort to identify any places where the flow of the sentences needs to be corrected. Eventually, after revisions, the manuscript is sent off to an appropriate editor.

Bunting was forty-three years old and her children were teenagers before her first book, *The Two Giants* (Ginn, 1972), was published. The book, with illustrations by Eric von Schmidt, told the story of a fight scheduled between the Irish giant, Finn McCool, and the Scottish giant, Culcullan. Their fight leads to the construction of the Giant's Causeway in the Irish sea. It was a story that Bunting thought everyone knew but quickly realized that although often told by the *Shanachies* (storytellers) in Ireland, it was not as well known in the United States.

That Irish folktale was the first of many Irish connections made by Bunting in her writing. Readers may not become aware of the connections, but the themes in Bunting's books often grew from Bunting's longing for her homeland or the rich heritage of the storytelling that surrounded her as she grew up. "Much of my background in Ireland finds its way into my books, as does a certain amount of Irish phrasing and Irish philosophy. In *Market Day* [HarperCollins, 1996], that is my little town in Ireland that I write about."

A book she calls her "Irish book" was published in 1995. That book *Spying on Miss Müller* (Clarion, 1995) was the book she says she "always wanted to write." Bunting says she "knew my experiences at the boarding school would make a pretty good book, and my editor at Clarion Books encouraged me, for years, to write the book. The school is real, although I did change its name. And a lot of people in it are real or a mixture of real people." At Alveara boarding school in Belfast, at the start of World War II, thirteen-year-old Jessie must deal with her suspicions about a teacher whose father was German. Bunting herself had been at boarding school during World War II when one of their teachers was treated horribly because she was suspected of being German. Bunting says, "In the book, *Spying on Miss Müller*, I am Jessie."

Bunting is acutely aware of the actions and events that go on around her. Since the beginning of her writing career, she has averaged six or seven books a year, and many of them reflect societal issues from the real world. There have been books about riots, the homeless, and illegal immigrants. Media accounts and discussions of those issues and events are like seeds that grow into full-fledged stories, stories that reflect the societal concerns of the times.

Latchkey children became the topic of *Is Anybody There?* (Lippincott, 1988), a book that focuses on Marcus Mullen. His mother, a widow, must work full time. One afternoon, just before Christmas break, Marcus discovers that his hidden key is missing. At first, Marcus suspects that the tenant in the garage apartment is responsible, but he discovers that the secret of his fear is something completely different.

Sensitive social issues and topics have not been restricted to Bunting's novels, and any appropriate issue may also creep into her picture books. Shortly after the Los Angeles riots, Bunting penned a title, *Smoky Night* (Harcourt, 1994) that dealt with a young boy, Daniel, and his mother who find themselves in the middle of a riot. When their apartment is set on fire and evacuation is necessary, Daniel loses his beloved cat, Jasmine. Daniel is left to wonder "Why?" and his mother has no good answer. The book's illustrations, created by David Diaz, earned a Caldecott Award. Bunting first got the idea for this book on the night of the Los Angeles riots. She had been speaking at a Pasadena library at an author program, and when she came out, she sensed something was different, even in Pasadena. By the time she got home, the television was filled with scenes from the rioting. She began to think about the effect the riots would have on a child caught in the middle of such horrible pandemonium. The day after the riots ended, she started making notes and writing the book. After several false starts, she finished it—in just one month's time. "That book and its subject matter are dear to my heart since I live close to Los Angeles."

The prejudice that is an undercurrent in that book is also the reason Bunting and her family left Ireland. She saw, first hand, the prejudicial relationships between the Catholics and the Protestants in her homeland and did not want to raise her children in "that kind of atmosphere." So, the family immigrated to the United States.

Homelessness is the topic of *Fly Away Home* (Clarion, 1991), a story that deals with a family unable to afford housing on the father's part-time janitor's pay. Andrew's mother has died, and Andrew and his father have taken up residence in the local airport. They wash in the airport bathroom and eat in the airport cafeteria. Andrew dreams of flying free to a new home, just as a bird trapped inside the airport is allowed to fly way.

The Wall (Clarion, 1990) deals with the aftermath of the Vietnam War, *The Wednesday Surprise* (Clarion, 1989) focuses on adult illiteracy, and *A Day's Work* (Clarion, 1994) deals with migrant workers. *The Wednesday Surprise* began as a story a librarian in Pasadena told about her grandmother, Patina. Bunting infused the subject of illiteracy into a novel, *Sixth-Grade Sleepover* (Harcourt, 1986), as well.

Bunting's favorite things creep into her writing. Her favorite holiday is Halloween, so it is no surprise that she has written books such as *Scary, Scary Halloween* (Clarion, 1986) and *In the Haunted House* (Clarion, 1990). Now her grandchildren give her ideas for books. *No Nap* (Clarion, 1989) and *Perfect Father's Day* (Clarion, 1991) feature a little girl named Susie whose reluctance to take a nap, and whose idea of a perfect father's day is to share her own favorite things, come straight from Bunting's grandchildren.

Bunting says her favorite book is impossible to identify. "Many of my books [26] have won state awards voted on by children." She says, "I love each of them for different reasons." And if she did not like what she had written she wouldn't have written the book at all.

Bunting and her husband live in Pasadena where they enjoy visits from their sons and daughter and four granddaughters, including a set of twins. When Bunting is not writing, she is likely swimming, reading, or walking. Wherever she goes, there is most likely a pencil and paper close at hand.

BOOKS AND NOTES

Eve Bunting has written for the picture-book audience and for older readers. Her fiction is laced with bits and pieces from events in her own life and the lives of her children. The range of her books has encompassed ghost stories (yes, Bunting does believe in ghosts), adventure stories, and books about sharks and whales. She has addressed homelessness, the Holocaust, the plight of migrant workers, the Vietnam War, the death of a friend, and urban violence while providing books that engage young readers and motivate them to reach out to reading. At the time of this writing, a complete list of Bunting's work would include more than 180 titles. The following are selected picture-book titles.

The Blue and the Gray. Illustrated by Ned Bittinger. (Scholastic, 1996).

Can You Do This, Old Badger? Illustrated by LeVyen Pham. (Harcout, 2000)

The Day the Whale Came. Illustrated by Scott Menchin. (Harcourt, 1998).

A Day's Work. Illustrated by Ronald Himler. (Clarion, 1994).

December. Illustrated by David Diaz. (Harcourt, 1997).

Doll Baby. Illustrated by Catherine Stock. (Clarion, 2000).

Dreaming of America: An Ellis Island Story. Illustrated by Ben Stahl. (Bridge Water, 1999).

Ducky. Illustrated by David Wisniewski. (Clarion, 1997).

Flower Garden. Illustrated by Kathryn Hewitt. (Harcourt, 1994).

Fly Away Home. Illustrated by Ronald Himler. (Clarion, 1991).

Ghosts Hour, Spooks Hour. Illustrated by Donald Carrick. (Clarion, 1987).

Happy Birthday, Dear Duck. Illustrated by Jan Brett. (Clarion, 1988).

I Am the Mummy Heb-Nefert. Illustrated by David Christiana. (Harcourt, 1997).

I Like the Way You Are. Illustrated by John O'Brien. (Clarion, 2000).

Market Day. Illustrated by Holly Berry. (HarperCollins, 1996).

The Memory of String. Illustrated by Ted Rand. (Clarion, 2000).

On Call Back Mountain. Illustrated by Barry Moser. (Blue Sky, 1997).

Peepers. Illustrated by James Ransome. (Harcourt, 2000).

The Pumpkin Fair. Illustrated by Eileen Christelow. (Clarion, 1996).

Smoky Night. Illustrated by David Diaz. (Harcourt, 1994).

So Far from the Sea. Illustrated by Chris Soentpiet. (Clarion, 1998).

Some Frog! Illustrated by Scott Medlock. (Harcourt, 1997).

Sunflower House. Illustrated by Kathryn Hewitt. (Harcourt, 1996).

Train to Somewhere. Illustrated by Ronald Himler. (Clarion, 1996).

The Wall. Illustrated by Ronald Himler. (Clarion, 1990).

FOR MORE INFORMATION

Articles

"Meet the Author: Eve Bunting." Supplement to *Instructor* (September 1992).

Raymond, Allen. "Eve Bunting: From Ireland with Love." *Early Years* (October 1986): 38–40.

Weiss, Stephanie. "Eve Bunting: Suitable for Children?" *NEA Today* (April 1995): 7.

Videos

A Visit With Eve Bunting (Houghton Mifflin/ Clarion, 1991). VHS 19 mins.

John Burningham

Farnharm, Surrey, England
April 27, 1936

Sharron L. McElmeel

📖 *Hey! Get Off Our Train*

📖 *John Patrick Norman
McHennessy—The Boy
Who Was Always Late*

📖 *Mr. Gumpy's Outing*

ABOUT THE AUTHOR/ILLUSTRATOR

John Burningham's early years were spent in as many as ten schools before he graduated from A. S. Neill's Summerhill experiment in education. The overall experience left Burningham with one major belief: No matter how responsive or stimulating a child's school is, the school's influence is secondary to the relationship and influence of that child's parents.

John Burningham was born in Farnharm, Surrey, England, the son of Charles and Jessie Burningham. The family lived in the country and moved a lot during the war years. The moves and changes in schools left John Burningham with substantial gaps in his education. When he was finally enrolled in Summerhill, he put a considerable amount of time and energy into his art classes. After completing his schooling, he was required to register for military service. He registered as a conscientious objector and was assigned two years' alternative military service. Those two years were spent working on farms doing forestry work. He also worked in hospitals and work camps, renovated slums, and helped build the nation's infrastructure. Part of the time was spent on assignments in Southern Italy, Yugoslavia, and Israel.

Once his period of military service was complete, he had to make a decision about what to do for his life's work. A friend was enrolled in the Central School of Arts and Crafts in London, and he decided to apply as well. He ended up studying illustration and graphic design for three years, earning a diploma with distinction. He was a "qualified book illustrator and graphic designer." He soon found out that his diploma did not ensure a job, however. He went to publishers and advertising agencies and did manage to get a few commissions to create advertising posters for the London Transport, but he was unable to obtain work from publishers. Eventually, he found work in animated films, designing backgrounds and puppets. The work temporarily took him to the Middle East.

Burningham's continued efforts to work for publishers were unsuccessful. Frustrated, he decided to write and illustrate his own book. The result was a book titled *Borka: The Adventures of a Goose with No Feathers* (Random House, 1963; Crown, 1994). That book was published in England in 1963 and earned him England's Kate Greenaway Medal in 1964. The Greenaway Medal is presented annually for the most distinguished work in the illustration of children's books published in the United Kingdom. The success of that book convinced Burningham to continue writing and illustrating children's books. Other artistic opportunities opened up for him as well, however. He has created friezes for children's rooms, murals, and exhibitions and has worked in animated films. He also has developed advertising and magazine illustrations and has had his work exhibited by the American Institute of Graphic Arts.

On August 15, 1965, John Burningham married Helen Oxenbury. They had both been students at the Central School of Arts and Crafts in London and had spent some time together in Israel. Burningham returned to England, while Oxenbury stayed in Israel to finish her work in Tel-Aviv. She rose as a designer in the National Theatre of Israel. Eventually she returned to England, they married, and they became the parents of two children. Lucy was born in 1967, and William Benedict was born in 1968.

The success of Burningham's first book and his subsequent success have brought him satisfaction. When he began as a creator of children's books, he had no children of his own, nor were there any other writers in his family. In fact, there was not the usual "apprenticeship" in writing and illustrating that helped him sharpen his skills in those areas. His first efforts, however, seemed to confirm that he was a natural children's writer. With the exception of a few novels that Burningham has illustrated for other authors, he has written each book that he has illustrated.

During Burningham's more than thirty-five years creating children's books, his technique and focus have shifted. In the earlier years, during the middle 1960s and early 1970s, his drawing was "hit or miss" and often dealt with the adventure of some animal. Gradually, he began to focus more on the relationships between the adults and children. In general, children come to understand the relationship but sometimes the adults reading the book do not. One of his earliest books that deals with this theme is *Granpa* (Crown, 1985). In this tale, a child shares a special relationship with his grandfather. When Granpa's chair is suddenly empty, the child knows his grandfather has died, but the memories of him have not.

Another title that deals with a young girl's relationship with her parents is *Come Away from the Water, Shirley* (HarperCollins, 1977). In the book, Shirley is fantasizing on one side of the page, and on the other side, the parents are saying, "Don't touch that dog," and cautioning her not to get near the water. Adults who read the book tend to infer that the parents are uncaring and don't want Shirley to have any fun. Burningham says that the book is not intended to present a moral lesson, however. The simple fact is the family has to get back on the bus, and wet feet will be bothersome. The book tells a story from two perspectives: the child's, who is oblivious to the problems that having wet shoes or boots will cause, and the parents', which focuses on not getting wet shoes.

Burningham's books have evolved to a simpler form over the years. Earlier, he wanted to put more and more detail and color into his books, but in the last decade he has moved toward simpler forms. His illustrations have just enough detail to move the story, but not so much that the book is overburdened by its elements.

Burningham's children's books begin with his mental plans. He develops a story line that works through pictures. Then, when the pictures are laid out, he develops the text. He revises his text and illustrations on mock pages, and as the revisions progress, the words and pictures begin to evolve. The simpler books actually take him longer to develop. It is more difficult to fit fewer words into a simple format. He does acknowledge that simplification can go too far. The people who buy books seem to want more than one word on a page. "They want a pound of words for their money," says Burningham.

Burningham likes to develop something new and to work with something he hasn't done before. Nonetheless, he has written two books about Mr. Gumpy. A publisher has asked him to write yet another book about the popular character, but he hasn't done so.

In the late 1960s and early 1970s, John Burningham spent two-and-a-half years creating an illustrated version of Jules Verne's *Around the World in Eighty Days* (Jonathan Cape, 1972). The book garnered an audience in the adult picture-book market. Afterward, he worked on developing a sketchbook of sorts in which he was "trying to define England." He views producing books as similar to repertory theater, so for several years, he "learned the part" for the England book. In 1992, Jonathan Cape publishers in England published *England*. The book was referred to as a book of "wit and humor," and it deals with the social life and customs of England.

Burningham has also developed a similar book for France. His book, *John Burningham's France* (DK, 1998) is a pictorial representation of life in modern-day France as seen through his eyes. While Burningham and Oxenbury have maintained a home on Hampstead Heath near London for all their married life, they also have lived a portion of each of the past twenty years in the hills of southwest France. In *France*, Burningham has fun with his view of life in his adopted home. He takes a look at the Moulin Rouge and the Cannes Film Festival. His caricatures poke fun at the driving practices in France, the concierge who sees all and reveals nothing, and the strange regulations sometimes imposed by the French government.

After a hiatus from children's books, Burningham returned with *Whadayamean* (Crown, 1999), a title that has God viewing the mess everyone has made of Earth and focusing on two children who implore "everyone to help make it a lovely place." It is clearly an environmental title with a message.

John Burningham and Helen Oxenbury both have studios in their London home. Their children are now grown. Burningham and Oxenbury continue their artistic endeavors with the luxury of being able to pick and choose projects that please them, while working at a pace that produces work they feel pride in producing.

BOOKS AND NOTES

John Burningham has had his art in several major exhibits. His watercolors are simple and direct. His one lament concerning the creation of art as a children's book illustration is that people are influenced in what they consider to be art by the circumstances in which they see the rendering. He has said, "If they see something in a book for children, it is 'child-like,' but put a frame around it and pop it in a gallery" and it is considered "serious art." Burningham's art is filled with humor and subtle jokes, the same elements that characterize his writing. The following selected list includes books written and illustrated by John Burningham.

Cannonball Simp (Candlewick, 1994).

A homely dog is followed as she strays away from her home and becomes the famous partner of a circus clown.

Cloudland (Random House, 1996).

When Albert falls off a cliff, the cloud children rescue him by uttering the magic words to make him light, preventing him from falling.

Come Away from the Water, Shirley (Harper-Collins, 1977).

A walk viewed from two perspectives. Shirley is adventurous and has fantasies along the way. Her parents are more concerned that she not get her feet wet.

Harvey Slumenburger's Christmas Present (Candlewick, 1996).

Santa returns home and realizes that he has left Harvey's present in his bag. The reindeer are not feeling well and have already gone to sleep, so Santa makes his own way back to the Slumenburger's home. Along the way, he catches a ride on a snowmobile, in a jeep, on a motorbike, on skis, and even uses a mountain climber's rope.

Hey, Get Off Our Train (Crown, 1989).

A boy rescues several endangered animals.

John Burningham's ABC (Crown, 1993).

This delightful alphabet features plump pigs on the "p" page and an exploding volcano on the "v" page.

John Patrick Norman McHennessy—The Boy Who Was Always Late (Crown, 1987).

A young boy arrives at school each day with an outrageous story to explain his tardiness. In the end, the tables are turned.

FOR MORE INFORMATION

Limited information can be found on book jacket flaps. No articles, books, or Web sites were located.

Virginia Lee Burton

Newton Centre, MA
August 30, 1909–October 15, 1968

📖   *The Little House*
📖   *Mike Mulligan and His Steam Shovel*

ABOUT THE
AUTHOR/ILLUSTRATOR

   Virginia Lee Burton was born in Newton Centre, Massachusetts. Her father was the first dean of the Massachusetts Institute of Technology. She spent her childhood and adolescent years in Massachusetts and California. She studied art at the California School of Fine Arts in San Francisco. She also studied ballet and at one point planned to become a professional dancer. Her natural understanding of rhythm contributed to the rhythmic patterns found in her drawing and painting.

   Later, at age 21, Burton enrolled in art classes at the Boston Museum of Fine Arts where she studied with George Demetrios, one of the few great teachers of life drawing at that time. A few months later, in 1932, Burton married Demetrios. It was not long before she was working on a picture book. Houghton Mifflin published her first, *Choo Choo*, in 1937. By then, she and Demetrios were living in Folly Cove, between Rockport and Gloucester, Massachusetts, on Cape Ann. Her inspiration for the book came from her elder son's interest in trains.

   At times, Burton would "go up the hill to George's studio and join his summer classes." She was able to refresh her artistic eye and hand as her husband critiqued her work. Art played a major role in Burton's life, but she also remained interested in dance. She enjoyed participating in a dance class that a well-known dancer and teacher taught in Cape Ann. Parties in Folly Cove with Burton and her husband often included square dancing. Burton, known to her friends as Jinnee, drew in much the same way that she danced: quickly, rhythmically, and with clarity.

Burton began using double-page spreads to full advantage in her second book, *Mike Mulligan and His Steam Shovel* (Houghton, 1939). She began using the two pages as a unit and put the text in specially designed spaces within the illustration. She felt the illustrator should command all the elements of the page. The book, *Mike Mulligan and His Steam Shovel*, was written for her second son, Michael Burton Demetrios. Those who knew the family will attest to the fact that the blond boy who races up to see Mike Mulligan and Mary Anne (the steam shovel) in Popperville was surely modeled after Michael.

Calico, the Wonder Horse; or, the Saga of Stewey Stinker (Houghton, 1941) came about during the time when her boys became interested in comic books, which began to gain popularity during the 1940s. Burton considered them to be of marginal value, and she sought to present an alternative comic-book format with *Calico, the Wonder Horse; or, the Saga of Stewy Stinker*. Burton received criticism for the book's title; after all, said critics, children should not be saying "stinker." Burton's publisher reissued the book in 1950 with a new title: *Stewy Stinker Triumphant*.

Burton did much of her illustrative work using scratchboard and linoleum block prints. She began by making sketches for each page and hanging them sequentially around her studio. As she created the final works, she replaced each of the sketches with the finished illustrations. As she continued to work, she could look continuously at the pages she had completed. Often times, she would look up and notice a line or an area that needed to be fixed. She continually reevaluated her work.

Burton used a flow of design in her illustrations to impart a specific perspective point. In the process, she used black and white lines and dots to create several "tones" in her illustrations. Another design element was her use of proportion to create a feeling of motion. Larger and smaller figures of the same type provide a perspective that gives a sense of the movement of the figures. These three elements—flow of design, tones, and proportion—combined to create what became known internationally as "Folly Cove Design."

Burton taught her techniques to other artists in design classes that she first taught in her Folly Cove barn from 1939 to 1941. The student group later became known as the Folly Cove Designers and began to sell hand-painted textiles beginning in 1941. For twenty-one years, from 1948 to 1969, the group had a shop in Folly Cove. It finally closed because the demand for the textiles was far too great for the few active members. The Cape Ann Historical Association in Gloucester has a permanent collection of the fabrics.

The Little House (Houghton, 1942), winner of the 1943 Caldecott Medal, put Burton's name firmly in the annals of children's literature. This book is so well known that even today, it is used in classrooms around the world. The book came about when Demetrios bought a piece of land in Folly Cove and moved the family's small house from its original position, which was too close to the street. In the book, Burton made the house small and simple. She gave the book a traditional shape to emphasize the house's survival through the cycle of seasons, through the years, and through its movement from one location to another. Their yard provided the model for the country setting.

In *Life Story* (Houghton, 1962), Burton used *The Little House* theme again in the last twenty pages of her book. The professor-lecturer in the earlier pages of the books changes to Burton herself in the later pages. Readers share the past twenty-five summers with Burton, near the orchard, meadow, and woodland area where they moved the house and her barn studio. It is there, Burton said, that she and her husband "raised our children until they grew old enough to begin living a life of their own."

Burton's work on *Life Story* took more than eight years and was exhausting both physically and creatively. Her charming surroundings and family life inspired many images in the work. The sheep shed on pages 66 and 68 of *Life Story* actually did exist on the family's acreage and even graced one of the Burton's family Christmas cards. For many years, the family held a picnic for their friends. It always came at the end of August, in honor of Burton and her son Michael, who shared the same birthday. There was always a baseball game in the meadow, dancing, and plenty of song singing. In December, caroling sessions were held in the barn studio. Burton kept a small spinet piano in the barn. The entire studio was decorated with green boughs and red ribbon. In later years, her sons sent large paper ornaments in brilliant colors from San Francisco's Chinatown. Many images from their home became part of her artwork. Even George's wood piles made their way into her books. A wonderful apple tree, the "swing tree," stood in the yard; through the years, it provided a wonderful motif for many of her drawings. George Demetrios was a sculptor, and many of his sculptures graced their lawn and terrace. Their son, Aristide, became a fine sculptor as well.

Burton did much of her work in black and white, but she did use color, too. *The Little House* was her first work in color and was followed by her retelling of *The Emperor's New Clothes* (Houghton, 1949). *Maybelle, the Cable Car* (Houghton, 1952) focused on the San Francisco cable cars. Burton often visited her sons in the western city and came to love the famous cable cars. Some people have said that her book helped to preserve them. In 1967, Burton presented the original art for *Maybelle, the Cable Car* to the San Francisco Public Library. She also donated the preliminary sketches and some discarded versions that she did not use. Some of the sketches for *Life Story* are held at the Free Library of Philadelphia, and the original illustrations for *Song of Robin Hood* (Houghton, 1947) are in the Boston Public Library.

Many of Burton's books were translated into Japanese, and Burton wanted to create a book with a Japanese theme, so she traveled to Japan in the spring of 1964. The book was never created.

Unfortunately, Burton was not in good health during her last five years. She had always felt that illness was a sign of weakness, but her "mind-over-matter" attitude could not overcome her ebbing stamina. Nonetheless, she enjoyed walking in the woods near her home and continued to swim and relax in the sun on what became known as "Jinnee's rock." In her later years, she purchased a small studio and a piece of land at the end of Folly Point. There she could retreat, spend time alone, and enjoy the sea. *Life Story* turned out to be her last book, providing an ambitious, all-encompassing work befitting the role of her final creation. Virginia Lee Burton Demetrios died on October 15, 1968.

BOOKS AND NOTES

Most of the books illustrated by Virginia Lee Burton were illustrated using black and white linoleum blocks or scratchboard. They demonstrate the use of the Folly Cove Design principles that she developed. Her use of color in *The Little House* earned the Caldecott Medal in 1943. Her career was filled with work as a textile artist and teacher, and it seems that she created her books primarily for her two sons, Michael and Aristide. Her technique of personifying objects brought readers the personable Mary Anne (steam shovel), Maybelle (cable car), Little House (house), and Choo Choo (engine). Even though her books first were published more than thirty years ago, they are still found in libraries and have been included in several reading anthologies.

Calico, the Wonder Horse; or, the Saga of Stewy Stinker (Houghton, 1941).

Choo Choo: The Story of a Little Engine Who Ran Away (Houghton, 1937, 1988).

The Emperor's New Clothes. Written by Hans Christian Andersen. (Houghton, 1949).

Katy and the Big Snow (Houghton, 1943).

Life Story (Houghton, 1962).

The Little House (Houghton, 1942, 1988).

Maybelle, the Cable Car (Houghton, 1952, 1996).

Mike Mulligan and His Steam Shovel (Houghton, 1939, 1967).

FOR MORE INFORMATION

Articles

Burton, Virginia Lee. "Making Picture Books." *Horn Book* 19 (July–August 1943): 228–29.
Describes how she made *The Little House* and other books, emphasizing Burton's belief in the importance of books for children.

Burton, Virginia Lee. "Symphony in Comics." *Horn Book* 17 (July–August 1941): 307–11.
Describes Burton's experiment of working with her son to create *Calico, the Wonder Horse; or, the Saga of Stewy Stinker* in comic-book style. Also analyzes the appeal of comics.

Kingman, Lee. "Virginia Lee Burton's Dynamic Sense of Design." *Horn Book* 46 (October–December 1970): 449–60, 593–602. (Reprinted in Hoffman, Miriam, and Eva Samuels. *Authors and Illustrators of Children's Books: Writings on Their Lives and Their Works.* [Bowker, 1972, pp. 41–55].)
Provides in-depth analysis of Burton's texts and art.

Web Sites

Houghton Mifflin: Trade and Reference Division. "Mulligan." URL: <http://www.Hmco.com/trade/mike_mulligan/biohome.html> (Accessed March 2000).

Eric Carle

Sharron L. McElmeel

Syracuse, New York
June 25, 1929

📖 *The Very Busy Spider*
📖 *The Very Hungry Caterpillar*

ABOUT THE AUTHOR/ILLUSTRATOR

Eric Carle lived the first five years of his life in the United States, spent the next decade in Germany, and finally returned to the United States as a young man in 1952. Carle was born in Syracuse, New York, on June 25, 1929 and began kindergarten there. Eric's father, Erich Carle, had immigrated to the United States from Stuttgart, Germany, in 1925. He was twenty-one years old. He found a job with a washing machine company, and two years later, he sent for a young woman, Johanna Oeschläger, whom he had met before leaving Germany. The couple was married in Syracuse in 1928.

When Eric's Grandmother Carle visited the family in the United States, she spoke of how wonderful life in Germany was. Carle's mother began to think about her homeland, and soon the family moved back to Germany. During the next decade, they lived in a four-story home. Relatives lived on each floor.

Adolf Hitler's control of the country created an atmosphere in which many artists' work was forbidden. A kindly teacher took Eric Carle to his house and showed him some of that forbidden artwork; paintings by Matisse, Picasso, Braque, Kandinsky, Klee, and others. He was told not to tell anyone what he had seen but to always remember the freedom of these artists' styles.

Carle's father was conscripted into Hitler's army and later became a prisoner of war. For months, Carle crawled out of bed, two or three times a night, and made his way to shelters to avoid Allied bombing. Stores and homes were bombed. When schools were threatened, many children were sent to the country where they would be safer. Carle was among these children and was sent to live with a foster family. At the end of the war, Carle returned home, but his father languished in a prisoner-of-war camp.

Carle attended art school after the war. One of his professors recommended that he study commercial and graphic art at the Akademie der bildenden Künste in Stuttgart. He entered the school at the age of sixteen, two years younger than the minimum age for students. He put on airs because he believed his art ability to be superior to that of the other students. One of his teachers, Professor Schneidler, recognized that Carle's attitude could ultimately hurt his work and demoted him from an art student to an apprentice in the typesetting room. He soon realized how perceptive Professor Schneidler was and set about learning everything he could about typography. The school later allowed him to resume his role as a student.

Carle included autobiographical stories from this era in *Flora and Tiger: 19 Very Short Stories from My Life* (Philomel, 1997). The stories introduce readers to Carle's Uncle August, who told Carle stories, and to other family members who influenced Carle's artwork and storytelling.

Although not yet twenty-three, Carle felt he was ready to return to the United States. He had a fine art portfolio and $40.00 in his pocket. He landed in New York on a beautiful day in May 1952. His father's younger brother opened his home to Carle, and he stayed there for a brief time until he was offered the chance to take care of an apartment near Broadway and 57th Street. Carle became acquainted with Leo Lionni, who was working for *Fortune* magazine. Lionni mentored Carle, and Carle ended up with a well-paying job at *The New York Times*.

Five months after arriving in New York, Eric Carle was drafted into the U.S. Army. Soon he was on his way back to Germany, where he was assigned to be a mail clerk for his unit. Each night, he was allowed to go to his mother's home to sleep in his old bed. His mother made him breakfast before he returned to the base. During one weekend pass in Wiesbaden, Carle ran into an old colleague from his days working for a German fashion magazine. The colleague's nineteen-year-old sister, Dorothea Wohlenberg, was with her, and she and Carle developed a relationship. A year later, in 1954, Eric and Dorothea were married—just one month before Carle's discharge from the army.

Dorothea accompanied Carle to New York, and they settled in Queens and had a daughter, Cirsten. When she was two years old, they moved to Irvington-on-Hudson, where their son, Rolf, was born. Four years later, the couple separated, which caused Carle much pain and anguish. For the next ten years, he lived alone except for regular weekend visits from his children. During that time, he began to create books for children.

Carle was a struggling artist and could not entertain friends very often. Nonetheless, he decided he could afford to host a pancake breakfast, and he made an invitation. That invitation became the start of a book, *Pancakes, Pancakes!* (Knopf, 1970; Picture Book, 1992). Carle has created many innovative books, including his most beloved, *The Very Hungry Caterpillar* (Crowell, 1969; Philomel, 1994). *The Very Hungry Caterpillar* came about when Carle was thinking about bookworms. He began playing with a paper punch, and as he punched the holes, he began to wonder how he could put his idea into a book.

He wrote the text and created sketches for a book called *Willy the Worm*. Ann Beneduce, Carle's editor, liked the idea but wanted him to examine other possibilities for the main character. When she suggested a caterpillar, Carle, without hesitation, said, "butterfly." *The Very Hungry Caterpillar* was born in that moment. When Carle took that first prototype to Beneduce, the end pages were tissue papers that had hundreds of holes punched into them.

Carle creates his trademark illustrations in collage with tissue paper. During his first years as an artist, he used commercial tissue paper. Later he developed a technique creating his own tissue paper colors. Today he uses acid-free, white tissue paper, painted a base color with acrylic paints, and then he paints with other designs and strokes to make the paper more interesting. He stores the colored papers in drawers according to their basic colors. Later, he cuts and tears the papers into shapes and glues them with polymer wallpaper paste to create his pictures. The materials he now uses are intended to help his art to be of archival quality.

Before he begins to create a book, Carle cleans his studio and chooses the papers he will use. He always finishes one book before beginning another. Children and their parents in England, Scotland, Holland, Germany, Finland, Italy, Japan, and France read Carle's books.

In 1971, Carle met Barbara Morrison. She was a teacher of children who had special needs. He invited her to dinner one evening. She brought him a single-stemmed anthurium cradled in white translucent paper. A year-and-a-half later, in 1973, they married.

The following year, they moved to a new house on fifty wooded acres in the Berkshires, in the northwest corner of Massachusetts. Their home sat atop a mountain at the end of a quarter-mile drive. A meadow stretches down the slope in front of this house. During the winter, they needed a sturdy vehicle to reach their home. More than a decade later, they decided that they would rather spend the winter months in nearby Northampton, where they were close to shops, friends, movie houses, the library, a post office, and a Chinese restaurant. They purchased an older home in town, and Carle has a 1,700-square-foot studio with plenty of room for the creation of his specialized tissue papers. Carle has even found time to serve on the school board in Northampton.

Carle's children, Rolf and Cirsten, are grown. Both have been involved in art-related careers. Rolf studied art in Philadelphia; Cirsten graduated from Syracuse University and has worked as a photographer. Many of Carle's books have his children's names or initials in the illustrations. Occasionally, his dog, Tock, was included in the illustrations. Carle has had many cats and named them all Mizi, except for one, named Delicat, who was the most graceful, charming, delicate, and murderous cat Carle has ever known.

Currently, Eric and Barbara Carle live in Northampton, Massachusetts, where he continues to create picture books and be involved in the community.

BOOKS AND NOTES

Eric Carle's books generally contain surprises. Occasionally, the pages have holes in them, others have flaps that hide something underneath, or magnificent foldouts that delight readers of all ages as they pop from the pages. Carle is fascinated by "paper engineering," and he believes most children enjoy his surprises.

His books help encourage literacy, as well as an interest in art.

As Carle has evolved as an artist, making his own tissue paper colors and using museum-quality materials, he has looked at his earlier books with an eye toward improving on them. He has reillustrated several of his books, including *The Mixed-Up Chameleon* (Crowell, 1975). This book was first illustrated with crayon in six basic colors. In 1984, he reillustrated the book using collage. The collages mimic the form and relationship to text as the original crayon drawings but have muted the boldness of the rainbow colors, helping the reader focus on the ever-changing composition of the mixed-up chameleon. In addition to the new illustrations, the text underwent revision. In both editions, the illustrations enhance and complement the text, but in the reissue, the illustrations have become an integral part of the book and no longer merely reflect the text but add information as well. Several books have undergone a similar type of reworking; sometimes even earning a new title. *The Very Hungry Caterpillar* was reissued in 1989 with all new art. The improvements are subtle; the colors are more vibrant, and some of the textures are more interesting. In April 1999, Eric Carle was awarded the 1999 Regina Medal by the Catholic Library Association. The award recognized the body of work that Carle has contributed to children's literature.

Books Written and Illustrated by Eric Carle

Many of these books have been published in one or more editions.

Do You Want to Be My Friend? (Philomel, 1988).

Does a Kangaroo Have a Mother, Too? (HarperCollins, 2000).

Draw Me a Star (Philomel, 1992).

Eric Carle's Dragons & Other Creatures That Never Were. Compiled by Laura Whipple. (Philomel, 1991).

Eric Carle's Treasury of Classic Stories for Children by Aesop, Hans Christian Andersen, and the Brothers Grimm (Orchard, 1988).

Flora and Tiger: 19 Very Short Stories from My Life (Philomel, 1997).

From Head to Toe (HarperCollins, 1997).

The Grouchy Ladybug (HarperCollins, 1996).

Hello, Red Fox (Simon & Schuster, 1998).

Little Cloud (Philomel, 1996).

My Apron: A Story from My Childhood (Philomel, 1994).

1, 2, 3 to the Zoo: A Counting Book (Philomel, 1996).

Pancakes, Pancakes! (Knopf, 1970; Picture Book, 1992).

Stories for All Seasons: Rooster's Off to See the World, A House for Hermit Crab, The Tiny Seed. (Simon & Schuster, 1998).

Today Is Monday (Philomel, 1993).

The Very Clumsy Click Beetle (Philomel, 1999).

The Very Hungry Caterpillar (Crowell, 1969; Philomel, 1994).

The Very Lonely Firefly (Philomel, 1995).

The Very Quiet Cricket (Philomel, 1990).

Walter the Baker (Simon & Schuster, 1995).

Books Illustrated by Eric Carle

Brown Bear, Brown Bear, What Do You See? Written by Bill Martin Jr. (Holt, 1992).

Polar Bear, Polar Bear, What Do You Hear? Written by Bill Martin Jr. (Holt, 1991).

FOR MORE INFORMATION

Articles

Klingberg, Delores R. "Profile: Eric Carle." *Language Arts* 54 (April 1977): 445–52.

Books

Carle, Eric. *The Art of Eric Carle* (Philomel, 1996).

Videos

Eric Carle: Picture Writer (Putnam, 1993). VHS 25 mins. Also available from Scholastic Book Clubs.

Web Sites

The Official Eric Carle Web Site. URL: <http://www.eric-carle.com/> (Accessed March 2000).

Lorinda Bryan Cauley

◆ Folklore

Washington, D.C.
July 2, 1951

📖 *The Pancake Boy: An Old Norwegian Folk Tale*
📖 *The Town Mouse and the Country Mouse*
📖 *Treasure Hunt*

ABOUT THE
AUTHOR/ILLUSTRATOR

Bright, humorous, and playful illustrations are the hallmark of Lorinda Bryan Cauley's books. As a child in Washington, D.C., she enjoyed art and often illustrated her school reports and projects. At home, she used art to keep busy and have fun.

Lorinda Bryan was born on July 2, 1951, in Washington, D.C. and says she cannot remember a time when she did not want to be an artist. One of her uncles was a mural painter. She was fascinated watching him standing high on a ladder, dabbing his long brushes into the paint pots and creating roomfuls of scenery or characters from faraway places. Her parents encouraged her efforts. After high school, she attended Montgomery Junior College and the Rhode Island School of Design (RISD). She earned her undergraduate degree in 1974, and on June 15 of that year, she married Patrick Dennis Cauley, a painter and an art professor.

At RISD, Cauley studied painting, drawing, and sculpting. Cauley is said to have settled on illustration because she could deal with a specific subject, focusing on an assignment, rather than the wide choices that were available in painting. Her training in illustration prepared her to work in the area of commercial art, but she began to feel that the field was too "slick" for her. She turned to children's book illustration as a showcase for her illustrative work.

When Cauley illustrates a book, she prefers to concentrate on making the settings interesting by including a lot of action, creating colorful images, and adding special details to make unique and fun books for children to read. At first, she wrote her own stories to illustrate. They centered on things she enjoyed—making and doing. Her first titles, *Things to Make and Do for Thanksgiving* (Watts) and *Pease-Porridge Hot: A Mother Goose Cookbook* (Putnam) were published in 1977. The following year, Putnam published *The Bake-Off*. Soon, Cauley began to retell folk and classic tales from authors such as Hans Christian Andersen and Rudyard Kipling. As the Cauley children, Ryan and MacKenzie, grew older, Cauley renewed her interest in writing her own stories. Many of her retellings, as well as her original stories, include animals.

Cauley's illustrations are filled with light, color, and energy. She attempts to draw animals as true to life as possible. Cauley's illustrations often show the animals with human characteristics and emotions. She spends many hours researching every detail of how the animal looks, how it moves, how it is structured, and anything else that might help her depict the animal correctly. She feels that children who go back to a book time and time again will surely notice if there are any visual errors.

The Cauleys have lived in upstate New York, Philadelphia, various cities in New Jersey, and Escondido, California. Both of the Cauleys are artists and have designed and hand-screened "beachy" clothes to sell in their clothing store in New Jersey.

The Cauleys' two children are now grown, and Patrick and Lorinda live in New Jersey. When she is not working on a book, Lorinda enjoys jogging and cooking.

BOOKS AND NOTES

Lorinda Bryan Cauley has written original tales and has illustrated retellings of some of her favorite nursery rhymes and folklore.

The Beginning of the Armadillos. Written by Rudyard Kipling. (Harcourt, 1985).

The Elephant's Child (Harcourt, 1983).

Jack and the Beanstalk (Putnam, 1983).

Old MacDonald Had a Farm (Putnam, 1989).

The Owl and the Pussycat. Written by Edward Lear. (Putnam, 1986).

The Pancake Boy: An Old Norwegian Folk Tale (Putnam, 1988).

Puss in Boots. Written by Charles Perrault. (Harcourt, 1986).

Three Blind Mice: The Classic Nursery Rhyme (Putnam, 1991).

The Town Mouse and the Country Mouse (Putnam, 1984).

FOR MORE INFORMATION

Web Sites

University of Southern Mississippi, de Grummond Collection: Lorinda Bryan Cauley Papers. URL: <http://www.lib.usm.edu/~degrum/findaids/cauley.htm> (Accessed March 2000).

Eileen Christelow

Washington, D.C.
April 22, 1943

📖 *Don't Wake up Mama!*

📖 *Five Little Monkeys with Nothing to Do*

📖 *The Great Pig Escape*

Karen Hesse

ABOUT THE AUTHOR/ILLUSTRATOR

At the age of three or four, Eileen Christelow dreamed that she could read. She read all the words, page by page. When she woke up, she realized it had only been a dream. She had to wait until first grade before she could make it come true. Christelow's parents read their children bedtime stories every night. Their home was filled with books, newspapers, comic books, and anything else that was interesting. Birthday and Christmas presents were often books. When Christelow had her appendix taken out, her parents gave her *Madeline* by Ludwig Bemelmans. Like Madeline, she saw cracks in the ceiling.

Christelow alphabetized and catalogued her growing library, and she loaned books to friends, fining them when the books were returned late. Television did not come into her life until she was twelve and then only for an hour and a half each week. She chose her programs very carefully.

Eileen Christelow was born in Washington, D.C., but grew up in homes there and in New Canaan, Connecticut, and Tokyo, Japan. Her father, Allan Christelow, was born and raised in England and worked for the United Kingdom British Treasury delegation. Her mother, Dorothy Beal Christelow, was an economist with the U.S. government.

As Christelow grew, she learned to love art. She made a horse with a black tail out of clay and a wedding cake from scraps of wood. She helped paint a volcano on the lunchroom wall at school. While she was discovering clay and paints, her father was discovering pastels. He created portraits of Eileen and her younger brother. Then, after creating a drawing of a vase of flowers, he put the pastels away. Christelow still has them. Along the way, her father discovered a magic shop near their home and became something of an amateur magician. He also brought home comic books about Mickey Mouse, Donald Duck, Uncle Scrooge, and many other wonderful characters. These books influenced Christelow's development, in later years, as an illustrator.

Eileen's maternal grandparents, "Daddy Harry" and "Damma," retired to a farm in Vermont and invited their twelve grandchildren to fill up the eleven bedrooms in their rambling farmhouse. Eileen and her brother, Allan, often spent summers on the farm. If more than two or three young grandchildren were there at a time, the adults hired a teenage live-in babysitter. The grandchildren and the babysitter often traded pranks back and forth, and these activities later became Christelow's inspiration for *Jerome and the Babysitter* (Clarion, 1985).

When Christelow was about ten, her family traveled to England to visit with her paternal grandparents and other relatives. On the ship, Christelow bought an autograph book and started to keep a journal of the trip. She was more interested in reading tales of King Arthur and the Knights of the Round Table, however. At the age of thirteen, the family traveled across the United States to San Francisco on their way to Japan. Then they sailed across the Pacific on the ship, *President Wilson*. When they arrived in Japan, she and her brother walked down the gangplank, and children on the pier pointed and giggled at them. Eileen realized that she was an oddity in this new country. She was several inches taller than other children, and instead of black hair and dark eyes, she had brown hair and brown eyes. At first, she wondered if she was going to spend an entire year having people stare at her, but the country was so interesting that she soon paid no attention.

Christelow's early interest in books did not translate into an interest in writing until she reached the eighth grade and encountered a "dynamic and demanding English teacher." She wrote many stories for the high school magazine and planned to major in English in college. However, her freshman English class was so tedious that she lost all enthusiasm for the idea. She turned to history and to drawing and design courses, which were part of a prearchitecture degree. She was headed toward three years of graduate work in architecture when she discovered photography during her senior year. During the years following her graduation, she photographed buildings for architects and created photo essays for magazines. Topics for her essays included skid row, Chinatown, inner-city schools and other aspects of urban life. During her time as a freelance photographer, she became interested in children's picture books. She began to experiment with writing and illustrated her stories with drawings and photographs.

During 1971 and 1972, Christelow and her husband, Ahren Ahrenholz, were living in Cornwall, England, where Ahrenholz studied pottery. Their daughter, Heather, was born while they were there. At the end of their year abroad, they had only $50.00 left in the bank and weren't sure where they were headed. For four months, they lived with family and friends and built up their bank account. One of their friends called from Berkeley, California and told them they were moving out of their house, which had a pottery wheel and kiln, and suggested that Christelow and Ahrenholz might wish to move in. The rent was low, so the family moved to Berkeley. Christelow picked up her work as a graphic designer and photographer. One of her design jobs included creating a poster about camouflage for a science museum. The poster work gave her the idea for the book *Henry and the Red Stripes* (Clarion, 1982).

The family decided to move to New England and ended up in Dummerston, Vermont, where they found twelve acres on which they could build a house, a place where Ahrenholz could pursue his pottery and Christelow could develop her career in children's books.

In 1981, Christelow sold two books and developed several more. Ideas came from everywhere, often from unexpected places. Once while visiting schools in Iowa, she read a newspaper headline, "Hog Wild Day on the Road." A farmer's hogs had escaped on the way to auction. The seed of the idea was planted for her book, *The Great Pig Escape* (Clarion, 1994). *The Robbery at the Diamond Dog Diner* (Clarion, 1986) came out of frequent stops at a diner in Whatley, Massachusetts, where Christelow often stopped when traveling to New York. It seemed a perfect setting for a mystery.

Christelow keeps "idea folders" where she searches for ideas to resurrect when she is at a loss for an interesting subject. Searching through her folder one day, she came across the rhymes enjoyed years earlier by her daughter, Heather. "Five Little Monkeys Jumping on the Bed" was one of them. Christelow did not want to start the book with the monkeys jumping on the bed, so she began the book with the monkeys brushing their teeth, taking a bath, putting on pajamas, and so forth, just like Madeline had done with the other girls in *Madeline*. And just like in *Madeline*, the shenanigans began when the lights went out.

Christelow's early books were anthropomorphic. *Jerome and the Babysitter* began with human characters, but it seemed implausible that children would misbehave with a crocodile babysitter. So the book became one about a family of ten little alligators. To Christelow, some animals seem to personify specific human characteristics better than others.

The first story Christelow wrote about humans was *The Five-Dog Night* (Clarion, 1993). The story came about when Christelow heard a retelling of a story on Vermont Public Radio. John H. Mitchell first reported the story in *Sanctuary*, the Massachusetts Audubon Society's magazine. The story is of an old man living in Vermont who relied on his dogs for warmth on cold winter nights. The book tries to pass on the idea that animals are more than mere pets.

One of Christelow's friends told of their eight-year-old daughter who had wrapped presents for all the family members, including the family dog, who was getting dog biscuits. It seemed the dog could not wait; the next morning, the family found chewed wrapping paper and dog biscuit crumbs under the tree. The Christelow dog, Ophelia, became the model for the canine hero of *Not Until Christmas, Walter!* (Clarion, 1997). The dog died just as Christelow finished the final illustrations for the book.

Christelow has authored several books about an alligator, Jerome, who is well known for his babysitting misadventures. One day, while visiting a second-grade class in Ogdensburg, New York, she began to develop a story about Jerome camping out. That day, while driving the seven hours home, the story went around and around in her head and actually went through several versions. The story finally became *Jerome Camps Out* (Clarion, 1998).

Eileen Christelow is a full-time illustrator and author. When she is not writing, she enjoys gardening and walking in the woods surrounding her home. In 1998, she was busy training their puppy, Emma, a task she says she did not enjoy. She reads both fiction and nonfiction. She also hangs out in coffee shops reading newspapers, which often provide her with ideas for her books. She frequently travels to visit schools across the United States.

BOOKS AND NOTES

Christelow's own writing and illustrating is showcased in her books *What Do Authors Do?* (Clarion, 1995) and its companion title, *What Do Illustrators Do?* (Clarion, 1999). Of her stories, she says, "I write about characters who are resourceful and self-reliant." Her books do not preach, and each character has his or her own flaws and quirks—just like the children who read them. Christelow writes books to entertain. She wants to show children that reading is enjoyable.

Books Written and Illustrated by Eileen Christelow

Don't Wake up Mama! (Clarion, 1992).

The Five-Dog Night (Clarion, 1993).

Five Little Monkeys Wash the Car (Clarion, 2000).

Five Little Monkeys with Nothing to Do (Clarion, 1996).

Gertrude the Bulldog Detective (Clarion, 1992).

The Great Pig Escape (Clarion, 1994).

Jerome Camps Out (Clarion, 1998).

Not Until Christmas, Walter! (Clarion, 1997).

The Robbery at the Diamond Dog Diner (Clarion, 1986).

What Do Authors Do? (Clarion, 1995).

What Do Illustrators Do? (Clarion, 1999).

Books Illustrated by Eileen Christelow

The Completed Hickory Dickory Dock. Written by Jim Aylesworth. (Atheneum, 1990).

A Fish Named Yum: Mr. Pin, Vol. IV. Written by Mary Elise Monsell. (Atheneum, 1994).

The Flimflam Man. Written by Darleen Bailey Beard. (Farrar, 1998).

No Room for Francine. Written by Maryann Macdonald. (Hyperion, 1995).

The Pumpkin Fair. Written by Eve Bunting. (Clarion, 1997).

FOR MORE INFORMATION

Web Sites

Picture Book Author and Illustrator Eileen Christelow. URL: <http://www.christelow.com/> (Accessed March 2000).

Joanna Cole

◆ Science, Nonfiction ◆ Family Relationships ◆ Folklore

Sharron L. McElmeel

Newark, New Jersey
August 11, 1944

📖 *Bony-Legs*
📖 *Don't Tell the Whole World*
📖 Magic School Bus Series
📖 *Norma Jean Jumping Beans*

ABOUT THE AUTHOR

Joanna Basilea was born in Newark, New Jersey, on August 11, 1944. Her parents, Mario and Elizabeth Basilea, raised their children in nearby East Orange. Even as a young child, Joanna enjoyed hunting for bugs, insects, and all sorts of creepy-crawly creatures. The family had a small backyard, and it was Joanna's exploration lab. The yard was filled with ferns, poison ivy, and mulberry trees. Joanna loved to read and investigate her surroundings. The neighborhood where she grew up was filled with children; there were fifty on her street alone. The children played street games late into the darkness of night.

Joanna says, "[my childhood was] quite ordinary. I grew up in the 1950s in a small city in northern New Jersey. My father had a house-painting business and my mother was a secretary. From my father I learned to be enterprising, and from my mother I learned to be sensitive to language. I don't think there was ever a meal in our house when either I or my sister wasn't sent to fetch the dictionary to check a word."

Joanna's love of both reading and of science was encouraged. The elementary school was just around the corner from her house. She loved writing school reports, especially when she could write about science. One of Joanna's favorite books was a gift from her aunt and uncle titled *Bugs, Insects, and Such*. She read and reread the book. She also "read many factual books, especially science books." Her interest in reading, writing, and science continued throughout her school years. After high school, she entered the University of Massachusetts and later attended Indiana University.

In 1965, she met her future husband, Philip Cole, on a street corner. They had known each other as teenagers and once they renewed their acquaintance, they became friends and married within one month. They moved to New York City where Joanna Cole worked part time at *Newsweek* and attended City College. She graduated from City College with a degree in psychology in 1967. Graduate courses in education led to a year as a librarian in a Brooklyn elementary school, P.S. 46. She shared many books with the students and learned to appreciate children's literature. She decided she would like to write children's books.

Because many of the children at P.S. 46 had reading difficulties, she decided to focus on writing easy-to-read books. Her goal was, and still is, to make the text as simple as possible while keeping it interesting and saying exactly what she needs and wants to say. Those goals make writing a real challenge. She says, "[The effort] is worth it . . . [when I] know that almost every child can read most of my books."

After her year as a librarian, Cole went to work as a correspondent at *Newsweek* and later became a senior editor at Doubleday Books for Young Readers. She also wrote books during this time. She admired the books written by Herbert Zim and Millicent Selsam and wanted to write similar works. Her father's chance comment about an article in *The Wall Street Journal* that focused on the cockroach and the belief that it was a living fossil motivated Cole to research the subject and to write a manuscript that Morrow published in 1971. *Cockroaches* was the first of many books that she wrote during the next ten years while continuing her work as an editor. She finally left Doubleday to become a full-time writer.

She does not write about events in her life but rather about things that interest her. Many of her books focus on subjects researched because of her own curiosity. She has written books about frogs, horses, snakes, birds, and cats. In addition to many nonfiction titles, Cole has also written fictional books. Her fiction tales and retellings of folk stories generally feature characters who figure out how to get along with others and, in the process, how to make life more satisfactory to themselves. She writes adventure stories and scary stories. One of her stories *Bony-Legs* (Four Winds/Macmillan, 1983; Scholastic, 1986) retells a Russian story about a girl who escapes from a horrible witch. Another tale, *Doctor Change* (Morrow, 1986) tells the story of a young boy outwitting a mean wizard. Her easy-to-read funny books include *Norma Jean, Jumping Bean* (Random House, 1987) and *Monster Manners* (Scholastic, 1995), the latter of which tells about a young monster who does not act monstrous. Instead, she acts sweet and is a great disappointment to her parents.

Her nonfiction books include books about evolution (*Evolution: The Story of How Life Developed on Earth*; Crowell, 1987); insects (*Find the Hidden Insect*; Morrow, 1979); nighttime and daytime animals (*Large As Life Animals: In Beautiful Life-Size Paintings*; Knopf, 1990); and a host of other topics. Several of her books are collaborations with her friend, Stephanie Calmenson. Together they have authored *Marbles* (Morrow, 1998); *The Any Day Book* (Morrow, 1997); *Rockin' Reptiles* (Morrow, 1997), and several other titles including collections of easy-to-read stories and poems, tongue twisters, card games, and party games.

In 1985, an editor at Scholastic suggested to Cole that she combine her talent for writing fiction with her interest in nonfiction. That editor, Craig Walker, suggested she intertwine a story with a class field trip. Cole liked the idea, and the concept of The Magic School Bus series evolved. The result was humorous tales through which information and facts are woven. The first book in the series was *The Magic School Bus at the Waterworks* (Scholastic, 1986). At the time she started the book, she had done extensive research on water systems but did not know exactly how the book would evolve. She did know that she wanted to write a coherent science book that would make young readers laugh. When first conceived, this idea seemed plausible, but it began to seem like an impossible task.

Cole tried to avoid starting the project. "I did everything but write," she says. "I answered mail, I went shopping, I even cleaned my apartment—which shows how truly desperate I was! Finally, one morning I said to myself, 'Okay, Joanna, this is it. Today you *must* start this book!' I sat down and wrote: 'Our class really has bad luck. This year we got Ms. Frizzle, the strangest teacher in school. We don't mind Ms. Frizzle's strange dresses, or her strange shoes. It's the way she acts that really gets us.'" The character of Ms. Frizzle began to emerge. Cole knew Ms. Frizzle would be a science enthusiast who would encourage the students in her class to learn science through hands-on activities. The students would build models, create experiments, and read science books. At the time, Cole did not know who the illustrator would be, so she did not have any idea what the strange dresses and shoes would look like. Eventually, she came up with the idea that "the

Friz" would wear dresses with outlandish patterns on them and shoes with "weird ornaments." Ms. Frizzle's student school reports included in the books are actually written by Cole on big yellow legal tablets.

The publishers asked Bruce Degen to illustrate the series. Cole and Degen began their collaboration with the first book. For each new title, Cole first writes the text and then makes a dummy by taping in the text, the word balloons, and the school reports. When the dummy is ready, she and Degen meet with the editors at Scholastic. Together, they work out any parts that need attention, and as Degen works on the illustrations, he might make suggestions for changes in the text to make the whole work better together. Cole also gives her comments about the illustrations. The series has enjoyed tremendous success with parents, teachers, and young readers. It even has become the subject of a Public Broadcast System program for children. The series uses television writers to create new episodes that are based on Cole's characters. Scholastic has used the television series to produce additional books based on the television episodes. The original Cole–Degen Magic School Bus books are rectangular in format, whereas those created from the television series are square; they lack much of the charm and excitement of the Cole–Degen titles.

Ms. Frizzle has inspired teachers to dress up like her. Classes decorate their rooms to look like the Magic School Bus. Young writers create their own Magic School Bus books, complete with pictures and jokes. Many of Cole's fans have sent their own "bus" books to her. Bruce Degen also gets plenty of mail. *The Magic School Bus at the Waterworks*, was so popular in New York City that the school district asked Cole and Degen to revise the book specifically to relate to the waterworks system in New York City. The book is used in New York City schools.

Cole once assumed that the image of Ms. Frizzle and her frizzy hair came from her first meeting with Degen because she had frizzy, permed hair at the time. Degen says Ms. Frizzle actually is based on a geometry teacher he had in tenth grade. The teacher had blond, frizzy hair and a face that beamed with the pure logic of the material she was presenting to her class.

Sometimes Degen attempts to slip funny things into his illustrations. When he attempted to put "Burp" on the sign on the front of the bus in *The Magic School Bus Inside the Human Body* (Scholastic, 1989), the editors asked him to remove it. They also had conversations on the color of the "goosh" inside the stomach and how the children should get out of Arnold's body. After discussions about various ways that the children could emerge, Cole, Degen, and the editors decided a sneeze would be acceptable. The editors then requested that nothing in the picture be colored green.

Cole and Degen have collaborated on Magic School Bus books that tell of field trips to the waterworks, inside the earth, inside the human body, through the solar system, inside a beehive, and into the world of electricity. At the end of each book, Ms. Frizzle's dress and shoes foreshadow the next field trip and the next Magic School Bus book. After writing ten Magic School Bus books, Cole and Degen have now created a spin-off book, *Ms. Frizzle's Adventures in Egypt* (Scholastic, 2000). In this book Ms. Frizzle is with a tour group in Egypt.

During the many years she made her home in New York City, Cole lived close to the Museum of Natural History. The museum was a wonderful source of information. She frequented the museum and made trips to bookstores, went to movies, saw friends, and wrote.

In addition to collaborating with Bruce Degen and Stephanie Calmenson, Cole and her husband authored *Hank and Frank Fix Up the House* (Scholastic, 1988) and *Big Goof and Little Goof* (Scholastic, 1989). Just as she did during her childhood, Joanna Cole enjoys her backyard and garden. Joanna writes most of the jokes for the Magic School Bus books, but her daughter, Rachel, has contributed some as well.

After nearly twenty-three years in New York City, the Coles moved to Sandy Hook, Connecticut. Rachel was able to ride horses and enjoy the family pets. The Coles still live in Connecticut, and Joanna Cole continues to collaborate with both Degen and Calmenson, as well as write her own fiction and nonfiction books.

BOOKS AND NOTES

Joanna Cole is a prolific writer and writes in many different genres. She has written both fiction and nonfiction picture books. Bruce Degen has illustrated many of her books, and she has written a number of books with Stephanie Calmenson.

Books Written by Joanna Cole

The Any Day Book. Co-authored by Stephanie Calmenson. Illustrated by Alan Tiegreen. (Morrow, 1997).

Bony-Legs. Illustrated by Dirk Zimmer. (Macmillan, 1983; Scholastic, 1986).

Bug in a Rug: Reading Fun for Just-Beginners. Co-authored by Stephanie Calmenson. Illustrated by Alan Tiegreen. (Morrow, 1996).

Bully Trouble. Illustrated by Marylin Hafner. (Random House, 1989).

The Clown-Arounds Have a Party. Illustrated by Jerry Smath. (Gareth Stevens, 1995).

Don't Tell the Whole World. Illustrated by Kate Duke. (Crowell, 1990).

Evolution: The Story of How Life Developed on Earth. Illustrated by Aliki. (Crowell, 1987).

Find the Hidden Insect. Photographs by Jerome Wexler. (Morrow, 1979).

Get Well, Gators! Co-authored by Stephanie Calmenson. Illustrated by Lynn Munsinger. (Morrow, 1998).

Give a Dog a Bone: Stories, Poems, Jokes, and Riddles About Dogs. Co-authored by Stephanie Calmenson. Illustrated by John Speirs. (Scholastic, 1996).

How I Was Adopted: Samantha's Story. Illustrated by Maxie Chambliss. (Morrow, 1995).

I'm a Big Brother. Illustrated by Maxie Chambliss. (Morrow, 1997).

I'm a Big Sister. Illustrated by Maxie Chambliss. (Morrow, 1997).

It's Too Noisy. Illustrated by Kate Duke. (Crowell, 1989).

Large As Life Animals: In Beautiful Life-Size Paintings. Illustrated by Kenneth Lily. (Knopf, 1990).

Marbles. Co-authored by Stephanie Calmenson. Illustrated by Alan Tiegreen. (Morrow, 1998).

Monster and Muffin. Illustrated by Karen Lee Schmidt. (Grosset, 1996).

Monster Manners. Illustrated by Jared Lee. (Scholastic, 1995).

Ms. Frizzle's Adventures in Egypt. Illustrated by Bruce Degen. (Scholastic, 2000).

Riding Silver Star. Illustrated by Margaret Miller. (Morrow, 1996).

Rockin' Reptiles. Co-authored by Stephanie Calmenson. Illustrated by Lynn Munsinger. (Morrow, 1997).

The Magic School Bus Series, Created in Collaboration with Bruce Degen

The Magic School Bus and the Electric Field Trip (Scholastic, 1997).

The Magic School Bus at the Waterworks (Scholastic, 1986).

The Magic School Bus Explores the Senses (Scholastic, 1999).

The Magic School Bus in the Time of the Dinosaurs (Scholastic, 1994).

The Magic School Bus Inside a Beehive (Scholastic, 1996).

The Magic School Bus Inside a Hurricane (Scholastic, 1995).

The Magic School Bus Inside the Earth (Scholastic, 1987).

The Magic School Bus Inside the Human Body (Scholastic, 1989).

The Magic School Bus Lost in the Solar System (Scholastic, 1990).

The Magic School Bus on the Ocean Floor (Scholastic, 1992).

FOR MORE INFORMATION

Articles

Cleghorn, Andrea. "Children's Book Scene: Aboard the Magic School Bus." *Publishers Weekly* (January 25, 1991): 27–28.

Lewis, Valerie. "Meet the Author." *Instructor* (July/August 1992): supplement.

Phelan, Carolyn. "The Inside Story: Joanna Cole and Bruce Degen's Magic School Bus." *Booklinks* 4, no. 1 (September 1, 1994): 44–46.

Books

Cole, Joanna, and Wendy Saul. *On the Bus with Joanna Cole: A Creative Autobiography* (Heinneman/Creative Sparks, 1996).

Barbara Cooney

◆ Community ◆ Environment

Brooklyn Heights, New York
August 6, 1917–March 10, 2000

📖 *Chanticleer and the Fox*

📖 *Hattie and the Wild Waves*

📖 *Island Boy*

📖 *Miss Rumphius*

ABOUT THE
AUTHOR/ILLUSTRATOR

Barbara Cooney's own life comes alive in the books she wrote and illustrated. Cooney and her twin brother were born in room 1127 of the Hotel Bossert, one of the largest hotels in Brooklyn Heights, on August 6, 1917. The family lived there for two weeks until moving to Long Island. The twins' immigrant grandfather, who had arrived in the United States with only thirty cents in his pocket, had built the hotel. Cooney's father was a stockbroker, and her mother was an artist, as was her great-grandfather.

Cooney spent most of her childhood summers in Maine. She attended art school and took every course available in studio art and art history before receiving an undergraduate degree in art history from Smith College in 1938. She studied lithography and then studied etching at the Art Students' League in New York City. In 1940, she began illustrating children's books. Two years later, she joined the Women's Army Corps. That was the same year she met and married her first husband, Guy Murchie.

Murchie was a war correspondent and author. The couple had two children, Gretel and Barnaby. The marriage ended in divorce after only five years, and in 1949 Cooney married a country doctor, Dr. Charles Talbot Porter. Two more children were born, Charles Talbot Jr. and Phoebe.

Although Cooney's mother was an artist, the only art lesson she ever offered was to teach Cooney how to clean her paintbrushes. She did take her daughter's painting seriously, however. She gave her the encouragement to make art a life-long passion. Cooney's art mirrored her own life. When she drew chickens, they were borrowed from those of a neighbor. She even traveled to other countries to gather images for books.

Ox-Cart Man (Viking, 1979), written by Donald Hall, is one of the hallmarks of Cooney's illustrative work. She created the illustrations in the early American tradition by using wood as the foundation of the paintings. At the time, Cooney was building a house by the seashore near South Bristol, Maine. She met a carpenter, Leon, who had a beautiful, red beard. Cooney wanted the beard to be in the book, so that dictated that the book's setting would be between 1803 and 1847, when beards were popular. The time setting also had to be a period when turnstiles were in existence, and there had to be a brick market still standing in Portsmouth. Research helped Cooney settle on the year 1832. Another carpenter, Markie, posed for the scene in which the ox-cart man kissed an ox. He actually posed kissing a lamp. When Cooney finished the illustrations, Markie created a mahogany box that was used to ship the illustrations to the publisher. Cooney painted an ox on the top of the box, placed the illustrations into it, and mailed them.

In 1979, Cooney was presented the Smith College Medal. It was about this same time when Cooney and one of her sons designed and built her home studio on the Damariscotta River in Maine.

The story of Barbara Cooney's life is perhaps best told in her semi-autobiographical trilogy, which she both wrote and illustrated. *Miss Rumphius* (Viking, 1982), tells of a young girl who learns that a life can include travel and adventure, a return to a place you love, and acceptance of the responsibility for making the world a more beautiful place to live. The young boy in *Island Boy* (Viking, 1988) leaves the island off the coast of Maine but eventually returns to work the land that is home for him. *Hattie and the Wild Waves* (Viking, 1990) tells the tale of a girl set apart from those around her who tries to decipher a message in the breaking ocean waves. The girl later becomes an artist.

Miss Rumphius is one of Cooney's most popular books. The illustrations include an embroidered shawl, a favorite armchair, a picture of her grandson, New England sites where Cooney has lived, and a conservatory much like the one at Smith College where she was a student. The idea for the story itself came from a woman Cooney met named Hilda, who was born July 5, 1898 and grew up to plant lupine seeds to make the world more beautiful, much in the same manner that Johnny Appleseed planted apple seeds wherever he went. Hilda became the book's Alice Rumphius, who passes on to her grandniece her own grandfather's advice to make the world a more beautiful place. The visualization of the connections between generations is made through the inclusion, in the illustrations, of items once seen in Cooney's grandfather's house and with items from her many travels. Like Miss Rumphius, Barbara Cooney has traveled far and wide and for a number of years lived by the sea.

Island Boy grew out of Cooney discovering an account of a man's life in late-nineteenth-century Maine. Cooney researched all aspects of the man's life. In the fall of 1987, the story was finished, and Cooney began to create acrylic paintings on fine Chinese silk. She used the finest sable brushes because she always believed that artists need to use perfect tools. Prisamacolor pencils and pastels helped Cooney to create wispy clouds and gusts of smoke.

The inspiration for her work came from the natural world. Growing up, she played with her cousins in woods and fields; they were "outdoor" children. When she lived in an urban environment, she "always felt trapped." She needed to live where she could run through the fields and walk along the shore and "mess around" in boats. Her trilogy is a slice of life that reflects the life she wanted to live. In fact, when asked if there was another direction her life could have taken, Barbara Cooney replied, *"Island Boy,* that's the kind of life I would have liked to have. . . . I would have been happy living out on an island, one of those Maine islands."

All of Cooney's four children are grown. They are as independent as their mother was. One daughter was a rigger in an Indiana Coke plant. Charles Talbot Jr., the younger son, once navigated around Cape Horn in a kayak and then became a glacial geologist in Patagonia.

Barbara Cooney's favorite place was the Maine coast, in Damariscotta, where, in her studio/cabin, she had an immense drawing board just a few feet away from the sea and where she enjoyed lobsters and making the world more beautiful, just like Miss Rumphius. In 1997, Cooney donated a total of $850,000 to build a new library in Damariscotta.

Barbara Cooney had a long and celebrated career in the field of children's books. At the time of her death, on March 10, 2000, she had written or illustrated 110 books. She was survived by her husband, Dr. Charles Talbot Porter, her four children, three grandchildren, and one great-grandchild.

BOOKS AND NOTES

Barbara Cooney's early illustrations were created mostly with scratchboard. Later she began to experiment, illustrating with pen and ink, pen and ink with wash, casin, collage, watercolor, and acrylic. She illustrated her own books and those written by others. She won her first Caldecott Award for *Chanticleer and the Fox* (Crowell, 1958) in 1959 and her second, in 1980, for the illustrations she created for Donald Hall's *Ox-Cart Man*.

In 1989, the Maine Library Association created the Lupine Award to recognize outstanding children's books that are either written or illustrated by state residents or that are set in Maine. Their opening ceremony honored Barbara Cooney and *Miss Rumphius*. In 1997, the governor of Maine declared Cooney "a State Treasure."

Books Written and Illustrated by Barbara Cooney

Chanticleer and the Fox (Crowell, 1958).

Eleanor (Viking, 1996).

Hattie and the Wild Waves (Viking, 1990).

Island Boy (Viking, 1988).

Miss Rumphius (Viking, 1982).

Books Illustrated by Barbara Cooney

Basket Moon. Written by Mary Lyn Ray. (Little, Brown, 1998).

Emily. Written by Michael Bedard. (Doubleday, 1992).

Emma. Written by Wendy Kesselman. (Doubleday, 1980).

Kildee House. Written by Rutherford Montgomery. (Walker, 1993).

Letting Swift River Go. Written by Jane Yolen. (Little, Brown, 1992).

Only Opal: The Diary of a Young Girl. Selected and adapted by Jane Boulton. (Philomel, 1994).

Ox-Cart Man. Written by Donald Hall. (Viking, 1979).

Roxaboxen. Written by Alice McLerran. (Lothrop, 1991).

Seven Little Rabbits. Written by John Becker. (Walker, 1994).

Snow-White and Rose-Red: A Story by Brothers Grimm (Delacorte, 1991).

Spirit Child: A Story of the Nativity. Written by John Bierhorst. (Morrow, 1984).

Squawk to the Moon, Little Goose. Written by Edna Mitchell Preston. (Morrow, 1984).

FOR MORE INFORMATION

Articles

Cooney, Barbara. "Caldecott Medal Acceptance." *Horn Book* (August 1989): 378–82.

McClellan, Constance Reed. "Barbara Cooney." *Horn Book* (August 1989): 383–87.

Smith, Julia. "Barbara Cooney's Award-Winning Picture Books 'Make the World More Beautiful.' " *Instructor* (March 1985): 94–96.

Web Sites

University of Southern Mississippi, de Grummond Collection: Barbara Cooney Papers. URL: <http://www.lib.usm.edu/~degrum/findaids/cooney.htm> (Accessed March 2000).

Floyd Cooper

Velma Cooper

Tulsa, Oklahoma
January 8, 1956

📖 *Coming Home: From the Life of Langston Hughes*

📖 *Cumbayah*

📖 *Mandela: From the Life of the South African Statesman*

ABOUT THE AUTHOR/ILLUSTRATOR

Floyd Donald Cooper was born and raised in Tulsa, Oklahoma. He recalls being interested in art very early in his life, around three years of age. One day, during a time when his father was building their house, young Cooper noticed a piece of sheet rock lying on the ground. He picked it up and started scribbling on the clean white surface. He remembers drawing a picture of a bird, a duck of some sort. He continued drawing throughout his childhood. The family lived in the projects and was of very modest means. He credits his mother, Ramona, with instilling in him a sense of value that he says, "I carry with me today." His mother was a storyteller and helped him develop his imagination.

After high school, Cooper received a four-year scholarship on the condition that he attend an in-state college or university. He went to the University of Oklahoma. The University was near the historically African-American college, Langston University. This school sparked Cooper's interest in Langston Hughes, although Langston University actually was named after Congressman John Mercer Langston, Hughes's uncle and the first black American to hold office in the United States. Cooper often visited Langston University. His visits reinforced his pride in both his Midwestern roots and his cultural heritage.

As a college student, Cooper began a freelance art career. After graduating with a degree in fine arts in 1980, he moved to Missouri and worked for Hallmark, a greeting-card company. The job was stifling, and Cooper began to look for something that would allow him more creativity. For a time, he worked for a toy designer but finally settled on freelancing as an illustrator. He wanted freedom and spontaneity as an artist.

Cooper, in a search for creative outlets, moved to the East Coast in 1984. He went to New York with the hope of becoming a "fancy illustrator like [his hero] Mark English." He tried to obtain work for about six months and eventually "stumbled into an agent's office"; the agent was associated with children's books. That day, Cooper discovered children's book illustrating. The field seemed to be just what he was looking for, and he brought a new sense of energy to his book illustration. The first book he illustrated, *Grandpa's Face* by Eloise Greenfield (Philomel, 1988), was acclaimed for its "family scenes of extraordinary illumination." Cooper's second book, *Laura Charlotte* by Kathryn Galbraith (Philomel, 1990), solidified his emerging reputation as a children's book illustrator. Both books were named best books of the year by *School Library Journal*.

Cooper's illustrative technique is subtractive in nature. The illustrations are oil-washed paintings to which he adds highlights and light spaces by using an eraser to subtract color. His illustrations are realistic and rendered in rich, warm tones. Although his artwork is filled with details, and its creation must consume many hours, the technique itself can be described simply. He paints a brown oil wash on artist's board. Once the board is completely dry, he uses a kneadable eraser to remove parts of the oil paint. Color is added in much the same fashion. In the advertising world Cooper's art technique is called "oil-wash-on-board technique."

Cooper says that he tries to stay "true to the culture." Through his illustrations, he attempts to help readers know what the setting feels and smells like and what the light looks like. He wants them to hear the same sounds the characters hear. The goal of his illustrations is to appeal to all the senses and hopefully to capture a memory to which the reader can connect. He keeps in mind that the experiences of African Americans are diverse and unique. The experiences of those in the South are not necessarily reflective of those living in the North or vice versa. The experiences of blacks living in places such as the Caribbean, Africa, and Great Britain are more different still. Cooper does not limit himself to illustrating only the experience of blacks, however. He has illustrated books that have included the Japanese culture and stories of caucasian children. Cooper has the insight to invoke the affection and compassion needed to help a reader find the positive images from within a culture, regardless of the setting or the characters' background. Cooper feels his work can illuminate the multicultural experience.

The inspiration for Cooper's art comes primarily from the text. The text seems to take Cooper into the story and transports him to the place where the story takes place. He says that he wants the reader to come into the story with him, to be transported to the place where the story takes place. When Cooper is not able to actually visit a location, he relies on his research and imagination. In preparation for illustrating *Satchmo's Blues* (Doubleday, 1996), Cooper visited New Orleans several years before he actually started the artwork. During his trip, he recorded things in his memory so that he could use the images when he did begin to work on the book. Cooper says the experience of being there enabled him to develop some sense of what it must have been like for the book's subject, Louis Armstrong, as a boy. Those images of New Orleans also provided him background for Fatima Shaik's *On Mardi Gras Day* (Dial, 1998).

The books he has authored as well as illustrated have come from his own interests and background. His interest in Langston Hughes emerged from his university days and his interest in Louis Armstrong, the subject of *Satchmo's Blues*, came from his love of music. Cooper says, " . . . although I have two left ears, I have been a fan of blues and jazz." Cooper considers Louis Armstrong one of the "major players" in the area of music.

Floyd Cooper, his wife, Velma, and their two sons, Dayton (b. 1989) and Kai Noah (b. 1996), currently live in West Orange, New Jersey, where they enjoy their pet fish, Little Foot. Among Cooper's hobbies are basketball, tennis, bicycling, nature walks, movies, laser discs, and all types of music. Pasta and pizza are among his favorite foods, and he is often seen wearing western boots. Among his favorite types of books are coffee-table photo and picture books. He now says that his favorite colors are those that are not usually seen. Once he said that his favorite colors were orange and blue, but as he visited schools, he began to be greeted by orange and blue posters and art displays and was even fed orange and blue pasta. Now he just says he enjoys all colors.

BOOKS AND NOTES

Floyd Cooper has illustrated books on many topics. One of his books, *One April Morning: Children Remember the Oklahoma City Bombing* by Nancy Lamb (Lothrop, 1996), presented conversations with the children who survived the Oklahoma City bombing. He has illustrated fictional picture books and historical titles. He says, "it is always fun to illustrate historical things." His illustrations complement each book he works on. The beauty of the Japanese landscape is incorporated into *The Girl Who Loved Caterpillars* (Philomel, 1992), along with details of the culture. He reflects Danitra Brown's thoughts through the expression on her face in *Meet Danitra Brown* (Lothrop, 1994) and is able to capture the festive mood of each holiday in *Gingerbread Days* by Joyce Carol Thomas (HarperCollins, 1995). His meticulous research and interest in historical details helped him create a culturally authentic representation for his in-depth look at the history of the African American woman in *Ma Dear's Aprons* (Atheneum, 1997). Although maintaining historic accuracy, he used his wife as the model for Ma Dear and his son, Dayton, as the model for David Earl, who become the focus in many of the illustrations for *Ma Dear's Aprons*.

Books Written and Illustrated by Floyd Cooper

Coming Home: From the Life of Langston Hughes (Philomel, 1994).
Langston Hughes's grandma told him stories about black heroes, such as Booker T. Washington and his own buffalo soldier uncles. This is Hughes's story, the story of how he began to write and how he reached people all over the world.

Cumbayah (Morrow, 1997).
An illustrated version of a popular folksong.

Mandela: From the Life of the South African Statesman (Philomel, 1996).
Nelson Mandela is the subject of this storybook biography.

Books Illustrated by Floyd Cooper

Danitra Brown Leaves Town. Written by Nikki Grimes. (Lothrop, 1996).
Poems in the form of letters tell of Danitra's summer experiences.

I Have Heard of a Land. Written by Joyce Carol Thomas. (HarperCollins, 1997).
The story of an African American pioneer woman who staked a claim for land in the Oklahoma Territory.

Laura Charlotte. Written by Kathryn O. Galbraith. (Philomel, 1990).
A young daughter now has the well-worn and loved stuffed elephant that once belonged to her mother. The story tells how a little girl was given the name "Laura" for her grandmother; and the name "Charlotte" because it was the most beautiful name in the world.

Miz Berlin Walks. Written by Jane Yolen. (Philomel, 1997).
Tells the fictionalized story of the author's own grandmother and the relationship of a young girl and an elderly neighbor who tells stories as she walks around the block of her Virginia home.

On Mardi Gras Day. Written by Fatima Shaik. (Dial, 1998).

Children experience Mardi Gras and observe the Zulu and Rex Parades.

Pulling the Lion's Tail. Written by Jane Kurtz. (Simon & Schuster, 1995).

An Ethiopian tale about Almaz and her father, who grieve the death of her mother and his wife. They wear black clothing and "faces like rain." Then comes Almaz's father's new wife. How can Almaz win her new mother's affection? Slowly, a little at a time . . . just like pulling the lion's tail.

Sea Girl and the Dragon King: A Chinese Folktale. Written by Ziporah Hildebrandt. (Atheneum, 2000).

Two girls save a village from a drought by stealing the magic key that opens the water gates.

Shake Rag. Written by Amy Littlesugar. (Philomel, 1998).

A story of Elvis Presley's childhood, during which he was introduced to the soulful music of the Sanctified church as it traveled through town.

The Story of Jackie Robinson, Bravest Man in Baseball. Written by Margaret Davidson. (Gareth Stevens, 1996).

Jackie Robinson became a hero when he joined the 1947 Brooklyn Dodgers to become the first black athlete to play in baseball's major league.

FOR MORE INFORMATION

Web Sites

Penguin Putnam Web Site. "Floyd Cooper." URL: <http://www.penguinputnam.com/yreaders/appear/bios.htm> (Accessed March 2000). Go to "C" then "Floyd Cooper."

Donald Crews

◆ Community ◆ Family Relationships

Sharron L. McElmeel

Newark, New Jersey
August 30, 1938

📖 *Bigmama's*
📖 *Freight Train*
📖 *Shortcut*

ABOUT THE AUTHOR/ILLUSTRATOR

As a youngster, Donald Crews spent his summer days on his grandparents' farm near Cottondale, Florida. It was there that his mother took Donald and his two sisters and one brother to keep them off the streets during the summer vacation. The four siblings were able to play with their cousins, explore the fields, feed the animals, and enjoy the country setting. During the school year, the family lived in Newark, where Crews's father worked for the railroad. It was that job that supplied the transportation for the yearly trip to Florida. Crews used memories of those trips years later to create *Freight Train* (Greenwillow, 1978).

Crews had not thought about making a career out of art until he attended Arts High School, a specialized school that required a competitive

128

examination for admission. He still might not have considered it if a teacher had not encouraged his abilities. When Crews finished high school, his brother was in medical school. Crews knew that his father's railroad salary would not stretch to cover college for both sons, but Crews was willing to set aside his own college so that his brother could finish. Fortunately, with help from a teacher, Crews was able to enter Cooper Union Art School tuition-free, courtesy of the advancement of Science and Arts in New York City.

It was at Cooper Union that Crews met his future wife, Ann Jonas. After completing college and working for two years, Crews entered the military and served in Germany as a military policeman. Jonas joined him in Germany, and they were married there on January 28, 1964. Their first daughter, Nina Melissa, was born in Germany. Crews also created his first picture book while the family was there. He created a book titled *We Read: A to Z* (Harper, 1967; Greenwillow, 1984). The book was intended to become a part of his design portfolio, but Harper liked it well enough to publish it in 1967. By this time, Crews and his wife were parents to a second daughter, Amy Marshanna. Crews's next book was *Ten Black Dots*, a companion volume to his earlier alphabet book. When Scribner published the book in 1968, other publishers took notice and began to request that he illustrate books for them.

For ten years, Crews illustrated books written by other writers, and he also accepted freelance art projects. He designed a book jacket for *Jazz Country*, written by Nat Hentoff (Harper, 1965), and one for a book of ethnic poetry edited by David Kherdian. He illustrated two books by Harry Milgrom, *ABC Science Experiments* (Macmillan, 1973) and *ABC of Ecology* (Macmillan, 1976). In the ecology title, he used a photograph of his older daughter, Nina, on the "I" page (she had an "idea").

As he grew dissatisfied with the books he was illustrating for others, he decided to create some of his own. He says that the fact that he would get to keep all the royalties did not escape him. He set out to develop a topic and thought about the trips he had made to Florida with his parents. He loved watching the moving trains and remembered the freight trains pulled by steam locomotives. He actually had spent hours counting the trains that passed by the porch of the house by Cottondale. He knew he wanted to introduce a spectrum of color and simple shapes. Using the images from his youth and his design skills, Crews was able to create *Freight Train*. The book is a riot of color. Crews created a sense of anticipation with the use of white background pages of track as the reader waits for the train to pass. Each brightly colored freight car passes on its own page. A concise and accurate description of each car follows the red, orange, yellow, green, blue, and purple cars. The grayish clouds of smoke and tunnels of black and gray provide contrast. This book introduces a technique that Crews would often use in the future: vivid colors outlined in black.

Crews offered the book to an editor at Greenwillow, Susan Hirschman. After seeing just two or three pages, she offered to publish the book. It was a good choice. *Freight Train* (Greenwillow, 1978) was named a Caldecott Honor Book in 1979. The book's success and the royalties that accompanied that success helped convince Crews that he might be able to make a living creating his own children's books.

At the time, he and his family were living in a loft on lower Broadway in New York City. There was a truck depot nearby where trucks loaded and were dispatched. The scene gave him the idea for his next book, *Truck* (Greenwillow, 1980). He wanted to extend the book so he investigated where the trucks went after they left the depot. He created thumbnail sketches to lay out the book. He wanted to emphasize the size of the trucks, and he also wanted young readers to identify with the vehicle's journey, so he loaded the truck with tricycles. He used proportion and size to suggest movement as the trucks traveled from New York to California. To accurately portray the interstate travel, he obtained photographs of the countryside in New York, Colorado, and other places along the way. He took a lot of photographs so he could study what trucks did and where they went.

Light (Greenwillow, 1981) showed the contrast of city and country. The finished art for the book began, as he begins all of his books, with thumbnail sketches. In a scene showing lights in the city, he used as a backdrop the clock tower at Cooper Union where he attended art school.

Each of his books demands that he do some research. He says that when he is "on the streets walking around during the day, I am not really playing hooky, I am doing research." *Parade* (Greenwillow, 1990) was the result of a New York City parade. Crews observed a marching band and nine soldiers standing in rank. He had not created human figures up to this time, so he decided to render the people abstractly and to concentrate his detailed artwork on the background for the parade. When Crews began *Bicycle Race* (Greenwillow, 1985), he went to Central Park and took photographs of a bicycle race. The photographs show the same streaks of color as Crews's final illustrations.

Before completing his artwork, Crews creates color thumbnail sketches of each proposed illustration. Only when Crews and his art editor are satisfied with the thumbnail sketches does he begin to create the finished product. It took him over a year to conceptualize and carry to completion the idea for *Bicycle Race*. In this minimal-text book, Crews's art helps the reader focus on number nine; and the reader is encouraged to cheer for number nine as the cyclist weaves between the other racers. Number nine does win the race.

Crews moved from Manhattan to Brooklyn to a four-story brownstone. He often traveled across the Brooklyn Bridge and decided to do a book about rivers, from mountains to floods. Crews says, "I thought it was terrific, they [the editors] hated it." Crews took the manuscript and expanded the harbor pages. The editors at Greenwillow liked it a little bit more, but not enough more. So Crews took the manuscript back again and expanded the harbor pages even more. They bought the book. Then they decided they didn't like it, but Greenwillow finally used the harbor pages, and the book became *Harbor* (Greenwillow, 1982).

Coney Island is the setting for *Carousel* (Greenwillow, 1982). Crews designed a simple carousel collage. He photographed the carousel and, by moving the lens, created a blur of color and made the carousel seem as if it were moving. Crews used the photographs to make his illustrations. That technique opened up other possibilities for creating illustrations. *Flying* (Greenwillow, 1986) came after Crews had flown just once or twice. He took a lot of photographs, many from the top of the World Trade Center. As is his practice, Crews placed himself in this book. He put himself in the lower left-hand corner of the page that shows passengers boarding the plane. Observant readers will also spot a truck and a tugboat or two from other Crews's books.

After writing several "concept books," Crews turned to writing about his own growing-up experiences. *Bigmama's* (Greenwillow, 1991) shares some of the adventures Crews and his siblings and cousins had at his grandmother's (Bigmama's) in Cottondale, Florida. A second book about the going-ons in Cottondale, *Shortcut* (Greenwillow, 1992), relates a scary afternoon when Crews, his brother, and their cousins were caught on a railroad bridge with an approaching train bearing down on them. Other writers authored his next few books, but in 1998, he released another book that he both wrote and illustrated, *Night at the Fair* (Greenwillow, 1998).

Many of Crews's other books contain bits and pieces of his family experiences. In *Bicycle Race,* Crews drew himself with his arm around his wife. In *School Bus* (Greenwillow, 1984), Crews can be seen crossing the street, carrying his portfolio. In *Freight Train,* the black steam engine carries the name of the railroad, N & A, the initials of his two daughters, Nina and Amy. The black train car bears, in large orange numerals, the date the book was published. In *Truck,* published in 1980, the numeral "79" appears on a van in a long line of vehicles traveling through the countryside. The seventy-nine is for the year Crew created the artwork. Similarly, the numeral "81" appears on a pier in *Harbor*; and "1982" is conveniently split between the street sweepers cleaning up before and after the festivities in *Parade*.

Dedications also provide some interesting bits of information. The dedication for his first book, *We Read: A to Z*, reads simply, "Particularly for Ann, Nina, Amy, Donna, Janine, Michael, and Zönke." His dedication for *Freight Train* is not as poetic as it is informative, "With due respect to Casey Jones, John Henry, the Rock Island Line, and the countless freight trains passed and passing the big house in Cottondale." Eventually, his dedications become a little more poetic and reflective. The dedication of *Flying* states that the book is "For those who make my heart soar." The dedication for *Carousel* is a visual treat, "For 'MAMANNINAMY' spinning together." Strung together are the names of his mother, his wife, and his two daughters: Mama, Ann, Nina, and Amy. His dedication for *Light* includes a long string of names with the concluding statement, "Bright Lights one and all." *Bigmama's* is dedicated to, appropriately enough, his grandmother, Bigmama, and all those in Cottondale.

Ann Jonas, Crews's wife, is also an artist with several picture books to her credit. For many years, Jonas and Crews lived in a brownstone home in Brooklyn, where the family lived on the top three floors and each of the artists had a studio. Jonas's studio was at the back of their second floor. Upstairs, on the very top floor, were two bedrooms and Crews's studio. Crews spent time each day sketching and creating his final illustrations. In the backyard was a large garden, and they enjoyed cooking on their six-burner gas range that sat in the kitchen. Crews and Jonas moved to Germantown in upstate New York where they both still enjoy cooking and gardening. At various times, they have shared their home with a very large dog and a very tiny kitten. Their two daughters, Amy and Nina, both attended Yale. Nina, who studied art, has followed in her parents' footsteps and is a children's book author and illustrator. Her first book, *One Hot Summer Day*, was published by Greenwillow in 1995. Since then, she has had eight more books published.

BOOKS AND NOTES

Characteristic of Donald Crews's artwork is vivid colors, graphic lettering, city signs, and diagonal lines. He often uses accents of black verticals, horizontals, circles, and squares. Much of his art shows the influence of well-known pop artists, especially Robert Indiana. They are simple and realistic and present easily identifiable characters. He uses Conté crayons, pencils, and pastels to create his illustrations, and when applying paint, he often uses an airbrush to gently apply the layers of color.

Crews's earlier books were printed from color-separated art, but beginning with *Carousel*, they have been printed from Crews's full-color artwork. From the beginning of his career, Crews has published with Greenwillow. In 1999, however, Harcourt released *Cloudy Day Sunny Day*, which he both illustrated and authored.

Books Written and Illustrated by Donald Crews

Bicycle Race (Greenwillow, 1985).

Bigmama's (Greenwillow, 1991).

Cloudy Day Sunny Day (Harcourt, 1999).

Light (Greenwillow, 1981).

Night at the Fair (Greenwillow, 1998).

Parade (Greenwillow, 1990).

Sail Away (Greenwillow, 1995).

School Bus (Greenwillow, 1984).

Shortcut (Greenwillow, 1992).

Truck (Greenwillow, 1980).

Books Illustrated by Donald Crews

Each Orange Had Eight Slices: A Counting Book. Written by Paul Giganti Jr. (Greenwillow, 1992).

More Than One. Written by Miriam Schlein. (Greenwillow, 1996).

This Is the Sunflower. Written by Lola M. Schaefer. (Greenwillow, 2000).

Tomorrow's Alphabet. Written by George Shannon. (Greenwillow, 1995).

When This Box Is Full. Written by Patricia Lillie. (Greenwillow, 1993).

FOR MORE INFORMATION

Articles

"Meet Donald Crews." *Frank Schaffer's SCHOOLDAYS* (April/May/June 1989): 32–33.

Bodmer, George. "Donald Crews: The Signs and Times of an American Childhood—Essay and Interview." *African American Review* 32, no. 1 (Spring 1998): 107.

Videos

Trumpet Video Visits Donald Crews (The Trumpet Club, 1992). VHS 20 mins.

Pat Cummings

◆ Biography ◆ Family Relationships

Sharron L. McElmeel

Chicago, Illinois
November 9, 1950

📖 *Clean Your Room, Harvey Moon*

📖 *C.L.O.U.D.S*

📖 *My Aunt Came Back*

📖 *Talking with Artists Series*

ABOUT THE AUTHOR/ILLUSTRATOR

During her childhood, Pat Cummings lived in Illinois, Virginia, Kansas, and in such faraway places as Germany and Japan. Her father was in the military, and his family moved with him to posts around the world. Cummings seldom spent more than three years in any one location. Each new home meant that she had to make new friends, and she used her art to get acquainted. By the time she was in fifth grade, her art was good enough that she was selling drawings to her classmates. Ballerinas were one of her favorite things to draw. Living in Germany put her in touch with fairy-tale castles, and living in Okinawa left her with a sense of mysticism and tradition. One of the books she remembers her librarian mother reading to her was a book of German fairy tales, *Tales of the Rhine*. Other books she remembers are C. S. Lewis's Chronicles of Narnia, especially *The Lion, the Witch, and the Wardrobe*, and *A Wrinkle in Time* by Madeleine L'Engle. At the time, Pat did not realize that her love of art would result in her becoming a book illustrator and author. Cummings does not remember having any picture books illustrated with black characters while she was growing up.

In the late 1970s, Pat Cummings and her husband, H. Chuku Lee, moved to Brooklyn, where the two of them settled into a huge loft in a building that was once a sculpture factory. At the time, there were no street signs or doorbells in sight. All the buildings in the neighborhood were once factories, and even though people, many of them artists, had been moving into the buildings, the cobblestone streets seemed deserted much of the time. Cummings and Lee still live in their loft today. It overlooks the waterfront, where they can see ships coming in from all over the world. When Cummings is working at her desk, she can see all of lower Manhattan, the World Trade Center towers, and the South Street seaport—a great location to enjoy Independence Day fireworks. She says she actually can watch fireworks on the seaport all summer long.

Cummings and Lee both work from their home. He is a real estate appraiser and has a trade business. He deals with people from all over the world, buying and selling such diverse things as brake pads for construction vehicles and ginger. The fax machine is apt to ring at any time of the day or night.

For several years, Cummings was a freelance artist. She worked in advertising and created advertisements for magazines and newspapers. She did some illustrations for different children's theater groups in New York and was taking her portfolio around to publishers when the Council of Interracial Books for Children featured her in their "Upcoming Artists" section. The article prompted an editor to offer her a book to illustrate, *Good News* (Coward, 1977) by Eloise Greenfield. Tom Feelings, another noted illustrator, became Cummings's mentor and guided her by giving pointers and explaining procedures. She also became friends with illustrators Leo Dillon and Diane Dillon. Over the next nine years, she illustrated nine more books. Sometimes other authors wrote the books she illustrated; other times, she authored them herself. In 1983, Cummings received a Caldecott Honor Book Award for the illustrations created for Jeannette Caines's *Just Us Women* (Harper, 1982). The following year, she was honored with the Coretta Scott King Award for the illustrations she created for Mildred Pitts Walter's *My Mama Needs Me* (Lothrop, 1983). *Storm in the Night* by Mary Stolz (HarperCollins, 1988) and *C.L.O.U.D.S.* (Lothrop, 1986) also were honored with the Coretta Scott King Award following their publication. Her books are illustrated with black characters. Cummings says that the stories are about "humans who happen to be black."

Pat Cummings says that the story in each book is the guiding factor to which style and medium she will use for the illustrations. During a speech at a conference in Iowa City, Iowa (October 28, 1989), she said that she reads the story over and over and imagines how she thinks the illustrations should look. Sometimes she does about seventy-three variations for a single page. For Jeannette Caines's *Just Us Women,* Cummings chose to create realistic illustrations. Cummings's sister and her niece, Kali, were the models for the two main characters in the book. Cummings used her husband as a model for one of the family members. He also appears as the painter in *Jimmy Lee Did It* (Lothrop, 1985), as the boss in *C.L.O.U.D.S.,* and as the father in Joyce Durham Barrett's *Willie's Not the Hugging Kind* (Harper, 1989). Cash, Cummings's cat at the time, made an appearance in *Storm in the Night.*

Jimmy Lee Did It was written about Cummings's brother, Artie, and their sister, Barbara. When Barbara was four years old she said, "Call me Angel." Everyone did. Artie and Angel are the book's stars, and Angel is the narrator. She tells about the trouble that Artie's imaginary friend causes. In the doughnut scene, the photograph is of Cummings's mother. Her mother was originally supposed to flip the pancakes, but it was the 1980s, and Cummings wanted to show that men have responsibilities at home, too, so she added a mustache and made the character the father. Artie and his messy room was also the inspiration for *Clean Your Room, Harvey Moon* (Bradbury, 1991). Cummings's studio and view from her loft make an appearance in *C.L.O.U.D.S.*

Black-and-white pencil sketches were used to create the illustrations, and a photocopy of an authentic road map was pasted onto one of those drawings to create an illustration for *Just Us Women.* Cummings's favorite media, and those with which she is most comfortable, are watercolors and colored pencil. She has, however, experimented with a variety of media. She has tried oil, and a friend, illustrator Diane Dillon, suggested she use pastels. When an editor suggested that she experiment, she used rubber stamps and collages.

When Cummings begins to formulate her plans to illustrate a book, she makes sketches and then a dummy. Sometimes she takes photographs of people and places to use as models for her drawings or paintings. Later she makes a final outline, and when the drawings suit her, she transfers the outline onto watercolor paper, a fairly heavy type that won't buckle if she loads it with paint. Once the outline of her sketch is transferred to the watercolor paper, she begins painting. Each painting takes two to three days. With paintings that she particularly enjoys, she tends to "noodle endlessly." Sometimes the most difficult part is stopping. Cummings also has used an airbrush, a technique used in *C.L.O.U.D.S.* to achieve a continuous tone. The resulting illustrations have an iridescent, luminous effect. Cummings describes her technique by saying, "using pencil on top of watercolor or airbrush allows me to get layers of colors; that something might seem to glow because your eye sees the color behind the surface color." The result is stunning.

Cummings's work schedule is sporadic at best. She has been known to work around the clock to make a deadline and, as a freelance artist, has used holidays and weekends to complete projects. However, she can also take an afternoon off to attend a movie or just to hang out.

Cummings has taught creative writing at Queens College and often visits schools and libraries to talk about writing and illustrating. She holds an undergraduate degree in fine arts from Pratt Institute in Brooklyn. She has worked as an assistant director of an art gallery and has been an instructor at both Queensborough Community College in New York and in the graduate school of education at Queens College.

Today most of Cummings's illustrative work is for children's books. In the last few years, she has created several books for which she has collected biographical information about a common group of people. She has written three volumes of her Talking with Artists series. The first volume was published under the Bradbury Press imprint in 1992, the second by Simon & Schuster in 1995, and the third by Clarion in 1999. Each volume features children's book illustrators. She has also interviewed adventurers for a book titled *Talking with Adventurers* (National Geographic Society, 1998). When Cummings is not working, she enjoys traveling, visiting her family, going to the gym, swimming, and going to the movies. Her favorite foods are seafood, spinach, cheese, bread, and popcorn.

BOOKS AND NOTES

For the most part Pat Cummings's books are stories about people doing everyday things, but she offers something unique in each book. In *Storm in the Night*, the story takes place in the dark of night, but Cummings challenged herself to create illustrations with a lot of color. When she made the illustrations for *I Need a Lunch Box* (Harper, 1988), she experimented with watercolors and rubber stamps. A snake shows up among the shoelaces in *Clean Your Room, Harvey Moon* (Bradbury, 1991). In her collections of interviews with artists, Cummings has gathered a sample of artwork from each artist, along with a childhood drawing. Photographs of the artist as a child and as an adult are also included. After publishing two volumes of *Talking with Artists* with Simon & Schuster—one under the Simon & Schuster Bradbury Press imprint—Cummings developed a third volume for Clarion to publish. Among the artists featured in *Talking with Artists III* are Paul Zelinsky, Jane Dyer, Peter Catalanotto, Lisa Desimini, and Ted and Betsy Lewin.

Books Written and Illustrated by Pat Cummings

The Blue Lake (Harper, 1997).

Carousel (Bradbury, 1994).

Clean Your Room, Harvey Moon (Bradbury, 1991).

C.L.O.U.D.S. (Lothrop, 1986).

Dear Mabel (Celebration Press, 1996).

Jimmy Lee Did It (Lothrop, 1985).

My Aunt Came Back (Harper, 1998).

Petey Moroni's Camp Runamok Diary (Bradbury, 1992).

Talking with Adventurers: Conversations with Christina Allen, Robert Ballard, Michael Blakely, Ann Bowles, David Doubilet, Jane Goodall, Dereck & Beverly Joubert, Michael Novacek, Johan Reinhard, Rick West and Juris Zarins. Compiled and edited by Pat Cummings and Linda Cummings. (National Geographic Society, 1998).

Books Illustrated by Pat Cummings

Barry and Beanie. Written by Angela Shelf Medearis. (Celebration Press, 1996).

"C" Is for City. Written by Nikki Grimes. (Lothrop, 1994).

Go Fish. Written by Mary Stolz. (Harper, 1991).

I Need a Lunch Box. Written by Jeannette Caines. (Harper, 1988).

Lulu's Birthday. Written by Elizabeth Fitzgerald Howard. (Greenwillow, 2000).

Pickin' Peas. Retold by Margaret Read MacDonald. (Harper, 1998).

Storm in the Night. Written by Mary Stolz. (HarperCollins, 1988).

Two and Too Much. Written by Mildred Pitts Walter. (Bradbury, 1990).

Willie's Not the Hugging Kind. Written by Joyce Durham Barrett. (Harper, 1989).

FOR MORE INFORMATION

Articles

Robb, Laura. "Talking with . . . Pat Cummings." *Booklinks* 6, no. 3 (January 1, 1997): 21.

Web Sites

HarperCollins Listserv Subscribers' Interview with Pat Cummings. URL: <http://www.manhattan.lib.ks.us/kail/'cummipa.html> (Accessed March 2000).

Tomie dePaola

◆ Family Relationships ◆ Friends

Meriden, Connecticut
September 15, 1934

📖 *Nana Upstairs, Nana Downstairs*
📖 *Strega Nona*
📖 *Tom*

© Suki Coughlin

ABOUT THE AUTHOR/ILLUSTRATOR

Tomie dePaola has lived in New Hampshire for more than two decades. He was born on September 15, 1934, in Meriden, Connecticut. dePaola learned to love cooking from his Italian father, Joseph, who often cooked Italian food and his Irish mother, Florence, who prepared American dishes. His mother also loved books and spent many hours reading to Tomie, his older brother, Joseph Jr., and his two younger sisters, Maureen and Judie.

It was from his mother that dePaola learned to love books and reading. As a four-year-old boy, he thought he "would grow up and write and draw pictures for books." He decided that if that did not work out, he would sing and dance on stage. He was excited about going to school and wanted to learn how to read. When the long-awaited day arrived, dePaola found out that all they did in kindergarten was play. He did not want to go back. His mother convinced him that he had to go back so he could get to first grade the next year, where he finally would learn to read.

In first grade, he discovered that there were three reading groups: red, yellow, and blue. It was not long before everyone figured out that the kids in the blue group were the smart ones, the reds were okay, and the children in the yellow group were the "dumb bells." In the first book he read, Tomie met a family of four, including a dog named Spot and a cat named Puff. Of course, regardless of which group any student was in, no one could touch a second-grade book.

His experience in art class was not much more encouraging. For his sixth birthday, he received a box of sixty-four crayons. His favorite color was flesh. His art teacher, Miss Bowers, was a large woman with braided hair around her head and long, dangling earrings. During one class, Miss Bowers wanted Tomie to draw a pilgrim. He did not want to "copy dumb pictures." He was so insistent that Miss Bowers finally negotiated a deal with him. If he drew the pilgrim, he could have a second piece of paper on which he could draw anything he wished. He agreed, and when he completed his second, elaborate picture, Miss Bowers asked if she could have it. He politely and quickly told her, "No, I'm saving it to sell." That was the beginning of his artistic and literary career. Years later, the incident became the basis for a story titled *The Art Lesson* (Putnam, 1989).

After growing up in Meriden, Connecticut, Tomie attended Pratt Institute in New York, where he earned an undergraduate degree in fine arts in 1956. While at Pratt, his classmates included Anita Lobel and Arnold Lobel. dePaola learned about composition and learned how to draw everything from tin cans to dogs to people, houses, and trees. He also learned about lettering and how to use different colors. He went on to earn a masters of fine arts from the California College of Arts and Crafts in 1969 and a year later had completed postgraduate work at Lone Mountain College in San Francisco. His art training helped him become a professional artist. Many of his paintings and murals were created for churches and monasteries in New England. He has designed greeting cards, posters, magazine and catalog covers, record album covers, and theater and nightclub sets.

In the 1970s, Tomie dePaola taught at New Hampshire colleges. For many years, he lived in a mid-nineteenth-century farmhouse and studio home in Wilmot Flats, a picturesque village down the road from New London. The thirteen-room house was built in the early 1830s and was once used as a library. A building, which had once been a barn, was connected to the main part of the house and became dePaola's studio. He added a greenhouse to the studio in 1980. In the years that dePaola lived in Wilmot Flats, he used the greenhouse to start more than 4,000 flowers from seed. The seedlings were transplanted to the flower gardens that surrounded his home. To dePaola, it seemed that his white house sprouted wings as it settled back into the country side, so he named the house Whitebird after the white dove of Greek legends. In June 1985, this home was featured in a ten-page article in *Better Homes and Gardens Country Home* ("Artist in Residence" by Linda Joan Smith [June 1985]: 31–41).

Shortly after the photographs were taken for this article, dePaola moved from Whitebird into a vintage house. The property included an old shed that he wanted to convert into a studio, but the projected expense of the conversion caused him to rethink the project, and he bought a newer house in New London. Near this house was an old barn that he finally did convert into a studio and where today he does all of his drawing. Because of the building's red-painted exterior, he calls this home Redwing Farm.

Two well-known book illustrators, Wally Tripp and Trina Schart Hyman, have been neighbors of dePaola. Some of his other neighbors have shown up in his books. For example in *Pancakes for Breakfast* (Harcourt, 1978), the woman who went in search of pancakes was one of his neighbors at Whitebird. Whitebird also provided the New England setting for his illustrated version of Clement Moore's *The Night Before Christmas* (Holiday House, 1980). dePaola's collection of quilts provided the patterns that form the borders on every page of that book.

Throughout his books there are recurring symbols and images. Two personal images recur frequently in each of dePaola's books: heart-shaped objects and white doves.

At one time dePaola had cats. He had one named Satie, after music composer Erik Satie, for fifteen years. When Satie, an Abyssinian, first came to live with dePaola in New Hampshire, he arrived by airplane from New York. dePaola arrived at the airport to pick him up and heard a piece of Satie's music. He decided Satie would be a good name for a cat.

Over the years, Satie shared her quarters with Token and later with Conrad. Unfortunately, dePaola developed allergies and can no longer have cats at home. He does have four dogs, however. He raised three Welsh Terriers: Madison, Moffat, and Morgan. He "adopted" a fourth dog, Markus. A fifth dog is often around the house, too. Tomie dePaola gave his very good friend Bob Hechtel, an Airedale terrier as a fortieth birthday gift. They named the dog Bingley. Hechtel has worked for (and with) dePaola since the fall of 1979. In one way or another, the dogs often end up in dePaola's books.

Events in dePaola's life have had a significant effect on his art and writing. dePaola's religious heritage encouraged him to create books that have religious themes. He visited many of the churches in Italy before completing the text and illustrations for *Francis, the Poor Man of Assisi* (Holiday House, 1982). Each year, he completes a Christmas book. One title features his beloved Italian folk character, Strega Nona. In *Merry Christmas, Strega Nona* (Harcourt, 1986), Big Anthony surprises Strega Nona by inviting all the townspeople to a special Christmas Eve party. dePaola and Bob Hechtel used to entertain his neighbors and literary friends at an extraordinary holiday party. His house and grounds were elaborately decorated, and guests came from all over the country. The annual party was so successful that friends began to invite friends, and dePaola didn't even know some of those in attendance. The number of guests swelled beyond what dePaola and Hechtel could handle so the large party was discontinued in favor of much smaller gatherings.

Many of dePaola's books are based on his own experiences. A story based on his grandmothers helped create *Nana Upstairs, Nana Downstairs*. Putnam originally published the story in 1973. The story is that of his grandmother and great-grandmother. dePaola's grandparents lived in a house where they cared for his eighty-four-year-old great-grandmother. Much of the time, great-grandmother is upstairs and bedridden. Tomie is very close to his great-grandmother and shortly after she dies, he sees a falling star. His mother tells him that it is a "kiss from Nana Upstairs." Later when his grandmother dies, he sees another falling star, and he concludes that both grandmothers are "now Nana Upstairs."

Tomie dePaola works full time illustrating and writing books. When he does have an evening free, he enjoys just staying at home and relaxing. He loves books and always reads a few pages of a book before he goes to sleep. He enjoys visiting with friends, cooking, and gardening. His favorite food is popcorn. He was served spaghetti with tomato sauce and meatballs so often as a youngster that he doesn't eat it anymore. He does make other kinds of pasta, however, and he likes plain noodles with cheese and butter. Tomie dePaola lives in New London, Connecticut.

BOOKS AND NOTES

Tomie dePaola's early books, prior to 1973, featured simple, two-color line illustrations. As dePaola's art developed over the years, his stylized depictions of his characters and the full-color illustrations became identifiable, as did his flamboyant signature. In 1998, dePaola reillustrated *Nana Upstairs, Nana Downstairs* with full-color illustrations "echoing the original art." The reillustrated book, published by Putnam, became dePaola's 200th illustrated book. For most of his life as a children's book illustrator, dePaola often answered questions about which of his books was his favorite by saying it was whichever one he was working on at the time. Since the reissue of *Nana Upstairs, Nana Downstairs,* however, he has admitted that it is his favorite.

Putnam had planned to release a reillustrated version of *Now One Foot, Now the Other,* but in 1998, that reissue was postponed indefinitely. He based that story on events in his life. His experiences also are the basis for a new series of early chapter books, which he is writing for Putnam. The series, 26 Fairmount Avenue, has been named for the address of the first house where dePaola and his family lived after living in several apartments. The first title, *26 Fairmount Avenue* (Putnam, 1999), is the anchor book and was honored with a 2000 Newbery Honor Award. It will be joined by other books about the neighborhood children. Among dePaola's well-known characters are Strega Nona, Big Anthony, and Bill and Pete. Those characters continue to populate his books.

Books Written and Illustrated by Tomie dePaola

The Baby Sister (Putnam, 1996).

Bill and Pete Go Down the Nile (Putnam, 1987).

Bill and Pete to the Rescue (Putnam, 1998).

Charlie Needs a Cloak (Prentice-Hall, 1973).

Helga's Dowry: A Troll Love Story (Harcourt, 1977).

Jamie O'Rourke and the Big Potato (Putnam, 1992).

The Knight and the Dragon (Putnam, 1980).

The Legend of Bluebonnet: An Old Tale of Texas (Putnam, 1983).

My First Thanksgiving (Putnam, 1992).

Nana Upstairs, Nana Downstairs (Putnam, 1973, 1998).

Pancakes for Breakfast (Harcourt, 1978).

The Popcorn Book (Holiday House, 1978).

Strega Nona Series and Big Anthony Series

Big Anthony and the Magic Ring (Harcourt, 1979).

Big Anthony, His Story (Putnam, 1998).

Merry Christmas, Strega Nona (Harcourt, 1986).

Strega Nona (Prentice-Hall, 1975).

Strega Nona, Her Story (Putnam, 1996).

Strega Nona Meets Her Match (Putnam, 1993).

Strega Nona's Magic Lessons (Harcourt, 1982).

Tom (Putnam, 1993).

26 Fairmount Series

Here We All Are (Putnam, 2000).

On My Way (Putnam, 2001).

26 Fairmount Avenue (Putnam, 1999).

Books Illustrated by Tomie dePaola

Alice Nizzy Nazzy: The Witch of Santa Fe. Written by Tony Johnston. (Putnam, 1995).

Can't You Make Them Behave, King George. Written by Jean Fritz. (Coward, 1977).

I Love You, Sun; I Love You, Moon. Written by Karen Pandell. (Putnam, 1994).

Mice Squeak, We Speak. Written by Arnold L. Shapiro. (Putnam, 1997).

The Tale of Rabbit and Coyote. Written by Tony Johnston. (Putnam, 1994).

FOR MORE INFORMATION

Articles

Campbell, Jane. "On Tour with Tomie dePaola." *Classroom: The Magazine for Teachers* 18, no. 5 (1998): 20.

"dePaola: A Veritable Industry." *Booklist* 86, no. 17 (May 1, 1990): 1705.

Elleman, Barbara. "Tomie dePaola." *Booklinks* 4, no. 6 (July 1, 1995): 11.

Books

Elleman, Barbara. *Tomie dePaola, His Art and His Stories* (Putnam, 1999).

Videos

Tomie Live in Concert (Whitebird, 1999).

A Visit with Tomie dePaola (Whitebird, 1999).

Web Sites

Hechtel, Robert. *Tomie dePaola.* URL: <http://www.bingley.com> or <http://www.tomiedepaola.com> (Accessed March 2000).

Diane Dillon
Leo Dillon

◆ Folklore

Glendale, California
March 13, 1933

Brooklyn, New York
March 2, 1933

📖 *Ashanti to Zulu: African Traditions*

📖 *To Every Thing There Is a Season: Verses from Ecclesiastes*

📖 *Why Mosquitoes Buzz in People's Ears*

Pat Cummings

Pat Cummings

ABOUT THE ILLUSTRATORS

"A spectrum of styles," "stunningly beautiful," and "extraordinarily varied" are all phrases used to describe the artwork of Leo Dillon and Diane Dillon. The two of them have collaborated on more than 40 illustrated books and have won numerous awards for their artistic work. They are the only artists to win the Caldecott Medal for two consecutive years. In addition to those two Caldecott Medals and a Hugo Award for science fiction and fantasy cover art, they have earned four Boston Globe–Horn Book Awards, three *New York Times* Best Illustrated Awards, two Coretta Scott King Awards for illustrations, and the Society of Illustrators Gold Medal.

In 1991, Leo Dillon and Diane Dillon received honorary doctorates of fine arts from Parsons School of Design. They were the U.S. nominees for the 1996 Hans Christian Andersen Award. Two years later, they were inducted into the Society of Illustrators Hall of Fame. Their collaboration has produced book jackets and illustrations, advertising material, posters, record album covers, magazine illustrations, boxes for soap, fine art paintings, and children's books. They have illustrated African folktales, American Indian legends, Egyptian tales, Greek myths, and a Chinese folktale. They have illustrated poetry, biblical passages, and fiction. They have worked in watercolor, acrylic, pastel, tempera, and sepia. They have painted with many different tools, including cotton, airbrushes, and conventional paint brushes. In addition to their paintings, they have worked in wood relief, inlaid wood, mosaic, crewelwork, mobiles, sculpture, collage, and stained glass. The diversity of their work and the variety of their styles are astounding.

Leo Dillon was born in Brooklyn, New York on March 2, 1933. Eleven days later, and across the country, Diane Sorber was born in Glendale, California on March 13, 1933. Leo's father was the owner of a trucking company. Diane's father was a teacher. Their childhoods were quite different. Diane and her brother spent their childhood in Van Nuys, North Hollywood, and Morristown, New Jersey. Leo and his sister spent their childhoods in Brooklyn. Diane began college in California, and Leo joined the Marines, where he served during the Korean War. Eventually they both ended up at Parsons School of Design. Competition between the two artists was fierce during their first encounters. As their competition grew, so did their respect for one another. After graduation from art school, they broke up briefly and later reconciled. They married in March of 1957 and began working as commercial artists.

As the two artists made the rounds to publishing houses and other commercial-art establishments, they faced disappointment. Their individual styles were so diverse that art directors could not categorize either of them. Leo and Diane decided to establish their own company. They called it Studio 2 so that art directors would think there was a complete studio of artists when the studio actually consisted only of Leo and Diane.

At the beginning of their art careers, they worked as individual artists, but the competition was wrenching. Finally, they both displayed art at an important show. After agonizing hours spent wondering who would sell more art, they learned that the work of both artists had completely sold out. They realized that they should become an artistic team and never again try to compare their work. For more than three decades, they have collaborated on every work of art. The work is passed back and forth until both have contributed to the whole. It is often impossible for even Leo and Diane to know how the work was divided. The artist that emerges is actually a third artist who has created a piece of art that neither of them could have created as an individual.

Leo Dillon and Diane Dillon's first picture book was *The Ring and the Prairie: A Shawnee Legend* by John Bierhorst (Dial, 1970). Six years later, in 1976, they were awarded the prestigious Caldecott Medal for the art in *Why Mosquitoes Buzz in People's Ears* by Verna Aardema (Dial, 1975). Vellum cutouts, frisket masks, and watercolors applied with an airbrush were used to create the art for that book. The next year, they became the first (and thus far only) artists to win the coveted Caldecott Medal for two consecutive years. This time the award came for *Ashanti to Zulu: African Traditions* by Margaret Musgrove (Dial, 1976). The illustrations for that book were created with pastels, watercolors, and acrylics.

Their work appeared steadily in picture books through 1980 when they took a hiatus from illustrating children's books. By 1985, they were back. Their reentry into children's books came with the offer to illustrate Mildred Pitts Walter's *Brother to the Wind* (Lothrop, 1985). Walter's story is an original African American tale written to bring the beauty of African culture to American children. It tells the story of Emeke, a boy who wishes to fly. Because the story did not concern a specific tribe or locale, the Dillons were able to draw on their knowledge and feeling for African cultures in an interpretive manner.

Shortly after the publication of *The Tale of the Mandarin Ducks* by Katherine Paterson (Lodestar, 1990) and *Aida* by Leontyne Price (Harcourt, 1990). Betsy Hearne, the editor of *The Bulletin of the Center of Children's Books*, spoke in *USA Today* about Leo Dillon and Diane Dillon's versatility: "Those two books were done in the same year and you would not recognize them as being done by the same artist except for the high quality of the work" (October 30, 1990). *The Tale of the Mandarin Ducks* was cited for the 1991 Boston Globe–Horn Book Award, and *Aida* was cited for the 1991 Coretta Scott King Award. The illustrations for *The Tale of the Mandarin Ducks* were inspired by *ukiyo-e*, a Japanese art form that uses woodcuts. The final paintings were created using pastels, watercolors, and ink.

Leo Dillon and Diane Dillon do exhaustive research, when needed, to produce authentic images. They spent months researching the setting and artifacts that could be used in *Ashanti to Zulu: African Traditions*, so it is no surprise that one of their most treasured compliments came from a Nigerian who, upon seeing the book, declared that, "this is my country." Each of their illustrations for that book include a man, a woman, a child, their living quarters, an artifact, and an animal generally found in that area of Africa. The Dillons have never visited Africa, but their research has served them well.

Leo Dillon and Diane Dillon have collaborated with Virginia Hamilton to create three collections of African American stories: *The People Could Fly: American Black Folktales* (Knopf, 1985); *Many Thousand Gone: African Americans from Slavery to Freedom* (Knopf, 1993); *Her Stories: African American Folktales, Fairy Tales, and True Tales* (Scholastic/Blue Sky, 1995).

The Dillons have one son, Lee, who is also an artist. The three of them collaborated on the illustrations for *Pish, Posh, Said Hieronymus Bosch* by Nancy Willard (Harcourt, 1991). Lee hand-crafted a frame for each of the illustrations using silver, bronze, and brass. Willard's book was inspired by the artist Hieronymus Bosch, who was born in the 1450s in Hertogenbosch, Netherlands. The meaning of his unusual art remains a mystery even to this day. Bosch died in 1516. The artwork of Diane Dillon and Leo Dillon recalls Bosch's own unusual style and extraordinary images.

In 1998, Scholastic released *To Every Thing There Is a Season: Verses from Ecclesiastes.* Each phrase is illustrated by one of sixteen panels, and each panel, spanning a two-page spread, stems from the artistic style of a different culture. The Dillons have referenced Egyptian tomb friezes, Japanese harvest scenes, Aboriginal bark paintings, Greek red-and-black vase paintings, kiva painting, medieval woodcuts, Russian icons, Inuit art, Thai shadow plays, and the Book of Kells.

The text for the book is from the King James Version of the Bible: The Book of Ecclesiastes; Chapter 1, Verse 4 and Chapter III, Verses 1–8. Diane Dillon says, "The idea came about over dinner with our editor, Bonnie Verburg. We expressed our desire to do a book that included a variety of cultures showing the things people share rather than differences. We weren't sure how to tie it all together. Bonnie suggested Ecclesiastes and all the pieces came together."

Diane Dillon, Leo Dillon, and their son live in a brownstone in Brooklyn, New York. For more than forty years, they have been remodeling the house brick by brick, floorboard by floorboard, and they have replaced walls they once tore out. They have a plan for the house, but the plan keeps changing. They live and work in the house where they create the many works of art, make marbleized paper, bind books, and enjoy building and woodworking. At one time, Leo and Diane worked in the same studio, but now they have separate studios on different floors of the house. Although they have to go a little farther to pass the art back and forth, they can listen to their own music without disturbing each other. In the early 1990s, their son Lee also established a studio in their home. Lee paints, sculpts, and makes jewelry. Leo especially enjoys working with bookbinding and sculpting. Diane likes to sew and makes her own clothing; she also loves to read. "Other than the demands of living, shopping, cleaning, going through catalogues, and trying to keep from being buried under the mail," Diane says, "we spend most of our time at the drawing boards. We enjoy working out at the gym, and of course, love reading. We love what we do and feel lucky we can work at home."

Each book or illustrative assignment brings to Leo Dillon and Diane Dillon a new challenge, a new opportunity to perfect their unlimited styles and techniques—traits that make them two of the most interesting and exciting artists in the field of books for young readers.

BOOKS AND NOTES

Leo Dillon and Diane Dillon were each born in the third month of 1933, and they have often consciously included motifs based on the number three. The number three often is found in folklore, so their connection with that genre is personal as well as literary.

They often use their illustrations to create visual subplots in the books they illustrate. In *Why Mosquitoes Buzz in People's Ears* they put a little red bird in each scene. The bird witnesses the story as it unfolds. In *Who's in Rabbit's House* by Verna Aardema (Dial, 1977), lions watch the activities of humans, who seem to be very foolish.

Not all of the images they create come from research. The gray tabby cat that belongs to the witch in Michael Patrick Hearn's *The Porcelain Cat* (Little, Brown, 1987) is Spats, one of their cats. Many other illustrations come straight from their imaginations. Their favorite subject matter is fantasy, which they feel gives them more freedom to use their imaginations. Of the books they have illustrated, there are five that Leo and Diane list as their favorites: *Aida* by Leontyne Price, *Brother to the Wind*

by Mildred Pitts Walter, *The Porcelain Cat* by Michael Patrick Hearn, *The Tale of the Mandarin Ducks* by Katherine Paterson, and *Why Mosquitoes Buzz in People's Ears* by Verna Aardema. Their versatility as artists was showcased in *To Every Thing There Is a Season: Verses from Ecclesiastes* (Scholastic, 1998). Among the Dillons' recent books is a fictional account of the nomadic wanderings of the boy who grew up to become Mali's great fourteenth-century leader, Mansa Musa. That book, *Mansa Musa: The Lion of Mali*, written by Khephra Burns, was published by Harcourt in 2000. They have collaborated with Virginia Hamilton on an African-American retelling of *Rumpelstiltskin* titled *The Girl Who Spun Gold* (Blue Sky, 2000). It is the story of Lit'mahn who must spin thread into gold cloth for the King's new bride.

Aida. Retold by Leontyne Price. (Harcourt, 1990).

Ashanti to Zulu: African Traditions. Written by Margaret Musgrove. (Dial, 1976).

Brother to the Wind. Written by Mildred Pitts Walter. (Lothrop, 1985).

Children of the Sun. Written by Jan Carew. (Little, Brown, 1980).

The Color Wizard. Written by Barbara Brenner. (Bantam, 1989).

The Girl Who Dreamed Only Geese, and Other Tales of the Far North. Written by Howard Norman. (Harcourt, 1997).

The Girl Who Spun Gold. Written by Virginia Hamilton. (Blue Sky, 2000).

Mansa Musa: The Lion of Mali. Written by Khephra Burns. (Harcourt, 2000).

Pish, Posh, Said Hieronymus Bosch. Written by Nancy Willard. (Harcourt, 1991).

The Race of the Golden Apples. Written by Claire Martin. (Dial, 1991).

The Sorcerer's Apprentice. Written by Nancy Willard. (Blue Sky, 1993).

Switch on the Night. Written by Ray Bradbury. (Knopf, 1993).

The Tale of the Mandarin Ducks. Written by Katherine Paterson. (Lodestar, 1990).

To Every Thing There Is a Season: Verses from Ecclesiastes (Scholastic, 1998).

What Am I? Looking Through Shapes at Apples and Grapes. Written by N. N. Charles. (Blue Sky, 1994).

Who's in Rabbit's House? A Masai Tale. Written by Verna Aardema. (Dial, 1977).

Wind Child. Written by Shirley Rousseau Murphy. (Harper, 1995).

FOR MORE INFORMATION

Articles

Cummings, Pat. "Leo and Diane Dillon." *Talking with Artists* (Bradbury, 1992): 22–29.

Dillon, Leo, and Diane Dillon. "The Art of Illustrating Picture Books." *Washington Post Book World* (February 28, 1988): 4.

Donahue, Deirdre. "Drawing on Each Other's Art Abilities." *USA Today* (October 30, 1990): 1D.

"Meet the Artists: Leo and Diane Dillon Show How Teamwork Pays Off." *Instructor* 102, no. 7 (March 1, 1993): 57.

Books

Preiss, Byron. *The Art of Leo & Diane Dillon* (Ballantine, 1981).

Web Sites

Amazing Artists: Leo and Diane Dillon URL: <http://www.best.com/~libros/dillon/> (Accessed March 2000).

Leo and Diane Dillon: Resource File URL: <http://falcon.jmu.edu/~ramseyil/dillon.htm> (Accessed March 2000).

Lois Ehlert

◆ Birds ◆ Gardening

Lillian Schultz

Beaver Dam, Wisconsin
November 9, 1934

📖 *Eating the Alphabet: Fruits & Vegetables from A to Z*

📖 *Feathers for Lunch*

📖 *Planting a Rainbow*

ABOUT THE AUTHOR/ILLUSTRATOR

As a child growing up in Beaver Dam, Wisconsin, Lois Ehlert gathered scraps of cloth from her mother's sewing projects and used them for her own creations. Her mother taught her to use the sewing machine when she was about eight years old. The wood from her father's woodworking projects let her create in three dimensions. She always had materials to create artwork, although they were not necessarily paper and pencil. She did not like painting and drawing as much as she liked cutting and pasting. Collages, even then, were a favorite art medium.

Ehlert's parents provided her with a place to work by setting up a card table in the "music room" of their house. It was the room that most families would have used for a dining room, but they kept a piano in the room, so it was the "music room." Her table fit between the closet and the piano. Her table was very special to her. If she was working on a project, she was allowed to leave it on the table rather than put everything away before she went to bed. That table was her workspace through high school, and then she took the table with her when she entered Layton School of Art on a scholarship. She converted it into a drawing table with a can and a wooden breadboard propped on top of the table. Throughout her career as an artist she has used the table; in fact, she still uses it. It now has a new wooden top complete with holes that have been drilled into it, ink spills, and razor-blade cuts.

Lois Ehlert was born on November 9, 1934, in Beaver Dam, the daughter of Harry and Gladys Ehlert. She graduated from the Layton School of Art in 1957 and received an undergraduate degree in fine arts from the University of Wisconsin in 1959. For a time, she worked as a teacher, a graphic artist, and a designer. Some of her first work after art school was on children's picture books, but she did not really enjoy the work because she was not given the opportunity to approve the color selections when the books went to the printers. She left the children's book field and turned her concentration to her graphic design.

At one time, Ehlert designed toys and games for children. Eventually, her friends convinced her to return to illustrating children's books. One of the deciding factors was the emergence of graphics in picture books. Observing that trend helped convince Ehlert that she should try illustrating once more. She also noted that more care was taken in the production of the books. She first illustrated books written by others and then decided to try her hand at both writing and illustrating. The result of her first efforts was *Growing Vegetable Soup* (Harcourt, 1987). The book focused on the steps involved in growing a vegetable garden. She continued to combine her love of gardening and growing things into her writing and illustrating and produced *Planting a Rainbow* (Harcourt, 1988), which deals with the cultivation of a flower garden. Bold colors and strong graphic shapes began to be a signature of sorts for Ehlert's books. Shortly after her success with *Growing Vegetable Soup*, Ehlert took a class at the University of Wisconsin and learned about new methods of design, which she subsequently used in *Color Zoo* (Lippincott, 1989) and *Color Farm* (Lippincott, 1990). These methods included cutting holes in the pages and using different combinations of the light and dark. She also began to use a wide range of colors and shapes.

Many of her illustrations are created with a collage technique, which allows her to move parts around until she gets an illustration just the way she wants it. She paints her own papers to get the exact colors she wants. After the paintings dry, she uses rubber cement to adhere the shapes together to create the total image. She paints the edges of the pieces so that the illustration looks like it is all one piece. She actually manipulates colored photocopies of her paintings so that she can arrange and rearrange the objects in the sequence and positions she wishes. Once she is pleased with the composition, she uses the fragile original paintings to create the final collages.

Even though her books are considered simple concept books, a lot of time and effort goes into research to help her create work that is accurate in terms of what it shows and tells. For example, when she was creating *Planting a Rainbow,* she spent a lot of time looking at flower gardens, garden centers, and parks. She checked her facts regarding flowers before she began to work. In *Eating the Alphabet: Fruits and Vegetables from A to Z* (Harcourt, 1989), each kernel of Indian Corn is a separate piece of paper. When she created the art work for *Red Leaf, Yellow Leaf* (Harcourt, 1991), she created all of the art for the book using a white background. But after a few weeks, she realized that it didn't look right. She got all the art back, redid the background, and reworked all the colors.

A special area for making art has always been important to Ehlert. As a youngster, her special place was her table; now she has a studio in her home. She has a huge drawing room with large windows. Cabinets and work surfaces surround her. The cabinets on the left hold jars bursting with brushes, pens, pencils, erasers, tape, rubber cement, a desk calendar, and a telephone. Even while on the phone, she can continue working. The drawers of the cabinets hold her marking pens and pencils, paints, and colored papers. Her desk calendar helps her stay organized and remember appointments, such as visits to schools and museums. At the end of the week, the pages are filled with paint and ink spots. Her office does not get cleaned daily. If Ehlert has ideas, she wants to keep working rather than stop to pick up after herself. She says, "There will be days with no ideas, and plenty of time to clean."

Many of her ideas come from her own interests. Certainly the books involving gardens and growing fruits and vegetables emerged from her love of gardening. *Nuts to You!* (Harcourt, 1993) came about after a squirrel sneaked into her house through the window. The origin of other ideas is difficult to identify. Some just come from her imagination and creativity.

Ehlert's work has appeared in various publications and in many books written by other authors as well. She currently lives and works in Milwaukee, Wisconsin. She doesn't have any live pets, but she has a clay deer in her kitchen and her bathroom is home to cloth mice. Fourteen carved birds dwell in her studio's birdcage, and a painted turkey guards her sewing machine.

BOOKS AND NOTES

Lois Ehlert's creates her books with simple shapes, bold graphics, and vibrant colors. Although her books are not written, to instruct they do provide information to young readers. Children can develop an understanding of geometric shapes and colors and the occurrence of shapes in nature. Her research allows her to include information that is not always the focus of the book. For example, in *Feathers for Lunch* (Harcourt, 1990), Ehlert presented a dozen birds, painted their actual size, with faithful attention to accurately portraying their colors. She also was able to put the birds in natural settings with flowers that harmonize with the bird's coloration and setting. To verify that the birds were the right color and size, Ehlert researched at the Field Museum in Chicago.

Ehlert wants children to learn from her books, but she does not view herself as an educator. She just wants to communicate what she feels is important. She says she would like her readers to "look for birds! Plant a garden or a tree! Grow some flowers!"

Books Written and Illustrated by Lois Ehlert

Circus (Harper, 1992).

Color Farm (Lippincott, 1990).

Color Zoo (Lippincott, 1989).

Eating the Alphabet: Fruits and Vegetables from A to Z (Harcourt, 1989).

Feathers for Lunch (Harcourt, 1990).

Fish Eyes: A Book You Can Count On (Harcourt, 1990).

Growing Vegetable Soup (Harcourt, 1987).

Lois Ehlert's Animals (Harper, 1996).

Market Day: A Story Told with Folk Art (Harcourt, 2000).

Mole's Hill: A Woodland Tale (Harcourt, 1994).

Nuts to You! (Harcourt, 1993).

Planting a Rainbow (Harcourt, 1988).

Red Leaf, Yellow Leaf (Harcourt, 1991).

Books Illustrated by Lois Ehlert

Chicka Chicka Boom Boom. Written by Bill Martin Jr. and John Archambault. (Simon & Schuster, 1989).

Crocodile Smile: 10 Songs of the Earth As the Animals See It. Written by Sarah Weeks. (Harper, 1994).

Cuckoo: A Mexican Folktale. Written by Gloria Andujar. (Harcourt, 1997).

Moon Rope: A Peruvian Folktale/Un Lazo a La Luna: Una Leyenda Peruana. Written by Amy Prince. (Harcourt, 1992).

A Pair of Socks (A Mathstart Book). Written by Stuart J. Murphy. (Harper, 1996).

Plumas Para Almorzar. Written by Alma Flor Ada. (Voyager, 1996).

FOR MORE INFORMATION

Articles

Ehlert, Lois. "The Artist at Work: Card Tables and Collage." *Horn Book* 67, no. 6 (November–December 1991): 695–704.

Goddard, Connie. "Alive with Color: An Interview with Lois Ehlert." *Publishers Weekly* 239, no. 9 (February 12, 1992): 18.

Books

Ehlert, Lois. *Under My Nose* (R. C. Owen, 1996). Illustrated with photographs by Carlo Ontal.

Videos

Get to Know Lois Ehlert (Harcourt, 1994). 20 mins.

Lisa Campbell Ernst

◆ Community ◆ Folklore (Literary)

Bartlesville, Oklahoma
March 13, 1957

📖 *Little Red Riding Hood: A New Fangled Prairie Tale*

📖 *Sam Johnson and the Blue Ribbon Quilt*

📖 *Stella LouElla's Runaway Book*

ABOUT THE AUTHOR/ILLUSTRATOR

One of Lisa Campbell Ernst's first memories of drawing goes back to her preschool years when she drew on paper in her church's Sunday school room. While hymns filtered into the room from the church service nearby, she drew pictures. Now she draws in a studio five minutes from her home in Kansas City, Missouri. Her studio is above a music store, so music still filters in as she creates her drawings.

Lisa Campbell was born in Bartlesville, Oklahoma on March 13, 1957, and spent her childhood there. Her older brother was the family athlete. Her older sister was good at the piano, and young Lisa was the "artist of the family." As a kindergartner, one of her drawings—a bird pecking a tree— was exhibited in the town's annual art show. Somehow, her drawing was hung sideways and became a bird digging in the dirt. Despite the disappointment,

Lisa continued to draw, and later she began to earn ribbons for her work. Lisa's mother encouraged her drawing by making a list of objects for her to draw. She drew pictures and made up stories about the things she drew.

Lisa's parents often read to her when she was little. She remembers hearing the Winnie-the-Pooh books by A. A. Milne and books by Margery Flack about a delightful Scottish terrier named Angus. She also enjoyed books by H. A. Rey, Dr. Seuss, and Robert McCloskey. Many of those early books featured animals, such as bears, dogs, monkeys, ducks, and some made-up creatures. As Lisa grew older, she drew many animals too. She drew the family dog, one of their neighbor's cats, and any bird, snake, rabbit, turtle, mouse, or lizard that she could find in the Oklahoma countryside. When she couldn't find an animal to draw, she drew creatures from her imagination—just like Dr. Seuss. Her early drawings were done in wax crayons.

During her school days, Lisa took art lessons. She learned to use watercolors and charcoal. She did not spend all of her time drawing, however. She was a typical child riding her bike, selling Kool-Aid from a sidewalk stand, baking cakes, collecting stamps, and playing street games in her neighborhood. She tried to learn to play the piano but was less than successful.

After completing school in Bartlesville, Lisa entered the University of Oklahoma and earned an undergraduate degree in fine arts. She moved to New York City and spent her first year there working in advertising. Her attention soon turned to children's books. She says that New York City was a good place to get started. She didn't really know how to begin but figured that a first step was to gather some samples of her artistic work together and get appointments to show her work to art directors at some of the publishing houses. She looked up the addresses and phone numbers for publishers she recognized from her own favorite books. She called and made appointments and then began making the rounds. An offer to illustrate a book came from one of those appointments.

By the time her first book was published, Lisa was married to Lee Ernst. Lisa Campbell Ernst first illustrated four titles by other authors, which were published in 1980. She illustrated three more titles that were published in 1981. The first book that she both wrote and illustrated, *Sam Johnson and the Blue Ribbon Quilt* (Lothrop, 1983), was widely acclaimed. Since its publication, she has continued to focus on illustrating books she has written, although she also has illustrated books by other writers.

After more than eight years in New York, the Ernsts returned to the Midwest. From her Kansas City studio, she continued to change a blank piece of paper into an exciting new world. While driving through the Missouri countryside, she spotted some cows standing in the shade under a big tree. The scene was nothing new to Ernst, but that day she began to think that perhaps the cows were "up to something." Her imagination did the rest, and soon she had the story of Bluebell, Swenson, and Big Eddie, the characters from *When Bluebell Sang* (Bradbury, 1989).

Ernst's imagination also allowed her to play with the traditional tale of "Little Red Riding Hood." She decided to create a new setting—both time and place—for a familiar character. Before she knew it, she had Little Red Riding Hood riding a bike down a path through a cornfield and grandmother roaring through the fields on a tractor. Then came *Duke, the Dairy Delight Dog* (Simon & Schuster, 1996), *The Letters Are Lost!* (Viking, 1996) and *Bubba and Trixie* (Simon & Schuster, 1997).

Her experience with lost library books brought her to write and illustrate *Stella LouElla's Runaway Book* (Simon & Schuster, 1998). From the end papers to the pages of the story itself, Stella LouElla shares her love of reading and her dismay in not being able to find a library book that "disappeared, as if in a magic act." The resulting search brings many neighbors and friends, all who have their own perspective on the lost book, its title, and where it might be. In the end, the lost book is found, but not before a rollicking search ensues. Along the way, readers get clues as to the title of the book that has been lost—an interesting subplot to the main story line.

Ernst works at a giant antique drawing board made of oak. It came from a school in New York. She sometimes wishes that the board could tell her its stories, but Ernst seems to have plenty of her own. Her drawing and writing schedule usually consumes eight or nine hours a day unless a deadline is near, and then the days may stretch into fourteen or fifteen hours spent at the drawing board. Most of her illustrations are created with pastels, pen, and ink. She often soaks up ideas from other books, which she finds on her frequent afternoon visits to the library or the "great bookstore" nearby.

Sometimes when Ernst works in her studio at night, the family's Scottish terrier, Sally, goes with her. Sally loves going on walks and riding in cars. At her studio, Ernst has a gray-and-white rabbit named Penny. Penny lives at the studio. Both Sally and Penny love to eat carrots and broccoli.

Lisa Campbell Ernst lives and works in Kansas City, Missouri, where she and her family, husband Lee Ernst and daughters Elizabeth and Allison, live in a big old house that they are "fixing-up." When she is not writing or drawing, Ernst is likely to be reading, gardening, or just enjoying being with her family and playing with her pets.

BOOKS AND NOTES

Lisa Campbell Ernst enjoys drawing animals, and she depicts in words and pictures the bond between animals and humans. Ernst also is fascinated with the past and feels that our present culture is a result of that which came before us. For that reason, many of her stories are set in the past. Those settings are meant to help young readers compare and contrast today with yesterday. Ernst's illustrations are not intended to include family and friends but once her illustrations are drawn, she may recognize a character who looks exactly like someone she knows. Her drawings are made first with a quill pen and ink. Line shading and cross-hatching is done with pencil, and the coloring of the illustrations is done with colored chalks and pastels.

Books Written and Illustrated by Lisa Campbell Ernst

Bubba and Trixie (Simon & Schuster, 1997).

Duke, the Dairy Delight Dog (Simon & Schuster, 1996).

Goldilocks Returns (Simon & Schuster, 2000).

The Letters Are Lost! (Viking, 1996).

Little Red Riding Hood: A Newfangled Prairie Tale (Simon & Schuster, 1995).

The Luckiest Kid on the Planet (Bradbury, 1994).

Sam Johnson and the Blue Ribbon Quilt (Lothrop, 1983).

Squirrel Park (Bradbury, 1993).

Stella LouElla's Runaway Book (Simon & Schuster, 1998).

The Tangram Magician. Co-authored with Lee Ernst. (Abrams, 1990).

Walter's Tail (Bradbury, 1992).

When Bluebell Sang (Bradbury, 1989).

Zinnia and Dot (Viking, 1992).

Books Illustrated by Lisa Campbell Ernst

Breakfast Time! Written by Harriet Ziefert. (Viking, 1988).

Feed Little Bunny. Written by Harriet Ziefert. (Viking, 1988).

Gumshoe Goose, Private Eye. Written by Mary DeBall Kwitz. (Puffin, 1996).

Potato: A Tale from the Great Depression. Written by Kate Lied. (National Geographic Society, 1997).

Who Says Moo? Written by Ruth Young. (Puffin, 1997).

FOR MORE INFORMATION

Articles

Cummings, Pat. "Lisa Campbell Ernst." *Talking with Artists* (Bradbury, 1992): 42–47.

Web Sites

Lisa Campbell Ernst. URL: <http://authors.missouri.org/ernst-l.html> (Accessed March 2000).

Mem Fox

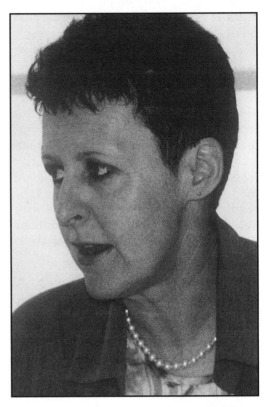

Sharron L. McElmeel

Melbourne, Australia
March 5, 1946

📖 *Koala Lou*

📖 *Night Noises*

📖 *Possum Magic*

📖 *Wilfrid Gordon McDonald Partridge*

ABOUT THE AUTHOR

Merrion Frances Partridge was born in Melbourne, Australia on March 5, 1946. She says that she has been "known as 'Mem' all of my life." At the age of six months, her parents, Wilfrid Gordon McDonald Partridge and Nancy Walkden Brown Partridge, took Mem to Rhodesia, now the country of Zimbabwe, where they were missionaries. Early in her school career, Mem was the only white child both at the missionary and in school. Eventually, the authorities insisted she attend an all-white school. She was caught between two worlds—her black friends and her white schoolmates. The intolerance in Rhodesia was stifling. She says, "I was living a double life . . . I could no longer tolerate the political and social repression in Rhodesia and decided to go to England to attend drama school."

At the age of nineteen, Mem left Rhodesia for England, where she met and married Malcolm Fox. It was after her marriage in 1970 that she returned to Australia. They were lured by incentives offered by the Australian government to migrants who would come back and the fact that Mem Fox's grandfather, age ninety, was alone in Australia. Malcolm and Mem Fox moved to Adelaide, South Australia, and thought they would stay there for two years. They have lived and worked there ever since.

In 1977, when their daughter, Chlöe, was seven, Fox decided to enroll in a children's literature course to refresh her knowledge of children's books. In that course, she was required to write a children's book. Out of that assignment came a book called *Hush, the Invisible Mouse*. Her instructor encouraged her to send the story to publishers. Fox thought that before she could do that, she had to find an illustrator. She asked a friend, an art professor, for a recommendation. He recommended a former student of his, Julie Vivas. Vivas made several illustrations, and Fox sent the book with the illustrations to publishers. Over a period of five years, the book received nine rejections. Some thought the story was "too Australian." Finally, an editor at Omnibus Books, the tenth publisher, read the story and liked it. The editor did ask Fox to rewrite the story, however, to make it shorter and more lyrical and to make it *more* Australian. The editor also asked that the mice characters be changed to possums. Australian possums are very soft and cute. The book includes references to Australian geography, food, and animals. Julie redid the illustrations, and the book was called *Possum Magic* (Omnibus/Harcourt, 1983). The book was published early in 1983 and was an immediate success. The publisher had to reprint the book ten times in the first year. All types of promotional items were spawned: T-shirts, stationery, buttons, calendars, bedding, pottery, baby books, and birthday books. In its first ten years, the book sold more than 1 million copies.

Fox writes many drafts for each of her books. *Koala Lou* (Harcourt, 1989), for example, underwent forty-nine drafts, even though the story was only 488 words long. The story was originally written for Olivia Newton-John to help promote her clothing stores, Koala Blue. It was to be marketed with a toy Koala. By the time the story was ready for publication, Newton-John and her partner decided they did not have the resources to publish the book and returned it to Fox, who was free to publish the story elsewhere if she did not use the name Koala Blue. Because the story had repeatedly used the phrase "Koala Blue, I do love you" Fox had to come up with another name that would rhyme with "you." She rejected "Koala Koo," "Koala Sue," and "Koala New," and finally settled on "Koala Lou." Fox has said that this book is her favorite but that she has gotten the greatest response from readers for her book *Wilfrid Gordon McDonald Partridge* (Kane-Miller, 1983, 1985). This book and its main character were named after Fox's father. Another character in the book, Miss Nancy, was named after her mother, Nancy. The rest of that character's name, Alison Delacourt Cooper, is a combination of her two sisters' names.

Not all of her books take as many rewrites as *Koala Lou*. *Hattie and the Fox* (Bradbury, 1986) only took four drafts and was finished in two days. Since her first book was published in 1983, more than twenty of Fox's books have been published in the United States. Many more of her books have been published in the Australia.

Mem and Malcolm Fox have lived in the capital of South Australia since first returning to the country in 1970. Their daughter lives in Paris, where she is the editor of *Elle Online*. The family home is nestled in a hilly, wooded area south of Adelaide. Mem Fox sometimes uses the kitchen table to write but more often spends her writing time in her study, which she designed herself. Her first drafts are constructed with a 4B pencil, and then the text is transferred to her computer where she can make final changes and rewrites. For many years, she was a senior lecturer in language arts at Flinders University and wrote at night and on weekends. Finally, in 1996, she left the University and is now writing and traveling in the United States and Australia to teach others about reading and literacy.

The Fox household has at various times included fish, dogs, a cat, and guinea pigs. Fox's favorites include food from India and the color pink. When she is not writing, she says her two favorite things to do are sleeping and traveling.

BOOKS AND NOTES

Shortly after her first book was published, readers wrote Mem Fox letters in which they frequently referred to Hush as a male, even though Fox had clearly referred to her as "she" in the book, *Possum Magic*. Realizing the impact of role models in children's fiction, Fox decided to write only about female heroes. The only exception she has made to that is her story about Wilfrid Gordon McDonald Partridge.

Boo to a Goose. Illustrated by David Miller. (Dial, 1998).

Feathers and Fools. Illustrated by Nicholas Wilton. (Harcourt, 1996).

Great Scott! Illustrated by Terry Denton. (Harcourt, 1996).

Harriet, You'll Drive Me Wild. Illustrated by Marla Frazee. (Harcourt, 2000).

Hattie and the Fox. Illustrated by Patricia Mullins. (Bradbury, 1986).

Koala Lou. Illustrated by Pamela Lofts. (Harcourt, 1989).

Night Noises. Illustrated by Terry Denton. (Harcourt, 1989).

Possum Magic. Illustrated by Julie Vivas. (Harcourt, 1983).

Shoes from Grandpa. Illustrated by Patricia Mullins. (Orchard, 1989, 1990).

Sleepy Bears. Illustrated by Kerry Argent. (Harcourt, 1999).

Whoever You Are. Illustrated by Leslie Staub. (Harcourt, 1997).

Wilfrid Gordon McDonald Partridge. Illustrated by Julie Vivas. (Kane-Miller, 1983, 1985).

Wombat Divine. Illustrated by Kerry Argent. (Harcourt, 1996).

FOR MORE INFORMATION

Articles

Fox, Mem. "Notes from the Battlefield: Towards a Theory of Why People Write." *Language Arts* 65, no. 2 (February 1988): 112–25.

Fox, Mem. "The Teacher Disguised As Writer, in Hot Pursuit of Literacy." *Language Arts* 64, no. 1 (January 1987): 18–32.

Fox, Mem. "Writing Picture Books: A Love/Hate Relationship." *The Horn Book Magazine.* (May/June 1990): 288–96.

Manning, Maryann and Gary Manning. "Mem Fox: Mem's the Word in 'Down Under.' " *Teaching PreK–8* 20, no. 6 (March 1990): 29–31.

See, Lisa. "On Tour with Mem Fox." *Publishers Weekly* 237, no. 3 (January 19, 1990): 71–72.

Books

Fox, Mem. *Dear Mem Fox, I Have Read All Your Books Even the Pathetic Ones and Other Incidents in the Life of a Children's Book Author* (Penguin Australia, 1990; Harcourt, 1992).

Fox, Mem. *Mem's the Word* (Penguin, 1990).

Videos

Trumpet Video Visits Mem Fox (Trumpet Club, 1992). 25 mins.

Web Sites

Mem Fox. URL: <http://www.memfox.net/> (Accessed March 2000).

Dick Gackenbach

◆ Animals

Allentown, Pennsylvania
February 9, 1927

📖 *A Bag Full of Pups*
📖 *Beauty, Brave and Beautiful*
📖 *Hurray for Hattie Rabbit*

ABOUT THE AUTHOR/ILLUSTRATOR

As a child during the Depression, Dick Gackenbach did not have books to read, but as an adult he became a collector of children's books. His collection includes all the works of Maurice Sendak, contemporary books by Shel Silverstein, and an early edition of *The Wizard of Oz*. His collection led him to a love of children's books and a desire to enter the field as an illustrator. In 1972, after twenty-two years as a paste-up artist and then a creative director for the J. C. Penney Company, Dick Gackenbach left his corporate job and moved to Washington Depot, an artists' and writers' community in Connecticut.

Dick Gackenbach was born in Allentown, Pennsylvania, on February 9, 1927 and grew up on a farm in the Pennsylvania Dutch Country. His parents, Gertrude Reichenbach and William Gackenbach, were hard workers, but the family had no books and little time to read. They listened to the radio instead. Dick Gackenbach's favorite show was *The Shadow*. He often entertained himself by tracing the comics that appeared in the newspaper.

After a tour of duty with the U.S. Navy, Gackenbach planned to go to New York City to become a fashion illustrator. With the help of the G.I. Bill, he enrolled at the Abbott School of Art in Washington, D.C. Eventually, he decided to use his artistic talent in other ways, so he transferred to Jameson Franklin School of Art in New York City. After studying advertising for two years, he obtained a job as a paste-up artist at the J. C. Penney corporate headquarters in New York.

In 1954, Gackenbach submitted some of his artwork to a publisher and obtained a job illustrating Gertrude Norman's *The First Book of Music* (Watts, 1970). He did not attempt to publish again until after he resigned from J. C. Penney.

His next efforts at getting illustrative assignments were unsuccessful. He decided to attempt to write his own books to illustrate. In 1974, an editor at Seabury Press accepted his first book, *Claude the Dog*. His years as a corporate artist had allowed him to learn the technique of color separation, and that knowledge proved to be an asset. He was able to prepare his illustrations for publication quickly, and the book was published that same year. His illustrations have always been the anchor for his work, and after that first book was published, Gackenbach continued to write his own books, as well as accept assignments to illustrate books written by other authors.

Much of Gackenbach's writing comes from the love and warmth he enjoyed in his childhood home and from his own love of children and dogs. "As with all writers," Gackenbach says, "my own life's experiences make their way into all my books. *Do You Love Me?* (Seabury, 1975) is a story of an event that happened to me when I was a boy. I write about dogs often because I love dogs. My stories always reflect my own values." When he was small, of the books he did have the chance to read, his favorite was *The Happy Prince* by Oscar Wilde. "It still is my favorite book, it made me cry when I was young, it makes me cry still. It is a story of kindness, gentleness, generosity, friendship and love. I wish I had written it, but I can only use it as a guide for my own stories."

Claude the Dog features a well-loved pet that gives away his own Christmas presents to a homeless mutt who has nothing. Claude does not miss his presents because, after all, he has his family. Claude continued to be a character in several more books by Gackenbach. In *A Bag Full of Pups* (Clarion, 1981), Mr. Mullin attempts to find homes for a dozen puppies. Various strangers, including a hunter, a policewoman, and a boy who just wants a dog to love, take a puppy.

In the late 1980s, Gackenbach wrote a book titled *Beauty, Brave and Beautiful* (Clarion, 1990). That book came about, says Gackenbach, because, "All my adult life I have had dachshunds, dogs that were a credit to their breed. But, one day in the late 1960s as I was walking down 2nd Avenue in Manhattan, I happened to look into a pet store. Normally I don't buy dogs from a store, rather from a kennel, but a dachshund pup caught my eye. I bought her and took her home. I called her Lottie. Lottie was the poorest excuse for a dachshund I had ever seen, but there was something about her that tore at my mind and heart. Over the years I've loved all my dogs, but I've always loved Lottie the most. Her love, her loyalty, her courage, her sweet nature made her most endearing. All these qualities made her the most beautiful dog in the world in my eyes. And so, my dear Lottie became the inspiration for my book *Beauty, Brave and Beautiful*."

Gackenbach says that his writing comes easily and that he feels like he is a very, very lucky writer. He does the entire draft of a story and then goes back to revise and polish the story. He generally revises five or six times over a period of several days. His final drafts are typed on a typewriter. As he writes, he begins to visualize the pictures, which come later. Most of his illustrations are done first as line drawings in pen and ink. He overlays with gray ink and water. Later he may add a color wash. His book dummies generally are submitted to publishers in an almost finished form. He feels it gives the editor a better feel for what the actual book will look like. When he was still writing and illustrating, his schedule usually yielded three books a year. After finishing those three books, he took two months off just to relax before he started working on new projects. He has not published a new title since 1994.

Gackenbach says, "I live a quiet life and have always shared it with one to several dogs." Before circulatory problems necessitated the amputation of both of legs below the knee, he enjoyed morning walks along the river. Now he continues to enjoy classical music, his dogs, collecting antiques (when he finds a piece he can afford), and gourmet cooking.

BOOKS AND NOTES

Animals often are featured as main characters in Dick Gackenbach's books. His illustrations have been called droll and colorful. Each book's text has a gentleness and warmth that leaves young readers with a perspective on the situation that may broaden their thinking and influence their behavior. Although many of Gackenbach's books impart positive attributes, they are first and foremost great stories. His books with dogs come from his love of dogs, and his rabbit stories are based on "talking to and watching small children. They wish for very funny things. They have a charming way of conning friends and parents into doing things." He has written and illustrated more than sixty books for young children.

Books Written and Illustrated by Dick Gackenbach

A Bag Full of Pups (Clarion, 1981).

Barker's Crime (Harcourt, 1996).

Beauty, Brave and Beautiful (Clarion, 1990).

Claude Has a Picnic (Clarion, 1993).

Hurray for Hattie Rabbit (Harper, 1986).

Mighty Tree (Harcourt, 1992).

The Perfect Mouse (Macmillan, 1984).

Tiny for a Day (Clarion, 1993).

What's Claude Doing? (Clarion, 1984).

Where are Momma, Poppa, and Sister June? (Clarion, 1994).

With Love from Gran (Clarion, 1989).

Books Illustrated by Dick Gackenbach

The Baby Blues: An Adam Joshua Story. Written by Janice Lee Smith. (Harper, 1994).

Serious Science: An Adam Joshua Story. Written by Janice Lee Smith. (Harper, 1993).

When I Am Eight. Written by Joan Lowery Nixon. (Dial, 1994).

FOR MORE INFORMATION

Web Sites

University of Southern Mississippi, de Grummond Collection: Dick Gackenbach Papers. URL: <http://www.lib.usm.edu/~degrum/findaids/gackenba.htm> (Accessed February 2000).

Wanda Gág

New Ulm, Minnesota
March 11, 1893–June 27, 1946

📖 *Gone Is Gone*
📖 *Millions of Cats*
📖 *Tales from Grimm*

ABOUT THE AUTHOR/ILLUSTRATOR

Wanda Hazel Gág was born on March 11, 1893, in New Ulm, Minnesota. She was the eldest of seven children of artist and photographer Anton Gág and his wife Lissi. The family home, built in 1894, was a unique home with skylights, an attic artist's studio and open turrets. Her parents were originally from Bohemia in Eastern Europe, and Wanda did not speak English until she went to school. The children were exposed to European music and oral storytelling. Their parents encouraged interest in drawing, painting, reading, and music. Her father made a humble living as a painter, and he encouraged Wanda to draw from a young age.

When Anton Gág died of tuberculosis, Wanda was fifteen. On his deathbed, he urged her to finish the work that he could not. Wanda spent half days at home helping with the younger children because her mother had never regained her strength after the birth of her youngest child. In an attempt to help with family finances, Wanda drew postcards and place cards, and instead of simply writing and illustrating stories for her own pleasure, she attempted to sell them. Her writings and illustrations became a mainstay on the pink pages of the *Journal Junior*, a supplement to the *Minnesota Journal*. In 1908 and 1909, she wrote and illustrated "postals" and place cards for private buyers. She also created twelve illustrations to decorate a "birthday book," which she designed so that people could write their names and birthdays in the book. In addition to the local sales she made, Gág also submitted material to other publications. Her work appeared in the *Youth's Companion* and in "Aunt Janet's Pages," a section of the *Women's Home Companion*. For four years, from the age of fifteen until she was a nineteen-year-old, she sold her stories, poems, jokes, and illustrations.

After graduating from high school, Gág taught in a one-room school house for a year and then left New Ulm to attend art schools in St. Paul and Minneapolis. In 1917, while still in school, she was commissioned to create eleven illustrations and a cover for a book to be published by Augsburg Publishing House. In September of that year, she was asked to go to Minneapolis to see the reproduction of her book, *A Child's Book of Folklore*. She received a scholarship for study in New York, so she moved there to study art.

Gág's mother died in February 1918, leaving Wanda with the responsibility of her younger siblings. She gave up her scholarship and returned to New Ulm to settle her siblings with families in New Ulm and in Minneapolis. She then returned to New York and began to solicit work at various publishing, advertising, and engraving companies. She could not find work in those fields and thus took a job painting designs on lampshades.

Gág began to experiment with art and designed boxes that could be folded, stacked, and read in sequence. She produced story boxes for "The House That Jack Built," "Little Black Sambo," and "Four Little Happy Workers on the Farm." The attempt to make this a commercial success failed and took all of her savings. In 1925, she was creating imaginative "Cross-Word Puzzle Fairy Stories." The puzzles were published in a variety of publications. She was boarding with a family with two children who often asked her to tell them stories. She invented stories to tell them and would repeat them time and again. Eventually, she put the stories on paper and illustrated them and then tried to sell them to children's publishers. She received many rejections, including some for her first drafts of *Millions of Cats*.

Wanda Gág continued to create her artwork, producing sketches, lithographs, and watercolors, and many of her works were displayed in galleries throughout the East Coast. In 1927, she moved to Tumble Timbers near Glen Gardner, New Jersey, and began working diligently to develop ideas for children's books. In 1931, she moved permanently to her own farm, which she named All Creation, near Milford, New Jersey. Some sources indicate that Gág married her long-time companion, Earle Marshall Humphreys, in

1930; other sources indicate that she was "in her late thirties" when she married. Those statements are consistent with one another. Other credible sources—including individuals who have examined her diaries and letters held by Special Collections at the University of Pennsylvania at Philadelphia that have been only open to the public since 1993—mention her independent nature. These sources indicate that she married Humphreys when she was fifty, which would make the date 1943. It is clear that Humphreys was her companion and often offered advice and encouraged her quest to build a reputation as a commercial artist. She spent much of her adult life on her New Jersey farm, which she shared with her brothers and sisters, and where she worked on her art.

Gág's art was exhibited at the New York Public Library in 1923 and at the Weyhe Gallery in New York City in 1926, 1930, and 1940. It was by happenstance that the head of the newly created juvenile department at Coward-McCann saw Gág's lithographs at the Weyhe Gallery in 1926, and through the gallery founder was able to contact Gág and look at her art portfolio. The editor inquired if Gág had ever written children's books. Gág mentioned the story she had told earlier and which had been typed in about 1923 by her sister Dele. Within a month, the manuscript for *Millions of Cats* (Coward-McCann, 1928) was in the publisher's editorial offices. The editor, Miss Evans, asked Gág to revise the story and to finish the illustrations. As models for the cats, her friend Jack Grass brought two kittens from a local farmer's wife. Earle Humphreys offered some text suggestions. Gág experimented with several illustrations. She tried red lettering with chocolate brown cats and other color compositions. In the end, the artwork was black and white. Her concept of a two-page spread with the text flowing along the illustrations helped to revolutionize picture books. When the illustrations were complete, Gág's brother Howard hand-lettered the text for the finished books. Gág kept a scrapbook of the reviews for *Millions of Cats*, many of them proclaiming that the book sure to be a perennial favorite. The reviews noted the illustrations and the originality of the folk-like text.

Published in a variety of editions and translations, *Millions of Cats* has remained in print since its initial introduction. After this initial success, more of Gág's books were published: *The Funny Thing* (Coward-McCann, 1929), the story of an old man who weans a dragon from eating young children's dolls; *Snippy and Snappy* (Coward-McCann, 1931), the story of two field mice who have adventures in a house; *The ABC Bunny* (Coward-McCann, 1933), an unconventional alphabet book which was one of the first to include a story line that continued from letter to letter; and *Gone Is Gone* (Coward-McCann, 1935), a retelling of a Grimm tale that features a man exchanging places with his wife who he feels just putters around the house all day.

A collection of Grimm tales with Gág's illustrations appeared in 1936, and in the following years, she illustrated individual selections from the same source. Her last original picture book was *Nothing at All* (Coward-McCann, 1941). It was the story of an invisible dog.

Gág's work earned her a Newbery Honor Book Award for *Millions of Cats* in 1929, and for *The ABC Bunny* in 1934. She earned a Caldecott Honor Book Award for *Snow White and the Seven Dwarfs* in 1939 and for *Nothing at All* in 1942. Gág died of lung cancer in 1946. She received the Lewis Carroll Shelf Award posthumously for *Millions of Cats*, and the Kerlan Award in 1977. Each year in March, the residents of New Ulm, Minnesota, along with many visitors, celebrate the anniversary of her birth. Her childhood home at 226 N. Washington is on the National Register of Historic Places. The Wanda Gág House Association owns the property and is restoring it to its early-1900s condition. During the summer months, the house is open on weekend afternoons and is open throughout the year for special events or by appointment.

BOOKS AND NOTES

Wanda Gág was considered a fine artist and continued to produce work throughout her career. She worked with graphite and charcoal, watercolor, lithographs, and a number of other media. Her lithographs and paintings won her international renown. Nonetheless, it is her books that have kept her name etched in the annals of our cultural development. *Millions of Cats* is cited as a picture book that defined the genre and was hailed as a classic from the beginning. It has been translated into many languages and published for over seventy years in many editions. Her illustrations, all in black and white except for those in *Nothing at All* (Coward-McCann, 1941), complement and enhance the mood created by her words. Her translations of the Grimm tales is what she described as "free translations." She felt one should never write down to children but that the stories might need to be simplified by removing or rewording confusing or complicated passages. She often inserted repetitious phrases to enhance a story's appeal to young readers. Much of the charm of her books rests in the illustrations that advance the mood. For example, in *Snow White*, each time the queen visited Snow White, Gág included clouds in the illustration; as the queen becomes more dangerous, the clouds get lower and darker.

Books Written or Retold and Illustrated by Wanda Gág

The ABC Bunny (Coward-McCann, 1933).

The Funny Thing (Coward-McCann, 1929).

Gone Is Gone (Coward-McCann, 1935).

Millions of Cats (Coward-McCann, 1928).

More Tales from Grimm (Coward-McCann, 1947).

Nothing at All (Coward-McCann, 1941).

Snippy and Snappy (Coward-McCann, 1931).

Snow White and the Seven Dwarfs (Coward-McCann, 1938).

Tales from Grimm (Coward-McCann, 1936).

FOR MORE INFORMATION

Articles

Hoyle, Karen Nelson. "A Children's Classic: *Millions of Cats.*" *Language of the Land Project CD-ROM. Manuscripts* 31, no. 4 (Fall 1979).

Web Sites

Language of the Land Project: A Children's Classic; Millions of Cats. URL <http://www.mnbooks.org/lol/au2-knh.htm> (Accessed March 2000).

University of Southern Mississippi, de Grummond Collection: Wanda Gág Papers. URL: <http://www.lib.usm.edu/~degrum/findaids/gag.htm> (Accessed March 2000).

Wanda Gag House. URL: <http://newulmweb.com/citylights/gag/gag.htm> (Accessed March 2000).

Paul Galdone

◆ Folklore

Budapest, Hungary
June 2, 1914–November 7, 1986

- 📖 *The Gingerbread Boy*
- 📖 *Henny Penny*
- 📖 *The Little Red Hen*

ABOUT THE AUTHOR/ILLUSTRATOR

Any child who has read nursery tales in the past four decades is sure to have read at least one title illustrated by Paul Galdone. He became a master of the illustrated poem and story, rendering the illustrations in simple yet detailed drawings that enhanced the text.

Paul Galdone was born in 1914, although some sources indicate it may have been 1907, in Budapest, Austria-Hungary (later Hungary). His family immigrated to the United States in 1914 (or 1921) when Galdone was fourteen. An aunt who was living in New Jersey arranged their emigration, so the family settled there, and Paul was enrolled in school. He could not speak a word of English, and despite attending three English classes a day, he found school frustrating. He did learn to rote read, however, and when he was asked to read Shakespeare aloud, he did so with a heavy accent and without understanding most of what he was saying. Nonetheless, he enjoyed biology class. It was there that he found out his drawing of grasshoppers made him a class attraction. Soon he was drawing grasshoppers for his classmates.

After a short time, the family moved to New York City. Galdone took odd jobs to help the family financially. He took day jobs as a busboy, an electrician's helper on unfinished skyscrapers, and a fur dyer. At night, he attended art school where he studied industrial design. He became acquainted with book design when he worked for four years in the art department at Doubleday & Company. During those years, he had his first opportunity to design a book jacket and began his freelance career. At the time, he was living in Greenwich Village in New York City. He continued to freelance and to build a career in jacket design. He was also a fine artist and continued to draw and paint and take long sketching vacations in the Vermont countryside.

His father had brought Paul to the United States to avoid war, but Paul ended up in the U.S. Army for four years. He was a member of the Army Engineer Corps but also contributed to their tabloid publication, *Yank*, in his spare time. At the end of the four years, Galdone returned home and with his wife, Jannelise (Elise), settled on sixteen acres in New City, Rockland County, New York. The rambling house, designed by Jannelise and Paul with the help of Jannelise's architect brother, was surrounded by woods, gardens, an apple orchard, and trout streams. Over the years, Galdone decorated his home with a large, silver grasshopper on the chimney. He also decorated the bathhouse at the pool with an oversized flying fish. He continued his work as a painter and sculptor, but his attention turned more and more to his freelance career in book illustration.

His first big break came in the early 1950s when he was asked to illustrate Eve Titus's books about Anatole, the French cheese-tasting mouse. Titus's economically written texts and Galdone's exquisitely restrained drawings were considered powerful. The first two titles, *Anatole* (Whittlesey, 1956) and *Anatole and the Cat* (Whittlesey, 1957), earned Galdone a Caldecott Honor Book Award. Those books began a long association with Titus. Galdone was asked to illustrate books by many other authors and began to illustrate well-known poems and nursery tales. It is those retellings that have become standards in many libraries. His illustrated versions of such stories as *The Little Red Hen* (Clarion, 1973), *The Gingerbread Boy* (Clarion, 1975), and verses and poems such as *Little Bo-Peep* (Clarion, 1986), and Edward Lear's *The Owl and the Pussy Cat* (Clarion, 1987) put him firmly in the annals of children's literature.

In later years, he and his family—including a daughter, Joanne, and a son, Paul Ferencz—spent time at his Rockland County home and on a farm in Tunbridge, Vermont. Both locations allowed him to help visualize settings and to sketch the many animals that populated his books. He sketched cows at the Tunbridge World's Fair in Vermont to help with his farmyard concert scenes in *Cat Goes Fiddle-I-Fee* (Clarion, 1985). It was also in Vermont where he visited a neighbor's sheep pasture to prepare the illustrative sketches for *Little Bo-Peep*. Every year his family planted a number of vegetables on their Vermont farm. Among the vegetables were the beans and beanstalks that made their appearance in his illustrated version of "Jack and the Beanstalk." In the Galdone's forest, he found just the right tree for the Queen's messenger to hide behind while observing Rumpelstiltskin singing and dancing round the bonfire.

Galdone's son, Paul Ferencz, became an architect, and his daughter, Joanne, became a teacher and a writer. Among the stories she has retold are *The Little Girl and the Big Bear* (Clarion, 1980), *Amber Day: A Very Tall Tale* (McGraw-Hill, 1978), and *The Tailypo: A Ghost Story* (Clarion, 1977), all illustrated by her father. Paul Galdone died of a heart attack on November 7, 1986.

BOOKS AND NOTES

Paul Galdone's illustrative work was usually in pen and ink and wash. He made his own color separations by hand, often with the help of his wife, Jannelise. His illustrative interpretations of the many nursery tales, classic poems, and classic verses became his trademark. There are more than 100 books in print illustrated by Galdone.

Books Written/Adapted and Illustrated by Paul Galdone

The Amazing Pig: An Old Hungarian Tale (Clarion, 1981).

Cat Goes Fiddle-I-Fee (Clarion, 1986).

The Elves and the Shoemaker (Clarion, 1984).

The Gingerbread Boy (Clarion, 1975).

The Greedy Old Fat Man: An American Folk Tale (Clarion, 1983).

Henny Penny (Clarion, 1968).

The History of Mother Twaddle and the Marvelous Achievements of Her Son Jack, later published as *Jack and the Beanstalk* (Clarion, 1974).

Little Bo-Peep (Clarion, 1986).

Little Red Hen (Clarion, 1973).

Magic Porridge Pot (Clarion, 1976).

The Monster and the Tailor: A Ghost Story (Clarion, 1982).

Puss in Boots (Clarion, 1976).

Rumpelstiltskin (Clarion, 1985).

The Teeny-Tiny Woman: A Ghost Story (Clarion, 1984).

Three Little Kittens (Clarion, 1986).

The Turtle and the Monkey: A Philippine Tale (Clarion, 1983).

What's in Fox's Sack: An Old English Tale (Clarion, 1982).

Books Illustrated by Paul Galdone

The Owl and the Pussycat. Written by Edward Lear. (Clarion, 1987).

Three Ducks Went Wandering. Written by Ron Roy. (Clarion, 1979).

The Three Sillies. Written by Joseph Jacobs. (Clarion, 1982).

FOR MORE INFORMATION

Limited information can be found on book jacket flaps. No articles, books, or Web sites were located.

Theodor Seuss Geisel

◆ Rhyming ◆ Humor

Springfield, Massachusetts
March 2, 1904–September 24, 1991

📖 *The Cat in the Hat*
📖 *The 500 Hats of Bartholomew Cubbins*

ABOUT THE AUTHOR/ILLUSTRATOR

Theodor Seuss Geisel, better known to millions of readers as Dr. Seuss and Theo LeSieg, was born in Springfield, Massachusetts, on March 2, 1904. He went on to become one of the most beloved figures in children's literature. His first book was rejected twenty-seven times. He was literally carrying it down the street when he, by happenstance, met an old college friend who was now a children's book editor at Vanguard. His friend agreed to publish his first book.

Geisel grew up in Springfield. He was a second-generation German and learned German before English. His father, Theodor Robert Geisel, was a brewery worker. After thirty-five years, the prohibition era forced the closing of the brewery, and the elder Geisel found a job redesigning the parks. Later he ran the city zoo. During World War I, Geisel's German heritage did not endear him to many of the other children.

After graduating from Central High School in Springfield, Geisel went to Dartmouth College, where he became interested in cartooning. He spent a lot of his time at the offices of the *Jack-o-Lantern*, a college publication. His grades were not stellar, but when his father inquired as to his plans after college, Geisel told him that he planned to go to Oxford University on a

Campbell Scholarship. There was never a scholarship, but because his dad had proudly announced the news to the local paper, they figured out a way to send Geisel to Oxford. It was in London, at Oxford, that he met Helen Palmer. He soon decided that he would never teach literature, and his tutor convinced him that he should withdraw from the university. He returned to the United States, not long after he married Helen. They moved to New York City where he worked as a freelance illustrator. His pay was low, and sometimes he was paid in merchandise such as nail clippers or shaving cream.

Geisel's first well-paying job came when he was asked to write advertising for a bug spray. His "Quick Henry, the Flit!" was highly successful. He was paid $12,000; during the Depression, that was very good money. His pleasure with his success in advertising did not last beyond a few years. He decided to try writing a children's book. After taking a Paris vacation on an ocean liner and listening to the hum of the ship's motors, he wrote the rhythmic text for *And to Think That I Saw It on Mulberry Street* (Vanguard, 1937). The book almost did not get published. After twenty-seven rejections, Geisel was not optimistic. But as luck would have it, he ran into the friend from Dartmouth. The rest is history.

Geisel's books immediately started selling well. Some were in rhyme, and others were in prose. His fundamental formula for his books included a tight story, personable characters with funny names, rhyme, and a magnificent imagination.

Characters such as Bartholomew Cubbins and Horton the elephant first appeared in magazines and later were developed into characters for books: *The 500 Hats of Bartholomew Cubbins* (Vanguard, 1938), *Bartholomew and the Oobleck* (Random House, 1949), *Horton Hears a Who!* (Random House, 1954), and *Horton Hatches the Egg* (Random House, 1940).

Along the way, Geisel had fun with his writing. He made Yertle of *Yertle the Turtle and Other Stories* (Random House, 1958) a caricature of Adolf Hitler. The story was a deliberate parody of Hitler and the totalitarian form of government. Other tales, such as *Horton Hears a Who!*, made a statement of the worth of all people "no matter how small"—a reference to the Japanese people defeated in war and seeking their own democracy. He also dealt with the commercialization of holidays in *How the Grinch Stole Christmas* (Random House, 1957).

Geisel's first books were published before World War II. During the war years, he continued his writing career and also continued as a cartoonist. He frequently targeted Hitler, Mussolini, and the Japanese, as well as domestic concerns such as inflation, racial inequality, and isolationism. Early in 1943,

Geisel was commissioned as a captain in the information and education division of the U.S. Army and sent to Hollywood, California, where he was to produce films for the military. One of his films, titled *Your Job in Germany*, was released to the public by Warner Brothers under the title of *Hitler Lives*. In 1945, Geisel won an Academy Award for the best documentary short subject of the year. Two years later, he won another Academy Award for the best documentary feature for *Design for Death*, a history of the Japanese people that he wrote with his wife, Helen Palmer Geisel. After three years with the army, Geisel was discharged as a lieutenant colonel.

Geisel continued to write children's books after he left the army. It was during this time that he wrote *If I Ran the Zoo* (Random House, 1950) and *If I Ran the Circus* (Random House, 1956), a book he dedicated to his father: "For my dad, Big Ted of Springfield, the finest man I'll ever know."

In 1950, Geisel won another Academy Award, this time for the animated cartoon, *Gerald McBoing Boing*. Fifty years later, several years after Seuss's death, this film provided the basis for the book *Gerald McBoing Boing* (Random House, 2000). Mel Crawford adapted the film's images to create the book's illustrations. It was also in the 1950s when Geisel's publisher challenged Geisel to write a book to help address the problem of "Why Johnny Can't Read." The book had to be written using only the words on a list of one-syllable words. Geisel thought he could write it in two or three days; it took him more than two years. He was almost ready to give up the challenge when he came across two rhyming words on the list: "cat" and "hat." Those words became the beginning for his enormously popular early reader, *The Cat in the Hat* (Random House, 1957). The book also spawned a whole new division, Beginner Books, at Random House. Geisel became president of the division and Helen Palmer Geisel became the editor-in-chief.

On October 23, 1967, Helen Palmer Geisel died. She and Geisel had no children. The following year, on August 5, 1968, Theodor Seuss Geisel married Audrey Stone Diamond, who had two daughters.

In addition to the early reader books, Geisel continued to write other books as well. One day while at a Democratic dinner, Geisel sat next to Liz Carpenter, former President Lyndon Johnson's press secretary. First lady Lady Bird Johnson was extremely active in efforts to beautify the environment and to prevent pollution. When Carpenter realized she was sitting next to the author of *The Lorax* (Random House, 1971), which dealt with environmental issues, she excused herself. In a short time, she returned to call Geisel to the phone. On the other end was President Johnson. He said he wanted to thank Geisel for offering to donate the manuscript for *The Lorax* to his presidential library and accepted Geisel's offer. Geisel was somewhat surprised, but the pencil-and-crayon and pen-and-ink drawings for *The Lorax* did become part of the Collection of Lyndon Baines Johnson Library and Museum in Austin, Texas.

Geisel continued to write more books. His *Cat in the Hat* had all the makings of a classic, and the rest of the Beginner Books were enormously popular. He began to contribute some books to the series using yet another pseudonym, Theo LeSieg (Geisel spelled backward). Other artists illustrated these books, emulating the cartoonish fun of the first Beginner Books. Geisel even used his wife's birth name "Stone" as inspiration for a third pseudonym, Rosetta Stone. He wrote only one title, *Because the Little Boy Went Ka-Choo* (Random House, 1975), using that pseudonym. Writing as Dr. Seuss, he produced *The Lorax*, *There's a Wocket in My Pocket* (Random House, 1974), *Oh, the Thinks You Can Think!* (Random House, 1975), *Oh Say Can You Say?* (Random House, 1979), *The Butter Battle Book* (Random House, 1984), and a host of other highly successful titles.

During the Watergate scandal of the Richard Nixon presidency, Geisel's friend, Art Buchwald, noted that Geisel had never written a political book. In response, Geisel wrote *Marvin K. Mooney, Will You Please Go Now!* (Random House, 1972). The child in the book is really Nixon in disguise. The day following the book's publication, Nixon resigned the presidency.

Audrey and Ted Geisel lived in a home they called "The Tower," which sits atop Mount Soledad in LaJolla, California. It could only be accessed by a narrow, winding road. Geisel's license plate read "GRINCH." He lived with more than 400 cats—most of which were not real but were part of his collection of pictures, statues, and other cat items. There was one live cat; for a number of years, Thing 1 lived in the Geisel residence.

On September 24, 1991, at the age of 87, Theodor Seuss Geisel died after an illness of several months. Geisel was survived by his wife and stepdaughters, Lea and Lark, his niece, Peggy Owens, and her son, Theodore Owens. At Geisel's request, no funeral was planned, and there is no memorial stone. Audrey Geisel has used the monetary legacy to contribute to a number of causes. She donated $1 million to the city of Springfield, Massachusetts, to help fund The Dr. Seuss National Memorial, which will consist of six bronze statues and will be placed in the Springfield Library and Museums Quadrangle. One of Geisel's stepdaughters, sculptor Lark Grey Diamond-Cates, is working with a landscape architecture firm to plan the memorial. The six statues will include: Theodor Geisel and the Cat in the Hat; Horton the Elephant with other Seuss characters; a storytelling chair backed by a massive book with the text of *Oh, the Places You Will Go!*; a small statue of the Lorax on a stump with the environmental warning, "Unless"; a tower of turtles from *Yertle the Turtle* above a shallow reflecting pool; and a bas relief of the entire book, *And to Think That I Saw It on Mulberry Street*.

In 1995, Audrey Geisel contributed $20 million to the main library at the University of California at San Diego. The library was renamed in honor of Audrey and Ted Geisel in December of 1995. Papers, manuscripts, illustrations, and other items relating to Geisel's lifetime of work are housed in a Dr. Seuss Collection within the Mandeville Special Collections Library located at the Geisel Library. There are approximately 8,500 items in the collection, beginning with his work as a high school student in 1919 and concluding with his death in 1991. Absent are papers dealing with *The Lorax*, which are in the Johnson Presidential Library, as well as *And to Think That I Saw it On Mulberry Street* and *Daisy-Head Mayzie* (Random House, 1994). A Detroit newspaper reported that Theodor Geisel had admired the library's whimsical eight-story building, which had opened in 1970, because it resembled a pyramid turned on its tip. He thought that if he had designed a building, it might have looked similar to the library. The building was renovated, and an addition was completed in 1992.

Audrey Geisel also established a Dr. Seuss Foundation, which funds charitable activities in the San Diego area. She continues to live in the area and to be active as a member of several boards and as an advisor to several charitable groups. She has also allowed several illustrations to be used in conjunction with the annual Read Across America day. The day, originated by the National Education Association in 1994, is designed to motivate reading and is celebrated on March 2—Theodor Geisel's date of birth. The memory of Theodor Geisel and Dr. Seuss will long live in the memories of book lovers.

BOOKS AND NOTES

Since Theodor Seuss Geisel's death, some unfinished manuscripts and previously unseen artwork have been published with Audrey S. Geisel's cooperation. The majority of the sketches and drawings for his many other books are part of Geisel's personal collection or are part of the collection of the Department of Special Collections, University Research Library at the University of California in San Diego.

Books Written and Illustrated by Theodor Geisel As Dr. Seuss

And to Think That I Saw It on Mulberry Street (Vanguard, 1937; Random House, 1989).

Bartholomew and the Oobleck (Random House, 1949).

The Butter Battle Book (Random House, 1984).

The Cat in the Hat (Random House, 1957).

The Cat's Quizzer (Random House, 1976).

The 500 Hats of Bartholomew Cubbins (Vanguard, 1938; Random House, 1990).

Hop on Pop (Random House, 1963).

Horton Hatches the Egg (Random House, 1940).

Horton Hears a Who! (Random House, 1954).

How the Grinch Stole Christmas (Random House, 1957).

I Can Lick 30 Tigers Today, and Other Stories (Random House, 1969).

If I Ran the Zoo (Random House, 1950).

If I Ran the Circus (Random House, 1956).

The Lorax (Random House, 1971).

Marvin K. Mooney, Will You Please Go Now! (Random House, 1972).

McElligot's Pool (Random House, 1947).

Oh, Say Can You Say? (Random House, 1979).

One Fish, Two Fish, Red Fish, Blue Fish (Random House, 1960, 1987).

The Sneetches, and Other Stories (Random House, 1961).

There's a Wocket in My Pocket (Random House, 1974).

Thidwick, the Big-Hearted Moose (Random House, 1975).

Yertle the Turtle and Other Stories (Random House, 1958).

You're Only Old Once (Random House, 1986).

Books Written by Theodor Geisel As Theo LeSieg

Hooper Humperdink . . . ? Not Him! Illustrated by Charles E. Martin. (Random House, 1976; reissued with illustrations by James Stevenson, Random House, 1997).

I Wish I Had Duck Feet. Illustrated by B. Tobey. (Random House, 1967).

The Many Mice of Mr. Brice. Illustrated by Roy McKie. (Random House, 1973).

The Pop-up Mice of Mr. Brice. Illustrated by Roy McKie. (Random House, 1989).

Ten Apples on Top! Illustrated by Roy McKie. (Random House, 1961).

The Tooth Book. Illustrated by Roy McKie. (Random House, 1981).

Wacky Wednesday. Illustrated by George Booth. (Random House, 1974).

Would You Rather Be a Bullfrog? Illustrated by Roy McKie. (Random House, 1975).

Books Published Posthumously, Based on the Work of Theodor Geisel

Daisy-Head Mayzie (Random House, 1994). A discovered manuscript.

Gerald McBoing Boing. Illustrations adapted by Mel Crawford. (Random House, 2000).

Hooray for Diffendoofer Day! Written by Dr. Seuss and Jack Prelutsky. Illustrated by Lane Smith. (Knopf, 1998). Based on an unfinished manuscript by Dr. Seuss and completed by Prelutsky.

My Many Colored Days. Illustrated by Steve Johnson with Lou Fancher. (Knopf, 1996). A discovered manuscript.

The Secret Art of Dr. Seuss. With an introduction by Maurice Sendak and a foreward by Audrey Geisel. (Random House, 1995).

Contains whimsical paintings created for his pleasure. Outlandish characters in otherworldly settings. Colors extend past the primary colors he characteristically used in his children's books.

FOR MORE INFORMATION

Articles

Butler, Francelia. "Seuss As a Creator of Folklore." *Children's Literature in Education* 20, no. 3 (1989): 175–81.

Wilder, Rob. "Catching up with Dr. Seuss." *Parents* 54, no. 6 (June 1979): 60–64.

Books

Greene, Carol. *Dr. Seuss: Writer and Artist for Children* (Children's Press, 1993).

Krulak, Victor H., et al. *Theodor Seuss Geisel: Reminiscences and Tributes.* With an introductory statement by Audrey S. Geisel. Edited by Edward Connery Lathem. (Dartmouth College, 1966, 1996).

Morgan, Judith, and Neil Morgan. *Dr. Seuss and Mr. Geisel: A Biography* (Random House, 1995; Da Capo Press, 1996).

Weidt, Maryann N. *Oh, the Places He Went: A Story About Dr. Seuss—Theodor Seuss Geisel.* Illustrated by Kerry Maguire. (Carolrhoda, 1994).

Web Sites

Lister, D. *Cyber-Seuss.* URL: <http://www.afn.org/~afn15301/drseuss.html> (Accessed March 2000).

Random House Inc./Books @ Random. URL: <http://www.randomhouse.com/> (Accessed March 2000). Search for "Seuss."

Gail Gibbons

◆ Animals, Nonfiction ◆ Community, Nonfiction

Oak Park, Illinois
August 1, 1944

Kent Ancliffe

📖 *Soaring with the Wind: The Bald Eagle*

📖 *Up Goes the Skyscraper!*

📖 *Yippee-Yay! A Book About Cowboys and Cowgirls*

ABOUT THE AUTHOR/ILLUSTRATOR

In the early 1970s, Gail Gibbons was working for John Chancellor's nightly news show on NBC. Then she began to work as a freelance artist. She soon became involved with books for children. Her curiosity has lead her to visit the seventeenth story of a skyscraper that was under construction, to learn how to drive big trucks while her family's home was under construction, and to visit a bald eagle's nesting site.

Gibbons was named Gail Ortmann when she was born on August 1, 1944, in Oak Park, Illinois. Her parents were Harry George Ortmann and Grace Johnson Ortmann. Her father was a tool and dye maker whose work took the family to Palos Heights and Blue Island, Illinois. Encouraged by several of her teachers, Gibbons developed an interest in drawing early in her childhood. She says, "I put together my first book when I was four years old. It was only four pages long and was a wordless picture book." She also remembers how she bound the book with yarn. A kindergarten teacher was one of the first people to notice that Gail had artistic talent and called it to her parents' attention. Soon they arranged for Gibbons to take art lessons. Gibbons began writing stories and drew pictures to "fit the words."

After graduating from high school, she entered the University of Illinois to study graphic design. There she met Glen Allen Gibbons, whom she married on June 25, 1966. Gail Gibbons received a degree in fine arts and began working as a graphic artist for WCIA, a CBS affiliate, in Champaign, Illinois. She worked on several programs, developing on-air graphics, animations, and printed promotional material. She also did some freelance work in animation for NBC in Chicago. She continued in that line of work when she and her husband moved to New York City in 1970, where she worked for NBC's local programs, particularly a network children's program called *Take a Giant Step*. The show was the forerunner of *The Electric Company*. The children participating on the show suggested that Gibbons should create children's books, and soon thereafter, she began to work on writing and illustrating stories for children.

Glenn Gibbons was killed in an accident in 1972. As a widow, Gail Gibbons decided that she would reduce her workload and try to get her life in order once again. She began working on John Chancellor's nightly news show on NBC and resumed her freelance artwork. In her Manhattan apartment near the Metropolitan Museum of Art, she began to illustrate and write. In 1975, her first book, *Willy and His Wheel Wagon* (Prentice-Hall) was published.

The following year, she married Kent Ancliffe and became a stepmother to Rebecca and Eric. With the help of a friend, they built a large home in Corinth, Vermont. The house, which is powered by solar power, sits on 300 acres of land. While the family was building their home, they used trucks to dig holes, haul logs, and shovel snow. Although Gibbons had not yet learned how to drive a car, she learned to drive a truck. Some of those experiences led to her book *Trucks* (Crowell, 1981). Since her husband was in the maple syrup business, it was natural for her to write a book about it. *The Missing Maple Syrup Sap Mystery: or, How Maple Syrup Is Made* (Warne, 1979) is a fictional work about Mr. and Mrs. Mapleworth who try to find out who is stealing the maple sap they are gathering to make maple syrup. Another book, *The Seasons of Arnold's Apple Tree* (Harcourt, 1984), was written about her son Eric's special relationship with an apple tree on a hilltop near their home in Corinth. The book is dedicated to Eric. It identifies the tree as his secret place and follows Arnold (Eric) and the tree through four seasons of the year. As Arnold builds a tree house and shades himself from the summer rains, the tree develops blossoms and produces ripened fruit.

Gibbons's curiosity and interest in learning about the events and activities around her have led to many other books. In a promotional brochure from Holiday House she says, "I love working with bright, bold, beautiful colors because that is what I enjoyed so in television art. I also have a real love for nonfiction writing. The research for any of my books takes a great deal of time and effort. To me, putting a nonfiction book together is like watching the pieces of a puzzle finally fitting together." Gibbons has researched many topics. She has learned that a honeybee visits up to 10,000 flowers in one day and that making one pound of honey takes nectar from more than one million flowers. This and much more information about honey bees is included in her book *The Honey Makers* (Morrow, 1997). Research visits to a dairy farm near her home where she often bought milk led to *The Milk Makers* (Macmillan, 1985). To learn more about the bald eagle, she visited a nesting location and then wrote *Soaring with the Wind: The Bald Eagle* (Morrow, 1998). Visits to the Florida Everglades helped her compile information for *Marshes and Swamps* (Holiday House, 1998). She has taken apart every clock in her house, talked to truckers about their rigs, and investigated the treasures hidden beneath the sea. She has traveled to Key West, Florida, to experience first-hand the efforts to locate the seventeenth-century Spanish galleon *Nuestra Señora de Atocha*. The treasure was one of the richest cargoes ever found on a sunken vessel. Only the turbulent sea waters kept Gibbons from donning scuba diving gear and going to the depth of the ocean to see what was down there. The information she gathered helped her to write *Sunken Treasure* (HarperCollins, 1988). Her body of nonfiction writing earned the *Washington Post* Children's Book Guild Award in 1987. At the time of the award, she had written and illustrated 38 books; in the decade that followed, she doubled the number of books she had written and illustrated.

Gail Gibbons and her husband spend most of the year in their house in Vermont, but they also have a house on an island off the coast of Maine. Puffins inhabit a nearby island. Her island home brought about *Surrounded by Sea* (Little, Brown, 1991) and *Christmas on an Island* (Morrow, 1994), and her captivation with puffins encouraged *The Puffins Are Back!* (HarperCollins, 1991). Their homes are shared with cats, a dog, and plenty of wild animals. Milton, her golden retriever, actually appears in several of her books.

Gibbons often is involved with the creation of three books at one time: researching one, writing another, and illustrating a third. When she is not working on one of the books in progress, she enjoys traveling, boating, and "lots of things."

BOOKS AND NOTES

One only needs to take a look at the titles of Gail Gibbons's books to surmise where she has been and what she has been up to. Visits to the local potter, the country diner, and the nearby newspaper bring a lot of questions, and she seeks out answer to create books that help young readers learn. Gibbons is consistently asking, "How does that work?" and her books share the answers she uncovers. She uses bold, bright, graphic illustrations to explain and clarify concepts that she writes about.

Apples (Holiday House, 1999).

Bats (Holiday House, 1999).

Beacons of Light: Lighthouses (Morrow, 1990).

Cats (Holiday House, 1996).

Check It Out! The Book About Libraries (Harcourt, 1985).

Christmas on an Island (Morrow, 1994).

Click! A Book About Cameras and Taking Pictures (Little, Brown, 1997).

Country Fair (Little, Brown, 1994).

Deadline! From News to Newspaper (Crowell, 1987).

Deserts (Holiday House, 1996).

Dinosaurs (Holiday House, 1987).

Flying (Holiday House, 1986).

Frogs (Holiday House, 1993).

From Path to Highway: The Story of the Boston Post Road (Crowell, 1986).

From Seed to Plant (Holiday House, 1991).

The Great St. Lawrence Seaway (Morrow, 1992).

Gulls—Gulls—Gulls (Holiday House, 1997).

Happy Birthday (Holiday House, 1986).

The Honey Makers (Morrow, 1997).

How a House Is Built (Holiday House, 1990).

Knights in Shining Armor (Little, Brown, 1995).

Marge's Diner (Crowell, 1989).

Marshes and Swamps (Holiday House, 1998).

The Milk Makers (Macmillan, 1985).

Monarch Butterfly (Holiday House, 1989).

My Baseball Book (HarperCollins, 2000).

My Football Book (HarperCollins, 2000).

My Soccer Book (HarperCollins, 2000).

The Pottery Place (Harcourt, 1987).

The Puffins Are Back! (HarperCollins, 1991).

The Pumpkin Book (Holiday House, 1999).

Rabbits, Rabbits, and More Rabbits (Holiday House, 2000).

The Seasons of Arnold's Apple Tree (Harcourt, 1984).

Sharks (Holiday House, 1992).

Soaring with the Wind: The Bald Eagle (Morrow, 1998).

Spiders (Holiday House, 1993).

Surrounded by Sea: Life on a New England Fishing Island (Little, Brown, 1991).

Trains (Holiday House, 1987).

Up Goes the Skyscraper! (Four Winds, 1986).

Valentine's Day (Holiday House, 1986).

Weather Forecasting (Macmillan, 1993).

Wolves (Holiday House, 1994).

Yippee-yay! A Book About Cowboys and Cowgirls (Little, Brown, 1998).

Zoo (Crowell, 1987).

FOR MORE INFORMATION

Articles

"The Booklist Interview: Gail Gibbons." *Booklist* 91, no. 7 (December 1, 1994): 676.

Web Sites

Gail Gibbons Home Page. URL: <http://www.gailgibbons.com> (Accessed March 2000).

Paul Goble

◆ Folklore (Literary) ◆ Native American Legends (Literary)

Haslemere, Surrey, England
September 17, 1933

📖 *The Girl Who Loved Wild Horses*

📖 *Iktomi and the Coyote: A Plains Indian Story*

Photograph of Paul Goble by Janet Goble. Reprinted courtesy of Paul Goble and Bradbury Press, an affiliate of the Macmillan Children's Book Group

ABOUT THE AUTHOR/ILLUSTRATOR

Since the time his mother, Marion Elizabeth Goble, read Paul Goble stories of Grey Owl and Ernest Thompson Seton, he has felt the pull of the Native American tradition. For more than three decades, Paul Goble's name has been associated with Native American stories, and many have assumed that he is Native American himself. In fact, Goble is a native of England. He was born in the town of Haslemere, a small town in the county of Surrey in England on September 17, 1933. His father, Robert John Goble, was a harpsichord maker, and his mother was a musician, author, and painter.

From the time he was very little, Goble wanted to know everything about Native Americans. He cut out pictures of Indians from magazines and books and collected them in scrapbooks. His mother made him an Indian outfit—a fringed shirt, leggings, and war bonnet—which he wore around his suburban English neighborhood. His mother even made him a teepee. Goble's interest in art and in Native Americans pleased his parents. He often combined the two interests in his drawings of Indians, but he also drew pictures of plants and animals. By the time Goble was twelve years old, the family had moved to Oxford. He attended boarding school during the week. On weekends, he often biked into the countryside. His interest in reading about Native Americans followed him into his teenage years as he read *Black Elk Speaks: Being the Life Story of a Holy Man of the Oglala Sioux* (republished by University of Nebraska Press, 1961), a famous autobiography of a visionary Sioux healer. He also met Joseph Epes Brown, a man who had recorded Black Elk's account of the sacred rites of the Sioux in a book titled *The Sacred Pipe: Black Elk's Account of the Seven Rites of the Oglala Sioux* (republished by University of Oklahoma Press, 1989). After completing school, Goble spent two years in the military in Germany, where he was able to go horseback riding whenever he wanted. He continued his hobby of reading about Native Americans.

At the age of twenty-three, Goble enrolled in the Central School of Arts and Crafts in London, where he met his first wife, Dorothy. Three years later, when he was twenty-six, Goble arranged to spend the summer on reservations in South Dakota and Montana.

After he returned to England, he and Dorothy ran an industrial design business while he served as a lecturer at design schools. His furniture designs earned several awards. The couple became the parents of two children, Richard and Julia. Goble searched for books about Native Americans to read to his children. Many of the books he found contained incorrect information, almost always told from the perspective of a non-Indian who had intruded on the Indian lands. After seeing a television serial that glorified the military and General Custer, Goble decided to write an account of that battle, an account that would attempt to accurately represent the Native American perspective. In 1969, *Red Hawk's Account of Custer's Last Battle: The Battle of the Little Bighorn, 25 June 1876* (Pantheon) was published. Goble shared the author credits with his wife Dorothy, although at the time, Dorothy viewed her role as one of adviser and encourager. During the next few years, Paul returned to reservations in the United States each summer. He often took his son with him. They camped in the Black Hills of South Dakota and visited national parks, forests, and reservation areas. He visited the Sioux, Crow, Shoshoni, and other plains Indian tribes. With him during these trips was a Swiss professor of comparative religions, Frithjob Suchon, who was also a painter and a friend of many medicine men of the plains Indian tribes. The two men visited the tribes in the area, and Goble was able to take part in ceremonies, help build the Sun Dance lodge, and observe sacred Sun Dances. Eventually, he became an adopted member of the Yakima and Sioux tribes and was given the name Wakinyan Chikala (Little Thunder) by Chief Edgar Red Cloud, an Oglala Sioux and the great-grandson of the famous war chief.

Paul and Dorothy Goble share credit for the authorship of two more books: *Brave Eagle's Account of the Fetterman Fight, 21 December 1866* (Pantheon, 1972; University of Nebraska Press, 1992) and *Lone Bull's Horse Raid* (Macmillan, 1973). All three books were illustrated by Paul Goble. He studied the historical records that Indians had painted on buffalo robes and attempted to emulate the style, using a magnifying glass to bring as much precision to his paintings as possible. His style of illustration is sometimes referred to as "Indian ledger book painting."

Goble continued to design furniture, which earned him several awards. He continued his teaching and became senior lecturer at Ravensbourne College of Art and Design in London, a position he kept until 1977 when he moved to the Black Hills of South Dakota with the intent of establishing permanent residence in the United States. His marriage to Dorothy ended, and in 1978 he married Janet Tiller. In 1984 he became a citizen of the United States. For almost thirteen years, Paul Goble lived in the Black Hills, working in a small room, his "studio." All but one side of this room had windows from which he could see pine trees, the meadow, and the forest wildlife. Not waiting for inspiration, Goble would sit down every day after breakfast and begin work. For breaks he often took trips to meet with Indians on reservations, attended ceremonies, and visited historical museums around the country. His home was close to the Crow and Cheyenne reservations to the west in Montana and to Sioux reservations to the north and east. In museums, he studied historical Indian paintings and old Indian beadwork. While driving through the countryside, he often stopped to view the flowers or to identify birds. He recorded his observations so that he could use certain details in his paintings. Rather than glorify or romanticize the image of animals and birds, he always wanted simply to promote respect for all beings. Paul Goble came to write books about Native Americans out of a deep interest and respect for their culture. Several of Goble's books feature Iktomi (eek-TOE-me), a Sioux name for a trickster character, who is the hero of many amusing stories. He is characterized as being very mischievous and as having unusual magical powers, but he is also very stupid and untruthful. He often tries to outsmart others but generally ends up being outsmarted. Goble has followed the tradition of Native American storytellers with these trickster tales; knowing there is no correct version of the stories, the storytellers are careful to keep to certain familiar themes and to weave variations of the theme into a story. Goble's story has a moral but is not didactic in the sense that it gives a sermon. All Iktomi stories start the same way, "Iktomi was walking along . . ." implying to the reader that Iktomi is more interested in making mischief than in doing any useful work.

Paul Goble has received various awards for his books, including a 1979 Caldecott Honor Book Award for his illustrations in *The Girl Who Loved Wild Horses* (Bradbury, 1978).

In the early 1990s, Paul and Janet Goble moved to Lewiston, New York, while their teenage son, Robert, attended boarding school in Canada. After a few years, the Gobles moved back to the plains. The family lived in Lincoln, Nebraska for a time and then relocated in Black Hawk, South Dakota, a small town north of Rapid City.

BOOKS AND NOTES

Paul Goble creates his artwork with India ink and watercolor. His technique produces a flat appearance, much like that of Indian paintings that were created by artists who made no attempt to achieve perspective and shading. Goble applies the brightly colored watercolors in layers and leaves a thin white line between the black outline and the colored inlay to suggest brilliantly colored bead and quill work. Goble thoroughly researches his topics and his artwork. He explains, in the author's notes for his books, the background and sources for his stories. Although Goble is serious about instilling in Native American children a sense of pride in their cultural heritage, he strives also to insert a few light touches into his illustrations. In his tales about Iktomi, Goble manages to bring the trickster from the past into the present by featuring Iktomi in jogging clothes. In one scene, Iktomi is seen hanging upside down from a tree branch wearing a T-shirt that declares, "I'm Sioux and Proud of It."

Books Written and Illustrated by Paul Goble

Adopted by the Eagles: A Plains Indian Story of Friendship and Treachery (Bradbury, 1994).

Beyond the Ridge (Bradbury, 1989).

Brave Eagle's Account of the Fetterman Fight, 21 December 1866. Co-authored with Dorothy Goble. (Pantheon, 1972; University of Nebraska Press, 1992).

Buffalo Woman (Bradbury, 1984).

Crow Chief: A Plains Indian Story (Orchard, 1992).

Death of an Iron Horse (Bradbury, 1987).

Dream Wolf (Bradbury, 1990).
   Based on a story originally published as *The Friendly Wolf* by Dorothy Goble and Paul Goble. (Macmillan, 1974).

The Gift of the Sacred Dog (Bradbury, 1980).

The Girl Who Loved Wild Horses (Bradbury, 1978).

The Great Race (Bradbury, 1985).

The Great Race of the Birds and Animals (Macmillan, 1991).

Her Seven Brothers (Bradbury, 1988).

I Sing for the Animals (Orchard, 1992).

The Legend of the White Buffalo Woman (National Geographic Society, 1998).
    A Lakota legend in which a woman gives her people the means to pray to the Great Spirit: a Sacred Calf Pipe.

Paul Goble Gallery: Three Native American Stories (Simon & Schuster, 1999).
    Includes *Her Seven Brothers*, *The Gift of the Sacred Dog*, and *The Girl Who Loved Wild Horses*.

Red Hawk's Account of Custer's Last Battle: The Battle of the Little Bighorn, 25 June 1876 (Pantheon, 1969; University of Nebraska Press, 1992).

Remaking the Earth: A Creation Story from the Great Plains of North America (Orchard, 1996).
    The Algonquin version of the creation myth, woven from the ideas of several traditional tales.

The Return of the Buffaloes: A Plains Indian Story About Famine and Renewal of the Earth (National Geographic Society, 1996).
    Lakota legend which explains the return of the buffalo and other animals to the Indian people.

Iktomi Series

Iktomi and the Berries: A Plains Indian Story (Orchard, 1989).

Iktomi and the Boulder: A Plains Indian Story (Orchard, 1988).

Iktomi and the Buffalo Skull: A Plains Indian Story (Orchard, 1991).

Iktomi and the Buzzard: A Plains Indian Story (Orchard, 1994).

Iktomi and the Coyote: A Plains Indian Story (Orchard, 1998).

Iktomi and the Ducks: A Plains Indian Story (Orchard, 1990).

Iktomi Loses His Eyes: A Plains Indian Story (Orchard, 1999).

FOR MORE INFORMATION

Articles

"Meet Paul Goble." *Frank Schaffer's Classmate.* (November/December/January 1989–1990): 44–45.

Books

Goble, Paul. *Hau Kola = Hello Friend* (R. C. Owen, 1994). Photographs by Gerry Perrin.

Gail Haley

◆ Folklore

Bob Caldwell

Shuffletown, North Carolina
November 4, 1939

📖 *Jack and the Bean Tree*
📖 *A Story, A Story*

ABOUT THE AUTHOR/ILLUSTRATOR

Gail Einhart was born in Shuffletown, North Carolina, near Charlotte on November 4, 1939. World War II had just begun, and her father George Einhart, a G.I., was headed to the West Coast. Gail's mother, Louise, smuggled Gail and herself aboard a troop train so they might travel to the West as well.

When she was two years old, the family returned to Shuffletown. She spent much of her time playing barefoot along the banks of the Catawba River, where she imagined people hunting, singing, or playing with their children. Gail spent time dreaming and telling stories in her head. At this time, George Einhart was the art director for *The Charlotte Observer*. The typographers set the newspaper using a letterpress. On Saturdays, after her dance lessons, Gail would drop by the newspaper office. She would hang around the artists and talk to the writers. Early on, she knew she wanted to work with the printed word.

Gail had a make-believe playmate named Sally when she was five years old, and together they played all kinds of games. She also used to imagine and talk to fairies and other little creatures. Gail rode the bus to a school ten miles away. The school librarian always allowed her to borrow books reserved for older students. Gail was a voracious reader, and by the time she was eight, she knew that she wanted to be a writer. She was nine years old before the first of two younger sisters, Beth and Carol, was born. When she became a big sister, Gail helped care for her little sister. As they grew older, Einhart took her sister on long walks in the woods and told her stories about the imaginary friends.

During high school, Gail worked at a print shop and developed a working knowledge of offset printing, as well as the preparation of art and film necessary for that process. At the age of seventeen, she left North Carolina, intending never to return. She attended art school and married Joseph A. Haley in 1959. He was working on a doctorate in mathematics at the University of Virginia in Charlottesville, so Gail Haley transferred there and studied under Charles Smith, a graphic artist who became her mentor. He taught her woodcutting and printmaking.

Before Gail Haley completed her college degree, she self-published her first book—with the help of a semi-retired printer in Crozet, Virginia—*My Kingdom for a Dragon* (Crozet Print Shop, 1962). She used $500 worth of pine planks to make the wood blocks for her illustrations, and she hand set the type. She printed a thousand copies of the book. It took another three years before a publisher offered to publish a book she wrote and illustrated.

Her marriage to Joseph Haley ended, but her book career began to flourish. By 1966, she was married for a second time and immersed in her work as a children's book writer and illustrator. She lived in England for eight years, in New York City, and in the Caribbean. It was on the island of Saint Thomas where she began to hear the Ananse tales that she later retold and illustrated in *A Story, A Story* (Atheneum, 1970). Often, when she was on the waterfront, she would hear people tell these trickster stories. She collected and wrote down as many as she could. Once she was back in New York City, she traced the stories' origins back to Africa. African woodcarvings provided her the inspiration for the wood cuts. Haley retold the legend of Ananse, who brought stories from the Sky God, Nyame. Haley is credited with being the first children's author/illustrator to portray a black God. The illustrations took almost two years to complete. Each one was hand separated for the color printing. Haley printed the originals on her own press, a Pocco proof press, using one block for each color. A printer later reproduced the originals in the book.

In 1971, Haley was awarded the Caldecott Medal for the illustrations she had created for *A Story, A Story*. At the time, she had two young children. Her daughter, Marguerite, was almost old enough to go to school and wanted "to write stories." Haley says she drew "very clever pictures." Her son, Geoffrey, was "just big enough to enjoy stories and pictures." Her marriage was ending.

A few years later, Gail Haley was honored with England's Kate Greenaway Medal for illustrations, awarded for her book, *The Post Office Cat* (Scribner, 1976). She became, and still is, the only illustrator who has been awarded both the United States Caldecott Medal and England's major award.

Meanwhile, her two young children were growing up in a playpen next to her drawing board. They traveled with her and her costume trunk as she publicized *Costumes for Plays and Playing* (Metheun, 1978). Her children's images appear in almost every book she has created.

Eventually Haley's writing and illustrating took her back home to North Carolina where she married David Considine, a professor of media studies and instructional technology at Appalachian State University. Together they collaborated on some professional titles for educators, and Haley continued writing and illustrating picture books. She turned her attention to many of the North Carolina tales she had heard during her youth and those she continued to hear as a resident of the Appalachian region of the south. She used Poppyseed, a traditional Appalachian storyteller, to retell tales of Jack. Her first retelling was *Jack and the Bean Tree* (Crown, 1986). Haley created the illustrations in acrylic paints and oil on wood using built-up gesso textures to get a three-dimensional effect. Modern color separation techniques require that artwork be created in such a way that it can bend around the drum that makes the photographic color separation negatives. For that reason, the art had to be photographed before it could go through the separation process, thus muting the colors to some degree.

Many of the images created in the illustrations are based on people and events in Haley's life. The storyteller, Poppyseed, was based on Haley's maternal grandmother, Ethel Bell. The house in the illustration is really her great-grandmother's house in King's Mountain. Typical of the mountain setting are the hanging leather britches beans, the morning glories, and the fireflies. The cat shown is Pyewacket who belonged to the Haley household. The little girl sitting on Poppyseed's knee is Haley herself as a young child.

Some of these images show up again in Haley's *Jack and the Fire Dragon* (Crown, 1988). This time she was able to show the cabin's interior, which she researched and portrayed authentically. The sleeping quarters were in the loft, and the items the brothers brought back were researched and are authentic to the pre-Civil War times.

For *Birdsong* (Crown, 1984), Haley took the skeleton of a Grimm tale about a witch who lures and cages birds, beasts, and innocent maidens into an enchanted forest. From this outline, Haley created a story of love's triumph over greed and wickedness. The idea came to Haley in a rush. She is said to have sat down to write it at 4:00 A.M. and to have called her editor at 10:00 A.M. The tale is set in medieval times, so she chose an art technique that simulates the rich artwork of the illuminated manuscripts of the time. The actual paintings were created using gouache and waterproof brown ink. Using the ink, she sketched three or four versions of each illustration. She chose the one she liked best and added the color with a resist and brilliant inks to create the illuminated feeling.

The story of *Jack Jouett's Ride* (Viking, 1973) came about when she was living in Virginia. A retired librarian told Haley about a local hero who had ridden forty miles at night to warn Thomas Jefferson and other signers of the Declaration of Independence about the arrival of Banastre Tarleton and his British troops. To render the illustrations accurately, Haley traveled to England and researched the uniforms of Tarleton's raiders and the uniforms Americans wore. During the American Revolution, wood engravings were common. One of the most notable engravers was Thomas Bewick. Haley studied his work to get a feel for the illustrative details and then executed her illustrations on linoleum blocks in such a way that the illustrations looked very much like a greatly enlarged wood engraving.

Haley was living in England when she heard a piece on the *Today Show* that told about Parliament debating whether or not post office cats were receiving a large enough salary and equal rights. The item intrigued Haley, so she did some research and ended up writing *The Post Office Cat* (Scribner, 1976). One of her kittens, Clarence, became the prototype for the cat illustrations.

England also provided the source material for a book titled, *The Green Man* (Scribner, 1979). While she was in London, she passed a pub with a sign out front that said "The Green Man." Told that the name was based on a local legend, she spent six months researching the legend of a man who could tame animals and control the changing seasons. He was a nurturer, a gatherer of the land's bounty, and a protector of children. In the fifteenth and sixteenth centuries, the Green Man often had been represented in the tapestries of the period. Haley's acrylic paintings on canvas board illustrations have a tapestry-like effect.

Linoleum blocks proved to be Haley's medium of choice again when she created the illustrations for *Go Away, Stay Away!* (Scribner, 1977). She used white ink for the naughty creatures—Bunshee, Kicklebucket, and friends—who cause trouble for Peter and his family. They were printed in black ink. As Haley was working on these illustrations, she mounted them on frames to keep the illustration paper from wrinkling. The finished illustrations carried cat-claw marks in the corners of the blotting paper. It was her cat Clarence's way of telling her it was time for Haley to stop working on the illustrations and to make dinner.

As she had in *Go Away, Stay Away!*, Haley used linoleum cuts and color to differentiate between types of characters and actions in her book *Sea Tale* (Dutton, 1990). Haley wrote the story when she woke early one morning with the beginnings of a tale about a seafaring man, Tom O'Shaunessy, who falls in love with a mermaid. Haley wanted to distinguish the events that took place above water from those that took place underwater, so she used brown and white oil based inks for the outlines. She filled in the outlines with color washes of gouache and brilliant inks. The castle she portrayed was one that she and her son had made at the beach.

When Haley begins to create her books, she does thumbnail sketches on index cards and then arranges the cards in different sequences. Next, she moves the various sequential groups around until she finds the best sequence to tell the story. From her preliminary thumbnail sketches, she produces layout sketches for a dummy book. Those sketches are the same size that will appear in the book.

Haley has earned a reputation as a meticulous illustrator who researches details and styles to best represent the tale she is telling. In addition to her writing and illustrating, she served on the faculty at Appalachian State University as writer-in-residence from 1980 to 1995. Many of her illustrative works are included in The Gail E. Haley Illustration Collection, created through a gift of the Blumenthal Foundation. The collection is housed in the main library at the Public Library of Charlotte and Mecklenburg County (North Carolina).

Gail E. Haley has visited classrooms, libraries, and media centers in Australia, England, Canada, and throughout the United States. In 1997, she traveled the African continent for the American International Schools. Her visits to Mozambique, South Africa and Swaziland gave her material for a manuscript titled *My Wall*. The story builds on the traditions and visual arts of the Ndebele women.

Haley lives in Blowing Rock, North Carolina, with her husband, David Considine, a native of Australia. Together Considine and Haley have written professional titles focusing on visual literacy including *Visual Messages: Integrating Imagery into Instruction* (Libraries Unlimited, 1992; 1999). Both of her children are grown. In 1998, Gail Haley and David Considine became grandparents for the first time when Ellen Morgan Considine, the daughter of Geoffrey and Michelle Considine, was born.

Haley is a storyteller and full-time creator of books, media, and puppets. When she is not working on one of those projects, she is most likely visiting classrooms and libraries. She says that there is not "a big distinction between my professional and personal life." Even while she watches television, Haley is apt to be sewing or gluing together a puppet. Her first CD-ROM is based on three-dimensional puppet characters that she created and carried around for years. Even when she "escapes" to someplace exotic such as the island of Bali, one is likely to find her seeking out the puppet masters to look and listen to their ancient stories. She says that just like Poppyseed, "I'm just a storytellin' woman and there ain't no two ways about it."

BOOKS AND NOTES

Historically, Gail Haley's books have been aligned to the genre of folklore and folktales. She is always interested in archetypes and the work of Joseph Campbell. In all her travels, she has gathered tales.

She works with whatever medium pleases her or seems right at the time. She has created illustrations using woodcuts, linoleum blocks, and paint on wood or canvas. Her husband, David Considine, appears in the illustration on the last page of *Birdsong*. Books are frequently dedicated to one or both of her children. The family's cats are frequently present in her illustrations as well.

Books Written and Illustrated by Gail Haley

Birdsong (Crown, 1984).

Dream Peddler (Dutton, 1993).

The Green Man (Scribner, 1979).

Jack and the Bean Tree (Crown, 1986).

Jack and the Fire Dragon (Crown, 1988).

Mountain Jack Tales (Dutton, 1992).

The Post Office Cat (Scribner, 1976).

Puss in Boots (Dutton, 1991).

Sea Tale (Dutton, 1990).

A Story, A Story: An African Tale (Atheneum, 1970).

Two Bad Boys: A Very Old Cherokee Tale (Dutton, 1996).

FOR MORE INFORMATION

Articles

"Gail Haley . . . A Whimsical Visionary." *Early Years PreK–8* (November/December 1985): 24–25.

Haley, Gail E. "From the Ananse Stories to the Jack Tales: My Work with Folktales." *Children's Literature Association Quaterly*. 11, no. 3 (Fall 1986): 118–21.

Web Sites

The Gail E. Haley Illustration Collection. URL: <http://www.plcmc.lib.nc.us/whatsnew/art/haley.htm> (Accessed March 2000).

University of Southern Mississippi, de Grummond Collection: Gail E. Haley Papers URL: <http://www.lib.usm.edu/~degrum/findaids/haley.htm> (Accessed March 2000).

Kevin Henkes

◆ Family Relationships ◆ Friends ◆ School Stories

Sharron L. McElmeel

Racine, Wisconsin
November 27, 1960

📖 *Chrysanthemum*
📖 *Julius, the Baby of the World*
📖 *Lilly's Purple Plastic Purse*

ABOUT THE
AUTHOR/ILLUSTRATOR

Kevin Henkes often uses the ears and tails of his mice characters to convey the emotion. The mice generally are coping with problems that are typical of childhood, and Henkes works through the problems with humor, ending on a hopeful note. He jokes that although the characters "have long skinny tails, they are remarkably human." They reflect vivid, sensory images from Henkes's own childhood.

Henkes grew up in Racine, Wisconsin, where he was born in 1960 to Bernard E. and Beatrice Henkes. Kevin was the next to the youngest child in a family of five children. He has one sister, Peggy, and three brothers. He was the baby of the family for six years, and although he says he did not tease his younger sibling as his character Lilly teases Julius, he did feel jealous. Lilly reflects many of those feelings.

Henkes always enjoyed reading. His family made regular visits to the library, and there he learned to love books. One of his favorite books was *Rain Makes Applesauce* by Julian Scheer, featuring the illustrations of Marvin Bileck (Holiday House, 1964).

The five Henkes children took art lessons at the local museum. Kevin's older brother, Peter, was considered the family artist. Peter always selected the fine, highest quality brushes; Kevin was left with the coarse, fat ones. When Peter was in eighth grade, their parents framed and hung one of his paintings in the living room. Kevin looked forward to the day when they might hang one of his paintings, too.

Eventually Peter and the rest of the children abandoned the art classes. But Kevin Henkes, who loved drawing, kept on taking lessons. His maternal grandmother used to use oil paints to create folk art on wood, and she gave him his first set of oil paints. His grandfather was a photographer, and he gave Henkes some paints used to tint his photographs. In high school, Henkes selected art classes as electives. He says, "I never thought I'd be lucky enough to be a real author and illustrator."

In high school, Henkes had an English teacher who helped him learn to like writing. Henkes found he could both draw and write, so he began to think about creating picture books. He visited the library and checked out books about writing and illustrating picture books. He began to create dummies of some of his ideas. In fact, he had the dummy for his first book, *All Alone* (Greenwillow, 1981), completed by the time he finished his senior year.

After graduating from high school, Henkes choose to attend the University of Wisconsin at Madison. He knew that Nancy Ekholm Burkett and Ellen Raskin had gone to school there and that the university was the home to the Cooperative Children's Book Center. As a youngster, he often wondered about the authors and illustrators that created the books he liked, but in college, he began to think seriously about his own career. Ginny Moore Kruse encouraged him to examine picture books by specific publishers. He made stacks of books organized by publisher. Using that criteria, he began to examine and categorize what types of books each one published. He tried to decide which publisher might be the most interested in the type of books he wanted to create, but he also assessed the quality of the publications. Greenwillow was Henkes' first choice among a list of his top-ten choices.

By the time he was nineteen, he had developed a portfolio. He gathered together all the money he had and flew to New York City with the idea of spending a week there. He was determined to get a book contract before he left. He made appointments with the publishers but had Monday free, so he decided to visit two publishers that were not his top choices—mostly to take the edge off his nervousness. The visits made him somewhat more at ease, even though they did not like what he had to show them. He had an appointment with Susan Hirschman at Greenwillow Books on Tuesday. When he got there, she looked through his portfolio and asked him several questions unrelated to his books or portfolio. Finally, she asked where he was going next. He said that his next visit was scheduled for Harper. She responded that they would just have to take him before Harper did, and she offered him a contract.

The next semester, Henkes took time off from school and worked on his book. He then returned to school but continued to create books—and to finish school as well. The confidence Henkes instills in his characters reflects his own confidence and persistence—one of the traits that helped earn him a book contract. To work with Susan Hirschman while he was still in school was a thrill—and he says it still is today. His first book, *All Alone* was published when he was just twenty-one.

Although most of his characters are rodents, this does not come from any personal experience. He did not have rodents as pets but once in awhile, there were uninvited house mice. He was, however, a Mickey Mouse fan. The characters in Henkes's first four books were people, but as he began to inject more humor into his books, he decided that animals might help him convey that humor. His next books used rabbit characters. In *Bailey Goes Camping* (Greenwillow, 1985), Bailey was too young to go camping with the Bunny Scouts, so his parents set up a camping experience right at home. Then Henkes turned to rodents when he created *A Weekend with Wendell* (Greenwillow, 1986, 1992) and *Chester's Way* (Greenwillow, 1988). It was in *Chester's Way* that the irrepressible Lilly made her first appearance. Lilly was based on his niece Kelly, his sister Peggy's daughter. She was the new girl in the neighborhood and made a splash with her bizarre costumes and ever-present squirt gun. Two other characters, Wilson and Chester, do not think too much of Lilly at first, but when she shows bravery in a confrontation with some bullies, they decide that Lilly may be someone with whom they want to be friends. The two pals make Lilly part of their group and set about to teach her a few tricks, such as double-knotting shoes, and Lilly shows them that toast does not always call for peanut butter and jelly. She shows them how to use fresh fruit and cereal to make faces on their peanut butter toast. And just when the three are getting along famously, along comes Victor, the new boy in the neighborhood. The final illustration on the back cover of the book shows what appear to be four friends getting along just fine.

Lilly shows up again as the jealous older sister in the household with *Julius, the Baby of the World* (Greenwillow, 1990). Julius's arrival came about when Henkes's niece Kelly got a new baby sister, Kristine. She became the prototype for Julius. In the story, Lilly thinks Julius is ugly. She is also quite jealous. Lilly does everything to sabotage Julius's becoming clever and smart. She sings him the alphabet backward and jumbles up numbers. But when Lilly's cousin begins to point out Julius's shortcomings, Lilly is quick to defend him and to declare that Julius is actually "the baby of the world." Henkes's niece actually asked, "When Kristine dies, can we have hot dogs?" In the book, Henkes changed the line to have Lilly say, "When Julius goes away, can we have hot dogs?"

One of the most loved tales about Lilly portrays her with a purple plastic purse. It was just the right accessory to go with her red cowboy books. The inspiration for *Lilly's Purple Plastic Purse* (Greenwillow, 1996) came one day when Henkes was on a book tour early in the 1990s. In the Boise, Idaho airport he observed a young girl "driving her father crazy" with a purse just like the one Lilly shows off in the book. Henkes knew right away that the purse would be just right for Lilly, so when he got on the plane, he started writing.

Lilly's purse plays music when it is opened and holds movie-star, rhinestone-studded sunglasses. The plot of the story involves Lilly's admiration for her teacher, Mr. Slinger, who is somewhat offbeat. Mr. Slinger asks Lilly to give up her purse when it becomes a distraction in the classroom. Lilly finds herself making some unfortunate decisions and puts herself in a situation for which she must apologize. Henkes said, "It is my intent that Lilly will benefit by being in Mr. Slinger's class and that Mr. Slinger's view of the world will expand by having Lilly in his class."

There are many lovable rodents in Henkes's books, each with their own predicaments in Henkes's rodent community. There is Chrysanthemum, who loves her name until she goes to school and children make fun of her. Owen loves his fuzzy blanket, but his neighbor convinces his mother that he is getting too big for it. Fearless Sheila Rae eats the eyes of bears (cherries in her fruit cocktail) and kisses spiders, but she has not yet met Lilly—such a meeting would be interesting and may come about in a future book.

After using mice as characters for several books Henkes went back to humans for two additional books. One of those was *Grandpa & Bo* (Greenwillow, 1986). Bo has been used to seeing his grandfather every other Christmas, but this year he is going to spend the entire summer with his grandfather. Their friendship grows quietly and gently as they walk through the cornfields, play ball, fish, and listen to records. When summer ends, they have forged a new relationship.

Human characters also populate *Jessica* (Greenwillow, 1989). Henkes said it would have been difficult to have a mouse character in a book with the opening line, "Ruthie Simms didn't have a dog. She didn't have a cat." Ruthie has an imaginary friend, Jessica, who seems to always be with her. Ruthie's parents are bothered that Ruthie insists on playing with Jessica and including her in every activity. They are just sure that this will be a problem when Ruthie finally goes to school. But when Ruthie shows up for her first day of kindergarten, who should be there except a live Jessica. They soon become fast friends.

Henkes has created many endearing characters for his books. He says that some readers tell him the characters in *Jessica* remind them of Maurice Sendak's characters. He remembers with fondness buying *Where the Wild Things Are* (Harper, 1963) from the school book club even though some would have considered him "too old" for the book. He bought it and loved it and says he still "hasn't outgrown it." Early on, Henkes was a great fan of Crockett Johnson. As an adult, he also admires Sendak's work, along with that of Rosemary Wells, James Marshall, Arnold Lobel, William Steig, and Margot Zemach.

When Henkes creates a picture book, he finds that most of the time it is the words that come first. The book might take him from a week to two months to write. His first drafts are written on legal pads. Sometimes he writes three lines and then finds that three hours have passed. He doodles and thinks and rewrites. He often has the opening and knows how he wants the story to end, but then he has to work on the middle. That, he says, "always takes the most time." As he writes, Henkes continually reads his words out loud because he says, "A good picture book is often read out loud and must read well. It must have a rhythm that is in tune with the oral language." The text is later "pecked out" on a typewriter. Once his text is as good as he thinks it will get, he sends it off to Susan Hirschman and then begins to put pictures with the words. Sometimes the illustrations show things that can be eliminated from the text, so there are adjustments as the process goes along. He has to be careful that eliminated words do not break the flow of the text.

Henkes works in his home studio. He creates illustrations with pen and ink and watercolor. He has a red container for his water—the same red Imperial margarine container that he has used for this purpose since the fourth grade. He creates pencil sketches for the entire book and sends them off to Hirschman for her perusal and suggestions. Once Hirschman approves them, Henkes retraces the sketches on good paper using India ink, and then he goes back and paints each of the inked sketches. Early in his career, he created each illustration from sketch to painting, one at a time. Now he finds that it works better to sketch the entire book and then finish the paintings in sequence. It helps him show the growth and change in the characters from the beginning of the story to the end. Henkes manages to impart a subtle humor in his picture books that bring smiles to the faces of the young readers, as well as adults who share them. In addition to picture books, Henkes creates novels, which allow him to develop a character more fully and tend to be more serious than his picture books.

Kevin Henkes married artist Laura Dronzek on May 18, 1985. They live in Madison, Wisconsin, where both have their own separate studios in their homes, created out of spare bedrooms. Each has made creative work a full-time career, although since the birth of their first child, Will, they have shared child-care duties. Both Henkes and Dronzek work four hours a day; although Henkes is working fewer hours than before, his books keep coming. He once developed two books a year, but he has found that slowing down a bit allows him to reflect on his writing and illustrating a bit more.

Of all his books thus far, Henkes says, "*All Alone* will always be special," perhaps because it was his first book. The spunky, sometimes outrageous, but always delightful Lilly remains close to his heart. "I love Lilly . . . she's my favorite character."

BOOKS AND NOTES

Kevin Henkes's cartoonish illustrations have been compared with those of James Stevenson and Steven Kellogg. They are colorful, full of emotion, and humorous. Taking a look at how Henkes's art illustration has evolved over the period of his book career is fascinating. From humans to rabbits to mice, his art has evolved to become more cartoonish. His realistic renderings for *Grandpa & Bo* gave way to human characters in *Jessica* which foreshadow the development of his rodent characters. Ruthie's eyebrows are created with the same expressive, arched black line as some of his popular mouse characters, Lilly, Sheila Rae, and so forth. But it is Henkes's mouse characters that have captured the imagination of most of his readers. Their tails droop, curl saucily, or stand up proudly, depending on the emotion they are experiencing. He has written and illustrated most of his books, but other artists have illustrated a few of his picture books as well. Henkes also has written several novels for eight- to twelve-year-old readers. Most of them, he says, mirror his own experiences in childhood.

Books Written and Illustrated by Kevin Henkes

Chester's Way (Greenwillow, 1988).

Chrysanthemum (Greenwillow, 1991).

Jessica (Greenwillow, 1989).

Julius, the Baby of the World (Greenwillow, 1990).

Lilly's Purple Plastic Purse (Greenwillow, 1996).

Owen (Greenwillow, 1993).

Sheila Rae, the Brave (Greenwillow, 1987).

A Weekend with Wendell (Greenwillow, 1986, 1992).

Wemberly Worried (Greenwillow, 2000).

Books Written by Kevin Henkes

Biggest Boy. Illustrated by Nancy Tafuri. (Greenwillow, 1995).

Good-bye Curtis. Illustrated by Marisabina Russo. (Greenwillow, 1995).

Oh! Illustrated by Laura Dronzek. (Greenwillow, 1999).

Once Around the Block. Illustrated by Victoria Chess. (Greenwillow, 1987).

FOR MORE INFORMATION

Articles

Cooper, Ilene. "The Booklist Interview: Kevin Henkes." *Booklist* 93, no. 9/10 (January 1, 15, 1997): 868.

Henkes, Kevin. "The Artist at Work." *Horn Book Magazine* 68, no. 1 (January/February 1992): 38–47.

Web Sites

Cary, Alice. *BookPage Children's Interview.* "Lilly's Purple Plastic Purse." URL: <http://www.bookpage.com/9609bp/childrens/lillyspurpleplasticpurse.html> (Accessed March 2000).

Hurst, Carol. *Carol Hurst's Children's Literature Site.* "Kevin Henkes." URL: <http://www.carolhurst.com/authors/khenkes.html> (Accessed March 2000).

Lillian Hoban

◆ Picture Book

Barbara Burger

Philadelphia, Pennsylvania
May 18, 1925–July 17, 1998

📖 *Arthur's Camp-Out*
📖 *Arthur's Christmas Cookies*

ABOUT THE AUTHOR/ILLUSTRATOR

Lillian Aberman was the youngest of three children in the Aberman family. She was born May 18, 1925, in Philadelphia. The family moved so many times while she was young that Aberman was always the "new kid" in school. She made few friends until she was older. Many of her childhood days were spent in libraries. She once said, "the art in the comics in the Philadelphia newspapers is the art I remember most vividly and certainly the first artwork that inspired me to be an artist."

Even as a child, she was interested in illustration. At age fourteen, she enrolled in classes at the Graphic Sketch Club at the Philadelphia Museum of Art. She later earned a scholarship to art school and majored in illustration. Lillian also studied dance at the Hanya Holm School of Dance. But it was at the sketch club where she met her future husband, Russell Hoban. Both studied art at the museum school. They married in 1944, just before Russell went overseas as a member of the U.S. Infantry. Lillian Aberman Hoban moved to New York. She gave up illustration to study and teach dance professionally. She appeared on television in the 1950s.

When Russell Hoban returned to New York City in 1945, they settled into a small apartment. She continued to dance and began to work once again in commercial art. He worked as a magazine illustrator, an advertising studio artist, and in various other art-related positions until he began to focus on his freelance career. The couple's first collaboration was in 1961, when they worked on *Herman the Loser* (HarperCollins).

Eventually Russell Hoban shifted his career emphasis from illustrator to writer, while Lillian Hoban shifted her focus from dancer to illustrator. Russell created the insatiable Frances, a little badger who experiences many of the family predicaments that children do: sibling rivalry, jealousy over a sibling's birthday, delay tactics at bedtime, and so forth. Garth Williams illustrated the first Frances book, but Lillian Hoban illustrated all of the subsequent titles. Eventually, she illustrated about twenty-five of Russell Hoban's books.

The couple lived and worked in New York and in Wilton, Connecticut. In Connecticut, the Hobans lived in a home that was once a barn overlooking a pond. In 1969, they moved to London. They were to stay for two years, but their marriage broke up. Lillian Hoban and the couple's children returned to Wilton, and Russell stayed in London. Their collaboration came to an end with their marriage.

Lillian went on to illustrate books for other authors and created a lovable chimp named Arthur and his younger sister, Violet. Arthur and Violet became the popular heroes of several easy-to-read books. Most of the incidents that happen to the two chimpanzees are things that had happened in the Hoban household. She did not deliberately model any of her animal characters after a specific child but the expressions on her animals' faces did seem to reflect expressions that were seen on the faces of her children.

In *Arthur's Christmas Cookies* (Harper, 1972), Arthur accidentally puts too much salt (instead of sugar) into the cookie dough. He finds that his security toy may be a problem in *Arthur's Honey Bear* (Harper, 1974). But as the times changed, so did the situations with which Arthur and Violet contended. In *Arthur's Camp-Out* (Harper, 1993), Arthur declines to allow Violet to accompany him on a camping trip, until a group of girls invite Violet to go camping. Then Arthur feels he must go along as their protector. The girls are very assertive and let him know that they are capable of taking care of themselves. In the end, Arthur follows along and is scared by bats, which do not scare the girls in the least because they know some scientific facts that he does not.

Lillian Hoban continued to live in the country near Wilton, and when she wasn't writing, she enjoyed the country sounds. Sometimes, the surroundings contributed ideas for her books. For example, when one of her daughters was young, she had a horse named Shandy. It was in Shandy's feed bin that Hoban first found Everett Mouse and the idea for the Easter story of *The Sugar Snow Spring* (Harper, 1973) Her last book, *Arthur's Birthday Party* (Harper, 1999), was written at the Villa Serbelloni at Bellagio in Italy during spare moments when she wasn't working on a series of paintings for a book about otters.

The Hobans had three daughters together—Phoebe, Esmé, and Julia—and one son, Abrom (Brom). Phoebe collaborated with her mother on two books in the early 1980s, and Julia became a children's author as well. Abrom has illustrated one of his father's books.

Lillian Hoban continued to write and illustrate books for more than three decades. She had homes in New York and Connecticut and traveled extensively. She spent much time in both Israel and London. She enjoyed reading and going to the theater and concerts. Most of all, she enjoyed "playing with my grandchildren." Lillian Hoban died suddenly of heart failure in New York City on July 17, 1998. She was 73.

BOOKS AND NOTES

Lillian Hoban said that she learned to draw from still life and began to write her own stories after she had children. Her first title in the Arthur series, *Arthur's Christmas Cookies*, was published in 1972 and has continued to be a favorite among young readers ever since. While Hoban illustrated books by other authors, her own series about Arthur, an irrepressible little chimp, is the perennial favorite.

Books Written and Illustrated by Lillian Hoban

Arthur's Back to School Day (Harper, 1996).

Arthur's Birthday Party (Harper, 1999).

Arthur's Camp-Out (Harper, 1993).

Arthur's Christmas Cookies (Harper, 1972).

Arthur's Funny Money (Harper, 1981).

Arthur's Halloween Costume (Harper, 1984).

Arthur's Honey Bear (Harper, 1974).

Arthur's Loose Tooth (Harper, 1985).

Arthur's Pen Pal (Harper, 1970).

Arthur's Prize Reader (Harper, 1978).

Case of the Two Masked Robbers (Harper, 1986).

Silly Tilly and the Easter Bunny (Harper, 1987).

Silly Tilly's Valentine (Harper, 1998).

Books Illustrated by Lillian Hoban

Best Friends for Frances. Written by Russell Hoban. (Harper, 1969, 1994).

A Birthday for Frances. Written by Russell Hoban. (Harper, 1968, 1995).

Bread and Jam for Frances. Written by Russell Hoban. (Harper, 1964).

Elisa in the Middle. Written by Johanna Hurwitz. (Morrow, 1995).

Ever-Clever Elisa. Written by Johanna Hurwitz. (Morrow, 1997).

I Never Did That Before: Poems. Written by Lilian Moore. (Atheneum, 1995).

Laziest Robot in Zone One. Written by Lillian Hoban and Phoebe Hoban. (Harper, 1983).

Ready . . . Set . . . Robot! Written by Lillian Hoban and Phoebe Hoban. (Harper, 1983).

FOR MORE INFORMATION

Web Sites

University of Southern Mississippi, de Grummond Collection: Russell and Lillian Hoban Papers. URL: <http://www.lib.usm. edu/~degrum/findaids/hobanrus. htm> (Accessed March 2000).

Nonny Hogrogian

◆ Folklore

New York, New York
May 7, 1932

- 📖 *Always Room for One More*
- 📖 *The Devil with the Three Golden Hairs*
- 📖 One Fine Day

ABOUT THE AUTHOR/ILLUSTRATOR

Twice a winner of the Caldecott Medal, Nonny Hogrogian has illustrated several books for older readers and many picture books. She won the Caldecott Medal in 1966 for the illustrations she created for Sorche Nic Leodhas's *Always Room for One More* (Holt, 1965), and in 1972, she won again for her illustrations accompanying the text she wrote based on an old Armenian folktale, *One Fine Day* (Macmillan, 1971).

Nonny Hogrogian was born in the Bronx on May 7, 1932. Her family was of Armenian descent and very artistic. Her mother, Rachel Ansoorian Hogrogian, was a painter and, according to Hogrogian, "could do almost anything." Her father, Henry Mugerditch Hogrogian, dabbled on Sundays copying the works of Renoir, Homer, and Monet.

Hogrogian has been drawing as long as she can remember. She began to putter with her father's paints when she was just three years old. When she reached high school, she attempted to gain admission to a special high school called Music and Art. Her portfolio of artwork paled in comparison to those of the other students who were seeking admission, but she was assured that a "test of her talent" would really determine whether she would be admitted. A school administrator asked Hogrogian to create a contour drawing—something she had never done. Her first efforts resulted in what she describes as a stiff, ugly little squiggle on the page, but Hogrogian got a feel for the task and felt she could draw it well on a second try. The administrator would not allow her to try again, and she failed the test.

This was one of the major traumas of Hogrogian's life, but she dreamed of becoming a good artist, and that goal helped her overcome the hurt. She was determined to develop her drawing and painting skills on her own. First, she made sure she could do a really fine contour drawing. Then she taught herself to letter. She learned dry-brush technique from an artist who sold cards to a card shop. Hogrogian helped color the cards for a nickel each—and she learned as she worked. Her aunt taught her to paint, and then she studied etching, lithography, and woodcutting. She later studied at Hunter College in New York and majored in art, studying various techniques, including fabric design, stage set design, and illustration.

Next, Hogrogian studied with Antonio Grasconi at the New School of Social Research and then studied in Maine at the Haystack Mountain School of Crafts. Finally, she began to work for a book publisher in New York as a designer.

Sometime in late 1965, Hogrogian became discontented with her work. She loved illustrating, but to make a living, she had to devote more than half of her time to designing and directing other people's artwork for Scribner. She wanted to spend more time on her own work. Hogrogian decided to apply for a scholarship to work on a master's degree in painting, hoping that she could take charge of her creative energy. Just before she sent in the final paperwork, she received word that she had won her first Caldecott Medal for *Always Room for One More*. Once she won the award, she was able to devote all her time to illustrating children's books, painting, and sketching.

Hogrogian was living in a small, fifth-floor apartment in New York City, overlooking a Russian Church across the street. The church had seven cupolas, each complete with cherubs, blue ties, and pigeons. Hogrogian created her illustrations working at a small table in that apartment, admiring the view.

Hogrogian created the art for *Always Room for One More* in pen-and-ink lines with crosshatching. She created the backgrounds for the images using one of two techniques: gray wash dabbed with paper napkins for the cloudy-day backgrounds and pastels in heather and green for other backgrounds.

Hogrogian already had illustrated a book with Scottish characters before those featured in her Caldecott-Medal-winning book. But Alger LeClaire who wrote *Always Room for One More* under the pseudonym Sorche Nic Leodhas told Hogrogian that some of the facial features of the Scottish men in the previous book, *Gaelic Ghosts* (Holt, 1963) looked more Rumanian than Scottish. Hogrogian took the comment to heart and says, "I promised myself I would never make a mistake like that again."

When she began work on *Always Room for One More,* she spent hours in the library finding pictures of the clothes that Lachie and his friends might wear. She found costumes for all but the fishing lass and the gallowglas. Sorche Nic Leodhas provided descriptions of those costumes. Hogrogian studied photographs of Scottish people, as well as the face of a Scottish friend. Together, Hogrogian and her friend spent an evening viewing slides of cottages on the isle of South Uist to find one with a but and a ben. She had books about Scotland open on the floor, and in the background she listened to the Scottish music, the ballads of Robert Burns, the energetic songs from the Jacobite Wars, or Ewan MacColl records. Because she felt that her favorite medium—woodcuts—would result in illustrations that would be too strong for the gentleness of the heather, she pulled out her watercolors, chalks, and pen and ink. She created the necessary mood, and the illustrations seem to flow.

Shortly before Hogrogian learned about the award for *Always Room for One More,* she was working on the illustrations for a collection of Armenian folk tales, *Once There Was and Was Not* (Little, Brown, 1966). The collection was one retold by Virginia Tashjian. After the 1966 Caldecott Medal, she felt a real sense of responsibility to live up to her reputation. Her work received more attention, and her books were in bookstores across the nation.

David Kherdian, a man of Armenian descent, was in a bookstore in Santa Fe, New Mexico, when he found one of Hogrogian's books. He liked her work and contacted her. After the exchange of a few letters and a phone call, she agreed to create the jacket cover for a book of his poems. They finally met when Kherdian traveled to New York early in 1971 to attend a reception in his honor as the new editor of *Ararat* magazine.

On March 16, 1971, Hogrogian finished etchings for a collection of Grimm tales, *About Wise Men and Simpletons: Twelve Tales from Grimm,* translated by Elizabeth Shub (Macmillan, 1971). The day after, on March 17, she and David Kherdian were married. They moved to an old farmhouse in New Hampshire where Kherdian was part of the state's Poet-in-the-Schools program. They had a garden and animals and enjoyed the company of family and friends.

Hogrogian continued her freelance work, attempting to complete four books a year. The stress of making ends meet and attempting to be creative on demand almost made her turn to a job that would provide a steady income—an income that would allow her to have more control of her artistic time. She decided to try teaching. But before she could find a job, she was notified that she had won her second Caldecott Medal, and her life changed drastically.

Hogrogian received word of the award on January 25, 1972. It was a stormy evening in New Hampshire, and the electricity had gone out. She and Kherdian were huddled around the fire in an attempt to keep warm and were talking about "what ifs." During the evening, she was drinking brandy, and when she had a touch more than she needed, she suggested to Kherdian that it would be wonderful if she won another Caldecott Medal. Kherdian commented that she was being silly, but she protested saying she deserved it. The conversation went back and forth until the heat and the lights came back on, and the two of them went to work for another hour or two. Hogrogian was just finishing her day's work when Anne Izard called her with the news that she had, indeed, won her second award. She had won the Caldecott Medal for the illustrations in *One Fine Day*. That award allowed her to reduce her output—to concentrate on doing fewer but better books—and to have time for painting, gardening, and other pursuits that were important to her.

The Kherdians moved to Aurora, Oregon, to live on a farm. This setting allowed them the solitude to pursue their creative endeavors. Kherdian turned to children's books, too. He wrote the Newbery Honor Book *The Road from Home: The Story of an Armenian Girl* (Knopf, 1979). The story is set in Turkey and is told in the first person from the point of view of his own mother. His mother actually witnessed the death and destruction portrayed in the book. She was forced to travel into Syria, lost most of her family in a cholera epidemic, and immigrated to the United States as a mail-order bride in 1924. She is a teenager when the story ends. The sequel, *Finding Home* (Knopf, 1981), continues her story. Two novels tell of his own recollections of his childhood in Racine, Wisconsin. He credits his entrance into the world of children's books to his marriage to Hogrogian, who has illustrated several of his books. Together they have published several books reflecting their common Armenian heritage.

In the late 1960s, Hogrogian used her favored woodcuts to create the illustrations for Robert Burns *Hand in Hand We'll Go* (Crowell, 1965) and *Ghosts Go Haunting* (Holt, 1965). She has also used colored pencils to illustrate a wordless fable, *Apples* (Collier-Macmillan, 1972). In 1970, Hogrogian used pen-and-ink drawings, with blue and olive green washes to illustrate Virginia Haviland's *Favorite Fairy Tales Told in Greece* (Little, Brown, 1970).

Over the years, Hogrogian created illustrations in a large variety of styles. When she created the illustrations for Kherdian's *The Dog Writes on the Window* (Four Winds, 1977), she created small framed watercolors for each of the 22 poems in the collections. The paintings for *The Devil with the Three Golden Hairs* (Knopf, 1983) were set against white backgrounds. The paintings seem to spill out of their frames. Most of the two-page spreads are illuminated with a full-page, framed illustration on one of the pages and an unframed illustration on the other. Each of the paintings is brilliantly colored, particularly the vibrant red of the devil's cape and the red wine flowing from the fountain.

By the publication of *The Glass Mountain* (Knopf, 1985), Hogrogian was experimenting with marbleized background paper. In this tale, originally written as "The Raven" by the Grimm Brothers, Hogrogian used the marbleized paper as the backdrop for her luminous illustrations.

Hogrogian's story ideas come from all around her, many from her childhood and stories that swirled around her as she read and searched for tales to retell. She first heard the story of *Rooster Brother* (Macmillan, 1974) from her husband, who's father had told him the tale when he was a child. Hogrogian's end papers foreshadow the illustrations within. Giant red poppies grace green fields. Traditional homes decorate the backgrounds. The bandit in the story has the same general physical characteristics as Nonny Hogrogian's husband, David Kherdian. The heathery garments in vibrant blues, magentas, oranges, and browns are colors familiar to the Armenian culture.

In the 1990s, Hogrogian concentrated on illustration. She illustrated several of David Kherdian's books. She created only one book that she both wrote and illustrated. Hogrogian and Kherdian no longer live in Oregon; several years ago, they returned to New York State, to Spencertown. Nonny Hogrogian has not published a book in the past decade, but the books published previously continue to delight young readers.

BOOKS AND NOTES

Nonny Hogrogian has authored and illustrated more than seventy books. She has twice won the Caldecott Medal for her illustrations. The media she uses range from woodcut to gentle, soft watercolor. She has retold folk stories, written original tales, and created literary folktales from the fabric of stories she heard long ago. Her illustrations often have red-orange tones and Persian blue as dominate colors, and her own facial features or those of David Kherdian often turn up in her illustrations.

Books Written and Illustrated by Nonny Hogrogian

The Cat Who Loved to Sing (Knopf, 1988).

Cinderella: Retold from the Brothers Grimm (Greenwillow, 1981).

The Devil with the Three Golden Hairs: A Tale from the Brothers Grimm (Knopf, 1983).

The First Christmas (Greenwillow, 1995).

One Fine Day (Macmillan, 1971)

The Renowned History of Little Red-Riding Hood (Crowell, 1967).

Books Illustrated by Nonny Hogrogian

Always Room for One More. Written by Sorche Nic Leodhas. (Holt, 1965).

By Myself. Written by David Kherdian. (Holt, 1993).

Feathers and Tails: Animal Fables from Around the World. Written by David Kherdian. (Philomel, 1992).

The Golden Bracelet. Written by David Kherdian. (Holiday House, 1998).

Juna's Journey. Written by David Kherdian. (Philomel, 1993).

Lullaby for Emily. Writen by David Kherdian. (Holt, 1995).

FOR MORE INFORMATION

Articles

Hogrogian, Nonny. "Caldecott Award Acceptance." *Horn Book Magazine* (August 1966): 419–21.

Hogrogian, Nonny. "Caldecott Award Acceptance: How the Caldecott Changed My Life—Twice." *Horn Book Magazine* (August 1972): 352–55.

Itta, John Paul. "Nonny Hogrogian." *Horn Book Magazine* (August 1966): 421–25.

Kherdian, David. "Nonny Hogrogian." *Horn Book Magazine* (August 1972): 356–58.

Deborah Hopkinson

◆ Historical Fiction

Michele Hill

Lowell, Massachusetts
February 4, 1952

- 📖 *Birdie's Lighthouse*
- 📖 *Maria's Comet*
- 📖 *Sweet Clara and the Freedom Quilt*

ABOUT THE AUTHOR

Little in Deborah Hopkinson's background would hint at her ability to weave a powerful story of African Americans and slavery, but that is exactly what she did when she authored *Sweet Clara and the Freedom Quilt* (Knopf, 1993). Since that picture book was published, Hopkinson has authored additional titles, each focusing on an event or person from history. Her New England childhood has brought her settings for the stories she has published since Sweet Clara, but the plots seem to be woven from her passion for learning about people and places from the past.

Deborah Hopkinson was born on February 4, 1952 and grew up in Lowell, Massachusetts. She was the oldest in a family of three girls. Her childhood in Lowell left her with memories of visiting the school librarian before spring vacations and taking home an armload of books to read. Her parents often read aloud to her and her sisters. She loved the Doctor Doolittle books and *The Secret Garden*. Later she enjoyed the nineteenth-century titles by Dickens, Elliot, Austen, and the Brontës. The school's "large geography books" were just right for hiding a novel behind. She was not very good at team sports, and she says, "I think I hid behind books in more ways than one. I remember being the only kid in seventh grade who liked Ivanhoe." From her childhood, Hopkinson wanted to be a writer, but it took her more than a decade to see her dreams come true.

After high school, Hopkinson earned an undergraduate degree from the University of Massachusetts and a master's degree in Asian Studies from the University of Hawaii at Manoa. She settled down in Hawaii and married an artist named Andy Thomas. They had their first child in 1984, a daughter named Rebekah.

When Rebekah was three years old and Hopkinson was working as an administrator, Hopkinson decided that if she really wanted to be a writer, she'd better start writing. She was reading many children's books to Rebekah at that time, and writing something short seemed more plausible than a full-length novel, especially with her busy schedule as a mother, homemaker, and full-time development director. Hopkinson says, "I guess my inspiration here is the Australian writer Patricia Wrightson, who wrote one of my favorite books, *The Nargun and the Stars*. Wrightson worked for years as a hospital administrator and raised two children as a single mom. I've enjoyed my 'day career' very much, though of course it would be wonderful to have more time to write."

Hopkinson could not fit her writing into a regular time slot because of her schedule, but she set goals and learned to find corners in her life to fit it in. She often stayed up late at night, working from 10:00 or 11:00 P.M. into the early morning. Sometimes she worked on weekends. Hopkinson wrote for two full years without selling anything. *Cricket* magazine was the first to publish any of her work. "Skate, Kirsten, Skate," appeared in the January 1990 issue.

Hopkinson says that *Sweet Clara and the Freedom Quilt* came about when "One morning getting ready for work, I heard a story on National Public Radio about the centennial of the first African American graduate of Williams College. For the event, the college was hosting a quilt exhibition. Just in passing, someone mentioned something about 'escape routes being sewn into quilts.' I can remember standing there and getting goose bumps—chicken skin as we say in Hawaii. It was as though, for a moment, I was standing in a tall cornfield myself, lost, looking for a route to freedom."

Hopkinson was clearly aware that she was writing about ethnic groups and cultures that were not inherently hers. She says that she has been "so lucky, though, to have this book [*Sweet Clara and the Freedom Quilt*] welcomed by children all over the country. I think my experience of race was certainly affected by living in America's most multicultural city, Honolulu. Everything in Hawaii is so mixed up, race is important but not that important. Interracial marriage of one sort or another is prevalent in Hawaii. In our neighborhood, our neighbors were Japanese American on one side, above us was a Hispanic/Filipino Armenian couple, and on the other side, an African American/Chinese-Hawaiian-Scottish couple. Chop suey, as we say. I miss that a lot here on the mainland."

Hopkinson says that she has "always felt *Sweet Clara* was a gift. Whenever I worked on it in the revision process, I would close my eyes and I could almost be there. At the time I wrote it, I hadn't even had one story appear in print. I was just this unknown aspiring dreamer in the middle of the Pacific Ocean."

Hopkinson wrote the book in the summer of 1989 and had sent it out to several publishers before Anne Schwartz, an editor at Alfred A. Knopf, (she is now at Atheneum) bought it in the fall of 1990.

Sweet Clara and the Freedom Quilt brought Hopkinson several honors, including the 1994 International Reading Association's award for a first picture book. Clara is an eleven-year-old slave who is sent away from her mother to work in the fields at another plantation. One of the plantation's house slaves, Aunt Rachel, teaches Clara to sew and become a seamstress—a skill that earns Clara her own place as a house slave. As a slave in the house, Clara is able to save bits of cloth and to gather, from other slaves, bits of information about routes to freedom. Clara uses the bits of cloth to fashion a quilt that provides a map to freedom. Many slaves come to see her quilt to learn about the freedom route and make their way to freedom.

When Clara and her friend, Young Jack, run away, Clara leaves the quilt behind for others to use as a map north. James Ransome's full-page illustrations are the ultimate complement to Hopkinson's text. His dedication on the book's title page shows the connection he made with Hopkinson's text: "For Emma Ransom, the first slave of Pattie and General Matt W. Ransom, and all the other Ransom slaves on Verona Plantation." (Sometime after James Ransome's ancestors were freed, they added an "e" to their surname.) In the book, Clara is a house slave on the Home Plantation, but some of the slaves who provide her with information about the location and terrain of the surrounding plantations, ponds, and so forth are from Verona Plantation— a detail that lends credibility to the story. Hopkinson says, "Of course we put the Verona Plantation in to reflect the fact that his [Ransome's] family were slaves there. James researched the book in part at Colonial Williamsburg's Carter's Grove Plantation, but he also traced down Verona."

Hopkinson lived in Hawaii for nineteen years before moving to Washington State, where she now lives with her family. Her stories have been set in Rangley, Maine; Leningrad, Russia; and on a southern plantation. *Birdie's Lighthouse* (Atheneum, 1997) is set in Maine in 1855, the subject of another book grows up in Nantucket, and yet another title focuses on the Jubilee Singers, who tour the United States and England. When asked where she gets her ideas and settings for her stories, she responds, "I keep my antenna up most of the time. My reading is usually some kind of 'fishing expedition.' I look at anthologies, travel books, first-person accounts, histories. I'm especially drawn to the nineteenth century, and I've found that the more I read and learn, the more it comes to life.

"One of my favorite things in the world is to walk into a huge research library! And somehow, over the course of time, I've become a sort of amateur historian.

"One of my stories in *Cricket*, 'Silversmith's Daughter,' was written because I was wandering the stacks at the University of Hawaii library one day and found a picture of the inkstand used to sign the Declaration of Independence."

After reading a travel book about a lighthouse in Iceland, Hopkinson was inspired to read further. Eventually, *Birdie's Lighthouse* evolved, telling the story of a tiny lighthouse island that is Birdie's new home. Birdie's only friend is the diary in which she writes everything down—the changes of seasons, rhythms of the sea, and all the things her father, the lighthouse keeper, is teaching her. During a very fierce storm, Birdie's father falls ill and ensuring the safety of the ships at sea falls to Birdie—she is the only person who knows how to direct the lighthouse's strong beam. Her mother thinks it is too dangerous for Birdie to go to the tower, and Birdie herself wonders if she is brave enough to guide the boats safely into the harbor. Yet, what else can she do? She is the lighthouse keeper now.

Another of Hopkinson's books, *Maria's Comet* (Atheneum, 1999), came about when she "discovered Maria Mitchell's name on an Internet calendar of women in history and thought—wow, I don't know anything about her." Mitchell grew up on Nantucket Island in the first part of the nineteenth century and was fascinated with astronomy—a fascination nurtured by her father. *Maria's Comet* tells the story of Maria Mitchell's early yearnings to learn about the stars. Mitchell became America's first woman astronomer and the first professor of astronomy at Vassar. She was also the first woman to discover a comet.

A Band of Angels: A Story Inspired by the Jubilee Singers (Atheneum, 1999) tells the story of Ella Shepherd and the Jubilee Singers of Fisk University, who, in 1871 faced prejudice but persevered in introducing the songs of slaves while on a fund-raising tour of America and Europe. Their tour raised enough money to save their school. Hopkinson's books and stories often feature strong female protagonists. Those come about, Hopkinson says, because, "in a way I'm writing the stories I wanted to read as a child. But even more, as in the case of Ella Shepard in *A Band of Angels* and Maria Mitchell, I find their stories so compelling. When I discover stories like this, I always think: 'How come I never knew about them before? Why doesn't everyone else know about them, too?' Writing [about them] is one way to share this excitement with others."

Hopkinson has written several titles which will be published in the early 2000s. A book about Fannie Farmer titled *Fannie Farmer in the Kitchen: The Whole Story from Soup to Nuts, or How Fannie Farmer Invented Recipes with Precise Measurements*, illustrated by Nancy Carpenter will be published by Atheneum. Atheneum will also publish *Under the Quilt of Night*, illustrated by James Ransome, *Girl Wonder: A Baseball Story in Nine Innings*, illustrated by Terry Widener, and a Ready-to-Read title, *Billy and the Rebel*, illustrated by Bethanne Andersen. Andersen will also illustrate Hopkinson's *Bluebird Summer* to be published by Greenwillow.

Deborah Hopkinson and Andy Thomas live with their children, Rebekah and Dimitri, in Walla Walla, Washington. Dimitri joined their family from Taldom, Russia when he was six years old. Because English is his second language, he has a difficult time with reading, but he enjoys books a great deal and likes animals. It comes as no surprise that among the books they have read aloud to him are the Doctor Doolittle books. Together the family has tried out skiing, and Deborah has taken up gardening since they purchased a house. The second spring that the family spent on the mainland, Deborah planted 100 tomato seedlings and then wondered "what am I going to do with them all?" She also planted about eight different kinds of sunflowers. Two cats are part of the household, one of which likes to sleep on Deborah's back all night. The family also had one dog until Hopkinson's 1997 birthday, when a birthday puppy, which is now huge, joined the family. All of the family's pets, except for one, have Hawaiian names.

BOOKS AND NOTES

Deborah Hopkinson's books—by chance or design—feature strong, independent women who achieve their goals. Hopkinson finds interesting women and then creates historically accurate tales of the events that might have surrounded their lives.

A Band of Angels: A Story Inspired by the Jubilee Singers. Illustrated by Raul Colon. (Atheneum, 1999).

Birdie's Lighthouse. Illustrated by Kimberly Bulcken Root. (Atheneum, 1997).

Maria's Comet. Illustrated by Deborah Lanino. (Atheneum, 1999).

Sweet Clara and the Freedom Quilt. Illustrated by James Ransome. (Knopf, 1993).

FOR MORE INFORMATION

Articles

McElmeel, Sharron L. "Author Profile: Deborah Hopkinson." *Library Talk* 11, no. 5 (November/December 1998): 20–21.

Web Sites

Amazon.com Author Interview. "Amazon.com Talks to Deborah Hopkinson." URL: <http://www.amazon.com/exec/obidos/show-interview/h-d-opkinsoneborah/102-3929558-9196018> (Accessed April 2000).

Deborah Hopkinson. URL: <http://people.whitman.edu/~hopkinda/> (Accessed February 2000).

Patricia Hutchins

◆　Friends　◆　Family Relationships　◆　Folklore (Literary)

Laurence Hutchins

Yorkshire, England
June 18, 1942

📖　*The Doorbell Rang*
📖　*Rosie's Walk*
📖　*Titch*

ABOUT THE AUTHOR/ILLUSTRATOR

Patricia Hutchins's love of drawing began when she was very young and exploring the fields near her home with her six siblings. Born in England during World War II, her early years were spent on the grounds of an army training camp. It was not unusual for the children to be swinging on the gun turrets of a tank or maneuvering through an assault course. Her mother decided they should move shortly after she found Pat and one of her brothers wandering across a rifle range during target practice. The family moved five miles away, to a nearby village.

Hutchins's mother was a naturalist of sorts. She cared for fledgling birds who fell from their nest, rescued injured animals from traps, and saved kittens from drowning. In addition to the seven children, the family included a cat, a dog, a crow, five pigeons, several white mice, and a hedge-hog. On many afternoons, Pat could be found wandering through the fields with the pet crow, Sooty. She spent hours sketching the animals and scenery that she observed while Sooty grubbed for worms. Her art was good—good enough that a couple who lived nearby often gave her a chocolate bar for each picture she drew for them.

When Hutchins was sixteen, she received a scholarship to study at a local art college. Later she entered Leeds College of Art to specialize in illustration. After graduation, she focused her work in the field of commercial art and worked for a London advertising agency. Patricia met Laurence Hutchins at Leeds, and they married in 1965. Five days after their marriage, they moved to New York City where Laurence Hutchins's company had transferred him. Finding herself in New York City, Pat Hutchins wasted little time in organizing her art portfolio and making the rounds of the publishers.

For a long while, Hutchins did not have any success getting illustrative work in the children's book field. Susan Hirschman, an editor at Macmillan at the time, liked her work, however, and suggested that she should attempt to write her own stories. Hutchins decided to try, and by 1968, two of her books, *Rosie's Walk* (Macmillan, 1967) and *Tom and Sam* (Macmillan, 1968), had been published. By that time, the Hutchins family was on their way back to London, where Pat Hutchins continued to write and illustrate.

Hutchins's picture books are simply written with vivid illustrations that manage to convey the depth of the most complex emotions. They encompass the basic concepts of time, growth, change, and visual perspective. Many of her story ideas come directly from her life or the lives of her children. *Happy Birthday, Sam* (Greenwillow, 1978) was written for her son Sam, who had a chair he used to carry around to stand on to reach things. *Titch* (Macmillan, 1971) was inspired by Morgan, Hutchins's older son. When Morgan was still "in his pushchair [stroller]," recalls Hutchins, "whenever we passed a playground, he always wanted to get out and join the fun." But he was really too little, and the other children wouldn't let him. Her novel *Rats!* (Greenwillow, 1989) is about Sam and his pet rats. In an interview, she described the beginning of *Rats!* "Sam, my son, wanted a rat," said Hutchins. "He went on and on about it for so long I finally gave in. He looked after the rat so well, it got fatter and fatter. The rat was supposed to be male, so we were all very surprised when it gave birth to ten baby rats. I wrote a story about Sam and his rats, and my husband Laurence illustrated it."

Hutchins is always on the watch for good story ideas from other sources, too. Her book, *The Very Worst Monster* (Greenwillow, 1985), came about when her niece told her that she wanted to give her baby brother away. That was a pretty harsh reality to use in a children's book, but Hutchins softened the theme of sibling rivalry by using soft watercolors. The softness made the monster family more lovable than scary. Most readers would like this monster family to live nearby.

The idea for *Shrinking Mouse* (Greenwillow, 1997) came from Hutchins's art bag. She says, "I'd been visiting schools in Yorkshire, and I'd taken my art bag with two examples of my work in it to show children. On the train back to London, I put my art bag on the rack above my head. When I arrived in London, it wasn't there. I assumed that perhaps I'd been mistaken, and placed it behind one of the seats. I started looking for it.

"The other passengers in the coach kindly joined in. A gentleman pointed out a bag on the rack, but it was at the other end of the coach. I told him it couldn't be mine—mine was much bigger—but as it was the only bag left on the rack, I walked along the corridor to look at it, basically to prove it was too small to be mine. As I got closer and closer to the bag, the bag got bigger and bigger. It was my art bag. This gave me an idea to do a book on spatial perspective, and the result was *Shrinking Mouse!*"

Rosie's Walk and *Changes, Changes* (Macmillan, 1971) have been animated for television, at least two of her novels have been read on BBC, and another was dramatized on Australian television. A London theatrical company has produced other titles for the stage. Hutchins's books about Titch are the basis for a model-animated series for four- to seven-year-olds. The television programs feature the adventures of Titch and his family: brother Peter, sister Mary, Mum, Dad, and Grandpa. Titch, as he did in the books, tries to do everything that adults do but with chaotic results. One episode has Titch helping his "Mum" make biscuits, but he ends up needing a lot of help. In another episode, he annoys his entire family when he accidentally knocks over the Christmas tree. The series has been photographed from Titch's perspective to emphasize the view he has of the activities. The entire adult world is only seen from the chest down. In 1997, a series of thirteen ten-minute programs was broadcast on national television (in England), and a second series of programs began airing in 1998. Pat Hutchins has created both picture books and novels for publication. Her first novel was *The House That Sailed Away* (Greenwillow, 1975).

When she is writing, Hutchins often sits on the sofa at her home; if she is illustrating a book, she works at her drawing board. From concept to finish, creating a book generally takes about six months. Her books are published extensively in the United States and in England. Many of her books have been translated into several languages. She schedules visits to the United States at least once a year to meet with her publishers and visit U.S. schools.

Pat Hutchins and her family live in London, but she dreams of having a small cottage in Yorkshire. When she is not writing or illustrating, she paints, collects momentos of the Victorian era, and putters around in the garden.

BOOKS AND NOTES

Hutchins's use of patterned fur and feathers has made her animal illustrations distinctive. Her earlier illustrations were quite stylized, whereas those for her more recent stories tend to be more realistic. Her full-color illustrations often are described as action filled. Many of her books have a strong pattern in the illustrations and the text as well. Because of the patterning, many of Hutchins's books are good books for connecting to math concepts.

In addition, each of Hutchins's books is designed to show a continuity of action from illustration to illustration and to create movement. She carefully positions details on the pages to reflect the overall action of the narrative. In *The Wind Blew* (Macmillan, 1974), for example, as the wind victimizes each of twelve people, the right side of the illustration becomes progressively more cluttered, while the left side of the two-page spread cleverly shows the next unsuspecting victim of the wind. Hutchins used a similar technique when she illustrated *Rosie's Walk*. Each two-page spread has Rosie appearing at the right edge walking toward the scene to be depicted in the following spread. Rosie appears unaware of the fox and the peril behind her.

The Doorbell Rang (Greenwillow, 1986).

Good Night, Owl! (Greenwillow, 1972).

Little Pink Pig (Greenwillow, 1994).

My Best Friend (Greenwillow, 1993).

Our Baby Is Best (Greenwillow, 1991).

Rosie's Walk (Macmillan, 1967).

Shrinking Mouse (Greenwillow, 1997).

Silly Billy (Greenwillow, 1992).

The Surprise Party (Macmillan, 1986).

Ten Red Apples (Greenwillow, 2000).

Three-Star Billy (Greenwillow, 1994).

Tidy Titch (Greenwillow, 1991).

Titch (Macmillan, 1971).

Titch and Daisy (Greenwillow, 1996).

The Very Worst Monster (Greenwillow, 1985).

What Game Shall We Play? (Greenwillow, 1990).

Where's the Baby (Greenwillow, 1988).

Which Witch Is Which? (Greenwillow, 1989).

FOR MORE INFORMATION

Web Sites

Pat Hutchins URL: <http://www.library.ubc.ca/edlib/hutchins.html> (Accessed March 2000).

Titch by Pat Hutchins. URL: <http://www.titch.net> (Accessed March 2000).

Trina Schart Hyman

Jean Aull

Philadelphia, Pennsylvania
April 8, 1939

📖 *Little Red Riding Hood*

📖 *Snow White and the Seven Dwarfs by the Brothers Grimm*

ABOUT THE AUTHOR/ILLUSTRATOR

It took Trina Schart Hyman more than twenty-six years to become an "overnight success." In 1959, she and her husband, Harris Hyman, were living in Boston. She was making the rounds of publishers, attempting to find one who would commission her to illustrate a book. The following year, they moved to Sweden, where Harris studied mathematics and Trina studied art and continued to look for a publisher.

While in Sweden, Hyman illustrated one book; when she returned to the United States in the early 1960s, she managed to get work illustrating two Little Golden Books. By then, Trina and Harris had divorced and she continued to struggle, looking for work as an illustrator to support herself and her daughter Katrin. Then, in 1986, she found herself on stage to accept the Caldecott Medal, the most prestigious award in children's books, for her illustrations created for Margaret Hodges's *Saint George and the Dragon* (Little, Brown, 1985).

Trina Schart was born in 1939 in Philadelphia. She grew up in Wyncote, Pennsylvania, northwest of Philadelphia, attended school, and eventually headed off to art school. In fact, she began studying art while still in high school and then went to three different art schools for a total of five years to learn about being an artist.

Astrid Lindgren, author of *Pippi Longstocking*, gave Hyman her first illustrating job. The job came while Hyman was living in Sweden. The manuscript was in Swedish. It took her two months to read it and then only two weeks to make the illustrations. Before returning to the United States in the early 1960s, Trina and her husband traveled 3,000 miles on bicycle through the Netherlands and England. When they returned to the United States, they settled in Boston. She took a portfolio with all of her best work and made appointments to see "all the children's book editors in the world." After about three years of rejections, she was finally given a Little Golden Book to illustrate. Very slowly, she began to get more work. Helen Jones, editor at Little, Brown, was very helpful in getting Trina started in the field. In 1963, she illustrated another. It was published by Houghton Mifflin in 1964.

Hyman says, "My illustrations are full of 'real' people who are my friends, family and neighbors. They're also full of places I've been to, chairs I've sat on, cats and dogs I've known, and things I like to have around me." By the time Hyman created the illustrations for *Snow White and the Seven Dwarfs by the Brothers Grimm* (Little, Brown, 1975), she was no longer married to Harris Hyman, but that did not stop her from portraying him as one of the dwarfs. He is the bald man seen through the door. The man behind him are other characters: a dwarf who looks like Hyman's father, one who looks like a neighbor, and even one who looks a lot like Trina. That dwarf plays with his hair, just like Trina does. Snow White is Hyman's daughter Katrin, and Snow White's stepmother—the Queen—is Hyman's friend Nancy. A scarf on a dresser is Nancy's. The Prince is Hyman's friend and fellow author, Jane Yolen's husband. "He is," says Hyman, "a gorgeous real man." When one critic called attention to the fact that the apple's seeds, as portrayed, were not as they were in real apples, Hyman replied that the apple was a magic apple.

When Hyman created the illustrations for *Sleeping Beauty* (Little, Brown, 1977), she made the illustrations a little softer and more romantic than her previous work. Anne Waggoner, Katrin's friend, was the model for Sleeping

Beauty. The monk pictured in the tale is Hyman herself, with no hair. The fairies include her editor, Helen Jones, and writer Gertrude Stein. The evil fairy is Michael Patrick Hearn, a children's book reviewer. The good fairy is the daughter of one of her editors at *Cricket* magazine. Katrin is shown sleeping on the queen's lap. Hyman shows the monk taking books to a publisher. When she and Barbara Rogasky created *Rapunzel* (Holiday House, 1982), a project that Hyman's sister suggested, Hyman used Barbara as the model for the Prince's image.

Little Red Riding Hood (Holiday House, 1983) features another self-portrait of Hyman. The woodcutter who rescued Little Red Riding Hood is modeled after Hyman's own father. Hyman recalls that when she was a four-year-old child, she really *was* Little Red Riding Hood. Her mother made her a red cape, and her dog Tiffy played the wolf. In her rendering of Little Red Riding Hood, Hyman spared the character the buckteeth that Hyman had as a young child. Her cat, Arthur, is shown in the illustrations. Hyman says that the cat thought he was a dog. Hyman sucked her thumb just as Little Red Riding Hood does, and her grandmother and mother were the "models" for the those characters in the book. The setting is Hyman's house in Vermont and shows her own kitchen table. The huntsman is based on her friend Hugh O'Donnell, an eighty-five-year-old retired real huntsman whose heritage was three quarters Irish and one quarter American Indian. Hyman loved his jacket and put it on him in the book. "Some," she said, "gave me flak about Grandmother drinking wine." But Hyman's retelling is consistent with the Grimm version so, "Little Red Riding Hood doesn't take Kool-Aid, she takes wine and bread." The story is set in New England at the turn of the century, although some reviewers have thought the story is set in Bavaria.

As a model for St. George, in *Saint George and the Dragon* (Little, Brown, 1985), Hyman used a man, George Todd, who she had known for years. He was an art student and a firefighter in Alaska during the summers. She thought his "rosy-cheeked, tow-headed Saxon coloring" was "just right for George." Borders are part of the illustrations in many of her books, and this one is no exception. The wildflowers shown are those that were on the English Isles in the fourth century. The king is a little like Sleeping Beauty's father.

Other participants include John Denver playing the guitar, her friend Barbara Rogasky, and Hyman's daughter Katrin.

Hyman not only slips in people from her circle of friends and family but she has been known to include images that satisfy her own impish whims. The ornately carved banquet table in *Sleeping Beauty* holds secrets too intimate to reveal.

After *Snow White* was published, it received a critical review from Virginia Kirkus, a well-known reviewer. The review bothered Hyman, and because she was working on the illustrations for a book by Jean Fritz, *Will You Sign Here, John Hancock?* (Coward-McCann, 1976) she slipped in a tombstone with a message for Virginia Kirkus. The message inscribed on the tombstone was "Virginia Kirkus, a nasty soul is its own reward." The inscription was spotted several months after the Fritz book was published. Subsequent printings of the book showed the tombstone without any inscription; the message had been airbrushed away.

About herself, Trina Schart Hyman has said, "I am a daydreamer and an accomplished liar (some people call it 'storyteller'). I am also bossy and cranky, and a joker. I like animals and children better than people, but I like trees the best. We live in an old farmhouse, and we have cats, dogs and sheep, and lots of gardens."

When her daughter Katrin graduated from college in 1985, she joined the Peace Corps and went to Cameroon, Africa, where she met and married an African prince. For several years, Katrin and her husband Eugène Tchana lived in Cameroon, and Hyman visited them there. She later illustrated Lloyd Alexander's *The Fortune Teller* (Dutton, 1992). It seemed to be a fortunate match because the story was that of a carpenter in the West African country of Cameroon. Hyman's trips to visit her daughter provided her with first-hand knowledge. Those visits also provided her with the background to illustrate a collection of "feminist folktales and fairy tales collected and retold by my daughter." That collection, *The Serpent Slayer and Other Stories of Strong Women* retold by Katrin Tchana (Little, Brown, 1999), was one of two books Hyman worked on concurrently. The other title was a book of poems written by John Updike, *A Child's Calendar* (Holiday House, 1999). She used her grandchildren Michou and Xavier as models for the children whose activities throughout the year are illustrated alongside Updike's poetry. For those illustrations, Hyman was honored in 2000 with a Caldecott Medal. In some past years, Hyman illustrated as many as seven books but "because of rheumatoid arthritis in my wrists and hands," she has slowed her work down considerably. "It has been an adjustment," she remarks.

Trina Schart Hyman was *Cricket* magazine's first art director and continued in that role until the publisher wanted her to move from New Hampshire to Illinois. She declined. She still draws for the magazine but is no longer its art director. Hyman still lives in her century-old home in Lyme, New Hampshire. Her daughter Katrin and her husband and their two children, Michou and Xavier, left Cameroon and now live only eight miles away in Thetford, Vermont, in what was Hyman's mother's house. Hyman says, "It's nice having them close by." Hyman's family includes her partner, Jean, and her daughter and her family, "plus Michael, John, Mary, Cyn, John, Brown, Penny, Neal, Jerry, Dean, Emily, Oscar, Merlyn, and Dave," who she says are "extras."

Hyman says she and her partner Jean like "taking walks and eating and cooking. We drink wine and play music and argue about books."

BOOKS AND NOTES

Trina Schart Hyman often uses borders to provide more information about the story line and to include details that otherwise might not have been included in the illustrations. She also includes many symbolic uses of the "magic numbers" of three and seven in her illustrations. She says she "love(s) cozy, intimate, everyday things: pussycats, kitchens, flowerpots, baskets of apples, the patterns and textures of homely, familiar things." She tries to put those things into her illustrations, along with grander things such as the "weather, light, seasons, trees, mountains, sun, moon, stars, and rain."

Books Illustrated by Trina Schart Hyman

The Adventures of Hershel of Ostropol. Retold by Eric A. Kimmel. (Holiday House, 1995).

Bearskin. Written by Howard Pyle. (Morrow, 1997).

A Child's Calendar. Written by John Updike. (Holiday House, 1999).

Comus. Written by Margaret Hodges from *Maszue in Ludlow Castle* by John Milton. (Holiday House, 1996).

Iron John. Adapted from the Brothers Grimm by Eric A. Kimmel. (Holiday House, 1994).

Rapunzel. Retold by Barbara Rogasky. (Holiday House, 1984).

Saint George and the Dragon. Retold by Margaret Hodges. (Little, Brown, 1985).

The Serpent Slayer and Other Stories of Strong Women. Retold by Katrin Tchana. (Little, Brown, 1999).

A Smile So Big. Written by Kathleen Abel. (Harcourt, 1998).

Snow White. Translated by Paul Heins. (Little, Brown, 1975).

Books Written and Illustrated by Trina Schart Hyman

The Alphabet Game (SeaStar, 2000).
    Originally published as *A Little Alphabet* by Little, Brown in 1980 and by Morrow in 1993.

Little Red Riding Hood (Holiday House, 1983).

Sleeping Beauty (Little, Brown, 1977).

FOR MORE INFORMATION

Articles

Brodie, Carolyn S. "Author! Author!: Trina Schart Hyman: Gifted Creator." *School Library Media Activities Monthly* 15, no. 5 (January 1, 1999): 43.

Evans, Dilys. "The Art of Trina Schart Hyman in *Comus* and *The Golem*." *Booklinks* 6, no. 4 (March 1, 1997): 27.

Raymond, Allen. "Trina Schart Hyman: Winner of the 1985 Caldecott Award." *Early Years K–8* (May 1985): 34–37.

Tony Johnston

◆ Historical Fiction ◆ Poetry

Los Angeles, California
January 10, 1942

📖 *The Adventures of Mole and Troll*
📖 *The Quilt Story*
📖 *The Wagon*

ABOUT THE AUTHOR

Tony Taylor was born on January 10, 1942, in Los Angeles, California. She was one of three daughters born to David Leslie and Ruth Hunter Taylor. Her given name is "Susan," but she says, "nobody knows it except doctors, lawyers, and Indian chiefs [she's part Cherokee]. I've always been Tony with a "y" to match the Taylor. My family is most alliterative. Some say I was named for a cowboy's, Tom Mix's, horse. Frankly, I hope it's true, for the West is one of my passions—its history, its people, its lore." Her two sisters were named (or nicknamed) Terry and Vicky. Terry became an artist, and Vicky has been a bilingual teacher in the Los Angeles schools since 1989.

Tony Taylor Johnston says that she has "written stories and poems since I can remember." In fourth grade, she and her best friend wrote a school play. Nonetheless, she thought she wanted to be a veterinarian, a "bugologist," or some other medical thing.

At the age of seventeen, Johnston entered college at the University of California at Berkeley and then transferred to Stanford University. In 1963, she earned her undergraduate degree, and the following year she earned an M.A. in elementary education. At Stanford, she met Roger Johnston, a banker, whom she married on June 25, 1966. For two years, she taught elementary school in Pasadena, California, and it was a fellow teacher who suggested that she write for children. "I'm grateful to her, for I can't think of a more challenging or rewarding profession."

Roger Johnston was transferred to New York, and the family moved to Brooklyn Heights in 1969. Tony Johnston secured a job in publishing, first at McGraw-Hill and then at Harper & Row, where she worked with the legendary children's book editor, Ursula Nordstrom. At first she was a "slush" reader, reading the unsolicited manuscripts that came into the publisher, and later she became the personal secretary to Nordstrom. In that capacity, she met several authors who would become icons in the field of children's books. "John Steptoe was in and out, working on his first book, *Stevie*. Anita and Arnold Lobel were there, and I remember [Maurice] Sendak coming in with his father to have lunch with Ursula." Johnston also became acquainted with Charlotte Zolotow, an editor at Harper's. Zolotow liked Johnston's story *Five Little Foxes*, but did not buy it for Harper's. Years later, in 1977, Putnam published it; nine years after that, Harper bought the paperback rights.

In 1971, the Johnstons moved to Mexico City, where they lived for the next fifteen years. Their three daughters, Jennifer (Jenny), Samantha (Sammy or Sam), and Ashley were born in Mexico and that is also where her success as a published author came to be. Her first books were published while she was living in Mexico. She wrote some stories in Spanish and had several commissioned by the Mexican government. She calls her experience there "a rich and wonderful experience in a rich and wonderful country." She says she feels so "close to Mexico that the only plants I have in the house are cacti and poinsettias." *The Adventures of Mole and Troll* (Putnam, 1972) was the first of several books about Mole and Troll. She has published several books that are set in Mexico or that have the flavor of the Southwest in the book's plot or setting. *My Mexico = Mexico Mio* (Putnam, 1996) is a book of poems translated from the Spanish by Johnston. It took more than six years to get the book published. It contains references to her interest in textiles and the countryside of Mexico. The inspiration for the poems came from her careful records and notes gathered about the history of the handwoven Indian belts that she and her husband collected while traveling around Mexico.

Another poetry title about Mexico is *I'm Gonna Tell Mama I Want an Iguana* (Putnam, 1990). *Lorenzo, the Naughty Parrot* (Harcourt, 1992) is another bilingual title set in Mexico. Her interest in education and her experience in

Mexico have made her aware of the "enormous need" for more bilingual books.

Johnston says she writes "because I can't do otherwise." She jokingly says that for the opposite reason, she rarely irons; she feels that if there were a big earthquake, someone would get crushed by the ironing pile.

Johnston's writing is going on in her head even when she is not at her desk. She says, "I think about stories and poems while in the market, on the freeway, or cooking. If the right words come to me, I just write them on myself and transpose them to paper when I get home, for I always forget my notebook." Her ideas are not "generated" but sometimes she feels "like a human mud pot. All the input of my life: people, books, conversations, views, animals, bugs, smells, *everything* is just gurgling around inside. From time to time, it shoots skyward in a spray of mud [story]." For that reason, she says people cannot invent stories, they come to them. One example is the manuscript for *The Witch's Hat* (Putnam, 1984). Johnston says, "One day I heard the words in my head, sat at my desk, and in 20 minutes, the final book was there!" Unfortunately, that never happened again. *Yonder* (Dial, 1988) took her seven years to write. That book is the most dear to her.

Examples of other stories that have come from her past experiences include the Mole and Troll stories. Tony and her sister, Terry, have wild, "naturally curly" hair—which she says is really a euphemism for frizzy. "In the story, *The Visit*, it is not Troll's hair frizzing all over in the rain, it is I kinking-up and fuming all over the place." *Mole and Troll Trim the Tree* (Putnam, 1974) highlights "the two Christmas-tree-decorating factions in my family—the Neats and the Messies." *Lorenzo the Naughty Parrot* (Harcourt, 1992) "protects" the house of a family—a Mexican family that actually made the Johnstons' pottery. Johnston's grandfather, a businessman-turned-rancher, once gave a calf to a boy. Later, the boy started a ranch of his own. That story is told in *The Promise* (Harper, 1992). Memories of a beautiful Christmas morning in New Hampshire, after a newly fallen snow, led her to write *Five Little Foxes and the Snow* (Putnam, 1977).

Johnston is an avid quilter and enjoys music, so her collaborations with Tomie dePaola, *The Quilt Story* (Putnam, 1985) and *Pages of Music* (Putnam, 1988), drew on that enjoyment. *Isabel's House of Butterflies* (Sierra Club, 1997) arose from her childhood desire to become a "bugologist." She collected everything that crawled or flew. She even raised monarch butterflies.

For much of her writing career, Tony Taylor says she has written on an Olympia portable typewriter—"the only one left in the world." She writes with a fountain pen and says she would "carry the sand to dry it if sand weren't so heavy." She describes herself as "pathetically old-fashioned." The number of cakes she has made from a package is few, and sometimes she writes with a pencil (a Dixon Ticondergoa #2 soft). She loves "the look, feel, and *smell* of a pencil, just poised there ready to say something."

The Johnstons are very close knit, and while the daughters were growing up, the family skied in the winter, read together at night, and had "sit-down dinners" whenever possible. They also took a trip to Spain. When it was time to go off to college, Stanford, the alma mater of both Roger Johnston and Tony Johnston, was Jenny's choice. All three daughters are now grown.

In addition to collecting hand-woven Indian belts—her husband has more than 500—the Johnstons also collect antique Mexican furniture and Indian trade beads. These are the beads the Spanish brought from the Old World especially to trade in the Americas. Tony also loves sports. She says she "is a basketball freak and a Lakers fan." Her list of things that she likes includes people, animals—especially owls—nature, books, state names spelled out, chocolate-chip cookies, music, and school. Johnston is both a teacher and a student. She has taught a course on picture-book writing at UCLA and once took a poetry writing from the late Myra Cohn Livingston.

As of 2000, Tony Johnston has published more than seventy-five books. She continues to write, juggling several book ideas in her head at one time. She and her husband still live in the house in San Marino, California, where they moved when they returned from their fifteen-year stay in Mexico. The home has a large, glass-walled family room where Johnston writes with her wire-haired dachshund, Suzi, nearby.

BOOKS AND NOTES

Tony Johnston's books are grounded in her own experiences and interests. Her love of Mexico and the Southwest is evident in many of her stories. Many of her books are pieces that touch on the history of a family or a group. *Yonder* helped to chronicle the traditions of one family who planted a plum tree in honor of the beginning of a marriage. Another tale, *Pages of Music*, tells the origin of a tradition on the island of Sardinia. Her more recent writing focuses on historical events. *The Wagon* (Tambourine, 1996) chronicles the journey of a young boy born into bondage and his journey to his day of liberation. *Trail of Tears* (Blue Sky, 1998) tells of the Cherokees and their forced march to leave their village, enduring suffering and death as they walked along the route that came to be known as the Trail of Tears.

The Adventures of Mole and Troll. Illustrated by Wallace Tripp. (Putnam, 1972).
The first of four titles about Mole and Troll, two good friends who share adventures: *Mole and Troll Trim the Tree* (Putnam, 1974); *Happy Birthday, Mole and Troll* (Putnam, 1979); *and Night Noises: And Other Mole and Troll Stories* (Putnam, 1977).

Bigfoot Cinderrrrrella. Illustrated by James Warhola. (Putnam, 1998).

Set in the old-growth forest and featuring Bigfoot characters.

The Cowboy and the Black-Eyed Pea. Illustrated by Warren Ludwig. (Putnam, 1992).

A western version of the classic Andersen tale, "The Princess and the Pea." The wealthy daughter of a Texas rancher devises a plan to find a real cowboy among her many suitors.

Day of the Dead. Illustrated by Jeannette Winter. (Harcourt, 1997).

A Mexican family celebrates the Day of the Dead (All-Souls Day).

Desert Song. Illustrated by Ed Young. (Sierra Club, 2000).

Nocturnal animals of the desert search for food.

How Many Miles to Jacksonville? Illustrated by Bart Forbes. (Putnam, 1995).

The narrator describes the excitement of having the train pull into the town of Jacksonville, Texas, when he was a boy.

I'm Gonna Tell Mama I Want an Iguana. Illustrated by Lillian Hoban. (Putnam, 1990).

Twenty-three humorous poems.

Isabel's House of Butterflies. Illustrated by Susan Guevara. (Sierra Club, 1997).

Eight-year-old Isabel hopes that her plan will spare her favorite tree, keep the butterflies coming, and provide an income for her poor family in Mexico.

It's About Dogs. Illustrated by Ted Rand. (Harcourt, 2000).

Poems about dogs.

My Mexico = Mexico Mio. Illustrated by F. John Sierra. (Putnam, 1996).

Poetry collected in Mexico, about Mexico.

Once in the Country: Poems of a Farm. Illustrated by Thomas B. Allen. (Putnam, 1996).

Poems celebrating life on a farm.

Pages of Music. Illustrated by Tomie dePaola. (Putnam, 1988).

A tradition that originated on the island of Sardinia involving a thick, hard bread called *foglio di musica*, or pages of music.

The Quilt Story. Illustrated by Tomie dePaola. (Putnam, 1985).

Gouache paintings reminiscent of the paintings on wood done by the early itinerant painters illustrate this story of a pioneer mother who lovingly stitches a beautiful quilt for her daughter Abigail; many years later, another mother mends and patches it for her little girl.

Sparky and Eddie: The First Day of School. Illustrated by Susannah Ryan. (Scholastic, 1997).

Even though they are not in the same class, two young friends are glad that they decided to give school a try.

Trail of Tears. Illustrated by Barry Moser. (Blue Sky, 1998).

The story of the forced journey of the Cherokee Indians from their homeland.

Uncle Rain Cloud. Illustrated by Fabricio Vanden Broeck. (Charlesbridge, 2000).

Carlos helps his uncle adjust to a new life in Los Angeles and to a new language.

The Vanishing Pumpkin. Illustrated by Tomie dePaola. (Putnam, 1983).

A 700-year-old woman and an 800-year-old man want to make a pumpkin pie but cannot find their pumpkin.

The Wagon. Illustrated by James E. Ransome. (Tambourine, 1996).

The life of a baby boy, born a slave, and his journey to freedom as an adult.

We Love the Dirt. Illustrated by Alexa Brandenberg. (Scholastic, 1997). Hello, Reader series.

The people, animals, and objects on the farm explain their relationship with the dirt, which is used and needed by all.

Whale Song. Illustrated by Ed Young. (Putnam, 1987).

An unusual counting book that gives much information about whales and their habits in the ocean.

Yonder. Illustrated by Lloyd Bloom. (Dial, 1988).

A young man plants a plum tree in honor of his marriage. The years pass, and the plum tree chronicles the family growth as well.

FOR MORE INFORMATION

Web Sites

Penguin Putnam Catalog Biography. "Tony Johnston." URL: <http://www.penguinputnam.com/catalog/yreader/authors/257_biography.html> (Accessed March 2000).

Ann Jonas

Sharron L. McElmeel

Flushing, New York
January 28, 1932

📖 *Round Trip*
📖 *The Trek*

ABOUT THE AUTHOR/ILLUSTRATOR

Ann Jonas grew up making and doing things, hoping to sell them; as a last resort, her family would buy the things she made. She was born in Flushing, New York, on January 28, 1932. Her father was a mechanical engineer, and her mother was an artist and homemaker. She and her brother shared many activities from skiing to cabinet making to repairing the family car. Her drawing began as an incidental skill—one she used when planning a project—rather than an end in and of itself.

Jonas graduated from high school and held several "dead-end jobs" before deciding that some specific training might be a good idea—maybe even necessary. It was then that she entered Cooper Union. She met Donald

Crews while both were students there. After her graduation from Cooper Union in 1959, Jonas went to work, until 1962, in the studio of her former graphic design instructor. She and Crews developed a relationship, so when he was inducted into the U.S. Army and sent to Germany, she followed him. She found work with a German advertising company, and the couple married on her birthday, January 28, 1963. Their first daughter, Nina, was born while the couple was still in Germany. After returning to the United States, Donald Crews and Ann Jonas opened their own freelance business in their New York apartment. Their second daughter, Amy, was born soon thereafter.

Jonas continued to work as a graphic designer and care for the girls. The Donald and Ann Crews Design Company flourished and occupied the time of both artists.

Soon, Donald Crews began creating children's books and working with Susan Hirschman at Greenwillow Books. Jonas did not even consider creating her own children's books until her daughters were almost ready for college, and then it was only through the urging of her husband that she met with Hirschman. In 1982, Jonas's first book, *When You Were a Baby* (Greenwillow), was published. For that book, Jonas drew on her memories of her children and their friends at ages two and three and the children's pride in their own accomplishments. Next came *Two Bear Cubs* (Greenwillow, 1982) and *Round Trip* (Greenwillow, 1983).

In creating her books, Jonas relies heavily on her awareness of drawings and graphics. Each of her books is unique. She illustrates to fit the text, first creating a storyboard in color, taking it to her editor, and then creating a full-sized book dummy, a rough draft, that she sends to her editor for final approval. Each final illustration is completed one at a time, starting with the lighter shades and building to the reds. That sequence is necessary because reds are very tricky to work with when using watercolor. As she creates shades and variations of colors, she saves the leftover paint combinations in case she needs them to do touch-ups at a later time.

Jonas's goal for each book is to entertain and to develop children's imaginations. She enjoys working with visual play and wants to create opportunities for children to look at things in a different way while offering the fun of a game or a puzzle. If deeper concerns come into play that is an additional benefit.

Jonas's experiences with her children have assisted in the development of her books. When her daughter Amy was little, she often peeked through what the family called "good holes." That play game resulted in her book

Holes and Peeks (Greenwillow, 1984). Daughter Nina figured into *The Quilt* (Greenwillow, 1984) when Jonas created a quilt for her using the scraps from other things she had made for her. Nina used to have dreams about the quilt. Sally, the dog, really did exist and grew to an old age.

Jonas thought it might be interesting to do a book from beginning to end and back again. While she was thinking about a circular story, she noticed that the shapes between skyscrapers mimicked the actual shapes of the buildings themselves. She took some pictures of the Manhattan skyline from the Brooklyn Bridge, and the drawings that resulted showed her some great possibilities. She began to look at landscaping books, even looking at them upside down, to get more ideas. As she worked with negative and positive space, the images began to make sense. The result was *Round Trip*. She used her graphic design experience and developed an idea for making a bridge out of telephone poles. She didn't turn the sketch over until she had done a lot of work. When she did turn it over, she realized that it was going to take a lot more work to accomplish what she wanted to show.

The Trek (Greenwillow, 1985) came about as Jonas looked at children's magazines that contained hidden animals. Her illustrations created a story in which a little girl and her friend were oblivious to the animals. She did not want to make the story frightening. In retrospect, she wishes she had made the animals a little more difficult to find.

Jonas often asks her husband for his professional opinion, and he asks the same of her. She lets her story ideas simmer in her head until she "gets things sorted out," and then she goes into her studio to work. Jonas says she "doesn't work well just sitting at the art table." When she is working on a book, however, she works in her studio for four to five hours a day. In a book's final stages, Jonas often works continuously for fourteen hours a day, seven days a week.

In 1976, the family purchased a brownstone in Brooklyn. The house needed a lot of fixing up and they wanted it done "just right." She worked in a light, airy studio on the second floor of their home while Crews worked in a third-floor studio. Jonas and Crews have since moved to a home in upstate New York in Germantown. Their daughters are grown, and Nina has become a children's book writer and illustrator. Both Donald Crews and Ann Jonas enjoy cooking and often prepare meals with produce from their garden. Their home is shared with a very large dog and a very tiny kitten.

BOOKS AND NOTES

Bold, graphic designs are characteristic of Ann Jonas's many books. The text is often simple and direct but with a bent toward dealing with more serious issues and concerns of young readers. Although her earlier books used graphic images more boldly, her more recent books incorporate her drawing and illustration background. She has only illustrated books which she has written.

Aardvarks, Disembark! (Greenwillow, 1990).
Noah calls a variety of little-known animals out of the ark. Many of the animals are endangered.

Birdtalk (Greenwillow, 1999).
Portrays many birds and their calls.

Color Dance (Greenwillow, 1989).
Three dancers show how primary colors create other colors.

The Quilt (Greenwillow, 1984).
A quilt provides memories and adventures at bedtime.

Reflections (Greenwillow, 1987).
A child's busy day at the sea, in the forest, and then back home is depicted with illustrations that show a different adventure when turned upside-down.

Round Trip (Greenwillow, 1983).
From the city to the country and back again.

Splash (Greenwillow, 1995).
A Turtle, fish, frogs, a dog, and a cat jump in and out of a backyard pond, providing an ever-changing answer to the question, "How many are in my pond?"

The 13th Clue (Greenwillow, 1992).
A little girl follows thirteen clues to find a surprise.

The Trek (Greenwillow, 1985).
A child's walk through the city streets on the way to school is filled with animals hiding behind telephone poles and in other unlikely spots.

Two Bear Cubs (Greenwillow, 1982).
Two wandering cubs are grateful to have their mom close by.

Watch William Walk (Greenwillow, 1997).
An alliterative walk is described as William and Wilma take Wally the dog and Wanda the duck on a walk.

When You Were a Baby (Greenwillow, 1982).
Youngsters are reminded of the things they could not do when they were babies.

Where Can It Be? (Greenwillow, 1986).
A treasured blanket is the object of a search behind closed doors (flaps that fold out on the page).

FOR MORE INFORMATION

Articles

Marantz, Sylvia, and Kenneth Marantz. "Interview with Ann Jonas." *Horn Book Magazine* (May/June 1987): 309–13.

Raymond, Allen. "Ann Jonas: Reflections 1987." *Teaching K–8* (November/December 1987): 44–46.

Keiko Kasza

◆ Animals ◆ Family Relationships

Jerry Mitchell

Hiroshima-ken, Japan
December 23, 1951

📖 *A Mother for Choco*
📖 *When the Elephant Walks*
📖 *The Wolf's Chicken Stew*

ABOUT THE AUTHOR/ILLUSTRATOR

Keiko Kasza was born in Japan on the small island of Hiroshima-ken and grew up there in a typical Japanese family—an extended family that included her parents, two brothers, and grandparents. Uncles, aunts, and cousins lived nearby. She says her childhood years "were very normal." In her late teens, she came to the United States to obtain a degree in graphic design from California State University at Northridge. After college, she worked as a graphic designer for about ten years. She married an American, Gregory Kasza. Shortly after they married, Gregory's work took the family to Ecuador for a year. Keiko Kasza was unable to work there, but during that time, she came across *Frederick,* a picture book by Leo Lionni. The book impressed her so much that she decided to use her spare time to create a book of her own. At this point, the pursuit was just a hobby. The hobby became considerably more serious when her first book, *Omu no Itazura* (The Parrot's Trick), was published in Japan in 1981.

When the Kaszas' first son was born in 1986, Keiko did not have time to work as a graphic designer and create picture books at the same time. She had to decide to do one or the other. Her choice was to create children's books.

Kasza came to admire the great picture-book creators, such as Lionni and Maurice Sendak, but says, "the work of Arnold Lobel has influenced me the most." The subtle humor and warmth he created in his books inspires her. She often looks at Lobel's work when she gets discouraged and needs to build her own confidence.

In 1987, her first book, *The Wolf's Chicken Stew* (Putnam), was published in the United States. The clever and sly wolf spies a hen who will make a delicious meal, but he reasons that if the hen were fattened up, she would make more stew for him. So he sets out to do just that, but the results are not quite what the wolf expected. That book was followed by *The Pigs' Picnic* (Putnam, 1988) and *When the Elephant Walks* (Putnam, 1990). In *The Pigs' Picnic*, Mr. Pig, wishing to convince Miss Pig to accompany him on a picnic, picks a flower to give her. Along the way, he accepts other gifts for her from his friends, Fox, Lion, and Zebra. All the borrowed items make Mr. Pig seem like a monster when he arrives at her door. She threatens to call her friend Mr. Pig if the monster doesn't go away. *When the Elephant Walks* is a cumulative tale that has the elephant scaring the bear, who runs away and scares the crocodile who swims for his life; the crocodile scares a wild hog, and eventually a mouse runs away and scares the elephant who runs making the tale go full circle.

Each of her books tends to have a societal message for readers, but the story comes first, followed by a subtle moral. *A Mother for Choco* (Putnam, 1992) tells of Choco's search for a mother. In 1997–1998, a CD-ROM was created for this story. The impressive list of cast members includes Mary Tyler Moore, Paula Poundstone, Lily Thomlin, and Bea Arthur.

One day when Kasza was looking at one of her son's animal books, she read that possums have a strange behavior: playing dead. That bit of information helped her come up with the idea for *Don't Laugh, Joe* (Putnam, 1997). She says, "What a wonderful idea for a picture book! I created Joe, the possum, his mother and the bear immediately. Then I had to come up with Joe's friends to make the last punch line successful." When she created those friends, however, she had to make sure that none of them ate bugs!

Friendship was the theme for her book *Dorothy and Mikey* (Putnam, 2000). In this book, Kasza tells three stories of the two friends who play and compete with one another.

Kasza's books have been published in Spanish, Chinese, French, German, Japanese, Korean, Danish, and Dutch. Her illustrations are created with watercolors. She is striving to create not 100 books but "one really good book that will be kept on the family bookshelves for generations." She does acknowledge, however, that creating 100 "really good books" would be even better.

Keiko Kasza lives in Bloomington, Indiana with her family. Her husband teaches Japanese politics at Indiana University. When their two sons were preschoolers, Keiko took the boys to a day-care center and then returned home to reenergize herself with some strong coffee and to work from about 10:30 A.M. to 4:30 P.M. on her books. These days, however, their two sons are in school, so she writes during the school day. As a family, the Kaszas follow the Indiana University basketball team. Kasza enjoys playing tennis, even though, she says, "I'm not a great player." Every three years or so, the family goes to Japan and lives there for a year. The Kaszas feel that it is important for their sons to learn Japanese, but going back and forth is increasingly more difficult on the children as they get older.

Whenever Keiko gets bogged down on a difficult illustration, she says she "fantasize(s) about starting a restaurant." She says she is a "great cook" as long as she stays away from pastries.

BOOKS AND NOTES

Keiko Kasza has written and illustrated several books, just right for the primary-aged reader. She is equally as proficient at writing as she is at illustrating. The illustrations are created with bright watercolors and simple, realistic drawings. Each of the books has an underlying ethical theme and contains subtle humor to tickle the fancy of readers of any age.

Don't Laugh, Joe (Putnam, 1997).
Mother Possum is frustrated when her son cannot learn to play dead without laughing.

Dorothy and Mikey (Putnam, 2000).
Three stories about two friends: Dorothy and Mikey.

Grandpa Toad's Last Secret (Putnam, 1995).
The secrets of survival are the topic of Grandpa's lessons, but it is Little Toad who saves the day when a huge monster attacks them.

A Mother for Choco (Putnam, 1992).

In search of a mother, Choco finally finds someone who will care for her.

The Pigs' Picnic (Putnam, 1988).

Mr. Pig is going to ask Miss Pig to go to a picnic with him but when he shows up he is carrying handsome portions of some of his friends own bodies. He looks like a monster to her, and she threatens to call her friend Mr. Pig if he doesn't leave.

The Rat and the Tiger (Putnam, 1993).

Rat and Tiger are friends, but Tiger uses his size to bully Rat until Rat learns to stand up for himself.

When the Elephant Walks (Putnam, 1990).

The elephant scares the bear, and the bear scares the crocodile, who scares the wild hog . . . and finally mouse runs away and scares elephant. A cumulative circular tale.

The Wolf's Chicken Stew (Putnam, 1987).

A hungry wolf wants to fatten up a hen for his stew pot, but the results aren't quite what he expects.

FOR MORE INFORMATION

Web Sites

Penguin Putnam Catalog Biography: Keiko Kasza. URL: <http://www.penguinputnam.com/catalog/yreader/authors/582_biography.html> (Accessed March 2000).

Ezra Jack Keats

Brooklyn, New York
March 11, 1916–May 6, 1983

📖 *A Letter to Amy*
📖 *Peter's Chair*
📖 *The Snowy Day*

ABOUT THE AUTHOR/ILLUSTRATOR

Ezra Jack Keats was born Jacob Ezra Katz on March 11, 1916, the son of Polish immigrants, Benjamin Katz and Augusta Podgainy Katz. His parents were both born in Warsaw, Poland but did not meet until they emigrated to the United States. As was Polish custom, their marriage was arranged. They made their home in the Jewish section of Brooklyn, where the family lived in a two-family home at 438 Vermont Street.

Ezra was the couple's third child. He attended junior high school during the Depression. After finishing his homework, he did the household errands and often returned home with messages about unpaid bills—the messages were painful and humiliating. The household was filled with defeat. His parents' marriage, according to Keats's writings, was "bitter and unhappy." His artwork and the public library was his refuge.

Keats lived his entire life in the New York area and views of the graffiti on the streets of New York often show up in his books. The storefronts, street signs, and street art were all part of the neighborhood scenes. He became an artist when he was four years old. As he grew older, the children of the neighborhood followed him and begged him to tell them a story. One of his childhood friends was Martin Pope; together they would spend hours in the Arlington Branch of the Brooklyn Public Library. Art books intrigued Keats, but Pope explored the science books.

Keats's mother encouraged his interest in art, but his father thought his son would starve. His father worked at Pete's Coffee Shop in Greenwich Village, and he knew how hard earning a living could be. He did buy tubes of paint for his son but then told him that some starving artist had traded the tube of paint for a bowl of soup. On the day before Ezra graduated from high school in January 1935, his father died. Ezra had to identify his father's body. That was the day he realized how proud his father was of his artistic talent, for there in his wallet were worn and tattered newspaper clippings about the awards Ezra had received.

Keats was awarded three scholarships to art school but was needed at home to help support his family. By day he worked, and by night he attended art school. In 1937, he went to work for the Works Progress Administration (WPA) as a muralist. After three years, he was able to get a job as a comic-book illustrator. He moved to Fawcett Publications in 1942 to illustrate the backgrounds for the Captain Marvel comic strips.

The following year, he joined the U.S. Air Corps where he designed camouflage patterns. After two years, he was honorably discharged, and for a time he had health problems and suffered from depression. Shortly after World War II, Jacob Ezra Katz legally changed his name to Ezra Jack Keats—a reaction, most likely, to the anti-Semitic prejudices of the times.

In 1954, Keats illustrated a children's book, and over the next eleven years he illustrated fifty-four more. In 1960, he authored his first book, *My Dog Is Lost!* (Crowell, 1960; Viking, 1999). The main character was a Puerto Rican boy who lost his dog. Over the years, Keats became quite well known. In 1967, he was the Empress of Iran's guest of honor at the International Film Festival in Teheran. Seven years later, he was the guest of honor at the opening of a children's roller-skating rink in Tokyo, Japan. The rink has a plaque bearing his name and was the result of the enthusiasm generated by his book *Skates!* (Watts, 1973).

Keats's books have been translated into sixteen languages. Believing in the universality of characters, he felt that whether a character was black or white did not matter. In his 1963 Caldecott-Medal-winning title, *The Snowy*

Day (Viking, 1962), Peter is black, as are the characters in several of his books. Long before Keats thought about creating books for children, he clipped a series of photographs from a magazine. The photographs were of a black child. He tacked the pictures on the wall. After awhile, he forgot why he had saved the pictures, but he did like the images of the little boy, and the pictures remained on his bulletin board. Twenty-two years later, those photographs became the inspiration for the illustrations for *The Snowy Day*. Keats had been illustrating other people's books for ten years, and there had never been a black child as a hero in any of those books. So, when he felt confident enough to do his own book, he resolved that his book's hero would be black. Peter was the result, and the character later appeared in six other titles: *Whistle for Willie* (Viking, 1964), *Peter's Chair* (Harper, 1967), *A Letter to Amy* (Harper, 1968), *Goggles!* (Macmillan, 1969), *Hi, Cat!* (Macmillan, 1970), and *Pet Show!* (Macmillan, 1972).

Keats was noted for his illustrations, which represent an acute ability to observe, and for his technique of combining paint and collage with a mixture of textures and brilliant colors. The backgrounds of many of his illustrations were made of marbleized paper, which he made with floating oil paints on water. He swirled the paints to create the marbleized effect and then laid a piece of paper on the surface of the water to pick up the colors from the water. Once the paper was dry, it became the background paper or, in some cases, the paper used for some of the collage pieces. Most of his collages were created with objects and shapes cut from wallpaper, painted paper, or solid colors to emphasize the form.

The story line for *The Snowy Day* came to Keats one day while he was at a friend's house. It was snowing, and they were talking about the things they had done in the snow as children. The memories brought back the profound effect the shear joy of it all had on him. He resolved to write a book about fun in the snow.

In 1980, seventeen years after winning the Caldecott Medal, Keats was awarded the University of Southern Mississippi Medallion for the body of his work. A majority of Keats's papers relating to his work was donated to the de Grummond collection at the university. His friend, Dr. Martin Pope, a professor emeritus of chemistry at New York University, is the president of the Ezra Jack Keats Foundation, which was established after Keats's death in 1983.

Keats filled his studio walls with illustrations for new books so that he could see the sequence of his pictures. He got many letters and pictures from admirers of his books, and he kept many of those letters and pictures. He had a special admiration for the way children saw their environment and used that view to create the shapes, colors, and moods of his stories. For many years, Ezra Jack Keats lived in his New York apartment at 444 East 82nd Street. He never married, nor did he have children, but when he died of a heart attack on May 6, 1983, his children's books became his legacy. His books have been translated into sixteen languages and are read by children all over the world.

BOOKS AND NOTES

Ezra Jack Keats focused his books on the everyday events that occur in an urban environment. His illustrations were created with collages made of wallpaper and other colorful papers.

Apt. 3 (Macmillan, 1971).

Dreams (Macmillan, 1974).

Goggles! (Macmillan, 1969).

Hi, Cat! (Macmillan, 1970).

Jennie's Hat (Harper, 1966).

John Henry: An American Legend (Pantheon, 1965).

A Letter to Amy (Harper, 1968).

Louie (Greenwillow, 1975).

Louie's Search (Four Winds, 1980).

Maggie and the Pirate (Four Winds, 1979).

Pet Show! (Macmillan, 1972).

Peter's Chair (Harper, 1967).

Skates! (Watts, 1973).

The Trip (Greenwillow, 1978).

Whistle for Willie (Viking, 1964).

FOR MORE INFORMATION

Articles

Cohl, Claudia. "Keen on Keats." *Teacher* (November 1974): 45–47.

Keats, Ezra Jack. "Dear Mr. Keats . . . " *Horn Book* (June 1972): 306–10.

Keats, Ezra Jack. "Ezra Jack Keats Remembers: Discovering the Library." *Teacher* (December 1976): 40–41.

Books

Alderson, Brian. *Ezra Jack Keats: Artist and Picture-Book Maker* (Pelican, 1994).

Engel, Dean and Florence Freedman. *Ezra Jack Keats: A Biography with Illustrations* (Silver Moon, 1995).

Web Sites

University of Southern Mississippi—de Grummond Collection. "Keats Biography." URL: <http://www.lib.usm.edu/~degrum/Keats/biography.html> (Accessed March 2000).

Steven Kellogg

◆ Animals ◆ Folklore

Norwalk, Connecticut
October 26, 1941

📖 *The Island of the Skog*
📖 *Pinkerton, Behave!*
📖 *The Three Little Pigs*

ABOUT THE
AUTHOR/ILLUSTRATOR

Shortly after graduating from Rhode Island School of Design in 1963, Steven Kellogg began work on two picture-book manuscripts. Those two books were eventually published by Dial—*The Orchard Cat* in 1972 and *The Island of the Skog* in 1973. As a young boy, Steven Kellogg told "stories on paper" to his sisters, Patti and Martha. With one of them on either side, Kellogg would sit with a drawing pad in his lap and fabricate a story while busily telling the story that he was drawing. For more than twenty-five years, *The Island of the Skog* was the story he "told on paper" most often when he visited schools and libraries. He says that he "has done programs in schools in every one of the fifty states."

After he finished school, attended art school, and developed an art portfolio, he began to work in the field of children's books. In 1998, he said "Even after thirty years and ninety books, I still find the complex process by which an idea for a story evolves into tens of thousands of published copies is as magical as it seemed when my very first book came together."

Steven Kellogg was born on October 26, 1941, in Norwalk, Connecticut, to Robert and Hilma Kellogg. Steven credits his grandmother as the major influence on his decision to become an artist. His grandmother told him stories of her childhood from the late-nineteeth century. She also instilled in him a love for the flowers and animals that lived in the New England woods. Even now, he says he is surprised by how frequently images from the time shared with his grandmother show up in his illustrations. Her surroundings were filled with momentos, and Kellogg learned to fill his surroundings with momentos of his interests, too, especially moments of drawing and sketching.

As an elementary student, he loved drawing and often drew animals and birds. He tacked sketches from floor to ceiling in his bedroom. His interest continued through high school, and he earned the Pitney-Bowes Scholarship to the Rhode Island School of Design. He received a fellowship to study in Florence, Italy, during his senior year. When he returned, he entered graduate school at American University and began to exhibit his etchings and paintings in the Washington, D.C., area. He also submitted illustrated manuscripts to editors in New York City. In 1966, he was given his first job, illustrating George Mendoza's *Gwot!* (Dial, 1967).

While he was in the Washington area, he met Helen Hill at American University, and they married in 1967. Soon, the couple, along with her six picture-book-age children, moved back to Connecticut where Kellogg devoted himself to the writing and illustrating of children's books. He wrote and illustrated his own books and accepted illustrating jobs for books written by other authors. In 1976, *Steven Kellogg's Yankee Doodle* was published by Parents Magazine Press. The illustrations depicted the stanzas of the early Yankee song and some additional stanzas created by a Harvard College student, who served as a minuteman at Lexington. That same year, Kellogg wrote about the siblings Henry (the bigger, older, and wiser brother) and Martin in a book titled *Much Bigger Than Martin* (Dial, 1976). Many of his earlier books have become classics. His five books about Pinkerton, the Harlequin Great Dane, have brought laughter to many young readers. Many of his books deal with family relationships and antics involving pets in the household.

Although he enjoys creating his own books he says, "sometimes another person's story can be more fun to illustrate than my own." Margaret Mahy's *The Boy Who Was Followed Home* (F. Watts, 1975), a book he illustrated, is definitely one of his favorites. The following year his alliterative adventure, *Aster Aardvark's Alphabet Adventures* (Dial, 1987) made its appearance. Aster Aardvark's aversion to the alphabet literally appalls those at Acorn Acres Academy, who alert Aster's Aunt Agnes. Bertha Bear and her Brooklyn buddies, Canadian conductor Cyril Capon, Dr. Delphius Dog and his dozen disciples, and other alphabetical characters show off their antics via Kellogg's exuberant and rollicking illustrations taking readers from A to Z.

As he did in his bedroom years earlier, he now fills every corner of the pages of his books with details of clever additions to the central action. Unusual color combinations and many lines fill the space with a festival of activity. Some of Kellogg's books evoke comments about the sexist roles played by the characters. For example, in *Can I Keep Him?* (Dial, 1971), a story about Arnold's desire to turn every animal he meets into the family pet, Arnold's mother is depicted cleaning toilets and putting away groceries while imagining what havoc each pet would bring to the home. Meanwhile, Arnold's father seems to be indifferent to the situation. Kellogg's role models, however, seem to be evenly distributed. He features a strong female leader in *The Island of the Skog*, and in *Steven Kellogg's Yankee Doodle*, he actually changed a line to avoid the appearance of sexism. In *Won't Somebody Play With Me?* (Dial, 1972), Kim goes from one friend's home to another; finding no one to play with, she imagines all the things she could be pretending with them. The illustrations show her fantasies of becoming a famous general, superwoman, a doctor, and the owner of Kim's Construction Company, Inc. But right then, she just wants someone to play with her, and no one seems to be interested. So she returns to her home to find all of her friends and a surprise birthday party waiting for her.

Kellogg's illustrations are filled with images that depict a clear delight with animals of all types, as well as delight in the impish antics of young boys and girls. As a child, he admired the work of Beatrix Potter and N. C. Wyeth. He says, "I always found every kind of animal story irresistible."

Many of his recent books have been retellings of tales involving American tall-tale heroes. Stories of Paul Bunyan and Johnny Appleseed fill the reader with images of early days in America. A traditional 100-year-old song game, "A-Hunting We Will Go," was transformed into a playful bedtime game when Kellogg created, *A-Hunting We Will Go* (Dial, 1998), a story of two children and their wanderings into a fantasy wilderness where their "managerie of stuffed animals are routed one by one from imaginary hiding places. The pace quickens and builds to a high point, and then tapers off in a, cozy good-night ritual."

Throughout his career as a children's book artist, Kellogg and his family have lived in a vintage farmhouse buffered from housing developments by twenty acres of wooded land. The Kellogg home was originally built in 1742 and set in the woods near the geographic center of Connecticut. The house is filled, much as his grandmother's was, with early American antiques, four-poster beds, rockers, and old-fashioned desks. The home includes an addition that was built in the 1940s. The addition was made from materials salvaged, board by board, from a Massachusetts tavern built in 1720. The tavern was carefully torn down and trucked to the home in Connecticut. The three-story home once had six bedrooms on the second floor and two on the third floor. Eventually, the third floor became Kellogg's studio, where he has created the illustrations for many of the ninety or more books he has worked on, thirty of which he has written or retold.

In 1987, the Kelloggs built a new studio, which became the center of Steven's illustrative and writing endeavors. The building project was described as "chaotic, but exciting."

Steven Kellogg has been visiting schools and libraries for more than three decades, and others have written a great deal about his life. Several years ago, two reference books incorrectly listed Kellogg's birthday as October 6. While other sources do have the birthday correctly listed as October 26, there is enough confusion that he enjoys receiving birthday cards from readers throughout the month of October—from the 6th to the 26th. Most of Kellogg's early books have been dedicated to one of his six stepchildren: Pam, Melanie, Laurie, Kim, Kevin, and Colin. In recent years, dedications have included the names of his grandchildren. It was two of his granddaughters who inspired Best Friends (Dial, 1986). It is not difficult to imagine that many of the scenes in his books involving children and animals have been reflective of events in the Kellogg household which, in addition to the six children, has included several dogs and cats over the years and more recently, eight grandchildren. All of the children are now grown, and the grandchildren are reaching adulthood. Kellogg says, "When I am not working on picture books, I enjoy visiting schools and libraries. I've met many wonderful people in my travels. I also like to spend time hiking, reading, listening to music, and being with my family and friends."

BOOKS AND NOTES

Characteristic of Steven Kellogg's books are the illustrations that lead the reader into his story before the text actually begins. The end papers, dedication page, and half and full title pages usually contain illustrations that foreshadow or begin the action. Kellogg utilizes the final pages in much the same way, using the available space to add yet another twist to the story through his detailed, intricate drawings. For example, in *Pinkerton, Behave!* (Dial, 1979), the pages before the story actually begins show a young girl and her mother visiting a pet store to choose and purchase the Great Dane that becomes Pinkerton in the book. Margaret Mahy's *The Boy Who Was Followed Home* (F. Watts, 1975) is the story of a young boy plagued by the increasing number of hippopotami that follow him home from school each day. Once that is cured, everything seems to be just fine. Unfortunately, the final illustration shows that he is then plagued by giraffes. Readers can only imagine that the giraffes might be the "side effects" that were mentioned in the discussion of the cure involving the hippos.

Observant readers can often find humorous details in Kellogg's tales. Pinkerton, the star of five of his own books, can often be found in other tales. The many details of Kellogg's illustrations provide something new each time one reads the book. No detail is too small. The labels on tiny food cans and titles of the miniature books in *The Island of the Skog* are fun to read and appropriate to the theme of the tale itself. The humor in his illustrations is both subtle and sophisticated yet basic, a combination that holds the interest of adults and children alike. The artwork for each book is generally prepared in full-color using ink and pencil lines and watercolor washes. The artwork is then color separated and reproduced as red, blue, yellow, and black halftones.

Books Written and Illustrated by Steven Kellogg

Best Friends (Dial, 1986).
Kathy and Louise share everything until Louise goes away on a summer vacation to the mountains.

Can I Keep Him? (Dial, 1971).
Arnold is an animal lover, but his mother is not necessarily interested in having an animal in the house.

Chicken Little (Morrow, 1985).
A wacky version of the classic Chicken Little, Chicken Licken, and Henny Penny tales.

Give the Dog a Bone (SeaStar, 2000).
A variation on a classic tale.

The Island of the Skog (Dial, 1973).
Frustrated by the dangers of urban life, Jenny—a mouse—leads her fellow Rowdies to the sea, and they sail out to find a peaceful place to live.

Jack and the Beanstalk (Morrow, 1991).
Kellogg's own version of the events surrounding Jack's climb to the giant's home in the sky.

Johnny Appleseed (Morrow, 1988).
Includes some of the traditional lore surrounding this legendary hero while including Kellogg's twists on this favorite tall tale.

The Missing Mitten Mystery (Dial, 2000).
A new version of a story about Annie and her search through the neighborhood for her lost mitten—the fifth this winter. Original version was published as *The Mystery of the Missing Mitten* (Dial, 1974).

Much Bigger Than Martin (Dial, 1976).
A classic tale of sibling rivalry, focusing on the younger brother's envy of the status of his older, wiser, bigger brother, Martin.

The Mysterious Tadpole (Dial, 1977).

Imagine a special gift from a favorite old Scottish uncle. When the tadpole begins to develop into something mysterious, Louis begins to think Uncle McAllister's birthday gift may be more than a soon-to-be frog.

Pinkerton, Behave! (Dial, 1979).

Pinkerton, the Great Dane, has obedience problems with humorous results.

A Rose for Pinkerton (Dial, 1981).

Great Danes and kittens are quite different in size and character—and this book shows just how different.

Sally Ann Thunder Ann Whirlwind Crockett: A Tall Tale (Morrow, 1995).

Sally Ann is Davy Crockett's wife, and she is not scared of anyone or anything, including Mike Fink, who tries to intimidate her.

The Three Little Pigs (Dial, 1997).

Serafina Sow opens her own waffle-selling business to prepare her three offspring for the future, which includes an encounter with a surly wolf.

The Three Sillies (Candlewick, 1999).

A variation of *The Three Sillies* by Joseph Jacobs.

Books Illustrated by Steven Kellogg

A Beasty Story. Written by Bill Martin Jr. (SilverWhistle, 1999).

A, My Name Is Alice. Written by Jane Bayer. (Dial, 1984).

An alphabet book that combines a parade of feathered and furry animals and a ball bouncing rhyme.

The Boy Who Was Followed Home. Written by Margaret Mahy. (F. Watts, 1975).

Forty-three hippopotami follow a boy home. He tries everything to get the hippos off the lawn and out of the family's life. Nothing works until a woman with special powers produces a pill that will get rid of the hippos—but not without side effects.

The Day Jimmy's Boa Ate the Wash. Written by Trinka Hakes Noble. (Dial, 1980).

Somehow, Jimmy manages to take his pet boa constrictor on a class field trip to the farm. The boa creates havoc everywhere.

Frogs Jump: A Counting Book. Written by Alan Brooks. (Scholastic, 1996).

A book that counts from one frog to twelve whales.

Jimmy's Boa Bounces Back. Written by Trinka Hakes Noble. (Dial, 1984).

The snake is concerned that he might be made into snake steaks, so he leaves the farm with hilarious results.

Library Lil. Written by Suzanne Williams. (Dial, 1996).

A formidable librarian creates readers from resistant residents of her small town.

Parents in the Pigpen, Pigs in the Tub. Written by Amy Ehrlich. (Dial, 1993).

When the farm animals decide to move into the house, the family moves out to the barn.

The Rattlebang Picnic. Written by Margaret Mahy. (Dial, 1994).

The McTavishes, their seven children, and Granny McTavish set off in their rattlebang car for an adventure and a picnic on Mt. Fogg.

Snuffles and Snouts. Poems selected by Laura Robb. (Dial, 1995).

Pig poems are enhanced with Kellogg's zany depictions.

Yankee Doodle. Written by Edward Bangs. (Simon & Schuster, 1990).

Originally published as *Steven Kellogg's Yankee Doodle* by Parents Magazine Press in 1976; an illustrated version of a minuteman's song.

FOR MORE INFORMATION

Articles

Elleman, Barbara. "The Booklist Interview: Steven Kellogg." *Booklist* 85, no. 18 (May 15, 1989): 1640–41.

Kellogg, Steven. "Colleagues and Co-Conspirators: The Author-Illustrator Describes the Collaboration Essential in Bringing Books to Life for Young Readers." *The Horn Book Magazine* 66, no. 6 (November 1, 1990): 704.

Kellogg, Steven. "Thoughts Upon Slicing the 'Regina Pie'." *The Catholic World Library* 61, no. 1 (July 1, 1989): 21.

Videos

Trumpet Video Visits Steven Kellogg (Trumpet, 1993). 17 mins.

Web Sites

The Scoop. "Steven Kellogg Biographical Sketch." URL: <http://www.friend.ly.net/scoop/biographies/kelloggsteven/index.html> (Accessed March 2000).

Eric A. Kimmel

◆ Folklore ◆ Jewish Tradition and Culture

Brooklyn, New York
October 30, 1946

📖 *Anansi and the Talking Melon*

📖 *Hershel and the Hanukkah Goblins*

📖 *Onions and Garlic: An Old Tale*

ABOUT THE AUTHOR

Eric A. Kimmel grew up in Brooklyn, New York, the city where he was born on October 30, 1946, to Morris Kimmel and Anne Kerker Kimmel. His family included a younger brother, Jonathan. Their family enjoyed stories, especially those that Kimmel's grandmother told, which were Eastern European legends. Kimmel says, "I liked my father's stories, too, about growing up in a family of seven children in a tenement on Kosciusko Street in the 1920s. It was only when I was an adult and talked to my aunts and uncles [that] I realized . . . my father's childhood was actually pretty grim. It sounded like fun though. Playing baseball in a vacant lot, climbing up steel girders to the elevated subway platform to avoid paying the nickel fare, going to silent movies. Quite a different world than the world I knew."

Kimmel attended P.S. 193, where the children sang, "One ninety-three, one ninety-three, we hope the H bomb drops on thee." Kimmel says, "I had two wonderful teachers, Mrs. McGroarty in the first grade and Mrs. Miles in the third, who not only taught me how to read but taught me to love reading." Kimmel says he read "voraciously." His favorite books included Bible stories and stories by the Grimm brothers, *Treasure Island*, *Gulliver's Travels*, and anything by Dr. Seuss. As he got older, he turned to *Captains Courageous*, *Beau Geste*, *Captain Blood*, and two "weird and wonderful" books by H. Rider Haggard, *King Solomon's Mines* and *She*.

Kimmel attended J.H.S. 240, also known as Andries Hudde Junior High School, named after a notorious pirate. Kimmel believes that the school might be the only one in the United States named after a pirate. Hudde gained the favor of the English, who ruled America at the time, by attacking Spanish ships in the Caribbean during England's wars with Spain. As a reward, the governor of New York gave Hudde a land grant, where most of the neighborhood (and the school) stand today.

The high school Kimmel attended, Midwood, was located right across the street from Brooklyn College. By the time he was ready for college, however, he wanted to see what was beyond the Hudson River, so he went to school in Pennsylvania and has been "working my way west every since."

Kimmel said, "I grew up in the fifties in Brooklyn, New York, and attended the city's public schools, which were excellent. I don't believe a system like that exists anywhere today." From sixth grade on, Kimmel and his friends often used the subway system. "New York City was an exciting place to grow up in. For fifteen cents, you could ride the subway. It would take you anywhere." On a typical Saturday, the friends might go to the Museum of Natural History and the Hayden Planetarium, then down to Times Square or Greenwich Village to see what was happening, with a stop at the Prospect Park Zoo and the Botanical Gardens on the way home. Along the way, they might stop to eat huge delicatessen sandwiches, onion boards, pizza, or Chinese food, washed down with unique New York concoctions such as malteds, frappes, or egg creams.

Later, Kimmel and a friend, Danny Feld, volunteered one summer to work for the Democratic Party during a campaign for mayor. They also worked for the Republicans in the mornings; their job was to spy on them and to report back to the Democrats in the afternoon. Both campaign offices fed them lunch, so the two of them gained ten pounds that summer.

In the 1960s, the Vietnam War was looming, and young men were drafted into the service. Kimmel hated war and heard that teachers were not being drafted, so he decided to become a teacher. He taught in Harlem for a year and recalls that that was where he was when Martin Luther King Jr. was assassinated. In 1968, he saw the riots and strikes that resulted. Later, he taught in a school in St. Thomas, Virgin Islands. For more than three decades, he was involved in teaching in one way or another. After the Virgin Islands, Kimmel ended up in Oregon, "which," says Kimmel, "is as far as you can get from New York without a passport."

Kimmel was a storyteller long before he was a writer. His writing career began in 1969, but writing success did not come until 1986 when Holiday House agreed to publish *Hershel and the Hanukkah Goblins* (Holiday House, 1989). The story had been written several years earlier but was rejected so many times that Kimmel gave up on it and put it back in his files.

Then Marianne Carus of *Cricket* Magazine called. Isaac Basheveis Singer had agreed to write a Hanukkah story for their magazine but now could not meet the commitment. Carus wanted to know if Kimmel had a Hanukkah story that they might use for their December 1985 issue. He did. He decided that he would send her "Hershel and the Hanukkah Goblins," and if she did not like it, he would still have time to write another story. Carus did like the story, and the magazine's art director, Trina Schart Hyman, illustrated it for the magazine. The story caught the attention of Margery Cuyler, who decided that she wanted Holiday House to make the story into a picture book. Trina Schart Hyman also wanted a chance to fully illustrate the story as a picture book. Hyman's illustrations for the book garnered her a Caldecott Honor Award in 1990. That brought success to Kimmel as well.

Hyman is just one of the wonderful artists who have illustrated Kimmel's books; Janet Stevens, Giora Carmi, and Glen Rounds have also contributed their talents to his work. As a rule, the illustrator works for the publisher, so Kimmel is not able to direct the artist, or even suggest what the illustrations should be like. Ju-Hong Chen, who created the illustrations for Kimmel's *Aladdin and the Magic Lamp* (Holiday House, 1992), lived in Oregon, not far from Kimmel's home. However, during the time the illustrations were being prepared by Chen, Kimmel said, "I know [the illustrations] are going to be splendid, yet even though Ju-Hong lives in Portland too, I doubt if he's going to invite me over to his studio until the pictures are done." In another instance Kimmel and his wife, Doris, visited Colorado and, while there, called on Janet Stevens, who was working on the illustrations for *Nanny Goat and the Seven Kids* (Holiday House, 1990) at the time. In speaking of the visit he said, "Janet took me up to her studio . . . and showed me some of the illustrations she was doing for *Nanny Goat and the Seven Kids*. That's as close as I've ever come to the artistic side of making a picture book." Earlier, Stevens had illustrated *Anansi and the Moss-Covered Rock* (Holiday

House, 1988); later she illustrated *Anansi Goes Fishing* (Holiday House, 1992) and *Anansi and the Talking Melon* (Holiday House, 1994). The origin of the latter is a story in itself. Eric Kimmel tells it this way. *"Anansi and the Talking Melon is one of my favorite books. Unlike the other Anansi stories that Janet Stevens and I have done together, it doesn't have a strictly African origin. As a matter of fact, it began in Akron, Ohio.*

"Janet and I were doing a Young Authors Conference in Akron. Since we were staying at the same hotel—which, by the way, was hosting a championship bowling competition—we decided to meet for dinner to thrash out a new Anansi story. It was easy to find each other. We were the only ones who weren't wearing bowling shirts.

"Just to start off, I asked Janet if there was anything special she'd like to draw Anansi doing. Janet answered right away. 'Yes! I'd like to draw him getting stuck. Anansi gets into a tight place and can't get out.'

" 'That sounds like fun,' I said. 'You mean, something along the lines of what happens when Winnie-the-Pooh goes visiting Rabbit, eats too much, and can't get through the door until he gets thin again?'

" 'Exactly!' said Janet. 'What about you, Eric? Got any favorite ideas you'd like to see Anansi try?'

" 'Well,' I replied, 'I can't think of anything right away. But there's an Ashanti story that I've always liked to tell. It's called 'Talk!' What happens is that all these inanimate objects, like a hoe and a fishing net, suddenly start talking. It drives everybody crazy.'

" 'I like that!' said Janet.

"Needless to say, by the time we met for breakfast the next morning, we had a story outlined. And that was the one that eventually become *Anansi and the Talking Melon.*"

Originally the story's illustrations included Elephant holding a watermelon. That piece of art also was to be used for the cover illustration. Marjorie Cuyler at Holiday House was sensitive to the stereotype of an African story depicting a watermelon. The story and illustration was "run by some African writers," who suggested they not use the watermelon. So, says Kimmel, "Out went the watermelon." Stevens said she'd like to use a cantaloupe and inquired, perhaps tongue in cheek, if the story might be called "Anansi and the Talking Cantaloupe." The answer from Kimmel was "No!" He would go to the library and find an African melon. And he did.

Meanwhile Kimmel sent the story to *Cricket* magazine, and it was accepted for publication. It was to be published in the premier issue of a new children's magazine, *Spider*, to be published by *Cricket*'s parent company. The January 1994 issue of the magazine featured "Anansi and the Melon" by

Eric Kimmel. The problem was that the magazine had asked Victoria Chess to create illustrations for the story. When Kimmel found that out, he knew he was in trouble. What was he going to tell Janet? He felt that a "brave person would just call her."

But he didn't, at least not before Janet Stevens was at the American Library Association's conference and visited the Holiday House booth. At the same conference the publisher of *Cricket* and *Spider*, Open Court, also had a booth. They were making a big deal about the launching of *Spider*. "Janet saw it and hit the roof." Marjorie Cuyler called to relay Stevens's great displeasure. Kimmel says, "It took two days to call. I apologized to her. I said, 'I'll make it up to you.'" She said, "I'll just have to stew and meditate over it. Maybe I'll be able to finish the book, maybe not." She did finish the story, and it has sold more than 177,000 copies.

There are stories about the origin of other books by Kimmel as well. *The Three Princes: A Tale from the Middle East* (Holiday House, 1994) evolved through Kimmel's work at Portland State University, where he taught a class in storytelling. A class assignment was to tell a favorite story. Among the students were individuals from the Middle East. At first, they thought the assignment meant that they should tell a story that everybody knew. "No," said Kimmel, "I want to hear *your* stories." One student from Kuwait told a story that would later become *The Three Princes*. The student's English was a little shaky, and he chose simple words; the "three guys" he talked about became three princes in Kimmel's version of the tale. Kimmel also had a problem with what the "three guys" took, which was "an apple" in the student's version. The phrase, "road across the desert," wouldn't do either. Kimmel changed the road to a path, and after some research, he determined that an apple was a northern fruit that would not have been found in the story's dessert setting. He verified that an orange would be appropriate, so that was what he used in the final version of the story.

Cricket first published the story and for a long time received little attention. Then came the Persian Gulf War. The sheer animosity that evolved from that conflict created a demand for a tale from Kuwait that portrayed brave protagonists. Kimmel's editor at Holiday House was looking for a story, and she liked his. Leonard Everett Fisher based his illustrations on the landscape of North Africa and used images he brought back from that area.

The development of these tales exemplifies Kimmel's approach to storytelling. He does not necessarily tell stories only from his own background nor, he says, is he a folklorist. When he comes across a story he might like to write or tell, he doesn't really care about its appropriateness to the oral tradition. He simply wants a story that will work for him. There has to be something in the story that attracts his attention, something funny, unusual, surprising, or weird. He makes changes to a story to put a little bit of himself into it. That puts the challenge and the joy of writing into the process. Kimmel does not believe that an author or storyteller has to stick to his or her own background in selecting tales. Good storytellers can tell good tales, regardless of their background. Kimmel does like Jewish stories, however, because, "That's my background," he says, "and while I am not as fluent in Yiddish or Hebrew as I would like to be, I can read and express myself to a limited extent in both languages." He also likes to travel and meet people, always keeping his ears open for a good story. He has a collection of storybooks from all over the world, including some languages he cannot read or speak. He returned from a trip to Stockholm with a set of Swedish folktales in Swedish. He doesn't read Swedish but thinks that someday he might, and there just might be some good stories inside those books.

Among his own books, two themes stand out as his favorites. His Anansi stories bring to mind the year he spent living on St. Thomas in the Virgin Islands, which is where he first heard the stories of "that crazy spider." Because he is fond of Wyoming, Montana, and eastern Oregon, he also enjoys his two cowboy stories as well. Glen Rounds's illustrations helped make *Charlie Drives the Stage* (Holiday House, 1989) and *Four Dollars and Fifty Cents* (Holiday House, 1990) favorites among young readers as well.

Kimmel's activities and hobbies invariably find their way into his books. When he wrote *One Eye, Two Eyes, and Three Eyes: A Hutzul Tale* (Holiday House, 1996), his interest in knitting and spinning showed up. Kimmel is a very good knitter; he loves the classic folk patterns: Irish Arans and Guernseys. He also learned how to spin and has his own spinning wheel. He has dreamed of spinning his own wool and knitting it into a sweater. "So it is no accident," Kimmel says, "that the fiber arts played a role in my book, *One Eye, Two Eyes, and Three Eyes*. The heroine's climactic task is to spin stinging nettles into thread, which I learned can actually be done."

"Children," Kimmel says, "often ask me where I get my ideas. The world is full of ideas, full of stories, I tell them. It's just a matter of learning to keep your eyes and ears open, and knowing how to recognize a good yarn when it turns up."

When Kimmel is not working on a story he might be playing a banjo in the "three-fingered bluegrass style," and he and his wife love to bird-watch. Eric also enjoys making bread. He particularly likes heavy, coarse, peasant rye breads, although he has a whole library of bread books. He'd like to build an adobe oven in the backyard. He also rides a Yamaha 500 cc Virago. He loves to ride the motorcycle but would also like to ride horses. He has said that someday he'd get a horse of his own and recently has come closer to that goal. "My neighbor manages a stable," he says, "and is a terrific riding instructor. So after twenty years, she convinced me it was time to get on a horse again. I've always been horse-mad, but being a city boy, my opportunities to actually be around horses were limited. I ride a very kind and patient horse named Golly. He and I have a lot of fun together. I'm sure that one day he will turn up in a book too."

Eric Kimmel and his wife, Doris, were instrumental in raising the funds to put the bronze sculptures honoring Beverly Cleary's Ramona and Henry books. The sculptures are now in a park in Portland and remain as visual evidence of the commitment the Kimmels have to children and literature.

For more than twenty years, Eric and Doris Kimmel have lived in the Pacific Northwest. Daughter Bridgett, to whom *I Took My Frog to the Library* (Viking, 1990) is dedicated, is now grown and married to James Oren. The Cascade Mountains are just an hour away from the Kimmel home, and the Oregon coast is two hours away in the other direction. The Kimmels consider the coast to be a "place of spectacular beauty" and the Pacific Northwest to be the "greatest place in the world to live." There are rain forests and high deserts and glorious roses, azaleas, and rhododendrons in the spring. The rainy days are welcome if only to get Eric back to his writing tasks.

BOOKS AND NOTES

Eric Kimmel has written several tales about Anansi the Spider, the trickster from Africa, several tales from the Jewish tradition, and a number of other titles from various story sources. His version of the *Baba Yaga* (Holiday House, 1991) tale is a classic retelling, but he does not hesitate to put his own twists on tales. For example: *Bearhead: A Russian Folktale* (Holiday House, 1991) was adapted from "Ivanko the Bear's Son." He gave the protagonist a bear's head on a man's body instead of the reverse. The original tale had the son outwitting his stepfather. In Kimmel's version, he outwitted a witch. The changes make a

somewhat different story but result in a glorious tale of a bumbler, who takes instructions literally and who eventually ends up with vast wealth.

Kimmel used variations of two tales from the Brothers Grimm with traditional male heroes to create a tale with four gallant heroines. *The Four Gallant Sisters* (Holiday House, 1992) is a tale in which four orphaned sisters disguise themselves as men to go out in the world and learn a trade.

Kimmel does not waste time thinking about the authenticity of a tale—his concern is only that the tale interests him and the intended audience. He believes the storyteller tells the tale, and it doesn't really matter where the tale comes from or how the storyteller came to know it. The strength of the story is that it bridges cultures and breaks down barriers.

Books Written by Eric Kimmel

Anansi Tales

Anansi and the Moss-Covered Rock. Illustrated by Janet Stevens. (Holiday House, 1988).

Anansi and the Talking Melon. Illustrated by Janet Stevens. (Holiday House, 1994).

Anansi Goes Fishing. Illustrated by Janet Stevens. (Holiday House, 1992).

Jewish Tradition and Culture

The Adventures of Hershel of Ostropol. Illustrated by Trina Schart Hyman. (Holiday House, 1995).

Asher and the Capmakers: A Hanukkah Story. Illustrated by Will Hillenbrand. (Holiday House, 1993).

The Chanukah Tree. Illustrated by Giora Carmi. (Holiday House, 1988).

A Hanukkah Treasury. Illustrated by Emily Lisker. (Holt, 1998).

Hershel and the Hanukkah Goblins. Illustrated by Trina Schart Hyman. (Holiday House, 1989).

The Jar of Fools: Eight Hanukkah Stories from Chelm. Illustrated by Mordicai Gerstein. (Holiday House, 2000).

The Magic Dreidels: A Hanukkah Story. Illustrated by Katya Krenina. (Holiday House, 1996).

One Winter Night: A Hanukkah Story. Illustrated by Jon Godell. (Doubleday, 2000).

When Mindy Saved Hanukkah. Illustrated by Barbara McClintock. (Scholastic, 1998).

Other Titles

Bird's Gift: A Ukrainian Easter Story. Illustrated by Katya Krenina. (Holiday House, 1999).

Count Silvernose: A Story from Italy. Illustrated by Omar Rayyan. (Holiday House, 1996).

Easy Work! An Old Tale. Illustrated by Andrew Glass. (Holiday House, 1998).

The Goose Girl: A Story from the Brothers Grimm. Illustrated by Robert Sauber. (Holiday House, 1995).

The Greatest of All: A Japanese Folktale. Illustrated by Giora Carmi. (Holiday House, 1991).

Iron John. Adapted from the Brothers Grimm. Illustrated by Trina Schart Hyman. (Holiday House, 1994).

Montezuma and the Fall of the Aztecs. Illustrated by Daniel San Souci. (Holiday House, 2000).

Onions and Garlic: An Old Tale. Illustrated by Katya Arnold. (Holiday House, 1996).

Sirko and the Wolf: A Ukrainian Tale. Illustrated by Robert Sauber. (Holiday House, 1997).

The Three Princes: A Tale from the Middle East. Illustrated by Leonard Everett Fisher. (Holiday House, 1994).

The Valiant Red Rooster: A Story from Hungary. Illustrated by Katya Arnold. (Holt, 1994).

FOR MORE INFORMATION

Web Sites

Alaska Association of School Librarians (AkASL): Puffin Newsletter. "Eric Kimmel's 'Virtual' Discussion with Kama Mitchell." URL: <http://www.alaska.net/~akla/akasl/akaslpuffin/kimmel.html> (Accessed March 2000).

Amazon.com: Author Interview. "Amazon. com Talks to Eric A. Kimmel." URL: <http://www.amazon.com/exec/obidos/show-interview/k-e-immelrica/002-0023398-> (March 2000).

Texas Teller: Storyteller Newsletter Online. "Author As Storyteller." URL: <http://www.tejasstorytelling.com/kimmel.html> (Accessed March 2000).

Steven Kroll

Edie Bresler

New York, New York
August 11, 1941

📖 *The Boston Tea Party*
📖 *Happy Mother's Day*
📖 *Pony Express*

ABOUT THE AUTHOR

Steven Kroll lived his entire childhood on the Upper West Side of Manhattan where he was born to Anita and Julius Kroll on August 11, 1941. Bits and pieces of his childhood often find there way into his books for young readers. During his free time, he enjoyed "reading, playing stickball, and hanging out at the Optimo Candy Store on 78th and Broadway." He says that when he writes about a child's room, he often visualizes the room he had in the Manhattan apartment house where he grew up. For suburban or small-town settings, he has to draw on his memories of the home of a summer-camp friend he once visited—and longed to visit again.

Kroll attended Hunter College Elementary School and McBurney School and later attended Harvard. In 1962, he obtained an undergraduate degree in history and literature. He moved to London where for three years he worked for Chatto & Windus as an associate editor for *Transatlantic Review*. He was a book reviewer for *The Spectator, The Listener, The Times Literary Supplement*, and *The London Magazine*. By 1965, Kroll had returned to New York City, where he became an acquisitions editor at Holt, Rinehart & Winston publishers.

Back in New York, Kroll became acquainted with a variety of people who were involved in children's books. When he moved to Maine in 1969 for a four-year stint, it was to teach writing at the University of Maine and to concentrate on his own writing. His friends who were already in the children's book field encouraged him to think about writing for children. "At first I thought they were crazy. Then, one night, at a boring dinner party, I was noodling around in my head and came up with an idea for—would you believe—a children's story! The story I wrote wasn't very good, but it led to other, better ones, and a change in my life."

In 1973, Steven Kroll returned to New York City, where he wrote reviews for publications such as *The New York Times Book Review* and taught summer courses at the New York University's Writers' Conference. Within two years, Kroll's first book, *Is Milton Missing?* (Holiday House, 1975), was published with illustrations by Dick Gackenbach. His books have been published regularly since 1975.

Early in Kroll's writing career, he began to find ways to write fiction with nonfiction elements. In *Santa's Crash-Bang Christmas* (Holiday House, 1978) and *Big Bunny and the Easter Eggs* (Holiday House, 1982), Kroll feels he has "conveyed a certain amount of information about Christmas and Easter." Among his holiday books is one of his favorite titles, *One Tough Turkey* (Holiday House, 1982). No one knows whether turkey was really eaten on the first harvest feast, but in this book Solomon, a turkey ringleader, succeeds in outwitting the Indians and the Pilgrims. The Pilgrims and their guests must eat squash and pretend that they are eating turkey. *Oh, What a Thanksgiving* (Scholastic, 1988) blends the past and the present when David comes home from school—in 1621—to a home in Plymouth colony.

Kroll's interest in history slowly trickled into his children's books, and as his writing career progressed, he began to focus more and more on the historical aspect of the stories he was writing. In *The Hokey Pokey Man* (Holiday House, 1989), Kroll uses Joe, an ice-cream man, as a storyteller to pass the story on to two young friends. At the turn of the century, "hokey-pokey" was the name for ice cream. It was, according to Joe's story, a "hokey-pokey" man who worked in the Lower East Side of New York that hoped to be the first to introduce the ice cream cone in New York City after hearing news of the invention that took place at the 1904 World's Fair.

Kroll tells about the origin, in the late 1980s, of "one of the most beautiful books I have ever done." That book, *Looking for Daniela: A Romantic Adventure* (Holiday House, 1988), came about when "Anita Lobel showed me a sketchbook full of pictures of an eighteenth-century Italian clown. 'Could you think of a story to go with these?' she asked. The pictures were wonderful. I'd begun a story to go with them before I'd even put down the sketchbook. Along the way, the historical period shifted to Italy in 1810." Kroll says this story of collaboration has a moral: "Always expect the unexpected."

Even though Kroll delights in the details of historical events, he has not abandoned fun and humor in fiction. *Oh, Tucker!* (Candlewick, 1998) resulted when Kroll wrote a "long nonsense poem about a lunatic dog with a hyperactive tail." His editors at Candlewick, first Amy Ehrlich and then Mary Lee Donovan, felt the poem "really wanted to be a punchy prose narrative that would become increasingly absurd." Kroll had to go through several revisions to iron out the kinks until all were satisfied that they had exactly what they wanted. And according to Kroll, the book was given "just the right dash" with Scott Nash's illustrations.

Kroll has lived in New York City throughout his writing career. He has lived in a small, cozy apartment on a tree-lined street in New York's Greenwich Village, where his apartment faced onto quiet gardens. His study was complete with an old-fashioned, Olympia Standard office model typewriter. And because he is such a terrible morning person, he did all of his writing between lunch and dinner.

He is married to Kathleen Beckett, and they often travel together. "With all the school and conference appearances I make—both at home and abroad—and my wife's travel writing, it's a good thing we enjoy traveling together." In 1998, Kroll said, "We've just returned from two weeks in Brazil, where I spoke at schools in São Paulo and Campinas and she did articles on the renovations at the Copacabana Palace in Rio and on a guest house at the top of a high hill in a pretty resort town called Buzios."

He has played a lot of tennis and squash and enjoys going to the theater and to museums. He and Kathleen Beckett still live in New York City on West 11th Street.

BOOKS AND NOTES

Steven Kroll says, "I have discovered that in writing stories, one can include a number of facts that can relate to any area." Most of his books incorporate information about topics while dealing with them in a fictional manner. For example, his book, *Eat!* (Hyperion, 1995) deals with a third grader's decision to become a vegetarian, and *Looking for Daniela* provides information about the historical period in Italy in 1810. As he moved toward more details, his books entered the nonfiction category. He has written about the Boston Tea party, the Pony Express, Ellis Island, and the Lewis and Clark expedition, and he has told the story of a doctor who spent 25 years in India practicing medicine. Many well-known illustrators have illustrated Kroll's books, including Tomie dePaola, Hilary Knight, Kay Chorao, Janet Stevens, Nicole Rubel, and Evaline Ness. Kroll says, "I think visually. When I'm working on a picture book, I see the pictures before I write the words. How frustrating, then, that I've never been able to draw. But how fortunate that the illustrators of my books have all seen what I've seen and have captured the magic I wished to share."

Books Written by Steven Kroll

Holidays

Big Bunny and the Easter Eggs. Illustrated by Janet Stevens. (Holiday House, 1982).
Just before Easter, the Big Easter Bunny, Wilbur, gets sick.

Big Bunny and the Magic Show. Illustrated by Janet Stevens. (Holiday House, 1986).
Wilbur, the big Easter bunny, decides he'd rather be a magic show bunny instead.

The Biggest Pumpkin Ever. Illustrated by Jeni Bassett. (Holiday House, 1984).
Two mice fall in love with the same pumpkin and then figure out a way to share it.

Happy Father's Day. Illustrated by Marylin Hafner. (Holiday House, 1988).
Six children, with the help of their mother, plan a Father's Day surprise for Dad.

Happy Mother's Day. Illustrated by Marylin Hafner. (Holiday House, 1985).
Six children, with the help of their father, plan a Mother's Day surprise for Mom.

It's Groundhog Day! Illustrated by Jeni Bassett. (Holiday House, 1987).
Godfrey Groundhog is kidnapped so he won't see his shadow on February 2.

Mrs. Claus's Crazy Christmas. Illustrated by John Wallner. (Holiday House, 1985).
Santa inadvertently leaves behind a gift puppy. Mrs. Claus tries to deliver it and has an adventure of her own.

History, Nonfiction

The Boston Tea Party. Illustrated by Peter Fiore. (Holiday House, 1998).
Events before, during, and after the American Revolutionary War are discussed.

Doctor on an Elephant. Illustrated by Michael Chesworth. (Holt, 1994).
One vignette in a day in the life of Dr. John Symington in India. Dr. Symington rides a large male elephant to tend to a man wounded by a leopard.

Ellis Island: Doorway to Freedom. Illustrated by Karen Ritz. (Holiday House, 1995).
Chronicles the activity of the immigration station on Ellis Island. Over sixteen million immigrants moved through this gateway into the United States between 1892 and 1954.

Lewis and Clark. Illustrated by Richard Williams. (Holiday House, 1994).

Fascinating historical facts, from the supplies that the explorers took with them, to the meetings with Indian tribes. Vivid illustrations and vivid details share the spirit of Lewis and Clark's 1804–1806 expedition of the land from the Mississippi River to the Pacific Ocean.

Pony Express. Illustrated by Dan Andreasen. (Scholastic, 1996).

Tells the history of the ill-fated Pony Express, which existed for eighteen months. The Pony Express officially started delivering the mail between St. Joseph, Missouri and Sacramento, California on April 3, 1860.

Other Titles

Eat! Illustrated by Diane Palmisciano. (Hyperion, 1995).

Henry's decision to become a vegetarian causes problems for him in his third-grade class.

Oh, Tucker! Illustrated by Scott Nash. (Candlewick, 1998).

A dog causes chaos as he bounds through the house. No one schools him because he is such a nice dog.

Patrick's Tree House. Illustrated by Roberta Wilson. (Macmillan, 1994).

This sixty-two-page book has Patrick at his grandparents' home in Maine. When he discovers his very own tree house, he is thrilled but then has to figure out how to deal with the two boys who have taken it over.

The Pigrates Clean Up. Illustrated by Jeni Bassett. (Holt, 1993).

Pig Pirates work hard to clean up for their captain's wedding.

FOR MORE INFORMATION

Limited information is available on book flaps. No articles, books, or Web sites were located.

Anita Lobel

◆ Folklore ◆ Family Relationships

Sharron L. McElmeel

Krakow, Poland
June 2, 1934

📖 *Away from Home*

📖 *Princess Furball*

📖 *Toads and Diamonds*

ABOUT THE AUTHOR/ILLUSTRATOR

Anita Lobel's simple words, "I was pampered and overprotected as a child in Krakow, Poland," might give the impression that she experienced an idyllic childhood in her native country. But few things could be further from the truth. Born Anita Kempler just four years before World War II broke out in Europe, she was the daughter of Polish Jews who were comfortable merchants in the city of Krakow. When the war and the Nazis came, their very existence was threatened.

Anita did not understand when her father disappeared in 1939. She later found out that he had been sent to Russia. Her mother managed to obtain papers that "proved" she was not Jewish but felt the children should go into hiding so she sent Anita, then age five, and her three-year-old brother Bernhard to the countryside with their nanny, Niania. Separated from their parents, Anita and her younger brother posed as the children of their devoted Catholic nanny. Anita's brother spent those years disguised as a girl so as not to be discovered as a circumcised Jew. The two children learned the meaning of the words "transported," "deported," "concentration camp," and "liquidation." The children and their nanny spent years hiding in the country and then in the Krakow ghetto. Finally, Benedictine nuns hid them in a convent. In 1944, someone informed the Nazis that the nuns were hiding Jews; despite efforts to keep them safe, the two children, just eight and ten years old, were discovered. The Nazis took them first to Montelupi Prison and then to a series of other prison camps. They were sick with lice, diarrhea, and eventually tuberculosis.

Anita sheltered and protected her brother. One day, starved with hunger, she spotted a raw potato in the mud. She and her brother took turns taking bites of it. At Ravensbruck, she recalls, "Everyone was told to turn right," but Anita grabbed her brother's hand and dragged him with her to the left to escape the "chimneys." She knew that "something bad happened to the group that turned right."

The two children hid among the adults and survived three camps and a forced march. After they were liberated on April 15, 1945, the Swedish Red Cross sent them to sanitariums in Sweden so that they might recover from tuberculosis. It wasn't until Anita was twelve years old that she set foot in a school. She was the only brunette among the fair-haired Swedes. To her classmates, Anita was exotic and artistic.

Miraculously, her parents came to Sweden and were reunited with their children. Anita was irritated that her parents viewed Sweden as just a stopping-off point while awaiting visas for America. For Anita, Sweden represented the first place where she could "feel like a human person, to go to school and to make friends." The family lived in Sweden for several years before they were given permission to enter the United States.

At age sixteen, Anita, her younger brother, and her parents traveled to the United States. Anita had lived in Stockholm, a large city by her standards, but she was overwhelmed by the size of New York City. It was frightening and dirty. She has said that she was brought to the United States against her will because her parents wanted to reclaim some long, lost relatives. Her parents settled into the Jewish community, but Anita did not want that. For six years, she had been in the care of a nanny who was a devout Catholic; now "they had to be Jewish again." Always feeling somewhat distant from her parents, it was Anita's loss of her Niania, the Polish nanny who had sheltered and protected Anita and her brother, that made her the saddest.

Nonetheless, Anita grew to love New York City. She has said, "I love the city. I'm happy with all the concrete. I'm really a city person." She attended Washington Irving High School, where she took eight terms of English in just two terms because she was such a voracious reader. The school had a strong art program, which furthered her interest in painting and drawing. After high school, Anita Kempler entered Pratt Institute to continue her study of art. It was at Pratt that she met Arnold Lobel, a fellow student. They married in 1955, just ten years after her liberation from the concentration camp.

After leaving Pratt, Anita Lobel worked as a freelance textile designer. The work was difficult and exacting but helped her acquire the techniques and skills that she came to use in the illustration of her books.

Anita Lobel spent seven years designing textiles. She worked at home while caring for her two children, Adrianne and Adam. Arnold Lobel was a children's book illustrator, and one Christmas, Anita Lobel gave his editor, Susan Hirschman, three scarves that she had designed. Hirschman suggested that Anita Lobel consider illustrating a picture book, and Lobel agreed. But then Hirschman told her that she should write it too. So Lobel did just that.

The pictures came first, then Lobel wrote the story to go with the pictures. The first book that she created was *Sven's Bridge* (Harper, 1965). The book was her tribute to the folk designs of Sweden that she loved. She used the same decorative approach to the illustrations for *The Troll Music* (Harper, 1966) but by the time she created illustrations for her third book, *Potatoes, Potatoes* (Harper, 1967), she had turned to the emotional content of the story.

Early in their careers, the Lobels lived in a series of small apartments. Their "studio" was actually a drawing table that Arnold made from a door that they set up in the room that doubled as a bedroom and playroom. At the time, their children were young, and after Adrianne and Adam had fallen asleep in a cubicle nearby, the Lobels would work late into the night while listening to music or glancing at old movies on the television. They shared the table, each working at one end. The legs weren't too sturdy, so every time one of them would erase a line, the table wiggled and irritated the other. That led to much grumbling, but as soon as they were able to afford a larger apartment, they solved the problem by getting two normal-sized tables and setting them side-by-side. Eventually, they established themselves in a brownstone in Brooklyn and were able to have a real studio on the third floor. Once the children began school, they were able to work in the daytime and sleep at night.

Anita Lobel spent seven years designing textiles and working in the theater, but eventually her work turned more fully to children's books and her illustrative work. One of Lobel's most popular books, *On Market Street* (Greenwillow, 1981) evolved from a poster she created in 1977 for Children's Book Week. Lobel drew on her admiration of the seventeenth-century French trade engravings to create a poster of an ice cream vendor made of what else, ice cream cones. The poster led to the book. Each of the shopkeepers on Market Street is made up of his or her wares.

Lobel's interest in all things theatrical and her love of eighteenth-century clothing lead her to develop a Little Theater concept to unify the illustrations for *Singing Bee!* (Lothrop, 1982). At the time that Lobel created the illustrations, she still was appearing in the theater "in a small but serious capacity" as an actress and cabaret singer. It took more than a year for her to complete the illustrations for *Singing Bee!* The book contained 125 songs including titles such as *All the Pretty Little Horses*, *Merrily We Roll Along*, *Pop! Goes the Weasel*, and *Incey Wincey Spider*. Lobel's illustrations were described by reviewers as "extraordinary."

Anita Lobel and Arnold Lobel worked with some of the same authors, such as Harriet Ziefert, but the two never collaborated on the same illustrative project. They did, however, collaborate on their own books. Anita Lobel illustrated several books that Arnold Lobel wrote.

The Lobels had been married for more than thirty years when Arnold Lobel died in 1987. At the time of his death, both their children were grown. Lobel now lives in New York's fashionable Soho neighborhood in a third-floor loft with high ceilings, polished hardwood floors, and a wall full of shoes. She has a close relationship with her two children. Her son is a musician, and her daughter is a set designer. Her own father died in the early 1980s, but her mother lived into the 1990s, past her 95th birthday. The little brother that Lobel sheltered during the days in which they evaded the terror of the Nazis is living in Atlanta, where he has built a successful practice as a psychologist.

BOOKS AND NOTES

Anita Lobel's illustrative technique was influenced by her work in the textile industry, as well as by the peasant art she came to know while she was in hiding in the Polish countryside. The art in the Catholic churches she frequented with her beloved nanny was also very influential. It represented stories in art, told step by step just as she would later do in her picture book illustration.

Books Written and Illustrated by Anita Lobel

Alison's Zinnia (Greenwillow, 1990).
An alphabet book based on flowers that lead an all-female cast through the garden.

Away from Home (Greenwillow, 1994).
Adam arrives in Amsterdam, and later Vincent vacations in Venice. Michael mopeds in Moscow. An alliterative tour of the world with famous landmarks in the background of each scene. An all-male cast.

The Dwarf Giant (Greenwillow, 1996).
Set in Japan, Prince Mainichi and his beautiful princess, Ichinichi, are perfectly happy until the prince falls in love with a dwarf they have welcomed into their palace.

One Lighthouse, One Moon (Greenwillow, 2000).
A cat and the people in and around a lighthouse and their activities through the days of the week and month are presented.

Books Illustrated by Anita Lobel

Mangaboom. Written by Charlotte Pomerantz. (Greenwillow, 1997).
A tall-tale romance between a gorgeous Latina lady, Mangaboom, who is nineteen feet tall and weighs more than 600 pounds, and her friend named Daniel.

My Day in the Garden. Written by Miela Ford. (Greenwillow, 1999).
Friends dress up like insects and animals and play in the garden.

A New Coat for Anna. Written by Harriet Ziefert. (Knopf, 1986).
A mother trades her few valuables to barter for the services and goods needed so that her daughter, Anna, could have a warm winter coat.

The Night Before Christmas. Written by Clement C. Moore. (Knopf, 1991).
Traditional scenes show the Lobels' home as the setting for the quiet eve before Christmas.

Not Everyday an Aurora Borealis for Your Birthday: A Love Poem. Written by Carl Sandburg. (Knopf, 1998).
" . . . because I love you I give you for your birthday present the aurora borealis." A never-before-published poem by Carl Sandburg.

On Market Street. Written by Arnold Lobel. (Greenwillow, 1981).
Anita Lobel's 1977 poster of an ice cream vendor inspired the visual of the vendors along Market Street. Arnold Lobel provided the text to accompany her illustrations.

Princess Furball. Written by Charlotte Huck. (Greenwillow, 1989).
A Cinderella tale that has the princess using her wits to rescue herself from the work-worn situation in which she finds herself.

The Rose in My Garden. Written by Arnold Lobel. (Greenwillow, 1984).
Start with a single rose; add hollyhocks and marigolds, sunflowers and zinnias and you have a beautiful garden growing before your eyes.

Sven's Bridge. Written by Anita Lobel. (Harper, 1965; Greenwillow, 1992). Illustrated with Swedish folk art designs.

Toads and Diamonds. Written by Charlotte Huck. (Greenwillow, 1996).
Lobel's folksy and dense paintings bring an edgy realism to the French folk story of Renee, a sweet maiden with an evil stepfamily.

This Quiet Lady. Written by Charlotte Zolotow. (Greenwillow, 1992).
A young girl views photos of her mother from baby, to young girl, through adulthood, and then to motherhood; the book features large, expressive paintings.

FOR MORE INFORMATION

Articles

Lobel, Anita. "Arnold at Home." *The Horn Book Magazine* (August 1981): 405–10.

Raymond, Allen. "Anita Lobel: Up from the Crossroad." *Teaching K–8* (November/December 1989): 52–55.

Sanzeni, Becky. "Anita Lobel: A Stunning Autobiography." *Teaching K–8* 30, no. 4 (January 2000): 41–43.

Books

Lobel, Anita. *No Pretty Pictures: A Child of War* (Greenwillow, 1998).
The touching and poignant story of Lobel's horrific childhood spent fleeing the Nazis, in concentration camps, and finally as a reluctant immigrant to the United States.

Arnold Lobel

◆ Family Relationships ◆ Friends ◆ Poetry

Los Angeles, California
May 22, 1933–December 4, 1987

📖 *The Book of Pigericks: Pig Limericks*
📖 Frog and Toad Series
📖 *Whiskers and Rhymes*

ABOUT THE AUTHOR/ILLUSTRATOR

The year Arnold Lobel was born, his parents were living in California, and it was the middle of the Depression. He was born on May 22, 1933, and his parents were close to running out of money; when they did, they packed up and went back with Arnold to Schenectady, New York. Arnold was about six months old. His parents divorced shortly after, and Arnold stayed with his mother. His grandmother cared for him while he grew up. He spent many days wandering the spacious front lawn of the family's large but ramshackle house.

Arnold was a sickly child, and he has often described his childhood as "unhappy." He spent many of his preteen days in hospitals because he suffered from a series of illnesses. His small stature and sickly nature kept him apart from other children. He was "terrible in gym class," but when he started telling stories and drawing pictures, he was "pushed up the social ladder." He often converted his cellar into a theater, painting scenery on old bed sheets and putting on plays for his few friends.

By the time he was a teen, his health had improved. He began to dream of becoming an artist. After graduating from high school, Lobel entered Pratt Institute. It was at Pratt that he discovered children's book illustration and Anita Kempler. Anita, a native of Krakow, Poland, was a survivor of the holocaust and had been in the United States less than ten years. She, too, was an artist, and both were "mainstays of the school's drama club." They married in 1955 and were soon parents of a son, Adam, and a daughter, Adrianne.

Early in his career, Lobel worked for advertising agencies, but he was always interested in children's book illustration. In 1960, he began to take his illustration portfolio to publishers in New York City. He visited fifty publishers, and none of them were interested—except Susan Hirschman, then an editor at Harper & Row. She gave him the opportunity to illustrated *Red Tag Comes Back* by Fred Pflager (Harper, 1961). Soon after, she encouraged him to write his own book to illustrate. Although Lobel described writing as "very difficult," he decided to try his hand at it.

The result was the first book that he both wrote and illustrated, *A Zoo for Mister Muster* (Harper, 1962), which was followed by *A Holiday for Mister Muster* (Harper, 1963). The setting for the stories came from Prospect Park Zoo, which was just across the meadow from the Lobels' Brooklyn apartment. The family spent many hours at the zoo, where Adrianne and Adam were particularly fond of the vultures and of the ice cream that was sold there.

By writing his books, Lobel could keep 100 percent of the royalties rather than split them fifty-fifty with the author. He appreciated this fact and continued to both write and illustrate. His words came first, and while the writing was difficult, the drawing was "no problem," even though the amount of artwork that goes into a picture book is incredible. For each of his books, usually sixty-four pages in length, he created one illustration per page. Because photographic separation was very expensive and seldom used at the time, Lobel hand separated the colors. That meant for every illustration that was printed in three colors (black, green, and brown), Lobel had to create three pieces of art. That added up to 192 separate pieces of artwork for a sixty-four-page book.

From the beginning, Lobel insisted on being on site when the printing presses began to run the sheets for his books. He said, "Horrible things happened at the printers. The colors did not come out right. Sometimes the reproduction was poor." The press operator was able to control the amount of ink and the pressure on the press. Depending on the skill of the worker, sometimes the color was too strong, and sometimes there was too much pressure. Unfortunately, Lobel was not always notified when a book went into paperback production, and that resulted in some horrendous mistakes. In one printing of a Frog and Toad book, the animals appeared Kelly green.

For many years, the Lobels lived in Brooklyn, New York. Anita Lobel was an illustrator as well, and she and Arnold Lobel worked with some of the same authors—such as Harriet Ziefert—although they never collaborated on illustration projects for other authors. They did, however, collaborate on their own books. Arnold Lobel wrote the text for *How the Rooster Saved the Day* (Greenwillow, 1977) and decided he would "let [Anita Lobel] illustrate the book." It was difficult for Arnold to sit back and watch her illustrate his story. He observed the theater concept she developed for the story and asked her, "What are you doing with *my* story?" Nonetheless, it became increasingly less difficult to give a text to Anita to illustrate, and they collaborated on several titles, including their final collaboration, *The Rose in My Garden* (Greenwillow, 1984).

Arnold Lobel was awarded the 1981 Caldecott Medal for his illustrations for *Fables* (Harper, 1980). The chance to illustrate the book was not easy to come by. The project began as an offer from Charlotte Zolotow and Pat Allen, editors at Harper, for him to select and illustrate fables written by Aesop. He agreed to take the assignment and set out to search for suitable fables. He did a lot of reading and eventually came to realize that, in this opinion, "[Aesop's] fables were not intended for children at all." Eventually, after weeks of agonizing over the decision, he admitted to himself that he did not want to do the book. He made an appointment to give the news to Zolotow and Allen.

As he told them the news and returned the advance for the proposed book, he optimistically commented, "Maybe I can write some of my own. Who knows?" Then he wondered why he had said such a foolish thing. Months passed, and on one cold and snowy day, the phone went dead in the Lobels' apartment. When he returned from using a pay phone to report the outage, he slipped on a little patch of ice, just before he reached their front stoop, and he broke a bone in his ankle.

He was faced with five weeks of confinement. So he found himself sitting in a chair with an open notebook waiting for something to happen. Writing was difficult, but in this predicament, there was no more opportunity to procrastinate; there simply was not much else he could do with his time. So he decided to give those fables a try. He thought of some of his favorite animals that somehow had never made their way into any of his other books. He thought about an ostrich, the hippo, the crocodile, and a kangaroo. He made a list. Surprisingly, each of them began to tell their story. Arnold wrote the stories down on his special writing pad, using a ballpoint pen. The first day, he began at 1:00 P.M.; by 3:00 P.M., he had the first fable. On the second day, he started again at 1:00 P.M. and again was able to write a second fable by 3:00 P.M.

Each day, Anita Lobel went off to a dance class, and when she came home in the early evening, she would ask, "Did you do it again?" Then Arthur Lobel read the story to her. For fifteen days, Lobel wrote; the last five fables came more slowly, but when he was finished, he rushed to do the pictures.

For as much as Lobel procrastinated as a writer, he loved to draw. He decided to create his first drawings for the dummy as full-color paintings. A camel was shown in a tutu, a pig floated through the cosmos, and a baboon clutched a ventilated umbrella. It was not very long before he had a dummy prepared and was ready to present it to his editors at Harper. He was nervous about their possible reaction and chose to take the dummy to one editor at a time when he knew she would be away from her desk. He planned to slip it in and then be safely at home by the time she looked at it and reacted to his newest work.

Coincidentally, he found himself, the very next day, at a party with his editor Charlotte Zolotow. At first, he was ready to hide, but when he saw her walking toward him with a broad smile, he knew she had already seen the dummy and that he was "officially a fabulist." He was able to get his advance back from Harper.

Although Lobel admired Edward Lear, he considered his poems too "Learish" for children. He did find their rhythm and rhyme interesting. In the late 1960s, he had written some limericks of his own for *Humpty Dumpty* magazine. He had used pigs to make them seem less like a Lear imitation. He felt they were "awful, quite an embarrassment." But he did not discard the idea and later returned to it as a possibility for a book. He realized that Lear had used European geographic locations for his rhymes, so Lobel developed a list of "lovely delicious American names such as Duluth, Decatur, Moline, and Savannah. He then took the "lim" out of limericks and decided his rhymes would be "pigericks." He wrote five "pigericks" and liked them. But he had to write at least forty for a book. He got to fifteen quite easily then "he stopped dead." He couldn't seem to write any more. The project languished.

Then one summer day Lobel and his wife were at a beach house on Long Island. The weather was threatening a hurricane on the day of their arrival, so they took to indoor activities. That meant browsing through antique shops. In a dark corner of one shop, they found a large, heavy, gray, cast-in-solid-lead, life-sized pig. The pig was beautiful and expensive and heavy. But he had to have it. The pig was worth it. Lobel said, "I returned to writing the Pigericks with a renewed passion. I finished them and was able to begin on the pictures."

Arnold Lobel created children's books for more than twenty years. He wrote and illustrated more than 80 books for children and he collaborated with several other authors and illustrators. Illustrations in two books, *Frog and Toad Are Friends* (Harper, 1970) and *Hildilid's Night* by Cheli Duran Ryan (Macmillan, 1971) were named Caldecott Honor Books and another book, *Frog and Toad Together* (Harper, 1972) was named a Newbery Honor Book. Eight years later, Lobel's *Fables* earned the highest award, the Caldecott Medal.

One of Lobel's last projects was a collaboration with Jack Prelutsky. They created an illustrated book of poetry, *The Random House Book of Poetry for Children* (Random House, 1983). Then he worked for three years to illustrate a companion volume of Mother Goose rhymes. That book, *The Random House Book of Mother Goose* (Random House, 1986), contained 306 nursery rhymes selected and illustrated by Lobel.

Arnold Lobel lived for many years in Brooklyn. In the months before his death, he moved to Manhattan where he died at Doctor's Hospital of cardiac arrest on December 4, 1987. He suffered from AIDS for several months before his death. Anita and Arnold Lobel had been married for more than thirty years when he died. His wife, mother, and two grown children survived him.

BOOKS AND NOTES

Arnold Lobel was able to call upon a wide repertory of styles. He worked in wash and pencil, but pen and ink seemed to be his favorite medium. His work was inspired by some of his favorite authors and illustrators: Edward Lear, Beatrix Potter, James Marshall, Maurice Sendak, Chris Van Allsburg, Tomi Ungerer, and William Steig.

Books Written and Illustrated by Arnold Lobel

Frog and Toad Series

Although Frog and Toad, the two main characters in these books, dress like people and act like people, they retain some of their animal characteristics. For example, the color of each animal—brown for Toad and green for Frog—is consistent with each animal's natural color. These two animals are true friends and share experiences common to people. Each book contains four or more chapters, each a story complete in itself. These "I Can Read Books" are favorites of primary and early intermediate students. Each book is written and illustrated by Arnold Lobel.

Days with Frog and Toad (Harper, 1979).

Frog and Toad All Year (Harper, 1976).

Frog and Toad Are Friends (Harper, 1970).

Frog and Toad Together (Harper, 1972).

Fables (Harper, 1980).

Grasshopper on the Road (Harper, 1978).

Ming Lo Moves the Mountain (Greenwillow, 1982).

Mouse Soup (Harper, 1977).

The Turn Around Wind (Harper, 1988).

Uncle Elephant (Harper, 1981).

Books Written by Arnold Lobel and Illustrated by Anita Lobel

How the Rooster Saved the Day (Greenwillow, 1977).

On Market Street (Greenwillow, 1981).

The Rose in My Garden (Greenwillow, 1984).

A Treeful of Pigs (Greenwillow, 1979).

Books Illustrated by Arnold Lobel

Hildilid's Night. Written by Cheli Duran Ryan. (Macmillan, 1971).

I'll Fix Anthony. Written by Judith Viorst. (Harper, 1969).

More Tales of Oliver Pig. Written by Jean Van Leeuwen. (Dial, 1981).

Tales of Oliver Pig. Written by Jean Van Leeuwen. (Dial, 1979).

A Three Hat Day. Written by Laura Geringer. (Harper, 1985).

Poetry

Arnold Lobel was able to write some of his own poetry, and he also illustrated poetry written or selected by others. He enjoyed the humor of many of the poems he illustrated. When he was preparing the illustrations for the books of poetry, he most often sketched the whole book to create a dummy. For *The Book of Pigericks* (Harper, 1983), he created a succession of small pictures to build up a little narrative. Each painting showed a pig in Victorian garb as a kind of tribute to the gentleman who inspired the poetry. He used a similar illustrative technique when he illustrated *The Random House Book of Poetry for Children* and *The Random House Book of Mother Goose.* His ability to use his illustrations to unify a collection of poetry made his illustrations a marvelous complement to those collections of poetry selected by others as well as books of his own poems. The following titles are illustrated by Arnold Lobel.

The Arnold Lobel Book of Mother Goose. Selected by Arnold Lobel. (Knopf, 1997).
A reissue of a book originally titled *The Random House Book of Mother Goose* (Random House, 1986).

The Book of Pigericks: Pig Limericks. Written by Arnold Lobel. (Harper, 1983).

Circus. Written by Jack Prelutsky. (Collier, 1974).

Nightmare: Poems to Trouble Your Sleep. Written by Jack Prelutsky. (Greenwillow, 1976).

The Microscope. Written by Maxine Kumin. (Harper, 1968; 1984).

The Random House Book of Poetry. Selected by Jack Prelutsky. (Random House, 1983).

Tyrannosaurus Was a Beast: Dinosaur Poems. Written by Jack Prelutsky. (Greenwillow, 1988).

Whiskers and Rhymes. Written by Arnold Lobel. (Greenwillow, 1985).

FOR MORE INFORMATION

Articles

Lobel, Anita. "Arnold at Home." *The Horn Book Magazine* (August 1981): 405–10.

Lobel, Arnold. "Birthdays and Beginnings." *Theory into Practice* 21, no. 4 (Autumn 1982): 322–24.
Published remarks presented at the Ohio State University Conference on Children's Literature, May 22, 1982.

Lobel, Arnold. "Caldecott Medal Acceptance." *The Horn Book Magazine* (August 1981): 400–410.
Published remarks presented at the Caldecott-Newbery Dinner at the American Library Association Meeting in San Francisco, California, on June 29, 1981.

Books

Shannon, George. *Arnold Lobel* (Twayne, 1989).

David Macaulay

◆ Humor ◆ Construction, Nonfiction

Burton-on-Trent, England
December 2, 1946

📖 *Black and White*
📖 *Cathedral*
📖 *Why the Chicken Crossed the Road*

ABOUT THE AUTHOR/ILLUSTRATOR

David Macaulay is loyal to England, the country of his birth. He was born there in 1946 and spent the first eleven years of his life in Lancaster, in a "house in the north of England, the last house in a row of identical brick houses." There were only two rooms. One was where the family "lived"; the other room was for company. Each member of the family coexisted in that one room. Both parents were creators. His father worked with wood, and his mother sewed and knitted. The work was not a hobby; the Macaulays actually made things the family needed.

David did not play much with his sister or brother. He often played alone, a fact that Macaulay has said probably "helped develop an imagination." He made things out of cigar boxes, string, and tape. He constructed elevators and used yarn to create a system of moving cable cars. In his Caldecott Medal acceptance speech, he said, "By the time we got out of that kitchen, we actually believed that creativity and craftsmanship were desirable—even normal." Macaulay was immersed in a household where self-sufficiency was valued; one did not have to go to the store to get everything. If there were problems to be solved, he learned how to solve them.

When David was eleven years old, his father took a job in the United States, and the family immigrated there, settling in Bloomfield, New Jersey. Macaulay's transition from an idyllic English childhood to the fast-paced life in America brought him closer to drawing. His dreams helped him create sketches for all sorts of objects and gadgets. To this day, he says that it is the dreaming that is the most fun.

Five years after coming to the United States, the family moved to Rhode Island. Macaulay's interest in drawing and solving problems had continued, so he enrolled in the Rhode Island School of Design (RISD) to study architecture. He earned his undergraduate degree in 1969 and spent a fifth year at the school in the European Honors Program at Palazzo Cenci in Italy. During that year, he studied in Rome, Herculaneum, and Pompeii. Macaulay fell in love with Rome. He enjoyed its culture and its history. He says, "It was a wonderful, wonderful year." He thought the place seemed hot and smelly, but he enjoyed walking through the streets discovering things many people do not notice: furniture makers, pizza makers, little shops selling a variety of things, young people hanging out, and old people having coffee. He also noticed that Rome was filled with the columns, structures, sculptures, and reliefs that were similar to things he had admired in the United States. He recognized how Roman architecture had influenced buildings in America.

While he has always been grateful for his background in architecture, he knew by the fourth year of studying architecture that he was not interested in sitting in an office, doing an internship, or becoming a working architect. When he returned to the United States, he worked for a time as an interior designer while he worked on his first book, *Cathedral* (Houghton, 1973). The book began as a fantasy about a gargoyle beauty pageant. Macaulay has described the story as a "poor man's *Where the Wild Things Are*."

When he first showed it to a publisher, the story was rejected. He had drawn some of the people in front of a cathedral, and the editor suggested that he did like the picture of the cathedral. So Macaulay did what was logical and went back to what he knew: architectural history and the construction of gothic buildings. He thought he could explain the building process in pictures and could tell a story about it. Soon he was off to Amiens, France, to study and to make sketches of a real cathedral for the book.

The book was completed, accepted, and published in 1973. It was named a Caldecott Honor Book in 1974. While the book was achieving fame, Macaulay took a part-time job teaching art students at South Junior High School in Newton, Massachusetts. After teaching there for a year, Macaulay returned to Rhode Island and began to teach at Rhode Island School of Design (RISD). He taught art history and enrichment. At the time, he felt that a working illustrator needed a classroom in which he or she is forced "to find answers that make sense." Teaching helped him learn how to explain concepts without putting his listeners to sleep. He taught at RISD for more than twenty-five years before leaving to focus on his books and other projects.

While he was teaching at RISD, his family, which includes two daughters, lived on a quiet street in Providence, in a barn-red clapboard house. His third-floor studio was filled with light from two skylights. One interior wall was covered with floor-to-ceiling bookshelves that were filled with toys: a miniature coronation set with golden carriage and royal band on horseback; toy soldiers; model buildings, a Snoopy doll, and even a real skeleton. The shelves also held copies of his books, including those printed in other languages: Japanese, Spanish, Portuguese, Italian, German, and French. It was in this studio that he created the text for his books. He describes the writing as "laborious," and he writes and rewrites several times until he gets the words just the way he wants them. The art is very time consuming because his drawings are very detailed.

In 1989, Macaulay's Caldecott-Medal-winning book, *Black and White*, was published by Houghton Mifflin. The book was a unique departure from most picture books. It looked like a picture book but was designed to tell four stories at the same time. Each quarter of a page held the illustration and narrative for one of the stories. Macaulay says, "You can either go through the book and read the upper left hand corner of each page or you can read a little bit of all four stories, turn the page and read a little bit more about each story. In the end, the reader realizes that all the stories link together."

Macaulay spent three years working primarily on *Rome Antics* (Houghton, 1997). His love for Rome inspired the book. The eighty-page book is actually a tour of Rome, with an emphasis on the architecture of the city. Developing the story was, says Macaulay, "a frustrating experience." The original story centered around three characters: one who travels through Rome with her dog, a second who works at a pizzeria and delivers pizzas on his scooter, and a television repairman who sees Rome from yet another perspective.

Although Macaulay felt he was on the right track, the story was not working. A second story line involved a pigeon that lives in Rome and visits his pigeon relatives in various landmarks throughout the city. That story line was not working either so after six or seven tries, Macaulay changed the story one last time but keep the pigeons involved. In the final story, a woman releases a homing pigeon. The pigeon decides that instead of delivering the message immediately, it will take a scenic route to the destination. Eventually, Macaulay began making sketches for a book based on this story line. As with most of his books, he begins by making small sketches and then, as he develops confidence in how the story is going, the sketches get bigger.

David Macaulay created a book, *The Way Things Work* (Houghton, 1988), using words and more than 2,000 illustrations to take readers on a tour of the scientific principles behind hundreds of objects. The book includes simple devices, such as water meters, toilets, and levers, and much more complex things, such as the space shuttle. *The Way Things Work* grouped machines together by the principles that govern their actions, rather than by their uses. A new edition published in 1998 revised and expanded the original book to include twelve new machines on eighty pages, detailing the latest innovations in digital technology. *The New Way Things Work* takes readers into the digital age of modems, digital cameras, compact discs, bits, and bytes. He includes visual puns, running jokes, a cast of thousands of tiny participants in on and around the machines, choirs of angels and lots of big woolly mammoths.

Macaulay uses pictures to get his message across. These days, he works in his studio, housed in a two-story building that used to be a general store. The first floor holds all the "computer stuff," and the second floor holds his drawing boards, his toys, "and junk." His use of computers is only for word processing and design. He has a "Mac setup with a scanner and a PC setup." He used to design books by typing, cutting, and taping portions of his illustrations and text to get a sense of what the pages would look like. Now he doesn't have to "mess around with that any more." He feels like he has more control of his books. Macaulay's studio is on Water Street, situated behind his home in Warren, Rhode Island. It is an old whaling port that was prominent in the seventeenth century. The nearest large town is Providence.

BOOKS AND NOTES

David Macaulay's first book, *Cathedral*, was published in 1973. It was a spectacular book about the construction of cathedrals. He went on to write about the construction of a Roman city, the erection of the monuments to the pharaohs, the building of medieval fortresses, and the evolution of a New England town. While most of Macaulay's writing has been books enjoyed by children and adults alike, his 1999 book, *Building the Book Cathedral* (Houghton), is most appropriate for adults who have some knowledge of his earlier work, *Cathedral*. In the 1999 book, Macaulay explains how he developed the words and illustrations for his first book. The book provides readers with insight into his artistic process. Readers will enjoy the author's wry comments on his earlier work. In addition, he has written a book focusing on the architecture of Rome and an award-winning picture book. *The Way Things Work* has become the basis of an interactive CD-ROM that allows users to manipulate the images. Users are given a problem that has to be defined and a number of pieces, tools, or whatever else is needed to conduct a project, such as gild an object. Four of his architectural-building titles have been made into PBS videos, called the *David Macaulay Series*. Videos included in this series are *Castle*, *Cathedral*, *Pyramid*, and *Roman City*.

Books Written and Illustrated by David Macaulay

Building

Castle (Houghton, 1977).
Pen-and-ink illustrations detail the brick-by-brick assembly of a medieval castle.

Cathedral (Houghton, 1973).
Recreates the building of a French Gothic cathedral from the hewing down of forest wood to the placement of leaden sheets upon a spire.

City (Houghton, 1974).
Charts the planning and building of an imaginary ancient Roman city, Verbonia.

Mill (Houghton, 1983).
Details the planning, construction, and operation of imaginary mills at Wicksbridge. Although the mills are imaginary, they are typical of the mills developed in New England in the nineteenth century.

Pyramid (Houghton, 1975).
Details of the conception and construction of the great pharaohs' burial places.

Underground (Houghton, 1976).
Down through the manhole and into the labyrinth beneath the streets.

Fiction

Black and White (Houghton, 1990).
Four stories told simultaneously in a series of quarter-page panels on each page.

Great Moments in Architecture (Houghton, 1978).
A survey of architectural follies erected in Macaulay's own imagination.

Motel of the Mysteries (Houghton, 1979).
Chronicles the discovery and misinterpretation in the year 4022 of a typical twentieth-century American motel.

Rome Antics (Houghton, 1997).
A pigeon tours Rome and discovers that the past is very much a part of the present-day city.

Ship (Houghton, 1993).
A combination of drawings, maps, and diagrams detailing a ship's recovery and the clues to the past.

Unbuilding (Houghton, 1980).

A fantastical, yet accurate, view of the unbuilding of New York's Empire State Building. In this tale, the building is purchased by a foreign investor, dismantled piece by piece, and taken overseas.

Why the Chicken Crossed the Road (Houghton, 1987).

A hysterical foray into the realm of cause and effect, depicting the lives of imaginary villagers who are portrayed with bold, bright colors.

FOR MORE INFORMATION

Articles

Ammon, Richard. "Profile: David Macaulay." *Language Arts* 59, no. 4 (April 1982): 374–78.

"Meet Author-Illustrator David Macaulay." *Frank Schaffer's Classmate* (November/ December/January 1988–1989): 34–35.

Web Sites

Cafe Z. "An Interview with David Macaulay." URL: <http://www.viewz.com/ interview/dmacaulay/dmacaulay. shtml> (Accessed March 2000).

Hastings, Wally. *David Macaulay*. URL: <http: //lupus.northern.edu:90/hastingw/ macaulay.htm> (Accessed March 1999).

Houghton Mifflin Web Site. "The New Way Things Work: David Macaulay." URL: <http://www.waythingswork. com/bio.htm> (Accessed March 2000).

Rao, Vivek. *David Macaulay: Redefining Writing*. URL: <http://www.ultranet. com/~denebola/archives/vol38_ issue2/news/003.htm> (Accessed March 2000).

James Marshall

San Antonio, Texas
October 10, 1942–October 15, 1992

- 📖 *George and Martha*
- 📖 *Miss Nelson Is Missing*
- 📖 *The Stupids*

ABOUT THE AUTHOR/ILLUSTRATOR

James Edward Marshall was a native of Texas, and his love of the state found its way into many of his books. Marshall was born in San Antonio on October 10, 1942. His father, George E. Marshall, worked for the Southern Pacific Railroad. His mother, Cecille Harrison Marshall, was a homemaker. His childhood was spent on a large farm, off Fredericksburg Road, sixteen miles from town. Marshall's mother, who drove him to school in a Meteor hearse, read to him from many children's books, as well as some adult books including those by Charles Dickens and a twenty-four-volume history of England.

Marshall's interest in drawing began early and lasted until a second-grade teacher managed to discourage him when she laughed at a picture he had drawn of a pecan tree. By the age of nine, he had turned to music. Both of Marshall's parents were musical. His father had his own dance band in the 1930s and played on the radio. His mother sang in the church choir. Marshall was talented and played both the viola and the violin. His music ability earned him a scholarship to the New England Conservatory of Music in Boston, where he studied viola.

One of Marshall's teachers was the principal violist with the Boston Symphony Orchestra, and Marshall was considered to be on his way to a successful musical career. In 1961, however, while flying to a Pablo Casals festival in Puerto Rico, his hand was injured during a rough plane landing. The injury was not severe, but it was enough to dash his aspirations for a professional music career.

Marshall enrolled and attended six different colleges. He attended Lamar University in Beaumont, Texas, where his father had been transferred. He felt it was the "least-interesting town on earth" and soon left to attend San Antonio College and then Trinity. It was at Trinity, while studying French, that he met Harry Allard, a French professor at the school. Years later, Allard collaborated with Marshall to create several children's books, including the Miss Nelson books. Eventually Marshall moved back east and graduated from Southern Connecticut State College with a degree in French and history.

In 1967, he returned to San Antonio. He got his first bulldog, Sophia, and the first of his many cats, Lorraine. Marshall really wanted to live in Boston, so he applied to teach at a Catholic School in Boston's South End. The mother superior asked if he could speak Spanish, and even though he was a French major, he lied and soon found himself teaching both French and Spanish in the high school. He made a deal with his students. If they came to class, they would get a "C"; if they helped to teach him Spanish they would get an "A."

It was during this time that Marshall returned to drawing, this time for his own enjoyment and to relax after the long days of faking his language ability. As he developed a sequence of sketches, a friend persuaded him to create a portfolio and to take his sketches to Walter Lorraine at Houghton Mifflin in Boston. He did, and within just a few weeks, he was offered a contract to illustrate Byrd Baylor's *Plink, Plink, Plink* (Houghton, 1971). Although that book was a commercial failure, Marshall was not discouraged. His two-year teaching career ended at the conclusion of the 1969–1970 school year.

Some time later, while visiting in Texas, Marshall was lying in a hammock on the patio at his mother's home in the little town of Helotes, outside of San Antonio. His mother turned on the television, which was airing a play, *Who's Afraid of Virginia Woolf?* Marshall was sketching cartoon characters and listening to the dialogue from inside the house. The characters he was drawing began as two dots, which became the eyes for some nonde-script animal. The animals needed names, and the play provided them. The hippopotamuses were named George and Martha. Marshall did not realize they were hippos until someone pointed this out to him later. He said that he "knew 'who' they were before he knew 'what' they were." George and Martha became the anchor characters in a series of books about two best friends. The first book, *George and Martha*, was published in 1972 by Houghton Mifflin and became an immediate success. The *New York Times* named the book one of the ten best illustrated children's books of 1972.

Over the years Marshall wrote and illustrated many books, including more books about George and Martha and books about the Stupids. Although he preferred to write his own texts, he did illustrate books written by other authors. When Marshall illustrated the work of others, he wanted the text to have a strong plot, contain an element of humor, and be "in tune" with his own individual style.

One of his most popular collaborations was the partnership he formed with his former French teacher, Harry Allard, to create the series about the Stupids and the Miss Nelson series, which featured the very original Miss Viola Swamp. One of the stories that surrounds the creation of the Miss Nelson series is the assertion by Marshall that Harry Allard was an interesting collaborator and often had spurts of creativity. At 3:00 AM one morning, Allard phoned James Marshall; all he said, before hanging up, was "Miss Nelson Is Missing." That was the beginning of the first book in the series featuring Miss Viola Swamp. Allard most often came up with the title, and then the two of them worked on the story together. Originally, Allard envisioned the characters in the Miss Nelson books as alligators, but Marshall wanted to create the characters as children. Marshall was successfully able to portray characters in a way that made them humorous and endearing to his young readers.

Marshall's books and their illustrations have been described as being "profound in their simplicity." He often carried a sketchbook with him to sketch as he tried to develop a character. Once he was familiar with a character, he began to think about where the character lived and who the character knew and what she or he did. The dialogue came next, as he put the characters into unusual situations. He often said that he liked to "shock, to surprise my readers." His advice to new writers often included the comment that "a book must have a good beginning and a strong middle, but without a knockout ending, you're shot." He also strove to create incentives for the reader to turn the page. The dialogue and illustration had to lead to the next page.

At one time, Marshall wanted to write an easy-to-read book but was under an exclusive contract at a publishing house, so he used his middle name and invented his cousin, Edward, who would write the book. When a publisher called to get some information about this new author, Edward Marshall, James made up a story about Edward living in a crematorium with his eighteen children. That bogus story was eventually put into publication. His own self-portrait appeared in *The Cut-Ups* (Viking, 1984). In that book, Marshall cast himself as the archcurmudgeon Lamar J. Spurgle, a former assistant principal who was portrayed as having "had enough kids to last him a lifetime." In contrast, Marshall himself was bookish and kindly, with a fine sense of humor.

Among the last books Marshall created were illustrated versions of several folktales: *Red Riding Hood* (Scholastic, 1987), *The Three Little Pigs* (Dutton, 1989), and *Hansel and Gretel* (Dial, 1990). His illustrations for *Goldilocks and the Three Bears* (Scholastic, 1988) earned a Caldecott Honor Book award. At the time of his death in 1992, Marshall had completed the illustrations for his final project, an illustrated version of Edward Lear's *The Owl and the Pussycat* (Houghton, 1992). In 1998, Houghton Mifflin released a facsimile edition of the book.

Marshall was a true lover of Texas, especially West Texas. Nonetheless, he claimed to have became a "New Englander, too. But I've never gotten warm." For a number of years, he divided his time between New York City and a former mill town in rural Connecticut, Mansfield Center. His home in Connecticut was once a general store. It had a pot-bellied Franklin Stove that dominated the living room of the small-but-efficient home with two bedrooms and a kitchen on the first floor. One or more of Marshall's several bulldogs and cats often visited the attic studio.

When Marshall set out to create, his goal was to create a "funny book." He wanted to entertain, and he did. His books are filled with twists, turns, and humorous events. Even though Marshall earned a Caldecott Honor Book award, he never received the Caldecott Medal. However, his books did win many awards, and his books consistently sold between 30,000 and 50,000 copies. In fact, at one bookshop signing he sold two thousand books in one day.

Maurice Sendak was Marshall's good friend. In the introduction to *George and Martha: The Complete Stories of Two Best Friends* (Houghton, 1997), Sendak said, "James the perfect friend was indistinguishable from James the perfect artist," thus paying tribute to a friend who raised friendship to an art and who contributed immeasurably to the world of children's books.

James Marshall died on October 15, 1992.

BOOKS AND NOTES

James Marshall's bulldogs and his cats often showed up in the illustrations in his books, but those who read and enjoy his books can often observe Marshall's love of Texas. In Marshall's *The Night Before Christmas* (Scholastic, 1985), Santa Claus wears cowboy boots with a Texas star on them. Boys dancing around the Mulberry Bush in his Mother Goose wear a bolero tie, a style that often is seen in Texas. Red Riding Hood picks large Texas sunflowers instead of the traditional small forest flowers often found in her story. In one of her stories, Martha can be seen fanning herself with a small souvenir paper fan from the Alamo. But most noticeable is the depiction of Miss Nelson's classroom as a Texas classroom. Miss Nelson has a small souvenir replica of the Alamo on her desk. A Texas map and Texas flag hang in the room. In many of the illustrations, James Marshall appears as a character, often with his trademark mustache.

Books Written and Illustrated by James Marshall

Goldilocks and the Three Bears (Scholastic, 1988).

Hansel and Gretel (Dial, 1990).

James Marshall's Mother Goose (Farrar, 1979).

Portly McSwine (Houghton, 1979).

Red Riding Hood (Scholastic, 1987).

Taking Care of Carruthers (Houghton, 1981).

Yummers, Too (Houghton, 1986).

George and Martha Series

George and Martha: The Complete Stories of Two Best Friends (Houghton, 1997).

George and Martha (Houghton, 1972).

George and Martha Rise and Shine (Houghton, 1976).

George and Martha One Fine Day (Houghton, 1978).

George and Martha Tons of Fun (Houghton, 1980).

George and Martha Back in Town (Houghton, 1984).

George and Martha Round and Round (Houghton, 1988).

Books Written by Edward Marshall and Illustrated by James Marshall

Owl and the Pussycat (HarperCollins, 1998).

Space Case (Dial, 1980).

Three by the Sea (Dial, 1981).

Troll Country (Dial, 1980).

Fox Series

Fox and His Friends (Dial, 1982).

Fox in Love (Dial, 1982).

Fox at School (Dial, 1983).

Fox on Wheels (Dial, 1983).

Fox All Week (Dial, 1984).

Fox Be Nimble (Dial, 1990).

Fox Outfoxed (Dial, 1992).

Fox on Stage. (Dial, 1994).

Books Illustrated by James Marshall

Cinderella. Retold by Barbara Karlin. (Little, Brown, 1992).

The Frog Prince. Retold by E. H. Tarcov. (Houghton, 1974).

The Night Before Christmas. Written by Clement C. Moore. (Scholastic, 1985).

Miss Nelson Series by Harry Allard

Miss Nelson Is Missing (Houghton, 1977).

Miss Nelson Is Back (Houghton, 1982).

Miss Nelson Has a Field Day (Houghton, 1985).

The Stupids Series by Harry Allard

The Stupids Step Out (Houghton, 1974).

The Stupids Have a Ball (Houghton, 1978).

The Stupids Die (Houghton, 1981).

FOR MORE INFORMATION

Articles

Harrigan, Stephen. "Growing Up with George and Martha." *Texas Monthly* (December 1987): 126–27.

Books

Holzschuher, Cynthia. *James Marshall* (Teacher Created Materials, 1998).

Bill Martin Jr.

◆ Rhyming ◆ Animals

Hiawatha, Kansas
March 20, 1916

📖 *Barn Dance!*

📖 *Brown Bear, Brown Bear, What Do You See?*

📖 *Chicka Chicka Boom Boom*

ABOUT THE AUTHOR

William Ivan Martin was born in Hiawatha, Kansas, on March 20, 1916. His grandmother was a storyteller who delighted the Martin family with her tales of family history. Martin grew up loving the language, but he could not read it. He says the first time he read a book came when he was twenty and had been admitted to college. In those days, he says, "nonreaders were admitted to college if they could muster tuition fees."

Martin says he was blessed as a child to have been taught by Miss Davis, who never missed a day reading aloud to the class. He always felt as if she were reading just to him. Among the things she read were the writings of Jack London, including his story "To Build a Fire," and Robert Louis Stevenson, whose *Treasure Island* was a favorite.

298

Now Bill Martin Jr. is the author of more than 300 books. When he speaks of writing books, he speaks first of "talking" them. At some point, the words get put down on paper, but first he must talk a story through to see if he is saying what he means. He needs to hear the words. Typical of his "writing style" is the story of how one of his best-known books, *Brown Bear, Brown Bear, What Do You See?*, came to be. Martin was living in New York City and had gotten on the Long Island Railroad train at Plandome Station for the thirty-three-minute ride to Penn Station. During that train ride, Martin worked out the entire story in his head. Along the way, he had repeated the words of some phrases out loud, to hear how the words sounded. A passenger beside him had eyed his curious behavior a few times, but by the time he got to his office, he was feeling very good about the story.

That story, says Martin, "was a sort of a watershed for me." Not only did it catapult him into the world of children's books, but it marked the entrance of illustrator Eric Carle into children's books as well.

Eric Carle was an art director for an advertising agency in the mid-1960s when Bill Martin Jr. saw an ad of a red lobster that Carle had designed; based on that illustration, Martin asked Carle if he would illustrate *Brown Bear, Brown Bear, What Do You See?* Carle has said that his mind immediately saw large sheets of paper, colorful paints, and the fat brushes of his earlier style and that the "opportunity changed my life."

Children's books have had a profound influence on Martin's work as well. He does not recall books in his childhood home and could not read as a child. The only children's book that left an impression on him was a copy of *The Brownies* by Palmer Cox that he had checked out of the Morrill Free Public Library in Hiawatha, Kansas. Martin could not read the verses Cox wrote, but his pen-and-ink illustrations of wee brownies engaged Martin in the "happy dreams of childhood."

Martin conquered his inability to read and eventually earned an undergraduate degree from Kansas State Teacher's College of Emporia. He began his teaching career at St. John and Newton high schools in Kansas, where he taught English, journalism, and dramatics. Eventually, he went on to earn both a master's degree and a doctoral degree in early childhood education from Northwestern University. His major graduate work included reading, creative writing, and elementary education. Martin moved to Winnetka, Illinois, where he became principal of Crow Island Elementary School.

In 1961, Martin moved to New York City where he went to work for Holt, Rinehart, & Winston and helped develop literature-based reading materials. He worked for the publisher for seven years before he launched his own career as an author and consultant. During the next twenty-five years, while living in New York City, Martin wrote books, traveled all over the United States, and shared his love of reading and writing with thousands of educators. He was invited to many college campuses as a visiting professor. He lectured, combining storytelling, reciting, singing, and philosophizing, across the United States from the University of California at Riverside to Northeastern University in Boston and to international audiences in Canada, Great Britain, Europe, and New Zealand.

Martin has collaborated with other writers. Among his most successful collaborations are the several titles he has created with John Archambault: *Chicka Chicka Boom Boom* (Simon & Schuster, 1989), *The Magic Pumpkin* (Holt, 1989), *Barn Dance!* (Holt, 1986), and *The Ghost-Eye Tree* (Holt, 1985). One of Martin's collaborations with Archambault, *Knots on a Counting Rope* (Holt, 1987), has been listed on many lists of Native American picture-book titles, although the Native American community has not embraced it as authentic. However, Martin's books generally gain favor because of the poetic, rhythmic language that helps to transfer the words on the page to the voice of the text. The words in his books are likely to figuratively swirl, zoom, or rock rhythmically across the page.

Martin began writing in an era when authors had more control over who was chosen to illustrate the text. He would often visit art galleries and scour publications in search of artists who might bring a fresh perspective to the pages of his books. Some of the best artists in the children's book field have illustrated his books, including Eric Carle, Ted Rand, Bruce Degen, Lois Ehlert, Steven Kellogg, Richard Egielski, and Martin's brother, Bernard Martin.

In the late 1990s, the Kansas Reading Association established the Bill Martin Jr. Award for picture books to honor the Kansas native. Among his more recent collaborative efforts are books with Michael Sampson, a professor at Texas A&M University. Sampson has authored several professional books in the area of literacy and has worked with Martin to conduct Pathways to Literacy workshops across the United States. In 1990, Sampson began writing children's books as well.

As a natural outgrowth of their professional association, the Sampson family and Martin became friends. One day, Michael Sampson and his wife, Mary Beth, were leaving their Texas home to visit Martin in New York City. On the way to the airport, Mary Beth convinced Michael to make a short stop to see a plot of land. The family had been searching, for five years, for a site to build a new home. Michael relunctantly agreed to stop and turned out to be very glad he did. The land seemed to be untouched by humans, and gigantic oak trees covered the area. The land was available, and Michael was excited. All the way to New York City, he thought about the land. When he landed, he immediately called back to hold the land. They took a taxi to Martin's apartment at 55th and Broadway and shared their good news with him. Michael sketched out the area, the lakes and the streams. Martin picked out a lake and said "Here's where I want to live." The lake was eventually named "Lake of the Blue Huron," and Martin moved to Texas and built a house in the spot he had chosen. In 1993, he moved to Woodfrost, the area that Martin named in honor of Robert Frost and his poetry about the woods.

Martin's home is nestled among the trees on a quaint, woodsy road. The front of his house is spanned with windows. The study where he handles correspondence faces out with two windows, and other windows allow him to craft his stories at the kitchen table and be greeted by the morning sun.

Martin's travel schedule is minimal these days, but he continues to write. He lives and works in his home in Woodfrost, near Commerce and Campbell, Texas.

BOOKS AND NOTES

Bill Martin Jr.'s books are creative in both text and form. The words virtually flow across the pages. The text is filled with song, poems, songs, and riddles that assist young readers to read and comprehend the words. The illustrations are as varied as his stories. Martin's books hold some of the finest art being executed in children's books—a virtual showcase of artists.

Barn Dance! With co-author John Archambault. Illustrated by Ted Rand. (Holt, 1986).

A Beasty Story. With co-author Steven Kellogg. Illustrated by Steven Kellogg. (Silver Whistle, 1999).

A Beautiful Feast for a Big King Cat. With co-author John Archambault. Illustrated by Bruce Degen. (HarperCollins, 1994).

Brown Bear, Brown Bear, What Do You See? Illustrated by Eric Carle. (Holt, 1967; 1992).

Chicka Chicka Boom Boom. With co-author John Archambault. Illustrated by Lois Ehlert. (Simon & Schuster, 1989).

Fire! Fire! said Mrs. McGuire. Illustrated by Richard Egielski. (Harcourt, 1996).

The Ghost-Eye Tree. With co-author John Archambault. Illustrated by Ted Rand. (Holt, 1985).

The Happy Hippopotami. Illustrated by Betsy Everitt. (Harcourt, 1970).

Knots on a Counting Rope. With co-author John Archambault. Illustrated by Ted Rand. (Holt, 1987).

Listen to the Rain. With co-author John Archambault. Illustrated by James Endicott. (Holt, 1988).

Old Devil Wind. Illustrated by Barry Root. (Harcourt, 1993).

The Maestro Plays. Illustrated by Vladimir Radunsky. (Harcourt, 1994).

The Magic Pumpkin. With co-author John Archambault. Illustrated by Robert J. Lee. (Holt, 1989).

Polar Bear, Polar Bear, What Do You Hear? Illustrated by Eric Carle. (Holt, 1991).

Si Won's Victory. With co-author Michael Sampson. Illustrated by Floyd Cooper. (Celebration Press, 1996).

Swish. With co-author Michael Sampson. Illustrated by Michael Chesworth. (Holt, 1997).

The Turning of the Year. Illustrated by Greg Shed. (Harcourt, 1998).

The Wizard. Illustrated by Alex Schaefer. (Harcourt, 1994).

Words. With co-author John Archambault. Illustrated by Lois Ehlert. (Simon, 1993).

FOR MORE INFORMATION

Web Sites

The Scoop—Bill Martin, Jr. Biographical Sketch. URL: <http://www.Friend.ly.Net/scoop/biographies/martinbill/index.html> (Accessed March 2000).

The Bill Martin, Jr. & Michael Sampson Homepage. URL: <http://tiill.com/authors.htm> (Accessed March 2000).

Jacqueline Briggs Martin

◆ Biography ◆ Community ◆ Historical Fiction

Sharron L. McElmeel

Lewiston, Maine
April 15, 1945

📖 *Green Truck Garden Giveaway*

📖 *Snowflake Bentley*

📖 *Washing the Willow Tree Loon*

ABOUT THE AUTHOR

Jacqueline Briggs Martin first read of Wilson A. Bentley when her own two children were youngsters. Bentley's story appeared in a children's magazine. She remembers reading that Bentley had said that he could not "remember a time when he did not love snow more than anything else in the world, except his mother." Several years later, she and her children were walking in a snowfall, and one of them mentioned that Snowflake Bentley would have loved the weather. When Martin began to think about another book to write, she turned to Wilson A. Bentley. She spent hours researching this man who spent his life studying snow and taking pictures of individual snow crystals. The result was the book *Snowflake Bentley*. Mary Azarian illustrated the book and her handpressed woodcuts earned her the 1999 Caldecott Medal. The woodcuts reflected the strength of the rugged farm life, as well as the delicate snowflakes that Bentley had photographed. This book was Martin's eleventh book for children and provided a highlight in a career that began with a series of books about a lovable little mouse named Bizzy Bones.

Jacqueline Briggs was born April 15, 1954, in Lewiston, Maine. Her childhood was spent on a dairy farm near Turner, Maine, where her parents raised five children. The farm has been in her family for seven generations. Her father, Hugh, loved the land and loved his work; he "tended the meadow." Her mother, Alice, was "a full-time mother and bookkeeper for the farm. She is also a wonderful cook and baker and once, with friends, prepared and baked fifty apple pies in her kitchen in one day." She has also made beautiful quilts.

Jacqueline Briggs Martin's life has always contributed bits and pieces to her writing. In her first three books, the beloved meadow, which held an apple orchard, was the setting for the stories. The first of Martin's stories, *Bizzy Bones and Uncle Ezra* (Lothrop, 1984), came about when her son Justin was just four years old and declared he wouldn't get out of bed. He was afraid that the wind would blow him away. Justin's childhood fears helped Martin create the first draft. Writing in her daughter Sarah's partially used school tablet, Martin began the story about a little boy afraid of the wind. Along the way, the boy in the story became a mouse who lived in a work shoe with his Uncle Ezra. The mouse, like Justin, was afraid of the wind. Two more Bizzy books followed. Other childhood memories and her family made their way into the Bizzy books. Martin remembered visiting her aunt during her own childhood and hearing her uncle sing about "rovers and riverboat riders." That showed up in *Bizzy Bones and Moosemouse* (Lothrop, 1986), as did her daughter Sarah's name and the French horn that Sarah played during high school. In *Bizzy Bones and the Lost Quilt* (Lothrop, 1988) Martin's mother's quilts make an appearance on the clothesline of the pack rats who befriend Bizzy and Uncle Ezra and help them to find Bizzy's lost quilt.

By 1992, Martin had moved on to write a tale sparked by information she gathered one summer about two of her aunts who had operated a dry goods store in Maine at the turn of the century. Few people in the town remembered her aunts, but one elderly watchmaker did remember that the sisters had "the finest horse in town."

From that small bit of information, Martin began to think about who might have cared for the horse while her aunts operated the dry goods store. The book presents three fictional scenarios that answered the question. Her aunts' names were Stella Prince and Zilpha Prince, but in the book Martin used her grandmother's name, Cara, for one aunt. The horse was named Prince. *The Finest Horse in Town* (HarperCollins, 1992) was published the same year as *Good Times on Grandfather Mountain* (Orchard, 1992), which was inspired by an article she read called "Homer Ledford: Making Music." She found the article in a 1989 catalog from the clothing company Lands' End. Ledford used a pocketknife to whittle parts of his instruments, and Martin used that concept to develop the main character, who is so good he can whittle "a spider out of wood." His optimism is evident at every turn—even when his house is blown down. In the end, neighbors show up to help him rebuild and to enjoy his music.

While Jacqueline was growing up in Maine, she and her brother tried to rescue injured birds by putting them in shoeboxes lined with handkerchiefs. "As if there would be good vibrations just from the shoe box that would be healing. Of course we ended up burying these casualties." Years later, a visit to her sister's lakeside house in Maine, where the families could hear the call of the loons as they dropped off to sleep, helped her capture those memories. The result was *Washing the Willow Tree Loon* (Simon & Schuster, 1995). Martin's husband, Richard, grew up watching birds, and Jacqueline Martin learned to share his interest. "My family and I have bird feeders, and we always watch for herons as we are driving or hiking by water. These were parts of my life but not my writing until I read an article about volunteers who go to the sites of oil spills and wash injured birds." As she researched the rescue of these birds, she began to look for people who would populate her story as volunteer bird washers. Martin remembered a woman who visited her classroom when she was in third grade. The woman showed the children a hummingbird nest and talked about hummingbirds. Martin decided that someone like her should be in the story.

While she was working on the book, the Martins had their house painted. The housepainter was a wonderful, kind, gentle man, and he went into the book, too. Then Martin remembered the family who had lived up the avenue, when they first moved to their present house. The family had two pet ducks that wandered up the avenue. Martin put someone who might have been in that family in the book. Martin took her quest for information about rehabilitating injured birds to Tri-State Bird Rescue and Research, a group in Delaware. They provided Martin with a lot of help, and she said, "I learned a lot writing this book and had a wonderful time thinking about the kinds of people who love and care for birds."

As a young child Jacqueline often walked through the fields or along the lanes lined with stone walls and wondered about people who had been there before. Her curiosity brought about *Grandmother Bryant's Pocket* (Simon & Schuster, 1995), the story of a young girl, Sarah, who visits her grandparents' home after her dog Patches is killed in a fire. The small, gold scissors; healing herbs; and pieces of cloth for bandages that Grandmother Bryant keeps in her pocket are important in helping Sarah accept the loss of Patches and learn to overcome her fears. While researching this story, Martin discovered a book about a midwife who had lived in Maine during the eighteenth century and who had kept a diary. The diary provided information about the daily life in that time and gave Martin the basis for the midwife character, Sarah's grandmother, who used herbs in the healing process.

Many of Martin's books are set in rural settings that bring to mind the dairy farm where she grew up. But Martin has "always wanted to live by the water." So when she got the idea for writing *Higgins Bend Song and Dance* (Houghton, 1997) about Simon Henry, an old fisherman, his friend Potato Kelly, and a wily catfish that Simon was determined to catch, Martin sensed that what she really had was, "a good reason to walk along rivers, talk to river people, watch fish, and sit in the sun." As part of her research, she "collected pictures of fish and rivers and imagined rivers and river people."

Her interest in gardening and how things grow encouraged her to write *Button, Bucket, Sky* (Carolrhoda, 1998), a story of acorns and growing trees. When Martin begins writing a book, she prefers to write by hand. Writing by hand, she says, "keeps me from writing too fast and, for me, gives the story a better foundation." Each new book is begun in a new notebook and with a new pen. She takes all the notes for the book, from reading or just ideas, in that notebook. Once the first draft is composed, Martin transfers the story to her computer. Revision is much easier on the computer, and she revises, revises, and revises. Finally, when she thinks she has revised a story as much as she can, she puts it away for several months. This is very difficult because she is always excited and wants to send the story off immediately, but whenever she has given in and has sent the story off, she ends up being embarrassed. When she reviews a story after a couple of months, she finds the blemishes, writing mistakes, shallow characters, and other flaws that she did not see in the initial writing stage.

Her interests often lead her to read or observe something that brings about a story idea. When Martin's daughter was a youngster and reading the Laura Ingalls Wilder books, they planted a wildflower garden together, much as Laura might have had when she was growing up. The Martin home has wonderful garden patches filled with interesting plants and flowers. Sharing cuttings from her plants or collecting seeds to give to someone who admires a particular flower is a common occurrence. So when Martin read of the real-life Home Gardening Project, begun by Dan Barker in Portland, Oregon, the story caught her interest. Barker started out with a pickup truck, dirt, and plants; in the years since he began the project, he has given away thousands of gardens. Many of those who received his gardens are still growing food and plants. Martin says, "When I read of these green gifts, I knew I wanted to write a children's book about them. I added the almanac so readers could begin their own gardens, in buckets, tubs, or the ground." *Green Truck Garden Giveaway: A Neighborhood Story and Almanac* (Simon & Schuster, 1997) tells the story of two generous people who use their green truck to give away gardens, just as Dan Barker did.

Jacqueline Briggs Martin began writing when her daughter and son were preschoolers and she was staying home with them. She wrote while they napped; when they gave up their naps, she got up at 4:00 AM to write. She wrote for nine years before she saw one of her books in published form. She had enjoyed writing as a high school and college student but the interest had lapsed while she began her family. Reading books with her children rekindled the interest. For a few years, Martin taught preschool in her home-town and wrote during the time when she wasn't teaching. Now she is a full-time writer; her children are grown, so her writing time is not restricted. Martin says, "I love writing, but I can't write all day. When I'm not writing I read, or walk outside, or do the things we all have to do—cook, wash dishes, sweep the floors. I like making quilts, but only if I'm doing it with someone I love. In the warm seasons, I like to work outside. I grow roses, chilies, and herbs for tomato sauce. And I work in the prairie that Sarah started in fourth grade when she was reading the Laura Ingalls Wilder books. I also enjoy tent camping, hiking, and canoeing. I love watching rivers and watching fish."

Jacqueline Briggs Martin lives in Mt. Vernon, Iowa, with her husband, Richard, an English professor on the Cornell College Campus. Justin still plays the drums as Bizzy did in Martin's first book. Jacqueline Briggs Martin continues to write in the hope that her "stories will remain with people like the memories of old friends or good melodies and will make them smile on a quiet afternoon or a rainy day."

BOOKS AND NOTES

Ideas for Martin's books come from almost everywhere—from her family, magazine articles, and her surroundings. Regardless of the topic, Martin does extensive research about any topic included in her books. Even though she does not have direct input on the illustrations, her research has, at times, aided the illustrator to create accurate illustrations. When Petra Mathers was preparing the illustrations for *Grandmother Bryant's Pocket*, the project editor sent some of the pictures of the Maine landscape and the houses and barns of the period that Martin had found. In another instance, the art editor and illustrator, in an effort to draw in young readers, had agreed to illustrate a very young boy as one of the bird washers in *Washing the Willow Tree Loon*. Fortunately, Martin was apprised of the decision before the book went to press because that illustration would have compromised the accuracy of her research. Federal law prohibits underage youngsters from handling contaminated animals. The illustrator revised the illustration to show the young man as a youthful-but-adult male handling the bird.

Books Written by Jacqueline Briggs Martin

Button, Bucket, Sky. Illustrated by Vicki Jo Redenbaugh. (Carolrhoda, 1998).

At the turn of the century, Prince was the finest horse in a small town in Maine. Martin imagines three situations concerning who cares for Prince while his owners, two sisters, are operating their dry-goods store.

Good Times on Grandfather Mountain. Illustrated by Susan Gaber. (Orchard, 1992).

Old Washburn lives on the mountain with his animals. One by one, the animals leave, but Old Washburn retains his positive attitude as he makes music and whittles a fiddle from a log or a spider from a stick.

Grandmother Bryant's Pocket. Illustrated by Nancy Carpentar. (Simon & Schuster, 1995).

Grandmother Bryant's pocket contained her most important possessions, and those possessions help her granddaughter Sarah deal with the loss of her dog. Set in 1787.

Green Truck Garden Giveaway: A Neighborhood Story and Almanac. Illustrated by Alec Gillman. (Simon & Schuster, 1997).

A gardening story of two friends who give away gardens to their neighbors and in the process help build a community of friends.

Higgins Bend Song and Dance. Illustrated by Brad Sneed. (Houghton, 1997).

A fishing story about two friends who live next to a river where the friends watch for herons—that is, until Simon Henry decides he wants to catch the wily catfish, Oscar.

The Lamp, the Ice, and the Boat Called Fish. Illustrated by Beth Krommes. (Houghton, 2000).

The story of a 1913 Canadian Arctic expedition that explored the high north.

Snowflake Bentley. Illustrated by Mary Azarian. (Houghton, 1998).

A narrative biography of Wilson A. Bentley, who lived in Jericho, Vermont, in the 1870s. Sidebars fill in the gaps with statistics and additional information about Bentley and his love of snow.

The Finest Horse in Town. Illustrated by Susan Gaber. (HarperCollins, 1992).

A story sure to inspire the youngest naturalists to save some acorns and to plant their own oak tree in the spring.

Washing the Willow Tree Loon. Illustrated by Nancy Carpenter. (Simon & Schuster, 1995).

An oil spill off the New England coast threatens the well-being of many animals along the coast. This story concerns itself with the plight of one hapless Loon and the many people who are involved in rescuing the oil-soaked bird.

Bizzy Bones Series

Illustrated by Stella Ormai. Each of the books features a little mouse who makes his home with Uncle Ezra.

Bizzy Bones and Moosemouse (Lothrop, 1986).

Bizzy is apprehensive about staying the weekend with Uncle Ezra's friend, Moosemouse.

Bizzy Bones and the Lost Quilt (Lothrop, 1988).

Bizzy Bones loses her favorite quilt, but with the help of friends his quilt, although tattered, is found and repaired.

Bizzy Bones and Uncle Ezra (Lothrop, 1984).

Uncle Ezra helps Bizzy Bones overcome his fear of the wind.

FOR MORE INFORMATION

Articles

McElmeel, Sharron L. "Author Profile: Jacqueline Briggs Martin." *Library Talk* 8, no. 5 (November/December 1995): 19–21.

Web Sites

Jacqueline Briggs Martin Home Page. URL: <http://www.geocities.com/Athens/Forum/1090> or <http://www.geocities.com/jbmartin_2000/> (Accessed March 2000).

Mercer Mayer

◆ Family Relationships ◆ Folklore ◆ Humor

Little Rock, Arkansas
December 30, 1943

📖 *A Boy, a Dog, and a Frog*

📖 *Little Critter's Camp Out*

📖 *There's a Nightmare in My Closet*

ABOUT THE AUTHOR/ILLUSTRATOR

Mercer Mayer was born December 30, 1943, in Little Rock, Arkansas. His father, who was in the U.S. Navy, did not see him until Mercer was two years old. Mayer spent most of his childhood in the southern part of the United States. On one base in Arkansas, he spent time wandering off to mud holes, through the forest, and wrestling with his dog into mud holes. He caught lizards, snakes, turtles, frogs, and anything else that he could. His pockets were often filled with his found treasures. By the time Mayer was a teenager, his father was transferred to Hawaii, so the family moved there. After finishing high school, Mayer went on to study at the Honolulu Academy of Arts. His art teacher felt that children's books were a dead end, so the students spent only one week learning about children's book illustrating. Mayer thought that was the best week of school and certainly the most fun he had ever had.

Mayer moved to New York and continued his studies. In 1964, he did not have money to pay for classes at the Art Students League in New York, so he became a monitor of one of the painting classes. Part of his job was to assist new students when they arrived. In that capacity, he met Marianna Ammirati. Within one week, the two classmates were married. They lived in a section of Long Island called Sea Cliff. Mayer took a job working at an advertising agency, but what he wanted to do was write and illustrate books.

One day, he saw one of his parents' friends from their time in Hawaii, Martha Alexander. She was a very good friend of his mother, and he hadn't seen her for ages. Mayer stopped by her studio, and she showed him what she was doing—illustrating children's books. When he told her that was "all [he] ever wanted to do." She told him to "just do it."

So Mayer took her advice and went home and began drawing the things that meant something to him: fanciful, funny characters. He drew little boys playing in a mud hole, dogs pulling kids into the mud, and kids wrestling with dogs. Then he added some funny little monsters. He drew anything that popped into his head. He saved all of the drawings and began walking around to publishers without appointments. He walked in and dumped his drawings down on the editors' desks of many publishers.

Within two weeks, Mayer had a contract to illustrate a book—John D. Fitzgerald's *The Great Brain* (Dial, 1967). His first book of his own was the wordless *A Boy, a Dog, and a Frog* (Dial, 1967). The following year, seven titles that Mayer illustrated were published by Dial and Harper & Row publishers. Among those books was one of his most popular, *There's a Nightmare in My Closet* (Dial, 1968). That book catapulted him firmly into the world of children's books. During the next three decades, he wrote or illustrated dozens of other books. His decade-long marriage to Marianna ended, but their collaboration remained. Together he and Marianna Mayer created several books, including: *Me and My Flying Machine* (Parents, 1971), *A Boy, a Dog, a Frog, and a Friend* (Dial, 1971), and *Beauty and the Beast* (Four Winds, 1978; SeaStar, 2000). For the most part, Mayer illustrated all of his books, but there was one exception. In the late 1970s, Mayer began writing a manuscript, *Appelard and Liverwurst* (Four Winds, 1978), a story about a farmer who has many wild adventures with his new farm hand, a rhinoceros. He said, "It [the manuscript] sounded and felt like it should be Steven Kellogg's story. So I sent the story to him and asked him if he would like to illustrate it, and that if he didn't like it my feelings wouldn't be hurt." Kellogg agreed and did illustrate the book. He made a few changes, with Mayer's approval. They worked so well together that they worked on another title, *Liverwurst Is Missing* (Four Winds, 1981). Many of Mayer's books have been reissued over the years and these two titles were reissued ten years after they were first published.

By 1973, Mercer Mayer had married his second wife, Jo, and they had one daughter. A son was born in 1980. During their childhood, Mayer told many stories to his children. They loved to hear any story he made up; Mayer said that many of them were the kind of stories "that were unpublishable." But the stories Mayer submitted for publication had to make sense to him. In 1976, Mayer joined Golden Publishing, and in the years that followed, he created the Little Monster series and a series of books about Little Critters and the Critter Kids. The Little Monster and Little Critter tales have been characterized as didactic. Children enjoy the zany illustrations, but the obvious "lesson about life" is not generally lost on the reader or the reader's parents.

In 1984, Mayer was cofounder of Angelsoft, Inc., a multimedia packaging company. His cofounder was John R. Sansevere, executive vice president with Deijon, Inc. The company set out to develop computer programs, books, toys, and games for the consumer market. Angelsoft was associated with Paperwing Press, the book packaging division.

Over the years, in addition to Marianna Mayer and Steven Kellogg, Mayer has worked with a few other authors. Mayer illustrated Jay Williams's *Everyone Knows What a Dragon Looks Like* (Four Winds, 1976) and continued to illustrate the Great Brain novels by J. D. Fitzgerald. In recent years, he has collaborated with his third wife, Gina, to write several more Little Critter books for Golden Books. In addition, he is illustrating some mini novels based on the Little Critter characters, which are written by J. R. Sansevere and Erica Farber. *Night of the Walking Dead (Part 1)* (Random House, 1997), *Night of the Walking Dead (Part 2)* (Random House, 1997), and *The Goblin's Birthday Party* (Random House, 1996) are among the titles.

Mayer's typical writing schedule is a seven-hour day, five days a week. He and his wife and co-author, Gina Mayer, live in Roxbury, Connecticut. Mayer's two children are adults. When Mercer Mayer is not drawing or reading, he likes to walk in the woods or sit on the riverbank.

BOOKS AND NOTES

When Mercer Mayer, writes he often starts with a picture he imagines. He uses his imagination to think of a particular thing and what the that thing might do. He says, "You can write a book from any point of view. You can start with something or an idea about something . . . all you have to do is imagine things and not edit them." Eventually, all of the pieces begin to fall into place, and a story comes together. He has sketched his boyhood memories, monsters and other frightening creatures, and tapestry-like paintings for the retellings of the time-honored stories. All the books in the following book list were written and illustrated by Mercer Mayer, unless otherwise indicated.

Books Illustrated by Mercer Mayer

Folklore

Beauty and the Beast. Written by Marianna Mayer. (Four Winds, 1978; SeaStar, 2000).
A traditional tale of romance and adventure set in the 1800s.

East of the Sun and West of the Woods. Written by Mercer Mayer. (Four Winds, 1980).
Mayer's retelling weaves the traditional plot elements with his own inventions along with some details from the story of the frog released from the witch's spell by a princess' kiss.

The Sleeping Beauty. Written by Mercer Mayer. (Macmillan, 1984).
A retelling of a traditional tale of a young princess who is enchanted until she is awakened with a kiss.

Wordless

Ah-choo (Dial, 1976).

A Boy, a Dog, a Frog, and a Friend. Co-authored with Marianna Mercer. (Dial, 1971).

A Boy, a Dog, and a Frog (Dial, 1967).

Bubble Bubble (Parents, 1973).

Frog Goes to Dinner (Dial, 1974).

Frog on His Own (Dial, 1973).

The Great Cat Chase: A Wordless Book (Four Winds, 1974).

Books About Monsters and Things

There's a Nightmare in My Closet (Dial, 1968).

There's an Alligator Under My Bed (Dial, 1987).

There's Something in My Attic (Dial, 1988).

Little Critter's Series

Little Critter: Just a Toy. Co-authored with Gina Mayer. (Golden Books, 2000).

Little Critter's the Best Present (Golden Books, 2000).

Little Critter's the Fussy Princess (Golden Books, 1989).

Little Critter's the Night Before Christmas (Random, 1992).

Little Monster at Home (Golden Books, 1978).

Mercer Mayer's Little Critter's Day (Golden Books, 1989).

Little Monster's Mother Goose (Golden Books, 1979).

Little Monster's Word Book (Golden Books, 1977).

Mercer Mayer's A Monster Followed Me to School (Golden Books, 1991).

Family Stories

Just Grandma and Me (Golden Books, 1983).

Just Grandpa and Me (Golden Books, 1985).

Just Leave Me Alone. Co-authored with Gina Mayer. (Reader's Digest Kids, 1995).

Just Say Please. Co-authored with Gina Mayer. (Western, 1993).

The School Play (Golden Books, 1999).

Shibumi and the Kitemaker (Marshall Cavendish, 1999).

Taking Care of Mom. Co-authored with Gina Mayer. (Western, 1993).

The Loose Tooth. Co-authored with Gina Mayer. (Reader's Digest Kids, 1995).

FOR MORE INFORMATION

Web Sites

Craig, Jason, and Inez Ramsey. "Internet School Library Media Center: Mercer Mayer." URL: <http://falcon.jmu.edu/~ramseyil/mayer.htm> (Accessed March 2000).

Educational Paperback Association. "Mayer, Mercer." URL: <http://www.edupaperback.org/authorbios/mayerme.html> (Accessed March 2000).

An article from H. W. Wilson's Junior Authors and Illustrators series © 1978.

Robert McCloskey

◆ Community ◆ Family Relationships

Hamilton, Ohio
September 15, 1914

📖 *Lentil*
📖 *Make Way for Ducklings*

Rodney Chadbourne

ABOUT THE AUTHOR/ILLUSTRATOR

Robert McCloskey is now well into his 80s and although he was once a full-time writer and illustrator, he now says, "Not anymore." But the legacy of books that he has given to readers is invaluable.

McCloskey was born in Hamilton, Ohio, on September 15, 1914, the son of Howard Hill and Mable Wismeyer McCloskey. He attended public school and was very interested in everything musical until he found out about electrical gadgets. From the time his fingers were long enough, he took piano lessons and next started to play the harmonica, the drums, and then the oboe. Later he began to collect old electric motors and bits of wire and old clocks. He became fascinated with the building of model trains and cranes and then operating them with remote controls. He made the family's Christmas tree revolve, twinkle, and buzz. He imagined himself as an inventor. But then he began to create drawings for his high school annual.

In 1932, McCloskey's drawings and other artwork earned him a scholarship to the Vesper George Art School in Boston. Every day on the way to school, he walked through the Boston Public Gardens and saw a family of ducks on their way to the pond. He didn't know it then, but these ducks would become very important to him in a few years. Meanwhile, McCloskey continued his studies and his pursuit of an art career. One of the commissions he received was to create some bas reliefs for the Hamilton, Ohio, municipal building. He later moved to New York City to study at the National Academy of Design. For two summers, he painted on Cape Cod. His art career, however, seemed to be a bust. He only sold a few watercolors and never did sell any of his oil paintings.

One day, he took his art portfolio, filled with "woodcuts, fraught with black drama," to May Massee, the children's book editor at Viking. She was not impressed. Massee suggested that he forget the dragons, Pegasus, and other creatures. Instead, the two of them talked of Ohio. He left and went into the commercial art field and eventually returned to Ohio. It was there that Massee's words began to make sense, and McCloskey began to draw images that were around him every day. The result was *Lentil* (Viking, 1940), the partly autobiographical story of a young boy and his harmonica in a small Midwestern town.

McCloskey returned to New York, where he took the manuscript and drawings back to Massee; she bought the book. On the basis of his new paintings, he obtained a job in Boston where he was to assist Francis Scott Bradford to create a mural of the famous people of Beacon Hill on the Lever Brothers' Building. It had been four years since he had been in Boston, but the ducks in the public gardens were still there. This time, McCloskey heard a few stories about them. McCloskey developed his own story idea about a family of ducks. He began to make sketches, and to render them accurately, he looked at stuffed specimens in the American Museum of Natural History in New York City, consulted with an ornithologist at Cornell University, and eventually purchased four live ducks and took them home to his Greenwich Village apartment and put them in the bathtub. At the time, he was sharing an apartment in an old house with illustrator Marc Simont. The ducks made a lot of noise, and McCloskey tried to keep the ducks quiet, but after a time the neighbors' complaints convinced McCloskey that the ducks had to go. Two of the ducks turned out not to be mallards, but McCloskey had already gotten his sketches. He had spent several weeks on his hands and knees following the ducks around with tissues and a sketchbook. The book *Make Way for Ducklings* was published by Viking in 1941, and the following year McCloskey was given the Caldecott Medal for his illustrations.

In 1943, McCloskey's third book, *Homer Price* (Viking), was published. He had written a humorous story about Homer Price, a small-town boy who was much like the young McCloskey had been. McCloskey's early interest in mechanical gadgets came in handy as he described Homer's Uncle Ulysses' famous doughnut-making machine. As the book was about to be printed, McCloskey's editor asked him to create an additional illustration for the book. He hadn't reread the story for a few months. He was being inducted into the army, but he took the time to create the additional drawing of five robbers in bed. Unfortunately, the text refers to only four robbers. As long as twenty-five years later, young readers were still writing McCloskey to tell him of their "discovery." The book's illustrations were never corrected in the United States printings, but when the book was translated into Japanese, "they took the fifth man right out of the bed." After McCloskey returned home from the war, he wrote a sequel titled *Centerburg Tales* (Viking, 1951).

McCloskey's service during World War II interrupted his career in children's books. He served as a sergeant in the Army and was stationed in Alabama, assigned to draw training pictures. During this time, he married Margaret "Peggy" Durand, the daughter of the world-renowned storyteller Ruth Sawyer Durand. Ruth Sawyer wrote *Roller Skates* (Viking, 1936; 1995) which won the Newbery Medal in 1937.

After the war, the McCloskeys spent a year in Italy and then returned to the United States. The McCloskeys' two daughters, Sally (Sal) and Jane, were born in the late 1940s and quickly became part of McCloskey's "everyday" life that he put into his books. Robert and Peggy McCloskey bought an island in Penobscot Bay, Maine, near Deer Isle, where they spent most summers May through October. His next three books developed from life on the island. *Blueberries for Sal* (Viking, 1948) was created with Sal as the berry picker and Peggy as the mother. The kitchen he illustrated on the book's end papers is his own except for the quaint stove that he drew from his mother-in-law's home in Hancock, Maine.

The second Maine title, *One Morning in Maine* (Viking, 1952), focuses on Sal and the loss of her first tooth. Jane is depicted as the baby, creeping around mischievously. McCloskey included the family's English setter, Penny, and their black cat, Mozzarella. When the family goes to the village to shop, the village shown is the very same one the McCloskeys went to when they rowed to the mainland for their supplies.

In between creating his own books, he illustrated his mother-in-law's classic tale, *Journey Cake, Ho!* (Viking, 1953). The title became an enduring one that still is found on many book lists for early primary grade readers. McCloskey's illustrations for this book included scenes from his mother-in-law's house.

Time of Wonder (Viking, 1957), the third Maine book, was McCloskey's first book illustrated in full color. The beauty of the Maine Island is the overall theme of this book, which shows the ever-changing scenes on the island. The illustrations took McCloskey three years to create and earned McCloskey his second Caldecott Medal. He was the first artist to be awarded the Caldecott Medal twice.

He created full-color illustrations for a fourth Maine book, *Burt Dow: Deep-Water Man* (Viking, 1963). This book actually was the last book that he both wrote and illustrated. McCloskey continued illustrating a few books by other writers, but he turned his interest to constructing puppets instead. In the late 1960s, he began creating a new type of puppet. His studio was turned into a machine shop, and he learned how to operate a lathe and how to cut rubber. His interest had been sparked by observing Morton Schindel at Weston Woods Studio and the studio's production of several of McCloskey's books into films.

McCloskey's art career brought him to illustrate the four titles in Keith Robertson's Henry Reed series, but his writing and illustrating career ended by the early 1970s. His books continue to please readers, however, so his contribution to children's literature remains vibrant.

In the next decades, the McCloskeys divided their time between their home in Maine, Connecticut, and the Virgin Islands. McCloskey received many honors including an honorary doctorate in literature degree from Miami University at Oxford, Ohio, in 1964; an honorary doctorate of letters from Mount Holyoke College in 1967, and the prestigious Regina Medal by the Catholic Library Association for his distinguished contributions to children's literature.

In 1987, the city of Boston installed a bronze sculpture of Mrs. Mallard and her eight ducklings. The sculpture was created by Nancy Schon, a sculptor who has become well known for her public art. Mrs. Mallard is thirty-eight inches tall, and the ducklings between twelve and eighteen inches tall. They are installed on a thirty-five-foot pathway of old Boston cobblestone in the Boston Public Garden. Many visitors each year "follow the ducklings" through the State House and Louisburg Square, across Charles Street, and into the Boston Public Garden, where they are able to see the ducklings. The inscription says, "This sculpture has been placed here as a tribute to Robert McCloskey, whose story "Make Way for Ducklings" has made the Boston Public Garden familiar to children throughout the world. 1987" As children "follow the ducklings," they might notice that the "lending library" referred to in the book is now a 7-Eleven store. Schon has commented that she likes public art because it allows young people to touch and feel the art, in contrast to art that is placed in a museum and is generally untouchable. It does have its disadvantages: She has had to cast a replacement for one of the ducklings, Quack.

Four years after the Boston sculpture was put in place, an identical casting was created and taken to the Soviet Union by Barbara Bush. She was accompanying President George Bush, and as part of the historic START Treaty ceremony, Mrs. Bush presented the sculpture to Raisa Gorbachev. The sculpture was installed across a pond from the famous sixteenth-century Novodevichy Monastery in Novodevichy Park, just fifteen minutes from Red Square in Moscow. It also sits on a pathway of old Boston brick cobblestones, coupled with black basalt stones exactly like those found in Red Square. The plaque in Moscow reads, "This sculpture was given in love and friendship to the children of the Soviet Union on behalf of the children of the United States." This second sculpture was installed in 1991.

The McCloskey daughters, Sal and Jane, have been gone from the household for more than three decades. Sal is a teacher in Maryland. Jane was attending Mount Holyoke the year her father was awarded an honorary doctorate from the institution. Most recently, the McCloskeys have spent much time in Florida, but they continue to live much of the year at their island retreat in Maine.

BOOKS AND NOTES

Robert McCloskey's books are drawn from his own life and set in places where he lived and worked. *Lentil, Homer Price,* and the *Centerburg Tales* seem to be right out of his childhood in Hamilton, Ohio. His award-winning picture books are set in Maine, clearly reflecting the influence of the family's island retreat. The books he illustrated are not clearly in one locale or the other but certainly do reflect the comfort and friendliness of the Midwestern background that shaped his own life. His most

popular title, *Make Way for Ducklings,* was set in Boston.

Books Written and Illustrated by Robert McCloskey

Blueberries for Sal (Viking, 1948).

Burt Dow, Deep-Water Man (Viking, 1963).

Centerburg Tales (Viking, 1951).

Homer Price (Viking, 1943).

Lentil (Viking, 1940).

Make Way for Ducklings (Viking, 1941).

One Morning in Maine (Viking, 1952).

Books Illustrated by Robert McCloskey

Journey Cake, Ho! Written by Ruth Sawyer. (Viking, 1953).

The Man Who Lost His Head. Written by Claire Huchet Bishop. (Viking, 1942).

FOR MORE INFORMATION

Web Sites

Educational Paperback Association. "McCloskey, Robert." URL: <http://www.edupaperback.org/authorbios/mcclosk.html> (Accessed March 2000).
An article reprinted from H. W. Wilson's Junior Authors and Illustrators series © 1951.

Horn Book Virtual History Exhibit—Anita Silvey. "Robert McCloskey Interview." URL: <http://www.hbook.com/exhibit/mccloskeyradio.html> (Accessed March 2000).

Public Art—Nancy Schon. "Make Way for Ducklings." URL: <http://www.schon.com/ducklings.html> (Accessed March 2000).
A photograph of a Boston Garden sculpture of Mrs. Mallard and her eight ducklings.

Patricia McKissack

◆ Biography ◆ Family Relationships ◆ Historical Fiction

Smyrna, Tennessee
August 9, 1944

📖 *Christmas in the Big House, Christmas in the Quarters*

📖 *Flossie and the Fox*

📖 *Mirandy and Brother Wind*

ABOUT THE AUTHOR

Patricia L'Ann Carwell, the daughter of Robert Carwell and Erma Carwell, was born on August 9, 1944, in Smyrna, Tennessee, near Nashville. She spent her first three years in Nashville, and later the family moved to St. Louis. Patricia remembers listening to her mother reading poems on hot summer nights. Among her favorites were poems by Paul Dunbar, especially "Little Brown Baby." When her parents divorced, Patricia's mother went back to Nashville. Patricia stayed in St. Louis with her paternal grandparents. When she was fourteen, she moved to Nashville to live with her mother and maternal grandparents.

For the first seven years of her life, Patricia was an only child and an only grandchild. She says she had "a wonderful childhood." She had two dogs, Buster and Smokey, that followed her everywhere. Her early school-ing began in a segregated school with forty children in a classroom and few books, but the teachers encouraged each student to do her or his best. Patri-cia says she "loved school." She also loved writing. She corresponded with pen pals in three countries. It thrilled her when her third-grade teacher told her that she liked a poem Patricia had written.

After she moved back to Tennessee and completed high school, she went on to Tennessee State University, where she earned her undergradu-ate degree in 1964. She married Fredrick McKissack on December 12, 1965. They had met years earlier, having both graduated from Pearl High School, but he was five years older than she was. After high school, he entered the U.S. Marine Corps. Once they both were adults and college graduates, the age difference did not matter any more. Fredrick McKissack proposed to her on their second date, and they were married four months later.

After Fredrick McKissack had earned a civil engineering degree, he worked for the city of St. Louis and the U.S. Army. Later he owned his own general contracting company in St. Louis.

During the early years of their marriage, Patricia McKissick went on to earn a master's degree from Webster University. She taught junior high English and wrote when she had the time. In addition to her teaching and writing, McKissick was also mothering three young sons. After nine years as a teacher, she ended that career and spent the next six years working as an editor for Concordia Publishing. It was during this time that the McKissacks established a writing service, All-Writing Service, in St. Louis. The company wrote technical manuals, promotional materials, and other commercial publications. Patricia McKissack also found time to write fiction. In 1981, she devoted herself full-time to writing.

McKissack wrote twenty nonfiction books before writing a picture book. She wrote *Flossie and the Fox* (Dial, 1986) and sent the manuscript off to Ann Schwartz, then an editor at Dial. Schwartz found the fifteen-page manuscript in the slush pile and said that there were too many words for a picture book, but McKissack didn't want to "give up any words." After Schwartz told McKissack that some of the descriptions she was trying to convey through the text could be shown in the illustrations, McKissack was able to shorten her text. For example, when the *Flossie and the Fox* manu-script was finally accepted, it was just six pages long. McKissack wrote that it was "hotter than a usual Tennessee day" in *Flossie and the Fox*, and then Rachel Isadora's illustrations in a warm palette tell the reader more about that day. In *Mirandy and Brother Wind* (Knopf, 1988), when McKissack wrote,

"It was spring," Jerry Pinkney's illustrations made sure the reader knew how a spring day looked.

Patricia McKissack became particularly well known for her nostalgic picture books, set in the rural South, that blended reality with a touch of fantasy. In many of her books, she created young black female protagonists who were assertive and who knew how to take care of themselves. *Flossie and the Fox* features just such a character: Flossie knows how to outfox the fox, who plans to steal the eggs she is carrying to her neighbor. McKissack also attempts to create books with positive images, and she lets the illustrations help her accomplish that. All elements—character, action, setting, theme—cannot be developed equally in the text alone because the average picture book has only 2,500 words.

McKissack created adaptations of classical folklore into abridged versions meant for the earliest of readers. These were not as successful as some of her other earlier reader titles for the Rookie Reader series. Original stories for this series were ingenious and popular. Her title *Who Is Who?* (Children's Press, 1983), co-authored with Fredrick McKissack, features twins based on her own sons. It is a clever tale that delineates the differences between identical twins and uses the concept of opposites very effectively. Her titles about Messy Bessy are equally clever.

As a wordsmith, McKissack plays with words and revises each sentence to get just the right sound. She uses her skills to tell stories about African American people. In addition to her picture books, Patricia McKissack also writes biographies of African Americans who have contributed to American society. Fredrick McKissick has been involved with the writing service and co-authored many of Patricia McKissick's books for older readers. One of his favorite projects was researching *Christmas in the Big House, Christmas in the Quarters* (Scholastic, 1994).

Although one of their goals has been to introduce children to African and African American history and historical figures, they have also written accounts of Native American tribes and have ventured into writing about the holocaust. When the McKissacks collaborate, they have no "magic formula." They talk about the idea and outline it as they talk. Fredrick most often digs into the research, and Patricia inputs the information he uncovers on the computer. Frederick fact checks a hard copy and refines it, then he gives it back to Patricia to make his changes and add changes of her own to the computer file. They repeat the process as long as it takes to generate a manuscript with which they are both comfortable.

Many of Patricia McKissack's stories come from her family. McKissack's great-grandmother Leanna inspired the story *Ma Dear's Aprons* (Atheneum,

1997). Leanna was a single mother of three and raised her children in Alabama during the first two decades of the twentieth century. She was a domestic worker who made her living doing chores for others. McKissack's strongest connection to her great-grandmother is a plain muslin apron. Leanna wore that apron as she did her work. McKissack transformed the apron into a badge of honor and hard work, a symbol of self-reliance. The aprons, one for each of the six days that Ma Dears works, show her creativity in balancing her long days as a household worker and as a mother.

A photograph that shows McKissack's grandparents participating in a traditional cakewalk inspired another story. Her grandfather boasted that his wife's dancing had captured the wind. The story that developed became *Mirandy and Brother Wind*. When McKissack began the story, she decided to use her husband's grandmother's name. The grandmother's name was Miranda, but that name jolted the flow of the language so she changed Miranda to Mirandy. The book also posed some illustration problems. Jerry Pinkney had to devise a way to illustrate Brother Wind. Some illustrations came more easily. As a child, McKissack was involved with the African Methodist Episcopal Church in Mississippi. At that church, she remembered a woman who scandalized the more conservative parishioners by wearing red on Sunday. Ms. Poinsettia is a lot like that woman. When Pinkney began to create an image for her, he drew a picture of a woman who looked a lot like his own wife, Gloria. The illustrations earned the illustrator, Jerry Pinkney, a Caldecott Honor Book Award.

Pinkney's illustrations are very authentic, but McKissack praises her other illustrators as well. Of Scott Cook, who created the illustrations for *Nettie Jo's Friends* (Knopf, 1989), she said, "He is white but was able to develop a love and a feel for the work of an African American." McKissack said he was knowledgeable about customs and even realized that the phrase "piney woods" is a southern phrase that indicates a stand of trees, not necessarily woods filled with pine trees. Rachel Isodora, illustrator of *Flossie and the Fox*, is a New Yorker whose grandfather told her stories in Yiddish. She was very careful to let her illustrations reflect the skill of the storyteller.

For many years, the McKissacks lived in a large, remodeled, inner-city home in St. Louis. Their office was not in their home but in a three-room suite in a high-rise office complex. One room is their library, one room is Fred's office, and one room is Patricia's office. They began work between 9:00 and 9:30 AM and worked until they had finished what they had to do that day.

In 1994, the McKissacks were each awarded an honorary Doctor of Arts and Letters degree from the University of Missouri at St. Louis. They now make their home in Chesterfield, Missouri, where they enjoy visits from their grandson and spend leisure time gardening and growing roses. Their sons Robert and John are in their thirties, and their older brother, Fredrick Jr., is a writer and journalist. He lives in Chicago and has collaborated with Patricia on an award-winning title for older readers, *Black Diamond: The Story of the Negro Baseball Leagues* (Scholastic, 1994). Fredrick Jr. collaborated with his father to write *Black Hoops: The History of African-Americans in Basketball* (Scholastic, 1999).

BOOKS AND NOTES

Patricia McKissack does not like the practice of putting age levels on books, many of which have varied uses. Simple books can often invoke some higher-order thinking skills in older readers. McKissack's stories often instruct while conveying a pride in African American heritage. Her books often feature strong female characters, and her nonfiction writing has been cited as evenhanded. Although she has contributed to a vast library of knowledge about African Americans through her biographies of such figures as A. Philip Randolph, Martin Luther King Jr., and Mary McLeod Bethune, it is her picture books that bring her inclusion in this volume. The selective book lists below represent her contributions to the body of picture books and early readers for children.

Books Written by Patricia McKissack

Picture Books

Christmas in the Big House, Christmas in the Quarters. Co-authored with Fredrick McKissack. Illustrated by John Thompson. (Scholastic, 1994).
A historical view of Christmas in two households.

Flossie and the Fox. Illustrated by Rachel Isadora. (Dial, 1986).
In a satisfying reversal of the action in "Red Riding Hood," Flossie shows that she has what it takes to outwit the fox. Isadora's illustrations are created with watercolor and ink.

Goin' Someplace Special. Illustrated by Jerry Pinkney. (Atheneum, 2000).
Set in the 1950s in segregated Nashville, Tennessee, a young girl only wants to be allowed into the public library.

The Honest-to-Goodness Truth. Illustrated by Giselle Potter. (Atheneum, 2000).
Libby's promise never to tell a lie creates even more problems than when she wasn't quite so truthful.

Mirandy and Brother Wind. Illustrated by Jerry Pinkney. (Knopf, 1988).
Mirandy is determined to catch Brother Wind and have him for her partner in the upcoming junior cakewalk.

Ma Dear's Aprons. Illustrated by Floyd Cooper. (Atheneum, 1997).
A portrait of an African American family set in the early decades of the twentieth century.

Nettie Jo's Friends. Illustrated by Scott Cook. (Knopf, 1989).
Nettie Jo has the cloth to make her doll a dress but has no needle, so she asks a rabbit, a fox, and finally, a panther for help.

Early Readers

Messy Bessey. Illustrated by Dana Regan. (Children's Press, 1987, 1999). Rookie Reader.

A gentle story about a little girl dealing with everyday situations. Other books about Messy Bessey include *Messy Bessey and the Birthday Overnight* (Children's Press, 1998); *Messy Bessey's School Desk* (Children's Press, 1998); *Messy Bessey's Garden* (Children's Press, 1991); and *Messy Bessey's Holidays* (Children's Press, 1999).

Monkey-Monkey's Trick: Based on an African Folk Tale. Illustrated by Paul Meisel. (Random House, 1988).

A Step Into Reading Book: Step 2. Monkey-Monkey asks for help in building his house, and when Hyena tries to trick him, Monkey-Monkey has a trick of his own.

Who Is Who? Co-authored with Fredrick McKissack. Illustrated by Elizabeth M. Allen. (Children's Press, 1983).

A Rookie Reader about twins, Bobby and Johnny.

FOR MORE INFORMATION

Articles

Bishop, R. "A Conversation with Patricia McKissack." *Language Arts* 69, no. 1 (January 1992): 69–74.

"Celebrate Black History Month with Patricia McKissack." *Instructor* 101, no. 5 (January 1992): 55+; photos.

Elliott, Ian. "Patricia C. McKissack: Going for a Dream." *Teaching Pre K–8* 23, no. 8 (May 1993): 36+; photos.

McKissack, Patricia. "Sojourner Truth: Ain't I a Woman? Acceptance speech for the *Boston Globe*-Horn Book Award for nonfiction." *Horn Book* 70, no. 1 (January 1, 1994): 53+.

Walters, Laurel Shaper. "Building Bridges to Black History." *Christian Science Monitor* 87, no. 62 (February 24, 1995): 14, 1c.

Books

McKissack, Patricia. *Can You Imagine?* (Richard C. Owens, 1997). Illustrated with photographs by Myles Pinkney.

David McPhail

◆ Bears ◆ Fantasy

**Newburyport,
Massachusetts
June 30, 1940**

Sharron L. McElmeel

📖 *Edward and the Pirates*

📖 *First Flight*

📖 *Lost!*

📖 Pig Pig Series

ABOUT THE AUTHOR/ILLUSTRATOR

David McPhail grew up in a poor family, but he says he really did not know they were poor because he was surrounded by people who loved him. In addition to his parents, there were two brothers, a sister, aunts, uncles, and many cousins. He had "a wonderful childhood." David was the big brother. His two brothers, Ben and Peter, where just a few years younger. He remembers his father as working all night and playing with the kids all day.

McPhail was born in Newburyport, Massachusetts, on June 30, 1940, and spent many of his childhood days exploring the fields and woods near his home. Much of his time was spent playing alone. Robin Hood was his favorite character, but he also imagined himself as Robinson Crusoe and

Hiawatha. He even built a tree house and a pit house, which he covered with sticks and leaves. Drawing occupied much of his time as well. When he was just two years old, his grandmother cut up brown paper bags and gave him a black crayon with which to draw. He drew everything he could think of on anything that was available. When he was five, he often filled a wagon with his drawings and took them over to his "girlfriend." Sometimes he got in trouble for drawing in school at times when he wasn't supposed to.

By the time he entered high school, he aspired to be a big league baseball player, despite the fact that he really wasn't very good at the game. During basketball season, he imagined himself a professional basketball player, but he wasn't very good at basketball either. Nonetheless, he loved sports and played them all year round.

Once McPhail had graduated from high school, he entered art school. After a year, he quit and decided to become a rock-and-roll star. He bought himself a guitar, took guitar lessons, and practiced and practiced. He spent six years playing in a rock band in small clubs. He never made more than ten dollars a performance, and the other odd jobs that he picked up paid minimum wage. His travels took him to California, where he played his guitar less and less and began to draw more and more.

He finally figured out that he wasn't going to get rich or become a famous musician, so, in 1963, he reentered the art school at the Museum of Fine Arts in Boston. He still wasn't very serious. He enjoyed parties with other students, made friends, worked some odd jobs, and drew a little. One of his roommates was Michael McCurdy, who became a renowned artist. A girlfriend of another roommate was an editor for a textbook company, and when the roommate showed her some of McPhail's drawings, she offered him a job illustrating textbooks. At the time, he was driving a truck delivering furniture and eggs for $35. McPhail was happy to illustrate for her company.

Every picture he drew for the textbook company earned him $100. In 1966, McPhail was working as a shipping clerk in a book clearinghouse when he rediscovered children's books. He spent lunch hours looking at the picture books that came across his desk and began his own collection of books. He began to write and illustrate stories of his own.

McPhail's first two books included *In the Summer I Go Fishing* (Little, Brown, 1971), a story about a little boy who sets up a lemonade stand after failing to attract any buyers for his fish, and *The Bear's Toothache* (Little, Brown, 1972). They marked his entry into the world of children's books. Since that time, he has created more than fifty picture books. He says he "loves writing and illustrating just as much today as I did then."

McPhail often works on two or three books at a time. His books have included wonderful bear characters, ingenious youngsters who get into interesting situations, and playful pigs. In *The Bear's Toothache*, the little boy who tries to help the bear pull his tooth is much like McPhail's own son, who was two or three years old when McPhail was creating the book's illustrations. McPhail often writes about bears in his books, and near Boston, Massachusetts, there is a bookstore named for McPhail's book *Henry Bear's Park* (Little, Brown, 1976).

He likes to draw pigs and used his neighbor's pig as a model when he drew the illustrations for his "Pig Pig" books. The book, *Pigs Aplenty, Pigs Galore* (Dutton, 1993), is dedicated to his friend, Jack, who owned the pig. Many of McPhail's books contain clever clues to events that will follow. For example, in *Fix-It* (Dutton, 1984), the family is concerned about why the television will not turn on. Mother and Father each take a turn at trying to figure it out. When the television repairman arrives, he finds that the television set was not plugged in. By then, the child has discovered a book to read and is much too engrossed to watch television. The title pages feature illustrations that give the reader a clue to the unplugged television.

Other than visiting the schools where his nieces and nephews attend, David McPhail does not usually visit schools or go on autographing tours. In 1998, however, he went on a multicity autographing tour for Little, Brown, and as part of the tour he visited Harrison Elementary School in Cedar Rapids, Iowa. At the time, one of his newest books was *Edward and the Pirates* (Little, Brown, 1998). In response to questions from the children, he revealed that when he is drawing, he does sometimes "mess up." He said, "Yes, sometimes if I do a drawing and it doesn't work out. I have to be pleased." He explained that when he draws in pen and ink and then paints over it, the lines still show up; the ink is waterproof and the watercolor is transparent, so the paint will not cover up the lines. He painted the illustrations for *Edward and the Pirates* using acrylic on canvas. Sometimes he puts himself in his books because, "It's my book, and I can do anything I want. So sometimes I put myself in." His book about Edward was dedicated to his oldest son, Tristan, and to his nephew, Patrick, who was the model for the boy in the story. McPhail likes to write and says it doesn't take long to write a story, but it takes longer to create the illustrations. It took him two to three months to create the illustrations for *Edward and the Pirates*. When he is creating the illustrations for a book, he sits at his drawing board, a drawing table, and he likes to listen to music. He draws with a basic #2 pencil and an ink pen.

For most of his life as an artist, McPhail has lived in the Northeast. For many years, he lived in Tamworth, New Hampshire. Once he endured a hurricane that threatened his beachfront home. Currently, he has returned to his hometown, Newburyport, Massachusetts, where he can wander through the fields and woods of his childhood. He has four children—Tristan, Joshua, Gabrian, and Jaime—and three stepchildren. He still loves baseball and music—including rock and roll. He enjoys the beach and wonderful books.

BOOKS AND NOTES

In the beginning of his career, David McPhail used a lot of cross-hatching as he created his illustrations. He created many of his later books using pen and ink with watercolor. He created some illustrations with pastels but then returned to pen and ink and watercolors. In some of his more recent books, he has created the illustrations with acrylics. Many of his books contain a visual or textual reference to reading. In *Fix-It*, the child is, at the end of the book, more interested in reading a book than in watching television. In many of his other titles, the characters are shown reading books. Learning to read is a focal point in *Santa's Book of Names* (Little, Brown, 1993). In that book, Edward learns to read during a special ride with Santa. In the sequel, *Edward and the Pirates* (Little, Brown, 1997), Edward reads everything he can—from cereal boxes to storybooks. The book is really a celebration of the power of reading and imagination.

Books Written and Illustrated by David McPhail

Annie & Co. (Holt, 1991).

The Bear's Toothache (Little, Brown, 1972).

A Bug, a Bear, and a Boy (Hello Reader! Level 1; Scholastic, 1998).

A Bug, a Bear, and a Boy Go to School (Hello Reader! Level 1; Scholastic, 1999).

Drawing Lessons from a Bear (Little, Brown, 2000).

Edward and the Pirates (Little, Brown, 1997).

First Flight (Little, Brown, 1987).

Fix-It (Dutton, 1984).

A Girl, a Goat, and a Goose (Hello Reader! Level 1; Scholastic, 2000).

Goldilocks and the Three Bears: A Retelling of a Classic Tale (Heath, 1989).

Henry Bear's Park (Little, Brown, 1976).

Lost! (Little, Brown, 1990).

The Magical Drawings of Moony B. Finch (Doubleday, 1978).

Mole Music (Holt, 1999).

The Return of Moony B. Finch (Doubleday, 1993).

Santa's Book of Names (Little, Brown, 1993).

Pig Pig Series

Pig Pig Gets a Job (Dutton, 1990).

Pig Pig Goes to Camp (Dutton, 1983).

Pig Pig Grows Up (Dutton, 1980).

Pig Pig and the Magic Photo Album (Dutton, 1986).

Pig Pig Rides (Dutton, 1982).

Pigs Aplenty, Pigs Galore (Dutton, 1993).

Books Illustrated by David McPhail

The Bear's Bicycle. Written by Emilie Warren McLeod. (Little, Brown, 1974).

The Nightgown of the Sullen Moon. Written by Nancy Willard. (Harcourt, 1983).

The Tale of Peter Rabbit. Written by Beatrix Potter. (Scholastic, 1989).

FOR MORE INFORMATION

Articles

Raymond, Allen. "David McPhail: He Leaps Over Chasms." *Teaching K–8* 23, no. 3 (November/December 1992): 40–42.

Books

McPhail, David. *In Flight with David McPhail* (Heinemann, 1996).

Web Sites

Harrison Elementary School: Visiting Authors. "David McPhail." URL: <http://www.cr.k12.ia.us/Harr/davidmc.html> (Accessed March 2000).

The Scoop. "David McPhail." URL: <http://www.friend.ly.net/scoop/biographies/mcphaildavid/index.htm> (Accessed April 2000).

Bernard Most

♦ Dinosaurs, Fiction ♦ Wordplay/Riddles

New York, New York
September 2, 1937

📖 *Four & Twenty Dinosaurs*
📖 *The Littlest Dinosaur*
📖 *When the Dinosaurs Come Back*

ABOUT THE AUTHOR/ILLUSTRATOR

Walt Chrynwski

Bernard Most's childhood was spent in New York City, where he was born on September 2, 1937. He grew up in East Harlem and eventually lived in an apartment building at First Avenue and 104th Street. He attended the High School of Art and Design and, in 1959, received an undergraduate degree in the fine arts from the Pratt Institute in Brooklyn. His career began in advertising, where he worked for many major New York advertising agencies. He and a partner established a creative consulting firm, Bernie and Walter, Inc. Meanwhile, he married Amy Beth Pollock on February 12, 1967. They became the parents of two sons: Glenn Evan and Eric David.

For more than two decades, Most worked in advertising and even rose to creative director and vice president of one firm before beginning his own business. Since college, however, Most had dreamed of writing and illustrating children's books. He always loved picture books, especially concept books such as Crocket Johnson's *Harold and the Purple Crayon* (Harper, 1955). He worked in the advertising and consulting business during the day and wrote at night.

Most says he came very close to having books published many times, but it was after his own children were born that he really focused on books for his two young sons. Reading books to them helped inspire him to persist in his efforts to create books. When in the first grade, his older son wrote about dinosaurs and how he wished that they would come back. That idea sparked Most's first published book, *If the Dinosaurs Came Back* (Harcourt, 1978; 1995). Since then, Most has had published a couple of dozen books, many about dinosaurs.

Even though his books seem fanciful and playful, Most does much research to make sure the information they contain is accurate. The ideas generally come when Most questions "What if?" The answers he comes up with are often the basis for his next book. When he wrote *The Littlest Dinosaur* (Harcourt, 1989), he visited the library to find out about small dinosaurs. He researched their size and habits. He explored his own home to find common objects that might be compared with the size of those small dinosaurs.

Most spends a lot of time in the library and has commented that "going to the library is like going on a treasure hunt." He is always amazed at the interesting information and ideas he finds at the library. When he is researching information for a book, he goes to the library often. Once he has all of his facts and information, he begins to write the text and create the illustrations in his studio. One thing he can do is make the dinosaurs any color he wants because no one really knows what color they were. Even in books that appear to be purely fanciful, Most has included information. For example, in *Where to Look for a Dinosaur* (Harcourt, 1993), Most has pictured an itemirus dancing with the ballerinas. That illustration is a clue as to where the dinosaur lived. The book links the dinosaurs with the countries in which fossils of that particular dinosaur have been found.

In one book, *A Dinosaur Named After Me* (Harcourt, 1991), Most makes dinosaurs named "Bernard-osaurus" and "Zach-iosaurus." He has also created books that use wordplay to interest readers. Many of them—such as *Zoodles* (Harcourt, 1992) and *Pets in Trumpets and Other Word-Play Riddles* (Harcourt, 1991)—encourage readers to join in the fun and to create other words-within-words riddles based on the patterns shown in the books.

Bernard Most and his wife Amy live in Scarsdale, New York. They share their home with pets, including many tropical fish, which have become a hobby for Most. Their two sons completed high school in Scarsdale and are on their own.

BOOKS AND NOTES

Bernard Most is best known for his books about dinosaurs. Some information, such as the color of dinosaurs, is not known, but researchers have ascertained a lot of other information about dinosaurs, and Most integrates many of those facts into his narratives about dinosaurs and animals.

A Pair of Protoceratops (Harcourt, 1998).
A pair of protoceratops engage in alliterative activities, such as packing for preschool, partying with pals, and peeling potatoes.

A Trio of Triceratops (Harcourt, 1998).
A trio of triceratops engages in alliterative activities, such as touching their toes, tooting trumpets, and telling tales.

ABC T-Rex (Harcourt, 2000).
A young T-Rex loves the ABCs so much that he eats them up.

Catbirds & Dogfish (Harcourt, 1995).
A fascinating collection of creatures with compound names—horseflies, squirrel monkeys, tiger sharks, elephant seals, and so forth. A small picture of the real animal and full-page whimsical illustrations of the animal.

Catch Me If You Can! (Harcourt, 1999).
Little Dinosaur is not afraid of the big dinosaur because he is her grandfather.

Cock-a-doodle-moo (Harcourt, 1996).
A cow attempts to help a rooster when he loses his voice.

Four & Twenty Dinosaurs (Harper, 1990; Harcourt, 1999).
Traditional nursery rhymes with dinosaurs as main characters.

If the Dinosaurs Came Back (Harcourt, 1995).
Speculation on what we might do with dinosaurs if such creatures actually came back to earth.

The Littlest Dinosaur (Harcourt, 1989).
A fanciful look at the smallest dinosaurs that lived. Dinosaurs are shown in relation to contemporary household objects.

Peek-a-moo (Harcourt, 1998).
Play peek-a-boo with a cow.

Row, Row, Row Your Goat (Harcourt, 1998).
A goat, a cow, and a pig, together with other farm animals, row their boat down the stream in a variation on a traditional song.

The Very Boastful Kangaroo (Harcourt, 1999).
A teeny tiny kangaroo cleverly wins the jumping contest.

Whatever Happened to the Dinosaurs? (Harcourt, 1995).
Speculation as to what really did happen to the dinosaurs.

Z-Z-Zoink (Harcourt, 1999).
A little pig has trouble finding a place to sleep because he snores so loudly.

FOR MORE INFORMATION

Limited information can be found on book jacket flaps. No articles, books, or Web sites were located.

Videos

Get to Know Bernard Most (Harcourt, 1993).

Helen Oxenbury

◆ Animals ◆ Humor

Ipswich, Suffolk, England
June 2, 1938

📖 *Farmer Duck*

📖 *The Three Little Wolves and the Big Bad Pig*

📖 Tom and Pippo Series

📖 *We're Going on a Bear Hunt*

ABOUT THE AUTHOR/ILLUSTRATOR

Helen Oxenbury turned to illustrating children's books when she found herself at home with two young children and wanted something to do. She "apprenticed" under the tutelage of one of the best children's illustrators/authors, her husband John Burningham.

The couple grew up in Suffolk, met at art college, and married. Now both John Burningham and Helen Oxenbury are involved in children's books, but they work separately in their Hampstead Heath home.

Helen Oxenbury was born June 2, 1938, in Suffolk, England, the daughter of Thomas Bernard Oxenbury and Muriel Taylor Oxenbury. She grew up in the Suffolk area and as a teenager enjoyed scene painting for local theaters and selected the Central School course in theater design. After college, Oxenbury traveled to Israel because Burningham was there doing alternative military service. When Burningham returned to England, Oxenbury remained in Israel to work as a designer for the National Theatre of Israel.

Eventually, she returned to England and found work in television and film as a scene designer. She and Burningham were married on August 15, 1965, and in the next few years their son, William Benedict, and daughter, Lucy, were born.

To care for her children, Oxenbury gave up her career in set design. She says that at that time, "It was jolly difficult to do two things, and we didn't have money for nannies." She wanted something to do at home, so she turned to book illustration, even though her work would be in direct competition with Burningham's work. According to Burningham, Oxenbury is very productive when faced with obstacles. During the first ten years of her career, she juggled motherhood and her illustrative work, in part because she was able to work at home. As the children grew, the juggling got easier, but Oxenbury's work slacked off. Then, when the children were ages twelve and thirteen, a third child, Emily, arrived. Again, with the challenge of juggling infant care with the work involved in maintaining her career, Oxenbury focused on her work and "started working very hard" again.

With the birth of "Em," the focus of Oxenbury's work changed. She turned to books that would please Emily. She pared down her own pictures to spare forms and bouncy babies. She became know for the books she created that were designed for infants, concept books with babies in the pictures. As Emily grew older, Oxenbury turned back to the type of books she had illustrated earlier, geared toward the primary child. Oxenbury doesn't want to be pigeonholed, however. She wants to be free to do the type of books that please her. In recent years, she has illustrated collections of nursery stories and classic poetry.

Oxenbury seldom writes her own texts, but she has authored some titles, the most notable of which are the Tom and Pippo series, which focuses on the interactions of a young boy named Thomas and his toy monkey companion, Pippo. Tom and Pippo have experiences similar to those that many young children have.

For more than a decade, John Burningham and Helen Oxenbury have maintained a home in the hills of southwest France and a home in north London. Their home in France provides a refuge from work. Their studios are in their Hampstead Heath home. Together they have built an interest in collecting antiques and rebuilding old houses and share an interest in tennis and good wine. Both hope to provide "good children's books" to young readers.

BOOKS AND NOTES

Helen Oxenbury's titles range from very simple concept books for the infant market to illustrated narratives of some of the most beloved titles in children's literature. Other authors have written most of the books that she has illustrated, but she has to "find the right text. It's like finding a house one likes—it can take a long time."

Oxenbury illustrated Eugene Trivizas's *The Three Little Wolves and the Big Bad Pig*. It is a "fractured" version of the classic "Three Little Pigs" tale that experienced a slight revision to show political sensitivity in the light of a tragic event. When the cuddly wolves go out on their own and build a good strong house, the pig comes along and uses his sledgehammer to knock it down. An even stronger house is destroyed by a pneumatic hammer. When they use concrete and armor to fortify their third house, the pig uses dynamite to blow the house down. When the three wolves build a house of flowers—with a "bluebell" as the doorbell, the pig "smells the flowers" and begins to dance on the lawn. The wolves decide to invite him in and, through their communication, they become friends. Oxenbury's watercolor illustrations have been described as clever and witty.

Unfortunately, after the publication of the trade edition of Trivizas's story, the United States experienced the trauma of the bombing of the Oklahoma Federal Building. So when the story was included in the Houghton Mifflin reading basal series, the text was revised. The original text and illustration showed the third house being exploded by dynamite. In the revision, the house is demolished by a wrecking ball.

Books Illustrated by Helen Oxenbury

The Dragon of an Ordinary Family. Written by Margaret Mahy. (Dial, 1992).
A very ordinary father gives his ordinary son a dragon as a pet; what was an ordinary family begins some extraordinary adventures.

Farmer Duck. Written by Martin Waddell. (Candlewick, 1992).
A hardworking duck takes care of the farm when the farmer is too lazy. The rest of the animals get together and chase the farmer out of town.

Franny B. Kranny, There's a Bird in Your Hair. Written by Harriet Lerner and Susan Goldhor. (HarperCollins, 2000).
Franny declines to cut her wild hair even when her family insists. Instead, she puts a bird in her hair when she attends a family reunion.

The Growing Story. Written by Ruth Krauss. (HarperCollins, 2000).
A young boy does not think he has grown during the summer, but when he tries on his winter clothing, he realizes that he has.

The Three Little Wolves and the Big Bad Pig. Written by Eugene Trivizas. (McElderry, 1993).
A fractured reverse version of the traditional tale about the conflict between pig and wolf—with a surprising ending.

Books Written and Illustrated by Helen Oxenbury

Helen Oxenbury's ABC of Things (Macmillan, 1971; 1993).
To introduce the letters of the alphabet, various objects are shown with appropriate labels.

I See (Candlewick, 1995).
An infant board book, filled with labeled objects. Part of a series of "Baby Beginner Board Books" that includes *I Can*, *I Touch*, and *I Hear* (All Candlewick, 1995).

It's My Birthday (Candlewick, 1994).

Several animal friends bring ingredients and help a "birthday child" to make a birthday cake.

Tom and Pippo Series

Tom and Pippo on the Beach (Candlewick, 1993).

Tom and Pippo on the Bicycle (Candlewick, 1993).

Tom and Pippo and the Dog (Candlewick, 1989).

Pippo Gets Lost (Candlewick, 1989).

Everyday adventures of Tom and his stuffed monkey, Pippo.

FOR MORE INFORMATION

Limited information can be found on book jacket flaps. No articles, books, or Web sites were located.

Bill Peet

◆ Animals ◆ Environment

Grandview, Indiana
January 29, 1915

- 📖 *Joel and Jethro Were a Troll*
- 📖 *The Whingdingdilly*
- 📖 *Zella Zach and Zodiac*

ABOUT THE AUTHOR/ILLUSTRATOR

Bill Peet spent twenty-seven years at a temporary job and then moved on to create some of the best-loved children's books on library shelves today. He was born on January 29, 1915, in a very small town on the banks of the Ohio River, Grandview, Indiana. Bill Peet's birth name was William Bartlett Peed. In 1947, at the age of thirty-five, he began to use "Peet" as his surname.

His memories of the town include the dull white pig and the rusty red pig that the family raised in their backyard. When Peet was three years old, the family moved to Indianapolis. It was during World War I, and there were many army tanks on railroad flatcars moving through the Midwest. The family's first home was just a block from the railroad yards, near the edge of the city. It was just a thirty-minute hike to the open countryside. On Saturdays, Bill, his two brothers, and several of the other children in the neighborhood went into the countryside and explored. They explored the dark woods filled with squirrels, chipmunks, weasels, opossums, and raccoons. Once in a while they would catch a glimpse of a fox disappearing into the brush. Peet and his brothers also spent much time on his grandfather's rustic old farm, which they found even more interesting than the countryside.

Peet's first visit to a zoo was memorable. He wanted to take a picture of every animal in the zoo, so he used all the money he had made selling newspapers and bought a small box camera and film. The day of the trip found him merrily clicking his way through the zoo. Unknown to Peet, the shutter wasn't working, so he got no pictures at all. While that was a disappointment, he did learn a lesson. From that time on when he went to the zoo, he always carried a sketch pad and pencils.

As he was growing up, he drew almost anything he saw or imagined. He drew the railroad trains that passed his house, airplanes, fire engines, and, most often of all, he drew animals. War and war scenes also interested Peet. He drew his visualization of the battles he heard about, and then he imagined the Revolutionary War. Football games, prize fights, and gladiators were other favorite topics.

He was able to draw during art class in "grammar school," but it was never enough for him. He keep a drawing tablet in his desk and every chance he got, he pulled it out and sketched. Often a teacher would take his notebook away and scold him for his inattentiveness, but one day a teacher snatched the tablet away and marched to the front of the room with it. She proceeded to open the pages and show the other boys and girls "what William has been doing." Then she continued by saying, "I hope you do something with your drawing." At that time, Peet did not realize that one could make a career of drawing, but after high school, he was awarded a scholarship to the John Herron Art Institute in Indianapolis. For the next three years, he studied drawing, painting, and design. In his spare time, he continued to draw and paint pictures of the animals he had seen on the farm, at the zoo, and circus. He drew farm buildings, the tumbledown shacks along the railroad, and he drew people. His art was earning him awards, but he still did not have a firm vision of how he would make a living with his art.

Sometime in 1937, he heard that Walt Disney was looking for artists to work in his film animation department, so he headed to California. The job was to be temporary. Peet hoped to earn enough money to marry Margaret Burnst, whom he had met in art school.

The job with Disney lasted twenty-seven years. He married Margaret the first year. Over his years with Disney, he developed a reputation for his character and story work. He developed many story sketches, including those for *Dumbo, Cinderella, Alice in Wonderland, Peter Pan, Sleeping Beauty, 101 Dalmatians,* and *The Sword in the Stone.* He wrote many original screen stories, including *Lambert the Sheepish Lion, Ben and Me* (based on the Robert

Lawson novel), and a series of popular Goofy short features. His drawing and writing was a part of the Walt Disney Company for all of those twenty-seven years. He also auditioned voice talent and directed the recording of the dialogue for many films.

Peet was one of Disney's earliest employees. During his career with Disney, others at the company observed a "clash" between Disney and Peet. The clash has been described as an "off-and-on" relationship. The two were both recognized as "creative geniuses," and often their creative ideas conflicted with one another. In many ways, they were alike. They both came from rural backgrounds, both preferred to work alone, and both took great pride in their work. Disney and Peet were both recognized for their storytelling ability; the competition among the two became legendary among the other studio employees.

The Peets had two sons, Bill and Steve, and when they were small, Peet made up stories for them each night. As his storytelling developed, Peet began to contribute more to the story lines at the Disney studio, but always through the illustrations. Over a period of years, Peet became Disney's top writer-illustrator for animated films.

Peet has described Disney as a "grouch" and the Disney studio as a factory, a factory where films were made by an army. Peet did not like the "factory" atmosphere. Once Peet created a story and the storyboard, many artists took on the completion of the task. The final product often, according to Peet, bore little resemblance to what he had envisioned as the story and images. The change in his creative design bothered Peet, and he decided that he wanted out.

In the late 1950s, Bill Peet had already begun to dabble in the world of children's books, writing at night and on weekends. His first book, *Hubert's Hair-Raising Adventure* (Houghton), was published in 1959. In 1963, Peet was working on completing the story and character work for Disney's *The Jungle Book*. Shortly after completing that work, on his forty-ninth birthday, Bill Peet resigned from the Walt Disney Company. He never returned but moved ahead to write and illustrate books for children. Twenty years later, more than one million of Peet's books were in print. In those twenty years, he had written and illustrated thirty books that had been published in America and in Europe, Africa, and Asia. Children in Sweden, Japan, South Africa, and elsewhere could read Peet's books.

During Peet's illustrative and writing career, he carried a notebook with him. His books began with an idea that he often sketched onto a yellow, lined pad. Those sketches were later transformed into book dummies, and the dummies were revised and used to create a manuscript that he sent to his publisher. When he finally sent off a manuscript for a new book, every page had been designed, every word finished, and every illustration sketched to exact size and in full-color.

Bill Peet loved creating children's books. He said it "was like having your cake and eating it too." Drawing the story was always easier than writing the books, but Peet did both. Many of his books were written in verse, using rhyming couplets to tell the story.

Peet said that he had many false starts, and sometimes he spent weeks or months mulling over an idea. *The Gnats of Knotty Pine* (Houghton, 1974) was to be a book focusing on hunting, from the animals' perspective. Peet could not formulate a way to have the animals outwit the hunters, however. Several years after the original idea for the story came into being, Peet was mowing his lawn and was swarmed by buzzing gnats. The solution was soon clear. He would have gnats swarm the hunters, forcing them into a hasty retreat. In this case, the writing was easier than the illustrating because he knew he would have to "dot" enough gnats that his literal-minded young readers would agree that there were indeed "billions" of gnats.

The Whingdingdilly (Houghton, 1970) came about as a result of guessing games that he used when he visited schools in the late 1960s. He would begin drawing an animal and the children would try to guess what animal he was drawing. He would extend the activity by deliberately putting off the completion of a critical attribute of the animal he was drawing. He found out that some animals were so recognizable that even if he began with an elephant's foot and toenails, the children were soon whispering "elephant." Peet wanted to be able to fool the children a little longer so he would begin drawing one animal and switch to another. If he started with an elephant's trunk the children would begin to shout, "Elephant, elephant!" At that moment, he would add a camel's hump and then continue with a lion's mane, a giraffe's neck, or whatever came to mind. The children always ended up laughing. The creature he ended up putting into a storybook was part rhino, giraffe, elephant, camel, zebra, reindeer, and part dog. Scamp was a dog who wanted to be someone or somebody else. Because he wished for the attributes of other animals, he became a hodgepodge animal who was captured and put on display in a circus sideshow. Scamp did not like his new role in life. Eventually, he escaped and returned to his farm home.

Over the years Bill Peet created a multitude of books. Some of them were sheer fun and adventure, whereas others were sheer fun and adventure *and* provided a social message. For example, *The Wump World* (Houghton, 1970) deals with environmental concerns; *Cock-a-Doodle Dudley* (Houghton, 1990) deals with envy and its effects on others, *Zella Zack and*

Zodiac (Houghton, 1986) tells a tale of a favor returned, and *Eleanor the Elephant* (Houghton, 1961) deals with finding a new focus in one's life.

One of the last books Peet created was his 190-page autobiography. The book, *Bill Peet: An Autobiography* (Houghton, 1989), was highly illustrated and earned him a Caldecott Honor Book award in 1990. Many feel that the autobiography was meant to set the record straight, to be a rebuttal to the many Disney histories that have ignored or underplayed his contribution to the success of the Disney empire.

For many years the Peets lived high on a hill in Studio City, a suburb of Los Angeles. His crowded studio loft above the garage was the site where he produced his books, and during his writing and illustrating career, the studio was stacked with every book dummy, his sketch pads, and other preliminary work associated with each of his books. Those who visited Peet in his studio usually noted that walking space was at a premium. Charcoal drawings of his characters were tacked onto one wall. Stacks of his books in foreign editions were in one corner; and other stacks included original manuscripts. Other boxes in his studio held Disney storyboards and sketches from his studio years.

In the late 1980s, Bill Peet was diagnosed with throat cancer, and Margaret often traveled with him to conferences and meetings so that she could respond to questions and help during autographing sessions. The early 1990s marked the end of Bill Peet's second career, and although he and Margaret still reside in California, they no longer live in their Studio City home. They are grandparents and enjoy visits from their sons, Bill and Steve, and their families and are enjoying the glow of Peet's having spent more than fifty years creating films and books for young children.

BOOKS AND NOTES

Bill Peet's books are characterized by personified animals and a strong connection to nature and environmental concerns. His book illustration career spanned more than twenty-five years.

Big Bad Bruce (Houghton, 1977).
A very independent witch diminishes a big bear bully, Bruce, into someone who thinks twice about picking on anyone again.

The Caboose Who Got Loose (Houghton, 1971).
Katy Caboose seeks a way to escape from always being the last car on the noisy, smoky freight train.

Cock-a-Doodle Dudley (Houghton, 1990).

A spiteful goose's malice almost destroys the popular rooster whose crow makes the sun rise.

Cowardly Clyde (Houghton, 1979).

Clyde decides that even if he can't *be* brave, he can *act* brave.

Eli (Houghton, 1978).

An old lion finally learns a lesson about friendship from the vultures he despises.

Encore for Eleanor (Houghton, 1981).

A retired circus star, Eleanor the Elephant, finds a new calling. She becomes the resident artist in the city zoo.

Fly, Homer, Fly (Houghton, 1969).

A sparrow talks a country pigeon into visiting the city. When the pigeon injures his wing, the sparrow and his friends help him home.

The Gnats of Knotty Pine (Houghton, 1975).

The small creatures manage to make the hunters turn tail and retreat by using very "sportsgnatlike" ways.

How Droofus the Dragon Lost His Head (Houghton, 1971).

The king puts a price on the head of all the fierce dragons in the land. Droofus, unlike his family, is a good dragon who does not deserve to lose his head.

The Kweeks of Kookatumdee (Houghton, 1985).

The Kweeks cannot survive if they don't find enough ploppolop fruit trees to feed them. Quentin saves the day with his amazing discovery.

The Luckiest One of All (Houghton, 1982).

A little boy dreams of being a bird but in the end decides that being a little boy may be better.

Jethro and Joel Were a Troll (Houghton, 1987).

A two-headed troll tramples through the countryside.

No Such Things (Houghton, 1983).

A variety of rhymes describe wonderfully fantastical animals: blue-snouted twumps, pie-faced pazeeks, and the fancy fandangos.

Pamela Camel (Houghton, 1984).

Long-sought after recognition comes to Pamela Camel, a tired and dejected circus camel.

The Whingdingdilly (Houghton, 1970).

Scamp, tired of his life as a dog, covets parts of the lives of other animals. His wishes are granted, and he becomes a whingdingdilly.

Zella Zack and Zodiac (Houghton, 1986).

Playing on the theme in Aesop's fable "The Rat and the Lion," Zella the zebra helps Zach the ostrich when he is young and helpless. Once Zach grows up, he manages to return the favor.

FOR MORE INFORMATION

Articles

Raymond, Allen. "Bill Peet . . . Whose Zany Characters Are Loved by Kids the World Over." *Early Years* (April 1984): 22–24.

Books

Peet, Bill. *Bill Peet: An Autobiography* (Houghton, 1989).

Bill Peet recounts his careers as a Walt Disney script writer and illustrator and as a children's author and illustrator. Winner of the 1990 Caldecott Honor Book award.

Web Sites

Province, John. "GoGraphics: Peetintr." URL: <http://gographics.com/funnies/peetintr.htm> (Accessed March 2000).

Andrea Davis Pinkney
Brian Pinkney

◆ Biography ◆ African American Culture

Sharron L. McElmeel

Washington, D.C.
September 25, 1963

Boston, Massachusetts
August 28, 1961

📖 *Bill Pickett: Rodeo-Ridin' Cowboy*

📖 *Dear Benjamin Banneker*

📖 *Duke Ellington: The Piano Prince and His Orchestra*

ABOUT THE AUTHORS/ILLUSTRATOR

Andrea Davis Pinkney and Jerry Brian Pinkney were both working for CBS magazines in New York when they met in the late 1980s. When they married in 1991, Andrea Pinkney was welcomed into one of the most revered families in the field of children's literature. As an editor and writer, she was soon focusing on writing for children; her husband who uses "Brian" or "J. Brian" on his books, was establishing himself as a children's book illustrator.

Brian Pinkney was born in Boston, Massachusetts, on August 28, 1961, the second child in the family of children's book artist Jerry Pinkney and his wife Gloria Pinkney. He and his three siblings, Troy Bernadette, Scott Cannon, and Myles Carter, enjoyed musical instruments and spent time creating artwork and building things. In school, Brian Pinkney often earned extra credit by creating posters and artwork to accompany assignments. He created posters depicting things he was interested in learning about, such as a tadpole turning into a frog or all the bones of the human body. He admired Leonardo da Vinci because da Vinci was an artist, musician, and inventor. Pinkney made illustrations of da Vinci's inventions and drew a portrait of him. "Because he (da Vinci) was left-handed, he wrote all of his notes backward. I started writing all of my notes backward, too." When it came time to study for a test, however, Pinkney found that he could not read the backwards notes and had to hold his notebook up to a mirror.

Pinkney remembers that in the second or third grade, he checked a book out of the library that told how to use pipe cleaners to make people figures. He took the directions a little further and began to create super heroes and action figures. He would smuggle the figures to school in his lunch box and set them up inside his desk. At one time, Pinkney was so busy that he had a tutor to help him organize his time.

Eventually the Pinkney family moved to Croton-on-Hudson, New York, where the parents, Jerry and Gloria Pinkney, still live. While he was growing up, Pinkney did everything his father did. He grew up wanting to be an illustrator because he "wanted to be just like him [his dad]." For his tenth birthday, he was given a miniature drafting table, just like his dad's. Pinkney's mother created a studio for him in a walk-in closet. "My mother would frame the work of myself and my siblings and hang them next to my father's. My family validated my drawings." Pinkney's desk was filled with paintbrushes and pencils that were too old or too small for his dad to use. His dad did not give Pinkney formal art lessons, but Pinkney watched and learned. Pinkney often stopped by his father's studio after school to discuss the school day. While they were talking, his dad would keep working as Pinkney watched.

Once Pinkney graduated from high school, he attended art school in Philadelphia at his father's alma mater, the University of the Arts, where he worked in pen and ink, watercolor, oil, and acrylic. He enjoyed printmaking and often worked in etchings and lithographs. Most of his illustrative work was in watercolors. Eventually, he began to search for a technique that might be more stimulating for him. While a graduate student at the School of Visual Arts in New York, one of his instructors suggested scratchboard.

He soon was using that technique in all of his illustrations. Scratchboard is a thin art board with black paint airbrushed onto the surface. Illustration is produced by using sharp nibs to create little strokes, or etches into the board. Oil paint makes the color brighter. Pinkney's earlier scratchboard work was colored with oil pastel; now he uses oil paint. Backgrounds are oil painted, and the etched portions are wiped with oil paints. The paint seeps into the etched scratch marks, and the excess is wiped away.

After attending art school, Pinkney went to work as an art assistant. In 1984, Pinkney was working at *Field and Stream* magazine; Andrea Davis was working as an editor for *Home Mechanix* magazine for the same publisher, and the two of them met.

By 1989, Brian Pinkney had made a firm entrance into the world of children's books when Robert San Souci's *The Boy and the Ghost* (Simon & Schuster, 1989) was published with Pinkney's illustrations. An art director at Simon & Schuster had spotted Pinkney's work in *Cricket* magazine and decided to ask him to look at a manuscript that had "been floating around" at the publishing house. When Pinkney first read the manuscript, he thought, "That's me. That's me as a little boy." He looked for a model that would be a little boy like he had been. But since the story was set in the rural south, Pinkney researched the area and began to form images. *The Boy and the Ghost* is the story of Thomas, a middle child of seven from a poor African American family who meets a stranger on the way to look for a job. The stranger, a ghost, has a treasure he'll give Thomas—but only on certain terms. Pinkney's illustrations, in line and watercolor drawings, depict the hot fields and the family's poor shanty in quiet, calm scenes. The model for the ghost was Pinkney's father. After the book was released, Pinkney learned that his father had turned down an earlier offer to illustrate the book.

Pinkney was also working in magazine illustration. His work appeared in *New York Times Magazine*, *Women's Day*, *Business Tokyo*, *Ebony Man*, and *Instructor* magazines. In 1990, he exhibited at the Original Art School at the Society of Illustrators, was honored with a solo exhibition at the School of Visual Arts Student Galleries, and was given the National Arts Club Award of Distinction. After *The Boy and the Ghost* was released, publishers offered him more book contracts.

During this time, Andrea R. Davis was working as a senior editor of contemporary living at *Essence* magazine and had written feature articles for several publications, including *Highlights for Children* and *The New York Times*. Her article about Katherine Dunham was awarded the 1992 Best Arts Feature Award by The Highlights for Children Foundation. Eventually, she and Brian Pinkney began to look for projects they could work on together.

Andrea Davis was born on September 25, 1963, in Washington, D.C. Her childhood was spent in Gaithersburg, Maryland; Syracuse, New York; and Wilton, Connecticut. She spent more time reading books than watching television. Her mother was an English teacher who "was always reading" and exposed Davis to many books. The family also enjoyed the performing arts. Her parents often took the children to see dance and theater performances. Among her childhood memories is seeing ballets performed by the Alvin Ailey Dance Company.

Her father was a master storyteller. Whenever the family gathered at holidays, everyone would swap stories. She says, "No one can top my dad. He usually has listeners in stitches over the most mundane events." Her love of books came from her mother, and her love of stories came from her father.

In her teenage years, Andrea Davis aspired to be a dancer, and upon completing high school, she entered the School of Visual and Performing Arts at Syracuse University. But she had also come to love the art of writing, and she soon transferred to the school of journalism. After her graduation, she moved to New York City where she began working for the CBS family of magazines. She and Brian Pinkney literally "met by the copier." For a time, she was an editor with *Home Mechanix* magazine and then became editor for *Essence*. Later she became a children's editor at Simon & Schuster. On October 12, 1991, Brian Pinkney and Andrea R. Davis married. Andrea Davis Pinkney was already involved in the publishing world, and she soon began to focus her efforts on children's books. She often modeled for her husband's illustrations. She was the mermaid in *Sukey and the Mermaid* (Macmillan, 1992) and Belle Dorcus in *The Ballad of Belle Dorcus* (Knopf, 1990). She also read the books that publishers sent for Brian to consider illustrating. He encouraged her to try her hand at writing a children's book.

Andrea Pinkney wanted to find a joint project, and finally the idea of writing about Alvin Ailey occurred to her. She remembered Ailey's dance theatre from her childhood. He had been part of the inspiration for her to enter Syracuse University's School of Visual and Performing Arts, and eventually Ailey inspired her first children's book.

Andrea Pinkney's background as a journalist made her a very thorough researcher. Both she and Brian Pinkney viewed videos of the Alvin Ailey Dance Troupe and studied the Katherine Dunham jazz technique with one of the original Alvin Ailey dancers, Ella Thompson Moore, who was a friend of Ailey when the company was founded in the late 1950s. The Katherine Dunham technique is the modern dance style that influenced Alvin Ailey.

Together Andrea Pinkney and Brian Pinkney learned all the choreography, so that in the illustrations all the hands and positions of the body are as Alvin Ailey would have performed the dance. Brian Pinkney had himself photographed for the dance scenes in the book. Brian often says that "even though it's Alvin Ailey's face, it's my body."

Andrea Pinkney interviewed a lot of the original dancers in the Alvin Ailey troupe and spent quite a bit of time speaking to Ailey's mother. She was the one who told Andrea Pinkney about Alvin Ailey in the True Vine Baptist Church.

The idea for the Bill Pickett book came when Andrea Pinkney and Brian Pinkney were in Denver on a business trip. They had a free morning, so they decided to pay a visit to the Black American West Museum and Heritage Center. When they arrived, the museum was about to open and they were the only ones there. They were greeted by a real modern-day cowboy who spent the morning with them, giving them their own private tour of the museum. As they walked through the museum, they were very taken by the stories, the incredible artifacts, and all the information about black cowboys. Bill Pickett was a big hero at the museum. Both of them knew that Bill Pickett would be the subject of their next book.

The Pinkneys often go to critical locations when researching material for a book, so when Brian Pinkney began to illustrate *The Faithful Friend* (Simon & Schuster, 1995), his fourth book with Robert San Souci, he and Andrea Pinkney traveled twice to the island of Martinique to research the setting and the culture on the islands. Brian cast himself as Clement, his best friend as Hypolite, and Andrea Pinkney as Pauline. The photographs that were taken helped him create the illustrations once they returned home.

When Andrea Pinkney was ready to begin a book about Kwanzaa, she wanted to sell it on her own. Then, when the writing was complete, the publisher commissioned Brian Pinkney to illustrate it. The tone of Andrea Pinkney's text is that of teacher as she takes readers through the seven-day holiday. She provides many ideas for celebrating each of the days. Brian's illustrations take on the colorful role of storyteller as he shows the thoughtful details of each family activity.

When they were working on *Dear Benjamin Banneker* (Harcourt, 1994), the couple visited the Banneker-Douglass Museum in Maryland. Although they had found, through their research, that the Banneker cabin was in the town of Oella, Maryland, a small town in Baltimore County, they drove around and never found the homestead. But they did find many pieces of information that they eventually used in their book. Brian Pinkney reached back into his childhood to a favorite painting, Van Gogh's *Starry Night*.

Because Banneker studied the stars, one of Brian's illustrations emulated Van Gogh's painting. The couple also found out that Benjamin Banneker once corresponded with Thomas Jefferson, who Banneker thought a hypocrite because he wrote the Declaration of Independence but owned slaves. One of the scenes was to show Banneker writing a letter to Thomas Jefferson. Brian Pinkney researched the kind and size of glass that would be in the windows during the early 1700s. Andrea Pinkney and Brian Pinkney studied old almanacs to determine the actual phase of the moon on the evening (August 17, 1791) that Banneker wrote a letter of Jefferson. Brian Pinkney had to determine whether the moon was waxing or waning on that date so that he could accurately depict the shining through the window.

Generally, Andrea Pinkney and Brian Pinkney come to a consensus on a book project, and once they have a proposal they both like, they begin to research. They read about their subject, find people to talk to, and learn as much as they can. Andrea Pinkney writes the text based on their research, and Brian Pinkney creates sketches. Eventually, he assembles models to create scenes he wants to illustrate and arranges for photographs to be taken.

The next step is for the two of them to create a book dummy based on her text and his sketches. They go through several versions of the dummy before they are satisfied with the text and the flow of the words. Once the dummy is sent off to the publisher, the editors make suggestions and create a color proof that can be changed, corrected, and adjusted to make the book just right. Once both writer and illustrator have approved the changes, the book is returned to the publisher for the final publication steps: printing and binding.

Andrea Pinkney always has pen and paper with her and says that she does some of her best writing on the subway, where she is alone and no one bothers her. She calls the constant grind of the subway wheels and the flurry of passenger activity a "wonderful stimulation." She also composes on the computer, but her ideas and prose usually "start out as chicken scratch—on an envelope, napkin, whatever." Andrea says that "Once, when I was at the pool swimming laps, I got a great idea, but had no paper. So I wrote with a pen on my plastic thong!"

When she is writing a longer book, she most often creates an outline and spends many months researching. With stories that have historical relevance, such as *Dear Benjamin Banneker*, she constantly researches during the writing process and sometimes for a period of years. She continually revises, working out how she wants to tell the story.

Since the birth of their daughter, Chloe, in June 1996, much of Andrea Pinkney's writing and research is done at 5:00 A.M. and on Sunday mornings. The Brooklyn Public Library is right across the street, so Andrea Pinkney often takes Chloe along on her research trips. She has to work quickly to locate the books she needs before Chloe gets too restless, so it helps that a good friend is a librarian and often gathers books on the topic Andrea is researching. Brian Pinkney often worked at night, so his schedule has not changed very much. To keep track of his projects, Brian Pinkney keeps a three-year calendar on which he tracks due dates for book projects. An eighteen-month calendar tracks his personal appearances, and shorter calendars provide more details about the projects and appearances. Brian Pinkney and Andrea Pinkney share an office-studio in their home and are able to bounce ideas off one another.

Together, the Pinkney team has developed a series of four board books for preschoolers, but each of them has worked on several independent projects as well. Brian's book, *The Adventures of Sparrowboy*, which Brian Pinkney both wrote and illustrated, "is about a boy with a paper route who becomes a superhero in his neighborhood." He also continues to illustrate the books of other authors.

Andrea Pinkney has written novels for middle-grade readers, *Hold Fast to Dreams* (Morrow, 1995) and *Raven in a Dove House* (Gulliver, 1998); an early chapter book, *Solo Girl*, illustrated by Nneka Bennett (Disney Press, 1997); and a historical novel set during the Civil War in Virginia, *Silent Thunder* (Hyperion Press, 1999). In 1998, Andrea Pinkney began a new publishing venture with Hyperion Press as editor of their "Jump at the Sun" imprint, which is devoted to books by African American writers and artists. She selected poems for a collection of Paul Dunbar poetry, *Jump Back, Honey: Poems* (Jump at the Sun, 1999), that the imprint published. The collection, illustrated by Ashley Bryan, includes "A Boy's Summer Song," "The Sparrow," and "Little Brown Baby."

Their family is very important to both the Pinkneys. Brian Pinkney often shows his work to his father and respects and values the feedback he receives. Andrea Pinkney tells of holidays and Sunday barbecues at which the family gathers to talk about each project. Both spend as much time as possible with their daughter, Chloe Grace.

BOOKS AND NOTES

Andrea Pinkney's writing is fluid, and each word is well chosen. She researches information to ensure historical accuracy in the details about each subject and event she is to write about. Brian Pinkney's illustrations are created with scratchboard, which gives them a vibrancy and dimension not achieved through some other techniques. His illustrations are researched to accurately reflect the details. For example, in *Bill Pickett: Rodeo Ridin' Cowboy*, Brian found out that in the 1920s cowboys mounted horses from the left and jumped off the left side. That fact was incorporated into the illustrations.

On books they create together, Andrea Pinkney generally needs six months to a year of revising to get the text just right. When the text is finished, Brian Pinkney begins the illustrations. The illustrations take Brian from six months to a year to go from rough sketches to finished artwork. Each book takes from one to two years to complete.

Several of their books have won awards, including Parents' Choice Picture Book Awards, A Golden Kite Honor, the Coretta Scott King Honor Award for Illustration, American Booksellers' Pick of the List, and in 1999, a Caldecott Honor Book award for *Duke Ellington: The Piano Prince and His Orchestra*.

Books Written by Andrea Davis Pinkney and Illustrated by Brian Pinkney

Alvin Ailey (Hyperion, 1993).
Honors the life and perseverance of one of America's foremost choreographers, the founder of a prestigious dance troupe in Harlem.

Bill Pickett: Rodeo-Ridin' Cowboy (Harcourt, 1996).
The life of an African American cowboy who invented the sport of bulldogging.

Dear Benjamin Banneker (Harcourt, 1994).
Traces the life of one of America's first surveyors, astronomers, and clock makers.

Duke Ellington: The Piano Prince and His Orchestra (Disney Press, 1998).
A biography of Edward Kennedy "Duke" Ellington.

I Smell Honey (Red Wagon, 1997).
A book about tasty foods and the five senses. Preschool board book.

Pretty Brown Face (Red Wagon, 1997).
A toddler discovers the unique characteristics of his face. Preschool board book.

Seven Candles for Kwanzaa (Dial, 1993).
Explains the origins, language, and daily themes of the festive seven-day holiday.

Shake Shake Shake (Red Wagon, 1997).
A mother and child play with an African instrument called the *shekere*.

Watch Me Dance (Red Wagon, 1997).
A preschooler amuses a baby in a playpen while they learn rhythm with the shekere.

Books Written or Selected by Andrea Davis Pinkney

Jump Back, Honey: Poems by Paul Dunbar.
Selected by Andrea Davis Pinkney and illustrated by Ashley Bryan. (Jump at the Sun, 1999).
An illustrated collection of favorite poems by Paul Laurence Dunbar (1872–1906).

Solo Girl. Illustrated by Nneka Bennett. (Disney, 1997).
Cass has a real gift for numbers. She is a math whiz, but she is a physical klutz. Finding a partner for the jump roping competition may be difficult.

Books Illustrated by Brian Pinkney

Cendrillon: A Caribbean Cinderella. Written by Robert San Souci. (Simon & Schuster, 1998).
A Creole version of *Cinderella* set in the Caribbean. It is a version derived from Perrault's French telling.

The Dark-Thirty: Southern Tales of the Supernatural. Written by Patricia McKissack. (Knopf, 1992).
Tales told in the southern tradition.

The Dream Keeper and Other Poems. Written by Langston Hughes. (Knopf, 1994).
A reillustrated volume of a classic collection of poems by the noted poet Langston Hughes.

The Faithful Friend. Written by Robert D. San Souci. (Simon & Schuster, 1995).
A folktale from Martinique Island.

In the Time of the Drums. Written by Kim Seigleson. (Little, Brown 1999).
Twi leads the insurrection at Teakettle Creek of Ibo people arriving from Africa on a slave ship. Told through the eyes of Mentu, an American-born slave boy and Twi's grandson.

Books Written and Illustrated by Brian Pinkney

Cosmos and the Robot (Greenwillow, 2000).
When his robot, Rex, malfunctions and threatens his sister, a boy knows he must do something. Set on Mars.

JoJo's Flying Side Kick (Simon & Schuster, 1995).
JoJo learns how to use Tae Kwan Do and gains confidence that helps her overcome her fears.

Max Found Two Sticks (Simon & Schuster, 1994).
Max, who loves to drum, finds two sticks that let him join in the rhythm of a marching band, and in the end he is given two drumsticks by the band's drummer.

FOR MORE INFORMATION

Bishop, Rudine Sims. "The Pinkney Family: In the Tradition." *The Horn Book Magazine* 72, no. 1 (January/February 1996): 42–49.

McElmeel, Sharron L. "Author and Illustrator Profile: The Pinkneys." *Library Talk.* 11, no. 3 (May/June 1998): 16–19.

Winarski, Diana L. "The Rhythm of Writing and Art." *Teaching PreK–8* 28, no. 2 (October 1, 1997): 38–40.

Gloria Pinkney
Jerry Pinkney

◆　Family Relationships　◆　Folklore

Lumberton, North Carolina
September 5, 1941

Philadelphia, Pennsylvania
December 22, 1939

📖　*Back Home*
📖　*Minty: A Story of Young Harriet Tubman*
📖　*The Sunday Outing*
📖　*The Talking Eggs*

ABOUT THE AUTHORS/ILLUSTRATOR

Jerry Pinkney has been creating children's books since 1964. Gloria Pinkney's first book, *Back Home* (Dial, 1992), was published in 1992. The first copies of that book arrived a few days before her fiftieth birthday. Now they are considered the matriarch and patriarch of a family tradition that includes their son Brian Pinkney, an illustrator; Brian's wife, Andrea Davis Pinkney, a writer; and Myles Pinkney. Myles is a photographer whose work has appeared in four books, including one by his wife, Sandra Pinkney, who has just entered the field of children's books with a book of "poetic text" titled *Shades of Black: A Celebration of Our Black Children* (Scholastic, 2000). Jerry Pinkney met Gloria Jean Maultsby in Philadelphia. They married on March 19, 1960.

Jerry Pinkney was born in Philadelphia on December 22, 1939. He was the middle child in a family of six children. The family lived in a small house, and one of the ways he defined his own space was to express himself on his drawing pad. He remembers drawing when he was as young as four or five. There were no artists in the neighborhood, but there were musicians. During his elementary school years, he struggled with reading and writing. In fact, Pinkney says, "I lagged behind." He became the class artist in first grade. One of his first drawings was of a red fire engine, drawn on a big sheet of brown paper. His two older brothers drew, and he mimicked them. When he was eleven years old, he sold newspapers to earn extra money, standing on a Philadelphia street corner. He often took his sketchbook with him. Selling newspapers would typically yield Jerry $6.00. He gave $3.00 to his mother to help the family and the other $3.00 went for cab fare to get to his assigned corner. One day, a cartoonist, John Liney, saw him sketching and invited Jerry Pinkney to visit his studio. That was his introduction to the idea that one could make money with art.

Pinkney's interest in art continued into high school. He never entered an art museum until he was in college. His mother recognized his talent and encouraged him, but his father was a working-class man and did not have any experience with successful black artists.

Pinkney's father was a handyman, and some of his clients told him about private art classes. During Pinkney's junior high school years, his father arranged for him to take some classes. Even so, he did not really encourage his son's art. Nonetheless, during high school Jerry Pinkney decided he would like to draw or paint for a living. He attended the Dobbins Vocational High School, where he took commercial art classes and learned how to letter, do technical drawings, use the airbrush, and experiment with many types of media.

During high school, a teacher handed out scholarship applications to all the white students but because there was "no use for any [African American] to go any further," he did not hand one to Jerry or to the other African American students in the class. Pinkney went to the counseling office and picked up some applications. Of the three scholarships students at that school received, Jerry received one and his friend, Warren, received another.

Pinkney entered the Philadelphia Museum College of Art (later called the University of the Arts) where he studied advertising and design. The classes he enjoyed most were the painting and printmaking classes. Drawing became very important to him.

After marrying eighteen-year-old Gloria Maultsby, twenty-year-old Jerry Pinkney began to work for the Rustcraft Greeting Card Company and then at the Barker-Black Studio in Boston. He and two other artists opened Kaleidoscope Studio. Much of their work was in the commercial art field, but he also did some textbook illustration, which made him realize that he liked illustrative work that was tied to a story. One of his earliest influences was the work of Arthur Rackham, an eighteenth-century English illustrator. Pinkney liked the quality of Rackham's drawings, as well as the way he used color. He began to look at the work of African American artists, and the strong, graphic drawings of Charles White and the photographs of James Van Der Zee particularly impressed him. Pinkney feels that the influence of these two artists is evident in his work.

Jerry Pinkney's first book was published by Little, Brown in 1964. He was in the Boston area, where there were a lot of book publishers. His art had been exhibited in several art shows, and his work had received favorable recognition. During that period, publishers were especially interested in publishing African American writers and illustrators. Little, Brown publishers were looking for a black artist to work on a collection of West African folktales. Pinkney showed them his portfolio, they liked his work, and he got the job.

Eventually, the Pinkneys moved to Westchester County, New York, and Jerry Pinkney established his own freelance studio in their home. His art has made a significant impact in the art community. He has created twelve postage stamps for the U.S. Postal Service's Black Heritage series, and he was a member of its Advisory Committee for ten years. He also was invited to join the NASA artist team for the space shuttle *Columbia.* He remains active at a national level in graphic arts, in part to present a strong role model for his family and other African Americans.

Jerry Pinkney has illustrated more than eighty books. He has won three Caldecott Honor Book awards and three Coretta Scott King Awards for illustration, and he has garnered a Coretta Scott King Honor Award twice.

Pinkney draws from real life or from photographs. He begins with thumbnail sketches and most often works in watercolor. Once he has agreed to work on a manuscript, he lays out the sequence and design of the book and creates a dummy. The dummy goes to the publisher for the editors' approval. The next step is to set up photography shoots so he has a reference point for his illustrations. To keep his watercolor paper from buckling when he applies the wet paint, he wets the paper and stretches it on his drawing board. As the paper dries, it becomes taut and ready for the application of paint.

Once the illustration has been sketched in pencil, Pinkney begins to apply the color. The paintings for each illustration are most usually 11 x 17 inches and created with pencil, watercolor, and pastel. Because he also designs his books, he can place the text and pictures where he wants them.

Pinkney uses the photographs to help him develop and create the thumbnail sketches and later for the final drawings. In one instance, he had a photograph of musicians playing cello and was using it to create a painting for *I Want to Be*, written by Thylias Moss (Dial, 1993). All the cello players were facing left, and he wanted the illustration to flow from left to right, so he wanted the musicians to face right. To achieve that, he merely flipped the drawing over so they faced the other direction. When the painting was finished, he realized that all of the musicians were playing their cellos with their left hands. He had to redo the illustration to show them playing with their right hands.

A similar scenario occurred when Pinkney was illustrating Patricia McKissack's *Mirandy and Brother Wind* (Knopf, 1988). In that book, Ezel is milking the cow from the wrong side. This book is also one of the books in which Pinkney's wife Gloria Pinkney appears. She modeled for Miss Poinsettia.

Jerry Pinkney does not usually write his own books, so most of his illustrative projects in children's books have been built in cooperation with the text of another author. He has created several books with a number of authors, including Robert San Souci and Julius Lester. He illustrated San Souci's *The Hired Hand: An African-American Folktale* (Dial, 1997) and *The Talking Eggs* (Dial, 1989), a tale that eighteenth-century French immigrants brought with them to Louisiana. The story became part of the American Creole culture and eventually spread throughout the southern United States. For *The Hired Hand,* Jerry found an eighteenth-century town, Waterford, which had harbored free slaves. There were many artisans and skilled people who had businesses. One of the businesses was that of a cabinetmaker. Jerry characterizes Robert San Souci as "a wonderful person to go back to tell stories from the past, and to tell them with a lot of flavor. He is a wonderful person to work with." Jerry Pinkney's son, Brian Pinkney, has worked with San Souci as well, illustrating *The Faithful Friend* (Simon & Schuster, 1995).

Julius Lester collected and retold three collections of the tales of Uncle Remus, from 1988 to 1994, and Jerry Pinkney illustrated each one of them. The project allowed him to go back and remember some of the tales he had heard as a child. Even when illustrating folktales, research is important. For one illustration in the Uncle Remus tales, Pinkney had to find out what an authentic rabbit trap would have looked like during the era in which the stories are set. During that period, Pinkney initiated one project that he wanted to do, a retelling of the "John Henry" legend. He wanted to draw the images, but he needed a writer. He solicited Julius Lester's expertise, and together they completed the book. Jerry was able to add information and complement the text through the illustrations. The illustrations took approximately five months to complete.

The link between the Uncle Remus tales and the John Henry legend was important. Bre'r Rabbit was a sly trickster that originated during slavery. Bre'r Rabbit represented the first African American folk hero. He represented slaves who, if they wanted to outsmart their master, had to be cunning and sly. The trickster was their hero. Later, John Henry, a free man, uses his strength and valor to gain fame. When Pinkney was creating the illustrations for the John Henry book, he put him on the C & O Railroad in West Virginia.

Pinkney and Lester later collaborated on a new version of the traditional story "Little Black Sambo." Pinkney was giving a presentation, and in response to a question, he mentioned that there should be a new version of the "Little Black Sambo" story. His offhand remark was eventually posted on an Internet Usenet group, rec.arts.book.children. Julius Lester saw the post and thought the message said that Jerry Pinkney was "working on a new version of Little Black Sambo." Lester says his first thought was, "Jerry wouldn't dare do that without asking me to write it." So, the next morning, he picked up the phone and called Pinkney, who recalled the comment but told Lester he was not, in fact, working on it. So Lester asked what he thought about doing such a project with him. While Julius Lester was writing the book, he read a rather lengthy discussion of the original Little Black Sambo story on the Usenet site, as well as a similar discussion group on child.lit. Because of those discussions on the Internet, Lester was able to think through a lot of the problems surrounding the book. Lester's dedication is "To the Internet and those on rec.arts.book.children and Child.Lit."

Lester and Pinkney took care to emphasize that the book was not set in Africa and that their book was a fantasy—just as the original author, Helen Bannerman, had intended. In fact, to emphasize its fantasy elements, Lester introduced other animals, in addition to the tigers, that could talk. Lester consciously set out to create a decidedly black fantasy. The first sentence begins, "Once upon a time there was a place called Sam-sam-sa-mara, . . . " It was a place where animals and people didn't know that they were not supposed to live and work together. Pinkney's illustrations represented a fantasyland where animals talked to people and Sam was a clever young boy.

The great majority of Pinkney's illustrative work in the children's book field has been done for Dial, although he also has published with several other companies and has worked with such notable authors as Patricia McKissack, Virginia Hamilton, Arnold Adoff, Mildred D. Taylor, and Verna Aardema. He also has illustrated the two books written by his wife, Gloria Jean Pinkney.

While Jerry Pinkney was developing his illustrative career, Gloria Pinkney was occupied with her own artistic endeavors, as well as being involved in the creation of children's books. She has been Jerry Pinkney's production assistant for many years, arranging for models, setting up photography sessions, and reading book manuscripts. In her own right, she is a fashion designer working as a silversmith and milliner. More recently, she has begun to write.

Gloria Maultsby was born in Lumberton, North Carolina, on September 5, 1941. Her father was an insurance salesman, and her mother, Ernestine, was a seamstress. When she was just eight months old, her parents divorced. Her father went to California, and Gloria moved to Philadelphia with her mother. They took up residence in an aunt's rooming house. It was the first stop for a family that moved north to find jobs and to take advantage of new opportunities. When the adults talked, Gloria listened. She mimicked their southern accents. Because Gloria was listening to their conversations, they often spelled words out, hoping she would not understand.

Gloria has said that she learned to read at a very young age. The adults would often give her children's books so that she would "keep out of grown-up business." When her mom remarried, Gloria Pinkney's bedroom was a former pantry—a tiny little room. One month after her eighth birthday, in October of 1949, her mother, Ernestine, was murdered. Shortly before she died, Gloria's mother had made her a yellow pinafore dress.

A few days after her mother's death, her father came and took her for a visit to a family farm in North Carolina. They traveled to Lumberton by train, and there she met a relative her own age, Jack. During that stay, she spent time with her grandfather as he harnessed his mule; when she was around the baby goat and other animals, she wore overalls. Her great-aunt, Alma, visited and said she did not approve of her niece wearing overalls.

Gloria's Aunt Alma became her guardian, and Gloria went back with her to Philadelphia. Aunt Alma was a stern woman and did not seem very affectionate, but Gloria knew her aunt loved her. The two of them often spent Sunday afternoons in the train station watching the comings and goings and dreaming of the trips they could take. Gloria kept diaries until she was sixteen, then she threw them away. Now she is sorry she did, but her books have helped bring the memories back.

Jerry Pinkney and Gloria Maultsby met at Dobbins Vocational School in Philadelphia, and during the years Jerry was attending college at the Philadelphia Museum College of Arts, they married. After their daughter, Troy, was born, the family moved to Boston, Massachusetts. Eventually they ended up in a home in Croton-on-Hudson, where they raised their four children and Jerry Pinkney established his studio. Gloria Pinkney began to pursue fashion design. In the 1980s, she established her own niche by creating "Jewelry by Gloria Jean" and "Hats by Gloria Jean."

As an elementary student, Gloria thought she could not write. Her "punctuation" grade was not as good as her other grades were. To compensate, she told her stories. She became the family storyteller, and over the years Jerry Pinkney tried to convince her to write. Gloria Pinkney read manuscripts, and she began to think about stories she might write. Pieces began to come together when the Pinkneys' daughter divorced and came with her daughter, Gloria Nicole, to live with them for awhile. Around the same time, Gloria moved her millinery shop to their home in Croton-on-Hudson. With Gloria Nicole in the shop and around the hats, Gloria Pinkney began to create a manuscript called "Vanessa's Hat." She tried to write the story in Gloria Nicole's voice but soon realized that she had to use her own voice. The story simply wasn't coming together.

Then came the invitation. She was invited to make a trip to a family reunion in Lumberton, North Carolina. She had not been back since her childhood, and she was hesitant to go. But she did, and memories flooded back. Her uncle told her that her mother never liked to go barefoot. Jack, who had resented her visit during their childhood, became a great friend and the cousin in Pinkney's book. When she returned home, the story came. Her grandfather became her uncle in the story, and her grandmother became her aunt. Ernestine became a mixture of fact and imagination.

Gloria wrote a voluminous text, and when it was offered to Phyliss Fogelman at Dial, it was forty pages long. It came back all marked up, but she was offered a contract. After many revisions, the manuscript was ready for Jerry Pinkney's illustrations. Many of the events that occur in *Back Home* (Dial, 1992) occurred during Gloria Pinkney's childhood visit to her grandparents' farm. Gloria named the girl Ernestine in honor of her mother. In the book, Ernestine's aunt gives her overalls to wear during the visit on the farm. They are patched and ironed and ready to take home after the visit, but Ernestine takes them out of the bag and puts them in a dresser drawer for her visit the next summer. Gloria was given a pair of overalls by her grandmother, and she took them home with her, but Aunt Alma threw them away. Similar to Ernestine, Gloria rode a goat but insists that she did not fall off. In the book, Ernestine wears a yellow pinafore dress, much like the one the real Ernestine—Gloria Pinkney's mother—had made for her daughter. A workman had an old truck, and Jerry Pinkney put that truck in the illustrations. Gloria Pinkney's Uncle Thomas had a cow named "Lizzie," so they named the truck in the book, "Old Lizzie."

The book is full of details from Gloria Pinkney's real visit to the farm when she was an eight-year-old girl. When Gloria was writing the book she named the depot in Lumberton the "Robeson County Depot." Gloria thought she was making up the name, but she found out later that a depot by that name really did exist. Because Jerry Pinkney illustrated the book, he was able to include images that he knew were significant to Gloria. As models for the illustrations, they arranged to photograph a child model from North Carolina and some members of the Star of Bethlehem Church.

A prequel to *Back Home*, *The Sunday Outing* (Dial, 1994), tells of Ernestine's efforts to gather enough money to make the train trip to the farm. The story takes place in Philadelphia. Ernestine greets her great-aunt, Odessa, at the railroad station. Her aunt is carrying a black bag just like Gloria Pinkney's aunt always carried when she traveled—a black bag with a fresh blouse, underwear, and food. Gloria Pinkney's real great-aunt, Alma, had been married to a railroad man. Gloria managed to remember her mother in the book as well; the dress form in the family's living room is like the form that stood in her mother's sewing area. When Ernestine set off for the farm, she boarded the train in her yellow pinafore dress, carrying her mother's wedding satchel.

Jerry Pinkney has taught a couple days a week at the University of Delaware, and both Jerry Pinkney and Gloria Pinkney travel and speak at schools and conferences about their role in creating books for children. On days allocated to working in his studio, Jerry begins around 8:30 to 9:00 AM and typically works until 8:30 or 10:00 PM. He takes breaks for meals and may take a walk or two, but in general he spends a lot of time focusing on his artwork. Both he and Gloria Pinkney have become mentors to other young book writers and illustrators, including their own children. Their daughter, Troy Bernadette, and three sons—Jerry "Brian," Scott Cannon, and Myles Carter—are grown. Troy is an art therapist in Boston. Brian is a children's book illustrator, and his wife, Andrea, writes children's books and young adult novels. Scott is an art director at a large advertising agency. After living for a time in England, he and his wife settled in Canada. Myles has studied photography. His photographic images are included in four books, including *Can You Imagine?* an autobiography by Patricia McKissack (R. C. Owens, 1997) and *It's Raining Laughter: Poems* by Nikki Grimes (Dial, 1997). Grimes's title features fifty-two color photographs of African American children. Myles has also used photographs to illustrate his wife Sandra's book. Myles and Sandra are parents to two of Jerry Pinkney and Gloria Pinkney's seven grandchildren.

BOOKS AND NOTES

When an artist illustrates the work of an author, they seldom meet or actually discuss the artwork and text as a whole. Each portion of the book is created without collaboration with the other's input. In these instances, the publisher accepts the manuscript for publication and arranges for an illustrator to illustrate the text. When Jerry Pinkney and Gloria Pinkney have created a book as illustrator and author, Jerry was able to consult with Gloria concerning some of the actual images, something that most likely would not have happened if another illustrator had worked on the book. Jerry Pinkney enjoyed a similar collaboration with Julius Lester when they created *John Henry, Sam and the Tigers* (Dial, 1996), and more recently *Black Cowboy, Wild Horses* (Dial, 1998). Gloria Pinkney has worked on a third book, yet unpublished, about Ernestine, *Grand Finalé*. In recent years, Jerry Pinkney has retold and illustrated several of Hans Christian Andersen's classic tales.

Books Written by Gloria Pinkney and Illustrated by Jerry Pinkney

Back Home (Dial, 1992).

The Sunday Outing (Dial, 1994).

Books Written/Retold and Illustrated by Jerry Pinkney

The Little Match Girl. Retold by Jerry Pinkney. (Dial/Phyllis Fogelman, 1999).

Rikki-tikki-tavi. Written by Jerry Pinkney. (Morrow, 1997).

The Ugly Duckling. Retold by Jerry Pinkney. (Dial/Phyllis Fogelman, 1999).

Books Illustrated by Jerry Pinkney

Albidaro and the Mischievous Dream. Written by Julius Lester. (Dial/Phyllis Fogelman, 2000).

Black Cowboy, Wild Horses. A True Story. Written by Julius Lester. (Dial, 1998).

Goin' Someplace Special. Written by Patricia McKissack. (Atheneum, 2000).

The Hired Hand: An African-American Folktale. Written by Robert San Souci. (Dial, 1997).

John Henry. Written by Julius Lester. (Dial, 1994).

I Want to Be. Written by Thylias Moss. (Dial, 1993).

Minty: A Story of Young Harriet Tubman. Written by Alan Schroeder. (Dial, 1996).

Mirandy and Brother Wind. Written by Pat McKissack. (Knopf, 1992).

More Tales of Uncle Remus. Written by Julius Lester. (Dial, 1988).

The Patchwork Quilt. Written by Valerie Flournoy. (Dial, 1985).

Rabbit Makes a Monkey of Lion: A Swahili Tale. Written by Verna Aardema. (Dial, 1989).

Sam and the Tigers. Written by Julius Lester. (Dial, 1996).

The Tales of Uncle Remus. Written by Julius Lester. (Dial, 1987).

The Talking Eggs. Written by Robert San Souci. (Dial, 1989).

Tanya's Reunion. Written by Valerie Flournoy. (Dial, 1995).

Uncle Remus, Tales from the Briar Patch. Written by Julius Lester. (Dial/Phyllis Fogelman, 1999).

FOR MORE INFORMATION

Articles

Bishop, Rudine Sims. "The Pinkney Family: In the Tradition." *The Horn Book Magazine,* 72, no. 1 (January/February 1996): 42–49.

McElmeel, Sharron L. "Author & Illustrator Profile: The Pinkneys." *Library Talk,* 11, no. 3 (May/June 1998): 16–19.

Web Sites

The Scoop. "Jerry Pinkney." URL: <http://www.friend.ly.net/scoop/biographies/pinkneyjerry/index.htm> (Accessed April 2000).

Patricia Polacco

◆ Family Relationships

Lansing, Michigan
July 11, 1944

📖 *Pink and Say*
📖 *Thank You, Mr. Falker*
📖 *Thunder Cake*

Sharron L. McElmeel

ABOUT THE AUTHOR/ILLUSTRATOR

Polacco was born Patricia Ann Barber in Lansing, Michigan, on July 11, 1944, and lived in nearby Williamston until she was three. That year, her parents, William Barber and Mary Ellen Gaw Barber, divorced, and each moved to their parents' homes. Patricia moved to Union City with her mother.

On her mother's side, Polacco is the descendant of Russian immigrants. They arrived on Ellis Island at the turn of the century and that is where the family name "Gaw" was obtained. It is believed that the name was Georgian, Guawgashvillie, and was shortened to "Gaw" or that the grandfather, George, was wearing a tag saying: "<u>G</u>eorge <u>a</u>nd <u>Wife</u>"—thus, the Gaw name. The family lived in New York and worked as "ragpickers" and at making artificial flowers until they had saved enough money to buy a small farm in Michigan.

Polacco's grandmother was born in New York but did not speak English until she was eighteen years old. When the family arrived in Michigan, they found only one other Jewish family in the area, but they did find other Russians. After a time, a section of her family started marrying Russian Orthodox Christians. "It was," said Polacco, "important to them to marry people from their homeland." Patricia was raised to reflect and respect the best of both traditions. Her father's family had come from Ireland and were "shanty Irish." Grandparents from both sides of the family were "incredible storytellers." Both the Russian and the Irish branches of the family passed on stories in the oral tradition. Because both Patricia's parents lived with their own parents after the divorce, she was surrounded by old, wise relatives.

For two-and-a-half years after her parents' divorce, Patricia lived in Union City, until her beloved grandmother (her *babushka*) died. Mary Ellen Barber was a schoolteacher, and she obtained a job in Coral Gables, Florida. She, her son, and her daughter lived in Florida for the next three years. From Florida, the family moved to Oakland, California, to Ocean View Drive in the Rockridge District. The neighborhood was filled with people of all colors and religions.

It was there that Patricia met Stewart Washington, who became her lifelong best friend. The Washingtons were African Americans, and Polacco says that her respect for other cultures grew during the time she lived in Oakland. The Washington family has become her own extended family, and she spent a great deal of time with Stewart and his younger brother Winston. She also spent a lot of time on her art.

From the age of four, Patricia could draw in perspective, but when she began school, she found reading and mathematics very difficult. She was dyslexic and did not learn to read until she was fourteen years old. A teacher finally recognized that Patricia had been pretending that she could read for all the years she'd been in school. The teacher, George Felker, used his own money to hire a tutor for her. Patricia began to realize that she wasn't dumb. But her memories of other children teasing her and of being a failure remained. She felt that art was the only thing that she could do well. She dreamed a lot, and her imagination provided a safe haven.

Nonetheless, Patricia did learn to read—and to excel. She attended colleges in Oakland, California. In fact, she obtained a Ph.D. in art history in 1978. During the course of her studies, she spent five years in Australia, where her particular area of interest became Russian and Greek painting and iconographic history. She became a historical consultant to museums in this specialized art field. Although she is no longer active in restoration of icons for museums, she does enjoy painting Ukrainian eggs, which are called *pysanky* or *pisanky*.

In Australia, she met and married Enzo-Mario Polacco, an Italian from Trieste. Daughter Traci Denise was born in 1966, and a son, Steven, was born in 1970. While her children were young, Patricia Polacco devoted much of her time to their upbringing. In 1985, when her children were in their teens, she began to write and illustrate children's books. She was forty-one.

Patricia's memories of family life have become part of the stories she writes. *The Keeping Quilt* (Simon & Schuster, 1988) tells the story of the quilt that preserved the memories of great-grandparents and their Russian origins through weddings, births, and other family events. Polacco's great-grandmother Anna's *babushka* (which means both grandmother and shawl) became part of the quilt, as did pieces of her Uncle Vladimir's shirt, her Aunt Havalah's nightdress, and her Aunt Natasha's apron. Over the years, the quilt was used as a tablecloth on the Sabbath, a blanket on the grass where marriage proposals were accepted, a wedding huppa (a canopy for the wedding couple during the ceremony), and a coming-home blanket for a new baby. The quilt welcomed Patricia the day she was born, and while she was growing up, it was part of her imaginary play in such places as the "steaming Amazon jungle." When she married, it served as her huppa and eventually welcomed her first child, Traci Denise. The pictures in the illustrations give readers a glimpse of Polacco's own family. A scene depicting her wedding shows her family members. Nearby is her best friend, Stewart Washington. She says, "He was my neighbor and dearest friend ever since I came to California. His grandmother became my 'Bubby' when mine died." The final picture in the book shows Patricia and Enzo-Mario and their new baby wrapped in the quilt.

The Keeping Quilt won the 1988 Sydney Taylor Book Award for Younger Children from the Association of Jewish Libraries and was nominated for the national Jewish Book Award in the Children's Picture Book category by the Jewish Book Council. On the tenth anniversary of the book's publication, the publisher reissued it with an author's note sharing some of the moments in Polacco's life that have occurred since the book's first publication, moments that she has shared with the Keeping Quilt, including the birth of her son. She says she is waiting patiently for grandchildren so that she might tell the story to them as well.

Her books reflect her deep respect for intergenerational relationships and for the diversity of cultures in the world. In the first five years of her writing career, she created more than thirty books. One of the first books was *Meteor!* (Putnam, 1987), which tells of a meteorite crashing into the Michigan farmyard of her Gaw grandparents. Polacco's present home sits just down the road from the site where it fell. The meteorite is now her family headstone in the village cemetery. When Polacco moved back to Union City in 1994, she renamed the "farm" Meteor Ridge Farm in honor of that memorable event. She lives at the edge of Union City on the twelve-acre estate where her Victorian house and gazebo sit. The house, which sits on the crest of a small hill, was built just before the outbreak of the Civil War and became part of the Underground Railroad.

Rechenka's Eggs (Philomel, 1988) showcases Babushka's gift for coloring eggs in patterns that come from folklore symbols and images—a gift that Polacco has inherited. Another story tells of Patricia and her grandmother's day during a thunderstorm. *Thunder Cake* (Philomel, 1990) tells the story of Polacco's childhood fear of thunder. She says, "I was the little girl and the recipe is the true one that was in my bubby's recipe box."

Other tales honor the flavor of diverse cultures. Polacco wrote many stories that took place in California and focus on events she shared with her friends Stewart and Winston Washington. *Mrs. Katz and Tush* (Bantam, 1992) tells the story of Larnel Moore and Mrs. Katz, who share a concern for an abandoned cat. Larnel, a young African American child, and Mrs. Katz, a Jewish woman, are brought together by Tush, the cat, and develop a lasting friendship. *Chicken Sunday* (Philomel, 1992) features Polacco's rich folk-art-style illustrations. A young Russian American girl is adopted into her neighbors' African American family in a backyard ritual, which makes Stewart and Winston her brothers and their grandmother, Miss Eula Mae Walker, her adopted grandmother. The three children often go to the Baptist church with Miss Eula Mae and share many special family times. Miss Eula Mae admires a very special hat in Mr. Kodinski's hat store, but the three children do not have enough money to purchase it. Later, the children are accused of misdeeds by Mr. Kodinski. That incident results in an opportunity for them to show Mr. Kodinski that they would never do such things and also gives them a chance to earn money to buy that special hat for Miss Eula Mae.

Polacco also has written books that are not related directly to her own life. *Just Plain Fancy* (Bantam, 1990) is an Amish story and came about during a breakfast that Polacco attended with Bantam representatives. They asked Polacco if she had an Amish story, and it just so happened that she had one "rattling around" in her head. Polacco told them about her idea, and they bought it on the spot. To write the story, she had to do a great deal of reading about the Amish, and she traveled to areas where the Amish live.

Polacco illustrated Ernest Lawrence Thayer's poem, *Casey at the Bat* (Putnam, 1988). Instead of the usual images of adults playing the ill-fated game, she sets the action at a Little League game. In an original introduction, Polacco has an arrogant red-haired boy—presumably her brother, Rich—whose sister prods him to get to the game on time. When the Mudville Nine's chances in the ball game are finished with Casey's final strike, he accepts his defeat humbly. He realizes that he was fairly beaten—even if it was his dad, the umpire, who called him out. Polacco's illustrations are large, bold, and brightly colored.

In recent years, Polacco has returned to subjects that are drawn from her own life. *Thank You, Mr. Falker* (Philomel, 1998) pays homage to the teacher who discovered Patricia's learning disability and helped her succeed at learning to read. The story tells of Trisha and her difficulty learning to read. In fifth grade, a new teacher helps Trisha overcome her problem. Another title, *Mrs. Mack* (Philomel, 1998), tells of the summer Patricia was ten years old and staying with her father in Michigan. She took lessons at a stable where the owner, Mrs. Mack, befriended her and actually ended up letting her keep a beloved horse at her own home for the summer.

Patricia was just five years old when her maternal grandmother died, but she says that the time she did spend with her Babushka was "the most magical time of my life." Her relationships with all of her grandparents were very important and have influenced the images in her books. Most of her books include a young person interacting with an elderly person. Many also reflect the good times and friendship she shared with her best friend in childhood, Stewart Washington, and tell of their exploits and childhood adventures. Virtually all of her books are autobiographical.

To create the illustrations for her stories, Polacco uses Pentel markers, acrylic paint, numbers 2B and 6B pencils, and oil pastels. She begins with a small rough dummy. She designs the dummy with drawings that are photocopied and sent off to the publisher for position corrections. When the drawings are returned, they are enlarged by 25 percent using a copy machine. Polacco then completes the color finishes by using a light box. At this point, she positions the text. Sometimes the visual part of the book comes first, but other times, the words come first. Polacco writes and draws every day that she is not at a school or on a publicity tour.

In the early 1990s, Patricia Polacco and Enzo-Mario Polacco divorced, and Patricia moved to Michigan on an acreage close to the Gaw farm. Polacco's house includes many rocking chairs, one in most every room. She shares her home on Meteor Ridge Farm with two cats, "Miss Chiff" and "Little Gray Thing." On the estate, there is a barn that holds her three other animal companions: her goats, William and Cherattie Mae, and a Suffolk lamb, Bundles. She sometimes puts the three animals onto leashes and takes them for long walks. There is a wading pond and plans to build a very large pond to attract Canada Geese to the area. Patricia Polacco's son and daughter are grown and live nearby.

BOOKS AND NOTES

As a child, Patricia Polacco spent almost every summer in Michigan with her father and paternal grandparents, who lived in a rural community. Many of her books come from that setting, including *Meteor! Boatride with Lillian Two Blossoms, Some Birthday, Picnic at Mudsock Meadow,* and *Mrs. Mack.* Her Jewish heritage is preserved in *The Keeping Quilt, Mrs. Katz and Tush,* and *Chicken Sunday.* The latter two titles are set in California. She pays respect to her Ukrainian, Russian, and Christian heritage in *Thunder Cake, Rechenka's Eggs, Uncle Vova's Tree, Babushka's Doll,* and *Luba and the Wren.*

Aunt Chip and the Great Triple Creek Dam Affair (Philomel, 1996).
Aunt Chip brings together a love of reading and her persistence in getting the townspeople to read books again. A tribute to librarians and teachers.

Babushka's Mother Goose (Philomel, 1995).
An eclectic collection of stories, poems, and verses the author heard at the knee of her Ukrainian babushka (grandmother).

The Bee Tree (Philomel, 1993).
Reenacts a tradition of honey as "sweet as the words" within the book. Symbolically the bees had to be chased to retrieve the honey, just as seeking the sweetness of reading has to be "chased."

Chicken Sunday (Philomel, 1992).
Based on incidents in the author's own life, incidents that she shared with her best friend, Stewart Washington, and his younger brother, Winston.

The Keeping Quilt (Simon & Schuster, 1988; rev. 1998).
Traces the author's family heritage through the moments shared with a homemade quilt. The revised edition updates the family's events during the ten years since the book's first publication.

Luba and the Wren (Philomel, 1999).
A Ukrainian variation of the "Fisherman and His Wife" tale.

Meteor! (Dodd, Mead, 1987; Putnam, 1992).
A story full of hyperbole, recounting the events that result when a meteorite lands in the author's grandparents' farmyard.

Mrs. Katz and Tush (Bantam Books, 1992).
A Jewish woman and an African American boy, with the help of a cat, form a bond and find out just how many similarities their two cultures share.

Mrs. Mack (Philomel, 1998).
The author remembers a summer when she was ten years old and spent hours at Mrs. Mack's horse stable.

My Rotten Redheaded Older Brother (Simon & Schuster, 1994).
A family story with her own older brother, Richard, as the older brother who has all the tricks.

Pink and Say (Philomel, 1994).
Sheldon Russell "Say" Curtis, a white Civil War soldier, describes his meeting

with Pinkus Aylee, a black soldier. The two are captured by Confederate soldiers and taken to Andersonville. Say survives, Pinkus does not. Based on a true story about the author's great-great-grandfather.

Rechenka's Eggs (Philomel, 1988).

Showcases the eggs that the author enjoys painting, *pisanky*. A young girl learns how to paint these beautiful eggs.

Some Birthday! (Simon & Schuster, 1991).

Set in Michigan, Patricia and her brother, Richard, are with their father, cousin Billy, and Gramma on the day of Patricia's birthday. Thinking everyone has forgotten her birthday, Patricia accompanies the others to Clay Pits Bottoms. When the legendary monster scares them home, they find Gramma has a birthday cake with whipped cream and a monster on top.

Thank You, Mr. Falker (Philomel, 1998).

Details the events in Trisha's life as her teacher discovers that she is learning disabled. A tribute to Polacco's junior high teacher, George Felker.

Welcome Comfort (Philomel, 1999).

A lonely foster child is assured that there is a Santa Claus and discovers the truth on a wondrous Christmas eve.

FOR MORE INFORMATION

Articles

Marantz, Sylvia and Ken. "Author & Illustrator Profile: Patricia Polacco." *Library Talk* 5, no. 5 (November/December 1992): 11–14.

Polacco, Patricia. "Author Letter: Meet Patricia Polacco." *Scholastic See-Saw Book Clubs* (March 1993): 2.

Books

Polacco, Patricia. *Firetalking!* Illustrated by Lawrence Migdale. (Richard C. Owens, 1994).

Web Sites

Polacco, Patricia. "Polacco's Web Site." URL: <http://www.patriciapolacco.html> (Accessed March 2000).

Vandergrift, Kay. "Patricia Polacco Page." URL: <http://www.scils.rutgers.edu/special/kay/polacco.html> (Accessed March 2000).

Beatrix Potter

South Kensington, London, England

July 28, 1866–December 22, 1943

📖 *The Tale of Benjamin Bunny*

📖 *The Tale of Peter Rabbit*

📖 *The Tale of Tom Kitten*

ABOUT THE AUTHOR/ILLUSTRATOR

Courtesy of the Victoria and Albert Museum. Reproduced by kind permission of Frederick Warne & Co.

Beatrix Potter is perhaps the best-known author and illustrator of children's books in the world. Her twenty-three tales have been translated into many languages and have been reissued over the years in various formats, including big books, board books, and pop-up books. Toy companies have produced stuffed animals, ceramic figurines, music boxes, and sundry other items based on the characters in Potter's popular titles. More than sixty-five million copies of her books are in print.

Helen Beatrix Potter was the first child born to Rupert Potter, a well-to-do attorney, and his wife Helen Leech Potter. The family lived in an elegant Victorian home in London. Beatrix Potter was tutored at home and spent much of her childhood in her nursery. When she was six years old, her brother, Bertram, was born. By then, Potter had become accustomed to entertaining herself. She spent hours in her schoolroom, drawing pictures of the little animals she observed in the family's backyard, making up stories about the animals, and reading.

The family nurtured Potter's interest in literature and the arts. They regularly visited art galleries and exhibits. The library in their home was filled with books. Rupert Potter's art collection included works by Randolph Caldecott and the painter John Everett Millais. Two Caldecott drawings were from *A Frog He Would A-Wooing Go* and included images of a gentleman frog and a fat smug rat. These animals could be relatives of Jeremy Fisher and Samuel Whiskers, characters that later appeared in Potter's own books. Millais was a family friend, and when he died in 1896, Beatrix Potter wrote in her journal of his encouragement. He had complimented her not only on her drawing, but on her ability to observe as well.

During summers from 1871 to 1881, the Potter family spent time in the Scottish Highlands at Dalguise House. The grown-ups fished and hunted while Beatrix and Bertram explored the wooded areas. When the children were older, in the 1880s, the family often went to England's Lake District.

During the school year, the Potter children kept pets in their nursery. At one time, the collection included a frog, a dormouse named Xarifa, a tortoise, black newts, lizards, and salamanders. Later the collection included a rabbit as well. Both drew many pictures of the animals and created page after page of drawings in their journals, carefully measuring and observing the pets' characteristics. When she was fifteen years old, Beatrix began a private journal, which she kept from 1881 to 1897. She created a secret code to write her entries.

Tutors came to the home and instructed the children in academic subjects. When Bertram turned eleven, his parents sent him to boarding school, and Mrs. Potter hired a young woman, Annie Carter, to be Beatrix's companion. Annie, who was just three years older, taught Beatrix German. The two girls became close friends. Potter described those days as among her happiest. In 1885, Annie married Edwin Moore. Potter often visited the Moores' home and wrote picture letters to entertain their young children.

Potter's pet rabbit, Benjamin H. Bouncer, was the subject of many of her drawings. Potter drew the animal from every angle. Bertram Potter encouraged his sister to send some of her drawings to Hildesheimer & Faulkner, a greeting card company. Upon receipt of Potter's work, the company requested more drawings from her. They used them to create cards and to illustrate a set of verses by Frederic E. Weatherly in a booklet called *A Happy Pair*. Beatrix Potter was just twenty-four and already a published professional.

When Benjamin H. Bouncer died, Potter purchased another rabbit, Peter Piper. Peter accompanied her when she went to the Lake District. At times, she took the rabbit for walks, using a string as a leash.

Potter continued to write story-letters to the Moores' children. During a "holiday" in Scotland, the Moores' young son, Noel, was five years old and ill. To cheer him up, Potter sent him a letter that was the first draft of a story that eventually became *The Tale of Peter Rabbit* (Warne, 1902). The letter began, "My dear Noel, I don't know what to write to you, so I shall tell you a story about four little rabbits whose names were Flopsy, Mopsy, Cottontail, and Peter." Potter decided to write a book, so she asked to borrow the letter from Noel. She copied the story into an exercise book, added forty-one black-and-white drawings (one for each page), and a color frontispiece. She submitted the story to six publishers and received as many rejections. Finally, Frederick Warne & Co. expressed an interest in it but wanted the book in a larger format and with color pictures. That would have increased the price, and Potter was firm that the book should be affordable. So, in 1901, she self-published the little story. The edition sold 250 copies. It was so successful that she was able to negotiate a commercial publishing with Frederick Warne & Co and did create illustrations in watercolor for Warne. That version came out in 1902 and quickly sold 8,000 copies. By the end of the year, almost 30,000 copies were sold. It marked the beginning of a decades-long relationship. Warne published all of Beatrix Potter's books. Many of them were translated into twenty-nine languages, from Latin to Japanese to Icelandic.

Color printing at the time often was done with chromolithography, which muted and muddied the colors in the illustrations. Potter adapted the colors she used and refined her technique to allow the printer to create a satisfactory reproduction. She used a very dry brush to create precise lines for the fur of her small animal characters. Because of later improvements in the color printing process, Potter was able to use more color washes. She created inventive illustrations for some of her favorite classic stories and poems. Illustrating the stories of other authors provided her with a pastime, but she was most comfortable drawing pictures to go with her own stories. Color printing was generally done using a three-color process until 1985. In 1987, Warne rephotographed the originals to Potter's almost two dozen books. The published books used new printing technology and no longer seem pastel but are vivid and more closely approximate the colors of Potter's original watercolors.

Eventually, Potter's friend Annie Moore had eight children. A story-letter to her son Eric in 1894 became the basis for *The Tale of Little Pig Robinson*. The book was not published until thirty-six years later, in 1930. A story sent to Norah Moore in 1901 was the first version of *The Tale of Squirrel Nutkin.*

Beatrix Potter's family lived near the Natural History Museum. Frequent access to that museum and all the summer days spent in the fields and forests of Scotland gave her a deep appreciation for nature. She observed and drew many plants and bugs and drew a vast variety of animal species from butterflies to weasels to rams. She created some of the finest watercolors of fungi. Many of her readers do not know that in 1897 a paper she wrote about the "Germination of the Spores of *Agaricineae*" was read to a scientific community, the Linnean Society of London. Members of the society were shocked that an amateur could have conducted the research. It seemed everything in the out-of-doors was of interest to Beatrix. She filled her drawing journals with drawings and copious notations. She drew pen-and-ink studies of a dormouse, magnified watercolors of the wings of small tortoiseshell and painted lady butterflies, and a watercolor of the fungi *Lepiota friesil.* She created literally hundreds of drawings from her early childhood through her career as a children's book illustrator and writer and into her mature years as a sheep farmer and breeder in the English Lake District.

During her negotiations with Frederick Warne & Co. publishers, Potter dealt through Norman Warne, the youngest of three brothers who ran the company. Warne and Potter became close friends and wrote letters to one another almost every day. By the summer of 1905, the couple was engaged to be married, but in August, Norman Warne contracted what was thought to be pernicious anemia and unexpectedly died. Later the illness was found to have been leukemia. The tragedy devastated Potter, and she went to the Lake District. She bought a farm, Hill Top, and immersed herself in the farm life. The farm was a working farm run by a manager, but Potter made the trip north from London to the farm whenever she could. She investigated the ins and outs of the farming operation and the process of butter making. She built on to the farmhouse so that she could spend extended lengths of time working on her writing and illustrations.

By this time Potter was in her forties, and she was writing her stories from the farm. She wrote and illustrated thirteen more books, and the stories began to reflect the area where she was living. Many are set in her Hill Top home, in Near Sawrey, or in the surrounding fields. *The Tale of Mrs. Tiggy-Winkle* is set in Newlands, and *The Tale of Squirrel Nutkin* is set in Derwentwater. The village of Sawrey is the setting for *The Pie and the Patty Pan* and *The Tale of Jemima Puddle-Duck.* Hill Top is the location for *The Tale of Tom Kitten* and *The Tale of Samuel Whiskers.*

In literary terms, the animals were personified as they took on the mannerisms and characteristics of those humans who lived in the Lake District. For example, Mrs. Tiggy-Winkle hid her key under the door sill just as most of the housewives in the area did. Mrs. Tittlemouse slept in a box bed as did most natives of the area. The animals, however, always were true to their animal nature.

Beatrix Potter began actively working her farm, and as the royalties rolled in for her books, she continued to amass more farmland. Her business dealings with the books and her farming interests were many, so she enlisted the help of a local attorney, William Heelis. She came to rely heavily on his advice, and they became close friends. On October 14, 1913, Beatrix Potter married Heelis. Beatrix's parents had opposed this marriage, as they had earlier opposed her engagement to Norman Warne. Nonetheless, Potter did marry, and after a honeymoon the couple settled in the Lake District. Potter became known as Mrs. Heelis, although her books are still published under the name Beatrix Potter.

Together for the next three decades, the two of them worked the farm, and Potter became known for her sheep-breeding activities. They moved into Castle Cottage, a farm that Potter had purchased in 1909. The property was larger and less primitive than Hill Top, located right across the road. Hill Top became a place for her to greet visitors and to write and draw. It had been furnished with seventeenth- and eighteenth-century furniture, and she used carved oak cupboards to hold her collection of fine china.

When Potter's father died the following year, she and her husband brought her mother to live in the Lake District. Less than ten months after Beatrix and William married, England was at war. The next four years were stressful for Potter. She had no immediate family members who were of the age to be sent to fight, but her plowman was drafted and went in the middle of plowing season. Potter worried about the young Warnes. Frederick Warne & Co. was in serious financial trouble. No books were published during this time, until the final year of the war. *Appley Dapply's Nursery Rhymes* (Warne, 1917) was published and helped the Warne company out of its financial problems.

From the 1920s on, Potter spent less and less time writing children's books and concentrated more of her time on sheep breeding. She was the first and only woman ever elected as the president of the Herdwick Sheepherders' Association. She regularly trudged through the sheep pens in a Herdwick tweed suit, down to her ankles. She wore heavy waterproof clogs and a shapeless brown felt hat tied under her chin.

During World War II, she suggested that people in Great Britain help ease the food shortage by breeding rabbits. She lived long enough to be satisfied that foreign interests would not overtake her beloved farms. When she died three days before Christmas 1943, she had provided in her will that upon the death of her husband, her fifteen farms and more than 4,000 acres of her Lake District property, including Hill Top Farm, would be put into the National Trust, a charity dedicated to preserving the British heritage. After William Heelis's death eighteen months later, the property was put into the National Trust, which opened Hill Top Farm to the public in 1946. The trust was also given the majority of the original illustrations for her books. They were exhibited at Hill Top for several years. The old farmhouse house nestles into the countryside. She used the unpretentious study, with its burnished wood surfaces, for writing and taking care of her accounts. More than 100,000 visitors pass through the farm each season. Since July 7, 1988, visitors have also been able to visit the Beatrix Potter Gallery and Museum in nearby Hawkshead, which now displays Potter's illustrations. The gallery is in William Heelis's old office. In 1988, an exhibit of more than 300 of her original watercolors was mounted at the Pierpont Morgan Library in New York City. The exhibit, "Beatrix Potter—The Artist and Her World," included many illustrations that had never been on display previously. Beatrix Potter's books are still published by her longtime publisher, Frederick Warne.

BOOKS AND NOTES

Beatrix Potter's original titles have been published in several formats and in various editions since Frederick Warne Publishers first released them. Twenty-three of her popular animal tales are listed in this bibliography with the date believed to be the first publication date by Warne.

Appley Dapply's Nursery Rhymes (Warne, 1917).

Cecily Parsley's Nursery Rhymes (Warne, 1922).

The Story of a Fierce Bad Rabbit (Warne, 1906).

The Story of Miss Moppet (Warne, 1906).

The Tailor of Gloucester (Warne, 1903).

The Tale of Benjamin Bunny (Warne, 1904).

The Tale of Ginger and Pickles (Warne, 1909).

The Tale of Jemima Puddle-Duck (Warne, 1908).

The Tale of Johnny Town-Mouse (Warne, 1918).

The Tale of Little Pig Robinson (Warne, 1930).

The Tale of Mr. Jeremy Fisher (Warne, 1906).

The Tale of Mr. Tod (Warne, 1912).

The Tale of Mrs. Tiggy-Winkle (Warne, 1905).

The Tale of Mrs. Tittlemouse (Warne, 1910).

The Tale of Peter Rabbit (Warne, 1902).

The Tale of Pigling Bland (Warne, 1913).

The Tale of Samuel Whiskers (Warne, 1908).

The Tale of Squirrel Nutkin (Warne, 1903).

The Tale of the Flopsy Bunnies (Warne, 1909).

The Tale of the Pie and the Patty-Pan (Warne, 1905).

The Tale of Timmy Tiptoes (Warne, 1911).

The Tale of Tom Kitten (Warne, 1907).

The Tale of Two Bad Mice (Warne, 1904).

FOR MORE INFORMATION

Articles

Taylor, Judy. "Beatrix Potter's Secret." *Cricket* 16, no. 4 (December 1988): 42–46. An excerpt from her book *Beatrix Potter, 1866–1943: The Artist and Her World.*

Books

Hobbs, Anne Stevenson. *Beatrix Potter's Art: Paintings and Drawings* (Warne, 1990).

Johnson, Jane. *My Dear Noel: The Story of a Letter from Beatrix Potter* (Dial, 1999).

Linder, Leslie. *A History of the Writings of Beatrix Potter*, rev. ed. (Warne, 1987).

Potter, Beatrix. *The Journal of Beatrix Potter, 1881–1897*, new ed. (Warne, 1989). Complete edition, transcribed by Leslie Linder.

Taylor, Judy. *Beatrix Potter, 1866–1943: The Artist and Her World* (Warne, 1988; Warne and The National Trust, 1987; reissued [rev. ed.] 1995). Commissioned as the official companion to the Beatrix Potter exhibition at the Tate Gallery in London (1987–1988) and the Pierpont Morgan Library in New York City (1988).

Taylor, Judy. *Beatrix Potter: Artist, Storyteller and Countrywoman.* (Warne, 1996).

Web Sites

Peter Rabbit Home Page. URL: <http://www.peterrabbit.com> (Accessed March 2000).

Jack Prelutsky

Brooklyn, New York
September 8, 1940

📖 *A Pizza the Size of the Sun*
📖 *Rolling Harvey Down the Hill*
📖 *Poems of A Nonny Mouse*

ABOUT THE AUTHOR

Jack Prelutsky always wanted to be the best at whatever he did. As a youngster, he was often paid to sing at weddings and was given free voice lessons by the choirmaster of the Metropolitan Opera. But then he heard Pavarotti sing, and he knew he could never be the very best singer, so he gave up that idea. He did eventually become, some readers would say, the very best poet.

Jack Prelutsky was born in Brooklyn, New York, on September 8, 1940. He has many stories about his childhood. As a child, he had thought about being a cowboy, but when he finally got to ride a horse in his teens, he was thrown off. Without hesitation, he admitted that he could not be a cowboy. His thoughts of being a jet pilot were dashed the first time he was on an airplane and found that air turbulence made him nervous. He didn't think the

U.S. Air Force would want a pilot who was afraid to fly. He even thought about being a baseball player, preferably for the New York Yankees. When he actually played ball, however, he was quickly convinced that he couldn't hit, run, throw, or catch.

Prelutsky has said that he was an oddity in his family. He wore (and still wears) glasses, was always difficult to deal with in school, and most of his family members are Republicans. He attended New York City public schools and studied voice at the High School of Music and Art. School often bored him. He says he "flunked" seven languages—eight if you count English. Since then, he has managed to translate books from German and Swedish into English.

Prelutsky says he also had unusual friends as a youngster. The Prelutsky family lived in a six-story apartment building where everyone knew everyone else. He says, "When I was a kid, I hung out with four best friends: Harvey, Lucky, Tony, and Willie." Willie was smart, strong, and fast, a good friend, and very handsome. "Willie was exactly like me. We were always competing. We had a secret agreement. If one did something different, the other one had to do it too—right there, right on the spot. One day, Willie spotted a worm. Prelutsky recalls what Willie did next: " 'That looks good,' he said and slurped it down. That meant that I had to eat a worm—a big, long, fat, red, juicy worm." That whole episode happened when Prelutsky was ten years old, but the memories became the beginning for "Willie Ate a Worm" from *Rolling Harvey Down the Hill* (Greenwillow, 1980).

Once he graduated from high school in 1958, Prelutsky entered Hunter College in Manhattan. School was no more exciting to him at this age than it ever had been. He joined the "beatnik" trend. Prelutsky did not seem destined to become a poet. In fact, as a youngster, he did not like poetry at all. While he was in school, he considered much of the poetry teachers read to him "the literary equivalent of liver. I was told it was good for me but I didn't believe it." He continues: "One teacher can take kids who love baseball and in forty-five minutes, they will want to sell their gloves and never play baseball again. And another teacher . . .!" As a result, Prelutsky did not particularly care for poetry until he rediscovered it in his twenties. He had a professor who was fond of poetry, and he also had a girlfriend who was working on a Ph.D. in literature. Her dissertation was on poets. These connections sparked Prelutsky's interest in poetry. During these years, he worked in a variety of jobs: he worked in construction, and he moved furniture and pianos. He was a service worker in a restaurant, an office worker, and a photographer. He even appeared on stage in a production of *Fiddler on the Roof*, sang in the New Mexico Symphony Chorus, and performed with several small opera companies. Later, when he fancied himself an artist and was working in a Greenwich music store, he added some poems to show-case sketches of two dozen little creatures that he had drawn. It had taken him six painstaking months to create pen-and-ink drawings of those creatures, creatures unlike any others. It took him about two hours to compose the verses, one per critter. A friend saw the illustrations and convinced him to take them to an editor. The first editor rejected his drawings (and his poetry), but a second editor told him that the publishing house would be interested in his poetry—but not his drawings. She told him that he had the talent to become one of the best poets for children in the world. More than thirty years later, that editor, Susan Hirschman, is still his friend and editor. Prelutsky feels that writing chose him.

Jack Prelutsky is probably the only author who has had a joint checking account with his editor. Once he began to write for Greenwillow Books and work with Susan Hirschman, she soon realized that he could not keep track of his money. So, as their friendship developed, she insisted that he put his royalty checks into a joint checking account from which he could not withdraw money without her signature. Now his wife, Carolynn, helps him organize and manage his finances. Prelutsky met his wife on a trip to visit schools in Albuquerque, New Mexico. She was a school librarian who met his plane. Prelutsky liked her immediately and asked her to marry him five minutes later. She did not give him her answer until the next day. The answer was yes, and a few months later, around Christmas in 1979, they married and settled down in Albuquerque. Carolynn resigned from her job and became Jack's assistant. She manages his schedule, books his speaking engagements, serves as his secretary, and assists him so he can concentrate on writing.

Much of Prelutsky's poetry builds on experiences from his childhood. Things that happen in the poems—being tied to a tree and having his pants pulled down—were things that happened to Prelutsky, or his friends, while they were growing up in the Bronx during the 1940s and 1950s. Prelutsky also loved ice cream—chocolate chip, peppermint chip, and many other flavors. In his mind, he created other innovative flavors. Those flavors became part of the poem he created about "Bleezer's Ice Cream" in *The New Kid on the Block* (Greenwillow, 1984).

As a child in New York, he loved anything to do with dinosaurs, and that interest came back in a book titled, *Tryannosaurus Was a Beast* (Greenwillow, 1988). "Gussie's Greasy Spoon" from *The New Kid on the Block* was based on a lunch he had in a small-town diner. He says, "It was one of the few meals I've ever consumed that was worse than school cafeteria food!"

Prelutsky has said that the "worse singer in the United States of America is my mother." When she sang, the plaster fell from the ceiling. The same type of "accident" happened in the street—and that took some doing because Prelutsky's family lived on the top floor of a six-story apartment building. She often sang her favorite song, "The Blue Danube Waltz." Prelutsky wrote a song about his mother and her singing, but he didn't want to tell her that it was about her.

Other poems come from his musings about events and people around him now. A package of boneless chicken sparked his curiosity about chickens in general. What would a whole boneless chicken be like? Would a boneless chicken lay scrambled eggs? Soon he had the makings for "Ballad of a Boneless Chicken." While taking a bath and reading an article about wolves in an issue of *National Geographic*, he began to think about wolves and water. The result: "A Wolf Is at the Laundromat" in *The New Kid on the Block*.

Prelutsky's writing schedule is rather sporadic—a day or two here or a week there—at times he writes around the clock. But when the words stop flowing, he may not write again for several months. For ten years, he kept notes about events and ideas for the poems that went into *The New Kid on the Block*. The actual writing was accomplished in seven weeks. He has said that he always has a notebook with him and tries to write down his ideas immediately. Sometimes an idea comes from a subject, a rhyme, or a word or two. Other ideas come from his dreams, and the scary ones come from his nightmares. Sometimes he's not sure where an idea comes from, but whenever one arrives, he writes it in his notebook. He has a stack of full notebooks that is taller than he is.

During one visit to a school, a boy told him he saved all of his fingernail clippings. When Prelutsky asked, "Why?" the child told him that when he had enough clippings, he took them to the zoo and threw them at the elephants because "It makes them crazy." Prelutsky saved that information and later created a poem, "I Toss Them to My Elephant." In the poem, however, the thrown objects are flowers. Each daisy that is tossed "makes him slightly crazy," but a tulip "always makes him sing."

In *A Pizza the Size of the Sun* (Greenwillow, 1996), Prelutsky talks about all sorts of "stuff" that might go on a pizza. His own favorite pizza has all types of toppings on it—extra cheese, sausage, pepperoni, roast garlic, olives, mushrooms. The only things he does not like on pizza are pineapple and anchovies.

Writing poetry finds Prelutsky in either his recliner or at his desk, where he uses a computer. His desk is situated under a large window that lets him see trees and many kinds of birds. He usually has his current favorite toy on his desk. It might be a gorilla pencil sharpener, some type of frog, or a wind-up toy. Some of the toys have turned into poems.

When he is not writing poetry, Prelutsky might be playing his guitar, singing, playing a game of chess or backgammon, or even playing a game of Scrabble. At one time, he even played Scrabble for money. Even though his first editor rejected his drawings, he still enjoys doodling, as well as woodworking and cooking. One of his favorite foods is chocolate chip cookies, but he also enjoys Vietnamese soups, sushi, chicken, and pasta. In 1990, the Prelutskys moved to the Pacific Northwest and settled into a home in Olympia, Washington. A couple of years later, when they moved to a different house three miles from their old one, they also had to move their more than 2,000 books and Prelutsky's collection of frogs, which includes drawings and statuettes and other nonliving artifacts. Prelutsky says he has at least two thousand frogs—and maybe more.

BOOKS AND NOTES

Jack Prelutsky always wanted to be the best at whatever he did. As a poet and anthologist he has achieved that goal. Many children enjoy and chuckle over his poetry. They also enjoy the poems he has compiled into collections for them to read. All of the following titles include poems written by Jack Prelutsky or selected by him for inclusion in a collection.

Awful Ogre's Awful Day. Illustrated by Paul O. Zelinsky. (Greenwillow, 2000).

Dinosaur Dinner with a Slice of Alligator Pie: Favorite Poems. Poems by Dennis Lee, selected by Jack Prelutsky. Illustrated by Debbie Tilley. (Random House, 1997).

Dog Days. Illustrated by Dyanna Wolcott. (Greenwillow, 1999).

The Dragons Are Sleeping Tonight. Illustrated by Peter Sis. (Greenwillow, 1996).

The Gargoyle on the Roof. Illustrated by Peter Sis. (Greenwillow, 1999).

Hooray for Diffendoofer Day. Co-authored with Dr. Seuss. Illustrated by Lane Smith. (Knopf, 1998).

This title was based on a manuscript by Theodor Seuss Geisel, which had not been published before he died in 1991. Prelutsky completed the manuscript.

Imagine That: Poems of Never-Was. Selected by Jack Prelutsky. Illustrated by Kevin Hawkes. (Knopf, 1998).

It's Raining Pigs and Noodles. Illustrated by James Marshall. (Greenwillow, 2000).

Monday's Troll. Illustrated by Peter Sis. (Greenwillow, 1996).

The New Kid on the Block. Illustrated by James Stevenson. (Greenwillow, 1984).

A Pizza the Size of the Sun. Illustrated by James Stevenson. (Greenwillow, 1996).

Something Big Has Been Here. Illustrated by James Stevenson. (Greenwillow, 1990).

Tyrannosaurus Was a Beast: Dinosaur Poems. Illustrated by Arnold Lobel. (Greenwillow, 1988).

FOR MORE INFORMATION

Articles

Raymond, Allen. "Jack Prelutsky . . . Man of Many Talents." *Early Years, Teaching K–8* (November/December 1986): 38–42.

Web Sites

Scholastic. "Authors Online." URL: <http://teacher.Scholastic.com/authorsandbooks/authors/Jprelsk/bio.htm> (Accessed March 2000).

Teachers@random. Resource Center: Author Bios. "Jack Prelutsky." URL: <http://www.randomhouse.com/teachers/rc/rc_ab_jpr.html> (Accessed March 2000).

James Ransome

◆ Historical Fiction ◆ Biography

Rich Square, North Carolina
September 25, 1961

📖 *Aunt Flossie's Hats (and Crab Cakes Later)*

📖 *Sweet Clara and the Freedom Quilt*

ABOUT THE ILLUSTRATOR

The Children's Book Council named James E. Ransome one of seventy-five authors and illustrators that everyone should know. He has received the Coretta Scott King Award and other honors for his illustration. Three of the books he illustrated have been selected as Reading Rainbow selections. His work is displayed as a mural for the Children's Museum of Indianapolis, in private and public collections, and in dozens of children's books.

James E. Ransome was born in Rich Square, North Carolina, on September 25, 1961, the son of Asrine and James Ransome. The town has, according to Ransome, just three traffic lights. The family name was derived from the slave owner, Matt W. Ransom, who owned James's ancestors on Verona Plantation. Along the way James Ransome's ancestors added an "e" to the end of the family name, making it "Ransome."

James Ransome grew up in a part of the rural south where there were few opportunities to meet artists or visit art galleries. There were not a lot of books, either. Behind the family home, where he lived with his grandmother, there was a swamp. Ransome seldom was punished physically, but the day he came back all muddy from the swamp, he received a spanking. Unbeknownst to him, there were alligators in the swamp, and it was a very dangerous place.

Ransome began drawing during his elementary school days. Some of those early drawings were hot-rod cars, and others were copies of comic book scenes. *Mad Magazine* became the inspiration for his own stories, which featured Ransome and his friends. The schools he attended did not have art classes, so he borrowed the few how-to-draw books that the school library owned. He kept an eye open for any television shows featuring art or artists. During his last years in elementary school, he found an offer in the back of a comic book for a correspondence school. The course, "How to Draw Gags and Cartoons and Get Rich, Rich, Rich!" taught him the rudiments of drawing cartoon characters but did not succeed in making him rich.

By the time Ransome was a sophomore in high school, his family had moved to Bergenfield, New Jersey, a suburb right across the river from Manhattan. Finally, art classes were available to Ransome. He was able to enroll in filmmaking and photography classes at Bergenfield High School. Those courses formed the foundation of his current style of illustration. Through his study of filmmaking, he developed a sense of perspective, value, and cropping and learned how those elements, along with framing and camera angles, could change an illustration's focus. During the course work, he was involved in the making of several student films and discovered that he preferred to work independently on his own projects. He began to dabble in animation and eventually was encouraged to take a drawing and painting class. Those courses renewed his interest in drawing and illustration.

After high school, he enrolled in the Pratt Institute of Arts in Brooklyn, New York. During his art history courses, he became acquainted with the work of Mary Cassatt, John Singer Sargent, Winslow Homer, Edgar Degas, and Joaquin Sorolla. The work of each artist had a major influence on Ransome's painting style. One of Ransome's instructors at Pratt was the renowned illustrator Jerry Pinkney. Pinkney's large body of illustrative work encouraged Ransome and helped him to realize that an African American artist could make a living as an artist. Pinkney befriended and mentored Ransome.

By Ransome's second year at Pratt, he had decided to become a sports illustrator and set his goals on working for major sports magazines, such as *Sports Illustrated.* By Ransome's senior year at Pratt, he had been exposed to Jerry Pinkney's wonderful illustrations for Valerie Flournoy's *The Patchwork Quilt* (Dial, 1985). He later created three paintings that included children in them. He found that he enjoyed creating those illustrations. Orchard published the first book Ransome illustrated, *Do Like Kyla*, in 1990. The book came about because James Ransome was attending a networking meeting of the Graphic Artists' Guild, and John Ward showed up. Ward suggested that Ransome take some of his illustrations to Richard Jackson at Orchard. As a result, the publisher offered Ransome a contract to illustrate Angela Johnson's book about two sisters. Ransome did not even read the manuscript; he knew he was going to take the book regardless of whether he liked it. Later Ransome illustrated another title by Johnson, *The Girl Who Wore Snakes* (Orchard, 1993). While Jackson gave Ransome his start, other editors have helped Ransome make his mark in the world of children's books.

For the most part, James Ransome has illustrated books written by other authors. His first introduction to a story is through the typewritten manuscript that the publisher sends him. He reads the manuscript and decides if he wants to accept the offer to illustrate it. Throughout the process of sketching and illustrating a book, he constantly assesses the effect of the layout and the images on the story as a whole.

When he constructed the illustrations for his second book with author Deborah Hopkinson, *Under the Quilt of Night* (Atheneum, 2000), he drew on his memory of that swamp from his childhood—only this one was immeasurably more menacing. His research also provides him with other images to include in his illustrations. For example, when African American slaves *fol*lowed the constellations and the North Star to freedom, they found safe haven along the way among people who would hide them during the day and help them along under the cover of night. An indigo spot on an article hung on a clothesline or near a door often signaled that the house welcomed slaves. In Ransome's illustrations, he incorporated an indigo spot in the middle of a log cabin quilt. The quilt illustration he created for *Sweet Clara and the Freedom Quilt* (Knopf, 1993) was one that he made up for the book, but slaves did make quilts that held secret symbols and information regarding slave routes. Some of the quilts were quite sophisticated in terms of accurate scales for distance and so forth. Ransome did not use any of those symbols, however; he attempted only to portray the map with landmarks mentioned in Hopkinson's text. In *Sweet Clara and the Freedom Quilt*, Clara is an eleven-year-old who is sent away from her mother to another plantation. As a house slave in the house, Clara is able to save bits of cloth and to gather, from visiting slaves, bits of information about routes to freedom. Clara uses the bits of cloth to fashion a quilt that provides a map to freedom. It is Ransome's illustrations that provide readers with an image for that quilt. His dedication on the title page provides a clue to the emotional connection that he made with Hopkinson's text. "For Emma Ransom, the first slave of Pattie and General Matt W. Ransom, and all the other Ransom slaves on Verona Plantation." Hopkinson says the reference in the book to the plantation was changed to actually refer to the Verona Plantation because of Ransome's family history. Ransome researched the book in part at Colonial Williamsburg's Carter's Grove Plantation, but he also traced the location of Verona.

Ransome uses photographs of models to make his illustrations, just as his mentor Jerry Pinkney does. The models pose, and photographs capture their actions. Ransome uses the photographs to help him create the paintings. At times, Ransome uses members of his family or friends to pose, but the models for the illustrations for *Sweet Clara and the Freedom Quilt* were "discovered" at a book fair in New Jersey. Danielle, the girl who ended up posing for Clara, was there with her mother, a reading teacher, who also posed for the book. Eventually the whole family—mother, brother, and dad—played a role in the book.

So far, of the books he has illustrated, Ransome's favorite is *Uncle Jed's Barbershop* (Simon & Schuster, 1993). He is also partial to *Bonesy and Isabel* (Harcourt, 1995). The subjects of these books were of particular interest to him. The title he found the most difficult to illustrate was Patricia McKissack and Fredrick McKissack's collection, *Let My People Go: Bible Stories of Faith, Hope, and Love: As Told by Price Jeffries, a Free Man of Color, to His Daughter, Charlotte, in Charleston, South Carolina (1806–1816)*. He had to take great care in making the clothing and objects in the illustrations appropriate to the time setting.

When Ransome illustrated William H. Hook's *Freedom's Fruit* (Random House, 1996), he used the illustrated end papers to show the slave plantation where Mama Marina, a conjurer, lived; he again used Verona Plantation as his model. Ransome also creates book jacket illustrations. One of his most notable is the jacket for Jane Kurtz's *The Storyteller's Beads* (Harcourt, 1998).

Most illustrators read manuscripts carefully before they accept a contract to illustrate a book. Various factors influence their decision: the manuscript itself, the publisher's deadline, and the vision the illustrator may have for the illustrations. Although publishers generally make an effort to have the same artist illustrate a sequel or companion book, that doesn't always happen. Among the books Ransome has illustrated is Elizabeth Fitzgerald Howard's *Aunt Flossie's Hats (and Crab Cakes Later)* (Clarion, 1991). It is the story of Susan and Sarah, two sisters who visit Aunt Flossie and try on her collection of hats. They also hear a story from Aunt Flossie before enjoying crab cakes. Although Howard wrote a sequel, *What's in Aunt Mary's Room* (Clarion, 1996), Ransome declined the offer to illustrate that book.

In 1999, Ransome's illustrations complemented a biography, *Satchel Paige* by Lesa Cline-Ransome (Simon & Schuster, 2000). The book, researched and written by Lesa Cline-Ransome, takes a look at the life of the first African American to pitch in a Major League World Series. Since Lesa is James's wife, the collaboration seemed to be a natural. In their personal life Lesa and James have collaborated to produce three children: Jaime, Maya, and Malcolm. The family lives in a large white house that used to be owned by a doctor who saw patients in his house. Ransome's studio is now situated in the area where the doctor's waiting room once was. In the hallway to the dining room are works of art. He continues to admire the watercolors of Winslow Homer and the pattern and design of Edgar Degas's work, as well as the work of Mary Cassatt, John Singer Sargent, and Joaquin Sorolla. In addition to his art studio, Ransome keeps an office where he deals with the business side of his illustrative work. He keeps extensive research files and books, a lot of magazines, and many photographs and pictures filed in categories. The Ransome family share their home, on the Hudson River, with their dog Clinton.

BOOKS AND NOTES

Once James Ransome accepts a manuscript to illustrate, he gets out his sketchbook and begins to sketch ideas of how the book might be divided and laid out in terms of illustration. He has been known to revise the sketched illustrations for an entire manuscript overnight. Once he is satisfied with the sketches, he uses them to create a dummy, which he sends to the publisher. The editors use the dummy to help decide on the book design and offer their comments. Ransome participates in the design of the book as well.

Ransome feels that his job as an illustrator is to "put the sprinkles on the ice cream." He most often works in oil or acrylic because that seems to result in more realistic images. His first four books were painted on canvas, but now he uses a special board covered with a wash that tones down the white. His pencil sketch is made directly onto the board, and then all the faces and arms are painted and then the background. He works across the page from left to right, working on each individual as they appear on the page. Each of the books in the following booklist were illustrated by James Ransome.

Freedom's Fruit. Written by William H. Hooks. (Random House, 1996).

Mama Marina uses her conjuring skills to cast a spell on the master's grapes and manages to win freedom for her daughter and the man she loves.

Let My People Go: Bible Stories of Faith, Hope, and Love: As Told by Price Jeffries, a Free Man of Color, to His Daughter, Charlotte, in Charleston, South Carolina (1806–1816). Written by Patricia McKissack and Fredrick McKissack. (Atheneum, 1998).

The daughter of a free man retells the stories her father, told to her during her childhood, and relates the stories to the experiences of African Americans.

Quinnie Blue. Written by Dinah Johnson. (Holt, 1999).

An intergenerational story in which Hattie's grandmother, Quinnie Blue, shares memories of her own childhood.

Rum-a-tum-tum. Written by Angela Shelf Medearis. (Holiday House, 1997). Sounds from Market Street.

Satchel Paige. Written by Lesa Cline-Ransome. (Simon & Schuster, 2000).

The first African American to pitch in a Major League World Series, Leroy Paige, is the subject of this biography.

The Secret of the Stones: A Folktale. Retold by Robert San Souci. (Dial/Phyllis Fogelman, 2000).

A childless couple discovers that it is two bewitched orphans who are doing their chores while the couple works in the fields.

Sweet Clara and the Freedom Quilt. Written by Deborah Hopkinson. (Knopf, 1993).

Clara fashions a quilt to lead fellow slaves to freedom in the North.

The Wagon. Written by Tony Johnston. (Tambourine, 1996).

A family keeps a wagon as they endure the hardships of slavery; when they are free, the wagon takes the family to the funeral of President Lincoln.

Uncle Jed's Barbershop. Written by Margaree King Mitchell. (Simon & Schuster, 1993).

Sarah Jean's Uncle Jed has a goal of opening a barber shop. When he finds that Sarah's family needs the money he has saved, he postpones his goal. But with perseverance, he establishes the only barbershop for African Americans in the county.

Under the Quilt of Night. Written by Deborah Hopkinson. (Atheneum, 2000).

A companion title to *Sweet Clara*, a young girl flees from the farm where she has been working as a slave. She makes her way to the North and to freedom along the Underground Railroad.

Your Move. Written by Eve Bunting. (Harcourt, 1998).

When the gang threatens to involve James's six-year-old brother Isaac, James realizes he must get the courage to say "no."

FOR MORE INFORMATION

Web Sites

Vandergrift, Kay. "Notes on James Ransome." URL: <http://www.scils.rutgers. edu/special/Kay/clara8.html> (Accessed March 2000).

H. A. (Hans Augusto) Rey
Margret Rey

◆ Animals

Hamburg Germany
September 16, 1898–August 22, 1977

Hamburg, Germany
May 16, 1906–December 21, 1996

📖 *Curious George*

📖 *Curious George Goes to the Hospital*

📖 *Curious George Takes a Job*

ABOUT THE AUTHORS/ILLUSTRATORS

Hans Augusto Reyersbach (H. A. Rey) was born in Hamburg, Germany on September 16, 1898. Margret Elisabeth Waldstein was born in the same city eight years later, on May 16, 1906. Together they created the mischievous monkey, Curious George, the subject of seven books and several CD-ROMS.

As a child, H. A. Rey spent as much time as possible at the Hagenbeck Zoo. When he was two years old, he started drawing and especially liked to draw horses. In 1900, horses could be seen all over Hamburg. He went to a humanistic gymnasium (in Germany, *gymnasium* is the term for what is called an elementary school in the United States). At this school, youngsters began to learn Latin in the fourth grade and later studied Greek, French, and eventually English. He had to learn to speak Portuguese when he later moved to Brazil. In addition to his native German, Rey could speak six languages.

When he was eighteen years old, he was drafted into the German army. He was sent to France and Russia with the infantry and medical corps. When he left the army in 1919, he wanted to go to art school but could not afford the tuition. Instead, he managed to attend the University of Munich and the University of Hamburg, earning his tuition by doing freelance artwork. One of his assignments was to design posters for a circus. He lithographed them directly on stone, an experience that proved helpful when years later he would have to create the color separations for his book illustrations.

Rey studied philology, as well as natural science. Before he could finish his degree, relatives offered him a job at their import firm in Rio de Janeiro, Brazil. The time was right for a move, because the postwar inflation was so bad that the fee Rey would receive for creating a poster was not even enough to buy lunch. So Rey traveled to Brazil. His job was to "sell bathtubs up and down the Amazon River." He worked at that job from 1924 to 1935. Just before he left Brazil, he met his future wife, Margret Elisabeth Waldstein. They shared a love of art and a dislike of the Nazis.

At the time H. A. Rey was selling bathtubs in Brazil, Margret Elisabeth Waldstein was attending Bauhaus (1927) and the Dusseldorf Academy of Art (1928–1929). During her years of study at the Academy, the well-known artists Paul Klee and Wassily Kandinsky were on the faculty. From 1929 to 1934, she had many one-artist shows in Berlin that featured her watercolors. Later, Margret got bored with art and switched to writing. She wrote for a newspaper and later wrote the lyrics for musical commercials. Because of that experience, she said that she developed an "undying hate for commercials." Eventually, she turned to photography and even opened her own studio in Hamburg, Germany, just before Hitler came into power. She decided to leave Hamburg and traveled from Hamburg to London and finally to Rio de Janeiro where she met H. A. Rey. They actually had become acquainted earlier in Hamburg when Rey had dated her older sister. In fact, H. A. first saw Margret when he attended a party for her older sister at which Margret slid down the banister.

Rey quit his job with the import business, and H. A. Rey and Margret Waldstein founded Rio's first advertising agency. They took wedding photos, generated newspaper articles (Margret wrote them and Rey illustrated them), and developed advertising campaigns. They married in 1935, four months after their meeting in Rio de Janeiro.

In 1936, the couple took a honeymoon to Europe and went to Paris, intending to stay two weeks. They rented a room in Montmartre and stayed for four years. Margret Rey did some freelance writing, and H. A. Rey did freelance illustration work for several French publications. H. A. Rey did a few humorous drawings of a giraffe for a Paris periodical. An editor at a French publishing house called to ask if he could make a children's book out of the drawings. They began to write and illustrate children's books. Together they wrote and illustrated their first book, *Cecily G. and the 9 Monkeys*. One of the monkeys was later the star of his own books, the Curious George series. Margret wrote and H. A. illustrated these books.

They were still living at Montmartre in June of 1940 when the Nazis began their advance on Paris. The Reys got on their bicycles and pedaled to the border only hours ahead of the invading troops, wearing warm coats and carrying their manuscripts, which they bundled and tied to the bicycle racks. They sold their bicycles to the custom officials at the French-Spanish border for money. Among the belongings they took with them was the partial manuscript for the first Curious George book. They made their way to Lisbon, and after a brief time in Rio de Janeiro, they eventually arrived in New York City on a clear crisp October morning in 1940. They became naturalized citizens in 1946.

Establishing themselves in a small apartment in Greenwich Village, they searched for a publisher for their books. The editor at Houghton Mifflin was interested in the book but wanted the name of the character changed. Grace Hogarth, the editor, said "My favorite [book is] *Cecily G. and the 9 Monkeys* (Houghton, 1942). But I also loved 'Zozo' and, above all, so did my children." Hogarth agreed to publish the books but felt that the title "seemed wrong." One day they hit upon the idea of renaming the little monkey "Curious George." The first title in the series was published by Houghton Mifflin in 1941.

The Reys lived in Greenwich Village for twenty-three years before moving to a house in Cambridge, Massachusetts. In the summers, they spent time in their cottage in Waterville, New Hampshire. Margret Rey enjoyed gardening, but H. A. Rey tried to avoid anything having to do with horticulture. Instead, he retired to his studio in the woods. He enjoyed watching nature, reading, making gadgets, swimming and snorkeling, and stargazing.

They eventually created six more books about Curious George. *Curious George Goes to the Hospital* (Houghton, 1966) was written in collaboration with the Children's Hospital Medical Center of Boston. The Curious George books are among those most often associated with H. A. Rey and Margret Rey. All of the Reys' books were not about monkeys, but with the exception of H. A.'s two books on astronomy, they were all about animals. The couple always owned animals. In Paris, they had turtles; in Brazil, they had monkeys; and in New Hampshire, they kept alligators, chameleons, and dogs. They always had a cocker spaniel, and H. A. often put a picture of one in his books.

After the success of Curious George in the United States, the books were translated for other countries. In England, Curious George was published with his original name, Zozo. Several years after the book's publication there, Grace Hogarth suggested to the British publisher that they might reap more sales if they renamed Zozo to Curious George. She was then informed that "curious" was not an adjective, except in the sense of "odd." Thus, in England, Curious George stayed "Zozo." In France, he was "Fifi," and in Denmark he became "Peter Pedal."

Hans Augusto Rey had an interesting sense of humor. When asked how old he was, he once said, "a first-grader is six years old; a second-grader is seven. I'd be a sixty-ninth grader if there were such a grade." After H. A. Rey's death in 1977, Margret Rey approved the publication of several additional Curious George books based on the Curious George film series. Those books never seemed to gain the success of the original series.

Margret Rey taught writing at Brandeis University in Waltham, Massachusetts, and oversaw a myriad of licensing agreements for products based on their book characters. After a time, she also became a "research associate in childhood studies" at the Harvard Erikson Center.

Margret Rey said there was no way she could go on creating books without her husband. Without him, it would be too hard. At the time of the 50th anniversary of George's birthday, Margret and her pet monkey, Coco, celebrated with a huge cake and plenty of balloons. Margret was eighty-one, and said she spent her time "yelling at manufacturers" to ensure that they kept up the quality of the Curious George merchandise. The merchandising that she oversaw included all types of "George merchandise"—hats, shirts, puzzles, and dolls. Margret Rey died at the age of ninety on December 21, 1996.

BOOKS AND NOTES

Together Margret Rey and H. A. Rey created other titles in addition to the Curious George titles. They had an interesting writing partnership. Margret was the one who most often wrote the books, and H. A. illustrated them. H. A. would get a story idea and Margret would turn the idea into a story. Sometimes the idea was entirely Margret's, such as, *Pretzel* (Houghton, 1944) and *Spotty* (Harper, 1945, 1997). In both of these instances, she wrote the story on her own and H. A. illustrated each of them. H. A. Rey was also a respected astronomer. In addition to his picture books, he wrote *Find the Constellations* (Houghton, 1954; rev. 1967) and *The Stars: A New Way to See Them* (Houghton, 1952; enlarged 1967), which was a book for adults. H. A. Rey wrote the astronomy titles, but Margret Rey sometimes rewrote passages so the section would be more understandable to the layman.

The books on astronomy came about, in part, because of World War I. When H. A. Rey was an eighteen-year-old soldier in the German army, he carried a pocket book on astronomy in his knapsack. He enjoyed studying the stars during the blackouts at night. But the book was not very helpful for a beginning stargazer, so years later he worked out a new way to show the constellations.

Books Written by Margret Rey and Illustrated by H. A. Rey

The Complete Adventures of Curious George. Introduction by Madeleine L'Engle. (Houghton, 1995).
A compilation of the seven books about Curious George with some additional notes.

Spotty (Houghton, 1945, 1997).
A book about a bunny that is different.

Pretzel (Houghton Mifflin, 1944).
A young dachshund named Pretzel seeks the friendship of Greta, another dachshund.

Pretzel and the Puppies (Harper, 1946).
Another story about the dachshund.

Curious George Series

Curious George (Houghton, 1941).

Curious George Flies a Kite (Houghton, 1958).

Curious George Gets a Medal (Houghton, 1957).

Curious George Goes to the Hospital (Houghton, 1966).

Curious George Learns the Alphabet (Houghton, 1963).

Curious George Rides a Bike (Houghton, 1952).

Curious George Takes a Job (Houghton, 1947).

Books Illustrated by H. A. Rey

Cecily G. and the 9 Monkeys (Houghton, 1942; 1989).
A story about nine monkeys; one of them is Curious George.

Don't Frighten the Lion. Written by Margaret Wise Brown. (Harper, 1942).
A playful tale about the not-so-frightening lion.

Katy No-Pocket. Written by Emmy Payne. (Houghton, 1944).
Katy, a kangaroo, has no pocket for her young offspring to ride in. But there is a solution.

Books Written and Illustrated by H. A. Rey

Elizabite: Adventures of a Carnivorous Plant (Harper, 1942).
A Venus flytrap wins fame by capturing a burglar.

Find the Constellations (Houghton, 1954).
A book about the stars.

Humpty Dumpty and Other Mother Goose Songs (Harper, 1943).
A collection of popular Mother Goose verses.

Look for the Letters: A Hide-and-Seek Alphabet (Harper, 1945).
An early alphabet book.

Tommy Helps, Too (Houghton, 1943).

A toy and moveable book, set in World War II.

FOR MORE INFORMATION

Articles

"Anniversary: Curious George and his literary Mama, Margret Rey, Celebrate a Half-Century of Monkeyshines." *People* 27, no. 22 (June 1, 1987): 98.

Web Sites

USM de Grummond Collection—Margret and Hans Augusto Rey Papers. URL: <http://www.lib.usm.edu/~degrum/findaids/rey.htm> (Accessed February 2000).

Faith Ringgold

Sharron L. McElmeel

New York, New York
October 8, 1930

📖 *Aunt Harriet's Underground Railroad in the Sky*

📖 *Dinner at Aunt Connie's House*

📖 *Tar Beach*

ABOUT THE AUTHOR/ILLUSTRATOR

Faith Willi Jones was born on October 8, 1930, at the Harlem Hospital in New York City. She was one of four children born to Willi Posey Jones and Andrew Louis Jones. When she was born, her parents had hoped for a boy because their eighteen-month-old son had died earlier of pneumonia. The baby girl came instead, and as a effort to "keep the faith," her parents named her "Faith." She joined Andrew Jr., then a seven-year-old, and Barbara, a four-year-old. Faith Jones grew up to be painter, a mixed media sculptor, a performance artist, and a writer, as well as a professor in the Department of Visual Arts at the University of California, San Diego.

During her childhood, Faith's siblings and parents doted on her. She was often tucked into a pram covered with a colorful quilt made of triangular shapes. When Faith developed asthma at age two, her mother began to make an extra effort to keep the air in their home moist, often rising before anyone else to boil water on the stove to bring moisture into the air. She would give Faith a warm bath and dress her in clothing that she had warmed on the radiator. Faith's hair was always carefully groomed, often braided with a special bow. She ate breakfast with her father, a New York City sanitation truck driver, and then again with her older sister and brother. Faith and her mother would walk Andrew and Barbara up the hill to their school. Once they arrived home again, Faith was left to her own devices. She colored and copied etchings onto blank paper. Her mother taught her to sew, and soon she was stitching together pieces of fabric. As she entered elementary school, her creations became more complicated. She attempted to make shoes, hats, pocketbooks, and even underwear. Sometimes the results were strange looking.

Faith often listened to the mayor of New York City read the comics over the radio each Sunday morning. She decided she wanted to learn to read, too, so her mother and siblings taught her. She was just four years old.

Faith Jones continued to be plagued by asthma, and when she entered school, her mother prepared health food for her to eat. Faith did not think much of the homemade lemon ice cream made with skim milk, nor the steamed vegetables and cornmeal gruel. Other foods her mother offered included fresh fruit, lamb, and chicken. Despite these efforts, Faith's asthma was so bad that she was unable to attend school, so Willi Jones taught her at home. She learned so quickly that when she finally could go to school, she was ahead of her classmates. She was also the best artist in the classroom.

Faith Jones's home-schooling days did not restrict her to her house. She and her mother often went to theater performances and museums. Faith learned of the work of Ella Fitzgerald, Duke Ellington, and Lena Horne. She admired the art she saw in the museums. When Andrew and Barbara returned from school, the children ate dinner together and then studied in their rooms. After their father came home, cleaned up from his job, and ate dinner, the whole family spent time together. Sometimes, especially on hot summer nights, the family and their neighbors gathered on the tar-paper rooftop of their tenement building. They played cards around an old green card table. The children, if they stayed quiet on the mattress, could stay up late. They created imaginary stories about the stars and the cities' glittering lights. Her brother enjoyed telling scary nighttime stories about the Boogie Man, especially in the dark when all the lights were out. Years later, as an adult, Faith Jones Ringgold created a quilt about her memories of those nights on the "Tar Beach."

In second grade Faith Jones's teacher chose her to paint an image of Santa Claus on the Christmas mural. That gesture helped her feel good about her artistic ability. Several years later, during World War II when Faith was twelve, her parents divorced, and her mother went to work in the garment industry. As a fashion designer and garment maker, she learned to operate powerful sewing machines. Even though Faith lived with her mother, brother, and sister, she also continued to see her father. He helped her to read and encouraged her in her art endeavors by giving her an easel and a drawing board.

When Faith was in high school, she stopped taking art classes and took only academic classes. But she continued to work on her art away from school. She drew portraits of family members and friends. At times, they did not like sitting still long enough for her to draw them, and sometimes they did not like the way they looked in her portraits. But Faith did not stop. She kept practicing. She graduated from high school in 1948 and set out to attend City College of New York. At the time, the college's school of liberal arts did not accept women. She could only enter the school of education. Faith's mother was pleased because her parents and several of her daughter's cousins had been teachers. Willi Jones thought that her daughter could earn a living as a teacher and could still find time to create her art.

Much of Faith Jones's art training involved copying the lines and forms of Greek busts. Throughout her art studies Faith's teachers had been white. She wanted to learn about African American art. She set about to create darker images. Her first results at mixing paints for different skin tones brought oranges and greens. Her instructors grew impatient, but she continued to experiment. She created African American images and used African American themes as subjects for her art. Before she graduated from City College in 1955, Faith married Robert Earl Wallace. He was a classical and jazz pianist. The marriage lasted only six years. They were the parents of two daughters, Michele Faith Wallace and Barbara Faith Wallace.

Upon graduation from City College, Faith embarked on a teaching career in the New York City Public Schools. During one of her first years teaching, a student told Faith about her brother, James Baldwin. He was a very highly respected writer. When Faith read his writing, it filled her with awareness of her African American culture, and she knew that she must work toward her dream of becoming a professional artist. To reach that goal, she began work on a master's degree from City College.

In 1961, she took her two young daughters, accompanied by her mother, Willi, and set off to tour the museums of France and Italy. They studied paintings and drawings and soaked in the bold vibrant colors of the paintings. She began to focus more and more on her art. Little could distract her until the following year, when her focus shifted to her friend, Burdette Ringgold. The couple married, and then they both turned their focus to Faith's art career. In 1959, Faith Ringgold obtained a master's degree in fine arts.

Although she spent hours making the rounds of art dealers, she met much discouragement. As an African American artist, her innovative techniques and bright colors were not viewed as "legitimate" art. Nonetheless, Burdette "Birdie" encouraged her to continue to explore her style and to persist in her efforts. As she explored her own artistic themes, she soon put aside the landscapes and ocean scenes and turned instead to the visual art of Romare Bearden, Jacob Lawrence, Louis Mailou Jones, Norman Lewis, and Hale Woodruff. Their art inspired her.

By 1966, Ringgold was participating in the first African American exhibition held in Harlem in thirty years. Some of her artwork was an outlet for her political beliefs. She became an outspoken advocate for women and African American artists. She participated in demonstrations in front of museums that did not acknowledge the contributions of women or African Americans. But it was while teaching at Bank Street College in New York City that she was moved to put aside her painted canvases and to begin to create artwork with the media of her ancestors: beads and cloth. Another traditional art form interested Ringgold: quilt making. The art of making quilts had been passed from generation to generation in her family. Her great-great grandmother, Susie Shannon, had been a slave. She taught her daughter, Betsy Bingham, to sew quilts. Betsy told her daughter, Willi Jones, about watching her own mother boil flour sacks until they were snow white. These sacks were used to line the quilts she made. Ringgold decided that she would use the sewing skills her mother had taught her when she was young.

During the following summer, Ringgold made another trip to Europe and discovered cloth frames for sacred paintings from Tibet. The frames, known as *tankas,* soon become a trademark for her own paintings. The cloth borders accented her pieces and were easily transported. Willi Jones helped Ringgold by creating *tankas* for her other paintings. Then Ringgold moved on to making soft sculptures of people she had admired in her childhood. Willi Jones helped make costumes for the sculptures. By now, it was 1973, and Faith Ringgold quit teaching to become a full-time artist. Art galleries and museums were still not very supportive of the work of women artists, and even less supportive of African American women's art. But Ringgold set out to show her work to the public. She sent her sculptures to campuses, packed into trunks. She toured, giving art lectures and art workshops. Her art career was thriving.

In 1976, Ringgold made her first trip to Africa and came back with many ideas from Ghana and Nigeria, ideas she would later weave into her art.

Ringgold's artistic career was moving at a fast pace when there was suddenly a turn. Ringgold's mother, Willi, died at the age of seventy-nine. Saddened by the loss of her mother, Ringgold turned more deeply into her art. The sadness manifested itself in a multitude of color spread on the canvas in irregular shapes. The following year bore more sorrow when Ringgold's sister Barbara died. Joy finally followed the grief when Ringgold's daughter, Barbara, gave birth to Ringgold's first granddaughter, named Faith. When little Faith was just eighteen-months old, she looked at a painting of her grandmother's and said, "Dah." Ringgold used that word as the title for a series of six abstract paintings that commemorated the sadness and joy of that time in her life.

As Ringgold developed her quilted paintings, she began to construct stories to accompany them. She "published" her stories by writing them onto the quilts. Those who saw her artwork also read her story quilts. One of the first story quilts created was *Church Picnic* (1988). It was a quilt of acrylic on canvas with a pieced fabric border (74½ x 75½ inches). The story was written on white cotton canvas sewn into the pieced border. This quilt now hangs in the permanent collection of the High Museum in Atlanta, Georgia. Another story quilt, *Harlem Renaissance Party* (1988) was larger (94½ x 82 inches) and became part of Ringgold's Bitter Nest series. The quilt depicted an elegant table setting and several famous artists and writers from the Harlem Renaissance period, including W. E. B. DuBois, Zora Neale Hurston, and Langston Hughes. Ringgold's *Tar Beach* quilt (1988) was part of her 1988 series, The Woman on the Bridge.

Ringgold has created quilts commemorating the efforts and results of her 100-pound weight loss, her fascination with the George Washington Bridge, and a trip to see the *Mona Lisa* (Leonardo da Vinci) at the Louvre in Paris. The trip to the Louvre inspired the first story quilt, *Dancing at the Louvre* (1991), in Ringgold's French Collection, which later came to include *The Sunflowers Quilting Bee at the Arles* (1991). The quilting bee quilt is in a private collection and depicts a group of women activists, including Sojourner Truth, Fannie Lou Hamer, and Rosa Parks. Included in the scene is an image of Vincent Van Gogh holding a bouquet of sunflowers. Another quilt in her French Collection is a quilt titled *Matisse's Chapel* (1991). The quilt depicts the art of the well-known European male artist, Henri Matisse. The basic scene is an imaginary gathering of Faith's own family in the chapel. In one section of the scene, Ringgold has the brother she never knew, Ralph, seated on her mother's lap. All the other characters are deceased members of her family, including Ringgold's mother and father, both of her brothers, and her sister, grandparents, and cousins. The fictional story refers to the family as being that of Willia Marie. Willia Marie is a character first introduced in Ringgold's story quilts in *Dancing at the Louvre*. After creating her French Collection, Ringgold ceased writing the stories onto the fabric of her quilts. Instead, she embraced the offer of publishers to write and illustrate her stories as children's books. From her earlier *Tar Beach* quilt came her award-winning book *Tar Beach* (Random House, 1991). Later came other stories inspired by more of her quilts.

For many years, Faith Ringgold's studio was in the garment district of Manhattan, where she first learned to sew. It was there that Faith accompanied her mother to factories to purchase fabric by the bolt. Now Ringgold and her husband are residents of Englewood, New Jersey, where Faith has a bright new studio across the George Washington Bridge from Harlem. Part of the year, Ringgold is in California, where she is a professor and artist. Among her pride and joys are her two daughters, Michele and Barbara, and her three granddaughters Theodora, Martha, and Faith. Faith's daughter Michele is Associate Professor of English and Women's Studies at the City College of New York. Leisure time is actually folded into Ringgold's work days. She says that she enjoys working and can find many ways to work that are almost play.

For a number of years, Ringgold has struggled to get her art represented in some of the major art museums in the world. There are permanent installations of her art in the Women's House of Detention on Riker's Island in New York City and on the platforms for the West 125th Street IRT Subway (on Lenox Avenue in Harlem). Ringgold's story quilt featuring the twelve major cultures that settled Crown Heights, *The Crown Heights Children's Story Quilt*, is installed in the school library at P.S. 90 in Crown Heights, Brooklyn, New York. A mural celebrating the life of Maria de Hostos, *Eugenio Maria de Hostos: A Man and His Dream*, is in the atrium of the Eugenio Maria de Hostos Community College in Bronx, New York. Her art is now exhibited or owned the world over and is included in such prestigious institutions as the Philadelphia Museum of Art; the Spelman College Museum in Atlanta, Georgia; and the Solomon R. Guggenheim Museum in New York City; and in the collections of private individuals.

BOOKS AND NOTES

Each of Faith Ringgold's books has a direct connection to a story told on a quilt. The quilts are Ringgold's art, tales fashioned of cloth and stories. She says that making story quilts takes varying amounts of time. Some quilts take several months, but *Tar Beach* took her only a month to make. She has been making art for more than fifty years and in those years has made more than ninety-five quilts and hundreds of other works of art. When an editor at Crown viewed Ringgold's *Tar Beach,* she asked Ringgold to think about creating a thirty-two-page picture book based on the quilt and its story. Ringgold's text for the book was published with very little editing, and the borders in the book are virtually identical to the original fabric borders because transparencies were made from the original story quilt. Faith Ringgold both writes and illustrates the books she creates.

Aunt Harriet's Underground Railroad in the Sky (Crown, 1992).

Bonjour, Lonnie (Hyperion, 1996).

Dinner at Aunt Connie's House (Hyperion, 1993).

My Dream of Martin Luther King (Crown, 1995).

Tar Beach (Crown, 1991).

Invisible Princess (Crown, 1998).

FOR MORE INFORMATION

Articles

"The Author As Artist." *Booklist* 87, no. 17 (May 1991): 28.

Books

Cameron, Dan, editor. *Dancing at the Louvre: Faith Ringgold's French Collection and Other Story Quilts* (University California Press, 1998).
Catalog to accompany exhibition of The French Collection and The American Collection.

Mazloomi, Carolyn, Faith Ringgold, and Cuesta Ray Benberry. *Spirits of the Cloth: Contemporary African American Quilts* (Clarkson Potter, 1998).

Ringgold, Faith, Linda Freeman, and Nancy Roucher. *Talking to Faith Ringgold* (Crown, 1996).

Ringgold, Faith. *We Flew Over the Bridge: The Memoirs of Faith Ringgold* (Little, Brown, 1995).

Turner, Robyn Montana. *Faith Ringgold* (Little, Brown, 1993).

Web Sites

Art in Context Center for Communications. "Faith Ringgold—Reference Page." Available at <http://www.artincontext.org/artist/r/faith_ringgold> (Accessed March 2000).

UCSD Visual Arts/Faculty. "Faith Ringgold." Available at <http://visarts.ucsd.edu/faculty/fringgol.htm> (Accessed March 2000).

Tony Ross

◆ Folklore ◆ Humor

London, England
August 10, 1938

📖 *The Boy Who Cried Wolf*

📖 *Foxy Fables*

📖 *Horrid Henry*

ABOUT THE
AUTHOR/ILLUSTRATOR

Tony Ross was just thirteen months old when England entered World War II. The war and the resulting bombs managed to destroy much of the art in England, but Ross found his art in books. By the time the war was over, Ross's fondness for art was firmly established.

Tony Ross was born on August 10, 1938, in London, England. He describes his father, Eric Turle Lee, as a conjurer and his mother, Effie Ross, as a marvel. The influence of his parents combined to give him an unusual view of the world and to make his imagination soar. Among his favorite books were those of his fellow English author and illustrator, Beatrix Potter. He loved *The Tale of Peter Rabbit* and *The Tale of Benjamin Bunny*, along with her many other tales. Ernest Shepard's illustrations in the magazine *Punch* and in A. A. Milne's *Winnie-the-Pooh* captured his imagination. The work of Arthur Rackham, Edward Ardizzone, and Gustave Dore also caught his eye. Ross spent hours copying the work of those artists whom he admired.

Dore's illustrations for *Don Quixote* were among Ross's favorites to copy. He focused on the illustrator's craft.

His interest in art continued through his school days. He entered the Liverpool College of Art in 1960 and received diplomas a year later. He was trained as an etcher but began his artistic career as a cartoonist and later entered advertising. His entry into illustrating children's books began when he realized that the field might give him an opportunity to "be totally self-indulgent and draw what I liked, and in as many colors as I liked." His first illustrations were submitted to English publishers in the early 1970s. *Mr. Toffy*, published in England, was followed by six more titles about the industrialist who didn't like industry and who wanted to do something silly. Mr. Toffy was a lot like Ross, and Ross was doing something "silly" too; he was creating children's books. After his books about Mr. Toffy, Ross went on to illustrate his version of *Goldilocks and the Three Bears* (Andersen, 1976). His illustrations were soon characterized as nontraditional and zany. His early books included his versions of *Little Red Riding Hood* (Andersen, 1978), *The True Story of Mother Goose and Her Son Jack* (Andersen, 1979), *Jack and the Beanstalk* (Andersen, 1980), *Puss in Boots* (Andersen, 1981), and *The Three Pigs* (Andersen, 1983). Several of these books were later published in the United States and in many other countries as well. For example, *Goldilocks and the Three Bears* (Overlook Press, 1992) retained Ross's unusual view of the tale. The unusually colored white bears "had lots to eat and a color television set." Goldilocks is a mop top in jeans. Artwork of different styles is displayed on the walls of the bears' house. The illustrations of Goldilocks jumping on the bed and the bears' fierce teeth grab the reader's attention.

One of his early and most popular titles was his fresh slant on the boy trickster fable, *The Boy Who Cried Wolf* (Dial, 1985). The tale follows the traditional route until the wolf shows up, and that is when Ross interjects his surprising twist to this far-out adaptation. His irreverence for the traditional is evident again in his modernization of six of Aesop's fables in *Foxy Fables* (Dial, 1986). Ross's illustrations are clearly humorous. *Lazy Jack* (Dial, 1986) is a tale of a boy who cannot please anyone. It is given new humor with Ross's wacky and sunny drawings.

Ross is a master at presenting old tales with new twists. He did just that when he made sure that the monster in *I'm Coming to Get You!* (Dial, 1984) was no threat at all. The classic blame game, "He did it" is played out by the supposedly invisible Billy and Oscar in *Oscar Got the Blame* (Dial, 1988). Ross puts his invariable twist once again when he shows a red-horned, wild-eyed, and visible Billy on the last page.

One of Ross's most masterful twists on a traditional tale is his rendition of *Stone Soup* (Dial, 1987). In this tale, Ross turns the tables on the fox. In the traditional stone soup story, the characters that wants soup manages to trick the soup maker. In Ross's version, the hen makes the soup for the wolf, but she is the trickster—managing to trick the wolf into chopping wood, taking down laundry, and fixing the television antenna. In the end, the wolf thinks he has captured the real treasure when he grabs the hen's soup stone and runs away.

Ross's pen-and-ink drawings are washed with brilliantly bold colors, each chosen to enhance the comic view to each zany episode. Ross's splendid sense of humor is showcased in his illustrations for his original tales and for the classic tales he retells with entertaining zest.

Ross's picture books are full of the humor, as are the book jackets and the line interior drawings that he has created for the novels of several popular authors. He illustrated the British edition of Sid Fleischman's *The Whipping Boy* (Methuen, 1988), the Puffin paperback edition of Roald Dahl's *The Magic Finger* (Puffin, 1989), and *Fantastic Mr. Fox* (Puffin, 1988); most recently, he illustrated the titles in Paula Danziger's Amber Brown series. A book he authored with Alison Sage, *The Family Who Won a Million*, was offered as a premium gift to those people who either sold or bought at least £450 of foreign currency at the government post offices.

Ross's work is published in England, the United States, and ten other countries. He has lived all of his life in the London area. He and his first wife, Carole Jean D'Arcy, had three children, Philippa, George, and Alexandra. The family lived in a chapel he renovated in Cheshire, England. Ross now lives in Devon with his second wife, Zoë. They are the parents of one daughter, Katy. He enjoys traveling and spending time collecting antiques and toy soldiers. He is fascinated by anything having to do with the monarchy, enjoys sailing, and loves cats.

BOOKS AND NOTES

Tony Ross is known for his comic illustrations and, in addition to retelling and illustrating a number of folk stories, he has contributed illustrations to a number of novels, the most notable of which is Paula Danziger's Amber Brown series. Some of his books have interesting credits. For example: *The Pet Person* (Dial, 1996) credits the "barking" to Jeanne Willis and the "scratching" to Tony Ross. The citations, as much as possible, reflect the publishers and dates of the books' publication in the United States. The books usually appeared in England the year before their publication in the States.

Books Written/Retold and Illustrated by Tony Ross

The Boy Who Cried Wolf (Dial, 1985).

A Fairy Tale (Little, Brown, 1991).

Goldilocks and the Three Bears (Overlook Press, 1992).

Hansel and Gretel (Overlook Press, 1994).

I Want a Cat (Farrar, 1989).

I Want My Dinner (Harcourt, 1996).

Lazy Jack (Dial, 1985).

Stone Soup (Dial, 1987).

Mrs. Goat and Her Seven Little Kids (Atheneum, 1990).

The Pop-up Book of Nonsense Verse. Paper engineering by David A. Carter and Roger Cublertson. (Random House, 1989).

Wash Your Hands (Kane/Miller, 2000).

Weather (Harcourt, 1994).

Books Illustrated by Tony Ross

Horrid Henry. Written by Francesca Simon. (Hyperion, 1999).

Meanwhile Back at the Ranch. Written by Trinka Hakes Noble. (Dial, 1987).

A Treasury of Pirate Stories. Chosen by Tony Bradman. (Kingfishers, 1999).

This Old Man: A Musical Counting Book. Paper engineering by Rodger Smith. (Collins, 1990).

Why? Written by Lindsay Camp. (Putnam, 1999).

FOR MORE INFORMATION

Web Sites

Library and Information Commission. "The Illustrator—Tony Ross." URL: <http://hosted.ukoln.ac.uk/stories/stories/illust/ross.htm> (Accessed March 2000).

Cynthia Rylant

◆ Family Relationships ◆ Poetry

Hopewell, Virginia
June 6, 1954

📖 Henry and Mudge Series
📖 *The Relatives Came*
📖 *When I Was Young in the Mountains*

ABOUT THE AUTHOR/ILLUSTRATOR

Raised in coal mining country, deep in the Appalachian Mountains, Cynthia Rylant ended up in Ohio, where she became a writer of children's books. She now lives in Oregon and enjoys the woods and collecting antiques. She is still writing children's books. In one recent year, her "forthcoming" list included seven titles.

Cynthia Rylant was born in Hopewell, West Virginia, on June 6, 1954. When she was four years old, her parents separated, and she was sent to live with her mother's parents, Elda and Ferrell Rylant, in Cool Ridge, West Virginia. Rylant's mother went off to nursing school. Her father had been in the armed services. She waited for her parents to come back. One did—her mother—and one didn't. Cynthia Rylant loved her grandparents, and her experiences in West Virginia strongly influenced her writing.

Rylant's grandfather worked in the coal mines for forty-two years. Each night, he returned home with coal dust covering him from head to foot. The family was living in one of the poorest parts of the Appalachian Mountains.

Their four-room house had no running water, and her grandparents grew or hunted the food they ate. Rylant learned to eat rabbit and squirrel and ochre, she actually draped a black snake across her friend's and her own shoulders, and observed baptisms in the creek. She read few books because her grandparents were poor and there were no libraries nearby. Rylant and her grandparents never traveled too far from home because they did not have a car, but every year aunts, uncles, and cousins would come from Virginia to help Rylant's grandparents fix up their property and just to visit and have a good time.

After Rylant had lived with her grandparents for four years, her mother came back for her and together they moved to Beaver, West Virginia. Rylant and her mother moved into a little three-room apartment beside the railroad tracks. The apartment was heated by old gas heaters. There was no carpet, and there were spiders in the bathtub. The view out the front door was Todd's junkyard. During the day while her mother was at work, Rylant attended school. She loved the school and remembers it as always smelling like fresh bread. The school had no library, but she did manage to get her hands on some Nancy Drew books and some of the Hardy Boys books. Comic books were also available. In the summertime, she spent time with her friends. They rode their bikes around town, picked up pop cans from the ditches to get some money, and bought Nehi Grape pop or Archie comic books at the little drugstore in town. Sometimes they bought penny candy at the hardware store. They played war and Tin Can Alley.

In high school, Rylant was a majorette in the band and even won a big trophy as "best majorette." She found the English textbook rather boring, preferring to read Harlequin Romances. Her boyfriend's name was Eddie, and he worked in a filling station. They had plans to marry and live "in a trailer" after finishing high school. Instead, the couple broke up when Rylant dropped him for a "cute boy" in town. By the time Rylant graduated from high school, there was no one she wanted to marry, so she went off to college in Charleston, West Virginia.

At first her goal was to become a nurse as her mother had, but later Rylant changed her major to English. During college, she learned to love books. She hoped to become an English teacher but could not find a job after graduating. For a time, she was a waitress and then got a job in the children's section of the library. Eventually, she reenrolled in college to obtain a master's degree in English.

Discovering children's books was, according to Rylant, an event that changed her life. One of the titles that influenced her from the beginning was Donald Hall's *Ox-Cart Man*, a book illustrated by Barbara Cooney.

Rylant decided that instead of just reading children's books, she wanted to write them. During this time, Rylant's grandfather died.

Rylant began to write stories and, using the *Writer's Market*, researched where to send her stories. After six months, she sold her first manuscript, *When I Was Young in the Mountains* (Dutton, 1982). At the time, her son Nate was nine months old. Her own life had been transformed. During her undergraduate days, she tried "to look like a hippie, but in grad school I tried to look intellectual." Once Rylant's son was born, she no longer had time to iron "India shirts" anymore. The changes in her life are also what allowed her to become a writer.

The publisher chose Diane Goode to illustrate Rylant's story. She took more than two years to create the illustrations. When it was finished, Rylant was less than pleased. The little girl on the cover did not look like Rylant, and the grandfather in the original picture had only a dirty hat on when he returned from work. Goode agreed to change the illustration of the grandfather to make him more like the image Rylant had of her grandfather.

After this first book, the stories came regularly. *Miss Maggie* (Dutton, 1983) was her second title. Rylant once described this book as the one that was "the most personal and more universal" in comparison with her other stories. The story was about a woman she really knew. Miss Maggie lived across the cow pasture and was the ugliest woman anyone would ever met. The dark house was rumored to have snakes in it. The main character is a boy instead of a girl, but in the book, he felt all of the feelings that Rylant once felt. The story describing the interaction between the two was constructed from her imagination. The illustrator, Thomas Di Grazia, used a photograph of the woman's log cabin to help him create the illustrations for the book. That helped Rylant make a personal connection to the house and to the book. When she saw the illustrations, she felt like she had walked through the doorway.

When Rylant moved to Beaver with her mother as an eight-year-old, it was the first time she had seen sidewalks or had indoor plumbing. Beaver Creek ran through town, and the main street was only about 500 feet long. Rylant says her mom was "a single parent, and I was a single kid." While her mother worked, she hung out on the streets. Her experiences resulted in poems collected into a book titled *Waiting to Waltz: A Childhood* (Bradbury, 1984). The poems reflected the eagerness of a fourteen-year-old to get out of Beaver. She wrote poems about the shoe shop and about the people in Beaver. Sixteen of those poems came to her in one day, and thirteen more came the next day. She sent the twenty-nine poems off to her editor, Richard

Jackson. He liked them but did not like the odd number of poems. He wanted her to write one more. She immediately knew what to write about.

She had known all along that she must write a poem about her father. Her mother had come back, but her father never did make it. He had left when she was four years old, and her only memories were of him tucking her, in striped pajamas, into bed and of a stuffed monkey that the two of them played with. He had been in the war and was an alcoholic. Both had taken a toll on her parents' marriage and on her own life. Then, her father's death took another toll. He died when Rylant was a teenager but had never returned to her. The poem came in a tidal wave and was sent in to complete the volume. The poem, titled "Forgotten," was perfectly complemented by Stephen Gammell's illustration of an empty chair. In its own way, *Waiting to Waltz* was a continuation of *When I Was Young in the Mountains*, even though the poems were meant for intermediate-aged readers.

The publisher also chose Steven Gammell to illustrate *The Relatives Came* (Bradbury, 1985). This story was special to Rylant, and she wanted just the right illustrator, so it sat at the publisher for four years. After Gammell illustrated *Waiting to Waltz*, Rylant felt that he could illustrate this story. She had sent him a postcard while he was illustrating *Waiting to Waltz*, and they had written every couple weeks after that. He was in Minneapolis, and Rylant was in Ohio. When Gammell received the manuscript for *The Relatives Came*, he called her and said, "Cynthia, this is the weirdest manuscript I've ever read. It sounds like aliens coming." Rylant dedicated the book to her aunt, and her family is sprinkled throughout the story, eating, hugging, and spending time together. She remembers that "When Uncle Leo got tired from all the good time, he would go out and sleep in the car." Gammell managed to incorporate his family into the story as well. Gammell himself appears in red sneakers playing a guitar. His wife is shown barefooted and with a camera hanging from her neck. His mother is on one of the last few pages, waving good-bye as the visitors leave in their car. Gammell's father is a gray-haired man giving a haircut to a youngster.

Another book of poetry, *Soda Jerk* (Orchard, 1990), came on Mother's Day 1988. The dog was barking in the next yard; it was seven o'clock in the morning. Rylant went into her yard, sat down in a lawn chair, and wrote sixteen poems. The next morning, she wrote seven more; the next day, she finished the poems for the collection.

For a while during the 1980s, Rylant was married to a man who enjoyed large dogs. One of those dogs became the prototype for Mudge in the series Rylant wrote about Henry and Mudge. Rylant's son gave her a lot of ideas for Henry. The books are early chapter books that attract an audience similar to those who are fond of Arnold Lobel's Frog and Toad series. Henry is the irrepressible young boy who romps through childhood adventures with his dog, Mudge.

While Rylant's son Nate was growing up, they lived in Kent, Ohio, where she loved the little shops and the old bridge over the river. Her first house was in Kent. It was an old house with a big attic and a front porch with a swing.

Much of Rylant's early writing was accomplished while she sat in that swing; she also wrote while sitting in her backyard, in bed, or on a couch. Rylant does not write at a desk. Her writing most often begins on yellow tablets. She writes quickly, but it is the culmination of months of thinking and living. Sometimes she will go months without actually writing, but when she does set pen to paper, her picture books might take only an hour. When she writes a novel, she might write a chapter and then not write another chapter for two or three weeks. But during that time, she thinks of what and how she wants to write. After completing the writing, she types the manuscript from her yellow tablets, revises it, and sends it off to her editor.

In Kent, Rylant and her son had a lot of pets: several cats and dogs, a parakeet, a guinea pig, a hermit crab, and even a squirrel who visited in their backyard. It was also in Kent, Ohio, where she met her friend Dav Pilkey. They both attended a writer's meeting in Kent, and Cynthia thought he was "the sweetest and funniest guy in the world." In 1993, the two of them got a feeling that it was time to live in a new place, so Nate, Dav, Cynthia, and all the pets trekked across the United States to Eugene, Oregon. They put the cats on a plane to fly across the country. Before they departed for Oregon, Rylant contributed her manuscripts and materials related to her published books to the library at Kent State University.

In Eugene, Rylant has a small, green house in the woods. She finds old cupboards, teapots, and quilts for her house. She collects stained glass lamps and puts stone angels, along with a gargoyle, in her yard. Her friend, children's author and illustrator Dav Pilkey, lives just down the street from Rylant. His house, surrounded by tall trees and more than 100 rhododendron and azalea bushes, is nestled into the same quiet wooded hills of Eugene. Nate has grown up and left home, and Cynthia shares her home with a new little dog, Gracie Rose, and two others, Leia and Martha Jane. Gracie Rose and Leia are corgis. Rylant still likes movies and sometimes sees a favorite seven or eight times. But she does not like to travel, preferring to stay at home with a cup of tea.

BOOKS AND NOTES

Many of Rylant's books are based on autobiographical incidents in her life. *When I was Young in the Mountains* describes her own life as a youngster in the mountains of West Virginia, as does *The Relatives Came*. Many of her books are set in the Appalachia region; especially of note is her book for older readers, *Appalachia: The Voices of Sleeping Birds* (Harcourt, 1991). Her earlier books were rooted in her own heritage and growing-up years. More recently, several early-chapter book series and individual books have sprung from incidents in her adult life. For example, when she and Nate moved from Kent, Ohio, to Eugene, Oregon, Rylant felt the trip was spectacular and wanted to share the wonderment of the experience. She wrote *Tulip Sees America* (Blue Sky, 1998), which tells of a young man and his dog as they drive west from Ohio across the farms of Iowa and come to view the skies of Nebraska, the wind in Wyoming, the mountains of Colorado, the desert in Nevada, and finally the ocean shore in Oregon. One wonders if this young man might possibly be her friend Dav Pilkey. Rylant liked Lisa Desimini's illustrations for the book so much that she sent her a small green Volkswagen model as a thank you.

When a friend of Rylant's lost a beloved dog, Rylant wrote *Dog Heaven* (Blue Sky, 1995) and later *Cat Heaven* (Blue Sky, 1997). Her own dog, Martha Jane, lent her name to the dog in *The Bookshop Dog* (Blue Sky, 1996). At times, Rylant does reach back into her childhood for another tale. When she was young, she was very poor. Each year her grandparents would take her to a place where children were given a single Christmas present. One year, she saw a nurse's kit and dearly wanted it because her mother was studying to be a nurse. Someone else got the kit. A similar incident occurs in *Silver Packages: An Appalachian Christmas Story* (Orchard, 1997).

Rylant has created several other series in addition to her most popular work, the Henry and Mudge series. Her later series include stories about cats and even a guinea pig.

Books Written and Illustrated by Cynthia Rylant

The Bookshop Dog (Blue Sky, 1996).
Martha Jane spends her days in her owner's bookshop. When the owner is taken to the hospital, the residents of the small town squabble over who will care for Martha Jane.

Cat Heaven (Blue Sky, 1997).
God created Cat Heaven with sweet grass and kitty toys.

Dog Heaven (Blue Sky, 1995).
God created Dog Heaven with ice cream biscuits and fluffy clouds to sleep on.

Books Written by Cynthia Rylant

All That I See. Illustrated by Peter Catalannotto. (Orchard, 1988).
The visions of an artist turn out to be something really special.

Bear Day. Illustrated by Jennifer Selby. (Harcourt, 1998).
Spend a day with little bear.

The Bird House. Illustrated by Barry Moser. (Scholastic, 1998).
A story about an orphan who is attracted to a house, which also attracts birds.

Margaret, Frank, and Andy: Three Writers' Stories (Harcourt, 1996).
In forty-eight pages, Rylant tells about Margaret Wise Brown (1910–1952), L. Frank Baum (1856–1919), and E. B. White (1899–1985).

The Relatives Came. Illustrated by Steven Gammell. (Bradbury, 1985).

When the aunts and uncles come from Virginia to visit and help the family in West Virginia, there's a lot "of new breathing" in the house.

Tulip Sees America. Illustrated by Lisa Desimini. (Blue Sky, 1998).

A young man and his dog drive across the midwestern and western United States to travel from Ohio to Oregon.

The Old Woman Who Named Things. Illustrated by Kathryn Brown. (Harcourt, 1996).

A woman has outlived all of her friends and so is reluctant to become too attached to the stray dog that shows up at her home each day.

When I Was Young in the Mountains. Illustrated by Diane Goode. (Dutton, 1982).

The story of a young girl's everyday life in the Appalachian mountains with her grandparents.

Series by Cynthia Rylant

Cynthia Rylant has created several series. Each of the series features central characters named in the titles. The following list include only representative titles in the series.

The Cobble Street Cousins Series

Illustrated by Wendy Anderson Halperin. Nine-year-old cousins Rosie, Lily, and Tess are living for a year with their Aunt Lucy, who has a boyfriend, Michael.

The Cobble Street Cousins: In Aunt Lucy's Kitchen (Simon & Schuster, 1998).

The Cobble Street Cousins: A Little Shopping (Simon & Schuster, 1998).

The Cobble Street Cousins: Some Good News (Simon & Schuster, 1999).

The Cobble Street Cousins: Special Gifts (Simon & Schuster, 1999).

Henry and Mudge Series

Illustrated by Suçie Stevenson. The Henry and Mudge series features a little boy named Henry and his big dog, Mudge. In recent books, Henry and Mudge's friend Annie has joined in the fun.

Henry and Mudge (Bradbury, 1987).

Henry and Mudge: Annie's Good Move (Simon & Schuster, 1998).

Henry and Mudge in the Family Trees (Simon & Schuster, 1997).

Henry and Mudge and the Funny Lunch (Simon & Schuster, 1999).

Henry and Mudge and the Great Grandpas: The Twenty-Third Book of Their Adventures (Simon & Schuster, 1999).

Henry and Mudge and the Sneaky Crackers: The Sixteenth Book of Their Adventures (Simon & Schuster, 1998).

Henry and Mudge in the Sparkle Days (Bradbury, 1988).

Henry and Mudge and the Tumbling Trip (Simon & Schuster, 1999).

Henry and Mudge and a Very Special Merry Christmas: The Twenty-Fourth Book of Their Adventures (Simon & Schuster, 1999).

Little Whistle Series

Illustrated by Tim Bowers. Little Whistle is the guinea pig that is the main character.

Little Whistle (Harcourt, 2000).

Little Whistle's Dinner Party (Harcourt, 2001).

Little Whistle's Medicine (Harcourt, 2001).

Mr. Putter and Tabby Series

Illustrated by Arthur Howard. The series features Mr. Putter and his cat friend, Tabby, enjoying activities and their friendship. A neighbor's dog, Zeke, often joins them.

Mr. Putter and Tabby Bake the Cake (Harcourt, 1994).

Mr. Putter & Tabby Paint the Porch (Harcourt, 2000).

Mr. Putter and Tabby Pick the Pears (Harcourt, 1995).

Mr. Putter & Tabby Take the Train (Harcourt, 1998).

Mr. Putter & Tabby Toot the Horn (Harcourt, 1998).

Poppleton Series

Illustrated by Mark Teague. Poppleton is a pig that has many experiences, sometimes with his friend Cherry Sue.

Poppleton in Fall (Blue Sky, 1999).

Poppleton and Friends (Blue Sky, 1997).

FOR MORE INFORMATION

Articles

Antonucci, Ron. "Rylant On Writing: A Talk with 1993 Newbery Medalist Cynthia Rylant. *School Library Journal* 39, no. 5 (May 1, 1993): 26.

Ward, Diane. "Cynthia Rylant." *The Horn Book Magazine* 69, no. 4 (July 1, 1993): 420.

Books

Rylant, Cynthia. *But I'll Be Back Again* (Orchard, 1989; Beach Tree, 1993).
A book about Rylant's life, written for young adults.

Rylant, Cynthia. *Best Wishes* (Richard C. Owen, 1992; Meet the Author Series). Illustrated by Carlo Ontal.

Robert San Souci

Mark Kane Photography

San Francisco, California
October 10, 1946

📖 *Kate Shelley: Bound for Legend*
📖 *Sootface: An Ojibwa Cinderella Story*
📖 *The Talking Eggs*

ABOUT THE AUTHOR

Robert San Souci was born into a household in which there was real excitement about literature. He grew up with a younger brother, Daniel San Souci, who became an illustrator of children's books. Every night, their mother would read to Robert and his younger brothers and sister. Daniel always loved the illustrations and would often sit at the dining room table drawing with his father. Robert always wanted to be the writer. Even before he could read and write, Robert San Souci was retelling stories. He would listen carefully to books that were read to him and then would retell his own version to his siblings. His versions generally included his own twists or omitted parts that he did not find interesting.

When Robert was in second grade and Daniel was in kindergarten, they created their first book. The story was about rabbits celebrating Christmas. Daniel's illustrations showed carrots in cowboy boots, holding pistols. Robert didn't know why Daniel had made the illustrations as carrots. Daniel solved the problem by adding little Santa Claus beards on the carrots. The story was to be titled "Crazy Bang," but by mistake the eight copies distributed had the title as "Carzy Bang."

The children often attended the Saturday matinee to see the latest cowboy movies. Robert says he would cheer for the Indians, who were much more colorful than the cavalry. Robert became interested in the stories behind the Native American people.

Robert San Souci was born in the Richmond District of San Francisco and spent his childhood in Berkeley and Walnut Grove, California. In elementary school, he wrote for his school newspaper and later in high school, he was part of the school's yearbook staff. He wrote stories and essays and was pleased when one of his essays was published in a book titled *T.V. As Art*. After high school, Robert entered St. Mary's College. He studied creative writing, English , and world literature. His interest in the study of folklore, myth, and world religions developed during graduate school.

San Souci entered the working world as a budding writer. He supported himself as a copywriter and book editor in the publishing field. As a freelance writer, he was writing articles for newspapers and magazines and reviews of books and the theater. He also worked in bookstores. All the while, he persevered in his efforts to succeed as a writer, while his brother Daniel San Souci was painting with watercolors for local shows. In the middle 1970s, the two brothers decided to get together again to collaborate on a children's book. Their first two attempts did not go far. One was a spin-off of a traditional fairy tale and the other was about a princess, a knight, and a dragon. Neither of them have ever been published. Their third attempt, however, did make it to the publisher. Robert traveled to the Blackfeet Reservation in Browning, Montana, and came home with the idea for *The Legend of Scarface: A Blackfeet Indian Tale* (Doubleday, 1978). Once Robert San Souci returned from his trip to Montana, he wrote the text for the story and Daniel San Souci created some sample illustrations. Then the two of them "hopped on a plane for New York City." The response to the manuscript was good, and a year later, the book was "hot off the presses." This success rekindled Robert San Souci's interest in Native American stories. Their next book was *Song of Sedna* (Doubleday, 1981), which has been called an Eskimo story. Later the two of them collaborated to create *Sootface: An Ojibwa Cinderella Story* (Delacorte, 1994).

Most of Robert San Souci's ideas come from his reading and traveling. He loves to travel by bus, where he can stare out of the window and observe the countryside and the events he passes. He also listens to people and seeks local stories wherever he goes. During one trip to speak at a conference in Iowa, he was having dinner with some friends near Des Moines. He asked them to tell any stories that were legend in their locality. The story they told him was that of Kate Shelley. When he returned home he began to research this story of a young woman from Moingona, Iowa. That is the site where Kate Shelley, in July of 1881, saved a trainload of people from a raging river. The story his friends told him became the basis for *Kate Shelley: Bound for Legend* (Dial, 1995).

Another time, he was working on a collection of folktales from different parts of the United States. He learned of Fa Mulan, a heroine who was known in every Chinese-American community. The story was fascinating. She dressed as a man and became a soldier as a substitute for her father who was too ill to honor the draft into the army. Fa Mulan fought in the great war against invaders on the other side of the Great Wall. She became a highly honored general. Meanwhile the Disney Company had spent years searching for an Asian story to use as the basis for an animated feature film. San Souci uncovered the fifth-century Chinese poem on which he based a mythical story, which he took to the Walt Disney Company in 1992. The story had a lot of action, and Disney purchased it. In 1998, the feature film, *Mulan*, was released. Robert San Souci received the third credit when the film *Mulan* was screened. San Souci also wrote the story for Hyperion Press. *Fa Mulan* was published in 1998. San Souci says it took fourteen outlines of the story and then eighteen versions of the film treatment to get to the place where they were ready to script the film. The addition of the small dragon as a fantasy element was said to have been created at the suggestion of an executive at Disney. It was San Souci, however, who actually had suggested the dragon. Some thought it would be too big, but San Souci relayed that in Chinese mythology, dragons can be huge or as tiny as one's thumb. He suggested a tiny dragon, and that became the seed of Mushu. San Souci worked both with the film department of Disney and their publishing arm, Hyperion Press, to create both the film and the book.

As with all folklore, each reteller makes additions and deletions to make what he or she feels is a more interesting story. In this case, San Souci says that Mushu isn't part of the original legend. That element was created for the Disney retelling. The earliest version of Mulan's tale spans ten or twelve years, but the film's time span is much shorter. The romance element is more developed in the film, but both the original tale and the Disney version, according to San Souci, focus on honor, love of family, loyalty, and doing one's best for one's county.

Two Bear Cubs: A Miwok Legend from California's Yosemite Valley (Yosemite Association, 1997) came about when Robert San Souci and Daniel San Souci were at a convention and someone from the Yosemite Association approached them about the story. Both thought the story sounded like an interesting project and eventually created the story for publication. The legend tells about the formation of El Capitan, one of Yosemite's most famous natural wonders. The illustrations depict authentic clothing and tools used by the Miwoks. The Yosemite National Park's research facility helped the San Soucis ensure that everything in the book, from basket patterns to the type of berries the tribe picked, was accurate. The nonprofit Yosemite Association published the book, and the national park benefits from the profits.

San Souci has written stories based on tales from diverse cultures, including the African American and Caribbean cultures; he also has penned classical tales, such as *Tarzan* (Hyperion, 1999) and stories from the King Arthur tradition. He has brought the "ogres in the Grimm Brothers' woods" alive in his retellings.

Robert San Souci actively supports libraries and literacy. In a twenty-year span, he has visited more than 1,000 schools and numerous bookstores and libraries. When he is not traveling, he writes every day. He often writes first drafts at his dining table because it is the sunniest place in the house. His writing schedule usually includes at least two hours of writing and many more hours researching his topics. He looks for the core elements in the stories that attract him. Once those core elements are uncovered, he fleshes out the story and works on making it something that children will enjoy. He tries to include extra depth that adults and teachers will recognize and appreciate.

Robert San Souci still lives in San Francisco and works in his home office in Eureka Valley. He spends time in Noe Valley, on 24th Street, two or three times a week to do his shopping and book buying. He is an enthusiastic uncle to nine nieces and nephews and enjoys travel, the theater, and taking long walks.

BOOKS AND NOTES

Robert San Souci has created more than fifty titles and has garnered several prestigious awards. One of the awards was the 1993 Aesop Prize, which is an annual award for a children's book that incorporates folklore in text and illustration. Many of his books have been named on the list of Notable Children's Trade Books in the Social Studies, the American Bookseller's Pick of the List, and the American Library Association's Notable Children's Book List, as well as many other lists. His stories draw on the traditions and legends of many cultures that he researches. The stories, however, are his own retellings with twists and elements that complement the retelling. In addition to picture books, Robert San Souci has developed collections of thematically related stories, such as *Cut from the Same Cloth: American Women of Myth, Legend, and Tall Tales.* (Philomel, 1993). The volume displayed the brilliant scratchboard illustrations of Brian Pinkney and an introduction by Jane Yolen. Another collection, *Larger Than Life: John Henry and Other Tall Tales* (Doubleday, 1991) includes tales of John Henry, Old Stormalong, Sluefoot Sue, and Paul Bunyan and is illustrated by Andrew Glass.

Brave Margaret: An Irish Adventure. Illustrated by Sally Wren Comport. (Simon & Schuster, 1999).
A brave young woman battles a serpent to rescue her beloved from a menacing giant.

Cendrillon: A Caribbean Cinderella. Illustrated by Brian Pinkney. (Simon & Schuster, 1998).
A Creole variant narrated by a godmother who helps Cendrillon find her true love.

Cinderella Skeleton. Illustrated by David Catrow. (Harcourt, 2000).
A rhyming tale of skeletons and a Cinderella who finds her prince at a Halloween ball.

Fa Mulan: The Story of a Woman Warrior. Illustrated by Jean and Mou-Sien Tseng. (Hyperion, 1998).
The legendary Chinese tale of a young woman who masquerades as a man to fight the Tartars in the Khan's army.

Feathertop: Based on a Tale by Nathaniel Hawthorne. Illustrated by Daniel San Souci. (Doubleday, 1992).
From a tale titled *Mother Rigby*, a witch creates a scarecrow to play a joke on a local judge. The judge's daughter falls in love with the scarecrow.

The Hired Hand: An African-American Folktale. Illustrated by Jerry Pinkney. (Dial, 1997).
When Sam hires a man for work at his saw mill, the man also teaches Sam's son about how to treat people.

Kate Shelley: Bound for Legend. Illustrated by Max Ginsburg. (Dial, 1995).
A fifteen-year-old Iowa girl becomes a hero in 1881 when she warns the station master of a broken bridge over a raging river.

The Legend of Scarface: A Blackfeet Indian Tale. Illustrated by Daniel San Souci. (Doubleday, 1978).
A young brave travels to the land of the sun to ask for the hand of his beloved.

Pedro and the Monkey. Illustrated by Michael Hays. (Morrow, 1996).
Retold from the Filipino folklore tradition. A monkey secures the fortune of his rather dimwitted young owner.

The Silver Charm. Illustrated by Yoriko Ito. (Doubleday, 1999).
From Japan's Ainu people, a pet puppy and a fox take back their young master's good luck charm from an ogre.

Six Foolish Fisherman. Illustrated by Doug Kennedy. (Hyperion, 1999).

A fishing trip has one thing after another go wrong, and six foolish fisherman try to figure out how to proceed.

Sootface: An Ojibwa Cinderella Story. Illustrated by Daniel San Souci. (Delacorte, 1994).

An Indian maiden wins the hand of a mighty, but invisible, warrior for her husband when she displays a kind and honest heart.

The Talking Eggs: A Folktale from the American South. Illustrations by Jerry Pinkney. (Dial, 1989).

A Creole tale of Blanche, who is kind and considerate to the witch she meets in the woods. Blanche reaps treasures for her kindness, in contrast to her greedy sister, whose deeds are also rewarded appropriately.

Tarzan. Illustrated by Michael McCurdy. (Hyperion, 1999).

Based on Edgar Rice Burroughs's original tale of a baby boy orphaned and left alone in the African jungle and adopted by apes.

Two Bear Cubs: A Miwok Legend from California's Yosemite Valley. Illustrated by Daniel San Souci. (Yosemite Association, 1997).

A little measuring worm saves two bear cubs stranded on top of a rock formation known as El Capitan.

A Weave of Words: An Armenian Tale. Illustrated by Raul Colon. (Orchard, 1998).

A lazy prince learns to read, write, and weave to earn his true love and then uses the talents to save himself from a three-headed monster.

Young Arthur. Illustrated by Jamichael Henterly. (Doubleday, 1997).

King Arthur's boyhood, the sword in the stone, and his first victorious battle.

FOR MORE INFORMATION

Web Sites

Penguin Putnam Site. "Robert San Souci." URL: <http://www.penguinputnam. com> (Accessed March 2000). Go to "Young Readers," then "Authors and Illustrators," and then "Author Bios."

Allen Say

Sharron L. McElmeel

Yokohama, Japan
August 28, 1937

📖 *Grandfather's Journey*

📖 *Tea with Milk*

📖 *Tree of Cranes*

ABOUT THE AUTHOR

Allen Say was born in Japan and then came to America, but he says, "I know I will always be rootless." His work is his home, his story, and most certainly his legacy. For Allen Say, life has been restless as well. He was born in Yokohama, Japan, in the city where his Japanese mother and Korean father had gone to escape the disdain of Say's maternal grandmother. The story of his Japanese-American family began when his grandfather discovered steamships.

Say's grandfather was a privileged Japanese gentleman from an ancient samurai family. In his early twenties, Say's grandfather traveled all over the world. He wanted to settle nowhere. During his travels, his own father's letter came ordering him to come home and marry a woman; it was a marriage that had been arranged by the two families. In *Grandfather's Journey* (Houghton, 1993), Say refers to this woman as his grandfather's childhood sweetheart, but that was untrue. She was, according to Say, a "horrible woman who ruined the lives of all those whose lives she touched." But Say's grandfather returned to Japan and married her; together they went to California, where Say's mother was born and where she went to school.

After graduating from high school in Oakland, Say's mother wanted to attend college at Stanford. Her mother would not hear of it. Stanford was not, according to Say's grandmother, a proper place for a Japanese young lady. So the entire family was uprooted to return to Japan so that Say's mother could get a proper education. This education involved special tutors who taught her how to arrange flowers and host a tea ceremony. Say's mother rebelled at the notion of entering a culture she did not like. She went out and got a job in a department store in the city of Osaka. She was doing something no woman had done in the 400-year history of the family. Her actions caused a great scandal, and she added to it when she ran off with the first man who spoke English to her. That was Say's father, a Korean orphan who had been raised by an English family in Shanghai. He spoke six languages, but the fact that he was Korean was reason enough for the family's displeasure with the marriage. The couple ran off to Yokohama, where Allen Say was born. Say's grandmother disowned his mother, and the clan was unforgiving. The couple faced many adversities.

Allen Say knew he wanted to be a cartoonist from the time he was six years old. He attended seven primary schools while B-29s dropped bombs on the cities of Japan. Say loved to draw, but his parents discouraged him. They felt that painters were irresponsible sissies and that artists gained fame only after death. An elementary teacher, Mrs. Morita, befriended Say and encouraged him to continue drawing. But Say's father wanted his eldest son to become a businessman. While Say did not actually draw in a closet, he always drew with a sense of guilt. Say felt that he did not meet his father's expectations.

When Say was eleven, his parents divorced, causing another scandal. Say's relationship with his father was never close, and his mother was unable to care for him in a society that did not look kindly on single mothers nor on children of "mixed heritage," so he was sent to live with his grandmother in Tokyo.

Say's relationship with his grandmother was explosive; they simply did not get along at all. His grandmother promised him that if he studied hard and got admitted to a special prep school, she would get him his own apartment. In his own apartment, he could read and draw all he wished. At first, he did not believe her, but she meant it. By the time he was twelve years old, he was living alone in a one-room apartment. Soon he met his mentor, Noro Shinpei. Say went to his studio seeking to apprentice himself, much in the tradition of his family's samurai history. Years later, Say realized that he was actually attempting to replace his own father. Shinpei took Say in and mentored him for the next four years. Shinpei was a great cartoonist and Say became his assistant. He trained Say in Western art.

Meanwhile, Say's father, whose dream had been to earn a lot of money and move to the United States, finally achieved his goal. He introduced the first hamburger stand in Japan, and by 1953, he had enough money to settle his new family in California.

Allen Say came to the United States to join his father. When Say arrived, he did not speak one word of English and had been on his own for four years. He did not fit into his father's new family, so his father abandoned him once again. Years before, Say's father had translated Japanese into English for a marine, who now was in charge of an American military academy. Say's father sent him to attend this exclusive military boarding school.

The war with Japan had been over for just a few years, and some bitterness remained. Say did not fit in with the wealthy students. The headmaster, the former marine, allowed Say to work for part of his tuition and board but did not treat him as if he belonged there. The headmaster quickly realized that Allen would be a four-year liability so, seemingly in an effort to get Say to leave, he provided a room for him above the kitchen. There were snakes outside the door and black widow spiders in the room. He wasn't allowed in the barracks with the rest of the cadets because of the pressure from the parents of the rich cadets. The headmaster told Say that he was a bad influence. He smoked, was rebellious, and did little to disprove the headmaster's perception of him.

One of the students offered to sell Say a 1946 Ford automobile for $50. Say accepted the offer, got in his car, and drove south to Mexico. Each time he filled the gas tank, he also had to put a quart of oil in as well. When he returned, his father was waiting for him in the parking lot. The headmaster, his sponsor, had gone into his room and found cigarettes. He then called Say's father telling him that Allen was not a desirable candidate. Say packed a cardboard suitcase and moved to a hotel for $8.50 a week. The hotel housed migrant fruit pickers. He went to the market and bought peanut butter.

Say knew he wanted to finish high school, so he went to Citrus Union High School and asked to see the principal. When Say walked in, he saw a man with a crew cut, glasses, and a tie. After his experience at the military school, Say felt like he was "climbing Mt. Fuji for the second time." There's an old Japanese saying, "You are a fool if you don't climb Mt. Fuji once, you are a fool if you climb it twice." When Say told the principal he had most recently been to Hardy Military School, the principal held his head.

Nonetheless, the principal, Mr. Petersen, was interested in helping Say finish high school. He requested Say's Japanese school to send his transcripts and then helped Say get a job cleaning machines at a print shop. Allen Say has said that he will "never forget Mr. Petersen." Say went to the school for a year and then managed to get a scholarship to an art school.

Once he graduated from high school, he received a letter from his mother saying, "Why don't you come home to visit?" He returned to Japan a year later, "not as an immigrant but as an exile." He eventually would return to California.

He attended Aoyama Gakuin in Tokyo for three years; Chouinard Art Institute for one year; and then returned to California to attend the Los Angeles Art Center School for one year; the University of California, Berkeley, for two years; and the San Francisco Art Institute for one year. In California, he met and married a Jewish woman, Deirdre Myles.

For several years after high school, Say had stopped drawing, but in an attempt to avoid the draft he enrolled to study architecture at Berkeley. He was drafted anyway and sent to Germany. When he returned to the United States, his marriage ended. Their one daughter, Yurioko, became a child with two households.

Say settled into a career in commercial illustration and photography. He became one of the highest-paid photographers in California. In 1968, Say began creating books for children. His first illustrations were mainly pen-and-ink illustrations. At first he avoided doing anything ethnic. He wanted to be known for his artistic ability, not as an ethnic artist. Allen Say was thirty-five when his first book, *Dr. Smith's Safari* (Harper, 1972), was published. At the time, he thought the book was evidence of a commendable sense of fair play and sportsmanship. In hindsight, he recognizes the book as a denial of his heritage—a denial spawned by the stereotyping that he had experienced. He also saw the story as a thinly veiled antigun tale. In a way, Dr. Smith was Say's own stereotype of a white male and the teenagers in the story were his own perception of southern California, where he had spent many unhappy days as a solitary young man with few friends.

Say's second book, *Once Under the Cherry Blossom Tree: An Old Japanese Tale* (Harper, 1974; reissued Houghton, 1997), was one of humor that borders on the grotesque. Say told the story of his childhood in a young adult novel, *The Ink-Keeper's Apprentice* (Harper, 1979; reissued Houghton, 1994).

In that story, he regrets portraying his grandmother as only a harsh but benign individual. Now he wishes he had portrayed her as she really was—a tragic figure.

True success came when Say's *The Bicycle Man* (Houghton, 1982) was published. It was a tale set in Japan after World War II. Two American soldiers, one black and one white, encounter a group of Japanese schoolchildren and engage in some bicycle tricks. Over the years, publishers had asked Say to illustrate Japanese stories. Say declined to illustrate most of them. Then, in 1987, Say decided that the next book he would illustrate would be his last. Walter Lorraine had convinced him to illustrate Dianne Snyder's *The Boy of the Three-Year Nap* (Houghton, 1988). During the illustration of that book, Say says that he was "transformed back to his childhood." With each stroke of his brush, he came a little closer to reconsidering his decision. It was with that book that convinced Say to become a full-time writer and illustrator of children's books.

Following that decision, Say created *A River Dream* (Houghton, 1988) and *The Lost Lake* (Houghton, 1989). Both had nothing to do with old Japan and everything to do with returning his Japanese heritage to his life.

Sometime earlier, Allen Say had read a newspaper article in a Sunday newspaper supplement, *California Living*, about a Billy Wong, a Chinese man who became a bullfighter. One day, he attended a first-grade school party with his daughter. There he met a Jewish woman whose last name was Wong. Since that was rather unusual, he struck up a conversation and discovered that Billy Wong, El Chino, was her husband's younger brother. El Chino had been killed in a car accident, but the family supplied Say with information that helped him write his story. The biographical story, *El Chino* (Houghton, 1990) told the story of the man's perseverance. When Say realized that the story was really about finding one's identity—a story that mirrored his own efforts—he told the story in first-person narrative. Billy Wong always wanted to be an athlete. His sights were set on being a basketball player, but realizing he was too short, he went to school to become an engineer. Wong's father had instilled in his six children the idea that each of them could be whatever they aspired to be. Wong was a top-notch engineer and saved his money for a trip to Spain; when he got there, he realized that he finally knew what he wanted to be: a bullfighter. He went to school for two years, but no one would let him participate in a bullfight. He was Chinese dressed as a Spanish bullfighter. When he realized that he was denying his own heritage, he dressed in traditional Chinese clothing and became El Chino, the Chinese bullfighter. Because the story reminds Say of his own denial of his heritage, the story remains close to his heart.

Tree of Cranes (Houghton, 1991) was his next book. It told the story of his own first Christmas. The year was 1943, when Say was six years old, just before the first Doolittle raid. The story is basically true. Say's mother was homesick for America, and Say was ill in bed. Both Say and his mother are dressed in traditional Japanese kimono. Say's mother cut down a small tree from the backyard and decorated it with traditional origami paper cranes. In the story, Say has his mother digging up the tree and repotting it. The next morning, Say received one present, a kite. In real life, says Say, the gift was probably a spinning top, but the kite, he thought, would best capture the theme of East meets West. That day, as it really happened, Say's mother shared many other stories about America. Her story of a vacuum cleaner fascinated Say—a machine that actually sucked up dust.

The 1994, the Caldecott Medal was presented to him for his illustrations of *Grandfather's Journey* (Houghton, 1993). This tale describes both his grandfather's journey to America and Say's own story as well. His favorite painting is the one he describes as "the picture of myself as the F.O.B. [fresh off the boat], standing in the sun-drenched, empty parking lot." Both Say and his grandfather were immigrants to the United States, and in a sense, his grandfather's experiences tell Say's own life story. They are mirror images of one another's lives, in a different era. He has pointed out that the most important phrase in *Grandfather's Journey* is: "After a time, I came to love the land my Grandfather loved . . . " His love for America was Say's inspiration for writing the story.

One of his most recent books, *Tea with Milk* (Houghton Mifflin, 1999), fills in the gaps in his mother's story. It is the story of a young woman who grows up near San Francisco but returns with her parents to their native Japan. In Japan, she feels as though she is the foreigner and very much out-of-place.

Allen Say is a writer and illustrator, a career he has embraced full-time since 1988. When he was awarded the Caldecott Medal in 1994 and met Lois Lowry, the 1994 Newbery Award winner, they discovered that they might very well have met one another on a school playground in Japan. Both had been in post war Japan in the same neighborhood at the same time. She was there as the daughter of the dentist assigned to General MacArthur's unit, and he was a Japanese child trying to survive the hardships of a life on his own. They both frequented the local school playground.

Although Allen Say appears at conferences and book signings, he doesn't usually visit schools. When he does, he sometimes tells children that his favorite food is raw fish, that he dislikes sports, and sometimes he shares stories about his twenty-pound cat, Tofu. He continues to work and live in San Francisco.

BOOKS AND NOTES

Allen Say's first illustrations were pen and ink. Later his illustrations began to be more photographic in nature. His paintings reflect the light and shadows found in the best of photographs, and while he once felt that the twenty years he spent as a photographer were squandered, he now feels that he learned a lot from that discipline. His paintings reflect that learning. He is fascinated by old photographs. When he first came to America, the students he encountered at the military school had never heard of Picasso or Matisse. Others were surprised that this young man who could speak no English could draw in the French academic way.

His proposals to his editor are generally in the form of half-page summaries. Many editors prefer to see the text before approving a book, but Say's drawings usually come first, fashioning the story before the words are written. Once the paintings are created, the stories seem to come quickly. It took Say eleven months to do the paintings for *El Chino* but only two days to write the text. The text for *Tree of Cranes* came in just three days. His editor, Walter Lorraine, accepts the way Say works.

Since the publication of *The Boy of the Three-Year Nap*, Say's writing has explored two basic themes: parent-and-child relationships and the relationship between Asian and American peoples. Several of his recent tales have been autobiographical, and all have been lushly illustrated with jewel-like paintings in a variety of artistic styles, calling to mind the work of artists from Monet to Ansel Adams to Andrew Wyeth.

Books Written and Illustrated by Allen Say

Allison (Houghton, 1997).
When Allison realizes she does not resemble her parents, she must deal with the information that she is adopted.

The Bicycle Man (Parnassus, 1982).
Two American soldiers borrow a bicycle and entertain young children at the finale of their school sports day by doing amazing tricks on the bicycle.

El Chino (Houghton, 1990).
Biography of Billy Wong, who believed what his father said, "In America, you can be anything you want to be."

Emma's Rug (Houghton, 1996).
Emma feels her special rug is her inspiration for her art but when the rug is destroyed she finds that the inspiration has really come from within.

Grandfather's Journey (Houghton, 1993).
The story of a Japanese man and his journey to America. Explores the feelings the man has for his country of birth and the country to which he has come. 1994 Caldecott Medal winner.

The Lost Lake (Houghton, 1989).
A trip to the mountains brings a young boy and his father closer together.

A River Dream (Houghton, 1988).
A fantastical fishing trip begins when a young boy opens a box from his uncle.

The Sign Painter (Houghton, 2000).
An artist's life is changed when he paints a large billboard in the desert.

Stranger in the Mirror (Houghton, 1995).
A young boy whose face ages overnight has difficulty convincing people that he is still who he says he is.

Tea with Milk (Houghton, 1999).

A young Japanese woman leaves her native United States and returns with her parents to their native Japan—a move she would not have chosen.

Tree of Cranes (Houghton, 1991).

A young Japanese boy tells of his first Christmas.

Under the Cherry Blossom Tree: An Old Japanese Tale (Harper, 1974; reissued Houghton, 1997).

A wicked landlord gets his just dues, and the poor villagers get a better life.

Books Illustrated by Allen Say

The Boy of the Three-Year Nap. Written by Dianne Snyder. (Houghton, 1988).

The lazy habits of a young boy are the subject of his mother's maneuverings to change his habits.

How My Parents Learned to Eat. Written by Ina R. Friedman. (Houghton, 1984).

An American sailor and a Japanese girl try to learn the other's method of eating.

FOR MORE INFORMATION

Articles

"An Interview with Allen Say: 1994 Caldecott Award Winner." *The Reading Teacher* 48, no. 4. (December 1, 1994): 304.

Marcus, Leonard S. "Rearrangement of Memory: An Interview with Allen Say." *The Horn Book Magazine* 67, no. 3 (May 1, 1991): 295+.

Rochman, Hazel. "The Booklist Interview: Allen Say." *Booklist* 90, no. 3 (October 1, 1993): 350–51.

Say, Allen. "The Boy of the Three-Year Nap." *The Horn Book Magazine* 65, no. 2 (March 1, 1989): 174+.

Say, Allen. "Caldecott Medal Acceptance." *The Horn Book Magazine* 70, no. 4 (July 1, 1994): 427+.

Say, Allen. "Grandfather's Journey." *The Horn Book Magazine* 71, no. 1 (January 1, 1995): 30+.

Say, Allen. "Musings of a Walking Stereotype." *School Library Journal* 37, no. 10 (December 1991): 45–46.

Say, Allen. "1994 Caldecott Acceptance Speech." *Journal of Youth Services in Libraries* 7, no. 4. (Summer 1994): 355+.

Web Sites

"Allen Say." *Houghton Mifflin Company Web Site.* URL: <http://www.eduplace.com/rdg/author/say/index.html> (Accessed March 2000).

Jon Scieszka

◆ Folklore (Literary) ◆ Humor

Sharron L. McElmeel

Flint, Michigan
September 8, 1954

📖 *Math Curse*

📖 *The Stinky Cheese Man*

📖 *The True Story of the Three Little Pigs by A. Wolf*

ABOUT THE AUTHOR

Jon Scieszka was the second oldest of six boys. He says he was "the nicest." Born on September 8, 1954, he was a year younger than the oldest child and two years older than the next child of Louis and Shirley Scieszka. His father was an elementary school principal, and his mother was a nurse. When he learned to read, reading the traditional "Dick and Jane" readers, he says he "suspected that the characters were not of this world." Nonetheless, he thought about becoming a writer from the time his mother first read Dr. Seuss's *Green Eggs and Ham* and Ruth Krauss's *The Carrot Seed* to him. His parents, however, hoped that he would enter a career associated with the medical field.

During his high school years, Scieszka attended Culver Military Academy in Indiana and later entered Albion College in Michigan. He was going to be a doctor until he "figured out he would have to work in a hospital." Sick people made him nervous. Even at Albion, he spent time "hanging out with the English majors, writing all sorts of stuff." He ended up with an undergraduate degree in chemistry but no credentials for a career in the medical field. And he still wanted to write.

At Albion, he met Jerilyn Hansen. They married, and the couple moved to New York, where she became an art director for a magazine and he entered Columbia University to obtain a master of fine arts degree in Fiction. Because writers have to eat, he became an assistant in a first-grade classroom. Next, he taught second grade for a couple years and then worked with third- through eighth-grade students in computers, mathematics, science, and history. His teaching was only one of the many jobs he held before he turned to writing as a full-time profession. He worked as a lifeguard; painted factories, houses, apartments; and wrote for magazines.

While he was still teaching, in 1987 or so, he began to play around with telling the real story of the three little pigs. He came up with the idea for a retelling while working with his second graders to rewrite their favorite fairy tales. After he finished the book, it was rejected a number of times before Viking finally agreed to publish it. Jon's wife was a good friend of Molly Leach and through her, Jon met Lane Smith. Smith and Scieszka became friends before they started working together. Eventually they thought they would make a good team because they both liked a lot of the same cartoons and books. They also laughed at each other's bad jokes. Together they created *The True Story of the Three Little Pigs by A. Wolf* (Viking, 1989). While he "was on a roll," he created another zany manipulation of a fairy tale. This time, he wrote *The Frog Prince, Continued* (Viking, 1991). That book was illustrated by Steve Johnson.

In 1992, Scieszka took a year's sabbatical from teaching to work with Lane Smith on developing some more ideas for books. They already had begun a series of books, The Time Warp Trio, about three adventurous kids who use magic to transport themselves back in time or into the future. Scieszka says that the three boys are a lot like the fourth- and fifth-grade boys he used to teach. He also says that the Stinky Cheese Man character is a lot like some other people he knows.

When people ask Scieszka how long a book takes to write, he does not have a specific answer. He says he is always writing down ideas, and when he writes a first draft, he finds that he must continually rewrite, rewrite, and then rewrite again. He scribbles an idea on paper, types the ideas up, changes them, types them up again, thinks some more, adds things, and keeps repeating the process until finally he has a story he thinks children will enjoy.

Jon Scieszka, his wife Jeri Hansen, their daughter Casey (b. 1984), and their son Jake (b. 1986) live on the best street in Brooklyn, New York, in a second-floor apartment that they share with their cat Potvin. The cat is named after the Toronto Maple Leaf's goalie, Felix "The Cat" Potvin. When Scieszka is not writing he is apt to be reading. He says his favorite things to read, in addition to fairy tales, myths, and legends, are comic books, books of all kinds, newspapers, codes, encyclopedias, dictionaries, advertisements, cereal boxes, matchbook covers, mattress tags, and scraps of paper with writing on them.

BOOKS AND NOTES

The first of the Time Warp Trio Series, *Knights of the Kitchen Table* (Viking, 1991), sets the stage for several more adventures when Joe receives a magic book for his birthday present from his uncle. The magic enables Joe, Fred, and Sam to transport themselves back in time. The second book, *The Not-So-Jolly-Roger* (Viking, 1991), featured the pirate Blackbeard. The series has been described as hilarious and as having great appeal to readers ages seven to eleven. Scieszka and Smith have created another book in the series every year or two. Although those books are enormously popular, it is Scieszka's picture books that have captured the attention of the public. In fact, the first printing or so of *Math Curse* created some additional interest when a fifth-grade honors class in Schnecksville, Pennsylvania, noticed that the prime numbers listed on the back cover of *Math Curse* were: 11, 100, 101, 111 and so forth. The list should have read; 11, 100, 101, 110, 111, 1000 and so forth.

Scieszka turned again to his love of folklore and created a comic revision of several fairy tales, which he intertwined in a madcap narrative. When Scieszka and Smith work together, Scieszka usually writes the story first and then Smith sketches and paints some ideas to accompany the tale. Then the two of them get together with Smith's wife, Molly Leach, and she figures out how the book should be designed so that the two of them can include all of their favorite jokes and puns. The two books by Scieszka that have been illustrated by other artists, *The Frog Prince, Continued* and *The Book That Jack Wrote* (Viking, 1994), were designed by his wife, Jeri Hansen.

The Book That Jack Wrote. Illustrated by Daniel Adel. (Viking, 1994).
    A variation of the cumulative tale, The House That Jack Built.

The Frog Prince, Continued. Illustrated by Steve Johnson. (Viking, 1991).
    The tale is not as we have always thought. The prince and the princess are not living happily ever after, so the prince sets out to find the witch to help remedy the situation.

Math Curse. Illustrated by Lane Smith. (Viking, 1995).
    When the teacher tells students that everything in the world can be viewed as a mathematical problem, one student develops a "math curse."

The Stinky Cheese Man and Other Fairly Stupid Tales. Illustrated by Lane Smith. (Viking, 1992).

Wacky variations of familiar fairy tales melded together into an even wackier narrative with familiar characters.

Squids Will Be Squids: Fresh Morals, Beastly Fables. Illustrated by Lane Smith. (Viking, 1998).

Contemporary fables with morals focusing on homework, curfews, and television commercials. A humorous perspective.

The True Story of the Three Little Pigs by A. Wolf. Illustrated by Lane Smith. (Viking, 1989).

Al Wolf's version of what happens when he goes to his neighbor to borrow a cup of sugar and accidentally blows down the pigs' house.

FOR MORE INFORMATION

Articles

Raymond, Allen. "Jon Scieszka: Telling the *True* Story." *Teaching K–8* 22, no. 8 (May 1992): 35–37.

Web Sites

"Author Chat with Jon Scieszka." *New York Public Library.* URL: <http://www.nypl.org/branch/kids/authorchat.html> (Accessed February 2000).

Jon Scieszka and Lane Smith Bring You . . . Chucklebait.com. URL: <http://www.chucklebait.com/> (Accessed March 2000).

Penguin Putnam Site. "Jon Scieszka." URL: <http://www.penguinputnam.com> (Accessed March 2000). Go to "Young Readers," then "Authors & Illustrators," and then "Author Bios." Text is also available at *The Scoop: Jon Scieszka Biographical Sketch.* URL: <http://www.Friend.ly.net/scoop/biographies/scieszkajon/index.html> (Accessed March 2000).

Pif Magazine. "One on One with Ryan Boudinet." (December 1998) URL: <http://www.pifmagazine.com/vol19/interview.shtml> (Accessed March 2000).

Interview with Jon Scieszka, author of the most subversive and intelligent children's books around.

Puffin Company, United Kingdom Site. "Author ID Card: Jon Scieszka." URL: <http://www.puffin.co.uk/living/aut_48.html> (Accessed March 2000).

Maurice Sendak

Brooklyn, New York
June 10, 1928

📖 *In the Night Kitchen*

📖 *Outside Over There*

📖 *Where the Wild Things Are*

ABOUT THE AUTHOR/ILLUSTRATOR

Maurice Sendak was born the same year as Mickey Mouse. The house where he lived in Connecticut included an intricate burglar alarm and a Mickey Mouse night-light. He placed Mickey Mouse memorabilia alongside family photographs. A backdrop curtain Sendak designed for the Brussels opera production of *Where the Wild Things Are* (Harper, 1963) was inspired by the huge face of Mickey Mouse. He was known to slip in an image of Mickey Mouse, among images of his own popular book characters, when he created jacket illustrations for reference books and posters. Some of his favorite childhood books featured Mickey Mouse.

Maurice Sendak was born on June 10, 1928, in Brooklyn, New York, where he spent his childhood with his sister Natalie, his brother Jack, and his parents, Philip and Sadie Sendak. His parents were immigrants from Poland; Maurice Sendak, his sister, and his brother were born in the United States. He knew he wanted to be a writer and illustrator before he ever went to school. His father made up wonderful stories to tell his children. His sister often took her two younger brothers to Radio City Music Hall or the Roxy in Manhattan. It was a big deal to go to the city and to eat there. Sendak read many comic books and spent hours at the movie theater. He was particularly interested in the work of Walt Disney. He remembers tagging after his older sister and copying every picture that his brother drew. Sometimes he even signed his name to Jack's drawings and presented them at school as his own work. Although Sendak says he had a very nice childhood, he wasn't particularly happy. Sendak's father was a dressmaker and partner in a shop, Lucky Stitching. During the Depression, the shop did not make much money. At age two and a half, Sendak contracted measles and then suffered with double pneumonia; later, at age four, he contracted a case of scarlet fever. His parents were overprotective, and Sendak seldom went outside to play with the other children. Instead, he stayed home and drew pictures. He was overweight, the family moved a lot, and he disliked school. The monsters in his "Wild Things" book are modeled after the people—relatives most likely—who came for Sunday dinner. He imagined them as "big people who would eat him up."

Sendak's relatives in Europe, including his paternal grandfather, perished in the Holocaust or shortly thereafter. The news of his grandfather's death arrived on the day of Sendak's bar mitzvah. His sister Natalie's fiancé, a soldier, was killed during World War II. Sendak's brother Jack was stationed in the Pacific during the war. At the same time, Maurice was attending Lafayette High School and excelled in art, but he disliked his other classes. He worked on the yearbook, the literary magazine, and the newspaper. He taught himself to draw illustrations for classic tales. He graduated from high school in 1946 but decided not to go to art school. He got a job with a window-design firm instead. He enjoyed the work and moved out of his parents' home for the first time. In 1948, he was promoted within the company, but he did not like the change. He left the company shortly afterward. He was out of a job but used his time to sketch children he observed in the street.

By this time his brother Jack had returned home, and the two teamed up to engineer six wooden mechanical toys. The prototypes were based on eighteenth-century, lever-operated toys from Germany. They took the toys to F.A.O. Schwarz, but they were rejected because they were too expensive to reproduce. Nonetheless, the trip resulted in a job offer for Maurice, and he became a window display assistant for the company. For the next three years, Sendak worked at F.A.O. Schwarz during the day and took art classes at the Art Student's League at night. At the toy store, he often used the children's book section to familiarize himself with the classic illustrators of children's books, such as Walter Crane and Randolph Caldecott. He also met Ursula Nordstrom. She was the distinguished editor at Harper and Brothers (later to be Harper & Row and then HarperCollins). When Nordstrom saw Sendak's drawings, she offered him an opportunity to illustrate *The Wonderful Farm* by Marcel Ayme (Harper, 1951). While that book marked his entry into the world of children's books, it was his illustrations for Ruth Krauss's *A Hole Is to Dig* (Harper, 1952) that became his first big success. Bolstered by the success of the book, he quit his job at F.A.O. Schwarz, moved to Greenwich Village, and became a freelance illustrator.

Sendak has referred to the years between 1951 and 1962 as his apprenticeship. During this time, he spent many weekends at the "big rickety frame house by a river with a boat" of Ruth Krauss and her husband David Johnson Leisk. Sendak was in his early twenties and has referred to Krauss and Leisk as his "weekend parents." Leisk wrote and illustrated children's books as Crockett Johnson. The couple helped shape Sendak into an artist. They often sat at the porch table, cutting and pasting together words and illustrations. Ruth Krauss and Sendak would arrange and rearrange. She would holler, and he would sulk. Leisk would act as referee. Sendak considered himself lucky to have been worked with them. He says, "I learned more than how to illustrate a book, I learned about the meaning of the book and how the text and illustrations work together and not against each other."

Sendak illustrated a number of books written by other authors. His first book as both author and illustrator was *Kenny's Window* (Harper, 1956). Kenny must answer seven riddling questions before he will be able to live in a magic garden where he will never have to go to bed. By the time Sendak had written his third book, *The Sign on Rosie's Door* (Harper, 1960), his illustrations were showing much humor. His next four books were published in 1962, comprising the "Nutshell Library." The books included *Alligators All Around*, *Chicken Soup with Rice*, *One Was Johnny*, and *Pierre* (Harper).The stories represented an unsentimental presentation of children's behavior and fantasy. All of these books were produced during the period of time Sendak considers his apprenticeship. By the time he was thirty-four, he was ready to try his first "picture book." That book was *Where the Wild Things Are*. The book began as "Where the Wild Horses Are." The original dummy had a young boy in search of wild horses, but over a series of rewrites, the book became the story of Max, who is banished to his bedroom, fantasizes about travels to the land of the Wild Things, and then returns to his room, homesick and famished. Despite some reservations from some parents and reviewers who felt it might disturb young readers, *Where the Wild Things Are* was a great success.

Many of Sendak's books included references to people and places in his life. Sendak had purchased a Sealyham terrier, Jennie, in 1954. For the next fourteen years, the dog was his best friend. Sendak created *Higglety Pigglety Pop!* (Harper, 1967) as a tribute to his friend. It was published just one month after Jennie died of cancer. In one illustration, she is shown with her paws on the table, in front of a dish marked with "Jennie." On the wall behind her is a picture representing the famous painting, the "Mona Lisa." Mona Lisa is the name that Jennie's breeders had given her before Sendak obtained her and changed her name to Jennie. Jennie is shown throughout the book and can be found in other of Sendak's books as well. Jennie first appeared in Betty Mac-Donald's *Mrs. Piggle Wiggle's Farm* (Lippincott, 1954) and appeared regularly in almost every one of Sendak's works in the following years.

In Else Minarik's *A Kiss for Little Bear* (Harper, 1968), Sendak slipped in a caricature of a wild thing as the picture drawn by Little Bear, as a gift for his mother.

In the Night Kitchen (Harper, 1970), Sendak has included references to his own life. As the boy, Mickey (a tribute to Mickey Mouse), falls out of bed and into the night, the words "Q. E. Gateshead" can be seen on the building outside the window. That is the hospital where Sendak recovered after he suffered a major heart attack during a trip to Europe in 1967. As a child, Maurice enjoyed many movies with his brother and sister. Among his favorites were those that featured Laurel and Hardy, who appeared as bakers in this book.

At the bottom of the page where the three bakers are shown, there is a sack of flour lying on its side. At the bottom of the sack is the name "Killingworth, Connecticut." That town is where his beloved Jennie was born. One of the bakers is holding a sack that has the partial name "Jennie" visible, along with the names of Jennie's breeders. The date 1953 is also on the sack. During the summer of 1953, Sendak was desperate for a dog and arranged to get the runt of the litter. Also, as Mickey flies over the top of the Milky Way in the night kitchen, he flies over "Jennie Street."

In the scenes where Mickey is turning his plane's propeller, there is a building in the background. Lettering on the building says, "Patented June 10th 1928." That is the date of Sendak's birth.

In the four-section illustration where "he kneaded and punched it and pounded and pulled," buildings in the background carry the phrases, "Eugene's," and "Philip's Best Tomatoes," and "Sadie's Best." Philip and Sadie were Sendak's parents. Eugene was a close friend who took Sendak's beloved Jennie to be put out of her misery when she was suffering from cancer.

As Mickey falls into the bowl of batter and "into the light of the night kitchen," a background building in the shape of a bottle has the name "Kneitel's Fandango." That refers to Kenny Kneitel, a collector and dealer of Mickey Mouse Figures and other nostalgia items from the 1930s. Kenny is also the namesake of Sendak's character in *Kenny's Window*.

On a following page, the salt tube held by another baker is labeled "Woody's Salt." That name is in reference to Wood Gelman, editor of the Nostalgia Press and a close friend. Another building has the name "Schickel." This is a reference to Richard Schickel, whose biography of Walt Disney prodded Sendak's memory of his childhood love of Mickey Mouse and of Disney himself.

Sendak's *Outside Over There* (Harper, 1981) includes pictorial references to Sendak's admiration of the famed composer Mozart. The setting is in Mozart's time, and in one illustration Mozart is in the background playing his flute.

Many of Sendak's books contain a lion. A Sendak lion appears first in Ruth Krauss's *A Very Special House* (Harper, 1953). He put lions next in his illustrations for Jack Sendak's *Circus Girl* (Harper, 1957), then lions appeared in his own *Pierre, Hector Protector and As I Went Over the Water* (Harper, 1965), and later in *Higglety Pigglety Pop!* The lions seem to bear some relationship to the many MGM movies Sendak saw from the age of six.

Alligators are also favorite animals, showing up in several of the books Sendak illustrated. *Alligators All Around* went through several drafts. The first draft featured a family of apes, but in later drafts, the animals became the more favored alligators. Alligators also show up in Else Holmelund Minarik's *No Fighting! No Biting!* (Harper, 1958).

Maurice Sendak received Caldecott Honor Book awards for several books that he illustrated for other authors. *What Do You Say, Dear?* (W. R. Scott, 1958), Sesyle Joslin's etiquette book, earned the honor in 1959; in 1960, he won another honor for *The Moon Jumpers* (Harper, 1959) by Janice May Udry. Two more Caldecott Honors came to him for his illustrations for *Little Bear's Visit* by Else Holmelund Minarik (Harper, 1961) and *Mr. Rabbit and the Lovely Present* by Charlotte Zolotow (Harper, 1962). In 1964, he won the top honor when he was awarded the Caldecott Medal for *Where the Wild Things Are*.

In 1996, Maurice Sendak was presented with the National Medal of Arts in a White House ceremony hosted by President and Mrs. Clinton. He was recognized for his efforts to promote parents' reading to their children and in getting youngsters to read. On May 18, 1998, in New York City, Maurice

Sendak was awarded the Jewish Cultural Achievement Award in recognition of the influence he has had—and continues to have—on the Jewish culture. In the last decade, Sendak has expanded his outreach and influence by designing sets and costumes and writing an operatic libretto. He has worked on videos and a children's television series. One of his most recent ventures is the founding of a children's theater company. In 1990, along with Arthur Yorinks and $1 million in seed money from HarperCollins, Sendak developed *The Night Kitchen*, a national children's theater. Subsequent deals have Sony Corporation providing management and support in exchange for its getting a first look at productions that the corporation might be able to develop. The company debuted with a comedy codirected by actor Bill Irwin and an operatic Hansel & Gretel.

In 1972, Sendak bought an eighteenth-century farmhouse in Ridgefield, Connecticut. At the time, the town had something that Sendak said was "essential to all artists—solitude, charm, and a warm community without the necessity of becoming too social. Ridgefield is considered "commutable" to New York City because it is only an hour-and-a-half train ride from Manhattan.

Maurice Sendak has never married, nor has he had children; nevertheless, he has devoted his life to children and helping them make connections to other people. In his rare speaking appearances, Sendak, in addition to the more obvious topics of illustration and children's literature, enjoys speaking about his three lifetime passions: opera, Herman Melville, and Mozart. He is represented by the Steven Barclay Agency in New York. He continues to live and work in the New York City area.

BOOKS AND NOTES

In 1963, Maurice Sendak's *Where the Wild Things Are* appeared among squeals from some self-appointed guardians of the purity of children's literature. Max, the hero in the book, not only defied his mother, but he had a fantasy with monsters so wild that they were sure to scare any young reader to death. Worse still was the fact that young Max was not properly punished for his behavior. He was sent to bed without any supper, but when he arrived back from his fantasy, there was a steaming warm supper waiting for him.

In the Night Kitchen followed in 1970. That book also created a fury from critics because naked Mickey fell into his surreal dream. In 1981, Sendak completed the trilogy when he published *Outside Over There*.

Sendak says the three books were "all variations of the same theme, how children come to grips with the realities of their lives, anger, boredom, fear, frustration, and jealousy."

Outside Over There is the story of a child transported out of reality and into a strange world of goblins in gray-hooded robes who have taken her baby sister. Ida conquers her fears to rescue her sister with her "wonder horn." The beautiful paintings show marvelous details rendered in softly hued colors: sunflowers, a glorious sea, and even Mozart playing a pianoforte in a tiny cottage by a stream, a subtle touch to establish the time.

In shades of Sendak's own childhood, Ida returns her sister to her mother, who is painting under a grape arbor much like the one a baby Maurice played under with his sister. The memory was not a conscious one until Maurice's sister noted the coincidence after the book was published.

Books Written and Illustrated by Maurice Sendak

In the Night Kitchen (Harper, 1970).

Kenny's Window (Harper, 1956).

The Nutshell Library (Harper, 1962). Includes: *Alligators All Around, Chicken Soup with Rice, One Was Johnny*, and *Pierre*.

Outside Over There (Harper, 1981).

Really Rosie: Starring the Nutshell Kids (Harper, 1975).

The Sign on Rosie's Door (Harper, 1960).

We're All Down in the Dumps With Jack and Guy (Harper, 1993).

Where the Wild Things Are (Harper, 1963).

Books Illustrated by Maurice Sendak

Hector Protector and As I Went over the Water. Written by Ruth Kraus. (Harper, 1965).

Nutcracker. Written by E. T. A. Hoffman. (Crown, 1984).

What Can You Do With a Shoe? Written by Beatrice Schenk deRegniers. (Margaret K. McElderry, 1997).

Originally published in two colors by Harper in 1955; reissued by McElderry with full-color paintings of the original line drawings.

Zlateh the Goat and Other Stories. Written by Isaac Bashevis Singer. (Harper, 1966).

FOR MORE INFORMATION

Articles

Devereaux, Elizabeth. "In the Studio with Maurice Sendak." *Publishers Weekly* 240, no. 44 (November 1, 1993): 28+.

Lodge, Sally. "Rediscovering What to Do with a Shoe." *Publishers Weekly* 244, no. 32 (August 4, 1997): 40+.

"Sendak's Scene." *Maclean's* 111, no. 4 (January 26, 1998): 6.

Books

Berg, Julie. *Maurice Sendak* (ABDO, 1993).

Lane, Selma G. *The Art of Maurice Sendak* (Abrams, 1984).

Sonheim, Amy. *Maurice Sendak* (Macmillan Library Reference, vol. 598, 1992).

Peter Sis

◆ Folklore ◆ Family Relationships ◆ Biographical Fiction

Brno, Czechoslovakia
May 11, 1949

📖 *The Scarebird*
📖 *The Three Golden Keys*
📖 *Tibet Through the Red Box*

ABOUT THE
AUTHOR/ILLUSTRATOR

Peter Sis was, as his father before him, a highly acclaimed Czech film-maker and book illustrator. He came to the United States in 1982, arriving in Los Angeles to produce a Czech-sponsored film about the Winter Olympics. The Czech government, along with the other Eastern Bloc nations, decided to boycott the Olympics. Thus, the film was never produced. Sis was ordered to return home, but he decided to request asylum in the United States. Asylum was granted.

Sis decided to find a place for himself in the world of American art, but he struggled in Los Angeles. His fame as a European filmmaker and illustrator did not follow him to America. He got a few illustration jobs but did not want to work in commercial animation or cartoon films. He even considered returning to Prague for a time, but the pull of his goal was stronger. He was determined to persist. A friend suggested that he write to Maurice Sendak. In a long-shot effort, he wrote to Sendak, enclosing some samples of his work and a copy of a children's book that he had illustrated in his homeland.

Sendak told Sis that if he was serious about book illustration, he should move to New York. Sis did not do that immediately, but several months later. Sis received a phone call from Sendak. Sis assumed he was calling from Connecticut. Instead, Sendak was at the Biltmore Hotel in Los Angeles and wanted to meet with him. Sis went to the hotel, and during their conversation, he told Sendak that he planned to take his advice and move to New York because all the major publishers were there. Sendak replied that at that moment, all the publishers were not in New York—they were right there in the hotel. The year was 1984, and the American Library Association was holding its annual convention in Los Angeles. After looking through Sis's portfolio, Sendak offered to introduce him to some of the book publishers. Sendak's assistance led to a meeting between Sis and the editor-in-chief of Greenwillow Books, Susan Hirschman, and its art director, Ava Weiss. Weiss coincidentally also had been born in Prague but had left as an infant. Hirschman and Weiss liked his work and extended an offer for him to illustrate *Bean Boy* by George Shannon (Greenwillow, 1984). Sis says that in just two hours, his life in the United States changed.

Sis did move to New York, allowing him to see some of the country. While traveling through Iowa, he gathered the idea for a book that eventually became *The Scarebird* (Greenwillow, 1988). Being in New York also afforded him the opportunity to solicit and obtain illustrative work in *The New York Times*, *Time*, *Newsweek*, *The Washington Post*, *The Boston Globe*, *Atlantic Monthly*, *Esquire*, *Forbes*, and other major publications. The work for magazines and newspapers was lucrative and seductive, but Sis wanted to succeed in the book world, so he persisted in his efforts to get published in that field. He relentlessly pursued book contracts. He took his portfolio from publisher to publisher, and when he found one who was interested, he would encourage them not to simply call him in the future, but to give him work immediately. In the five years following his first book, Sis illustrated and published fifteen more titles, including a collection of folktales retold by George Shannon, *Stories to Solve: Folktales from Around the World* (Greenwillow, 1985), and Sid Fleischman's Newbery-Award-winning title, *The Whipping Boy* (Greenwillow, 1986).

During this time Sis was living in a small walk-up Greenwich Village apartment that also served as his studio. He was not married, and his family was still in Czechoslovakia. If Sis were to return to visit them, the government would probably have taken his passport. Sis still loves his native country, but he had come to love America too. He became an American citizen in 1988. He worked day and night in an effort to prove himself after his "California experience."

Soon after his initial successes, Peter Sis met and married Terry Lajtha, a filmmaker. The year was 1991, and he was well on his way to making an indelible mark in the field of children's books. In the next few years, he wrote and illustrated several books and also continued to illustrate the work of other writers. His own book, *Follow the Dream: The Story of Christopher Columbus* (Knopf, 1991), was well received. In the introduction, Sis acknowledges that his previous awareness of Columbus was only that he had sailed the seas in 1492 and that he had reached the Western world. He alludes to the obstacles that Columbus faced as synonymous with the "iron curtain" that surrounded his homeland. He gave credit to Frances Foster (an editor) and Terry Lajtha (his soon-to-be wife) for helping him finish the book in time for the 200th anniversary of Columbus's voyage.

The following year, Knopf published Sis's tale of a folk hero from his native Czechoslovakia, Jan Welzl. The story, *A Small Tall Tale from the Far Far North* (Knopf, 1993), told of Welzl's adventures in the Arctic. One of those journeys was in 1893. Welzl worked on a trans-Siberian railway to earn enough money to buy a small horse and a cart with a false bottom to hide his valuables. After three years, he came to a place where he traded his horse for reindeer and sled. He thought he would find Eskimos living there but only found a cave that he made into a home. On an outing to check his traps, he has an accident and would have frozen to death had it not been for two Eskimos who rescued him and took him to their home. There he learned songs and tales while he recovered. He also learned how to live and survive in the harsh Arctic climate. In an epilogue, Sis explains that Welzl eventually formed a trading company and set sail for San Francisco to take furs there. The boat sunk, and the authorities sent him back to Monrovia, the country of his birth. It was there that Welzl, in an effort to earn enough money to get back to the northern region, wrote his memoirs. When he grew up, Sis realized that many of the stories Welzl told were too fantastical and that many bordered on tall tales. But the stories had impressed Sis and were still in his memory as an adult, ready to retell to a new audience. Welzl did make it back to the northern regions; his gravestone in Dawson, Yukon Territory, is inscribed with the date of his death, August 15, 1951.

In 1994, Doubleday published Sis's book, *The Three Golden Keys*. That book was the last book Jacqueline Kennedy Onassis edited. She had contacted him soon after seeing some of his art, including eggs he had decorated. She had suggested that they do "books together." Shortly after, she took a trip to Prague, and upon her return suggested that Sis write a book about that city. He agreed and wrote a tale of a cat who leads a man on a magical journey through the deserted streets of Prague. While on the journey, the man comes across some of the city's landmarks and locates the keys to his childhood home and to three traditional Czech tales. Onassis thought that the book was magnificent.

In the dedication to the book, Sis addresses his daughter, Madeleine, to tell her that one day she would wonder where her father had come from and that the book, *The Three Golden Keys*, would tell her. The book, says Sis, is about his childhood experiences in Prague, the city where he lived before coming to the United States.

Peter Sis was born in Brno, Czechoslovakia, in 1949, a few years after World War II and just a year after communists had taken over his country. His mother encouraged him to draw. Many people liked his pictures, but some, such as his art teacher, told him to draw in a different style. These people even suggested that he would never be successful if he drew in the style he chose.

He grew up in Prague, but he "never really liked living there." The city was a little bit scary. He remembers shadowy, dark, cobblestone streets and dark cellars. Life was different than in the United States. The Czech people celebrated St. Nicholas Day on December 6. That is when St. Nicholas came to see if children had been good or bad. If the child had been bad, St. Nicholas left a lump of coal; but if the child had been good, he left a present. A few days before Christmas, people purchased large living carp and kept them alive in the family's bathtub. On Christmas Eve, they cooked the fish for a special meal.

Sis's father traveled a lot and told Peter about the places he had been. Peter had an obsession with American books. His maternal grandfather had been to the United States when Peter's mother was a young girl in the 1930s. He was a railway engineer and designed railway stations in Cleveland and Chicago. The Czech government made him promise to return when the project was over, and although some of his friends told him it was foolish to return to Europe because Hitler had already taken power, he did anyway. Peter Sis says that his grandfather's life was never again as good as it had been in America. He brought back many American books. They were so precious that he kept them in a glass-front cupboard so they would not get dirty. At special times, he would take the books out and show them to Peter and his siblings.

Peter Sis's father was a well-respected documentary filmmaker. The communists drafted him into the army film unit and ordered him to go to China to make films and to teach filmmaking. He was only supposed to be gone for two months. Vladimar Sis had thought he would be allowed to return to Czechoslovakia to continue filming butterflies and rare plants. Instead, the Chinese wanted him to document the building of a highway in the Himalayas. Vladimar Sis found himself on the highest mountain range in the world in a remote area of China. What was described as the "western province" was actually Tibet. The highway was intended to open Tibet to China. Vladimar was, through an act of nature, separated from the project and became lost in Tibet. It is there that he met the Boy-God-King (the Dalai Lama) in the forbidden city of Lhasa. Eventually, the Chinese army arrived, after Vladimar Sis had been lost for more than two years. He witnessed China's invasion of Tibet. He kept a diary with writings and sketches of experiences that had occurred there. When he came home, the diary was locked in a red box. Peter and his brother David were not allowed to touch the box. Vladimar knew he dared not talk to his friends about the invasion and other experiences in Tibet, but he told many stories to Peter, who believed everything he was told. Years later, when Peter Sis was in America, he received a brief note from his father telling him that the "Red Box is now yours." Sis, now an American citizen, went back to Prague, where the contents of the red box explained the mystery of his father's long absence during the 1950s. His father's diary and his own memories of his father's incredible tales told in Peter's childhood became the basis for a tale Sis eventually put into a book, *Tibet: Through the Red Box* (Farrar, 1998).

After his father's return, Peter, then aged fifteen, entered art school and studied for four years. The next six years were spent studying at the Academy of Applied Arts. His work was recognized almost immediately in Czechoslovakia. It was also a time when he realized that what he produced might inadvertently have political intonations that could bring criticism; he would have to change his work to get it published.

Sis exhibited some of his paintings in Prague, and when a Swiss children's author, Eveline Hasler, saw that exhibit, she thought he would be the perfect illustrator for her book about "Little Witch Licorice." The book was part of a series that was popular in German-speaking countries. Sis was able to earn money in Switzerland. But as the iron curtain increasingly separated his country from the West, his ability to earn money outside of Czechoslovakia or to work on a Swiss television series or similar projects was curtailed. Because he was "serving the government," he was allowed out of the country, but he always had to get a permit. Eventually, when the government sent him to Los Angeles to work on the Olympics film, he took his chance to stay in the United States.

Peter Sis, a bachelor until he was forty-two, changed his schedule when his children were born. When his son was an infant and his daughter a toddler, he often got up at 6:00 A.M., gave his son a bottle, and changed his son's diaper.

Then he would make breakfast for his wife and finally take his daughter to her playgroup. Today Sis still spends much time with his children. When not caring for them, he spends time in the studio. Sis, a man who once worked day and night, says, "I never thought I would go to bed at 9:00 P.M." Peter Sis and his wife Terry Lajtha live with their two children—Madeleine, born in 1992, and Matej, born in 1994—in New York City.

BOOKS AND NOTES

Peter Sis most often uses pen and ink and watercolor to create his illustrations. Meticulously positioned dots blend to create the lines of the illustrations in varying degrees of intensity. His artwork is described as humorous, surreal, mystical, and filled with moods. He seems to demand perfection from himself and in his illustrations. He says the most enjoyable part of creating illustrations is being able to invent, that is, when he makes his first sketches. Once he finishes a project, he often has worked on it so long that he no longer feels it is good. His pictures can take him anywhere from half an hour, a day, or even an entire week to create. It all depends on the subject and how many objects the illustration contains.

When Sis creates his illustrations, the materials he uses depend on the space in which he works. For example, when he travels, he uses small compact materials, such as little pads and ink. His young children also influence his choice of material. He is conscious of whether or not a particular material is toxic or not. He now prefers to use pen and ink and watercolor instead of smelly, messy materials such as oil paints. He also makes up rubber stamps from some of his designs, which he uses in his paintings. His work has been exhibited in Prague, London, Zurich, Hamburg, Los Angeles, and New York in both group and one-man shows.

Books Written and Illustrated by Peter Sis

Fire Truck (Greenwillow, 1998).
Matt, who loves fire trucks, wakes up one morning and finds that he *is* a fire truck, with one driver, two ladders, and many other interesting things.

Follow the Dream: The Story of Christopher Columbus (Knopf, 1991).
A tale of Christopher Columbus's voyage to the Orient.

Rainbow Rhino (Knopf, 1987).
Rhino's friends, rainbow birds, decide to live elsewhere but discover that the places where they have gone hold hidden dangers.

Ship Ahoy! (Greenwillow, 1999).
A child on a sofa imagines his adventures on the sea.

Sleep Safe, Little Whale: A Lullaby (Greenwillow, 1997).
Animals from whales to eagles sleep safely.

A Small Tall Tale from the Far Far North (Knopf, 1993).
Jan Welzl (1868–1951) survives a perilous journey from central Europe to the Arctic regions.

Starry Messenger: A Book Depicting the Life of a Famous Scientist, Mathematician, Astronomer, Philosopher, Physicist, Galileo Galilei (Farrar, 1996).
A look at the life of Galileo Galilei (1564–1642).

The Scarebird (Greenwillow, 1988).

A farmer realizes the value of friendship when a young man helps him and his scarecrow on a Midwestern farm.

The Three Golden Keys (Doubleday, 1994).

A journey through Prague that unlocks the author's childhood memories of Prague.

Tibet Through the Red Box (Farrar, 1998).

A tale woven from the author's memory and from his father's tales of being lost in Tibet for two years.

Trucks, Trucks, Trucks (Greenwillow, 1999).

A child cleans his room using a variety of trucks. One word on each page describes the work the truck is doing.

Books Illustrated by Peter Sis

Alphabet Soup. Written by Kate Banks. (Knopf, 1988).

A boy takes a magical journey with a friendly bear as he uses the alphabet to guide the way.

The Gargoyle on the Roof. Written by Jack Prelutsky. (Greenwillow, 1999).

Poems about gargoyles, monsters, vampires, and other strange creatures.

Monday's Trolls. Written by Jack Prelutsky. (Greenwillow, 1996).

Poems about witches, wizards, goblins, and giants.

The Senses of Animals: Poems. Written by Diane Ackermann. (Knopf, 2000).

Poems about the five senses.

FOR MORE INFORMATION

Articles

Raymond, Allen. "The Creative Magic of Peter Sis." *Teaching PreK–8* 27, no. 6 (March, 1997): 34–37.

Raymond, Allen. "Peter Sis: A Creative Journey." *Teaching PreK–8* 18, no. 7 (April 1988): 44–46.

Sis, Peter. "The Artist at Work." Based on an Interview with Anita Silvey on September 9, 1991. *Horn Book Magazine* 67, no. 6 (November/December 1992): 681–87.

Web Sites

Puma, Joseph and Brandon Ng. "On the Job with Peter Sis." *Zuzu Organization.* URL: <http://www.zuzu.org/sisinterview.html> (Accessed February 2000).

David Small

◆ Humor

Detroit, Michigan
February 12, 1945

📖 *The Gardener*
📖 *Imogene's Antlers*

ABOUT THE
AUTHOR/ILLUSTRATOR

David Small was born on a cold and blustery day in Detroit, Michigan, on February 12, 1945. He grew up in the industrial city, and when he speaks of his childhood, he says that he was following a "firm, invisible thread through the forest." That thread was his art. The thread eventually led him to a "bright, wide, and verdant place." He says he always dreamed of being an artist, but it wasn't until the middle 1970s, when he was in his thirties and had several books published, that he felt he could say, "I am an artist."

In a search for an exotic location to study art, Small applied to the University of Mexico and actually had his plane tickets and a letter of acceptance in hand. The night before he was to depart was also the night the 1967 riots began in Detroit. The riots sparked Small's loyalty to his hometown. Even though it was a turbulent city, he suddenly had a great sense of Detroit being his home. So he stayed to complete his study of art and English at Wayne State University. Looking back, he says Wayne State had the best program in which he has ever taken part—either as a student or teacher. It was a professor at Wayne State, Stanley Rosenthal, who exposed Small to the great engravers, such as Piranesi, and the work of "those dark Germans." Rosenthal was Small's greatest influence at Wayne State. When Small graduated from Wayne State in 1969, Rosenthal encouraged Small to continue his studies at Yale, where Small earned a masters of fine art. For a time, Small taught at the State University of New York and Fredonia College. By 1978, Small was back in Michigan, teaching printmaking, painting, and drawing at Kalamazoo College. He taught there for six years and was anticipating a promising academic career when, on the evening before his tenure recommendation was to go before the University hierarchy, he was informed that his position was going to be eliminated. So, not only did Small not receive tenure, he had no job—and no health insurance and, because he was living in university housing, no home.

Small realized he would need to find other work, and the logical move was to literally go back to the drawing board. He had already written *Eulalie and the Hopping Head* (Macmillan, 1982), a book that had seen a small print run. The children's book industry did not seem to be too lucrative, but Small realized that he had to eat, so he embarked on the creation of a few children's books. He also cultivated clients in the commercial area, gaining clients that included: *Newsweek*, *The New York Times*, Young and Rubicon, Leo Burnett, and Crain Communications. He also taught two summers at the University of Michigan.

His first commercial success was *Imogene's Antlers* (Crown, 1985), which is still popular today. Imogene awakens one day to find that she has grown antlers. No one has the answer for how she can get rid of them. When she appears antler-free on a subsequent morning, her family and readers alike will be humorously surprised. After a spurt of creation, Small now consciously produces only one book a year. That pace allows him to think about all levels of a book in more detail. The layers allow adults and young readers alike to enjoy a book.

Small's books are filled with humorous threads. The always-clever texts are complemented by Small's invigorating watercolors. *Ruby Mae Has Something to Say* (Crown, 1992) introduces readers to Miss Ruby Mae Foote who, according to her neighbors, is a goofball. Aliens come to visit Moe and Shirley in *Company's Coming* (Crown, 1988). Their visit makes for a chaotic time.

One of Small's most prestigious honors came in 1998 when his illustrations for *The Gardener* by Sarah Stewart (Farrar, 1997) earned him a Caldecott Honor Book award. Sarah Stewart, who is married to Small, wrote the text about Lydia Grace Finch, a young farm girl who comes to the city to live with her uncle Jim. Uncle Jim is a hard-working baker during the Depression. When Lydia Grace comes to the city, she arrives at the train station, which Small modeled after an old photo of Penn Station. Lydia Grace looks small and unimposing as she stands at the edge of the station. After he had finished the drawing for *The Gardener*, Small realized that he had patterned the Uncle Jim character after his inspiration and mentor Stanley Rosenthal. Sarah Stewart and David Small had collaborated on two earlier books: *The Library* (Farrar, 1995) and *The Money Tree* (Farrar, 1991).

David Small and Sarah Stewart live in a large Victorian mansion set among Amish homes on a bend of the Saint Joseph River in Mendon, Michigan. It is an 1835 Georgian home that was the site of the signing of the first treaty between the United States and Native Americans in Michigan. The walls of the home are painted a warm ochre. Small's studio is in the former parlor. The room, once filled with horsehair-stuffed furniture, is now filled with Small's worktable, a chair, his desk, a stereo, and speakers. A wall of reference shelves hold a few publications he often turns to for ideas: a few art books, some of Walt Kelly's Pogo collection, and several references to dog breeds and architectural styles.

On the walls of Small's studio are pinned the pages of whatever work is currently in progress. He places sketches in various stages of completion, and when the project is completed, new sketches take their place.

While Small and Stewart decided that they would try to maintain their more than 150-year-old home in a traditional manner, they also acknowledged that times change. Although it was important to restore it to its state in 1835, they wanted to add unobtrusively modern conveniences and put "their own mark on the house."

Small began to paint some leaves and vines over a window, a group of dancing insects by a fireplace, and along one wall, he put a series of three cupboard doors. On a shelf in one cupboard is a tiny replica of the house, which shows yet another smaller house inside, and another inside, to infinity.

Small definitely has made his mark on his family home, and with more than two dozen books in publication, and several awards and honors, he has succeeded in making his mark on the world of children's literature.

BOOKS AND NOTES

David Small illustrates books that he authors, as well as books that others have authored. His interpretation of the text always adds layers to the story text and provides humor for both the young reader and for the adult who might be sharing the book with the child. He also has illustrated books for older readers. Two are by Norton Juster and are about similes: *As Silly As Knees, As Busy As Bees: An Astounding Assortment of Similes* (Beech Tree, 1998) and *As: A Surfeit of Similes* (Morrow, 1989). Others are books on politics, one by Milton Meltzer, *American Politics: How It Really*

Works (Morrow, 1989) and another, *So You Want to Be President*, by Judith St. George (Philomel, 2000). St. George's book presents an assortment of facts about the qualifications and characteristics of U.S. presidents from George Washington to Bill Clinton. Small has also illustrated a retelling of Carl Sandburg's tale about the Huckabuck family, which he first told in his *Rootabaga Stories* in 1923, published by Harcourt.

Books Written and Illustrated by David Small

Fenwick's Suit (Farrar, 1996).
Fenwick's new suit comes to life and takes over everything.

George Washington's Cows (Farrar, 1994).
Rhymes about Washington that have cows wearing dresses, pigs wearing wigs, and sheep that are scholars.

Hoover's Bride (Crown, 1995).
Until he marries a vacuum cleaner, Hoover's house is overrun with dust. But he soon discovers that human and appliances are not meant to be married.

Imogene's Antlers (Crown, 1985).
When Imogene wakes up with antlers growing out of her head, she finds that she is a sensation wherever she goes.

Paper John (Farrar, 1987).
Living in a paper house, this man makes paper boats for the village children and then manages to use his paper-folding skills to rescue himself from a situation with a devil.

Ruby Mae Has Something to Say (Crown, 1992).
Ruby Mae realizes her dream of speaking before the United Nations for world peace, when her nephew Billy Bob invents a device to help alleviate her speech problem.

Books Illustrated by David Small

The Christmas Crocodile. Written by Bonny Becker. (Simon & Schuster, 1998).
The Christmas celebrations of Alice Jayne and her family are thoroughly disrupted when a very hungry crocodile is delivered to the wrong address.

Company's Coming. Written by Arthur Yorinks. (Crown, 1988).
Aliens accompany Moe and Shirley to dinner with the relatives.

Fighting Words. Written by Eve Merriam. (Morrow, 1992).
Words such as lummox, kinkajou, and balderdash substitute for some harsher words that some might have expected two friends to use in a "fight."

The Gardener. Written by Sarah Stewart. (Farrar, 1997).
Written in the form of letters, this story is set in the Depression and is Lydia Grace's story of going to live with Uncle Jim when her own father loses his job. Lydia Grace takes along her love of gardening.

The Huckabuck Family and How They Raised Popcorn in Nebraska and Quit and Came Back. Written by Carl Sandburg. (Farrar, 1999).
A story of a family whose popcorn pops out of control, but they manage to make the best of it.

The Library. Written by Sarah Stewart. (Farrar, 1995).
Elizabeth Brown loves books, and when her book collection grows and grows, she knows she must make a change.

The Money Tree. Written by Sarah Stewart. (Farrar, 1991).
A strange tree yields green "leaves" during the summer; and while all of her neighbors flock to gather the leaves, Mrs. McGillicuddy goes about her work. In the winter she uses the tree for firewood.

Petey's Bedtime Story. Written by Beverly Cleary. (Morrow, 1993).

The story of the day Petey was born gets an imaginative twist when Petey comes up with his own version.

FOR MORE INFORMATION

Web Sites

Urban, Linda. *Wayne State University Web Site.* "David Small: The Illustrating Man." URL: <http://www.alumni.wayne.edu/magazine/fall98.htm> (Accessed March 2000).

Peter Spier

Amsterdam, The Netherlands
June 6, 1927

📖 *The Fox Went Out on a Chilly Night*

📖 *Noah's Ark*

📖 *We the People: The Constitution of the United States of America*

ABOUT THE AUTHOR/ILLUSTRATOR

Sharron L. McElmeel

Peter Spier began to draw early in his childhood. His father, a journalist and illustrator who worked at home, influenced his efforts. Spier was born on June 6, 1927, in Amsterdam, the eldest child of Joseph E. A. "Jo" Spier and Albertine van Raalte Spier. The family spent holidays and summers in Broek-in-Waterland, a country village and the literary home place of Hans Brinker. Spier and his brother and sister attended school in Amsterdam, and to get there, they had to travel by train, boat, the city tram, and finally on foot. On weekends, the family enjoyed sailing. After World War II, during Spier's teen years, the family moved permanently to Broek-in-Waterland. The village was the center for almost 2,000 farmers and ten times as many cows.

When Peter Spier was eighteen, he decided to make art his career. He entered Rijksacademie, an art school in Amsterdam, in 1945 and attended until 1947. During those years he made study trips to Italy and France. In 1947, he was drafted into the Royal Netherlands Navy and served until 1951. With the navy, he traveled to the West Indies and South America. He has said that he liked many things about being in the service—the discipline, the ships, the water, and the people. He loved to travel as well. But he never abandoned his desire to work in publishing, and after his stint in the navy, Spier went to work for *Elsevier's Weekly*, the largest Dutch weekly newspaper. He was based in Paris for a time and then assigned to Houston, Texas.

The Houston assignment came in 1951, after Spier and his father visited the United States. They both liked what they saw and decided to try to settle there permanently. *Elsevier's Weekly* had a branch office in Houston, so Spier was able to transfer there. Spier's mother and two younger siblings joined Peter and Joseph Spier in Houston. After a year in Houston, Spier moved to New York City and began to illustrate children's books. He took his portfolio to Doubleday, and when the editor asked if he could draw goats, he was able to produce one from his portfolio. He got the assignment and produced the illustrations for *Thunder Hill* by Elizabeth Nicholds (Doubleday, 1953). In the next decades, he illustrated more than 150 books written by other authors and created more than fourteen of his own as both author and illustrator.

On July 12, 1958, Spier married Kathryn M. Pallister, and the couple set up residence in Port Washington, Long Island. By the early 1960s, Spier's interest in writing and illustrating his books had blossomed. His first effort, *The Fox Went Out on a Chilly Night* (Doubleday, 1961), earned a Caldecott Honor Book award for 1962. That book was set in New England and is one of many that show Spier's love for American history and lore. He also shows his love for his homeland when he situates a story in The Netherlands. A book he illustrated, *The Cow Who Fell in the Canal* (Doubleday, 1957), written by Phyllis Krasilovsky, is filled with the humor and bustle of the Dutch countryside. Spier has also illustrated an edition of *Hans Brinker* by Mary Mapes Dodge (Doubleday, 1958). Interestingly enough, this book is not really known in The Netherlands, where it is supposedly set, but is a classic in the United States.

Between 1967 and 1969, Spier released four books in his Mother Goose Library. *London Bridge Is Falling Down!* (Doubleday, 1967) shows the building and rebuilding of the bridge and the hustle and bustle of the city. Readers are able to visit landmarks in London, and each detail is authentic—right down to the shingles over the storefronts. That is, all but one shingle. One of them, "M. Pallister, Maker of Scientific Instruments," honors Spier's father-in-law, M. Pallister. At the end of the book, Spier provides the music for the rhyme and the complete history of the bridge. Spier went to London to gather images for the illustrations. Later, he went to Delaware, Maryland, and Pennsylvania to collect the hundreds of details that went into *To Market! To Market!* (Doubleday, 1967). *Hurrah, We're Outward Bound!* (Doubleday, 1968) tells the story of a voyage between New York and Dartmouth, England, whereas *And So My Garden Grows* (Doubleday, 1969) is set in Italy. It begins in a resort town northeast of Florence.

By 1970, Spier had turned to Americana and produced *The Erie Canal* (Doubleday, 1970) and *The Star-Spangled Banner* (Doubleday, 1975). With *The Erie Canal* he wanted to record the historical details of the canal and to show the changes brought with each season, along with an essence of life on the canal. His book succeeded in providing a factual historical perspective of the construction and operation of the canal.

As the United States bicentennial approached (1976), Spier decided it was a timely opportunity to produce *The Star-Spangled Banner*. It became an oversized book with a blast of reds and blues and included a history of the naval battle that inspired the national anthem. Notes at the end of the book include the music for the song and documents relating to the battle. The end papers detail the historic development of the American flag.

Spier's next body of work involved producing concept books. His first concept books were *Gobble, Growl, Grunt* (Doubleday, 1971) and *Crash! Bang! Boom!* (Doubleday, 1972). The first book was about the noises animals make, and the second was about sounds from human and domestic activities. A third title, *Fast-Slow, High-Low: A Book of Opposites* (Doubleday, 1972), deals with concepts such as long and short, under and over.

Sometimes Spier's research reveals illustrations he should not use. While preparing for a book about the Erie Canal, Spier went to the area and found a stately old gingerbread house standing beside the canal lock. He found out the house was once the Canal Hotel. Later, after all his preliminary sketches had been completed, he found out the hotel had really been a house known for its bawdy occupants. Spier decided that would not be an appropriate image in a children's book. Another time, he had drawn an image of a Japanese couple in traditional kimonos and elevated sandals. The woman was wearing an obi, holding a dainty parasol, with an infant on her back. The book was *We the People* (Doubleday, 1987). The final cover art was finished and was being shown at a the Bologna Children's Book Fair in 1979 with the idea of getting some international publishing contracts. As the festival progressed, Spier became aware that something was amiss regarding the illustration. He subsequently was told that the Japanese woman he had shown with a baby was wearing a wedding kimono. Spier airbrushed the baby out of the cover illustration. The cover now has a small open space in the illustration; the space where the baby once was. Another incident concerning the same book occurred when some Arab visitors from Tripoli and Damascus came by. They searched the book for depictions of Arabs. Each illustration met with their approval. Then the pair came to the forty-five styles of writing from around the globe. After several minutes of studying the writing, the two explained to Spier that the five types of Arabic script that he had copied from a well-respected European encyclopedia were all upside down. Spier's dedication to accuracy and details warrant even last minute changes if new information is uncovered. He lost no time in making the corrections.

Each time Spier moves in a new direction, the results are outstanding. In the early 1980s, he produced several board books that, when standing on end, turn into small buildings that create an entire neighborhood. The Village Books, as the series was called, were primarily concept books for preschoolers.

One of Spier's most notable titles is surely *Noah's Ark* (Doubleday, 1977), which won the 1978 Caldecott Medal. When Spier thought about doing an illustrated version of the seventeenth-century Dutch poem by Joacobus Revius, he went to the public library and found dozens of titles already focusing on Noah's ark. He knew the idea was not new, but as he looked at the competition, he realized that all the versions depicted the journey as if it were a Caribbean cruise. He decided there was room for one more book, one that would attempt to show the devastation caused by the flood, the mess the animals made inside the ark, and other more realistic details that were associated with the ark's voyage.

During his childhood, Peter Spier's father had developed a collection of Caldecott Medal books—many of them first editions. When Peter was three, he used a red crayon to color on all the pages of one of the books in his father's collection. Nonetheless, when Spier was notified that he had won the Caldecott Medal, one of the first people to congratulate him was his father, Joseph. With Joseph's congratulatory comments came the gift of his Caldecott collection, which Peter now owns.

Peter Spier and his wife Kathryn live in Shoreham, New York. Spier has his studio in the lower level of his home. He is a full-time writer and illustrator. In his spare time, he enjoys sailing and building model ships. His models are built to scale—one quarter inch to the foot—which makes them from one to three feet long. Many of his models are of Dutch seagoing vessels;

others are British cruisers. Because the family enjoys sailing, the Spiers at times have owned their own boat. Other times, they charter a boat to sail around the Chesapeake Bay and Long Island Sound. The Spiers have raised a son, Thomas Pallister, and a daughter, Kathryn Elizabeth.

BOOKS AND NOTES

Peter Spier creates the illustrations for his children's books with pen and ink and watercolor. He began *The Fox Went Out on a Chilly Night* with pencil sketches and then translated them into pen-and-ink drawings. The final step was the watercolor process. He uses only blue, red, and yellow watercolors on non-photo blues of the black key—so that there is no black halftone in the books at all. This technique gives an impression of crispness.

To accurately depict a location for his books, he travels to the setting and sketches the details, recording images he will use in the illustrations. Sometimes images are viewed differently in other cultures. Spier's titles are published in the United States, as well as in several other countries. A middle-class house in the United States might be one in which only the very wealthy would live in another country. Thus, a scene depicting a homeowner painting his or her house might be interpreted as realistic or as a scene that would never happen, depending on who is reading the book. In one book Spier, portrayed a frog in a pet store. A French publisher felt the frog should have been in a food market rather than a pet store!

In an effort to make a scholarly presentation, Spier often includes diagrams, further information, and author notes as part of the book.

Books Written and Illustrated by Peter Spier

Crash! Bang! Boom! (Doubleday, 1972).

Fast-Slow, High-Low: A Book of Opposites (Doubleday, 1972).

Gobble, Growl, Grunt (Doubleday, 1972).

The Fox Went Out on a Chilly Night (Doubleday, 1961).

Noah's Ark. Includes Peter Spier's translation of "The Flood" by Joacobus Revius. (Doubleday, 1977).

Peter Spier's Christmas (Doubleday, 1983).

Tin Lizzie (Doubleday, 1975).

We the People: The Constitution of the United States of America (Doubleday, 1987).

Mother Goose Library

Hurrah, We're Outward Bound! (Doubleday, 1968).

To Market! To Market! (Doubleday, 1967).

London Bridge Is Falling Down (Doubleday, 1967).

And So My Garden Grows (Doubleday, 1969).

Village Books

Bill's Service Station (Doubleday, 1981).

Fire House, Hook and Ladder Company Number Twenty-Four (Doubleday, 1981).

The Food Market (Doubleday, 1981).

My School (Doubleday, 1981).

The Pet Store (Doubleday, 1981).

The Toy Shop (Doubleday, 1981).

FOR MORE INFORMATION

Articles

Chenery, Janet D. "Peter Spier." *Horn Book Magazine* 65, no. 4 (August 1978): 379–81.

"The Frog Belongs in the Food Market and Other Perils of an Illustrator." *Publishers Weekly* 218 (July 25, 1980): 93–94.

Spier, Peter. "Caldecott Award Acceptance." *Horn Book Magazine* 65, no. 4 (August 1978): 372–78.

Diane Stanley

◆ Humor ◆ Biography

Sharron L. McElmeel

Abilene, Texas
December 27, 1943

📖 *Bard of Avon: The Story of William Shakespeare*

📖 *The Month-Brothers: A Slavic Tale*

📖 *Shaka: King of the Zulus*

ABOUT THE AUTHOR/ILLUSTRATOR

It was reading to her two young daughters that interested Diane Stanley in becoming involved in children's books. She was living in Maryland in 1976, and a friend asked her, "What would you do if you could do it for a year?" Stanley's response was "I would want to be a children's book illustrator." Later that year, she put together a portfolio of work and took it to Boston, where she was able to meet with John Keller, then editor-in-chief of Little, Brown & Company. That meeting resulted in the publication of *The Farmer in the Dell* (Little, Brown, 1977). That book was published under her married name at the time, Diane Zuromskis. Three more books with Stanley's illustrations came in 1979, including Verna Aardema's *Half-a-Ball-of-Kenki: An Ashanti Tale* (Warne, 1979).

Diane Stanley was born two days after Christmas in 1943 in Abilene, Texas, where she spent much of her childhood and adolescence among her mother's family, the Grissoms of Abilene. Soon after Stanley's birth, her parents divorced, and her mother moved periodically from coast to coast. Consequently, Stanley also became familiar with New York City and La Jolla, California. Her mother suffered through two lengthy illnesses, and during those times, Stanley and her brother lived with her aunt's family in Abilene. Stanley's Grandmother Pearl was a stabilizing influence in her life. She was a storyteller and an adventurer.

In Abilene, Stanley attended high school and graduated in 1961. By 1965, she had earned an undergraduate degree in social studies from Trinity University in San Antonio. During her senior year at Trinity, Stanley excelled in two drawing classes. She seemed to have a natural ability. With the encouragement of one of her art professors, she turned her efforts toward a career in medical illustration. She continued with a year of postgraduate study at the University of Texas and a second year studying art at the Edinburgh College of Art in Edinburgh, Scotland. Those two years provided her with the background that earned her admittance to graduate school, and in 1970, she graduated from the Johns Hopkins University School of Medicine with a master's degree in medical and biological illustration.

Diane Stanley married a graduating medical student. Eventually, the Zuromskis family welcomed two daughters, Catherine and Tamara. While her daughters were young, Stanley did medical illustration on a freelance basis. But once she was introduced to the world of children's literature, she knew she had found her life's work. It was not that Stanley disliked medical illustration; rather, children's book illustrating was simply so inviting. In her customary style, she set out to learn as much as she could about illustrating children's books. She studied book illustration and production. Her first attempt at illustrating resulted in a series of woodcuts to illustrate nursery rhymes. She sent the illustrations to Little, Brown in Boston. The editor was not interested in publishing that book but invited her to stop by if she was ever in Boston. That was her cue to make a point of being in Boston.

By 1978, she had published her first book. That was also the year her marriage ended. Stanley moved with her two daughters to New York City, where she worked as a designer for Dell and later become an art director at G. P. Putnam's Sons. Once in New York, Stanley approached an editor at Frederick Warne, who offered her a text by Verna Aardema, an African tale, to illustrate. Her editor subsequently moved from Warne, to Macmillan, to Four Winds Press, and most recently to William Morrow. Stanley followed her editor to each of the publishers, and twenty years later, William Morrow is publishing her books, although she has illustrated books by other authors for other publishers.

Shortly after moving to New York City, Stanley met an old friend, Peter Vennema. They married, and the couple moved to Houston, Texas, where they still live today. Their son, John, was born in 1981. Meanwhile, Stanley continued illustrating books.

Stanley's studio is on the second floor the family's Houston home. It is there that she has written about Sweetness, one of the several orphans that populates two of her light stories about a good-hearted but bumbling sheriff who takes them in. She has created the images that portray Rumpelstiltskin's daughter, Joan of Arc, Shaka, and a host of other subjects from her drawing table. Her husband often helps with the research for the subjects of her biographies and thus gets co-author or contributor credit on those books. After writing and illustrating several biographies, Stanley illustrated a biography that was very important to her. Stanley's mother, Fay Stanley, wrote the biography about Princess Ka'lulani, the princess of Hawaii before the United States annexed the string of islands. With the help of Diane Stanley's illustrations, the biography documented the princess's life, as well as her efforts to keep her kingdom free. Diane Stanley and her mother were able to see the proofs together, but her mother died shortly before the book was actually published.

When Stanley writes the text for her biographies she does not back away from the flaws of the character but does attempt to project a character that readers will care about. When Stanley wrote *Shaka: King of the Zulus* (Morrow, 1988) she presented many facts about the warrior but intentionally left out the more gruesome details—even though, she says, "it was obvious that he was capable of doing those things."

When her publishers wanted something set in Texas, Stanley drew on melodrama and wrote *Saving Sweetness* (Putnam, 1996), which was illustrated by G. Brian Karas.

The next year, Stanley wrote and illustrated a humorous twist on the Rumpelstiltskin story when she penned *Rumpelstiltskin's Daughter* (Morrow, 1997). The king, depicted as a bug-eyed, pointy-nosed man with bad teeth and curly locks down to his shoulders, wanted to take Rumpelstiltskin's daughter for a wife. Instead, she showed him how to spread the wealth, instead of hoarding it, and gain his subjects' loyalty in the process. In response to his plea to marry him, she declines but becomes the kingdom's prime minister instead.

When her biographical subjects come from another culture or setting, Stanley often takes a trip to gather the appropriate images and background details she needs to augment the thorough library research she and Vennema do. For example, the French gold-leaf design found on the back cover of her Joan of Ark biography is an authentic design she got from the French heroine's coat of arms, which she photographed during a trip to France.

When she was completing research for the Charles Dickens biography, she traveled to London to find the pamphlets in which he published his stories as serials. She did not know what those pamphlets would look like but did know that they existed. She found some of the publications in London. They had pale green covers and included several images which she was able to use to help her create the illustrations for the biography.

Diane Stanley, Peter Vennema, and their son John live in Houston, Texas. Diane's two daughters, Catherine and Tamara, live on the coasts; one in New York City, the other in San Francisco.

BOOKS AND NOTES

For a number of years, Stanley produced as many as three books a year. She wrote both whimsical stories and more complex biographies that demanded meticulous research to authenticate the facts and information about the setting and people. Her husband, Peter Vennema, regularly assists with the research for her biographies, her current forte.

Stanley most often creates her illustrations using gouache, an opaque watercolor. Sometimes other artists illustrate the more humorous tales that she writes.

Books Written and Illustrated by Diane Stanley

Bard of Avon: The Story of William Shakespeare. Written with Peter Vennema. (Morrow, 1992).
A biography of William Shakespeare (1564–1616).

Charles Dickens: The Man Who Had Great Expectations. Written with Peter Vennema. (Morrow, 1993).
A biography of Charles Dickens (1812–1870).

Cleopatra. Written with Peter Vennema. (Morrow, 1994).
A biography of Cleopatra, Queen of Egypt (d. 30 BC).

Fortune (Morrow, 1990).
A poor man in Persia follows the advice of his betrothed and goes to the city to seek his fortune.

Good Queen Bess: The Story of Elizabeth I of England. Written with Peter Vennema. (Four Winds, 1990).
A biography of Elizabeth I, Queen of England (1533–1603).

Joan of Arc (Morrow, 1998).
A biography of Saint Joan of Arc (1412–1431).

Leonardo da Vinci (Morrow, 1996).
A biography of Leonardo da Vinci (1452–1519).

Peter the Great (Four Winds, 1986; Morrow, 1999).
A biography of Peter I, Emperor of Russia (1672–1725).

Petrosinella: A Neapolitan Rapunzel (Dial, 1995).
The heroine breaks the enchantment put on her by the ogress.

Rumpelstiltskin's Daughter (Morrow, 1997).
She is more than a match for the king who wants to marry her. She becomes the prime minister instead.

Shaka: King of the Zulus. Written with Peter Vennema. (Morrow, 1988).
Chief Zulu Chaka (1787?–1828).

Books Illustrated by Diane Stanley

The Last Princess: The Story of Princess Ka'iulani of Hawai'i. Written by Fay Stanley. (Four Winds, 1991; Aladdin, 1994).
Ka'iulani, Princess of Hawaii, 1875–1899.

The Month-Brothers: A Slavic Tale. Retold by Samuel Marshak. Translated from the Russian. Written by Thomas P. Whitney. (Morrow, 1983).
A young girl outwits her greedy stepmother and stepsisters with the help of the month brothers.

Books Written by Diane Stanley

The Gentleman and the Kitchen Maid. Illustrated by Dennis Nolan. (Dial, 1994).
Two paintings in a museum fall in love, and a resourceful art student finds a way to unite the lovers.

Saving Sweetness. Illustrated by G. Brian Karas. (Putnam, 1996).
The sheriff takes in a group of orphans to save them from nasty old Mrs. Sump and her terrible orphanage.

Woe Is Moe. Illustrated by Elise Primavera. (Putnam, 1995).
Moe's new advertising job at the ice cream factory brings him everything but happiness.

FOR MORE INFORMATION

Web Sites

Children's Book Council: Meet the Author/Illustrator. "Meet the Author/Illustrator. Diane Stanley." URL: <http://www.cbcbooks.org/navigation/autindex.htm> (Accessed March 2000). Go to "The Archives," then to "Diane Stanley."

Houston Public Library Web Site: National Children's Book Week. "NCBW@HPL!—Diane Stanley." URL: <http://www.hpl.lib.tx.us/youth/ncbw_dstanley.html> (Accessed March 2000).

National Center of Children's Illustrated Literature. "Diane Stanley: Journeys." URL: <http://www.nccil.org/exhibit/stanley.html> (Accessed March 2000).

John Steptoe

◆ Folklore ◆ Family Relationships

Brooklyn, New York
September 14, 1950–August 28, 1989

📖 *Mufaro's Beautiful Daughters: An African Tale*

📖 *Stevie*

📖 *The Story of Jumping Mouse: A Native American Legend*

ABOUT THE AUTHOR/ILLUSTRATOR

On July 24, 1989, John Lewis Steptoe wrote "I am proud to be one of the artists who will create the first and new lexicon of African images for children now in America. John Steptoe." Just one month and four days later, on August 28, 1989, John Steptoe died of AIDS. He left behind his son, Javaka, his daughter Bweela, and a legacy of African images in books for all the children in America.

John Lewis Steptoe was born at St. John's Hospital on September 14, 1950, in the Bedford-Stuyvesant section of Brooklyn, New York. He was one of three children of Elesteen Steptoe and John Oliver Steptoe. He had a brother, Charles, and a sister, Marica. From a young age, John Steptoe drew and showed a natural artistic ability. He considered himself an introvert, not one to play popular sports with his contemporaries or to find much comfort in friendships. He attended the High School of Art and Design in Manhattan. While in high school he was able to study with the painter Norman

Lewis. During this time, he also worked in HARYOU-ACT, an antipoverty program in Harlem.

Just three months before graduation, at the age of sixteen, he left school, and according to John Steptoe, he "learned to hitchhike." He felt he didn't fit in. He ended up in Camden, New Jersey, where he lived for a few months. Soon, however, he was back in New York looking for work. Steptoe first took his portfolio of artwork to Madison Avenue, hoping to interest the editors of *Harper's* magazine. When there was little interest, he decided that some of his illustrations would work in children's books. It was then that he connected with the Harper & Row's editors. He said, "I simply presented my work to an editor at Harper & Row. This was illustrations done in high school. Ursula Nordstrom, editor-in-chief, suggested I do a book."

John Steptoe was sixteen when he began to write that first book. The manuscript was to become *Stevie* (Harper, 1969). Steptoe said, "Stevie is largely autobiographical. My mother took care of friends' children, women with jobs outside the home." Steptoe's father was a transit worker, and Steptoe said the story was based on feelings he had about the children his mother cared for. He was just nineteen when the book was published.

The book was heralded as an immediate success. It was one of the first books to address a universal theme through the language and setting of an urban African American child. The narration was written in dialogue that African American children spoke. It was an insider's view of life in the city. *Stevie* centered on a child's experiences with peer jealousy. The thick, soft edges in black and deep browns frame brilliant colors. The loosely applied pastels give the illustrations a grainy texture. Critics have compared the illustrative work to that of George Rouault, finding similarity in the harsh but brilliant tones.

In the next two decades, John Steptoe created or illustrated more than a dozen books. In 1985, he won a Caldecott Honor Book award for his illustrations in *The Story of Jumping Mouse: A Native American Legend* (Lothrop, 1984) and for *Mufaro's Beautiful Daughters: An African Tale* (Lothrop, 1987). He became noted for his strong African American images and for the honesty and strength of his writing.

John Steptoe's career was off to a very successful start. He was just twenty years old when he was honored with the dedication of the John Steptoe Library in Brooklyn, New York. He had met Stephanie Douglas. His daughter, Bweela, was born, and his second book, *Uptown* (Harper, 1970), was published. *Uptown* is the story of John and Dennis, who walk through Harlem. They pass dead-end people on the street, junkies, cops, brothers, karate experts, and hippies. With each passing, the boys wonder what it would be like to be one of them. They decide they don't want to be a policeman ("cop") because they would not have any friends. And they discuss the way the army changes a man. In the end, they decide not to decide and "just hang out together for a while and just dig on everythin' that's goin' on."

Javaka, Steptoe's son, was born in 1971, the year Steptoe's third book for Harper & Row was published. *Train Ride* (Harper, 1971) tells the exciting story of Charles and his friends who take a subway to Times Square. Both *Uptown* and *Train Ride* contain strong black speech patterns and powerful paintings. Steptoe is one of the few artists and writers who have been able to portray life in a black community from an insider's point of view. His narration, illustrations, and the settings are characteristically African American. His stories would have to be changed considerably if the characters were of another cultural or ethnic heritage. While *Stevie* was heralded as universal in theme, *Uptown* and *Train Ride* moved away from a comfortable and safe universal theme. They more closely represented the specific experience of an African American child growing up in Harlem. Critics were slower to accept these two books.

In the late 1970s, Steptoe fled the hubbub of the city to reside in Peterboro, New Hampshire, where he lived in near seclusion. Steptoe had become noted for his character sketches of life in urban ghettos, strong forceful illustrations, and brilliant images. The work Steptoe continued to produce retained that focus. Steptoe did write some young adult titles, although the majority of his work was with picture books. His own life contributed much to his books. *My Special Best Words* (Viking, 1974) reflected the relationship between his son and daughter. *Daddy Is a Monster . . . Sometimes* (Lippincott, 1980) focused on the parent-child relationship. He used his two children as the main characters, and the father is an illustrative self-portrait.

His intricately drawn black-and-white pencil sketches for *The Story of Jumping Mouse: A Native American Legend* were drawn from the mouse's perspective. They won him a Caldecott Honor Book award in 1986. In 1987, Steptoe returned to his vibrant African motifs with the illustrations for *Mufaro's Beautiful Daughters: An African Tale*. Steptoe traveled to Zimbabwe and studied the flora and fauna, as well as the architecture of the ruins of the area. The paintings inspired by his research earned him another Caldecott Honor.

At the time of John Steptoe's death in 1989, he was "refurbishing a brownstone in Bedford-Stuyvesant in Brooklyn, New York." That house on Monroe Street is the home where he had spent his first sixteen years. Javaka

Steptoe, the son of John Steptoe and Stephanie Douglas is now an art therapist; he was just eighteen years old when his father died, but already many people asked if he would follow in his father's footsteps. A few years after John Steptoe's death, Pat Cummings, a children's book author and illustrator, suggested to Javaka that he take his portfolio to an editor at Lee and Low Books. They liked his work and later gave him a call to ask if he was interested in doing a book on fathers. The result was a collection of thirteen poems about black fathers with illustrations by Javaka. The book, *In Daddy's Arms I Am Tall: African Americans Celebrating Fathers* (Lee & Low, 1997) begins with an Ashanti proverb: "When you follow in the path of your father, you learn to walk like him." And Javaka Steptoe, a full-time artist and art teacher says, "I was able ... to give something to him by honoring his memory."

BOOKS AND NOTES

John Steptoe's books were heralded as the first for young children to utilize the language, setting, and culture of an urban child to portray universal themes. His works featured black dialogue and positive depictions of the urban environment and urban living. His earlier illustrative work bordered on expressionistic art with heavy outlines and bright colors. His later work moved to more subtle paintings and African motifs, and seeming more closely aligned to art deco style and surrealism.

His work was generally considered optimistic in nature and often focused on universal themes. His illustrations were noted for their technical brilliance.

Books Written and Illustrated by John Steptoe

Daddy Is a Monster . . . Sometimes (Lippincott, 1980).

A father deals with his two young children and becomes a "monster" when he feels he has "monster children."

Mufaro's Beautiful Daughters: An African Tale (Lothrop, 1987).

An African tale with Cinderella motifs, inspired by a tale that G. M. Theal first told in 1895. The cold, spiteful Manyara determines that it is she who will be chosen as the king's wife rather than her considerate sister, Nyasha.

My Special Best Words (Viking, 1974).

A tale of the relationship between siblings.

Stevie (Harper, 1969).

Robert develops a feeling of rivalry when Stevie, a foster brother, stays at his house. When Stevie is no longer there, Robert realizes his loss.

The Story of Jumping Mouse: A Native American Legend (Lothrop, 1984).

A Native American tale of transformation. The smallest and humblest of creatures can dream of greatness and, if faithful to himself and the dream, can become the noblest of creatures.

Books Illustrated by John Steptoe

All the Colors of the Races: Poems. Written by Arnold Adoff. (Lothrop, 1982).

Poems celebrating the many different cultures.

All Us Come Cross the Water. Written by Lucille Clifton. (Holt, 1973).

A thought-provoking tale emphasizing that all black Americans "crossed the water." Vibrant full-color paintings stress the unity of black Americans.

OUTside INside Poems. Written by Arnold Adoff. (Lothrop, 1981).

A collection of tales by an eminent poet.

FOR MORE INFORMATION

Books

Berg, Julie. *John Steptoe* (ABDO, 1994).

Janet Stevens

© 1997 Geoffrey Wheeler, Black Star

Dallas, Texas
January 17, 1953

📖 *Cock-a-Doodle-Do!*
📖 *Tops & Bottom*

ABOUT THE AUTHOR/ILLUSTRATOR

Her parents called her "the artist." Janet Stevens always felt her older brother and sister were smarter than she was, but she discovered art and used her ability in art to carve out her own niche. She loved animals and often drew them in her pictures; she still does.

Janet Stevens was born on January 17, 1953, into a family of three children. Her father was a naval officer, which necessitated frequent moves. They lived in Italy, Hawaii, and many other exciting places. Stevens was always the "new kid." She began drawing early in her childhood; it helped her make friends. She drew pictures for her book reports, on math assignments, on anything she could find. Sometimes her teachers did not appreciate her drawings; they wanted more writing. Once when she was asked to produce a book report on *The Diary of Anne Frank*, she drew each character in the book in great detail. It was the pictures that helped her understand the book. Her teacher "did not appreciate my lack of words." Later she created posters, yearbook covers, and anything else for her school that needed artwork.

After high school graduation, Stevens entered the University of Colorado to study art. During the summers, she "worked in Hawaiian fabric design in Honolulu." Many of her art projects in school resulted in finished drawings, and when she graduated in 1975, she had piles of art. She had pictures of "bears in sneakers, rhinos in ties, and rhinos in Hawaiian shirts." She was told that her art belonged in children's books. Her job, however, was to design fabric. She also worked as an artist in advertising and as an architectural illustrator.

By the time she was twenty-four, Stevens had decided to pursue a career in children's book illustration. She sent her portfolio to publishing companies and did get an offer to illustrate Myra Cohn Livingston's collection of poems, *Callooh! Callay! Holiday Poems for Young Readers* (Atheneum, 1978). Other requests for her illustrations were not numerous, but she persisted. In 1978, she went to an illustrator's workshop and met Tomie dePaola. He told her she was a good illustrator and showed some of her work to a book editor. An editor at Holiday House contacted her and asked her to illustrate some books for them. She illustrated *Big Bunny and the Easter Eggs* by Steven Kroll (Holiday House, 1982), and they gave her the opportunity to retell Hans Christian Andersen's *The Princess and the Pea* (Holiday House, 1982). Stevens's version featured animal characters and gave the story a different perspective. Eventually, in addition to Kroll's books, publishers offered her contracts to illustrate books by Arnold Adoff, Eric A. Kimmel, Marjorie Sharmat, Sheila Turnage, Barbara Shook Hazen, and Polly M. Robertus. She also has adapted or illustrated tales by Hans Christian Andersen, Edward Lear, and Aesop.

Animals in clothes most often populate Stevens's illustrations. She uses the words of stories to provide a stage for her animal dramas, dramas in which the animals come alive and dance through tales made humorous by Stevens's zany illustrations. Her animals invade her house and don clothing from her family's clothes closet. In *Lucretia the UnBearable* by Marjorie Weinman Sharmat (Holiday House, 1981), Lucretia is wearing Stevens's own shoes. In *The Tortoise and the Hare* (Holiday House, 1981), the hare is wearing a tie that belongs to Stevens's husband, Ted. The tortoise is sitting at Stevens's dining table eating breakfast cereal and wearing Stevens's daughter Linze's pink bunny slippers, which she wore when she was little. The town mouse in *The Town Mouse and the Country Mouse* (Holiday House, 1987) is depicted wearing some of Stevens's jewelry. When Stevens illustrated *Goldilocks and the Three Bears* (Holiday House, 1986), she put them in her living room.

Not only does Stevens use the clothes that are around her, but the people as well. When she began to draw the illustrations for Steven Kroll's *Big Bunny and the Easter Eggs* (Holiday House, 1982), she was pregnant, so she used herself as the model for the bunny. Her nephew, Jason, was a model for the little boy waking up in *Animal Fair* (Holiday House, 1981). Later, she used her father and mother as the models for Noah and Mrs. Noah in her story *How the Manx Cat Lost Its Tail* (Harcourt, 1990). One of her husband's graduate students became a model for Androcles in *Androcles and the Lion* (Holiday House, 1989). *The Gates of the Wind* (Harcourt, 1995) featured Stevens's husband playing the part of the grandmother. Stevens's daughter, at the time a preteenager, was the model for the granddaughter in the story.

Sometimes Stevens has to create her models. When she illustrated Edward Lear's nonsense verse *The Quangle's Hat* (Harcourt, 1988), she actually made the Quangle Wangle's hat to see what it would look like.

She often includes things in her books that she loves to draw, such as wingtip shoes, funny clothes, and the furniture in her own home. She loves to draw rhinoceroses and often sneaks them into books where they are not supposed to be. When her editor doesn't want the rhinoceros in the picture, he red-pencils the illustrations and writes, "Get the rhinoceros out of here!" So she does.

Stevens also enjoys putting details in books, details that she likes but that might be missed by readers. For example, when she drew the illustrations for *Wally, the Worry-Warthog* by Barbara Shook Hazen (Clarion, 1990), she has Wally worrying about his encounters with Wilberforce Warthog. Wilberforce's shirt carries the number 7, which was also longtime Denver Bronco quarterback John Elway's jersey number. Football players worried about their encounters with Elway, just as Wally worried about his encounters with number 7, Wilberforce.

When she got the manuscript for Anne Miranda's *To Market, To Market!* (Harcourt, 1997), she knew the woman in the story must be a very special person. So she called her good friend Coleen Salley, a well-known storyteller and children's book expert from New Orleans. Coleen modeled for photographs, which later were the basis for illustrations that Stevens created.

At times, Stevens has scoured thrift shops to find just the right garments for her characters. She purchased some red high-heeled shoes and some purple high-heeled shoes, and it is the purple ones that Coleen wears in the book.

When Stevens was looking for a setting to place the illustrations for *To Market, To Market!* she thought it was time to explore her own "mythology" for a change so she looked to her neighborhood. She had illustrated folklore in many other cultures and now felt it was time to do her own. She asked permission to use her local grocery store, the Ideal Market, as the backdrop for her illustrations and then began to take black-and-white photographs of the interior and exterior of the market. She thought the photographs would become the models for her paintings. Instead, she decided to digitize the photographs and superimpose the colorfully clad characters as illustrations onto the photographs. The result was an unusual and interesting juxapositioning of black-and-white and full-color images. Stevens shows her eccentric shopper returning to the market again and again to buy a pig, cow, fish, chicken, and other animals. Eventually, the animals invade the shopper's home, and the woman ends up returning to the store to buy vegetables to make soup for all of her new friends. The model for the interior settings in the woman's home was Stevens's own kitchen and living room.

Once she finished *To Market, To Market!* she turned even closer to home and with her sister, Susan Stevens Crummel, created a book that features her real-life dog Violet Samantha Scarlett O'Hara and focuses on the arrival of "Violet" through the eyes of Merl, one of the family cats. *My Big Dog* (Golden Books, 1999) focuses on the relationship between the new Golden Retriever puppy and the family's grouchy old tabby cat Merlin.

Janet Stevens and her sister Susan collaborated on another title that built on the classic folktale about "The Little Red Hen." In this tale, *Cook-a-Doodle-Do*, Big Brown Rooster gets tired of eating chicken feed, so he goes in search of this great-granny's cookbook. Big Brown Rooster had thought that his great-granny had only baked bread, but from the cookbook, he learns that she had made many other things. He found a recipe for strawberry shortcake. In this version, Rooster finds that Dog, Cat, and Goose decline to help him, just as his great-granny had been rebuffed. Nonetheless, Rooster does find some helpers in Turtle, Iguana, and a Potbellied Pig, who would have rather eaten the ingredients than to have made the shortcake, but still they work together, and the result is a delicious strawberry shortcake. The recipe is included in the book.

Janet Stevens and her husband, Ted Habermann, and their two children, Linze (b. 1982) and Blake (b. 1986) live in Boulder, Colorado, with their dog, Violet, and three cats, Abo, Domino, and Merlin. Stevens is a full-time writer and illustrator. When she is not working on her books, she enjoys hiking, skiing, walking the dog, reading, painting for fun, and outdoor activities with her family.

BOOKS AND NOTES

When Janet Stevens illustrates works written by others she begins by trying to capture the vision of the author. When she writes the stories herself, she has the freedom to portray her own ideas.

She begins by making the sketches of the characters and then progresses to making a storyboard, which she describes as a "comic strip of the book." From there, she makes the dummy or rough draft of the book. From that point in time, she has to make decisions about the illustrative medium that she will use. Depending on the story and illustrations she envisions, she may choose to use homemade brown paper or experiment with watercolor, acrylic, colored pencil, collage, or a mixture of the media. Some of her more recent books have been created using a digital camera, computer-generated images, and collages using fabric and colored paper. During the illustrative process for *Tops & Bottoms*, she inverted a drawing so that the spine is at the top of the book. She likes to use a variety of media and varies how she illustrates the books because, "doing each book in the same way would be boring."

Books Written and Illustrated by Janet Stevens

Androcles and the Lion (Holiday House, 1989).

The Bremen Town Musicians (Holiday House, 1992).

Cook-a-Doodle-Do. Co-authored with Susan Stevens Crummel. (Harcourt, 1999).

Coyote Steals the Blanket (Holiday House, 1993).

Goldilocks and the Three Bears (Holiday House, 1986).

How the Manx Cat Lost Its Tail (Harcourt, 1990).

My Big Dog. Co-authored with Susan Stevens Crummel. (Golden Books, 1999).

Old Bag of Bones (Holiday House, 1996).

Shoe Town (Harcourt, 1999).

The Three Billy Goats Gruff (Harcourt, 1987).

Tops & Bottoms (Harcourt, 1995).

The Tortoise and the Hare (Holiday House, 1984).

The Town Mouse and the Country Mouse (Holiday House, 1987).

Books Illustrated by Janet Stevens

Anansi and the Moss-Covered Rock. Written by Eric A. Kimmel. (Holiday House, 1988).

Anansi and the Talking Melon. Written by Eric A. Kimmel. (Holiday House, 1994).

Anansi Goes Fishing. Written by Eric A. Kimmel. (Holiday House, 1992).

The Dog Who Had Kittens. Written by Polly M. Robertus. (Holiday House, 1991).

The Gates of the Wind. Written by Kathryn Lasky. (Harcourt, 1995).

It's Perfectly True. Based on a story by Hans Christian Andersen. (Holiday House, 1988).

Nanny Goat and the Seven Little Kids. Written by Eric A. Kimmel. (Holiday House, 1990).

The Owl and the Pussycat. Written by Edward Lear. (Holiday House, 1983).

To Market, To Market! Written by Anne Miranda. (Harcourt, 1997).

Wally, the Worry-Warthog. Written by Barbara Shook Hazen. (Clarion, 1990).

FOR MORE INFORMATION

Books

Stevens, Janet. *From Pictures to Words* (Holiday House, 1995).

Web Sites

Janet Stevens Web Site. "Janet Stevens Illustrator." URL: <http://www.janetstevens.com> (Accessed March 2000).

National Center for Children's Illustrated Literature. "Janet Stevens." URL: <http://www.nccil.org/exhibit/stevens.html> (Accessed March 2000).

The Scoop—NAME Biographical Sketch. "Artist/Author At a Glance." URL: <http://www.Friend.ly.net/scoop/biographies/stevensjanet/index.html> (Accessed March 2000).

James Stevenson

◆   Family Relationships   ◆   Humor

New York, New York
July 11, 1929

📖 *Don't You Know There's a War On?*
📖 *The Great Big Especially Beautiful Easter Egg*
📖 *Popcorn: Poems*

ABOUT THE
AUTHOR/ILLUSTRATOR

The years between World War I and World War II were the years of James Stevenson's childhood, years during which he attended an elementary school that encouraged its students to be actively involved in the nation's political and social events. He also observed his father's work as an architect and watercolorist during that time. His childhood provided many experiences that later would become the basis for books he would create as a prolific children's book author and illustrator.

James Stevenson was born in New York City on July 11, 1929, the son of Harvey and Winifred Stevenson. The family lived in several small towns in New York State in the Hudson River Valley during the 1930s. His attitudes and perceptions regarding the social and political issues of the day were formed early. At the age of seven, Stevenson wrote a letter to President Franklin Roosevelt and asked him to lift the arms embargo on Spain. Later, he created political cartoons about Chamberlain. The school promoted the arts, "bohemianism," and a feeling that everybody could do everything:

sing, dance, act, play a musical instrument, write stories, create artworks, and change the world. Some of those early memories are recorded in the several autobiographical picture books that he created. In these books he shares memories of watching his Aunt Kate pickle peaches and put up raspberry preserves and make rhubarb pies and file recipes, which she called "receipts." He remembers watching the iceman deliver fifty-pound blocks of ice, seeing the coal truck come, riding on shiny woven wicker seats on the train to New York City, and being afraid of snakes, tough kids, and the dark. One of the autobiographical stories deals with his relationship as a father to his daughter.

Stevenson went to many movies and read comic books by the dozen. Those hobbies influenced his art style, and in several of his books, he has used the format and frames similar to those found in comic books. His stories are often similar to storyboards, and the various perspectives shown in his books are inspired by the various camera angles used in movies to show scenes from different angles.

Two years after the end of World War II, in 1947, James Stevenson entered Yale University and majored in English. He began selling his cartoon ideas to *The New Yorker's* art department. He graduated from Yale in 1951 and entered the United States Marines as an officer. He continued selling his cartoon ideas during the two years he was in the marines. He also helped develop cartoon ideas for other artists. Once his military duty was over, Stevenson joined the staff of *Life* magazine as a reporter. Two years later, his freelance work with *The New Yorker* led to his joining the staff as a member of the art department, where he created cartoon ideas for other artists. Stevenson continued to work in the art department while focusing on reaching his goal of becoming a writer. In 1960, he began to report, in addition to illustrating, for *The New Yorker*. In the late 1960s, Stevenson moved from reporting on suburban issues to lampooning national problems. He wrote a satire focused on the United States military. It was titled *The ABCs of Your ABM: A Public Service Pamphlet from Your Defense Department*.

In addition to his regular day job, James Stevenson began writing fiction in his spare time during the early 1960s, but even his fiction was touched by satire. He had three novels and a book of cartoons published before entering the field of children's books.

His first picture book was *"Could Be Worse!"* Another of his early books, *If I Owned a Candy Factory* (Greenwillow, 1968, 1989), was a collaboration with his then-eight-year-old son, James Walker Stevenson. James Walker dictated the text, and James illustrated the book. They split the royalties. He also collaborated on a title with his daughter Edwina. That book, *"Help!" Yelled Maxwell*, was published by Greenwillow Books in 1978.

Stevenson went on to create many memorable characters. Mary Ann, Louie, their baby brother Willy, and their grandfather are stars of several of Stevenson's books. Emma, an apprentice witch, is another character that populates Stevenson's books. She actually came to him via the *New Yorker*. Susan Hirschman spotted Emma in one of Stevenson's cartoons for the *New Yorker*. She suggested he develop a story about Emma. The first book that came from that suggestion was *Yuck!* (Greenwillow, 1984), featuring Emma and her two cranky rivals, Dolores and Lavinia.

James Stevenson is a prolific author and illustrator. Most of his time is spent on children's books. He and his wife still live in Cos Cob, Connecticut, where they raised nine children. Among those children were Edwina and James Walker, who collaborated with their father on books as youngsters; Harvey, a resident of Paris who has written and illustrated a number of children's books, including some titles written by his father; and Suçie Stevenson, who is also a children's book illustrator. Among Suçie Stevenson's illustrated titles are the *Henry and Mudge* series by Cynthia Rylant. Suçie lives "by the seashore with her two dogs."

BOOKS AND NOTES

James Stevenson's illustrations carry a comic-strip-style format. Illustrations for his autobiographical stories were executed with what Stevenson refers to as "minimal" art. While his usual style features black-line illustrations with color washes, he deliberately departed from that style in these books. Indefinite dabs of color represent family surroundings and are meant to force readers to supply many of the details of the stories. His early books were stories with pictures; his later books were stories in pictures.

Books Written and Illustrated by James Stevenson

Books Featuring Mary Ann, Louie, Willy, and Their Grandfather

When the children have a problem, they go to their grandfather, who helps them confront the problem with elaborate stories of his own childhood and stories of his relationship with his brother Wainwright. In these books, Grandfather has a mustache; when he tells his stories of his childhood, he is depicted as a young boy, but he still sports the characteristic mustache.

"Could Be Worse!" (Greenwillow, 1977).

Grandpa's Great City Tour: An Alphabet Book (Greenwillow, 1983).

Grandpa's Too-Good Garden (Greenwillow, 1989).

The Great Big Especially Beautiful Easter Egg (Greenwillow, 1983).

No Friends (Greenwillow, 1986).

That Dreadful Day (Greenwillow, 1985).

That Terrible Halloween Night (Greenwillow, 1990).

There's Nothing to Do! (Greenwillow, 1986).

We Can't Sleep (Greenwillow, 1982).

We Hate Rain! (Greenwillow, 1988).

What's Under My Bed? (Greenwillow, 1983).

Will You Please Feed Our Cat? (Greenwillow, 1987).

Worse Than Willy (Greenwillow, 1984).

Books Featuring Emma and Her Adversaries, Dolores and Lavinia

Little Emma just wants to emulate the two most rapturously gruesome witches around, but her potions bring glee to Emma and her friends: Botsford the cat and Rowland the owl. The exaggerated humor, obvious characterization, and straightforward plot line make these books perfect choices for bringing chuckles. All the text occurs as dialogue within cartoon balloons.

Emma (Greenwillow, 1985).

Emma at the Beach (Greenwillow, 1990).

Fried Feathers for Thanksgiving (Greenwillow, 1986).

Happy Valentine's Day, Emma! (Greenwillow, 1987).

Un-happy New York, Emma! (Greenwillow, 1989).

Yuck! (Greenwillow, 1984).

Autobiographical Titles

Most of Stevenson's autobiographical titles are humorous tales of his childhood memories. *Don't You Know There's a War On?* weaves a tale of Stevenson's reminiscences with watercolor sketches. His war memories included his dad in the army, a brother in the navy, food rationing, tinfoil collecting, and enemy-plane spotting. The family ate Spam®, and watched newsreels of the Allied battles. Other biographical sketches included remembrances of lunch at the automat, weekly ice deliveries, and coal in the cellar for the furnace.

Don't You Know There's a War On? (Greenwillow, 1992).

Fun—No Fun (Greenwillow, 1994).

Higher on the Door (Greenwillow, 1987).

I Had a Lot of Wishes (Greenwillow, 1995).

I Meant to Tell You (Greenwillow, 1996).

When I Was Nine (Greenwillow, 1986).

Poetry

Popcorn: Poems (Greenwillow, 1998).

Sweet Corn: Poems (Greenwillow, 1995).

Mud Flat Series

A group of animals does everything from celebrating spring, to preparing for Christmas, to playing tricks on one another on April Fool's Day, and finally creating a mystery when their curiosity about what is inside a large box delivered to Duncan brings speculation.

Christmas at Mud Flat (Greenwillow, 2000).

Heat Wave at Mud Flat (Greenwillow, 1997).

Mud Flat April Fool (Greenwillow, 1998).

The Mud Flat Mystery (Greenwillow, 1997).

The Mud Flat Olympics (Greenwillow, 1994).

Mud Flat Spring (Greenwillow, 1999).

Yard Sale (Greenwillow, 1996).

Miscellaneous Titles Written and Illustrated by James Stevenson

Everything from the experiences of the Worst Person on Crab Beach to the oldest elf working for Santa Claus. Zany and whimsical illustrations create humorous perspectives on events representing universal themes.

All Aboard! (Greenwillow, 1995).

The Oldest Elf (Greenwillow, 1995).

Worse Than the Worst (Greenwillow, 1994).

The Worst Goes South (Greenwillow, 1995).

Books Illustrated by James Stevenson

James Stevenson has illustrated books of humor and poetry authored by other writers. His illustrations always complement the humor and fun in the book. Sometimes the illustrations are washes of watercolor without any defining lines to restrict the form of the image.

Hooper Humperdick. . . ? Not Him! Written by Theo LeSieg. (Random House, 1997).

A Pizza the Size of the Sun: Poems. Written by Jack Prelutsky. (Greenwillow, 1996).

Grandaddy's Stars. Written by Helen V. Griffith. (Greenwillow, 1995).

Something Big Has Been Here. Written by Jack Prelutsky. (Greenwillow, 1990).

FOR MORE INFORMATION

Articles

Limited information is available on book flaps. No recent articles, books, or Web sites were located.

Nancy Tafuri

◆ Animal

Brooklyn, New York
November 14, 1946

📖 *Have You Seen My Duckling?*
📖 *Spots, Feathers, and Curly Tails*
📖 *What the Sun Sees, What the Moon Sees*

ABOUT THE
AUTHOR/ILLUSTRATOR

One of Nancy Tafuri's favorite activities as a child was listening to her mother read aloud. Nancy sat beside her mother, and they read books over and over again. When she wasn't reading or being read to, Nancy would use her crayons to create her own artistic "masterpieces" or would go outdoors to watch the animals and to enjoy nature. Now she uses those hours of observation to help her create children's books about animals and nature.

Nancy was born on November 14, 1946, in Brooklyn, New York, where she grew up and attended school. After high school, she planned to study children's book illustration, but when she enrolled in the School of Visual Arts in New York City, she found that many of the courses dealt with graphics, type, painting, and other topics that prepared her for a career in a graphics-related field. One of her fellow students was Thomas Tafuri. They married in 1969, and after graduation, they began to establish their art careers. Tom was focusing on book-jacket design, and Nancy was working full-time for publishers in the New York area. Three years later, the two of them established One Plus One Studio, and together they worked on everything from photography and logos to work on films. Their specialty remained book-jacket design.

Nancy periodically did some illustrative work for publishers, but it was not until 1980, when she walked into the offices of Greenwillow Books that she got a break. She asked to have her art portfolio reviewed and received her first illustrative assignment: the illustrations for George Shannon's *The Piney Woods Peddler* (Greenwillow, 1981). Tafuri spent months on the illustrations. She used Tom as her model for the bearded peddler. To get inspiration for the background setting, she secluded herself in an old stone mill in Millback, Pennsylvania. Many residents of Millback became models for characters appearing in the book. After that book became an American Library Association Notable Book, a publisher asked her to illustrate books by Mirra Ginsburg, and her career in children's books became a reality. She then began to create books that she both wrote and illustrated. Uncluttered illustrations were characteristic of her work.

In the mid-1980s, Tom and Nancy Tafuri moved their studio to Roxbury, Connecticut. Their home and studio sits in the middle of ninety-seven acres of fields and trees. Tom and Nancy Tafuri and their daughter, Cristina, enjoy being surrounded by nature. There are a lot of baby birds in nests around the property, a pond, and many small creatures who nibble the grasses, climb the trees, and frolic across the country meadow.

In 1985, one of her first books, *Have You Seen My Duckling?* (Greenwillow, 1984), earned her a Caldecott Honor Book award. That book came about when she and Tom, on a spring day, spotted two ducks down at their pond. They closely watched the little ducklings emerge. The mother duck seemed intent on proudly showing off her little brood—until one little duckling just could not sit still. *Have You Seen My Duckling?* became a series of expressive pictures and the story of a mother duck seeking to find her little duckling, told in a mere eight words. Readers see the little duckling in every illustration, but Mother Duck is not able to see the little duckling in the lushness of the stream and its water plants.

Rabbit's Morning (Greenwillow, 1985) came about "on a misty morning in the apple orchard while raking leaves from a tree that had come down with a fungus. I turned and heard a loud 'thump thump,' and lo and behold a huge jackrabbit went right by me—then another one scooted by. So I figured it would be wonderful to show . . . the early morning with lots of animal families through the eyes of a rabbit in the country meadow."

Tafuri also used the many meadow animals as she introduced a variety of animals and the numbers one to ten in *Who's Counting?* (Greenwillow,

1986). Similarly, the meadow and woods became an integral part of *Do Not Disturb* (Greenwillow, 1987), a book that has a family camping in the woods and the animals reacting by moving, scurrying, and making animal noises. In the next several years, Tafuri produced several additional concept books. *Two New Sneakers* (Greenwillow, 1988) dealt with common objects of clothing, baby animals were featured in *My Friends* (Greenwillow, 1987), and colors are the focus of *In a Red House* (Greenwillow, 1987).

Animals and basic concepts continued to be the focus of Tafuri's books. *I Love You, Little One* (Scholastic, 1997) featured mama animals telling their little ones all the ways that they are loved, forever and always.

Some of Tafuri's most memorable characters reappeared in *What the Sun Sees, What the Moon Sees* (Greenwillow, 1997). This book contained scenes of the sunny bustling daytime on the farm, in the woodland, in the city, and at school. If the reader turns the book over and goes through it again, one will see the same scenes under the light of the moon. In the scenes, readers see the gray-and-black-speckled hens from *Early Morning in the Barn* (Greenwillow, 1983), the marmalade cat from *Junglewalk* (Greenwillow, 1988), and the sweet brown dogs from *Who's Counting?* (Greenwillow, 1986).

In 1999, Scholastic published a rhyming text that takes a country family through the changes and surprises of the year's cycle. *Snowy Flowy Blowy: A Twelve Months Rhyme* (Scholastic, 1999) was a book based on an old poem by Gregory Gander.

Nancy Tafuri has a deep love of nature, and her dream to live in the country came true in the 1985 when she and her husband moved to their home in Connecticut. The eight-room country home dates to the 1790s and is filled with colonial antiques. It is splendid—from its tall French-style doors, to its 200-year-old windows, to its working fireplace. A remodeled chicken coop 200 feet away from the house serves as their artists' workplace. At art tables, side-by-side, the two of them work. Tom Tafuri designs more than 240 book jackets each year, and Nancy Tafuri creates books about ducks, rabbits, mice, and other animals, as well as books about fairies. She has created counting books, color books, and books about seasons and holidays. Tafuri loves to garden, and although she has a passion for white flowers, she has also eased in some colorful ones, too. On beautiful spring days, it takes all of her strength to keep herself at the drawing board. Tom Tafuri loves to cook (and Nancy declares that he is the best), and she loves to eat.

BOOKS AND NOTES

Nancy Tafuri's full-color illustrations are executed in watercolor paints and black line or black line with colored inks and dyes. The consistent element is the bold vivid colors of paints or inks. The illustrations are carefully rendered to reflect an accurate view of nature. Every detail seems to be carefully thought out. Even the endpapers reflect the central focus or an important element. For *Junglewalk*, the endpapers are an expanse of white topped by a jungle vine against a background wash of sky blue. *Have You Seen My Duckling?* has endpapers the color of the little ducks, a golden yellow, and the endpapers for *Do Not Disturb* are a solid pink—the same color as the flower on the book's title page. For Mirra Ginsburg's *Four Brave Sailors* (Greenwillow, 1987), Tafuri repeated the silhouette pattern of small white birds against a blue background. The same design, with a gray bird against the same blue background, appears on the first text page as the wallpaper in a small boy's room.

Books Written and Illustrated by Nancy Tafuri

The Ball Bounced (Greenwillow, 1989).

The Barn Party (Greenwillow, 1995).

The Brass Ring (Greenwillow, 1996).

Counting to Christmas (Scholastic, 1998).

Follow Me (Greenwillow, 1990).

Have You Seen My Duckling? (Greenwillow, 1984).

I Love You, Little One (Scholastic, 1997).

Junglewalk (Greenwillow, 1988).

One Wet Jacket (Greenwillow, 1988).

Snowy Flowy Blowy: A Twelve Months Rhyme (Scholastic, 1999).

Spots, Feathers, and Curly Tails (Greenwillow, 1988).

This Is the Farmer (Greenwillow, 1994).

Two New Sneakers (Greenwillow, 1988).

What the Sun Sees, What the Moon Sees (Greenwillow, 1997).

Who's Counting? (Greenwillow, 1986).

Books Illustrated by Nancy Tafuri

Across the Stream. Written by Mirra Ginsburg. (Greenwillow, 1982).

Asleep, Asleep. Written by Mirra Ginsburg, inspired by a verse by A. Vvedensky. (Greenwillow, 1992).

Biggest Boy. Written by Kevin Henkes. (Greenwillow, 1995).

Flap Your Wings and Try. Written by Charlotte Pomerantz. (Greenwillow, 1989).

Four Brave Sailors. Written by Mirra Ginsburg. (Greenwillow, 1987).

FOR MORE INFORMATION

Articles

Raymond, Allen. "Nancy Tafuri. Nature, Picture Books and Joy." *Early Years* (January 1987): 34–36.

Chris Van Allsburg

◆   Fantasy

Grand Rapids, Michigan
June 18, 1949

📖   *Jumanji*
📖   *The Polar Express*

ABOUT THE AUTHOR/ILLUSTRATOR

Chris Van Allsburg describes his illustrative work as surrealism. Others refer to his work as magical, mystical, strange, moving, and otherworldly. Whatever the description, most agree that his work has made him a favorite among young readers. He has earned the coveted Caldecott Medal twice, once in 1982 for *Jumanji* (Houghton, 1981) and again in 1986 for *The Polar Express* (Houghton, 1985).

Chris Van Allsburg was born in Grand Rapids, Michigan, on June 18, 1949. He grew up in Michigan, where his father ran a dairy. The dairy was the kind that made milk into ice cream. As a child, he entertained his friends with his ability to draw, but he later gave up drawing to pursue other more "socially useful" activities, such as playing ball.

Once he completed high school, he had ideas of going to college to study law or perhaps forestry. A recruiter came to his high school from the University of Michigan, and Van Allsburg enrolled at the university. During his freshman year, "as a lark," he took a figure drawing course and rekindled his interest in art. A sculpture course followed, and he eventually declared his major as fine arts. During his years at Michigan, he met his wife,

Lisa, and when he decided to pursue a master's degree in sculpture at the Rhode Island School of Design (RISD), they moved to Rhode Island. At RISD, he learned how to turn and laminate hardwood and to make molds of rubber, latex, silicone, and plaster. He also learned to cast metal in various ways. After completing the degree, he established a small studio in Providence, Rhode Island. Before long Van Allsburg had earned a reputation as a "witty and versatile" sculptor.

His road to children's books began with a series of events. In the early 1970s, he often spent twelve hours in his studio working on his sculpture. For relaxation and to help him generate new ideas, he began to make large narrative drawings. An admirer at RISD saw his drawings and recommended him to the school as a drawing instructor. In 1977, he joined the staff.

When he was teaching at RISD, he offered a course titled "Design Your Own Country." The participants were required to produce visual documents that represented the culture of their imagined country. They produced posters and postage stamps. The course demanded imagination and a thorough understanding of technical skills that would enable the student to effectively communicate and support the ideas developed as part of their country's culture.

Meanwhile Van Allsburg's wife was working as a teacher. She often brought home children's books with the comment that he could do as well. Later, Lisa Van Allsburg was producing a local television show and invited one of the guests home for dinner. The guest was David Macauley, who had already published three children's books with Houghton Mifflin. He and Lisa began to encourage Van Allsburg to submit some of his drawings to publishers. He was reluctant to make the rounds of the publishers, so his wife, who had already successfully promoted his sculptures to New York Galleries, stepped in and actually took his portfolio to publishers. She even secured illustrative assignments for him. When Van Allsburg read the manuscripts they had given him, however, he decided he really did not want to illustrate them. It was during a time that he was deeply involved in preparing for an exhibit of his sculpture in a New York art gallery. After the show, he pulled out the manuscripts again and reread the manuscripts. They still were not anything that interested him, so he decided to write his own story.

Van Allsburg wrote and illustrated his first book, and Lisa Van Allsburg took the book to Houghton Mifflin, one of the publishers who had expressed interest in his illustrative work. They liked the book and agreed to publish it. *The Garden of Abdul Gasazi* (Houghton, 1979) was designated as a Caldecott Honor Book in 1980.

The Van Allsburgs used to live in a "slightly Scandinavian-possibly-Bavarian woodman's cottage built just before 1920 by a neo-Victorian." The surroundings provide clues to the inhabitants' personalities. At the side of the front door was a well-maintained 4-H sign; on the other side was an out-of-order doorbell. It was a testament to the fallibility of the inhabitants, especially considering Van Allsburg's preponderance for order. At the time Van Allsburg's children's books were gaining popularity, the inside of his house featured a large stuffed raven holding court along with a smaller stuffed crow perched atop the glass-covered bookcase. Objects in his home have represented his interests at a given time. There have been a variety of ephemera, including a miniature Red Sox batting helmet, two carved giraffes, a lithograph of a lion, and a bust of Dante. He has a collection of cast-metal Statues of Liberty and bulldogs. His own "weird" sculptures are also displayed in their house. The home also included an unusual kitchen, the largest room in their house, that Van Allsburg restored in authentic 1930s style, complete with red-and-white-checkered tile above the counter and a raised four-seat booth.

The second largest room was Van Allsburg's seven-by-thirty-foot studio on the second floor. It was in this skylit space that Alan P. Mitz, Abdul G., Judy, Peter, and Ben first appeared on paper. It was there that Fritz, the name for a favorite sculpture, "Brancusi's Dog," which Van Allsburg owns, appeared in Van Allsburg's books. While it is Fritz who has appeared in most, if not all, of Van Allsburg's books, it is their real-life Siamese cat, Cecil, who got to hang out in Van Allsburg's studio. Sometimes Cecil sat on the drawing board, other times he hung by his front paws from a doorframe.

Van Allsburg's books fall into two general categories: quests and surrealistic mysteries. They each contain a puzzle element that either the hero or the reader must attempt to solve so that the story can end. Each of his books have a psychological, emotional, or moral premise. For example: *The Polar Express* is a story of faith and *Jumanji* deals with perseverance and finding a solution even if one is frightened. *The Garden of Abdul Gasazi* compares illusion to real magic; Alan is left with the unanswered puzzle of whether or not his dog was turned into a duck by his neighbor. *Two Bad Ants* addresses staying faithful to nature.

Jumanji is the source for an imaginative game that turns real and ends only when the children can successfully bring an end to the game. In *The Wreck of the Zephyr* (Houghton, 1983), there are two mysteries: how a sailboat came to crash on a mountain and if, in fact, the event really did occur.

The Mysteries of Harris Burdick (Houghton, 1984) consists of fourteen story beginnings left to the imagination of the readers to complete. Each of fourteen illustrations are captioned with a provoking sentence filled with ideas to allow the reader to take control of the stories.

Jumanji was a story that emerged out of an assignment Van Allsburg gave his students at the Rhode Island School of Design. He asked his students to find pictures of house interiors, then to find pictures of wild animals, and finally to create a drawing that would convince those who viewed the drawing that the animals were part of the interior space. Van Allsburg did the assignment along with his students, and once his were completed, he realized the power they had. He began to think of a story to go with his pictures.

When Van Allsburg created his illustrations for *The Alphabet Theater Proudly Presents the Z Has Zapped* (Houghton, 1987), it featured black-and-white, three-dimensional-like drawings of each of the letters of the alphabet. Van Allsburg actually carved letters that served as models for his drawings.

One day, Van Allsburg spotted two ants in the kitchen, trying to climb out of a sugar bowl. The next day, he dreamed up *Two Bad Ants* (Houghton, 1988), in which the adventures of the two ants—ranging from nearly getting sucked into a garbage disposal to being cooked in the toaster—are seen from the perspective of the two ants.

The ideas for his stories come, according to Van Allsburg, from random, even trivial, experiences. He often sees pictures of a story in his mind. He asks questions of himself: "what if—and what then?" *The Polar Express* came about with the idea of a train standing alone in the woods. Then he began to ask questions: What if a boy gets on the train? What does he do? Where does he go? After the boy got on, Van Allsburg thought of different destinations in his mind. When he finally decided the train should go north, he wondered who the boy would visit. The idea of visiting Santa Claus and including Christmas began to shape the story.

In the beginning of a project, Van Allsburg arranges the text in his mind, editing, recreating, and changing the perspective of his idea before sitting down to draw or write. Once he has a firm idea, he draws thumbnail sketches that detail one event, scene, or theme that he is trying to convey. After he completes the sketches, he determines the best composition and then begins the drawings. He uses models, but only for the figures. The rest is fabricated based on the perspective. He makes the backgrounds the way he wants them to be, not how they would be in reality. The entire process of creating a book—from idea to sketches to text to delivering the manuscript and drawings to the printer—takes about seven months.

Each of Van Allsburg's books allows him to explore new drawing techniques. *The Garden of Abdul Gasazi* was drawn in pencil with the fine, grainy look of a lithograph. The illustrations in *Jumanji* were created with waxy, pressed charcoal, a Conté-filled pencil, and dust grindings rubbed in with cotton. He used blacked-out scratchboard for *Ben's Dream*, scratching away sections from the black board to create whites spaces. He then drew on the white spaces with pen and ink. Other techniques have included pastels and charcoal and, in the case of *Two Bad Ants*, black line over color washes.

As he creates a drawing, Van Allsburg likes to leave an element of mystery in each drawing. For example, he might turn a face away a bit or crop a drawing with only part of a figure in a frame. Often he leaves something out of the story. He wants readers to have something to ponder at the end of the story. His stories generally do not begin with the posing of a question, nor does he end a book with the solution to a question. It is the reader who must pose the questions and who must resolve the question. Van Allsburg feels that by so doing, he invites readers to use their imaginations to fill in the gaps.

Van Allsburg has become a respected creator of picture books, which he views as being appropriate for all ages. In 1989 he began a collaboration with Mark Helprin to create illustrated narratives popular with older readers. The first book, *Swan Lake* (Houghton, 1989), was declared a marvel. *A City in Winter* (Viking, 1996) was a sequel, and the third book in the trilogy was *The Veil of Snows* (Viking, 1997).

Chris Van Allsburg is a magician of sorts, making strange things happen in his books. Artists and authors can make time stand still or change the sequence of events. Illustrations or stories in books tend to stay around a little longer. The creator's work becomes a permanent exhibit between two covers, a small gallery that reaches thousands of people. In addition to his work in books, Van Allsburg's illustrations and other art objects are sold through New York galleries.

In March 1989, the Van Allsburgs moved into a larger house in Providence. At the time of the move, Chris Van Allsburg had years of meticulous renovations planned for the house. The house was much larger than their previous home and allowed Chris the luxury of keeping his clothes in the bedroom instead of in the basement, as well as allowing him to take some of his own original artwork out of storage. In 1993, their daughter Sophia was born, and a second child was born within a couple of years. The family still lives in Providence, Rhode Island.

BOOKS AND NOTES

The main element with which Van Allsburg plays is light. In reality, light diffuses once reflected off an object, so there are inconsistencies in lights and darks that exist in nature. He manipulates light to create the surrealistic appearance found in his books, but when he began to work in the medium of painting, he encountered difficulties using the medium. Van Allsburg explains that when one draws with light and dark values, it is a matter of drawing darker or lighter. With color, it is not simply a matter of adding color; one has to think about such things as temperature and saturation changes. With any color, there are warm or cold tones that must be blended together to appear realistic.

His desire to use color grew from the need to experiment with other mediums and from the stories themselves. He found some technical difficulties when creating his first color work, *The Stranger* (Houghton, 1987). Initially, he treated pastels as though they were true oil paints. Most pastel artists place a shade of blue next to a shade of yellow and mix the two colors together to create green. Van Allsburg mixed the two colors together first and then applied them to the surface as an oil painter would. That made his colors meet at very precise boundaries rather than blending together as pastels generally do.

The Alphabet Theatre Proudly Presents the Z Was Zapped (Houghton, 1987).

Bad Day at Riverbend (Houghton, 1995).

Ben's Dream (Houghton, 1982).

The Garden of Abdul Gasazi (Houghton, 1979).

Jumanji (Houghton, 1981).

Just a Dream (Houghton, 1990).

The Mysteries of Harris Burdick (Houghton, 1984).

The Polar Express (Houghton, 1985).

The Stranger (Houghton, 1986).

The Sweetest Fig (Houghton, 1993).

Two Bad Ants (Houghton, 1988).

The Widow's Broom (Houghton, 1992).

The Wreck of the Zephyr (Houghton, 1983).

The Wretched Stone (Houghton, 1991).

FOR MORE INFORMATION

Articles

Allis, Sam. "Rhinoceroses in the Living Room." *Time* (November 13, 1989): 108.

Hubbard, Kim, and Dirk Mathison. "Chris Van Allsburg, A Rare Bird Among Illustrators, Brings His Art to a Fresh Christmas Treasure." *People* 32, no. 24 (December 11, 1989): 142–44.

Lane, Selma. "Story Behind the Book: The Wreck of the Zephyr." *Publishers Weekly* 230, no. 15 (April 8, 1983): 38–39.

Lessem, Don. "The Illustrator Man." *The Boston Globe Magazine*. (November 6, 1988): 21–23+.

Raymond, Allen. "Chris Van Allsburg." *Early Years K–8* (August/September 1985): 32–33.

Web Sites

HomeArts. Long, Marion. "Chris Van Allsburg: A Western Canon, Jr." <http://homearts.com/depts/relat/allsbuf1.htm> (Accessed March 2000).

Houghton Mifflin Eduplace. Loer, Stephanie. "About the Author: Chris Van Allsburg from Children's Books and Their Creator." URL: <http://www.eduplace.com/rdg/author/cva/article.html> (Accessed March 2000).

Houghton Mifflin Eduplace. Loer, Stephanie. "Ask the Author: Enter the World of Chris Van Allsburg." <http://www.Eduplace.com/rdg/author/cva/question.html> (Accessed March 2000).

Houghton Mifflin Interactive. "About Chris Van Allsburg." URL: <http://polarexpress.com/CVA/CVA.html> (Accessed March 2000).

Who 2. "Chris Van Allsburg Profile." URL: <http://who2.com/chrisvanallsburg.html> (Accessed March 2000).

Judith Viorst

◆ Family Relationships ◆ Humor

Newark, New Jersey
February 2, 1931

📖 *Alexander and the Terrible, Horrible, No Good, Very Bad Day*

📖 *Alexander Who Used to Be Rich Last Sunday*

📖 *I'll Fix Anthony*

ABOUT THE AUTHOR

Judith Stahl was born in Newark, New Jersey, the daughter of Martin and Ruth Stahl. She went to school in Maplewood and South Orange, New Jersey. In her childhood, she wrote and submitted poems, without success, to a number of publications. At the age of seven or eight, she composed an ode to her dead parents, although they were both still alive and well. Another poem was titled "Saint Marie," and another was a poem about a "Faithful Dog." Her writing continued through high school, where she wrote a tragic epic, "The Royalists and Roundheads," for a history paper and a gloomy sonnet called "Driftwood" for an art project. She wrote some rather mournful musings on nature for her science class and many woeful poems about life for her English courses. After graduation, she entered Rutgers University. Her writing was interrupted during her years at Rutgers when it became apparent that her roommate was a much better writer. In 1952, Judith graduated Phi Beta Kappa with a degree in history.

Following her graduation, Judith moved to Greenwich Village. Her mother thought she was living in the slums, but Judith was stepping into a career in publishing. In fact, she thought she was going to conquer the publishing world. Instead, she conquered shorthand and typing—rather mundane tasks in the publishing world. But in her spare time, she returned to writing. Her first job out of college was as a showroom model in New York's garment district. She read books during breaks in an effort to show that she wasn't just "an ordinary model [but that] she was this deep person." Later, she was employed as a secretary at *True Confessions* and then at *Women's Wear Daily*. When she was employed by *True Confessions*, she wrote confession stories. When she worked for *Women's Wear Daily*, she focused on writing fashion stories. Then she got a job as an editor in the children's department of a publishing house. Her writing began to turn toward children's stories. None of her employers ever opted to publish her writing, however.

During Judith's years at Rutgers, she met Milton Viorst. But he seemed "dramatically uninterested" in her—or so Judith thought. In late 1959, he was working for the *Washington Post*, and she was working as a children's book editor when he decided to call her. It was one o'clock in the morning. They prowled around Greenwich Village all night talking. Two months later, on January 30, 1960, they married—twice. They got married first by a minister friend in a civil ceremony in Washington and later by a rabbi in New Jersey. They moved away from the publishing industry, to Washington, D.C., where they have lived every since.

Milton Viorst is a writer whose fields are chiefly history and politics. Judith Viorst got a job as a stringer for the *New York Herald Tribune*, writing about the parties in Washington, D.C. She could never recognize anyone famous, so Milton had to go along everywhere she went. She often had to cover events at 2:00 AM and have the story written by 6:30 AM. She got a string of editorial jobs, including writing paperback science books.

Judith Viorst began writing children's books even before the births of her three sons, but none were published at the time. After three sons—Anthony Jacob (b. October 1961), Nicholas Nathan (b. August 1963), and Alexander Noah (b. March 1967)—were born, Viorst continued to write. Still nothing was published. Milton Viorst encouraged her to write and supported her morally and financially. He helped with the children and the dishes. Together, they wrote four science books for teenagers on space, nature, geology, and scientific experiments. She began to write poetry and newspaper and magazine articles. She obtained a contract to write a regular column for *Redbook*. Eventually, she turned to children's books, each one suggested by her children and their experiences.

When her children were little, Viorst wrote at night and when they were taking naps. When they went to play school, she could write during the two-and-a-half hours they were gone.

Today, Viorst writes on a computer in her office, but she travels with paper and pencil so she can write anywhere. She doesn't need a mood, inspiration, or the right place. She says she can "write in the airport, on the plane, in hotel rooms" or sitting in a chair. She tunes out the world and writes. She is extremely disciplined and makes herself lists and plans. Even when she is on a trip, she sets writing goals. For example, when she was writing one of her adult titles, she set a quota of finishing a page a day. That finished page included the necessary research and writing footnotes. When she took a few days to go to New York City, she kept her goals and did not go out shopping until she finished her page.

I'll Fix Anthony (Harper, 1969) came from a fantasy on brotherly love and revenge. Her son Nicholas actually adored his brother Anthony, but Anthony consistently took advantage of his size to beat up on Nick—thus came the fantasy of what Nick would do to Anthony when Nick became six. Nick's fear of the dark resulted in *My Mama Says There Aren't Any Zombies, Ghosts, Vampires, Creatures, Demons, Monsters, Fiends, Goblins, or Things* (Atheneum, 1973). Anthony's fear of death brought about *The Tenth Good Thing About Barney* (Atheneum, 1971, 1975). Tony was upset to find that his mother would actually kill a cat, even if it was only with her typewriter.

When Alexander's life seemed to be going badly, Viorst wrote *Alexander and the Terrible, Horrible, No Good, Very Bad Day* (Atheneum, 1972, 1976). For a time, Alexander felt his mother had told too much and wasn't sure he wanted his name splashed across the cover of the book. Viorst offered to change the name. But as a five-year-old, Alexander could not resist seeing his very own name in big bold letters across the cover of the book, so the name stayed.

When the three boys were growing up, their rooms were on the third floor of the Viorst's spacious three-story, century-old home. The upper floor was carpeted with thick plush carpet to reduce the noise from their activities. The second floor was the site of separate offices for Judith and Milton, both of whom were writers. Judith Viorst once described the first floor as being the DMZ (demilitarized zone). That floor (zone) was a common family area where they all met in the kitchen.

In 1981, when the last of her three sons went off to college, so did Viorst. She enrolled in classes at the Washington Psychoanalytic Institute—the only layperson among a group of psychiatrists. She wanted to keep doing what she was doing, writing about what goes on between people and inside people's heads. She wanted a different perspective but found that her new learning took her to a position where she wanted to write more directly about those relationships.

Viorst is an author of both children's and adult books, an Emmy winner, a lecturer, a mother, and a grandmother. In 1998, she wrote the lyrics for eight songs that were performed as part of the John F. Kennedy Center for the Performing Art's production of *Alexander and the Terrible, Horrible, No Good, Very Bad Day*. The production opened on November 27, 1998, and continued through December 23. Composer and arranger Shelly Markham composed the music for the production.

In 1998, Judith Viorst was also the recipient of the H. Louise Cob Distinguished Author Award, which was established in 1997 in conjunction with the Oklahoma State University's Speaker Series. Viorst was the second recipient; the first was Walter Buckley, Jr. A $10,000 honorarium accompanied the award, as did a piece of artwork chosen for the recipient.

Judith Viorst and Milton Viorst have lived for forty years in their Washington home, where both continue to write. Their children have all completed college. Anthony is a member of the bar in Denver, Colorado. After a stint in Hollywood where he worked as a writer, Nick is now living in Brooklyn and works in media projects as a developer. Alexander graduated from business school and is living in Chicago. There is a granddaughter, the reason Judith has started baking, although she never had before. Now she regularly "sifts flour."

BOOKS AND NOTES

Judith Viorst is a notable poet and an essayist whose writings have appeared in book format as well as in magazines. Her books of poetry for adults include *When Did I Stop Being 20 and Other Injustices: Selected Poems from Single to Mid-life* (Simon & Schuster, 1987) and *How Did I Get to Be Forty . . . & Other Atrocities* (Simon & Schuster, 1976). A humorous version of a classic poem for children, but written for adults, is her fractured version of "The Night Before Christmas." That book, *A Visit from St. Nicholas (to a Liberated Household): From the Original Written in 1823 by Clement Clarke Moore* (Simon & Schuster, 1976), was pub-lished as a "A Visit from St. Nicholas: To the Liberated Household of Richie and Joyce" in the December 1974 issue of *Redbook* magazine. She only recently wrote poems specifically for children when she penned the poems in *Sad Underwear: And Other Complications, More Poems for Children and Their Parents* (Atheneum, 1995). The majority of her books for children have been humorous picture books dealing with everyday incidents in the lives of young boys trying to make decisions about their lives and then dealing with the consequences, as in *Alexander Who Used to Be Rich Last Sunday* (Atheneum, 1978). Her book about the death of a pet, *The Tenth Good Thing About Barney* (Atheneum,

1971), is probably one of the books most often listed in bibliographies about death.

Absolutely Positively Alexander: The Complete Stories. Illustrated by Ray Cruz and Robin Preiss-Glasser. (Atheneum, 1997).

A single-volume collection of previously published stories about Alexander.

Alexander and the Terrible, Horrible, No Good, Very Bad Day. Illustrated by Ray Cruz. (Atheneum, 1972, 1976).

Alexander Who Used to be Rich Last Sunday. Illustrated by Ray Cruz. (Atheneum, 1978).

Alexander, Who's Not (Do You Hear Me? I Mean It!) Going to Move. Illustrated by Robin Preiss-Glasser. (Atheneum, 1995).

The Alphabet from Z to A (With Much Confusion on the Way). Illustrated by Richard Hull. (Atheneum, 1994).

Earrings! Illustrated by Nola Langner Malone. (Atheneum, 1990).

The Good-bye Book. Illustrated by Kay Chorao. (Atheneum, 1988).

I'll Fix Anthony. Illustrated by Arnold Lobel. (Harper, 1969).

My Mama Says There Aren't Any Zombies, Ghosts, Vampires, Creatures, Demons, Monsters, Fiends, Goblins, or Things. Illustrated by Kay Chorao. (Atheneum, 1973).

Rosie and Michael. Illustrated Lorna Tomei. (Atheneum, 1974).

Sad Underwear: And Other Complications, More Poems for Children and Their Parents. Illustrated by Richard Hull. (Atheneum, 1995).

Super-Completely and Totally the Messiest. Illustrated by Robin Preiss-Glasser. (Atheneum, 2000).

FOR MORE INFORMATION

Articles

Peterson, Karen. "Don't Look Now, Feminism, but Your Judith Viorst Is Showing." *Chicago Tribune* (December 12, 1977): Sec. 1, 16.

"PW Interview: Judith Viorst." *Publishers Weekly* 244, no. 5 (December 8, 1997): 51.

Books

Wheeler, Jill C. *Judith Viorst* (Abdo & Daughters, 1997).

Bernard Waber

Philadelphia, Pennsylvania
September 27, 1924

📖 *The House on East 88th Street*

📖 *Ira Sleeps Over*

📖 *Lyle, Lyle Crocodile*

ABOUT THE AUTHOR/ILLUSTRATOR

Bernard Waber's first successful children's book, *The House on East 88th Street* (Houghton, 1962), which introduced Lyle the crocodile, had a profound effect on the Waber household. Every since the success of the stories about Lyle the crocodile, the Waber household has been filled with "crocodilia"—crocodiles made from paper, wood, plastic, glass, and ceramic. Tables shaped like crocodiles, sofas, crocodile-decorated glass and dishware are everywhere. A bathtub with claw feet, just like the one that was in the Primm household, was found at a flea market and graces the foyer of the Waber home—with the obligatory stuffed crocodile.

Bernard Waber was born on September 27, 1924, in Philadelphia, Pennsylvania. His parents, Henry and Pauline Waber, had three other children, all older than Bernard. Henry had emigrated from Austria as a child. Pauline had come from Russia. Both had been very poor children, and times were still difficult for the Waber family during the Depression. The family had to move frequently, and with each move Bernard sought assurance from his parents that there was a neighborhood library and a cinema nearby. Playmates were important, too, but the library and cinema, by Waber's estimation, were life-giving. When he was about eight years old, he got a job at the movie theater, and in addition to a small wage, he received free admission to the movies. His job was to raise seats and pick up discarded candy wrappers after daily matinee performances. He enjoyed the work very much.

Waber's mother died when he was nine years old. She had worked very hard and liked to draw. As the youngest sibling, he often was the recipient of hand-me-downs. Interestingly, one of his older brothers also handed down his interest in drawing. Waber tried to copy photographs of film stars. After high school, he enrolled at the University of Philadelphia to study finance. Just one year into his studies, World War II interrupted his college days. He served in the U.S. Army from 1942 to 1945. During his years in the army, he had time to reconsider his life's goals. His interest turned to drawing and painting. After the army discharged him, he entered the Philadelphia College of Art and later the Philadelphia Academy of Fine Arts. He learned to draw landscapes, still lifes, figure drawings, and abstract designs. He also discovered that he could have fun making comic drawings. That may be where Lyle the crocodile was born.

When Waber completed his study at the Philadelphia Academy of Fine Arts, he moved to New York City to work. That same year, 1952, he married Ethel Bernstein. His first assignment was as a commercial artist for Conde Nast Publications and for *Seventeen* magazine. Later he worked as a graphic designer for *Life* magazine. By 1961, he also was writing children's books. In 1974, he moved to *People* magazine as a graphic designer.

His interest in children's books came slowly. Art editors often admired illustrations of children in his portfolio and suggested that they might be suited for children's books. But it was during his frequent read-aloud sessions with his three young children that he began to seriously enjoy the books and to formulate his own stories. Eventually, he began to send stories and ideas to publishers, accumulating many rejections, until one day an encouraging letter arrived from Mary K. Harmon, a children's book editor at Houghton Mifflin. A subsequent meeting resulted in a contract for Waber's first children's book, *Lorenzo* (Houghton, 1961).

As he began to create illustrations for children's books, he worked at the family's kitchen table, where the play of his three children, Paulis, Kim, and Jan Gary, caused wiggly and squiggly lines to become part of his drawings. He often had to remind his children not to rock the table. If Waber left his artwork on the table for a few minutes, he might return to find crumbs from someone's snack resting on the partially finished drawing. Everyone who visited the home—from the milkman to the neighbors—offered their evaluative comments about his work. Eventually, the Wabers moved to a larger apartment, and Waber was able to have his own quiet room in which to work.

Bernard Waber has created more than thirty books for children. He may be best known for *Ira Sleeps Over* and *Lyle, Lyle Crocodile*. Waber no longer works for New York publishing companies. He is a full-time writer and illustrator, and now—when he has time available—he visits schools and talks to children. He has spoken to hundreds of children about his books. They want to know if he is married. The answer is "yes." Does he have children? Again the answer is "yes, two girls and one boy." Where does he live and does he have any pets? In fact, Waber says that sometimes children want to know more about him than do evaluators at his health insurance plan. One young letter writer wrote: "Are you famous? If you are, do you know Wayne Gretzky?"

Waber loves to draw tall buildings, signs, moving vehicles—especially taxis, buses, flags, balloons, and traffic lights. When he begins his stories, he says, "I'm not always certain where I'm going or how I am going to get there." He most often writes first and then illustrates.

In the early 1960s, Bernard and Ethel Waber moved from New York City to Baldwin Harbor, Long Island. Among Bernard Waber's favorite things are ice cream, playing the piano, and playing tennis. But his "absolute favorite things" are to write and draw and to be with his family. He enjoys visits from his three children and his grandchildren.

BOOKS AND NOTES

Bernard Waber does not illustrate books written by other authors, preferring instead to write his own text. His best-known books are those about Lyle Crocodile and Ira. Lyle has become a very lovable character, and any book about him is almost sure to be a success. *Ira Sleeps Over* and its sequel have garnered much interest as well. In what seems to be a one-time departure from his normal humorous fare, Waber created a historical fiction book, *Just Like Abraham Lincoln* (Houghton,

1964). Waber most often writes about crocodiles, mice, and sometimes other animals, including hippopotami and rhinoceroses as he did in *"You Look Ridiculous," said the Rhinoceros to the Hippopotamus* (Houghton, 1966).

Bearsie Bear and the Surprise Sleepover Party (Houghton, 1997).
A cumulative story that has one animal after another seeking warmth in Bearsie Bear's big bed.

A Firefly Named Torchy (Houghton, 1970).

A little firefly's light is so bright all the plants and animals think it is daylight.

Funny, Funny Lyle (Houghton, 1987).

Lyle's mother moves in with the Primm family, and Mrs. Primm announces that she is expecting a baby.

Gina (Houghton, 1995).

When Gina moves to the new apartment building, she finds that there are only boys, no girls, her age.

The House at East 88th Street (Houghton, 1962).

The first of the books about Lyle the crocodile.

Ira Says Goodbye (Houghton, 1988).

Ira's friend Reggie is moving to a new town.

Ira Sleeps Over (Houghton, 1972).

Ira is worried about sleeping over at his friend's house. He is worried about how he'll get along without his teddy bear.

A Lion Named Shirley Williamson (Houghton, 1996).

A lion with an unusual name becomes a favorite at the zoo.

Lyle and the Birthday Party (Houghton, 1967).

Lyle celebrates with his friends.

Lyle at Christmas (Houghton, 1998).

Lyle helps Mr. Grumps find his lost cat and join in the festivities of the holiday.

Lyle at the Office (Houghton, 1994).

Officials representing Krispie Krunchie Krackles cereal attempt to recruit Lyle as spokesperson during a visit to Mr. Primm's office.

Lyle Finds His Mother (Houghton, 1974).

Lyle leaves the Primm home to search for his mother.

Lyle, Lyle Crocodile (Houghton, 1965).

Lyle is very happy at the Primm's household until Mr. Grumps changes all that.

The Mouse That Snored (Houghton, 2000).

A quiet house in the country has its inhabitants disturbed by the loud snoring of a little mouse.

Nobody Is Perfick (Houghton, 1971).

Eight vignettes showing imperfections that are shown even by good friends.

FOR MORE INFORMATION

Articles

Limited information can be found on book jacket flaps. No articles, books, or Web sites were located.

Wendy Watson

◆ Folklore ◆ Holidays

Paterson, New Jersey
July 7, 1942

📖 *Father Fox's Pennyrhymes*
📖 *Tom Fox and the Apple Pie*

ABOUT THE
AUTHOR/ILLUSTRATOR

Wendy Watson is the eldest of eight children who were raised on a farm in Vermont. Her mother was a writer, and her father was an illustrator; both of them worked at home. There were eight brothers and sisters, chickens, goats, cats, dogs, horses, and an occasional pig or two enjoying the country surroundings. Drawing and writing were a part of the children's everyday life.

Wendy was born on July 7, 1942, in Paterson, New Jersey. Her family resided in New Jersey and for a time in New York before moving to a farm in Putney, Vermont. Wendy attended the Putney School. During her school days, Wendy created hand-bound books, pen-and-ink drawings, and hand-printed greeting cards as gifts for her family and friends. Because her parents believed in giving their children a variety of educational experiences, each of the children spent at least one year going to "school" at home.

As her senior project during her high school years, she wrote and illustrated a fifty-eight-page book titled *Very Important Cat*. That book became her first published book when Dodd, Mead published it in 1958. She went on to enter Bryn Mawr College in Pennsylvania and majored in Latin. She studied art with Jerry Farnsworth on Cape Cod during the summers. In 1964, she graduated magna cum laude. In 1966 and 1967, she studied at the National Academy of Design.

A couple of years after college, Wendy Watson went to work as a composer and designer for a small press in New Hampshire before turning to freelance artwork. Along the way, Wendy learned to play the piano and the cello. She has played the cello with chamber music groups.

In 1970, Wendy Watson met and married the actor and opera singer Michael Donald Harrah. Their daughter, Mary Cameron Harrah, was born in 1973, and a few years later, their son James was born. During this time, Wendy was illustrating a book of thirty poems penned by her sister Clyde. The illustrations for *Father Fox's Pennyrhymes* (Crowell, 1971) were inspired by the sisters' childhood on a Vermont farm. The changing of seasons, the farm work, and the family fun were all incorporated into the illustrations. Even the garments that the foxes wear came from those memories. In fact, Wendy says some of those clothes "still hang in the closets in Putney." Almost every poem and picture depicted a special family occupation or occasion.

In the middle 1980s, Watson began to illustrate a collection of 200 authentic nursery rhymes. The result was published as *Wendy Watson's Mother Goose* (Lothrop, 1989). The rhymes were arranged to follow the cycle of a year and through a day—from the silvery winter's dawn to the sunny spring morning, a summer's afternoon, a fall evening, and a final festive midnight at New Year's Eve.

After living in Toledo, Ohio, with her family for "quite a few years," Wendy Watson returned to Vermont and settled in the East Corinth-Topsham area on Willey Hill Road. Reaching back to traditions that she felt gave her a sense of continuity, Watson worked on the illustrations for the Mother Goose collection for more than five years. She drew on her own homespun Vermont wedding when she illustrated the poem "Oh, rare Harry Parry/When will you marry?" The wedding was a community event—everyone was welcome to the potluck celebration. Guests wore overalls, aprons and danced while a country band played. The bride and groom, looking healthy in the fresh country air, rounded the bend up a grassy hill to the white-steepled church.

Wendy Watson has written and illustrated more than sixty titles in the more than thirty years that she has been working in the area of children's books. Her books have been named to several best book lists and notable book lists. As a full-time author and artist, she regularly visits schools, where she draws for her audience, invites participation, and shares the process of making a picture book with them.

As an alumnus of Bryn Mawr, Watson has designed a series of greeting cards and postcards for the college, each with a delightful cat image. She occasionally visits and lectures at Bryn Mawr. Wendy Watson lives in Vermont with her children, Mary Cameron Harrah and James Harrah.

BOOKS AND NOTES

Wendy Watson was known as a book illustrator before making her debut as an author and illustrator of her own books. Other than her high school project, her first book as author and illustrator was *Lollipop* (Crowell, 1976), a book for very young children. She has illustrated eleven titles by her younger sister, Clyde, and two books by her mother, Nancy Dingman Watson. One of the books written by Clyde and illustrated by Wendy Watson is *Father Fox's Pennyrhymes*, a book of thirty rhymes recording the various activities of Father Fox, his family, and friends. Watson has written and illustrated more than twenty books of her own, including *Fox Went Out on a Chilly Night* (Lothrop, 1994) and several holiday books.

Her illustrations are bright watercolors that often show round-eyed, chubby-cheeked children and scenes full of quiet rhythm and spirit. In addition to the many picture books that Watson has illustrated, she also has illustrated several novels, including Anne Pellowski's series of books about people of Polish descent who settle on a farm in the Midwest. One of those titles is *First Farm in the Valley: Anna's Story* (Saint Mary's Press, 1998), a title originally published by Philomel in 1982.

Books Written and Illustrated by Wendy Watson

Boo! It's Halloween (Clarion, 1992).

Fox Went Out on a Chilly Night (Lothrop, 1994).

Happy Easter Day (Clarion, 1993).

Hurray for the Fourth of July (Clarion, 1992).

Tales for a Winter's Eve (Farrar, 1988).

Thanksgiving at Our House (Clarion, 1991).

A Valentine for You (Clarion, 1991).

Wendy Watson's Frog Went A-Courting (Lothrop, 1990).

Wendy Watson's Mother Goose (Lothrop, 1989).

Books Illustrated by Wendy Watson

Applebet: An ABC. Written by Clyde Watson. (Farrar, 1982).

Belinda's Hurricane. Written by Elizabeth Winthrop. (Dutton, 1984).

Doctor Coyote: A Native American Aesop's. Written by John Bierhorst. (Macmillan, 1987).

The Night Before Christmas. Written by Clement C. Moore. (Clarion, 1990).

Valentine Foxes. Written by Clyde Watson. (Orchard, 1989).

FOR MORE INFORMATION

Web Sites

Author & Illustrators Who Visit Schools™ Homeroom. "Wendy Watson, Author and Illustrator." URL: <http://www. Teleport.com/~authilus/watson/watson. htm> (Accessed March 2000).

Bryn Mawr College Web Site. "Biography of Wendy Watson." URL: <http://www. brynmawr.edu/Acads/Langs/classics/ wendy_watson.htm> (Accessed March 2000).

Windham Library Web Site. "Wendy Watson Piece." URL: <http://www.windham. lib.me.us/wwpiece.htm> (Accessed March 2000).

David Wiesner

◆ Fantasy

Bridgewater, New Jersey
February 5, 1956

📖 *Free Fall*
📖 *June 29, 1999*
📖 *Tuesday*

Sharron L. McElmeel

ABOUT THE AUTHOR/ILLUSTRATOR

David Wiesner was the second son and fifth child of Julia Wiesner and George Wiesner. He was born on a Sunday, February 5, 1956, in Bridgewater, New Jersey, where he and his siblings grew up. David and his brother, George, shared many adventures and an inclination to be artistic. Their oldest sister was also artistic. David's older siblings passed down their used or unneeded art supplies and, in general, reinforced David's artistic endeavors. When David accompanied his parents to the paint and wallpaper store, he often could be found in the small section devoted to art supplies. He wanted to see, touch, and even sniff the offerings he found there.

When Wiesner was ten years old, he and his siblings who were interested in art watched the goatee-wearing "coolest-of-artists," John Nagey, who demonstrated painting techniques to anyone who cared to watch his weekly television show. Within the next few years, David is said to have completed every sequential exercise in the workbooks that accompanied Nagey's lessons.

The Wiesner household was filled with imaginative games and activities that stimulated their creativity. The neighborhood also encouraged creative play. The older children in the neighborhood became the game masters, teaching the younger ones the games they had invented. Trees and shrubs became forests, sidewalks became brooks and rivers. Armies of children chased one another through the forests and as they fjorded the waterways. As the children got older, their activities became more involved. They created hot air balloons using a coat hanger, a plastic bag, and hot gas. They tracked the balloons with walkie-talkies.

Eventually, as with many families, the older Wiesner children left the household, and David was able to have his own second-floor bedroom. His room became a studio when his father came home with a sturdy oak drafting table. The drawing table signified that his parents took his art seriously. Wiesner spent a lot of time at his artist's table. He was known as a shy person. It wasn't until high school that his recognition as the class artist helped him grasp an identity that moved him a bit out of his shyness.

During this time, he pored over the Time-Life Books of Great Artists and had become familiar with the work of da Vinci, Dali, De Chirico, Brueghel, and Dürer. These artists had created wonderful landscapes. Wiesner began to play with landscapes, and as he drew or painted each variation, he discovered that with a different perspective, the drawings allowed him to achieve more creativity. David created comics and even a live-action vampire film with his friends called *The Saga of Butchula*. It was a silent movie accompanied by a sound track.

One individual who had an impact on David's art career was his high school art teacher, Bob Bernabe, who taught at the Bridgewater Raritan High School. Bernabe found Wiesner an eager student whom he could motivate to reach beyond his present capabilities. Wiesner learned printmaking, photo silk screens, and watercolor. It was also during Bernabe's classes that Wiesner began to think about art school. David began to realize that there were places he could go and "not have a real job."

Wiesner graduated from high school in 1974 and left New Jersey to attend the Rhode Island School of Design (RISD). The mountain of drawings he had created before graduating was left behind in Bridgewater, but Wiesner took his incredible imagination and creativity. At RISD, he was able to explore his own unique points of view and create responses to assignments in unusual and creative ways. In his sophomore year, he was asked to depict "metamorphosis." He did so with a ten-foot-long by forty-inch-high mural with orange slices that turned into sailboats that turned into fish. The teacher chuckled when he saw the mural unfurled. This mural was transformed once again when, thirteen years later, it became the basis for Wiesner's Caldecott Honor Book, *Free Fall* (Lothrop, 1988).

The year Wiesner created the mural is also the year that he began oil painting. He went through the rigors of learning the techniques of using oil, but he never did enjoy it. He eventually returned to watercolor. At the time, his professor was Tom Sgouros, who continued to help Wiesner stretch his skills and techniques. Wiesner acknowledged Sgouros's contribution to his development as an artist when Wiesner dedicated his 1992 Caldecott Medal book, *Tuesday* (Clarion, 1991), to Sgouros.

Another assignment "series" resulted in eight drawings that began with an image of King Kong on top of the Empire State Building gradually becoming Leonardo's human proportion study. Assignments with the fewest restrictions often resulted in Wiesner's best work.

Wiesner's inspiration for wordless picture series was Lynd Ward. He was introduced to one of Ward's books by his first-year roommate at RISD. Michael Hays described the book to him, and Wiesner knew he had to see the book. It was in the rare book collection in the Hunt Library at Carnegie-Mellon University. Almost two years later, Wiesner visited his friend in Philadelphia and made sure that he visited the rare book collection. It was there that he first viewed the series of 130 woodcuts that Ward created for *Mad Man's Drum*. Being able to see that book helped him to begin to explore the possibilities of wordless storytelling. As his senior project, he created a forty-page, wordless book based on Fritz Leiber's short story "Gonna Roll the Bones."

As a 1974 graduate of the Rhode Island School of Design (RISD), David Wiesner embarked on his career. He moved to New York City and began to solicit illustrative work. At first he was offered manuscripts to illustrate. In March 1979, his work appeared on the cover of *Cricket* magazine. Then publishers commissioned book jackets.

In 1983, an apartment fire destroyed all of Wiesner's possessions. Those possessions included all of his accumulated work and the treasured oak drafting table given to him by his father. But the fire could not squelch Wiesner's quest to produce books. By 1987, he and his wife, a surgeon named Kim Kahng, had collaborated on a novel, *The Loathsome Dragon* (Putnam). Wiesner created the many watercolor landscapes for the book. A year later, his first book *Free Fall* (Lothrop, 1988) was published. It drew heavily on that ten-foot-long mural he had created at RISD. It also marked a reappearance of "The Loathsome Dragon" or at least a very similar looking sibling or cousin.

After a decade in the field of children's books, Wiesner was asked to create another cover for *Cricket*. He felt that the commission would be great as bookends to his ten-year career. The editors only requested that the cover be appropriate for the March issue, which would include stories about St. Patrick's day and frogs. Wiesner liked drawing frogs, so he gravitated toward that subject. He pulled out his old sketch books and copies of *National Geographic* and began to draw. Frogs on a lily pad took on a persona from a 1950s "B" movie that featured flying saucers. The lily pads seemed to have the flying power of a flying saucer. The cover ended up being a scene featuring frogs rising up and flying over a swamp, on their lily pads. His illustration appeared on the March 1989 cover.

In 1990, Wiesner's highly autobiographical book, *Hurricane* (Clarion), was published. The names of the boys, David and George, were indeed the Wiesner brothers, who really did weather a hurricane and play on the tree toppled by the high winds. The wallpaper on page thirteen of the book came directly off the walls of the room David played and slept in as a child. The same pattern of rockets, magnifying glasses, elephant heads, ships in bottles, books, and medals had been part of the first eleven years of his life.

Known to wonder what happened before and after the point of time captured in a painting, Wiesner began to wonder what happened to the frogs featured on his 1989 *Cricket* magazine cover. He wondered what happened before they began to fly and what happened afterward. Soon he was thinking seriously about a "frog book." The result was *Tuesday*. Because the action in the story spanned the times of day, Wiesner felt that the title should be a day of the week—but which one? He eliminated the weekends. They had too much associated with them and were not the funniest days. Neither was Friday. Monday, being the first day of the workweek, was eliminated, too. That left Tuesday, Wednesday, and Thursday. Wiesner did not like the way Wednesday was spelled. So Tuesday and Thursday were left. The sound of the way "Tuesday" was pronounced seemed to better match the nature of frogs. So the book became *Tuesday*—and the 1992 Caldecott Medal winner.

The following year, Wiesner's *June 29, 1999* appeared with another wacky scenario. In this book, on May 11, 1999, Holly Evans sends vegetable seedlings aloft as a part of her science experiment. By the end of June, the seedlings have grown to gigantic proportions. When vegetables she did not include in her experiment begin to appear in her garden, Holly is puzzled—until the author reveals a final twist that amuses readers. Readers will connect this book to *Tuesday* not only because of the interesting perspective, but also because May 11 and June 29, 1999, were Tuesdays.

As a child, David Wiesner followed the Howling Commandos across the pages of Marvel Comics and was inspired by the artist, Jim Steranko, who often drew several pages of wordless action in those comic books. Wiesner has used that inspiration to master his own talent for creating wordless stories. Most of his books have been wordless or minimal text books.

In 2000, Wiesner's *Sector 7* (Clarion, 1999), another wordless tale, was honored as a Caldecott Honor Book. Research for the book took David Wiesner to the New York Empire State Building on a cloudy day—he was the only one there. Within the book, there is a globe with "sector 7" highlighted. A major portion of that sector lies in the Atlantic Ocean, but the corner of the sector includes the area where Wiesner grew up and began his art career: New Jersey, New York, and more recently, Philadelphia. The book is dedicated to one of Wiesner's sons, Jaime, who always says, "Read a book."

After living in the New York area, Wiesner moved with his family first to Philadelphia and then to Wisconsin, where David and his wife, Kim, live with their two sons, Kevin and Jaime.

BOOKS AND NOTES

David Wiesner has illustrated several longer, novel-length books, including Avi's *Man from the Sky*; *Firebrat* by Nancy Willard (Knopf, 1988); and *Tongues of Jade* (HarperCollins, 1991) and *The Rainbow People* (HarperCollins, 1989) by Laurence Yep. Nonetheless, Wiesner remains most well known for his illustrated picture books, both those authored by others and those that he both wrote and illustrated. He wrote *The Loathsome Dragon* (Putnam, 1987) with his wife, Kim Kahng.

Books Written and Illustrated by David Wiesner

Free Fall (Lothrop, 1988).

Hurricane (Clarion, 1990).

June 29, 1999 (Clarion, 1992).

Moo! (Clarion, 1996).

Sector 7 (Clarion, 1997).

Tuesday (Clarion, 1991).

Books Illustrated by David Wiesner

Looking for Merlyn. Written by Dilys Evans. (Scholastic, 1997).

Night of the Gargoyles. Written by Eve Bunting. (Clarion, 1994).

Owly. Written by Mike Thaler. (Harper, 1982; Walker, 1998).

FOR MORE INFORMATION

Articles

Macaulay, David. "David Wiesner." *Horn Book Magazine* 68, no. 4 (July/August 1992): 423–28.

Wiesner, David. "Caldecott Acceptance Speech." *Horn Book Magazine* 68, no. 4 (July/August 1992): 416–22.

Web Sites

National Center for Children's Illustrated Literature. "David Wiesner." URL: <http://www.nccil.org/exhibit/wiesner.html> (Accessed March 2000).

Nancy Willard

◆ Community ◆ Folklore ◆ Poetry

Ann Arbor, Michigan
June 26, 1936

📖 *Cracked Corn and Snow Ice Cream: A Family Almanac*

📖 *The Nightgown of the Sullen Moon*

📖 *The Sorcerer's Apprentice*

Sharron L. McElmeel

ABOUT THE AUTHOR

Nancy Willard's *A Visit to William Blake's Inn: Poems for Innocent and Experienced Travelers* (Harcourt, 1981) was the first book of poetry to win the Newbery Medal. The book also was named a Caldecott Honor Book for its glorious illustrations by Alice and Martin Provensen. Nancy Willard's affection for William Blake began in her childhood during a time she was ill and an older friend gave her two volumes of Blake's poetry.

Nancy Willard was born on June 26, 1936, in Ann Arbor, Michigan, where she grew up listening to her mother tell stories, writing neighborhood newspapers with her sister, and telling stories to anyone who would listen. The girls' father was a professor of chemistry at the University of Michigan, and the family was able to spend the summers in a small town on the edge of a lake. On the opposite side of the lake stood a gravel pit, which employed nearly all the men in the town. The town had no library and no bookshop, but it was full of things to inspire gossip. So the girls set out to gather all the "news" of the town. They gathered the news and stored the articles under their bed in a shoebox. When the shoebox was full, they would publish an issue of the tabloid. In the course of gathering the stories, Willard heard many of the town's storytellers and learned the art of storytelling. She was also encouraged to develop her artistic talents. When Nancy was seven, her first published poem appeared in the children's page of a Unitarian church magazine. When she was a high school senior, a miniature book she wrote and illustrated included the text that appeared in *The Horn Book Magazine* as a story titled "A Child's Star." The editor of *The Horn Book Magazine*, Bertha Mahony Miller, sent Willard a letter telling her that Mr. Miller liked one of her illustrations so well that they wanted to offer ten dollars for the use of an illustration on their Christmas cards. During college, one of Willard's little illustrated books was published in the University of Michigan's literary magazine.

Art was also important to Willard. She painted angels over the cracks in their house's plaster walls, mermaids on the bathroom floor's patched linoleum, and huge sunflowers to cover the holes in the copper roof.

There was a great variety of guests in her childhood home. Willard's grandfather lived on the third floor. His room was filled with his clothes, his chewing tobacco, and some treasured books. Among those books were the Bible, *Pilgrim's Progress*, and the works of Edgar Allan Poe. When Willard arrived home from school, she often could hear her grandfather reciting the verses written by Poe. For a time, a cousin and the cousin's friend occupied a room across the hall from her grandfather's. They often "atoned for their sins" with loud prayers recited early in the morning before they left for class at 8:00 A.M. And then there was Nancy's grandmother. She hummed and stirred and talked all day long to people who had, fifty years before, helped her on her father's farm in Iowa. At night, she forgot her English and said her prayers in German, dreaming of a time when women sat on one side of the church and the men sat on the other side. Occasionally a wise cow waited outside the church.

After finishing high school, Nancy Willard attended the University of Michigan and obtained her undergraduate degree. She earned a master's degree at Stanford University in Palo Alto, California, and then returned to Michigan to earn her Ph.D. While Willard was a student at the University of Michigan, she met her husband, Eric Lindbloom, a philosophy professor. They moved to Poughkeepsie, New York, and Willard began teaching at Vassar College. When their son, James Anatole, was born in 1970, Willard began teaching part-time so that she could spend more time with him. For several summers, James accompanied his mother to Vermont, where she was on the staff of the Bread Loaf Writers' Conference.

Meanwhile, Willard was writing novels, poetry, and picture books. She wrote on trains, buses, or when she was doing household tasks. Many of the incidents in her life showed up in her books.

The idea for writing *The High Rise Glorious Skittle Skat Roarious Sky Pie Angel Food Cake* (Harcourt, 1990) came about when Willard reflected back on a story her mother told her about what happened when she (Willard's mother) sneaked down to the kitchen at night to bake her own mother a surprise birthday cake.

When she wrote *The Nightgown of the Sullen Moon* (Harcourt, 1983), she actually created a sullen moon, using a basketball, and hung it in a fanciful garden cottage in the family's backyard.

When Willard writes fantasy, she often makes a model of the place and the people who live in her setting. While she was writing *A Visit to William Blake's Inn*, she built a six-foot-tall model of his eighteenth-century English Inn. It was first built of cardboard boxes, and then a family friend, Ralph Gabriner, replicated the structure out of sturdy wood. Willard filled the inn with the moon and stars, angels, people, animals, and the mythical characters that inhabit the book. All the objects are made from scraps and bits and pieces of discarded objects. Willard's family and friends became part of the inn, as did Blake's friend and contemporary, Lewis Carroll, the author of *Alice in Wonderland*. Rooms in the inn were papered with Blake's engravings, Kate Greenaway illustrations, and Lewis Carroll's photographs of Alice. There were two green rabbits, some Dutch girls with silver shoes, and cooks with silver spoons monogrammed with moons, a Wise Cow, a dragon, a bear, and many other animals. All became part of the verses penned for Willard's award-winning book. The book is a book of poetry inspired by the poems of the copper engraver and poet William Blake.

When Willard retold *Beauty and the Beast* (Harcourt, 1992), she did not make a model for the Beast's mansion because she found a real mansion that seemed just right. The mansion was not far from her own home and was set on the Hudson River, where it had been built more than a hundred years before. Willard's version of *Beauty and the Beast* was similarly set at the turn of the century.

The names of her family have become the names of characters in many of her books. The Anatole series of books were named for her son James Anatole. Uncle Terrible, another character in the book, is the nickname of a family friend. Other stories feature a protagonist named James. Erik, a soldier in one of her tales, is a variation on the first name of her husband, Eric.

A figure of a Marzipan man, from *The Marzipan Moon* (Harcourt, 1981), often accompanied Willard as she visited schools or told stories at the public library in Poughkeepsie, New York. The Marzipan man, made of old discarded burlap sugar bags, rode double behind Willard on her bicycle. Willard's two cats often find their way into her books, too.

Willard's father was almost sixty years old when she was born. He was a man of few words, but he did write daily in pocket diaries. Most of the entries were short phrases, often focusing on the weather. The day he married Nancy's mother he simply entered, "Today I married Marge Sheppard." He told his wife that he never wrote anything personal. He had read as a child but Willard believes he "put away childish things" and did not read another piece for fiction beyond his freshman English class. The only piece of writing by Willard that her father read was an occasional birthday poem she wrote for him when she could not afford the traditional pair of socks. In his ninetieth year, however, he picked up a book of her stories and read it. He found himself in the book as a character. As with all her characters, he was part fiction and part real. Although Willard could never recall her father having cried during her childhood, he cried when he read her words. He died at the age of ninety-two.

Willard is a pack rat of sorts. Nothing gets thrown away. She fills closets and cupboards with boxes containing all kinds of materials. A single earring might be used as a decoration for a soft cloth sculpture. Scraps of cloth are kept in the event they are needed to make a garment or a curtain for a window in one of Willard's creations. Artwork continues to be an important part of her life. She paints chests, cupboards, and other art objects. Her herb garden is filled with laughing faces, and other images that laugh and sing.

Willard is a lecturer at Vassar College in Poughkeepsie, where she teaches writing, especially poetry writing. She writes books for adults and for children. Some books are prose, and some are poetry. When she visits schools, she listens to the stories her hosts tell, she tells stories she has heard, and she draws her visions of the tales. She and her husband, Eric Lindbloom, still live in Poughkeepsie, where he continues with his interest in photography. James Lindbloom, their son, is now grown. Willard's delight in creating whimsical objects is still evident in the furniture and decoration throughout the family's home and garden.

BOOKS AND NOTES

Nancy Willard is a versatile and creative writer. She has illustrated her own books, usually novels, but other artists usually illustrate her picture books. Her books feature a variety of subjects, including baseball (*The Highest Hit*; Harcourt, 1978), and imaginary cultures (*Sailing to Cythera, and Other Anatole Stories*; Harcourt, 1974; *The Island of the Grass King: The Further Adventures of Anatole*; Harcourt, 1979). She has retold folklore (*East of the Sun & West of the Moon: A Play*; Harcourt, 1989) and compiled stories and traditional beliefs, recipes, and ideas into an almanac (*Cracked Corn and Snow Ice Cream*; Harcourt, 1997) celebrating the culture of the Midwest. She writes both prose and poetry. Many of her poetry books are substantial volumes of original and selected poems, including *Swimming Lessons: New and Selected Poems* (Knopf, 1996).

Books Written by Nancy Willard

Cracked Corn and Snow Ice Cream: A Family Almanac. Illustrated by Jane Dyer. (Harcourt, 1997).

A combination of oral history, scrapbook, almanac, recipe sampler, and photo album arranged in a month-by-month format. The book is filled with photos and funny facts (thirty-three cows will fit into a classroom), poems and farming lore, home arts, jokes, moon phases, and riddles.

The High Rise Glorious Skittle Skat Roarious Sky Pie Angel Food Cake. Illustrated by Richard Jesse Watson. (Harcourt, 1990).

A young girl bakes her mother a special angel food cake. When three angels in heaven smell the cake, they suddenly appear.

The Marzipan Moon. Illustrated by Marcia Sewell. (Harcourt, 1981).

A hungry parish priest is given a gift of a broken crock, which magically produces a marzipan man each morning.

The Nightgown of the Sullen Moon. Illustrated by David McPhail. (Harcourt, 1983).

A fanciful tale of the moon, who wishes to have a nightgown like all the people on earth. When she comes down to find one, she succeeds by finding one the color of the sky and filled with the stars that surround her.

Shadow Story. Illustrated by David Diaz. (Harcourt, 1999).

Clever Holly Go Lolly lures the ogre Ooboo into her make-believe shadow forest.

The Tale I Told Sasha. Illustrated by David Christiana. (Little, Brown, 1999).

A yellow ball rolls over a bridge of butterflies to the place all lost things are found.

The Voyage of Ludgate Hill: Travels with Robert Louis Stevenson. Illustrated by Alice and Martin Provensen. (Harcourt, 1987).

Inspired by Robert Louis Stevenson's letters describing his transatlantic voyage in 1887 on a cargo steamer.

Poetry Written or Selected by Nancy Willard

Among Angels: Poems. With Jane Yolen. Illustrated by S. Saelig Gallagher. (Harcourt, 1995).

This collection of thirty-five poems about angels, sent back and forth between two brilliant poets over a period of several years, includes lyrical works about angels from the Christian and Hebrew traditions.

An Alphabet of Angels. Illustrated by Nancy Willard. (Scholastic, 1994).

A poetic text that showcases Nancy Willard's talent as a folk artist with photographs of her ceramic, stone, and metal angels.

Gutenberg's Gift. Illustrated by Bryan Leister. (Harcourt, 1995).

Relates in rhyme how Johann Gutenberg contributed to the printing process by perfecting movable type and creating a Bible for his wife, Anna. (Gutenberg did not have a wife; the information in the poem is fictional rather than biographical.)

Pish, Posh, Said Hieronymus Bosch. Illustrated by Leo Dillon, Diane Dillon, and Lee Dillon. (Harcourt, 1991).

A tale of the unconventional Flemish painter Hieronymus Bosch, who painted extraordinary surreal scenes. Willard imagines that Bosch's house is crowded with his own fantastical creatures, driving his housekeeper wild.

A Visit to William Blake's Inn: Poems for Innocent and Experienced Travelers. Illustrated by Alice and Mary Provensen. (Harcourt, 1981).

Original poems inspired by the poems of the eighteenth-century copper engraver and poet William Blake.

FOR MORE INFORMATION

Articles

Krim, Nancy. "When Things Invisible Become Visible: A Writer and Her Readers." *English Journal* 79, (April 1990): 16–19.

"Nancy Willard: Winner of the 1982 Newbery Medal." *Early Years.* (October 1982): 10–13.

Steinberg, Sybil. "PW Interviews: Nancy Willard." *Publishers Weekly* 226, no. 24 (December 14, 1984): 88–89.

Willard, Nancy. "The Well-Tempered Falsehood: The Art of Storytelling." *Top of the News* (Fall 1982): 104–12.

Vera B. Williams

Hollywood, California
January 28, 1927

📖 *A Chair for My Mother*
📖 *Something Special for Me*

ABOUT THE
AUTHOR/ILLUSTRATOR

Vera Baker was born in Hollywood, California, on January 28, 1927, but before her grade-school years, her family moved to the Bronx. During her childhood, her parents, Albert and Rebecca Baker, encouraged her to create pictures, tell stories, and to act. Her father had immigrated to the United States from Russia when he was sixteen. Her mother came from Poland when she was a small child. Both were from Orthodox Jewish families and retained their Jewish culture. They held dear the community aspirations for a better life for the working class and brought Vera up in a hopeful climate. Her mother was active and helped start the parents association at the local elementary school. She actively campaigned to remove teachers who were negative toward children from poor families. Vera frequented the Bronx House, a neighborhood center in New York, a place that nurtured her creative talents. When Vera was nine, one of her paintings, a piece titled "Yentas," was exhibited at a Works Progress Administration (WPA) show at the Museum of Modern Art. Eleanor Roosevelt came to the exhibit, and Vera was able to talk to her. Years later, in 1986, "Yentas" (the Yiddish word for busybodies) was exhibited again at the Bronx Museum's "Jewish Life in the First 50 Years of the Century."

A teacher at school referred Vera and her sister Naomi to The Clinic for Gifted Children at New York University. It was there that the two sisters studied with Florence Crane, who included Vera in her book *The Growth of the Child Through Art*. A full chapter was devoted to Vera. Crane used the pseudonym "Linda" for Vera. The girls traveled downtown by themselves every Saturday on the subway to study with Crane. There was never a charge for these lessons. Often, the girls went to the library, zoo, or park after the lessons, where one of their parents would met them.

Even though there were many positive aspects to their childhood, Vera and Naomi Baker were growing up in the Depression, and life with their family was not always easy. Their father had a difficult time—as did many people at the time—keeping a job, paying rent, and resisting despair. The girls were sent to foster homes and lived in a children's home for a time. They moved around a lot in California and in New York City. Vera resisted the mainstream culture, which included the Green Hornet, Superman, and hanging around the streets. Instead, she planted tomatoes, peas, and beets in a little plot in the neighborhood garden in Crotona Park.

When the family was together, Vera's father would hike with them from their home in central Bronx to a nearby beach or amusement area. They loved to walk, made little fires, and enjoyed picnics. Their father loved singing and dancing, as well as a good political argument. He was also restless and, at times, reckless and inconsiderate. The Bakers' family life was very intense and filled with competition and worry. It was their mother who held the family together.

Vera followed her older sister's lead and attended the New York High School of Music and Art, where she wrote and illustrated her first children's book. After high school, Vera enrolled in the Black Mountain School in North Carolina. At Black Mountain, she was part of an experimental institution where learning was an informal community activity. Students participated in hauling coal, discussing admissions, and analyzing Melville. She planted corn and produced the college's publicity on the printing press. She helped to build the house that she and her husband, Paul Williams, lived in. He was a student at the school as well. Every situation or activity was viewed as a learning opportunity. In 1949, Vera Williams graduated with a degree in graphic arts.

After obtaining her degree, the Williamses settled in Boston. Paul Williams studied architecture at Harvard, and Vera Williams continued her studies at the Boston Museum School. In a few years, the family moved to

Stony Point, New York, where they helped establish a cooperative community, Gate Hill Cooperative. They also established an alternative school for children called the Collaberg School. The Gate Hill Cooperative was nestled between the Bear Mountain ridge and the Tappan Zee Bridge, on the west side of the Hudson River, thirty-five miles north of New York City. It was a community built with other people who had attended Black Mountain: a poet, musicians, and potters. Paul, an architect, designed many of the homes. Everyone pitched in to build them. Vera, her husband, and their three children (Sarah, Jennifer, and Merce) lived at Gate Hill from 1953 to 1970. When Vera and Paul divorced, Vera moved to the Ontario countryside in Canada. She planned to stay for one year as a cook in a school that was very much like the Collaberg School. She ended up teaching topics that were important to her: nature study, art, writing, cooking. She cooked two meals a day for forty people, started a bakery, and even made butter. She helped preserve garden produce and butcher meat. She began canoeing during this period of time. She took many small trips with friends and eventually embarked on a 500-mile trip on the Yukon River. Those trips later became the inspiration for *Three Days on a River in a Red Canoe* (Greenwillow, 1981).

Williams was living on a houseboat in the bay at Vancouver, British Columbia, when she developed her first children's book, *It's a Gingerbread House: Bake It, Build It, Eat It!* (Greenwillow, 1978). That book grew out of her nursery school teaching while at Gate Hill.

Williams moved back to Ontario, to Toronto, after three years because she missed her family but was not yet ready to leave Canada. She lived in a cooperative household with two families and their children. She joined a Toronto Women's Writing Collective. By 1979, she was ready to leave Canada and moved to New York City.

During this time, she became an activist for woman's rights, as well as for nuclear freeze. She signed her name to a petition in the infamous "Baby M" case, protesting the judge's criteria for determining who is and who is not a "fit" mother. Her participation in a peaceful demonstration at the Pentagon in 1981 earned her a month's detention at Alderson Federal Penitentiary.

Williams does not carry politics into her children's books, but she says she deliberately depicts real life in her work. Her books show people of various races, women-centered families, and people working for a living. In many ways, some of her books are gifts to her mother's memory, her strength, and her perseverance as a woman.

An example of her effort to put images of many different kinds of faces in her books is *"More More More" Said the Baby: 3 Love Stories* (Greenwillow,

1990), which features Little Guy, Little Pumpkin, and Little Bird. The book is really three diverse stories of love, showing the relationships of father and son, grandson and grandma, and mother and daughter, all of varying races.

Vera B. Williams continues to live in New York, where she remains a political activist, concerned about human rights and the environment. Her three daughters are grown, and Williams is a grandmother.

BOOKS AND NOTES

Vera B. Williams's first book was not published until she was in her fifties. She had pursued other interests up to that time. She illustrated two books by other writers before embarking on her own writing and illustrating career. Her stories show the strength of females and their ability to set goals and to attain them. Illustrations are characteristically created in brilliantly hued watercolors. She often uses borders in her picture book illustrations to carry themes, make correlations with the images in the main illustrations, and bring continuity to the flow of the story.

In addition to her picture books, Williams also has created paintings to illustrate a collection of stories and poems put together by Grace Paley, *Long Walks and Intimate Talks* (Feminist Press, 1991).

Books Written and Illustrated by Vera B. Williams

A Chair for My Mother (Greenwillow, 1982).
A fire destroys the furniture of a young girl, her mother, and her grandmother. They work together to save dimes in a jar until they have enough to purchase a comfortable chair. Mother is able to use the chair to rest after she comes home from work.

Cherries and Cherry Pits (Greenwillow, 1986).
Bidemmi's attention turns to cherries as she draws and tells stories.

Lucky Song (Greenwillow, 1997).
A little girl has a kite-flying adventure and then finds a lucky song that her father sings to her. Home, clothing, food and love—all that a child needs most.

"More More More" Said the Baby: 3 Love Stories (Greenwillow, 1990).
Loving attention is given to three babies by a father, grandmother, and mother.

Music, Music for Everyone (Greenwillow, 1984).
When her grandmother is sick, Rosa's mother works to keep up with expenses. Rosa and her Oak Street Band try to earn money to help out.

Scooter (Greenwillow, 1993).
A child's adjustment to her new home is helped by the child's silver blue scooter.

Something Special for Me (Greenwillow, 1983).
As a birthday present for Rosa, her mother decides to let her use the coins from her tip jar to buy something she chooses. Rosa cannot decide until she hears a man playing beautiful music on an accordion.

Stringbean's Trip to the Shining Sea: Greetings. Co-illustrated by Jennifer Williams. (Greenwillow, 1988).
Stringbean and his brother embark on a trip across the country. As they travel in their pickup truck, Stringbean sends postcards home. Each postcard and its stamp reflect the theme of the place of origin.

Three Days on a River in a Red Canoe (Greenwillow, 1981).

Two women and two children make their way down the river in a red canoe.

Books Illustrated by Vera B. Williams

Hooray for Me! Written by Remy Charlip and Lilian Moore. (Four Winds, 1975; Tricycle Press, 1996).

Hooray for families, friends, and pets.

FOR MORE INFORMATION

Articles

Raymond, Allen. "Vera B. Williams: Postcards and Peace Vigils." *Teaching K–8* (October 1988): 40–42.

Audrey Wood
Don Wood

Sharron L. McElmeel

◆ Folklore (literary) ◆ Humor

Sharron L. McElmeel

Little Rock, Arkansas
1948
Atwater, California
May 4, 1945

📖 *King Bidgood's in the Bathtub*
📖 *The Napping House*
📖 *Quick As a Cricket*

ABOUT THE AUTHORS/ILLUSTRATORS

Don Wood met Audrey Brewer in Berkeley, California, in 1968. They married in 1969. After stops in Northern California, in Little Rock and Eureka Springs in Arkansas, and in Mexico, the couple settled in Santa Barbara, California. Audrey Wood already was writing and beginning to sell children's books. Don Wood began doing freelance magazine illustration. Eventually Don illustrated some of Audrey's books. Audrey Wood writes and illustrates some of her own titles, as well as writing books that are illustrated by other artists. One of the most recent illustrators of her work was their son, Bruce Robert Wood. By entering the field of art, Bruce became the fifth generation of artists in his family.

Audrey Brewer was born in Little Rock, Arkansas, the daughter of Cook Edwin and Maegerine Brewer. She was the oldest of three daughters whose family had been artists for three generations; Audrey Brewer would make the fourth generation and was to be the first female artist to carry on the family tradition. By the time Audrey was in fourth grade, she knew two things: She wanted to live in Dr. Doolittle's house, and she wanted to write and illustrate children's books.

Audrey's first memories are of being taken by her mother to watch her father paint the circus tents and sideshow murals at the Ringling Brothers Circus's winter quarters in Sarasota, Florida. Audrey was very young and thought of the people in the circus as her friends. Her first baby-sitters were a family of little people who lived in a trailer next to the Brewer family. They told her stories about the circus's chimpanzee, an elephant named Elder, and Gargantua the Gorilla. While Audrey watched her father repaint some of the twelve-foot murals, her mother would tell her stories about some of the circus performers shown on the mural: the tallest man in the world, the snake woman, and many other circus people.

Audrey learned to swim before she could walk and astounded some of the circus people when she scaled a seven-foot, chain-link fence when she was just one year old. When she was two years old, her family went to San Miguel de Allende, Mexico, where her parents studied art and Audrey learned to speak Spanish and English simultaneously. Her mother read to her every day. She became an avid reader and could read in both English and Spanish. The family lived in Mexico until Audrey was five.

Eventually, the family moved back to Arkansas, where Audrey spent most of her childhood and adolescence. Two more girls were born into the family, and together they sang, danced, and made up plays to stage on a makeshift stage in their family's basement. The girls had floodlights and a red velvet curtain on their stage.

Audrey's mother was very talented artistically but never pursued art as a career. She sewed all of the girls' ballet costumes and restored antiques. Her storytelling had a great impact on Audrey, and she became a storyteller for her two sisters. She often opened some of the lavish art books in her parents' library and would weave a story while looking at a painting. She also used the pictures in the nature encyclopedia to inspire her storytelling. Audrey especially liked the pages with snakes and other reptiles and amphibians.

Audrey attended a Montessori School and later public elementary school. But she was a student who either liked a subject or simply did not involve herself with it. As a result she either got A's or D's—there was no in between. When she was uninterested, she found ways to use the little objects she collected in a cigar box in her desk to amuse herself. For the most part, she was very different from the other pupils, and she was taunted and ostracized. Once Audrey completed elementary school, she attended a Catholic academy for girls. She was again an outsider because she was not Catholic, but the education was excellent and the teachers allowed her to create her art and to dream her dream.

She spent a lot of time in her grandfather's art studio. Audrey came to associate the sound of classical music playing and the aroma of paint, turpentine, and linseed oil with a "magical" place. Her grandfather mixed pigments from powders and oil for her, and in junior high, she entered a demonstration, showing where various pigments come from, in the science fair. She won third place.

Audrey also painted with her father, who guided her but allowed her to work freely. When her father and grandfather became involved in the formation of the Little Rock Art Center's art and drama institute, Audrey took advantage of the many opportunities to study with artists from all over the world.

During the early 1960s, Audrey moved to Berkeley, California and began to pursue an art career. She was teaching children's art part time and was creating art objects, mostly narrative paintings and large sculptures, and also writing some stories. She met Don Wood, and they married in 1969.

Don Wood had been born in Atwater, California on May 4, 1945. He was the son of Elmer B. and Elizabeth Wood. His father was a farmer in the central San Joaquin Valley who began as a grape picker, worked hard, and by the time he died was a very prominent man in California agriculture.

Wood's mother was a well-liked elementary teacher, but she died when he was in the second grade, and his father married Marjane Locher. His stepmother was an honors graduate in chemistry and had an interest in languages. Wood had older brothers and a half brother. All of them were working hard on the farm by the time they were twelve or thirteen years old. Because summers were busy times on the farm, winter was the season when Wood had time to draw. He always drew stories. His first story drawings were in pencil, but he later drew in ink and painted with watercolors. The family always sent their clothing out to be laundered, and Wood came to love laundry day. The clothing was always returned wrapped in tan paper, which became his artist's canvases.

During his high school years, Wood took art classes each year. The program was not ambitious, but his technical art skills improved, and the study did serve to bolster his confidence because he received many compliments. Wood entered the University of California at Santa Barbara and declared a major in fine arts. He was also interested in the theater and did so much work for the university's theater department that he ended up with a minor in theater. He studied art for six years and remembers just one teacher, Irma Cavat, whose work was narrative and illustrative. She was a strong influence on his work. Because the prevailing trend was to purge any literary content from one's artwork, Wood followed the trend, but it lessened his interest in art. He attended the California College of Arts and Crafts and graduated in 1969 with a master's in fine arts. For the following six years, he "hardly put pen to paper."

Don Wood and Audrey Wood, newly married, moved to Northern California, and Don became a logger. Because he was the only crew member "over the age of nineteen," he was designated the head chain saw operator. At summer's end, the couple moved to Little Rock. At first, Don Wood got a job stacking bricks in a factory but eventually was able to work as a substitute art teacher. The school where he taught had very little money, and he had few art supplies beyond pen and paper. But the students did have fun, getting much of their inspiration from music. Teaching was not what Don intended to do with his life, however, and soon he and Audrey went to Mexico, where they worked to bring native artwork to the United States. They traveled through Mexico, the Yucatan, and Guatemala. They got to know many of the artisans and learned the stories behind many of the pieces of art.

After a few months, they decided to investigate Eureka Springs, Arkansas, as a place to establish a shop that would sell Mexican and Guatemalan art and books. Audrey Wood had spent many of her childhood summers in the unique location; when Don Wood saw it, he was "knocked out." The Ozark location was built right into the mountains. There was not an intersection in the whole town. He fell in love with the town; Audrey Wood had always liked it. The couple stayed in Eureka Springs for five years. By then, Audrey Wood was beginning to write children's books. To maximize her opportunities in that field, the couple decided they needed to move to a location where they would be more accessible to the publishing industry.

It was at that junction in their lives that Don Wood and Audrey Wood made the move to Santa Barbara, California. Don Wood obtained work as a magazine illustrator, and Audrey Wood pursued her children's book career. At one point, Audrey sold a manuscript for *Moonflute* to Green Tiger Press. They were seeking an illustrator, and Audrey persuaded Don to send samples of his illustrative work to the publisher. He did, and they offered him the opportunity to illustrate the book. Green Tiger published that edition in 1980. After collaborating on a number of other titles and publishing them with Harcourt, the publisher purchased the rights to *Moonflute*, redesigned it, and published the title in hardback in 1986. *Moonflute* began the collaboration between Audrey Wood and Don Wood.

For a number of years, the two artists worked together in the same studio, back to back, but they now have a studio addition to the back of their house. The addition allows them to have separate-but-adjacent studios. Audrey Wood has room for writing and illustrating, as well as for her many pets, including Max, a lilac-headed Amazon parrot. She has been known to draw while Max is perched on her shoulder and a tortoise crawls along the floor.

Don Wood once spent weeks with a little mouse crawling around his drawing board. The mouse was the model for the mouse in *The Napping House* (Harcourt, 1984). Don uses his ample space to create his wonderful oil paintings. He has said that he prefers the control he is able to get with oil paints. They dry more slowly, allowing him more room for revision. In the early 1990s, he began to experiment and research computer art; in 1993 he began illustrating a book using the computer. *Bright and Early Thursday Evening* (Harcourt, 1996) took Don two-and-a-half years to illustrate. He says, "It took as long to paint the digital illustrations for [the book] as it did to make the oil paintings with fifteen layers of glaze for *Heckedy Peg*."

Generally, while Audrey Wood and Don Wood often work on a book together, their contributions are well defined in terms of one being the author and the other the illustrator. They did, however, co-author *Piggies* (Harcourt, 1991), and they co-illustrated *Elbert's Bad Word* (Harcourt, 1988). Audrey Wood drew the illustrations for that book and then Don Wood colored them. In 1998, the publication of Audrey's book *The Christmas Adventure of Space Elf Sam* (Blue Sky, 1998) marked their son Bruce Wood's entrance into the children's book field. Although he had illustrated more than twenty book covers, this was the first book he illustrated in its entirety. He attended California Institute of the Arts in 1991, where he studied drama and developed his interest in computer art. In 1993, he was among the first students to enroll in the San Francisco State Multi-Media center, where he studied animation and 3-D modeling. With his move into the field as an artist, he became the fifth generation of artists in his mother's family.

Authors and illustrators often are asked where their ideas come from, and the Woods are not ones to hedge the question. Their response is often, "From our idea box." In fact, whenever they come across a newspaper clipping or an incident that strikes them as having story potential, they clip the article, jot a note, or slip an object into their "idea box." When they need a story idea, they sift through the box and let their imaginations take over.

The idea for *The Napping House* (Harcourt, 1984) came when Bruce was young. When it was time for him to take a nap, he often did so at his maternal grandmother's house next door. That allowed Audrey Wood and Don Wood to work undisturbed for a period of time. Whenever it was time for Bruce's nap, one of his parents would take him by the hand and say, "Let's go to the napping house." That fact, an article about people sleeping with their animals but not talking about it, and Audrey Wood's observation of two young children reciting the story, "The House That Jack Built," all came together to create the cumulative story line for *The Napping House*.

King Bidgood was originally a gentle character in a book to be titled "Nightmare Pie." Every time Mr. and Mrs. Bidgood left their kitchen door open, the entire neighborhood felt a heat wave. Anything they did affected the entire neighborhood. The story idea did not go anywhere, so it went back into the idea box. But the image of the mischievous, stout, red-haired fellow stuck with Audrey Wood, and while she was sifting through the idea box for another story idea, she came across a slip of paper reading "the sultan's bath, a magical place, a fantastic bath experience where anything can happen." The idea did not immediately present a plot or even a story line, but after thinking about it for a while, Audrey Wood wondered why someone would ever want to get out of such a wonderful bath. Mr. Bidgood immediately became connected to the story, but because Audrey did not think his image was that of a sultan, she transformed him into a king. In the end, she had to think of a way to get the king out of the tub. She decided it would be the same way they enticed their son to get out of the tub—they pulled the plug.

When the Woods are working on the same project, Audrey plays the role of Don's art director; Don serves as initial editor and establishes the final authority.

The Woods still live in Santa Barbara, California, near both their families. Most of Audrey's family now live in Santa Barbara, and all are in the arts. Don's family is still involved in the agriculture business in California's Central Valley. When Audrey Wood is not creating books, she relishes her work with abandoned and wounded birds, an interest that led to *Birdsong* (Harcourt, 1997). She loves to read—everything from science fiction and fantasy to the classics, nature books, and poetry. Don Wood, who loved sports as a child, is an avid beach volleyball player. Their son, Bruce, has taught his dad to surf.

BOOKS AND NOTES

Don Wood and Audrey Wood work differently, but their visions of picture books seem very similar. Both see the creation of a book as at least half theater. Critical elements for both artists are the rhythm and the point of view.

When creating illustrations for a book, Don Wood prefers to work using photographs of models and staged scenes as the basis for his work. Audrey Wood draws from memory. When Don created the illustrations for *Heckedy Peg* (Harcourt, 1987), photographs were taken of Audrey posing as the mother, of Don as the witch, and of seven children from local schools. The children were preschool aged through seventh grade and included a niece as "Wednesday" and a nephew as "Saturday." Don Wood used the family's own house, with a changed roofline, as the model for the Napping House in *The Napping House* (Harcourt, 1984). Audrey Wood was the model for the queen in *King Bidgood's in the Bathtub* (Harcourt, 1985). Her sister was the wacky duchess, and her father was the bald-headed knight. A red-haired friend from college, Harry, posed for the king, and Bruce modeled for the role of the page. Bruce was also the model for the boy in *Quick as a Cricket* (Child's Play, 1990) and *Tickleoctopus* (Harcourt, 1994).

Since Audrey Wood's illustrations are created from her memory, she studies her subjects first. When she was illustrating *Little Penguin's Tale* (Harcourt, 1989), she went to Sea World in San Diego and was given a VIP pass to enter the Penguin's Encounter. She was able to sit on the ice in their environment and hold a baby penguin in her arms. Her illustrations for *Oh, My Baby Bear* (Harcourt, 1990) were based on her memories of a stuffed toy bear that she had loved as a child.

Books Written by Audrey Wood and Illustrated by Don Wood

Heckedy Peg (Harcourt, 1987).

King Bidgood's in the Bathtub (Harcourt, 1985).

The Little Mouse, the Red Ripe Strawberry, and the Big Hungry Bear. Co-authored with Don Wood. (Child's Play, 1990).

The Napping House (Harcourt, 1984).

The Napping House Wakes Up (Harcourt, 1994).

Moonflute (Green Tiger, 1980; Harcourt, 1986).

Piggies. Co-authored with Don Wood. (Harcourt, 1991).

Tickleoctopus (Harcourt, 1994).
Houghton Mifflin originally published this text in 1980 with illustrations by Bill Morrison.

Books Written and Illustrated by Audrey Wood

Little Penguin's Tale (Harcourt, 1989).

Rude Giants (Harcourt, 1993).

Silly Sally (Harcourt, 1992).

Books Written by Audrey Wood

Birdsong. Illustrated by Robert Florczak. (Harcourt, 1997).

The Bunyans. Illustrated by David Shannon. (Blue Sky, 1996).

The Christmas Adventure of Space Elf Sam. Illustrated by Bruce Wood. (Blue Sky, 1998).

The Flying Dragon Room. Illustrated by Mark Teague. (Blue Sky, 1996).

The Rainbow Bridge: Inspired by a Chumash Tale. Illustrated by Robert Florczak. (Harcourt, 1995).

Sweet Dream Pie. Illustrated by Mark Teague. (Blue Sky, 1998).

When the Root Children Wake Up. Illustrated by Mark Alan Weatherby. (Scholastic, 1995).

FOR MORE INFORMATION

Web Sites

Audrey Wood Website. URL: <http://www.audreywood.com> (Accessed March 2000).

The Scoop—Don Wood Biographical Sketch. "Artist at a Glance: Harcourt Brace & Company." URL: <http://www.friend.ly.net/scoop/biographies/wooddon/index.html> (Accessed March 2000).

Jane Yolen

◆ Folklore ◆ Fantasy ◆ Poetry

New York, New York
February 11, 1939

📖 Commander Toad Series
📖 *The Emperor and the Kite*
📖 *Owl Moon*

ABOUT THE AUTHOR

Jane Yolen was born on February 11, 1939, in New York City and lived there until she was thirteen years old. She was born into a family of storytellers. Her great-grandfather was an innkeeper who told *bubba meises*—Yiddish for "grandma tales"—in the Finno-Russian village that was his home before he immigrated to the United States. Her father, Wolf "Will" Yolen, was an author, and her mother was an unpublished writer. Yolen began writing when she was in first grade, when she wrote the class musical. The musical was about vegetables, and Yolen played the lead carrot; the finale was a singing salad. She studied ballet for eight years and often rode the subway for hours. She and her friends would check all the gum machines for pennies or dimes. She lived across the street from Central Park and often played there alone or with friends. Fantasy games such as Robin Hood or King Arthur were popular tales to act out. She and her friends frequented the nearby museums. The Museum of Natural History was just fifteen blocks away, and the Museum of the City of New York was across the park from the family's house.

Her father played the guitar and introduced her to folk songs. Jane was pleased that she learned every old English, Scottish, Irish, and Appalachian love song and ballad that she ever heard. She also developed a knack for creating puns, which became her forte. Later in life, they would be part of her Commander Toad series and her books about Piggins.

The family moved to Westport, Connecticut, when Yolen was thirteen, and although Westport was just an hour from New York City, they concentrated their attention on the Westport community. The town was filled with writers and artists, and the assumption was that when children grew up in that town, writing would be their chosen occupation.

During high school, Yolen was captain of the girl's basketball team and worked on the school newspaper and literary magazine. She was also a member of the jazz, Spanish, and Latin clubs and part of the school choir—"the best in the country." Yolen often wrote term papers in verse. She wrote her big class essay about New York State manufacturing in verse, with a rhyme for Otis Elevators. Verse seemed to come more easily to her than did prose. In college she even wrote a final exam in a history class in verse. The teacher gave her an A+, but in terms of content it was probably a C paper.

After graduating from Staples High School in Westport, she entered Smith College in Northampton, Massachusetts, and later attended the New School for Social Research in New York City and the University of Massachusetts in Amherst. She trained as a poet and a journalist. She was not happy during some of those college years but made them more bearable by singing with a guitar-playing boyfriend at college parties and mixers. They made a little money, but more important, they learned many folk songs. Those songs became part of her life. As part of her journalism assignments, she often had to interview people in poor situations. She would get so upset that she would cry and later would end up writing her news stories off the top of her head, making up some of the facts. It was clear she was not cut out to be a journalist, but a fiction writer instead. She also wrote poetry and actually had a poem published while she was in college.

After graduating from Smith College in 1960, she worked as an editor in New York City. She worked for *Saturday Review* and *This Week*; later she went to work for book publishers and ended up at Alfred A. Knopf Publishers as an assistant juvenile editor. During that time, she continued writing. She published poetry, stories and books. On September 2, 1962, she married David Stemple, a photographer, computer expert, and avid bird-watcher. In 1965, she left Knopf. The oldest of her three children, Heidi Elisabet, was born in 1966, Adam Douglas was born in 1968, and Jason Frederic was born in 1970. The family soon was living on "Phoenix Farm" in Hatfield, Massachusetts.

Yolen continued writing books for children, reviewing books for the *New York Times Book Review.* She was a columnist for the *Daily Hampshire Gazette.* Her leisure activities included an interest in kites. Her father had been interested in kites, and she became a member of the International Kitefliers Association and the American Kite Fliers Association. Kites began to show up in her stories. One of the best-known stories is *The Emperor and the Kite* (World, 1967), which told how the tiniest Chinese princess in a family of eight children saved her father by sending him a basket of food each day that he was imprisoned in a high tower. The basket reached him when she attached it to her kite. Eventually, she was able to rescue him when the kite carried a rope she lovingly wove from grasses, vines, and her own long dark hair. He used the rope to climb down the wall of the tower. Ed Young illustrated that book and earned a Caldecott Honor Book award.

Jane Yolen is a prolific and versatile writer. She has written science fantasy novels, historical fiction, original tales featuring folk- and fairy-tale motifs, picture books, and nonfiction works. Many feel her best work is her folk- and fairy tales, literary, and retold tales.

The third-floor attic of her family's huge, old New England farmhouse is the location of her writing studio. The attic has two rooms and is filled with bookcases. One room is for editing, and the other room is where she writes. The writing room has three "wings." One area is the actual writing area, another is the copier and filing cabinet area, and the third is her reading area, although at times the sofa there serves as an "in" basket.

Yolen's husband often took their three children owling near their rural Massachusetts home. Those owling nights inspired the book *Owl Moon* (Philomel, 1987), which became a Caldecott Medal book when John Schoenherr was recognized for his illustrations. Stemple is the "original" of Pa. The little girl is based on Yolen's daughter, Heidi.

When Yolen gets an idea that might have potential for a story or comes across an interesting inscription on a tombstone or an unusual photograph—anything that might lead to a story—it is put into an idea file. Those ideas or snippets of ideas are sometimes in the file for months or years before coming to the forefront when she is sifting through the ideas. Sometimes the ideas are never used. Sometimes they begin a story and then fade into the background when a stronger idea takes over. Sometimes ideas are in the file, and after a story is written, Yolen realizes that its genesis was in the idea file.

In 1980, Jane Yolen was awarded an honorary doctorate in law by Our Lady of Elms College in Chicopee, Massachusetts. The degree recognized that "throughout her writing career, she has remained true to her primary source of inspiration—folk culture." She says that she considers science fiction as the folklore of the future and that in addition to her young adult novels, she has used that interest to create the Commander Toad series. This series tells of the fantastic and comic adventures of a group of space explorers, led by Commander Toad, aboard the spaceship, Star Warts.

Yolen's husband is her greatest supporter. He reads everything she writes and in fact reads even more than her editors do because they don't read her failures. Sometimes she reads her writing out loud to him; other times she discusses problems with him.

In addition to their home in Massachusetts, Yolen and Stemple own a home in Scotland, where they live part of the year. When in the United States, the couple lives on their fifteen acres of farmland; twelve acres are typically rented to truck farmers. From her writing desk, she can view the acreage, a small forest, and an occasional fox. She loves to bake bread, sing folk songs, tell stories, write music, and enjoy the outdoors. She no longer travels to speak at schools but does support other writers by being actively involved in writers' conferences and by attending major conferences. When she attends those conferences, she is seldom, if ever, without pictures of her grandchildren. Her grown sons and daughter are all three accomplished writers. Each has collaborated with Yolen. Her daughter, Heidi, has co-authored *The Mystery of the Mary Celeste* (Simon & Schuster, 1999). Jason's photographs are an integral part of *House/house* (Marshall Cavendish, 1998), which he also helped to write. Adam created musical arrangements for several of Yolen's books, including *Jane Yolen's Old MacDonald's Songbook* (Boyds Mills, 1994), *Jane Yolen's Mother Goose Songbook* (Boyds Mills, 1992), and *Milk and Honey: A Year of Jewish Holidays* (Putnam, 1996).

BOOKS AND NOTES

Many of Jane Yolen's stories are about a girl trying to please her father. Jane has said that little girl is her. Her father, Will, liked to say Jane was a writer, but he never did read what she wrote; he seemed to feel that Jane's books were not "real" books because they were written for younger readers. Her brother, however, was a journalist, an economic and political reporter about South America. He was the "real" writer. Yolen continually tried to please her father. Two days after he died Yolen learned that his real name had been "Wolf." He changed it to Will to make it sound more American. That fact helped her to realize that part of the family's Jewish heritage was in danger of being forgotten and inspired her historical fiction novel *The Devil's Arithmetic* (Viking, 1988). It is one of the many non–picture-book titles that she has written. While she wrote in many genres earlier in her career, Yolen has commented that her most significant contribution to literature for children has been her literary fairy tales.

Yolen has also talked about the significance of many of her books. The manuscript for *Bird to Time* (Crowell, 1971) came about when Yolen misheard the song lyrics of a Righteous Brothers song. The song had nothing to do with birds or time, but by then Yolen was already wondering about a time bird. When the book was accepted for publication, she gave the manuscript to her mother to read. It was a short time later that her mother died of cancer. After the book was published, Jane remembered her mother's comments and realized the book was really about her mother—and Yolen's desire to make time stop.

Books Written by Jane Yolen

All Those Secrets of the World. Illustrated by Leslie Baker. (Little, Brown, 1993).

All in the Woodland Early. Illustrated by Jane Breskin Zalben. (Boyds Mills, 1997).

Alphabestiary: Animal Poems from A to Z. Illustrated by Allan Eitzen. (Boyds Mills, 1995).

Baby Bear's Bedtime Book. Illustrated by Jane Dyer. (Harcourt, 1990).

The Ballad of the Pirate Queens. Illustrated by David Shannon. (Harcourt, 1995).

Fever Dream. Illustrated by Jerry Pinkney. (HarperCollins, 1996).

Jane Yolen's Old MacDonald Songbook. Illustrated by Rosekrans Hoffman. Music arrangements by Adam Stemple. (Boyds Mills, 1994).

Little Mouse & Elephant: A Tale from Turkey. Illustrated by John Segal. (Simon & Schuster, 1996).

Milk and Honey: A Year of Jewish Holiday Houses. Illustrated by Louise August. Music arrangements by Adam Stemple. (Putnam, 1996).

The Originals: Animals That Time Forgot. Illustrated by Ted Lewin. (Philomel, 1998).

Raising Yoder's Barn. Illustrated by Bernie Fuchs. (Little, Brown, 1998).

Sleeping Ugly. Illustrated by Diane Stanley. (Coward-McCann, 1981).

The Three Bears Rhyme Book. Illustrated by Jane Dyer. (Harcourt, 1987).

Welcome to the Icehouse. Illustrated by Laura Regan. (Putnam, 1998).

Commander Toad Series
Illustrated by Bruce Degen

Commander Toad and the Big Black Hole (Coward-McCann, 1983).

Commander Toad and the Dis-asteroid (Coward-McCann, 1985).

Commander Toad and the Intergalactic Spy (Coward-McCann, 1986).

Commander Toad and the Planet of the Grapes (Coward-McCann, 1982).

Commander Toad in Space (Coward-McCann, 1980).

Commander Toad and the Space Pirates (Coward-McCann, 1987).

Commander Toad and the Voyage Home (Putnam, 1997).

Piggins Series

Piggins and the Royal Wedding. Illustrated by Jane Dyer. (Harcourt, 1988).

Piggins. Illustrated by Jane Dyer. (Harcourt, 1987).

Picnic with Piggins. Illustrated by Jane Dyer. (Harcourt, 1988).

FOR MORE INFORMATION

Articles

"Interview: Jane Yolen." *Storytelling Magazine* 8, no. 1 (January 1, 1996): 22.

"Interview: Jane Yolen: Telling Tales." *Locus* 39, no. 2 (August 1, 1997): 4.

Koch, John. "An Interview with Jane Yolen." *The Writer* 110, no. 3 (March 1, 1997): 20.

"Meet the Author." *Instructor* 105, no. 7. (April 1, 1996): 61.

Books

Yolen, Jane. *A Letter from Phoenix Farm* (Richard C. Owens, 1992). Illustrated with photographs by Jason Stemple.

Web Sites

Amazon.com Author Interview. "Amazon.com Talks to Jane Yolen." URL: <http://www.amazon.com/exec/obidos/show-interview/y-j-olenane/002-6230071> (Accessed March 2000).

Jane Yolen Official Web Site. URL: <http://www.janeyolen.com/> (Accessed March 2000).

Ed Young

◆ Folklore

Tientsin, China
November 28, 1931

  📖 *Lon Po Po: A Red Riding Hood Story from China*
  📖 *The Lost Horse: A Chinese Folktale*
  📖 *Yeh-Shen: A Cinderella Story from China*

ABOUT THE AUTHOR/ILLUSTRATOR

Ed Tse-Chun Young was born in China, two months after the Manchurian invasion. He was born in Tientsin, a coal-mining town near Peking, on November 28, 1931. His father, Qua-Ling Young, was a structural engineer who wanted his son to be an engineer as well. During Ed's childhood, his father sometimes held three jobs to support the family. His mother, Yuen Teng Young, became an entrepreneur in an attempt to keep the household running.

Three years after the Manchurian invasion, there was another impending threat to northern China, so the family moved south to the mouth of the Yangtze River, to Shanghai. Jurisdictions within the city were under a number of different European countries. It was in this city that Ed Young grew up. There were five children in the family, and often the children's friends came and stayed a while. They occupied themselves, and Young was often dreaming. He created plays and drawings. His mother often asked, "Eddy, I wonder what will become of you." His father hoped that his interests would take him into the field of architecture.

The family lived in Shanghai until the Communists took over. It was then that the family moved to Hong Kong, where Young continued his high school education. Two-and-a-half years later, he entered the United States to study architecture as his father had wished. For three years, he studied at the City College of San Francisco (1952) and at the University of Illinois (1952–1954), until he realized with certainty that the profession was not for him. In 1954, at the age of twenty-three, he entered the Art Center College in Los Angeles. Three years later, he graduated from that institution as an illustrator.

After graduation, Young moved to New York City and accepted a job with an advertising studio, Mell Richman Studio. He worked there as an illustrator and designer until the studio ceased doing business in 1962. He had already begun instructing in the field of visual communications at the Pratt Institute in Brooklyn and continued doing that until 1966. Meanwhile, he was also involved in the Shr Jung Tai Chi Chuan School in New York City's Chinatown as an instructor in Tai Chi Chuan, a form of moving meditation that is beneficial to the mind and body. He was the school's director in 1973.

In 1962, Young also embarked on a career aimed toward the children's book market. Friends encouraged him to show his sketches of animal movements to Ursula Nordstrom of Harper & Row. He did, and she offered him a contract to illustrate *The Mean Mouse and Other Mean Stories* by Janice May Udry (Harper, 1962). He found illustrating a children's book to be fun, and it transported him back to his childhood, when he imagined that animals behaved like humans. This first book won an award from the American Institute of Graphic Arts. His next contracts were with Holt, Rinehart & Winston, Follett, and World Publishing. In 1968, he made a firm mark in the field when he illustrated Jane Yolen's *The Emperor and the Kite* (World, 1967). That book was named a Caldecott Honor Book in 1968.

Young went on to illustrate many more books, inspired by Chinese painting that was often accompanied by words. He believes that the words and images must be complementary. There are things that words can do that pictures cannot and vice versa.

Ed Young and his wife, Natasha Gorky, whom he married on June 1, 1971, have lived in Hastings-on-Hudson in New York since the early 1970s. Young is still involved in Shr Jung Chuan and occasionally translates at seminars and presentations given by Chinese leaders in this discipline.

BOOKS AND NOTES

Ed Young has illustrated his books with pencil, pastel, and oil crayons, as well as with intricate cut-paper collages. When he illustrated *Yeh-Shen: A Cinderella Story from China* (Putnam, 1982), he depicted authentic costumes reflecting the area of China from which the story came. He used paneled pictures that resembled folding painted screens. The illustrations were executed in pastel and shimmering watercolors. His illustrations for Jane Yolen's *The Emperor and the Kite* (Putnam, 1988) were created in the authentic Chinese art form of cut-paper design. They are as delicate as the sensitive story of the Djeow Snow, who is so tiny she is often ignored. But this smallest of eight children persistently sends food to her father when he is captured and held in a high tower. She attaches a food basket to her kite and flies it to him. Finally, she is able to rescue him with a rope she has braided using vines, grasses, and her own long black hair. The collage illustrations for Yolen's *The Girl Who Loved the Wind* (Crowell, 1972) were reminiscent of Persian miniatures in their exquisite detail.

Young's illustrations are often sparse and depict characters in dark shadowy images. His illustrations showing the wolf in *Lon Po Po: A Red Riding Hood Story from China* (Putnam, 1989) use dark images that make the scenes with the wolf very foreboding.

Books Written or Retold and Illustrated by Ed Young

Cat and Rat: The Legend of the Chinese Zodiac (Holt, 1995).

Donkey Trouble (Atheneum, 1995).

Lon Po Po: A Red Riding Hood Story from China (Putnam, 1989).

The Lost Horse: A Chinese Folktale (Silver Whistle, 1998).

Mouse Match: A Chinese Folktale (Harcourt, 1997).

Seven Blind Mice (Philomel, 1992).

Books Illustrated by Ed Young

Bitter Bananas. Written by Isaac Olaleye. (Boyds Mills, 1994).

Chinese Mother Goose Rhymes. Written, selected, and edited by Robert Wyndham. (World, 1968; Paper Star, 1998).

Dream Catcher. Written by Audrey Osofsky. (Orchard, 1992).

The Emperor and the Kite. Written by Jane Yolen. (Putnam, 1988).

Foolish Rabbit's Big Mistake. Written by Rafé Martin and Ed Young. (Putnam, 1985).

The Turkey Girl: A Zuni Cinderella. Written by Penny Pollack. (Little, Brown, 1996).

I Wish I Were a Butterfly. Written by James Howe. (Harcourt, 1987).

Yeh-Shen: A Cinderella Story from China. Written by Ai-Lilng Louie. (Putnam, 1982).

FOR MORE INFORMATION

Web Sites

"Ed Young." *Penguin Putnam Catalog Biography.* URL: <http://www.penguinputnam.com/catalog/yreader/authors/468_biography.html> (Accessed March 2000).

Margot Zemach

◆ Folklore

Los Angeles, California
November 30, 1931–May 21, 1989

📖 *Duffy and the Devil*
📖 *Nail Soup*

ABOUT THE
AUTHOR/ILLUSTRATOR

Margot Zemach's childhood was spent traveling across the country with her Aunt Margie and Uncle Tom, who sold ink eradicator. Her mother was an actress and left Margot behind with her Aunt Margie. When she was two, Margot was sent to Oklahoma City to live with her grandparents. Both of her grandparents were doctors. Margot's Aunt Aggie was a doctor, too. Her Uncle Charles was too young to be a doctor yet, so they spent a lot of time together and became best of friends.

By the time Margot was five years old, she was traveling with her mother, Elizabeth Daily, and her stepfather, Benjamin Zemach, a director and dancer. Margot spent many hours alone backstage, where she amused herself by drawing pictures and telling herself stories. She loved the lights of New York City, but because she traveled with her parents, she attended many different schools. She did not like school but did manage to graduate from high school. She tried several different jobs. At one time or another, she was a movie usher, a typist, a file clerk, a salesperson, and a messenger. She was unsuccessful at all of these jobs.

537

One thing Margot could do was draw, so she decided to become an artist. She wanted to illustrate children's books. She studied at the Los Angeles Institute of Art and was awarded a Fulbright Scholarship to attend the Vienna Academy of Fine Arts in 1955–1956. The first night in Vienna, she met Harvey Fischstrom. For a year, they walked and talked in Vienna. Neither of them went to school. At the end of the year, they returned to the United States. She settled in California, and he entered graduate school in Massachusetts. In January 1957, Margot Zemach and Harvey Fischstrom married.

Fischstrom taught history and social sciences at Boston University and later at the University of Massachusetts. Zemach really wanted to illustrate children's books and convinced her husband to write one for her. As a writer, Fischstrom used the name Harve Zemach. They were both unemployed and expecting their first baby when they sold their first book, *A Small Boy Is Listening* (Houghton, 1959). It was the story of a small boy in Vienna, where the couple had overheard a small boy on his way home from school greet Mrs. Ditterdorf. The book was published shortly after their daughter Kaethe was born in 1958. For several years, Fischstrom and Zemach lived in the Cambridge, Massachusetts, area. They became parents of two more daughters, Heidi, born in 1960, and Rachel, born in 1962.

When the girls were ages six, eight, and ten, the family set out to see the world. They traveled to England, Denmark, and Austria. They traveled to Italy and saw red-poppy-covered fields shining in the sun. Their life was beautiful and carefree. Zemach and Fischstrom planned on teaching their children themselves as they continued to travel and work on books. Lessons for the girls were so sporadic, however, that they finally decided to settle in Denmark for a year. That is where their fourth daughter, Rebecca, was born in April 1970. That same year, they moved to London, where the family lived in Greenwich Park. They continued to travel in Denmark and Wales but spent most of their time working on books. The three older girls attended school in London, and Rebecca learned to walk and talk. They loved living in England. But tragedy struck on November 2, 1974, when Fischstrom died; he would have turned forty-one a month later. The older girls were sixteen, fourteen, and twelve. Rebecca was only four.

Zemach returned with her family to the United States, where they settled into an old house in Berkeley, California. Zemach continued to create books. Her daughter Kaethe co-authored a title, *The Princess and Froggie* (Farrar, 1975), with her father and later illustrated a few books. Kaethe's illustrative style was uniquely hers but clearly showed her mother's influence. Among the books Kaethe illustrated were *The Traveling Men of Ballycoo* by Eve Bunting (Harcourt, 1983) and The Purim Goat by Yuri Suhl (Four Winds, 1980). She also wrote and illustrated two books with her married name, Kaethe Zemach-Bersin: *The Beautiful Rat* (Four Winds, 1979) and *The Funny Dream* (Greenwillow, 1988).

Margot Zemach died in Berkeley on May 21, 1989, of amyotrophic lateral sclerosis (ALS).

BOOKS AND NOTES

Many of the Margot Zemach titles were folklore, particularly versions from various cultures. Her illustrations were created with pen and ink and full-color washes. Her images were fluid and spontaneous. She often used her daughters and husband as models for the people who populated her books.

Books Written/Retold and Illustrated by Margot Zemach

It Could Always Be Worse: A Yiddish Folk Tale (Farrar, 1976).

Jake and Honeybunch Go to Heaven (Farrar, 1982).

The Judge: An Untrue Tale (Farrar, 1969).

The Little Red Hen: An Old Story (Farrar, 1983).

Simon Boom Gives a Wedding (Four Winds, 1972).

The Three Little Pigs: An Old Story (Farrar, 1988).

The Three Sillies: A Folk Tale (Holt, 1963).

The Three Wishes: An Old Story (Farrar, 1986).

Books Illustrated by Margot Zemach

All God's Critters Got a Place in the Choir. Words and music by Bill Staines. (Dutton, 1989).

The Chinese Mirror. Written by Mirra Ginsburg. (Harcourt, 1988).
Adapted from a Korean folktale.

Duffy and the Devil: A Cornish Tale. Written by Harve Zemach. (Farrar, 1973).

The Enchanted Umbrella. Written by Odette Meyers. (Harcourt, 1988).
Based on a French folktale; a short history of the umbrella.

The Fisherman and His Wife: A Tale from the Brothers Grimm. Translated by Randall Jarrell. (Farrar, 1980).

Nail Soup, a Swedish Folk Tale. Retold by Harve Zemach. (Farrar, 1964).

A Penny a Look: An Old Story. Retold by Harve Zemach. (Farrar, 1971).

Salt: A Russian Tale. Retold by Harve Zemach. (Farrar, 1965).

The Sign in Mendel's Window. Written by Mildred Phillips. (Macmillan, 1985).

The Two Foolish Cats. Written by Yoshiko Uchida. (McElderry, 1987).
Suggested by a Japanese folktale.

FOR MORE INFORMATION

Books

Zemach, Margot. *Self-Portrait: Margot Zemach*. Illustrated by Margot Zemach. (Addison-Wesley, 1978; Harper, 1985).

Appendix

PHOTOGRAPHY CREDITS

Photograph of Verna Aardema by Courneye Tourcotte, Master Photographer, courtesy of Verna Aardema and reprinted with permission.

Photograph of Sue Alexander copyright by Marilyn Sanders, courtesy of Sue Alexander and Marilyn Sanders and reprinted with permission.

Photograph of Aliki Brandenberg by Val Lambros, courtesy of Aliki Brandenberg and reprinted with permission.

Photograph of Mitsumasa Anno, courtesy of Mitsumasa Anno and reprinted with permission.

Photograph of Caroline Arnold by Arthur Arnold, courtesy of Caroline Arthur and reprinted with permission.

Photograph of Frank Asch by Jan Asch, courtesy of Frank Asch and reprinted with permission.

Photograph of Jim Aylesworth by Scott Campbell, courtesy of Jim Aylesworth and reprinted with permission.

Photograph of Graeme Base by Earl Carter, courtesy of Graeme Base and Penguin Books Autralia and reprinted with permission.

Photograph of Jan Brett, courtesy of Jan Brett and reprinted with permission.

Photograph of Norman Bridwell by Mark Lovewell, courtesy of Norman Bridwell and reprinted with permission.

Photograph of Craig Brown, courtesy of Craig Brown and reprinted with permission.

Photograph of Marc Brown, copyright 1995 by Rick Friedman and reprinted with permission.

Photograph of Marcia Brown by Sharron L. McElmeel and reprinted with permission.

Photograph of Anthony Browne, courtesy of Anthony Browne and reprinted with permission.

Photography of Ashley Brown by Sharron L. McElmeel and reprinted with permission.

Photography of Eve Bunting by Hans Gutknecht, courtesy of Eve Bunting and reprinted with permission.

Photograph of John Burningham by Sharron L. McElmeel and reprinted with permission.

Photograph of Eric Carle by Sharron L. McElmeel and reprinted with permission.

Photograph of Eileen Christelow by Karen Hesse, courtesy of Eileen Christelow and reprinted with permission.

Photograph of Joanna Cole by Sharron L. McElmeel and reprinted with permission.

Photograph of Floyd Cooper by Velma Cooper, courtesy of Floyd Cooper and reprinted with permission.

Photograph of Donald Crews by Sharron L. McElmeel and reprinted with permission.

Photograph of Pat Cummings by Sharron L. McElmeel and reprinted with permission.

Photograph of Tomie dePaola copyright by Suki Coughlin, courtesy of Tomie dePaola and reprinted with permission.

Photograph of Diane Dillon and Leo Dillon by Pat Cummings, courtesy of Diane Dillon and Leo Dillon and reprinted with permission.

Photograph of Lois Ehlert by Lillian Schultz, courtesy of Lois Ehlert and reprinted with permission.

Photograph of Lisa Campbell Ernst, courtesy of Lisa Campbell Ernst and reprinted with permission.

Photograph of Mem Fox by Sharron L. McElmeel and reprinted with permission.

Photograph of Dick Gackenbach, courtesy of Dick Gackenbach and reprinted with permission.

Photograph of Gail Gibbons by Kent Ancliffe, courtesy of Gail Gibbons and reprinted with permission.

Photograph of Paul Goble by Janet Goble. Reprinted courtesy of Paul Goble and Bradbury Press, an affiliate of Macmillan Children's Book Group.

Photograph of Gail Haley by Bob Caldwell, courtesy of Gail Haley and reprinted with permission.

Photograph of Kevin Henkes by Sharron L. McElmeel and reprinted with permission.

Photograph of Lillian Hoban by Barbara Burger, courtesy of the late Lillian Hoban and reprinted with permission.

Photograph of Deborah Hopkinson by Michele Hill, courtesy of Deborah Hopkinson and reprinted with permission.

Photograph of Pat Hutchins by Laurence Hutchins, courtesy of Pat Huchins and reprinted with permission.

Photograph of Trina Schart Hyman by Jean Aull, courtesy of Trina Schart Hyman and reprinted with permission.

Photograph of Ann Jonas by Sharron L. McElmeel and reprinted with permission.

Photograph of Keiko Kasza by Jerry Mitchell, courtesy of Keiko Kasza and reprinted with permission.

Photograph of Steven Kellogg, courtesy of Steven Kellogg and reprinted with permission.

Photograph of Eric A. Kimmel, courtesy of Eric A. Kimmel and reprinted with permission.

Photograph of Steven Kroll by Edie Bresler, courtesy of Steven Kroll and reprinted with permission.

Photograph of Anita Lobel by Sharron L. McElmeel and reprinted with permission.

Photograph of Bill Martin Jr., courtesy of Bill Martin Jr. and reprinted with permission.

Photograph of Jacqueline Briggs Martin by Sharron L. McElmeel, courtesy of Jacqueline Briggs Martin and reprinted with permission.

Photograph of Robert McCloskey by Rodney Chadbourne, courtesy of Robert McCloskey and reprinted with permission.

Photograph of Patricia McKissack, courtesy of Patricia McKissack and reprinted with permission.

Photograph of David McPhail by Sharron L. McElmeel and reprinted with permission.

Photograph of Bernard Most by Walt Chrynwski, courtesy of Bernard Most and reprinted with permission.

Photograph of Andrea Davis Pinkney and Brian Pinkney by Sharron L. McElmeel and reprinted with permission.

Photograph of Patricia Polacco by Sharron L. McElmeel and reprinted with permission.

Photograph of Beatrix Potter, 1913. Courtesy of the Victoria and Albert Museum. Reproduced by kind permission of Frederick Warne & Co.

Photograph of Jack Prelutsky courtesy of Michelle Ross and reprinted with permission.

Photograph of James Ransome courtesy of William Morrow Publishers and reprinted with permission.

Photograph of Faith Ringgold by Sharron L. McElmeel and reprinted with permission.

Photograph of Robert San Souci by Mark Kane Photography, courtesy of Robert San Souci and reprinted with permission.

Photograph of Allen Say by Sharron L. McElmeel and reprinted with permission.

Photograph of Jon Scieszka by Sharron L. McElmeel and reprinted with permission.

Photograph of Peter Spier by Sharron L. McElmeel and reprinted with permission.

Photograph of Diane Stanley by Sharron L. McElmeel and reprinted with permission.

Photograph of Janet Stevens by Geoffrey Wheeler, Black Star, courtesy of Janet Stevens and reprinted with permission.

Photograph of David Wiesner by Sharron L. McElmeel and reprinted with permission.

Photograph of Nancy Willard by Sharron L. McElmeel and reprinted with permission.

Photograph of Audrey Wood by Sharron L. McElmeel and reprinted with permission.

Photograph of Don Wood by Sharron L. McElmeel and reprinted with permission.

Photograph of Jane Yolen, courtesy of Jane Yolen and reprinted with permission.

Genre Index

This index groups authors and illustrators according to the genres or themes with which their books are associated. This reference volume is arranged in alphabetical order by each author's or illustrator's last name; thus page numbers are not included with this index.

General Index

In this index, the page numbers that refer to the main entry for each author appear in bold. All titles written or illustrated by any subject in this book are included in the index, regardless of whether the title appears in a chapter's narrative or in the book list at the end of the chapter.

About the Author

Born in the heartland of the United States—Iowa—Sharron Hanson McElmeel spent her childhood days on a dairy/grain farm where she and three siblings enjoyed swimming in the farm creek, riding horses and eating picnic lunches on the "back forty," and enjoying idyllic days playing and reading in an abandoned stone cabin that stood in a cornfield. During her childhood, few books were in her life—the only two books she remembers owning as a child were collections of Grimm's fairy tales and the tales of Hans Christian Andersen. Those tales are still among her favorites. When she married and became a parent she knew that she wanted her children to have more exposure to the literature being offered to young people. Books by Virginia Lee Burton, Maurice Sendak, and Ezra Jack Keats became early favorites. Bill Peet, Beatrix Potter, and many others were added to the list of her family's favorites.

In addition to her career as a classroom teacher and library media specialist, she has authored more than twenty reference books for educators and parents focusing on books for younger readers and the people who create those books. Her own books have been described as "a gem of a book . . . wonderful, wonderful!" by the editors of *Teaching K–8* and as sources for "hundreds of ideas that will put literature into every curriculum area." She has consulted with school districts and professional organizations from Canada to Oklahoma to Arkansas to Kansas to Virginia and throughout Iowa, where she continues to write and teach. One of her most recent titles to be published is this book's companion title, *100 Most Popular Children's Book Authors* (Libraries Unlimited, 1999).

Sharron and her husband live in a rural area near Cedar Rapids where their sons and daughters, grandchildren, various relatives and friends, and pets often congregate for potluck meals, conversation about good books and movies, and their own "work-up" version of softball or card games played with "our rules." Sharron's Web site is at <http://www.mcelmeel.com>.